MANCHESTER UNITED

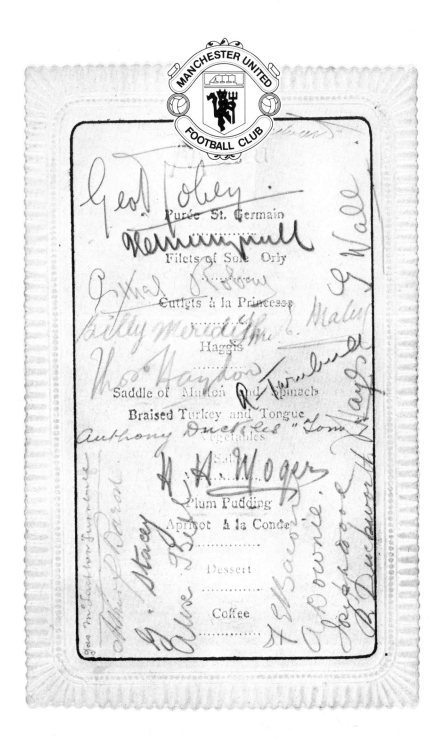

MANCHESTER UNITED

THE OFFICIAL HISTORY

TOM TYRRELL & DAVID MEEK

HAMLYN

Published by
The Hamlyn Publishing Group Limited
a division of
The Octopus Publishing Group
Michelin House, 81 Fulham Road
London SW3 6RB
and distributed for them by
Octopus Distribution Services Limited
Rushden, Northamptonshire NN10 9RZ, England

First published in 1988

ISBN 0 600 55703 0

Printed in Italy

Bibliography

Atkinson, Ron *United to Win* Sidgwick and Jackson, 1984

Green, Geoffrey *There's Only One United* Hodder and Stoughton, 1978

Morrison, Ian and Shury, Alan *Manchester United –
A Complete Record* Breedon Books, 1986

Roberts, John *The Team That Wouldn't Die* Arthur Barker, 1975

Stepney, Alex *Alex Stepney* Arthur Barker, 1978

Tyrrell, Tom *Manchester United* Hamlyn, 1984

Tyrrell, Tom *Manchester United – The Religion* Kaye
and Ward

Tyrrell, Tom *Twenty Five Years After Munich*
Stafford Pemberton, 1983

Young, Percy M *A History of British Football* Stanley Paul, 1968

Photographic acknowledgments

Although every effort has been made to trace the copyright
holders, we apologise in advance for any unintentional
omissions and would be pleased to insert the appropriate
acknowledgments in any subsequent edition of this publication.

Covers: (*left*) Colorsport (George Best);
(*centre*) David Smith Sports Photography (Munich clock);
(*right*) All Sport (Bryan Robson).

All Sport 130, 131, 133 bottom, 134 bottom, 138 bottom, 140,
(Simon Bruty) 191 top right, (David Cannon) 87, 161, 162,
166, 190 (bottom), (Russell Cheyne) 137 top and bottom, 138
top, (Tony Duffy) 149 bottom, (Michael King) 192-3 centre;
BBC Hulton Picture Library 42 top; Cheshire Press Photos
156; Graham Collin 56-7 top, 57 bottom, 66 top, 66-7 centre,
67, 69, 70 right, 80 top; Colorsport 88 top left and bottom;
Clive Cooksey 62; Daily Mirror 11 bottom, 12 bottom, 13, 15
top and bottom, 17, 24-5 centre, 26 top, 29 top right, 36 centre,
64 bottom right, 90, 95, 99, 100, 103, 105, 106, 114; Express
Newspapers 36 bottom; Harry Godwin 12 top; Dick Green 50
bottom, 50-1 top, 60 top, 61, 120, 136, 148 bottom right; The
Illustrated London News Picture Library 104; International
News Photos 71; The Keystone Collection 29 top left and
bottom, 31, 75; Manchester Evening News *endpapers*, 2, 8
(bottom), 11 (top), 18, 20 bottom, 23, 28, 44-5 bottom, 46, 53
bottom, 55, 89 top right, 97, 116, 122-3, 149 top, 153 top and
bottom, 155 bottom, 157, 159, 165; Manchester United
Football Club/Cliff Butler 40 bottom; David Meek 20 top, 24
bottom, 25 top, 30 top, 33 bottom, 48, 53 top, 64 bottom left,
84-5 top and bottom, 107, 110, 111, 135, 139, 164; Octopus
Group Picture Library/Frank Power 41; Oldham Evening
Chronicle 8 top, 68 top and bottom, 73, 80-1, 83 top right;
Harry Ormesker 76; Popperfoto 6 bottom; The Press
Association 118 top, 134 top, 144, 150 bottom; Provincial Press
Agency 21; Peter Robinson 84 top left, 88-9 centre, 142
bottom, 146 top, 146-7, 148 top left, 150 top; S & G Picture
Library 51 top and bottom; David Smith Sports Photography
192 top left, 192-3 top and bottom, 193 top right; Syndication
International 10 top right, 26 bottom, 36 top, 38 top, 42
bottom, 45 top, 47, 58, 60 centre, 118-9 bottom, 126, 133 top,
154 bottom, 155 top, 167; Tom Tyrrell *half title page*, 30
bottom, 33 top, 35, 38 bottom, 40 top, 50 centre and bottom,
60 bottom, 64 top, 66 bottom, 70 left, 81, 82-3, 98 top and
bottom, 102, 108, 109 left and right, 112, 121, 124, 128, 129,
142 top, 154 top, 190-1.

Contents

Foreword

by Bobby Charlton CBE

MANCHESTER UNITED seems to have been the focus of my sporting life for almost as long as I can remember.

When I think about it, I suppose it is really not so surprising considering that my association with the club now goes back some 35 years, even longer if you take into account my schooldays back home in Ashington in the north-east when Joe Armstrong, the United scout, first came round to our house. I shall always remember little Joe with the beaming smile because he was the first to take an interest, and later when there were a few more on the scene and I had to choose a club to go to, I thought I couldn't do better than stay with Joe. The fact that he represented Manchester United and Matt Busby came into it as well of course, but I think my first instincts were right.

I have had a most exciting and rewarding lifetime associated with Manchester United and the fact that I am now honoured to serve the club as a director has been the ultimate satisfaction. Outside my home and family, the club has been my life, and I guess there have even been times when Norma, my wife, has wondered whether football hasn't taken over at home as well. I have got to admit that the game fascinates me as much as ever, especially Manchester United, the club which gave me much of my education and most of my inspiration.

I was privileged to know and play alongside the Busby Babes, lucky to escape with my life when so many of those fine young players failed to survive that terrible crash at Munich. The experience perhaps left me a little more appreciative of the many good things which have happened to me since then, the successes and even the disappointments that make up a career.

Sir Matt Busby and Jimmy Murphy I hold in great affection and respect as the men who did so much to fashion me as a footballer and who led us to those achievements in Europe, to the League Championship and the FA Cup. I have so many memories of matches, friends and team-mates, not to mention opponents and the people I have met in my football travels. Now as I read this latest book on Manchester United my mind is refreshed as the events leap to life again, partly because I was there for 20 years as a player, but also because of the detailed touch of authority brought to a formidable task by Tom Tyrrell and David Meek.

For they were there as well! Tom reports for Piccadilly Radio and was writing about Old Trafford nearly 20 years ago. David has been the *Manchester Evening News* representative covering the club for more than 30 years.

There have been other fine books written about Manchester United, but not with quite the same insight and feel for the club and its many famous players. Even when they are writing about the early days I feel they have captured the essence and spirit of a club which so many of us hold so dear.

So it is with particular pleasure that I write this foreword to a book which I know will stand the test of time as a history of Manchester United.

Matt Busby: Birth of the Babes

Sir Matt Busby lent his name to the most romantic and tragic experiences of football. The 'Busby Babes' of Manchester United fired the imagination of the public as they came bounding onto the scene a few years after the Second World War. They were the creation of a remarkable manager, a man of genius and vision who was to change the face of English football.

Tragically, the Busby Babes were destroyed in the Munich air disaster of 1958 before they had reached their prime, and their manager came close to perishing with them. But he survived and Manchester United rose again from the ashes of their despair. Busby started all over again and produced more splendid teams so, as Bobby Charlton once put it, Old Trafford became a theatre of dreams.

United blazed a trail for English football in Europe. Winning the European Cup in 1968 just ten years after the tragedy at Munich was an incredible achievement and, of course, a testament to the life and work of Matthew Busby, born in 1909 in a two-roomed pitman's cottage in Orbiston, a small Lanarkshire mining village some miles from Glasgow.

The young Busby was no stranger to loss. His father and all his uncles were killed in the First World War. The result was that the remainder of the family, one by one, emigrated to America, looking for a better life than coal mining. Matt's mother was due to join her sister, and Matt himself was only waiting for a visa quota number. Then, just before he was 17, came the invitation to join Manchester City after he had played a few games for Denny Hibs, a local side.

Plans to go to the United States were scrapped, though Matt probably wished at times that he had gone, because life at Maine Road was not easy. He was homesick and he struggled to get into the first team. A switch of position to take the place of an injured player at wing half in the reserves finally launched him on a distinguished career with City and won him Scottish international honours.

He won a Cup-winners' medal in 1934 and by 1936 he was captain of City, but he decided he wanted a change and he signed for Liverpool.

Like most of the Liverpool team he joined the army when the Second World War started and served in the 9th Battalion of the King's Liverpool Regiment, and eventually in the Army Physical Training Corps. After the war Liverpool wanted him back as a player and as assistant to manager George Kay. But, as Matt says: 'I got this opportunity to go as manager of Manchester United. I had a soft spot for Manchester after my City days and it attracted me.'

So began a 25-year reign in which he produced three great teams, all different in character but reflecting his desire to create and entertain. In his time with United they won five League Championships, the FA Cup twice (from four finals), the FA Youth Cup six times, five of them on the trot as he fashioned the Busby Babes, and achieved crowning glory in 1968 with the winning of the European Cup. He was never naive in pursuit of honours, either on the field or in the transfer jungle, but he always set responsible standards. Busby took the appalling tragedy of Munich at both personal and club level with a quiet fortitude. The heady delights of football victory and the gloomy setbacks were alike treated with an admirable calm and sense of proportion.

His great gift was as a leader and manager of men. Obviously, he was a perceptive judge of players and a shrewd tactician, but he always had the additional advantage of being able to inspire. He enjoyed the respect of players, rather like the old type of headmaster. Some say Busby failed to handle George Best; but he did get nearly 500 first-team games from him – and some priceless performances – and it's quite possible that without Busby in the background Best might have burnt out in half the time he did.

Honours have been heaped upon him. He was awarded the CBE in 1958, he was given the Freedom of Manchester in 1967 and he was knighted the following year. Pope Paul conferred one of the highest civil awards in the Roman Catholic Church on him in 1972 by making him a Knight Commander of St Gregory

the Great. When he retired as manager of Manchester United in 1970 he was made a director and then the club's first president, a position he still holds. Over the years he has changed little; certainly success never swayed him. As Geoffrey Green, then a distinguished reporter for *The Times*, so admirably expressed it: 'Now he is a legendary eminence who has always been approachable and modest, with time to spare for everybody. It is a humility born of early struggle and given only to those who found the answer when the way ahead looked bleak and life itself seemed an insuperable mountain.'

Even after retirement, life posed great tests for Sir Matt and he again was not found wanting. For some years now he has supported his invalid wife with daily visits although Lady Busby has been unable to recognise him. Few outside his family guessed at the strength he needed, but then it took a strong man to wake the slumbering giant that was Manchester United when he was appointed manager in 1945. It must have been a daunting prospect as he looked at a bombed ground and examined the books.

United were £15,000 overdrawn at the bank, and it was impossible to play at Old Trafford. The dressing rooms were derelict and there were no facilities for training. The club offices were lodged at the nearby premises of the chairman. Matches had to be played at Maine Road, the ground of neighbouring Manchester City. Of the players on the books, some were still away in the services.

The first great team

The new manager wasted little time, and right from the start showed the character and judgement that eventually became legendary. To start with, he insisted on a five-year contract when

the chairman, James Gibson, offered him one of three years. Gibson was a man used to having his own way, but he gave Busby what he wanted . . . time to create a team using the ideas that had been simmering in his mind during his days as a player with Manchester City and as a Scottish international.

His next move was to don a tracksuit and go out on the field with his players. In those days this was revolutionary. As Johnny Carey, the captain when Busby was demobbed as a company sergeant-major, and later a manager himself, explains: 'When I joined United, Scott Duncan, with spats and a red rose in his buttonhole, typified a soccer manager. But here was the new boss playing with his team in training, showing what he wanted and how to do it. He was ahead of his time.'

Players on the books included Carey, Henry Cockburn, Jack Rowley, Johnny Morris, Stan Pearson, Allenby Chilton, Joe Walton, Charlie Mitten, John Aston and goalkeeper Jack Crompton. Some say Busby was lucky to start with such a promising nucleus of established players, but many a manager has taken over as good a squad and not made anything of it. He also soon showed the shrewdness in the transfer market that stood him in good stead over the years. He paid £4,000 to Glasgow Celtic in February 1946 for Jimmy 'Brittle Bones' Delaney, a fast right-winger. Delaney was no youngster and with a history of injuries he was regarded as past his best. But Busby saw something that others had missed, and as Carey says: 'It was like fitting the last piece in a jig-saw to complete the picture.'

Behind the scenes he had also made a good signing. Jimmy Murphy, a player in his day with West Bromwich and Wales, was brought to Old Trafford as assistant manager after a friendship formed during the war abroad, and he became

Above left: Matt Busby, his wife Jean and son Sandy at Buckingham Palace for the CBE award ceremony in 1958. The honour came in the Birthday Honours in June shortly after the manager's return home from hospital in Munich

Above: Matt Busby and his wife Jean arrive at Manchester Town Hall for the ceremony which granted the Manchester United manager the Freedom of the City in 1967 . . . a fitting recognition of his 21 years' service to football

Right: Matt Busby (right) gets in a header in a training session with Johnny Carey (number 3) and Henry Cockburn. Busby, home from the war, put his old playing gear back on and worked out on the pitch with his men as a coach as well as their manager. He moved soccer management into an entirely different era. The old style manager was mostly chairborne and wore suit and spats

Above: Old Trafford was blitzed on 11 March 1941, the main stand destroyed along with the dressing rooms and offices. By the end of the war there was even a small tree growing on the terraces. The club made a claim to the War Damage Commission for reconstruction, but it was not until August 1949 that they were able to play football again at Old Trafford. In the meantime they made an arrangement with Manchester City, hiring their neighbours' ground for around £5,000 a year with a percentage of the gate money also going to the Maine Road club

Busby's able lieutenant, the hard man to complement his own more fatherly role in an outstanding football partnership. Busby also showed an early appreciation of tactics, making international full-backs from modest inside-forwards John Aston and Johnny Carey.

When he took over the job in October 1945 United were 16th in the table but by the end of the season they had risen to fourth with a team which read:

Crompton, Hamlett, Chilton, Aston, Whalley, Cockburn, Delaney, Pearson, Rowley, Buckle, Wrigglesworth.

United were on their way, and the following season, 1946-47, as football returned to a national league instead of being divided into northern and southern leagues, they finished second, one point behind Liverpool, in the Championship. Busby's talented collection of experienced players, many of them seasoned by life in the services, were runners-up for two more years.

That was impressive consistency, even if they did miss out on the Championship itself. They were not to be denied a deserved honour, though, giving Busby his first trophy by winning the FA Cup in 1947-48. The 4–2 victory over Blackpool at Wembley was regarded as a classic final. United dominated the competition right from the start and reached Wembley by scoring 18 goals in five ties, indicating their great attacking strength.

They had a magnificent forward line. Jimmy Delaney played on the right wing with Charlie Mitten, one of the sweetest strikers of the ball in the game, operating on the left wing to give the

Reds a two-winged attack that was normal in those days and is only just back in fashion. The dashing Jack Rowley was a traditional centre-forward with a fierce shot. He was flanked by the delightfully skilful Stan Pearson at inside-left and the clever Johnny Morris at inside-right. The most commanding figure of all featured further back in the team at right-back – the captain, Johnny Carey, an influential man both on and off the field.

In the third round of the Cup United played at Villa Park and found themselves a goal down without touching the ball. Scoring after only 13

Left: Sir Matt Busby and Jimmy Murphy (seen here shortly before their retirement) formed one of the most effective partnerships in football management. Busby, a Scot, and Murphy, a Welshman, were quite different characters, but they shared a common ideal in football and the sum of their work roused the slumbering giant that was Manchester United. They worked together from just after the Second World War until they retired, still a partnership, in 1971

Below: One of Matt Busby's early teams. Back row: Walter Crickmer (secretary), John Aston, Tom Curry (trainer), Jack Warner, Joe Walton, Jack Crompton, Allenby Chilton, Jimmy Murphy (assistant manager), Billy McGlen, Matt Busby (manager). Sitting: Jack Rowley, Ronnie Burke, Johnny Morris, Johnny Carey, Johnny Hanlon, Stan Pearson, Charlie Mitten

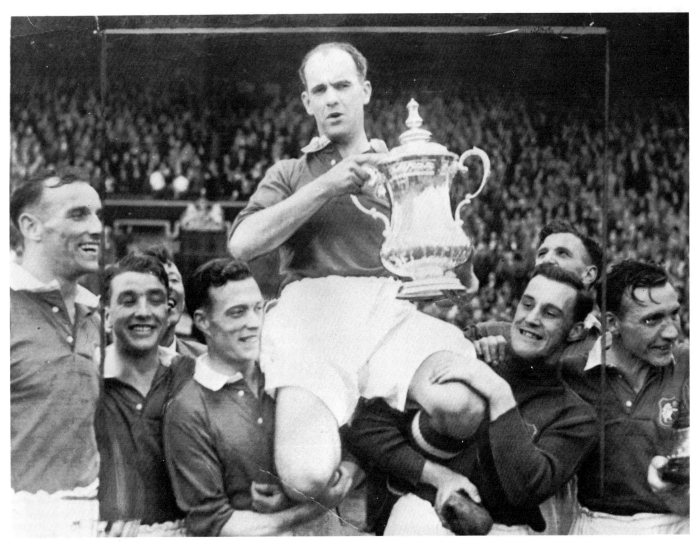

Above: Johnny Carey is hoisted shoulder high by his team-mates after leading United to victory in the FA Cup competition of 1948. The genial Irishman enjoyed many successes, including the captaincy of the Rest of the World when they played against Great Britain in 1947. He was voted Footballer of the Year in 1949, the season he skippered the Republic of Ireland to a notable 2–0 win against England at Goodison Park

seconds was, perhaps, the worst thing Villa could have done, for United's reply was to produce such devastating football that they were leading 5–1 by the interval. Villa creditably fought back in the rain and mud to cut United's lead to 5–4, but United still had the last word, with a goal from Pearson giving them a dramatic 6–4 victory.

United beat Liverpool 3–0, Charlton 2–0, Preston 4–1 and Derby County in the semi-final 3–1, with a hat-trick from Pearson. They arrived at Wembley for the final against Blackpool full of confidence but respecting an opposition that included players like Stanley Matthews, Stan Mortensen and Harry Johnston.

Blackpool gave early notice of their intentions. After only 12 minutes Mortensen broke clean through and was heading for goal when he was brought down by centre-half Allenby Chilton. He fell into the penalty area and Eddie Shimwell beat Jack Crompton with his spot kick. United were a shade lucky with their equaliser in the 28th minute, despite their pressure. For it was a misunderstanding between Blackpool goalkeeper Joe Robinson and centre-half Eric Hayward that let Rowley step in to walk the ball over the line. It was an evenly contested match with Blackpool taking the lead again in the 35th minute with a goal hammered home by Mortensen.

Blackpool led 2–1 until the 69th minute, soaking up a whole stream of punishing United raids. Then their defence cracked under the pressure with Rowley heading a free-kick from Morris into the roof of the net. The game was now 2–2 with both teams redoubling their attacking efforts. Crompton saved brilliantly from Mortensen and then within seconds the ball was in the other net to put United in front. Crompton's clearance was switched by Anderson to Pearson who scored off the post from 25 yards.

It was the 'killer' goal and three minutes later United clinched victory. Anderson shot from a long way out and with the help of a deflection Robinson was wrong-footed to give United a memorable 4–2 win. The team was:

Crompton, Carey, Aston, Anderson, Chilton, Cockburn, Delaney, Morris, Rowley, Pearson, Mitten.

The old sweats still had another shot in their locker, and after finishing runners-up in the League three years on the trot, then fourth followed by another second, the 'nearly men' finally cracked it. They won the Championship in 1951-52, four points ahead of Spurs. They were mean at the back and prolific up front, with 30 goals from Jack Rowley and 22 from Stan Pearson. The team which clinched the title read:

Allen, McNulty, Aston, Carey, Chilton, Cockburn, Berry, Downie, Rowley, Pearson, Byrne.

Rowley opened the Championship season in spanking form, scoring hat-tricks in the first two games for a 3–3 draw at West Bromwich and a 4–2 win at home against Middlesbrough. United weren't invincible, as they showed with a 1–0 defeat at Bolton in September. Then they lost successive games at the end of the month at Tottenham and at home against Preston.

Portsmouth were the early pace-setters, but they fell away to leave United, Spurs and Arsenal looking the strongest teams. Arsenal were, in fact, chasing a League and FA Cup double. They went all the way to Wembley, where they lost 1–0 to Newcastle after an early injury to their right-back Wally Barnes. In the League they hit Championship form with an unbeaten run from just after Christmas until the end of April. United matched them except for another double defeat in successive matches, losing at Huddersfield and again to Portsmouth.

United, Spurs and Arsenal were almost neck and neck on the last lap, with United having their noses just in front. The destiny of the title was decided on the last game of the season, with a grand finale between two of the top three teams. Arsenal came to Old Trafford on 26 April as outsiders because, thanks to the scoring prowess of Rowley and Pearson, they had an inferior goal average. In fact they needed to win 7–0 to become champions, which of course was asking a lot. In the event United established themselves as worthy champions by running rampant for a 6–1 victory.

What a shoot-out! Naturally, the scorers were led by a hat-trick from Rowley, with two goals coming from Pearson and one from Roger Byrne.

So United finished on 57 points, with Spurs and Arsenal level on points, four behind. Tottenham took second place on goal average. The big difference was in the scoring. United had notched a magnificent 95 as opposed to 76 from Spurs and 80 by Arsenal. It was a worthy climax for what was still largely the first post-war team. It was a fitting peak for them after coming so close for five years. And the first League Championship for Manchester United for 41 years established Matt Busby in the record books as a manager of style and perception.

Jack Rowley

Busby's team was packed with men not just of ability but also of character . . . people like Jack Rowley who was not nicknamed 'The Gunner' for nothing. For this man gunned his shots on the football field with the kind of ferocity and accuracy he had used as an anti-tank gunner with the South Staffordshire infantry. Perhaps for the fans of those days his two occupations as a gunner on and off the field made an obvious nickname. We don't know how many tanks he hit as part of the invasion force in France during his six-and-a-half years in the army, but he certainly made a habit of hitting the net as a footballer.

Until Dennis Viollet came along a few years later Rowley held the United League scoring record for a season with his 30 goals in 1951-52. Overall, he scored 175 goals in 359 League appearances, which is a remarkable record when you consider that the war deprived him of six of his peak years as a player. Not that he stopped scoring during the war. He played as a 'guest' for Spurs, Wolves and Distillery in Ireland among other clubs, and it's war-time football that provides him with one of his most cherished memories. He recalls: 'I played for Spurs one week and scored seven, and then a few days later I got eight out of eight for Wolves.'

Jack dominated the scoring in the post-war years. He hit two in the 1948 FA Cup Final win against Blackpool and he was in fact the team's top marksman in each of the first four seasons after the war. His record season helped win the Championship and he thrilled the supporters from the time he scored those hat-tricks in the first two games.

Rowley won six caps, playing in four different positions for England, with his highspot the scoring of four goals against Northern Ireland in 1949. His shot was reckoned to be the hardest of his day, a finish in keeping with the strong, aggressive style of the traditional centre-forward of the time.

Perhaps it is because of this physical nature of his game that if he is watching a match these days it is likely to be just down the road from his home in Shaw, Oldham, on the touchline at the local Rugby Union ground, or as a guest at Swinton Rugby League ground.

'I am still interested in soccer, but it's convenient to go three minutes down the road to watch the rugby. I like the way they take the knocks and shake them off and later are the best of pals in the bar,' he explains. 'I was always hard, but fair, as a player, and I see that these days more in rugby.'

Born in Wolverhampton, he was a junior at his local club under the legendary Major Frank Buckley, but made his League debut playing for Bournemouth. United signed him for £3,000 in 1937. He was soon among the goals, scoring four out of five against Swansea to help United win promotion to the First Division on the eve of the war.

Jack played for ten years after the war and then joined Plymouth as player-manager for a couple of seasons. His management career saw him twice at Oldham and with Ajax in Amsterdam, Wrexham and Bradford. During his second spell with Oldham he took a local post office and newsagency which became his job when he left the soccer scene until his retirement in the 1980s.

Stan Pearson

Stan Pearson, the other half of the high-scoring partnership, was the perfect foil for Rowley. They often say strikers are born in pairs, and these two players certainly complemented each other.

Stan Pearson was one of the most gifted inside forwards to play for United in post 1945 football. He struck a particularly effective partnership with Jack Rowley, and together they formed one of the highest scoring strike forces in football. Salford born, Jack joined the club before the war and returned with a number of his colleagues to provide Matt Busby with his first successful team

Pearson was the more subtle, and created a great many of Rowley's goals, while at the same time he himself profited from the big man's more forceful style. He was a lethal finisher as well as the traditional inside-forward of that period, good on the ball and skilful, with a deceptive body swerve. He made 345 League and FA Cup appearances, scoring 149 goals, a tremendous scoring rate. As with Rowley, the war took six years out of his United career.

Pearson was a Salford schoolboy who joined the club at the age of 15 in 1936. He made his debut at the age of 17 in a 7–1 win at Chesterfield, and he scored in each of the next two games. But he had only two seasons before the war interrupted normal football. He served in the Second/Fourth South Lancashires, ending up in India where he played in a British Army touring team with Dennis Compton to entertain the troops after the Japanese had been pushed back in Burma. Incidentally, Johnny Morris, another of United's post-war stars at inside forward, was touring India in another 'Select' side around the same time. One by one, United's soldier footballers came home after the war to play for Sergeant-Major Busby, and Stan Pearson remembers it well.

'For two or three seasons leading up to the Championship, the forward line picked itself. We all got to know each other so well that instinctively we knew what was going to happen next. For instance, if Johnny Aston had the ball at left-back I would come towards him, and I knew without looking that if I slipped it straight, Jack Rowley would be moving for it. He would then push it out to Charlie Mitten on the left wing and in seconds we had the ball in front of goal. They talk about one-touch football these days as if it is something new, but we were doing it in 1948, and in my view no team has done it better.'

Stan signed for Bury in 1954 after a 17-year association with United. He later played for Chester and managed them. Finally, he settled at Prestbury in Cheshire, running the local post office and newsagent's shop.

Johnny Carey

United were a star-studded team in that era, but they had one major, influential character, the captain, Johnny Carey. Carey took Busby's philosophy of attacking football out to the pitch. He had joined United in 1936 from the Dublin club, St James' Gate, for the modest sum of £250 after being spotted by Louis Rocca, a scout who was one of the founding fathers of the latter-day United.

Rocca had gone to Dublin to watch an entirely different player. It is said that Carey was playing only his third real game of soccer, but his natural ability shone through and Rocca quickly made arrangements for him to come to Old Trafford.

United played Johnny Carey in every position except on the wing. This included one game in goal after the usual goalkeeper had been taken ill on an away trip. He started as an inside-forward, made his name at right-back and then became a commanding wing-half. Louis Rocca brought him over from Dublin in 1936 for £250 and he didn't retire until 1953, when he was given a special vote of appreciation by the Old Trafford directors

Carey was 17 at the time and made his League debut the following year. He started as an inside-left, became an outstanding right-back, played centre-half, and finished his career as a polished wing-half. In fact he played in every position except wing for United, including a game in goal when Jack Crompton was taken ill on the day of a match. In all he played 344 League and FA Cup games spanning 17 years with the club. He would have made many more appearances for the club but for army service in Italy during the war. A fine international, he had the distinction of playing for both Northern Ireland and the Republic. Perhaps his greatest honour was captaining the Rest of Europe against Great Britain in 1947. Two years later he was voted Footballer of the Year by the Football Writers' Association.

Carey retired from playing in 1953 and started in management as coach at Blackburn. He was promoted to manager there before managing Everton, Leyton Orient, Nottingham Forest and Blackburn again. A genial, pipe-smoking man, he was known as 'Gentleman John' and as a manager the gist of his team talks would be to urge his players to 'fizz it around'.

He ended his managerial days by returning to Old Trafford as a part-time scout while working in the borough treasurer's office at Sale, Cheshire. Later golf took over from football to fill his sporting interests, though he says: 'I still think football is a terrific game. I perhaps wish people would accept defeat with a little more grace sometimes, and I would like to see players allowed to express themselves more, but soccer is super, the best game in the world.'

Jack Crompton

Another of the stalwarts in the post-war period was Jack Crompton, who joined the club in 1944 from the local works side, Goslings, having played for Oldham as an amateur. He was in Busby's first team and was prominent in the 1948 FA Cup win. His highlight was stopping a piledriver from Stan Mortensen when the score was 2–2 and then making the long clearance which saw Stan Pearson streak away to score.

Jack was born in 1921 and United was his only club as a professional. He made about 200 League appearances before joining Luton Town as their trainer in 1956. Just over a year later he returned to Old Trafford as trainer to help Jimmy Murphy in the crisis of Munich.

He served Matt Busby well as both player and staff man, and admits that in the early days he did not appreciate the impact Busby was going to make on the soccer world.

'He was such a quiet, unassuming and modest man that at first you didn't know the strength,' says Jack. 'The first thing I remember he did was to change the them and us of management and players to we, and he kept it that way. Naturally, when he first took charge he had to

fight to make his presence felt and he had still to win the great respect he enjoyed later.

'I think he had the sympathy of the players as someone fresh from our ranks in his first job as a manager and I am sure he would agree that the players were patient and understanding. But, of course, a manager must command more than that from his players and though his outstanding ability was apparent after only a few months, I think he was still feeling his way up to the 1948 Cup final win. Ironically, it was this first major trophy success, evidence to all and sundry that he was a man destined to do big things in football, that brought the one and only crisis between players and club that I can remember.

'We went on strike a few months after the final for something we thought we should have. Details don't matter now and I only mention the incident to show that he did not win his place as a master manager without his share of problems. It was finally sorted out though it took a little while before the trouble was forgotten. It was a big test for a comparatively new boss and it was probably only due to his ability as a manager of men that the problem was finally compromised.

'No doubt he had many a struggle to get his way at the board meetings, though as a player I could feel his presence becoming more widely felt all the time. I realised that he had really won his battle when another challenging problem arose in 1949 as we were heading for the Cup final again.

'Johnny Morris, our talented inside-forward was giving the Boss some headaches and after dropping him for one Cup-tie he had him transferred to Derby. To my mind, if Johnny had played we would have reached the final again. Naturally, the players thought the club should have kept him. I thought so, too, at the time. But this is where you live and learn and time proved that the manager was right to stick to his beliefs. Johnny Morris was transferred on a matter of principle. Matt must have had a tremendous fight with his own conscience and with other people before taking such a drastic step. I can appreciate now that he was right and it is this almost uncanny foresight and judgement, even if it involved an unpopular decision, that kept Manchester United at the front in post-war football.

'He was accurate in his assessment of players and always thoughtful. I remember our first flight to the Continent after the Munich disaster. After we had landed at Amsterdam, Bill Foulkes telephoned his wife to let her know we had arrived safely. Teresa Foulkes already knew. Busby had been on the phone to tell her. You can perhaps appreciate the concern behind this phone message when you stop to think about the aftermath of Munich.

'As a manager he had a tremendous memory for players' strengths and failings. He never lost the common touch, the knack of understanding, and being in touch with players. He never forgot a player, past or present, and his memory for people's names is uncanny. There are many facets to the character of Matt Busby.'

Jack Crompton later tried management himself at Barrow and Preston. A keen YMCA member in his youth, he was always fitness minded, and in the mid-1980s he was still coaching youngsters at Manchester's splendid Platt Lane sports complex used by Manchester City. To prove how young at heart he remains, his big present on his retirement birthday was a course of flying lessons to help him achieve his lifelong ambition to be a pilot.

The 1951-52 Championship side

Jack played only a handful of games in the Championship year after losing his place to Reg Allen, the first goalkeeper to attract a five-figure transfer fee. Busby paid Queen's Park Rangers £11,000 for him and he held the first-team job down for two seasons, including the Championship year, before he was overtaken by illness which finished his career.

John Anderson had gone from wing-half to prompt the masterly switch of Carey to form the dominating half-back line of Carey on the right, Allenby Chilton at centre-half and Henry Cockburn on the left. Tom McNulty took Carey's place at right-back with John Aston still on the

left, though starting to concede that place to Roger Byrne.

It was the balance and blend of the half-back line which was the key to the way the team took charge in so many games and managed to supply their marvellous front runners and wingers with quality service.

Henry Cockburn, recruited like Crompton from the local works team Goslings, which had become something of a United nursery, was the typical little guy who made up for lack of inches with fire and determination. He also had class and timing, which meant he often outjumped taller men for the ball.

He made his first-team debut in war-time football and he was there for the first League game after the war in a 2–1 win against Grimsby at Maine Road. He was still working in an Oldham mill and had played only a handful of League games when he was selected for the first of his 13 England caps. At international level he was part of another famous half-back line, featuring with Neil Franklin and Billy Wright. For United he played in the 1948 Cup-winning team and in the 1951-52 Championship side. In all he spent ten years at Old Trafford before moving in 1954 to Bury. Later he worked as a coach for Ian Greaves, the former United full-back, at Huddersfield.

Manchester at the start of the 1952–53 season complete with the League trophy and FA Charity Shield which they won by beating Newcastle United 4–2. Jack Rowley scored twice with the other goals from Johnny Downie and a young Roger Byrne. Back row: Tom Curry (trainer), Walter Crickmer (secretary), Alan Gibson (director), Dr W McLean (director), George Whittaker (director), Bill Petherbridge (director), Matt Busby (manager). Middle: Johnny Downie, Jack Rowley, John Aston, Reg Allen, Allenby Chilton, Roger Byrne, Stan Pearson. Front: Johnny Berry, Johnny Carey, Henry Cockburn, Tommy McNulty. They were champions for the first time under Matt Busby in 1951–52

The pillar of the team and the kind of player Matt Busby always preferred at centre-half was the remarkable Allenby Chilton, a man who played before the war yet lasted to see the Busby Babes settling in around him. After being signed from Seaham Colliery in the north-east, he made his League debut against Charlton in September 1939. War was declared the following day and sliced out seven years of his United career.

Chilton fought in France and was wounded at Normandy, and he was nearly 28 before he was able to resume his life with United. But he played in the first team for another ten seasons, with Busby always claiming that he played his best football in his later years. In all, he played nearly 400 League and Cup games and he was the only player ever-present in the Championship side, not that that was anything special to Chilton, who was as durable as he was big and strong. Towards the end he took over the captaincy from Johnny Carey, and when he lost his place to Mark Jones in 1955 he had achieved a club record of 166 consecutive League appearances.

Chilton played twice for England; he would have played more often if Busby had been manager of the national side. After Old Trafford, he led Grimsby to the Third Division North Championship as player-manager and then had spells in management with Wigan and Hartlepool.

Johnny Carey has been discussed already. His switch to right-half with Tommy McNulty

coming in at right-back was a masterly move in the second half of the Championship season.

Up front, Rowley and Pearson were still the scoring stars but Busby had brought in new wingers and changed one of the inside-forwards.

After sacrificing Johnny Morris from the 1948 team on a point of principle, selling him for a British record fee of £24,500 to Derby County, Busby bought Johnny Downie for a club record £18,000 from Bradford Park Avenue in 1949. Downie had established himself in the team the season before the Championship, and he is perhaps not so well remembered as some of the other players of that era. He simply wasn't there as long as most of the others, but he certainly played his part in bringing the title to Old Trafford after such a long absence, and he scored 35 goals in the 110 League appearances he made in his five seasons with the Reds. Later he played for Luton, Hull City, Mansfield and Darlington, yet another Scotsman with a good career in English football.

The 1948 wingers had also gone by 1951-52. Jimmy Delaney had been given something of an Indian summer when Matt Busby made him his first signing in 1946, and he played a total of 164 League games plus 19 in the FA Cup spread over five seasons. But there was still a lot more football left in him, despite his spate of injuries before coming down from Scotland. At the end of 1950 he went back home to Scotland to join Aberdeen. Later he played for Derry City to win an Irish FA Cup medal and complete a unique

Jimmy Delaney shooting for goal against Weymouth in the third round of the FA Cup in January 1950, when he scored in a 4–0 home win. Delaney was Matt Busby's first signing after becoming manager at the end of the Second World War. He was tagged Brittle Bones because of a number of broken limbs and he was generally regarded as being past his best, but he proved a brilliant buy at £5,000 from Glasgow Celtic. He was a speedy winger who played a key role in helping to win the FA Cup in 1948, United's first post-war success

hat-trick of winners' medals. In 1937, when he was with Glasgow Celtic, he had been in their Scottish Cup-winning team, and while with United he collected a medal with the 1948 team. Derry in 1954 gave him his third medal, and a couple of years later, at the age of 40, he was close to picking up a fourth. He was player-manager of Cork Athletic when they reached the final of the FA of Ireland Cup in the Republic, but this time he was on the losing side against Shamrock Rovers, despite Cork leading 2–0 at one point.

Delaney finally hung up his boots back home in Scotland with Highland League club Elgin City after 23 years as a player. Martin Edwards, the current chairman of Manchester United, went to Scotland in 1987 to talk to Delaney, the one remaining member of the 1948 Cup team he hadn't met. He was introduced by the United manager, Alex Ferguson, who had played football in his early days with Jimmy's son Pat. One of the happy outcomes of the meeting was a sportsmen's dinner at Old Trafford later in the year with 'Brittlebones', turned 70, the guest of honour among a reunion of virtually every member of Matt Busby's first honours team.

The transfer of Delaney came soon after the departure of his fellow winger, Charlie Mitten, though he left for a quite different reason. Charlie, one of the great characters of all time at the club, joined straight from school locally in 1936 and was just about ready for his League debut when war broke out. He made war-time appearances for the Reds as well as playing for Tranmere, Aston Villa and Chelsea. His debut proper came in the first League fixture after hostilities and he was one of the 'famous five' forwards who helped win the 1948 Cup. Always a speedy winger, he gave superb service from the left and he scored a lot of goals himself as well.

Then, in the summer of 1950, he became one of the 'rebels' of English football who rocked the boat to try for fame and fortune, especially fortune, in Colombia. United were on an end-of-season tour in South America when Charlie was approached by a representative of the Bogota club, Sante Fe, to play in Colombia. There was talk of a £5,000 signing-on fee, a lot of money in those days, plus wages of £60 a week, four times as much as the maximum pay at home. Neil Franklin, the England and Stoke centre-half, threw in his lot with the South American adventure, perhaps influencing men like Mitten.

Busby counselled caution, pointing out that playing outside FIFA jurisdiction would mean suspension at home. Charlie gave it a year, and with a lot of the promises unfulfilled returned to England. He was duly banned and had to be transfer-listed by United. After completing his suspension, he joined Fulham for five years, subsequently becoming player-manager of Mansfield.

The whole affair was a sad blow for United fans, who saw Charlie in their colours for only four seasons. His tally of 50 goals in 142 League appearances reflected his ability as a high-scoring winger. In all, he played nearly 400 League games. After Mansfield he became manager of Newcastle United where it seems he indulged his passion for dog racing. There are colourful stories of him at St James's Park, such as his having a hot line from his office to the dog track, and occasionally bringing in his dogs for medical treatment at the football ground!

Mitten later worked as a manager at Manchester's White City dog track. In more recent years he turned to sports promotion and, holding a UEFA licence, he arranged soccer tours, with Manchester United among his customers. His two sons, John and Charles, both played junior football for United.

So with both Delaney and Mitten gone, Busby had need of new wingers. He bought Harry McShane, a player who later became the club announcer and then a scout, from Bolton, and he also played Ernie Bond. But four games into the Championship season he was still casting around, when he recalled a match the previous season against Birmingham City. He remembered the performance of a little winger who had scored an outstanding goal against them at Old Trafford.

Busby swooped for Johnny Berry at a cost of £25,000 and was delighted with his capture. Berry's debut against Bolton ended in defeat, but he soon settled down to solve the right-wing position with his tricky, ball-playing ability, which also saw him net half-a-dozen goals. Berry made the position his own for the next seven seasons, making nearly 300 League and Cup appearances for 43 goals until he was severely injured in the Munich crash. He was critically ill with head injuries for some weeks and made only a slow recovery. There was never any chance of him playing again. He returned to his native Aldershot where he opened a sports shop with his brother Peter, a former Crystal Palace and Peterborough player. After that he worked in the parts warehouse of a television company.

By the end of the Championship season the new outside-left was Roger Byrne. He had made his League debut midway through the campaign at left-back but was switched to the left-wing with devastating effect, playing in the last six games and scoring seven times. Roger, later to become a distinguished captain, was the first of the home-grown kids to come pushing through the ranks as the Busby Babes concept gathered force behind the scenes and at junior level.

The season after the Championship Roger Byrne returned after a few games to left-back, where he played with great distinction using his instinct as a winger to attack down his flank. His flair took him into the England team at left-back in 1954 and he won 33 successive caps until he was a victim of the Munich disaster. He was only 28 when he died. His wife, Joy, gave birth to their son, Roger, eight months after his death.

In all Byrne made nearly 300 League and

Cup appearances involving three Championships. Few who were there at the time will forget, though, his dramatic impact on the wing to help clinch that first vital title in 1952.

Manchester United's achievement, perhaps because of its then rarity, was considered worthy of a tribute from the *Manchester Guardian* in their esteemed leader column, usually reserved for weightier matters. The leader writer eulogised:

'After an interval of forty-one years, Manchester United have regained the Championship of the Football League. The title has never been better earned.

'Not only has the team, in the five seasons before this one, finished second four times and fourth once in the League and won the FA Cup; it has been captained, managed and directed in a way that is a lesson to many others. J. Carey, the captain in this period, has been a model footballer – technically efficient, thanks to hard work; a fighter to the last, without ever forgetting that he is a sportsman; a steadier of the younger and inexperienced, an inspirer of the older and tiring, and at all times the most modest of men, though he has won every football honour open to him.

'M. Busby, the manager, has shown himself as great a coach as he was a player, with an uncannily brilliant eye for young local players' possibilities, whether in their usual or in other positions; a believer in the certainty of good football's eventual reward, and a kindly, yet, when necessary, firm father of his family of players.

'Between them they have built up a club spirit which is too rare in these days, a spirit which enables men to bear cheerfully personal and team disappointments and to ignore personal opportunities to shine for the good of the whole.

'Moreover, by eschewing the dangerous policy of going into the transfer market whenever a weakness develops and giving their chances instead to the many local citizens on the club's books they have made it likely that this club will persist, since the club today is a Manchester one

not in name only but in fact as far as most of its players are concerned.

'Manager and captain could never have brought about this happy state of affairs had they not had through these years such full authority and support from the Board of Directors as must be the envy of many other officials in all parts of the country.'

The emergence of the Babes

After winning the Championship in 1951-52, Busby naturally kicked off the following season with his winning team, but it was soon obvious that the first great post-war side had passed its peak. Six of the first 11 matches were lost, and Busby realised he had to start drafting in new players, and making changes. The situation did not take him altogether by surprise because he had already laid the foundations for the future.

Always in his mind had been the creation of a team based on youngsters he had taken from school and brought up in his ways. Right from the start he had paid a lot of attention to this aspect of the club and he had taken great care to appoint the right kind of men to make a success of his plan. The result was that in addition to having Jimmy Murphy as his right-hand man, he had Joe Armstrong busy signing the best schoolboy players he could find, with Northern Ireland and the Republic of Ireland proving rich recruiting areas.

Bob Bishop and Bob Harper in Belfast and Billy Behan in Dublin, three grand football men, didn't miss much. And when it came to persuading anxious parents to let their sons come to Old Trafford, Joe Armstrong was a charmer but honest and sincere with it.

Left: Roger Byrne clutching the cherished championship trophy after leading the Reds to success. He won three championship medals in his seven seasons of first-team football with Manchester United. He made his League debut in the November of season 1951–52 to share in the club's first post-war success as champions. Then he went on to become an integral part of the Busby Babes as their captain, leading the youngsters to the championship in two successive seasons before his tragic and untimely death at Munich. He won 33 consecutive caps for England

Below: Bill Foulkes, one of United's longest serving players, flanked on the right by his mentor, Bert Whalley (right), and assistant manager Jimmy Murphy (left), another of the highly influential figures bringing on the reserves at United. Foulkes had to play for two years as an amateur before he was invited to join the professional ranks in 1951. But he was always made to feel part of the club, and in his early days when he was away in the army on national service coach Bert Whalley used to write to him regularly commenting on his performances

Then Busby had Bert Whalley as a dedicated, gifted coach and Tom Curry as the kindly trainer. Helped by enthusiastic part-timers like Jack Pauline, they put great emphasis on grooming the youngsters. They had good material to work with, and they made sure the finished product had excellence. United dominated the game in this area, as can be seen in their FA Youth Cup record. They won the competition for five successive seasons, starting from its inception in the 1952-53 season, the year the first team started to come apart.

The result was that towards the end of that rather troubled season players such as David Pegg, Jeff Whitefoot, John Doherty, Jackie Blanchflower, Bill Foulkes, Dennis Viollet and Duncan Edwards started to get the occasional game.

Busby also went into the transfer market to pay £29,999 to Barnsley for Tommy Taylor. The team finished a modest eighth, but Busby knew he had talent in the making. He made his decisive move in October the following season. Busby explained: 'We played a friendly at Kilmarnock and I played half-a-dozen of the youngsters. They did well and we won 3–0. Then, as I walked the golf course in the next few days, I pondered whether this was the moment to play them all in the League team. One or two had already come into the side, and I decided that I would go the whole way with the youngsters.'

This meant that Edwards, Viollet and Blanchflower squeezed out three more of the veterans to give the team a more youthful look. Most things in football have to be worked for, and the Busby Babes didn't find overnight success. They finished only fourth in that 1953-54 season, and then, with more youngsters

like Albert Scanlon, Mark Jones and Billy Whelan occasionally drafted in, the best they could do in 1954-55 was fifth place.

But then everything began to click and the Busby Babes hit the headlines. They took the First Division by storm in 1955-56, winning the Championship by a devastating 11 points from Blackpool and with an average age of barely 22. By this time precociously talented youngsters were rolling out of the Busby academy. Eddie Colman, whose shimmy of the hips was said to send even the crowd the wrong way, had forced his way into the team while top-class reserves like Ian Greaves and Geoff Bent were ready in case there were any injuries.

The team which played most for the 1955-56 title lined up:

Wood, Foulkes, Byrne, Whitefoot then Colman, Jones, Edwards, Berry, Blanchflower or Doherty or Whelan, Taylor, Viollet, Pegg. Ian Greaves, Albert Scanlon and Colin Webster also played.

John Aston, who later became a chief scout at Old Trafford, was in both the 1948 Cup and 1952 League-winning teams, and was one of the men who had had to make way for youth.

'It was very disappointing for the players who had brought the Championship to Old Trafford for the first time in 40 years to have to give way to new men,' he says. 'But we were not blind to the fact that the Boss had also been busy creating a tremendously successful youth team, winning the FA Youth Cup five times off the reel when it was started.

'Matt Busby had also been at the club long enough to have established himself as a very far-seeing and shrewd manager. He had won the respect of all of us which meant that it was easier for him to put over these new ideas. We just

Left to right: Duncan Edwards, Ian Greaves, Ray Wood, Dennis Viollet, Mark Jones, David Pegg and Eddie Colman celebrate the victory against Blackpool which gave them the League championship in 1956. The achievement was remarkable in that it had come so soon after winning the title in 1952 with an almost entirely rebuilt team. This was the first trophy for the sensational Busby Babes who had nearly all graduated through the junior teams at Old Trafford to fulfil Matt Busby's dream of fashioning a team in his own image from schoolboys

accepted the changes because when he said it was for the good of the club we knew that it was. For Matt Busby is an amazing man. He is kind, he is gentle, but he can also be very strong and firm. He treats everyone with respect and he in turn is greatly respected. It is this quality which enabled him to move from one successful era to another with a team that became the great Busby Babes.'

Only right-winger Johnny Berry and left-back Roger Byrne bridged the four-year transition from the 1951-52 Championship side to the 1955-56 Championship.

Ray Wood had taken over in goal from Allen by this time. United had signed him as a teenager from Darlington in 1949 and he gradually worked his way through to the first team after providing cover for Allen and Crompton. He played in all but one of the 1955-56 Championship games. He collected a second Championship medal the following season and was the central figure in the controversy with Peter McParland in the 1957 FA Cup final.

Just before the air crash Ray lost his place to new signing Harry Gregg. He recovered from the relatively minor injuries he suffered to play again, but he was forced to move on, playing for Huddersfield Town, Bradford City and Barnsley. Later he turned to coaching with great success in Cyprus, the Middle East and Africa. He won three caps for England.

Roger Byrne was at left-back, but with a new partner. Bill Foulkes had dug in at right-back with the kind of dour tenacity associated with his coalmining background. His father was a miner at St Helens, and Bill was also working at the pit when he was picked up by United as an amateur with Whiston Boys Club. He became a full-time professional and won a regular place in 1953, going on to become one of the club's greatest ever servants.

Foulkes lasted a long course, playing First Division football for 18 years, involving some 600 games for the club. He won just about everything in the course of his career: four Championship medals, an FA Cup winner's medal and he went on to win a 1968 European Cup medal. As a survivor of Munich he played an important part in bridging the gap between the Babes and later teams, at one point captaining the club. He was never regarded as one of the more skilful stars, but he had them all licked for staying power, as Allenby Chilton had before him, and like Chilton he played at centre-half later in his career.

After retiring as a player in 1970 Bill became a youth coach at Old Trafford. Then he played and managed in the United States and more recently in Norway. Such is the esteem of his old team-mates that they elected him the first chairman of the association of former Manchester United players.

Jeff Whitefoot started the season at right-half, and indeed won a Championship medal, but such was the competition for places that he was forced to concede to Eddie Colman. Whitefoot was a schoolboy international and he was only 16 when he was given his League debut in 1950. He was a brilliant, cultured wing-half, yet he played only 95 League and Cup games for United before being squeezed out by the stream of starlets coming through. He underlined his great ability by going on to play nearly 300 games for Nottingham Forest, and win an FA Cup medal with them.

There was no holding back Colman, though. 'Snake Hips' played the second half of the season at right-half, striking up an uncanny understanding with Duncan Edwards at left-half. They both loved to attack, which is probably why Busby went for the rocklike steadiness of Mark Jones between them at centre-half.

Mark was a traditional 'stopper', arriving as a schoolboy from Barnsley and fitting perfectly into the mould established by Allenby Chilton. Together Colman, Jones and Edwards formed one of the finest half-back lines ever assembled. All three were to die tragically young at Munich.

Duncan Edwards is probably the player mentioned most often as the best-ever footballer to wear a Manchester United shirt. Certainly Jimmy Murphy, assistant to Sir Matt Busby until the day they both retired, has not the slightest doubt in his mind.

'When I used to hear Muhammad Ali proclaim to the world that he was the greatest, I used to smile,' he says. 'You see, the greatest of them all was an English footballer named Duncan Edwards.

'If I shut my eyes I can see him now. Those pants hitched up, the wild leaps of boyish enthusiasm as he came running out of the tunnel, the tremendous power of his tackle – always fair but fearsome – the immense power on the ball. In fact the number of times he was robbed of the ball once he had it at his feet could be counted on one hand. He was a players' player. The greatest . . . there was only one and that was Duncan Edwards.'

Jimmy tells the story of when he was manager of Wales and preparing a team to play against Duncan Edwards and England. He carefully went through all the England players, detailing their strengths and weaknesses. Then, at the end of his team talk, Reg Davies, the Newcastle and Welsh inside-forward, said to Jimmy that he hadn't mentioned Edwards, the player probably marking him. Replied Murphy: 'There is nothing to say that would help us. Just keep out of his way, son.'

Duncan Edwards played his first League game for United at the age of 15 and 285 days, against Cardiff City at Old Trafford on Easter Monday 1953. During the next five years he became the youngest England international, making his debut at the age of 17 and 8 months in a 7–2 victory against Scotland at Wembley.

He won two Championship medals and played 19 times for England. He would have been a natural successor as captain to Billy Wright.

'From the first time I saw him as a boy of 14,' says Jimmy Murphy, 'he looked like and played with the assurance of a man, with legs like tree trunks, a deep and powerful chest and an unforgettable zest for the game. He played wing-half, centre-forward, inside-forward and centre-half with the consummate ease of a great player. He was never bothered where he played. He was quite simply a soccer Colossus.'

By 1955-56 the attack had also taken on a new look, and not every player had come from the youth ranks. The gap at centre-forward caused by the absence of Jack Rowley was filled by a man they found at Barnsley, Tommy Taylor.

United were not his only admirers. Jimmy Murphy says that the last time he saw him play at Barnsley there were so many managers and club chairmen there that he thought it was an extraordinary general meeting of the Football League. Altogether 20 clubs were chasing the 21-year-old forward, and Murphy says that the biggest problem was trying to persuade him he was good enough to play for Manchester United in the First Division.

'He had this mop of black hair and a perpetual smile on his face which prompted one sportswriter of the time, George Follows, to christen him "the smiling executioner",' says Murphy. 'He didn't really want to leave Barnsley where everyone knew him. Eventually Matt Busby's charm won him over, and convinced him that if he came to Old Trafford to link up with the youngsters we had produced ourselves, the sky was the limit to his future in football.'

Taylor was signed for the odd-sounding fee of £29,999 so as not to burden him with a £30,000 tag, and he was an immediate success with his penetrating stride, fierce shot and powerful heading. He crossed the Pennines in 1953 and two months after signing he won the first of 19 England caps. He played 163 League games for United, scoring 112 goals. He scored 25 of them from 33 appearances to help win the 1956 Championship.

The inside-right berth was causing something of a problem, with first Jackie Blanchflower, then John Doherty and finally another exciting youngster, Billy Whelan, all sharing in the Championship race. Inside-left was more settled with Dennis Viollet now a regular, but more of him later as a Munich survivor who hit the scoring headlines in 1960.

Johnny Berry was still at outside-right, while the youthful David Pegg occupied the left wing for most of the title season. David was another of the successful youth team, a Busby Babe recruited at Doncaster. He was able to make only 127 League appearances in his five seasons before losing his life at Munich. He played just once for the full England team, joining team-mates Roger Byrne, Tommy Taylor and Duncan Edwards against the Republic of Ireland. Munich was England's loss as well as Manchester United's.

United were at the forefront of the 1955-56 Championship race right from the start, though it wasn't until around Christmas that the rest of the First Division felt their real power. They went to the top of the table in early December when they beat Sunderland 2–1 at Old Trafford. They lost only twice in the second half of the season. They clinched the title with two games to spare by beating their closest rivals, Blackpool, 2–1. They were a goal down at half-time and it looked possible that they would suffer their first home defeat of the season, but goals from Johnny Berry, representing the old guard, and Tommy Taylor, the comparative newcomer, saw them home.

Taylor's 25 goals were backed by 20 from Viollet and nine from Pegg. United's 11-point margin from Blackpool at the top of the table equalled the record shared in the previous century by Preston, Sunderland and Aston Villa.

All but three of the team had been nurtured as home-produced players. As Jimmy Murphy would say: 'As ye sow . . . so shall ye reap.'

Busby summed up: 'From the very start I had envisaged making my own players, having a kind of nursery so that they could be trained in the kind of pattern I was trying to create for Manchester United.'

The League champions were now in peak form and they won the title again the following season, this time romping home eight points in front of Spurs. The team had settled down to read:

Wood, Foulkes, Byrne, Colman, Jones, Edwards, Berry, Whelan, Taylor, Viollet, Pegg.

There was one other notable player who began to crop up in this season, playing whenever Taylor or Viollet was injured, another home-produced starlet, Bobby Charlton. Making his debut at Charlton Athletic in October, he scored twice in a 4–2 win. Altogether that season he made 14 League appearances, scoring ten goals. Clearly he was a youngster with a great future, as events subsequently bore out.

It was a high-scoring season, with United's goals topping the ton thanks to Charlton's youthful contribution, plus 16 from Dennis Viollet, 22 from Tommy Taylor and an outstanding 26 from Billy Whelan.

Billy, or back home in Dublin, Liam, was a ball-playing inside-forward, very gifted and a surprisingly good marksman for one whose main job was to create for others. But then most of this talented team were good all-rounders and Whelan was at the peak of his powers. He had joined the club as a youngster from Home Farm, the Irish team which served United well over the

Matt Busby leads out Manchester United for the final of the 1957 FA Cup at Wembley against Aston Villa. Roger Byrne follows him as captain of the team labelled the Busby Babes in tribute to their youth and precocious talent which had already earned them the championship. It was a team which had already taken Europe by storm, reaching the semi-finals of the European Cup in the first season in the competition

Below left: Manchester United's goalkeeper Ray Wood lies clutching his broken face watched by anxious team-mates. Jackie Blanchflower took over in goal, but though United fought bravely they couldn't prevent Aston Villa emerging 2–1 winners with the villain of the piece, Peter McParland, scoring Villa's two goals

Above: Ray Wood, his cheekbone shattered by Peter McParland, is taken off on a stretcher at Wembley. The injury also shattered Matt Busby's dreams of a League and FA Cup double. The manager, with the 1957 championship already won, said later that on the morning of the Cup final against Aston Villa he had come downstairs at the team hotel never more certain of anything in football than that Manchester United would complete the double . . . but that of course had not taken into account the injury to his goalkeeper in the days before substitutes were allowed

years. In four seasons at Old Trafford before the crash he played 96 League and Cup games for a total of 52 goals. He won four Republic of Ireland caps, and was a player with immaculate control.

United were named as League champions by Easter. Busby rang the changes for the following match because of Cup commitments and he played seven reserves. The Football League could hardly complain because United won 2–0 with a goal from Alex Dawson on his debut and another from Colin Webster. To illustrate the club's great strength in depth, the 'reserve' side made up mostly of youth team players won 3–1 at Burnley on the same day.

United's final points total of 64 was the highest for 26 years.

The 1956-57 season was notable not only for winning the Championship for the second successive season. The Busby Babes were also flying high in the FA Cup as well as storming along in the European Cup. In the FA Cup they went to Wembley and came within an ace of achieving the elusive League and FA Cup double. Matt Busby says now that when he came downstairs on the morning of the final against Aston Villa he had never been more sure of victory before in his football life. The Championship was already in the bag, and the form book pointed only one way for the winner at Wembley. But just six minutes into the match goalkeeper Ray Wood was carried off the field suffering from a smashed cheekbone. Peter McParland had headed the ball into Wood's arms and it seemed a routine matter for the goalkeeper to kick it clear. But McParland, perhaps fired up for the final, kept on coming to crash into the United man. Even allowing for the fact that in those days goalkeepers did not enjoy the kind of protection they get now from

referees, it was an outrageous charge, and in 1957 there were no substitutes.

Jackie Blanchflower took over in goal and, with the rest of the defence, performed heroically to keep the game goalless at the interval. Ray Wood bravely returned to the field for spells at outside-right, but could not do much and the team's pattern had been destroyed, even though Tommy Taylor managed to score with a fine header.

At half-time physiotherapist Ted Dalton took Wood to the back of the stadium and tested him with a few shots and throwing the ball at him, but, as Busby reports: 'Poor Ray saw no more than a couple out of every six balls sent to him.'

McParland the villain then became Villa's hero by scoring two second-half goals for a 2–1 victory. Towards the end Busby sent the dazed Wood back into goal in a desperate gamble to pull the game out of the fire. The players responded by giving a tantalising glimpse of what might have been but for the injury to their goalkeeper, but Wood was really in no condition to play. It was rough, tough luck for United, and the incident helped bring in the substitute rule, but that was little consolation at the time as the dream of the double collapsed.

There was no denying that Manchester United in 1957 were the outstanding team in the country, playing some majestic football and so young that they were only on the threshold of their full potential. At home and in Europe they had covered themselves in glory and there was a tremendous expectation and excitement as they readied themselves for another treble bid in season 1957-58. But all these hopes were to come crashing to the ground in the February snow and ice in what was to be one of the saddest seasons in English football history.

Munich: End of a dream

The team Matt Busby had built from the club's successful youth policy seemed destined to dominate football for many years. Such was the power of the Babes that they seemed invincible. The average age of the side which won the Championship in 1955-56 was just 22, the youngest ever to achieve such a feat. A year later, when they were Champions again, nothing, it seemed, would prevent the young braves of Manchester United from reigning supreme for the next decade.

United had taken their first steps into European football in defiance of the football authorities and it was on foreign soil that the final chapter in the story of the Babes was to be written. The aircraft carrying the United party back from a victorious visit to Yugoslavia crashed in the snow of Munich airport and the Babes were no more.

The young Champions flew out of Manchester to face Red Star Belgrade remembering the cheers of 63,000 intoxicated football fans. Five days before Munich, United had played Arsenal at Highbury and thrilled all those who witnessed that game with a display of the attacking football that they had made their trademark. Nine goals were scored . . . four by Arsenal, five by United.

That game, on Saturday, 1 February 1958, had typified the Busby Babes. They played with such flair and enthusiasm that they thought nothing of conceding four goals in their efforts to score five. United were trying to win the League Championship for the third successive season and by then had already reached the fifth round of the FA Cup.

To set the scene for the tragedy which was to shock football, let us consider how the 1957-58 season led up to a symbolic game with Arsenal and the fateful journey to Yugoslavia. For United, the season had started well, victories over Leicester at Filbert Street, then Everton and Manchester City at Old Trafford being the perfect launch towards the title. Their scoring record was remarkable with 22 goals coming in the opening six games. Yet when they lost for the first time it was not by just an odd goal, but

by 4–0 at Burnden Park, where Bolton Wanderers ran rampant in front of a crowd of 48,003.

As 1957 drew to an end the Babes lost 1–0 to Chelsea at Old Trafford, then picked themselves up to beat luckless Leicester 4–0. On Christmas Day goals from Charlton, Edwards and Taylor secured two points against Luton in Manchester. On Boxing Day they met Luton again at Kenilworth Road and drew 2–2 and two days later the 'derby' game with Manchester City ended in the same scoreline at Maine Road. A crowd of 70,483 watched that game as the old rivals battled for pride as well as points.

As the European Cup-tie with Red Star approached, the side also made progress in the FA Cup with a 3–1 win at Workington and a 2–0 victory over Ipswich at Old Trafford to see them through to the fifth round, where they were to meet Sheffield Wednesday.

But the third target for Matt Busby, success in Europe, was perhaps the greatest. In 1956 United had become the first English club to compete in the European Champions' Cup, falling at the semi-final to the might of Real Madrid, winners of the trophy in the competition's first five years.

That year, the European seed had been sown. Manchester had witnessed the skills of di Stefano, Kopa and Gento, had seen United score ten times against Belgian club Anderlecht, then hang on against Borussia Dortmund before a remarkable quarter-final against Atletico Bilbao. In this match the Babes defied the odds by turning a 5–3 deficit from the first leg into a 6–5 victory, with goals from Taylor, Viollet and Johnny Berry, to win the right to challenge Real Madrid in the penultimate round.

That was where the run ended, but when United qualified to enter the European competition again in the 1957–58 season it was clear where the club's priorities lay. Matt Busby wanted a side which was good enough to win everything. The FA Cup had been snatched out of his grasp because of an injury to goalkeeper Ray Wood in the 1957 final, but his Babes were capable of reaching Wembley once again, and having secured the League Championship in

1956 and 1957 they could certainly emulate the great sides of pre-war Huddersfield Town and Arsenal and win it for a third successive time.

United's second European campaign saw them stride over Shamrock Rovers before beating Dukla Prague 3–1 on aggregate to reach the quarter-final against Red Star.

The Yugoslavs came to Manchester on 14 January 1958, and played a United side which was smarting from a 1–1 draw at Elland Road against Leeds United, who had been beaten 5–0 at Old Trafford earlier in the season.

Bobby Charlton and Eddie Colman scored the goals which gave United the edge in a 2–1 first-leg victory over Red Star, but it would be close in Belgrade. The run-up to the second leg was encouraging. A 7–2 win over Bolton, with goals from Bobby Charlton (3), Dennis Viollet (2), Duncan Edwards and Albert Scanlon, was just the result United needed before visiting Highbury, then leaving on the tiring journey behind the Iron Curtain.

The great match at Highbury

The United side which faced Arsenal was the eleven which was to line up against Red Star four days later. With Irish international Harry Gregg, a new signing, in goal, United were without some of their regulars. Jackie Blanchflower, the centre-half who had replaced Ray Wood in goal in the FA Cup final, was missing from the side along with wingers David Pegg and Johnny Berry and the creative inside-forward Liam Whelan, all of whom were being rested by Busby.

The two full-backs were Bill Foulkes and captain Roger Byrne, with the half-back line of Eddie Colman, Mark Jones and Duncan Edwards supporting the forward line of Ken Morgans, Bobby Charlton, Tommy Taylor, Dennis Viollet and Albert Scanlon.

Jack Kelsey was in goal for the Gunners and he was first to feel the power of United. Only ten minutes had gone when Dennis Viollet laid off a pass to an advancing Duncan Edwards who struck the ball with such ferocity that it was past Kelsey and in the net despite the efforts of the Welsh international. The goal was typical of Edwards. His power and strength had become a hallmark of his game despite his youth. Duncan was just 21, yet had played for England 18 times and represented his country at every level. In his short career with United he played 151 games and that first goal on that February afternoon was his 19th and final League strike.

Arsenal fought back, urged on by the huge crowd, and it took a superb save by Gregg to prevent them from equalising. He somehow kept out a certain scoring chance by grabbing the ball just under the crossbar and his clearance led to United's second. The ball was pushed out to Albert Scanlon on the left wing and he ran virtually the full length of the field before crossing. Two Arsenal defenders had been drawn into the corner by the United winger and his centre found Bobby Charlton running into the penalty area from the right. Charlton's shot was unstoppable and all Kelsey could do was throw up both arms in a token gesture as he dived to his right, but the shot was past him and the young Charlton was turning to celebrate the Babes' 2–0 lead.

By half-time it was 3–0, and again Scanlon's speed had played its part. The winger broke down the left, rounded Arsenal right-back Stan Charlton and crossed to the far side of the pitch where right-winger Kenny Morgans met the cross and chipped the ball back into the penalty area. England centre-forward Tommy Taylor scored his 111th goal in the First Division after five seasons with United.

United seemed to be on their way to a comfortable victory, ready to take four points away from the London club following a 4–2 win in Manchester earlier in the season. High-scoring clashes between the two seemed commonplace, United having beaten Arsenal 6–2 on their way to the 1956-57 Championship. Was this to be another massive victory for the Babes?

For 15 minutes of the second half there was no further score, then Arsenal took heart when David Herd, later to be a United player, broke through and hit a fierce shot at Gregg's goal. The big Irishman tried to keep the ball out but Herd's power and accuracy beat him. It was 3–1 with half an hour remaining.

Within two minutes the scores were level as Arsenal staged a sensational fight back. Wing-half Dave Bowen was the man driving Arsenal forward. It was from his cross that Herd had got the first of the home side's goals and he was involved in the move which led to the second

Above: Action from the Babes' last game as Dennis Viollet (left) and Tommy Taylor attack the Arsenal goal. Jack Kelsey in the Gunners' goal runs to his left to cover as Dennis Evans, his full-back, glances the ball towards Jim Fotheringham his centre half. On the far left of the picture is United winger Ken Morgans, and in the background referee G. W. Pullin from Bristol

Above right: The flying Albert Scanlon, the speedy winger who had just begun to establish himself in the side when he was injured in the air crash. He returned to play in every League game the following season in the position previously filled by his uncle Charlie Mitten. In 1960 he was transferred to Newcastle, and ended his career at Mansfield in 1965 after a spell with Lincoln City

Left: A gymnasium training session for wingers Johnny Berry (left) and David Pegg as they prepare for a cup-tie. Berry suffered serious head injuries in the air crash which ended his career and Pegg was killed

Above: Duncan Edwards spreads his arms to appeal for a goal-kick as 'keeper Harry Gregg goes down to cover this Arsenal scoring attempt. Racing back to cover are Bill Foulkes and Mark Jones while on the far left captain Roger Byrne looks on

Arsenal strike. Vic Groves jumped above the United defence to head down a cross from Gordon Nutt which fell to Jimmy Bloomfield, who scored. It was Nutt again who made the pass to Bloomfield some 60 seconds later for the London-born striker to dive full length and head home a magnificent goal which turned Highbury into a deafening stage for the final drama.

No scriptwriter could have dreamt up the plot for the last chapter of the Babes' challenge for Football League supremacy. No-one in that arena knew that they were witnessing the last magnificent demonstration of sheer genius which had taken English – and to a certain extent European – football apart in that decade. Under Busby the Babes had created a new style, a game that was refreshing, flowing, entertaining, and a game which was putting England

back on the map after falling to the skills of the Hungarians and the Brazilians in the early and mid-1950s.

Would United collapse under the Arsenal onslaught? Lesser teams would have been forgiven if they had defended in depth to hold out for a draw, having seen a three-goal lead disintegrate, but Manchester United went all out in search of more goals, and got them.

The speed of Scanlon and the skill of young Charlton combined to give Dennis Viollet a goal. The Manchester supporters screamed their delight, and were in raptures a few minutes later when Kelsey had to retrieve the ball from his goal for a fifth time, after Eddie Colman had found Morgans with a precise pass and Tommy Taylor had scored his last goal.

Yet even then this magnificent game had not ended. Derek Tapscott ran through the centre of United's near exhausted defence to put Arsenal within one goal of United again. But it was the final goal of the afternoon. The referee blew for time and the players collapsed into one another's arms. United, their white shirts mud-spattered and clinging to their breathless bodies, shook hands with the opposition and each other. Supporters on the terraces embraced one another as a reaction to the sheer enjoyment of the game, and the massive crowd left the stadium with a feeling that they had witnessed something unique in football.

Fate had decided that for fans at home this game would be the epitaph to those young heroes of Manchester. In the weeks which were to follow many words would be written about the greatness of Busby's Babes and in the years which have passed since the Munich air disaster they have become legendary characters, but that

5–4 scoreline, in a game played with all the passion and creative expression those tens of thousands had watched, said all that needed to be said as far as the ordinary football fans were concerned. They knew they had seen something special in Busby's young cavaliers.

The fatal European Cup trip

After that symbolic game, all thoughts were now on Europe. Could United hold on to that slender lead from the first leg? For the supporters left behind it seemed a narrow margin, but they had faith in those young players – after all had they not proved themselves time and again in similar circumstances?

For the players the damp, grey smog of Manchester's winter was replaced by the fresh crispness of mid-Europe. They had seen snow on their journey to the Yugoslav capital yet they had been welcomed with warmth by the people of Belgrade who understood the greatness of Manchester United in the common language of football.

It was time for the game and as the two sides lined up in the stadium the roar of thousands of Yugoslav voices rang in the ears of the Babes. Cameras clicked as last-minute photographs were taken, and above the players in the press area British journalists filed stories which were to be read in England the following morning.

A SPECIAL EDITION OF THE OFFICIAL M.U.F.C. PROGRAMME
14th JANUARY, 1958
NUMBER SEVENTEEN

Manchester United VERSUS **Red Star of Belgrade**

EUROPEAN CUP COMPETITION
SECOND ROUND – FIRST LEG
KICK-OFF 7.45 PM
PRICE FOURPENCE

Among them was Frank Swift, a giant of a man who had kept goal for Manchester City and England, and who had a reputation of being **the** gentle giant. Big 'Swifty' had retired from the game and taken a job as a sportswriter with the *News of the World*, and his role in Belgrade was to write a column for the following Sunday edition.

Above: Over 60,000 copies of this programme were sold as Red Star of Belgrade came to Old Trafford for the first leg of the European Cup quarter-final in 1958. United won the game 2–1 thanks to goals from Bobby Charlton and Eddie Colman

The final team talk. Matt Busby chats to his players following their pre-match meal in Belgrade, shortly before the Red Star game. Listening to his words Bert Whalley rests an arm on the shoulder of Tommy Taylor as next to him stand Jackie Blanchflower and Duncan Edwards. Seated right is Dennis Viollet and in the foreground Bobby Charlton (right) and Ken Morgans

The last line-up in Belgrade. 5 February, 1958 and the Busby Babes are ready for their final game. Left to right: Duncan Edwards, Eddie Colman, Mark Jones, Ken Morgans, Bobby Charlton, Dennis Viollet, Tommy Taylor, Bill Foulkes, Harry Gregg, Albert Scanlon, and captain Roger Byrne who leans forward to shout encouragement to his colleagues before the European cup tie

Frank had played in the same Manchester City side as Matt Busby and was a team-mate of the United manager when City won the FA Cup in 1934. The big goalkeeper had made headline news in that game when, aged just 19, he had fainted as the final whistle was blown, overcome with the emotion of such an occasion. Perhaps he, more than any other spectator, understood the feelings of the young players as they stood together for the last moments before the start of the game.

Also looking out from that crowded press box were journalists who had travelled to Europe for each of United's previous games: Tom Jackson of the *Manchester Evening News* and his close friend and rival Alf Clarke of the now defunct *Manchester Evening Chronicle*. Both men loved Manchester United and lived to see their every game. Alf Clarke had been on United's books as an amateur, and was with the club before Matt Busby arrived to rebuild it after the war.

Because Manchester was a printing centre for the northern editions of the national newspapers, and also because of the tremendous popularity of the United side, most other daily newspapers were represented.

From the *Daily Mirror* was Archie Ledbrooke, who had only just made the trip having been on the point of being replaced by Frank McGhee because he (Ledbrooke) had still to complete an outstanding feature only hours before the flight had left England. Others included Eric Thompson from the *Daily Mail*, George Follows of the *Daily Herald* – the daily newspaper which was succeeded by *The Sun* following its closure – Don Davies of the *Manchester Guardian*, Henry Rose of the *Daily Express* and Frank Taylor from the *News Chronicle*, another publication which has since gone out of existence.

Don Davies wrote under the pen-name of 'Old International' and had been in the England

amateur side which played Wales in 1914, having been a member of the famous Northern Nomads side. On 5 February 1958 this is the story Davies filed back to the *Manchester Guardian* office in Cross Street, Manchester:

Who would be a weather prophet? At Belgrade today in warm sunshine and on a grass pitch where the last remnants of melting snow produced the effect of an English lawn flecked with daisies, Red Star and Manchester United began a battle of wits and courage and rugged tackling in the second leg of their quarter-final of the European Cup competition. It ended in a draw 3–3, but as United had already won the first leg at Old Trafford by 2–1 they thus gained the right to pass into the semi-final round of the competition for the second year in succession on a 5–4 aggregate.

Much to the relief of the English party and to the consternation of the 52,000 home spectators, Viollet had the ball in the net past a dumbfounded Beara in ninety seconds. It was a beautifully taken goal – a characteristic effort by that player – but rather lucky in the way a rebound had run out in United's favour. But, as Jones remarked, 'You need luck at this game'; and he might have added, 'a suit of chain mail also would not have come amiss'. A second goal almost came fourteen minutes later, delightfully taken by Charlton after a corner kick by Scanlon had been headed by Viollet, but this was disallowed, because of offside, by the Austrian referee whose performance on the whistle so far had assumed the proportions of a flute obligato. That was due to the frequency which fouls were being committed by both sides after Sekularac had set the fashion in shabbiness by stabbing Morgans on the knee.

But in spite of many stops and starts events in the first half ran smoothly for United, on whose behalf Taylor led his line like a true Hotspur from centre-forward. Other factors telling strongly in Manchester's favour at this time were the clean hands and sound judgement of Gregg in goal.

Further success for United was impending. Charlton this time was the chosen instrument. Dispossessing Kostic about forty yards from goal, this gifted boy leaned brilliantly into his stride, made ground rapidly for about ten yards, and then beat the finest goalkeeper on the Continent with a shot of tremendous power and superb placing. There, one thought, surely goes England's Bloomer of the future. Further evidence of Charlton's claim to that distinction was to emerge two minutes later. A smartly taken free kick got the Red Star defence into a real tangle. Edwards fastened on the ball and did his best to oblige his colleagues and supporters by bursting it (a feat, by the way, which he was to achieve later), but he muffed his kick this time and the ball rolled to Charlton, apparently lost in a thicket of Red Star defenders. Stalemate surely. But not with Charlton about. His quick eye detected the one sure route through the circle of legs; his trusty foot drove the ball unerringly along it. 3–0 on the day: 5–1 on the aggregate. Nice going.

As was natural, the Red Star players completely lost their poise for a while. Their forwards flung themselves heatedly against a defence as firm and steady as a rock; even Sekularac, after a bright beginning in which he showed his undoubted skill, lost heart visibly and stumbled repeatedly. Nevertheless there was an upsurge of the old fighting spirit when Kostic scored a fine goal for Red Star two minutes after half time. It ought to have been followed by another one only three minutes later when Sekularac placed the ball perfectly for Cotic. Cotic's terrific shot cleared the bar by a foot – no more. Next, a curious mix-up by Foulkes and Tasic, Red Star's centre-forward, ended in Foulkes falling flat on top of Tasic and blotting him completely out of view. According to Foulkes, Tasic lost his footing, fell over, and pulled Foulkes over with him. But it looked bad and the whistle blew at once with attendant gestures indicating a penalty. Tasic had the satisfaction of converting that one, although his shot only just evaded Gregg's finger tips.

The score was now 3–2 and the crowd broke into an uncontrolled frenzy of jubilation and excitement. So much so that when Cotic failed to walk the ball into a completely unprotected goal – Gregg was lying hurt and helpless on the ground – a miniature repetition of the Bolton disaster seemed to occur at one corner of the arena.

Down the terraces streamed a wild horde of excited spectators who hung limply along the concrete walls with the breath crushed out of their bodies, if indeed nothing else had befallen them.

A quarter of an hour from the end Red Star, with their confidence and self-respect restored, were wheeling and curvetting, passing and shooting in their best style, and the United's defenders had to fight their way out of a regular nightmare of desperate situations. It was significant hereabouts that United's inside forwards were not coming back to chase the ball as they had done so effectively in the first half and this, of course, threw added pressure on the rearguard. As soon as this fault was rectified the Red Star attacks, though frequent enough, lost something of their sting. In fact, United began to pile on the pressure at the other end and once Morgans struck a post with a glorious shot.

The furious pace never slackened, and as England's champions tried to find their flowing, attacking play of the first half, they were pelted by a storm of snowballs. Two minutes from time Harry Gregg came racing out of his goal, and hurled himself full length at Zebec's feet. He grasped it safely, but the impetus of his rush took him outside the penalty area with the ball, and Red Star had a free kick some twenty yards out.

Kostic watched Gregg position himself by the far post, protected by a wall of United players. There was just a narrow ray of light, a gap, by the near post, and precision player Kostic threaded the ball through as Gregg catapulted himself across his goal. Too late. The ball eluded his grasping fingers, and hit the back of the net. The score was 3–3.

It had always been Davies's ambition to be a football writer. For most of his life he had worked as an education officer with a Manchester engineering firm, but after it was suggested that he should try his hand at journalism he had been taken onto the *Guardian* staff when the editor saw a report of a fictitious match. It was the key he needed to open the door to a career of full-time writing. His style was that of the essayist, ideally suited to the *Manchester Guardian*, and contrasting totally with that of Henry Rose, the most popular daily writer of that time – certainly with the Old Trafford supporters.

Rose saw the game from the same vantage point as Davies, yet his description was totally different:

Red Star 3 Manchester United 3
Star Rating ★★★

Manchester United survived the Battle of Belgrade here this afternoon and added another shining page to their glittering history by drawing 3–3 with Red Star and winning the two-leg tie 5–4.

They had to fight not only eleven desperate footballers and a fiercely partisan 52,000 crowd, but some decisions of Austrian referee Karl Kainer that were double-Dutch to me. I have never witnessed such a one-sided exhibition by any official at home or abroad.

The climax of Herr Kainer's interpretations, which helped inflame the crowd against United, came in the 55th minute when he gave a penalty against Foulkes, United's star defender. Nothing is wrong with my eyesight – and Foulkes confirmed what I saw . . . that a Red Star player slipped and pulled the United man back down with him. A joke of a ruling it would have been had not Tasic scored from the spot.

Later in his report, Rose wrote:

Gregg was hurt, Morgans and Edwards were limping; Byrne was warned for wasting time. United players were penalised for harmless-looking tackles.

I thought Herr Kainer would have given a free-kick against United when one of the ballboys fell on his backside!

He described the United side as:

Heroes all. None greater than Billy Foulkes. None greater than Bobby Charlton, who has now scored twelve goals in the eleven games he has played since he went into the side at inside-right on 21 December. But all eleven played a noble part in this memorable battle.

The game over and the work completed, it was time to relax, and the party of journalists joined the United officials, players and their opposite numbers from the Red Star club at a banquet in the Majestic Hotel in Belgrade. It was a friendly affair, despite the disappointment felt by the host club at losing such an important game. There was a great friendship between the clubs in those early years of the European competition.

Roger Byrne, captain of the Busby Babes. The England full-back would have learned on his return home that he was to be a father. His wife was preparing to break the good news to Roger when she heard about the air-crash. Years later the son Roger never saw was one of the team of ball-boys at Old Trafford

Two young men drink to the future . . . Duncan Edwards (left) survived the air crash but died two weeks later from his injuries. The laughing Tommy Taylor was killed instantly and Manchester United and England had lost two great players

In a moving scene the meal ended when waiters entered the dining room carrying trays of sweetmeats lit by candles set in ice. The United party stood to applaud the skill of the Yugoslav chef, and Roger Byrne led his colleagues in song:

We'll meet again,
Don't know where, don't know when,
But we know we'll meet again
some sunny day. . . .

That scene was remembered clearly by Yugoslav writer Miro Radojcic in an article for his newspaper *Politika*, which he translated into English 20 years later for Geoffrey Green, and which was published in *There's Only One United* (Hodder and Stoughton, 1978). Part of it read:

Then followed the simple warm-hearted words of Matt Busby and Walter Crickmer as they said: 'Come and visit us, the doors of Old Trafford will always be open to you' . . . and after that lovely, crazy night as I parted from 'Old International' – Don Davies from the *Manchester Guardian* – he said to me: 'Why didn't you score just one more goal then we could have met for a third time?

Radojcic sat up throughout most of the night musing over a feature article he planned to write for his newspaper. *Politika* was not a sporting publication – in fact he was a political writer – but he had a great love for football and the flair of Manchester United's young side attracted him.

After chatting and drinking with Tommy Taylor and Duncan Edwards in a bar named Skadarija, Radojcic was left alone with his thoughts. He decided that he would arrange to fly back to Manchester with the team, and write his story from the Manchester angle, a look at England's top team seen through the eyes of one of Yugoslavia's most celebrated journalists.

The players had gone off to bed when Radojcic came to his decision so he went back to his flat, packed a bag and made his way to the airport only to discover that he had left his passport at home. He asked the airport authorities to hold the aircraft for as long as possible while he took a return taxi trip back to his hime. By the time he got back with his passport the twin-engined Elizabethan had taken off, bound for England via Munich where it was to stop to re-fuel.

The tragedy at Munich airport

Those on board were in a relaxed mood when the plane landed on German soil. They had played cards, chatted over the latest news, read any books and magazines which were around and passed the time away as best they could. There was the usual air of nervous apprehension about the flight, but card schools and conversation hid any fears of flying and some even managed to catch up on lost sleep rather than gaze out on the snowscape below.

By around 2 pm G-ALZU AS 57 was ready once more for take-off with Captain Kenneth Rayment, the second in command, at the controls. The man in charge, Captain James Thain, had flown the plane out to Belgrade, and his close friend and colleague was now taking the 'Lord Burleigh' home again.

At 2.31 pm the aircraft control tower was told that '609 Zulu Uniform is rolling' and Captain Thain later described what happened:

Ken opened the throttles which were between us and when they were fully open I tapped his hand and held the throttles in the fully open position. Ken moved his hand and I called for 'full power'. The engines sounded an uneven note as the aircraft accelerated and the needle on the port pressure gauge started to fluctuate. I felt a pain in my hand as Ken pulled the throttles back and said: 'Abandon take-off'. I held the control column fully forward while Ken put on the brakes. Within 40 seconds of the start of its run the aircraft was almost at a halt again.

The cause of the problem had been boost surging – a very rich mixture of fuel causing the engines to over-accelerate – a fault which was quite common in the Elizabethan. As the two men talked over the problem Captain Rayment decided that he would attempt a second take-off, this time opening the throttles gradually before releasing the brakes, and then moving to full power.

At 2.34 pm permission for a second take-off attempt was given by air traffic control and for a second time the plane came to a halt.

During their wait while the aircraft was being refuelled, the passengers had gone into a lounge for coffee. Now, after the two aborted attempts to take off, the party was in the lounge once more. It had begun to snow quite heavily. Full-back Bill Foulkes remembers:

We'd been playing cards for most of the flight from Belgrade to Munich, and I remember when we left the aircraft thinking how cold it was. We had one attempt at taking off, but didn't leave the ground, so I suppose a few of those on board would start to worry a little bit, and when the second take-off failed we were pretty quiet when we went back into the lounge.

Some of the players must have felt that they would not be flying home that afternoon. Duncan Edwards sent a telegram to his landlady back in Manchester: 'All flights cancelled returning home tomorrow'. The telegram was delivered at around 5 pm.

Bill Foulkes recalls how after a quarter of an hour delay the passengers were asked to board again but it was another five minutes before everyone was back in the aircraft.

Alf Clarke from the *Evening Chronicle* had put a call through to his office and we had to wait for him to catch up with us. We got back into our seats, but we didn't play cards this time. . . . I slipped the pack into my jacket pocket and sat back waiting for take-off.

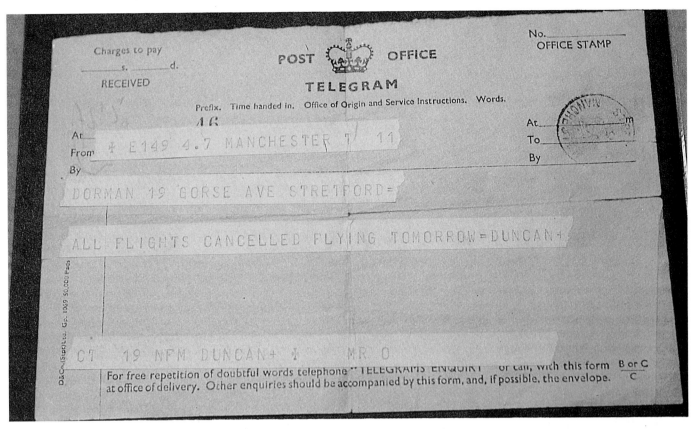

POST OFFICE TELEGRAM

Charges to pay

RECEIVED

No.

OFFICE STAMP

Prefix. Time handed in. Office of Origin and Service Instructions. Words.

E149 4.7 MANCHESTER T 11

DORMAN 19 GORSE AVE STRETFORD=

ALL FLIGHTS CANCELLED FLYING TOMORROW=DUNCAN+

CT 19 NFM DUNCAN+

For free repetition of doubtful words telephone "TELEGRAMS ENQUIRY" or call, with this form at office of delivery. Other enquiries should be accompanied by this form, and, if possible, the envelope.

After the second unsuccessful take-off the players and journalists decided that it would be impossible to leave Munich until the next day. Duncan Edwards sent this telegram to his landlady back in Manchester telling her of the delay . . . but a third attempt at take-off was made. The telegram was delivered after the crash

I was sitting about half-way down the aircraft next to a window, on the right-hand side of the gangway. Our card school was Ken Morgans, who was on my right, and facing us David Pegg and Albert Scanlon. Matt Busby and Bert Whalley were sitting together on the seat behind us and I remember how Mark Jones, Tommy Taylor, Duncan Edwards and Eddie Colman were all at the back.

David Pegg got up and moved to the back: 'I don't like it here, it's not safe,' he said and went off to sit with the other players. I saw big Frank Swift back there too, he also felt that the rear was the safest place to be.

There was another card school across the gangway from us, Ray Wood and Jackie Blanchflower were sitting on two of the seats, Roger Byrne, Billy Whelan and Dennis Viollet on the others with one empty seat amongst them.

Back on the flight deck Captain Thain and Captain Rayment had discussed the problem they were having with the station engineer William Black, who had told them that the surging they were having was quite common at airports like Munich because of its altitude. At 3.03 pm 609 Zulu Uniform was rolling again. Captain Thain describes the next attempt at take-off:

I told Ken that if we got boost surging again, I would control the throttles. Ken opened them to 28 inches with the brakes on. The engines were both steady so he released the brakes and we moved forward again.

He continued to open the throttles and again I followed with my left hand until the levers were fully open. I tapped his hand and he moved it. He called 'Full power' and I checked the dials and said: 'Full power'.

Captain Thain again noticed that there was a sign of boost surging and called this out to Captain Rayment above the noise of the engines. The surging was controlled and the throttle pushed back until it was fully open:

I glanced at the air speed indicator and saw it registered 105 knots and was flickering. When it reached 117 knots I called out 'V1' [Velocity One, the point on the runway after which it isn't safe to abandon take-off]. Suddenly the needle dropped to about 112 and then 105. Ken shouted, 'Christ, we can't make it' and I looked up from the instruments to see a lot of snow and a house and a tree right in the path of the aircraft.

Inside the passengers' compartment Bill Foulkes had sensed that something was wrong:

There was a lot of slush flying past the windows and there was a terrible noise, like when a car leaves a smooth road and starts to run over rough ground.

The Elizabethan left the runway, went through a fence and crossed a road before the port wing struck a house. The wing and part of the tail were torn off and the house caught fire. The cockpit struck a tree and the starboard side of the fuselage hit a wooden hut containing a truck loaded with fuel and tyres. This exploded.

Bill Foulkes had crouched down in his seat after tightening his safety belt. He remembered afterwards a terrific bang, then after being unconscious for a few moments, seeing a gaping hole in front of him.

The back of the aircraft had just disappeared. I got out as quickly as I could and just ran and ran. Then I turned and realised that the plane wasn't going to explode, and I went back. In the distance I could see the tail part of the aircraft blazing and as I ran back I came across bodies. Roger Byrne still strapped to his seat, Bobby Charlton lying quite still in another seat, and Dennis Viollet. Then Harry Gregg appeared and we tried to see what we could do to help.

The two team-mates helped the injured. Matt Busby, badly hurt, was taken away on a stretcher, Bobby Charlton had walked over to Gregg and Foulkes and was helped into a mini-bus, sitting alongside Dennis Viollet in the front seats as other survivors were picked up. They were taken to the Rechts de Isar Hospital in Munich. It was the following day before the true horror of the air crash became evident to Bill Foulkes and Harry Gregg:

We went in and saw Matt in an oxygen tent, and Duncan Edwards, who seemed to be badly hurt. Bobby Charlton had a bandaged head, Jackie Blanchflower was nursing a badly gashed arm which had been strapped up by Harry Gregg in the snow of the night before. Albert Scanlon lay with his eyes closed, he had a fractured skull, and Dennis Viollet had a gashed head and facial injuries. Ray Wood's face was cut and he had concussion and Ken Morgans and Johnny Berry lay quite still in their beds. I spoke to a nurse and she told me that she thought Duncan had a better chance of making a full recovery than Johnny did. . . .

We came across Frank Taylor in another bed; he was the only journalist around and he asked if we'd like to have a beer with him. Like us, he didn't know the full implications of what had happened the afternoon before.

We were about to leave the hospital when I asked a nurse where we should go to see the other lads. She seemed puzzled so I asked her again: 'Where are the other survivors?' . . . 'Others? There are no others, they are all here.' It was only then that we knew the horror of Munich.

The Busby Babes were no more.

Roger Byrne, Geoff Bent, Mark Jones, David Pegg, Liam Whelan, Eddie Colman and Tommy Taylor had been killed instantly. Club secretary Walter Crickmer had also died, along with the first team trainer, Tom Curry, and coach Bert Whalley.

Duncan Edwards and Johnny Berry were critically injured and fighting for their lives, Matt Busby had suffered extensive injuries and was the only club official to survive the crash.

Eight of the nine sportswriters on board the aircraft had also perished: Alf Clarke, Don Davies, George Follows, Tom Jackson, Archie Ledbrooke, Henry Rose, Eric Thompson and the gentle giant, Frank Swift.

One of the aircrew had been killed, together

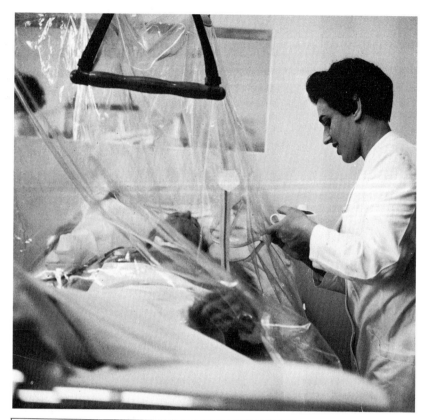

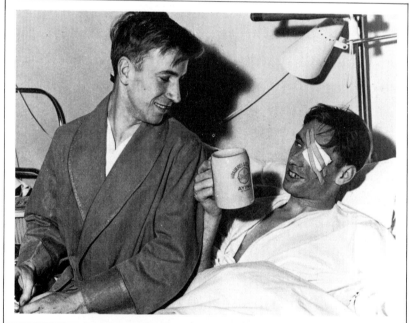

A last photograph of football writer Henry Rose (right), and Tommy Taylor as they share a moment together on the Elizabethan aircraft which crashed at Munich. Eight journalists died in the disaster, among them former England goalkeeper Frank Swift who was working as a correspondent for the *News of the World*

with two other passengers: the travel agent who had arranged the flight details, and a supporter who had flown out to watch the game. Nine players had survived, but two of them, Johnny Berry and Jackie Blanchflower – brother of Tottenham Hotspur's Danny – never played again.

Two photographers, the travel agent's wife, and two Yugoslav passengers, one with a young baby, had survived, together with Frank Taylor. On the afternoon of the crash 21 people had died, 18 had survived, of whom four were close to death.

Of those four, Duncan Edwards, Matt Busby, Johnny Berry and Captain Kenneth Rayment, two would survive. Three weeks after the aircrash which had become known simply as 'Munich', Duncan Edwards and Kenneth Rayment had lost their battle to live.

The news reaches Manchester

On the afternoon of the crash Alf Clarke had telephoned the *Evening Chronicle* sports desk to say that he thought the flight would be held up by the weather and made arrangements to return the following day. By three in the afternoon the paper had more or less 'gone to bed', and the final editions were leaving Withy Grove. In other parts of the city the daily newspaper staffs were beginning their routines. Reporters were heading out on diary jobs, sub-editors were looking through agency stories to see what was to form the backbone of the Friday morning editions.

That weekend United were to play League leaders Wolves at Old Trafford. Despite the long journey home it looked on form as if the Reds would close the four-point gap at the top of the table, putting them just one victory behind Billy Wright's side, and ready to increase their efforts for that third successive Championship. Could United emulate Huddersfield Town and Arsenal? Surely if they did it would be an even greater achievement than in those pre-war days. Saturday was coming round again. United would make the headlines.

Then on the teleprinter came an unbelievable message: 'Manchester United aircraft crashed on take off . . . heavy loss of life feared.'

The BBC interrupted its afternoon programming to broadcast a news flash. The football world listened to the words but few understood their meaning.

Jimmy Murphy, Matt Busby's wartime friend and now his assistant, was manager of the Welsh national side, and a World Cup qualifying game had coincided with the Red Star fixture. Murphy told Matt Busby that he would go to Yugoslavia rather than the game at Ninian Park, Cardiff, but his manager told him that his place was with the Welsh side.

'I always sat next to Matt on our European trips,' Murphy recalls, 'but I did what he said and let him go off to Red Star without me. Mind

you, I've got to be honest – my mind was more on our game in Yugoslavia than the match I was watching. When I heard that we were through to the semi-final it was a great load off my mind; I didn't like not being there.'

He had just returned to Old Trafford from Wales when news of the aircrash reached him. Alma George, Matt Busby's secretary, told him that the charter flight had crashed. Murphy failed to react.

'She told me again. It still didn't sink in, then she started to cry. She said many people had been killed, she didn't know how many, but the players had died, some of the players. I couldn't believe it. The words seemed to ring in my head. Alma left me and I went into my office. My head was in a state of confusion and I started to cry.'

The following day Jimmy Murphy flew out to Munich and was stunned by what he saw: 'Matt was in an oxygen tent and he told me to "keep the flag flying". Duncan recognised me and spoke. It was a terrible, terrible time.'

Murphy was given the job of rebuilding. Life would go on despite the tragedy, and Manchester United would play again: 'I had no players, but I had a job to do.'

After the agency newsflash had reached the Manchester evening newspapers, extra editions were published. At first details were printed in the Stop Press. By 6 pm a special edition of the *Manchester Evening Chronicle* was on sale:

About 28 people, including members of the Manchester United football team, club officials, and journalists are feared to have been killed when a BEA Elizabethan airliner crashed soon after take-off in a snowstorm at Munich airport this afternoon. It is understood there may be about 16 survivors. Four of them are crew members.

The newspaper, which was carrying Alf Clarke's match report and comments from the previous night's game, said on its front page: 'Alf Clarke was talking to the *Evening Chronicle* reporters in Manchester just after 2.30 pm when he said it was unlikely that the plane would be able to take off today.' Even though only three hours had elapsed since the crash the newspaper had a detailed report of how the disaster occurred.

Twenty-four hours later, as the whole of Europe reacted to the news of the tragedy, the *Evening Chronicle* listed the 21 dead on its front page under a headline: 'Matt fights for life: a 50-50 chance now'. There was a picture of Harry Gregg and Bill Foulkes at the bedside of Ken Morgans, and details of how the other injured were responding to treatment. The clouds of confusion had lifted – Munich had claimed 21 lives, 15 were injured and, of these, four players and Matt Busby were in a serious condition.

In the days following, Manchester mourned as the bodies of its famous footballing heroes were flown home to lie overnight in the gymnasium under the main grandstand before being passed on to relatives for the funerals. Today that gymnasium is the place where the players' lounge has been built, where those who succeeded the Babes gather after a game for a chat and a drink with the opposition.

Thousands of supporters turned out to pay their last respects. Where families requested that funerals should be private, the United followers stayed away from gravesides but lined the route to look on in tearful silence as corteges passed.

Cinema newsreels carried reports from Munich, and the game itself responded with memorial services, and silent grounds where supporters of every club stood, heads bowed, as referees indicated a period of silence by a blast on their whistles.

Desmond Hackett wrote a moving epitaph to Henry Rose, whose funeral was the biggest of all. A thousand taxi drivers offered their services free to anyone who was going to the funeral and there was a six-mile queue to Manchester's Southern Cemetery. The cortege halted for a moment outside the *Daily Express* offices in Great Ancoats Street where Hackett wrote in the style of Henry: 'Even the skies wept for Henry Rose today. . .'

Football returns to Old Trafford

Rival clubs offered helping hands to United. Liverpool and Nottingham Forest were first to respond by asking if they could do anything to assist. Football had suffered a terrible blow.

To give United a chance of surviving in football the FA waived its rule which 'cup-ties' a player once he has played in an FA Cup round in any particular season. The rule prevents him from playing for another club in the same competition, so that if he is transferred he is sidelined until the following season. United's need for players was desperate and the change of rules allowed Jimmy Murphy to begin his rebuilding by signing Ernie Taylor from Blackpool.

Manchester United took a deep breath. Football would return to Old Trafford.

Thirteen nights after news of Munich had reached Jimmy Murphy the days of torture ended when United played again. Their postponed FA Cup-tie against Sheffield Wednesday drew a crowd of 60,000 on a cold February evening of immense emotion. Spectators wept openly, many wore red-and-white scarves draped in black – red, white and black were eventually to become United's recognised colours – and the match programme added a poignant final stroke to a tragic canvas.

Under the heading 'Manchester United' there was a blank teamsheet.

Spectators were told to write in the names of the players. Few did, they simply listened in silence as the loudspeaker announcer read out the United team. Harry Gregg in goal and Bill Foulkes at right-back had returned after the traumas of Munich, other names were not so familiar.

UNITED WILL GO ON . . .

On 6th February, 1958 an aircraft returning from Belgrade crashed at Munich Airport. Of the twenty-one passengers who died twelve were players and officials of the Manchester United Football Club. Many others lie injured.

It is the sad duty of we who serve United to offer the bereaved our heartfelt sympathy and condolences. Here is a tragedy which will sadden us for years to come, but in this we are not alone. An unprecedented blow to British football has touched the hearts of millions and we express our deep gratitude to the many who have sent messages of sympathy and floral tributes. Wherever football is played United is mourned, but we rejoice that many of our party have been spared and wish them a speedy and complete recovery. Words are inadequate to describe our thanks and appreciation of the truly magnificent work of the surgeons and nurses of the Rechts der Isar Hospital at Munich. But for their superb skill and deep compassion our casualties must have been greater. To Professor Georg Maurer, Chief Surgeon, we offer our eternal gratitude.

Although we mourn our dead and grieve for our wounded we believe that great days are not done for us. The sympathy and encouragement of the football world and particularly of our supporters will justify and inspire us. The road back may be long and hard but with the memory of those who died at Munich, of their stirring achievements and wonderful sportsmanship ever with us, Manchester United will rise again.

H. P. HARDMAN, CHAIRMAN

Bare headed workmen pay their respects as a cortege leaves Old Trafford. Immediately after the disaster the bodies of those who died were brought back to Old Trafford where they lay in the club gymnasium until arrangements for the funerals were completed. Supporters kept vigil at the stadium as the football world mourned the passing of the Babes

At left full-back was Ian Greaves who had played his football with United's junior sides and found himself replacing Roger Byrne: 'I can remember the dressing room was very quiet. I couldn't get Roger out of my mind, I was getting changed where he would have sat. I was wearing his shirt. . .'

At right-half was Freddie Goodwin, who had come through from the reserve side after joining United as a 20-year-old. He had played his first League games in the 1954-55 season. Another reserve regular was centre-half Ronnie Cope, who had come from United's juniors after joining the club in 1951. At left-half was Stan Crowther, whose transfer to United was remarkable. He played for Aston Villa, and was not very keen to leave the Midlands club. Jimmy Murphy recalls: 'Eric Houghton was Villa manager at the time and he had told Stan that we were interested in him. He didn't want to leave Villa, but Eric got him to come to Old Trafford to watch the Sheffield Wednesday game. On the way up he told him he thought that he should help us out, but Stan told him he hadn't brought any kit with him. "Don't worry, I've got your boots in my bag," Eric said. We met at about half-past five and an hour before the kick-off he'd signed!'

Colin Webster at outside-right had joined United in 1952 and made his League debut in the 1953-54 season. He had won a League Championship medal in 1956 after 15 appearances, but had since been edged out of the side by Johnny Berry. Ernie Taylor was inside-right, and at centre-forward was Alex Dawson, a brawny Scot who had made his debut as a 16-year-old in April 1957, scoring against Burnley. Inside-left was Mark Pearson, who earned the nickname 'Pancho' because of the Mexican appearance his sideburns gave him. Like the Pearson who preceded him, Stan, and the one who was to follow him almost two decades later, Stuart, Mark was a powerful player and a regular goalscorer with the lower sides. That night he took the first steps of his senior career. The new United outside-left was Shay Brennan, who was a reserve defender. Such was United's plight that the 20-year-old was to begin his League career not as a right-back but as a left-winger.

Sheffield Wednesday had no chance. Murphy's Manchester United were playing for the memory of their friends who had died less than a fortnight earlier. The passion of the crowd urged them on. To say that some played beyond their capabilities would be unfair, but with Wednesday perhaps more affected by the occasion than the young and new players, the final score was United 3 Wednesday 0.

Playing in the Sheffield side was Albert Quixall, later to join United in a record transfer deal, who recalls: 'I don't think anyone who played in the game or who watched it will ever forget that night. United ran their hearts out, and no matter how well we had played they

would have beaten us. They were playing like men inspired. We were playing more than just eleven players, we were playing 60,000 fans as well.'

United scored in the 27th minute after two errors by Brian Ryalls in the Wednesday goal. Bill Foulkes had taken a free-kick from well outside the penalty area and his shot was going wide when Ryalls palmed it away for a corner. There had seemed no danger from the shot, but Brennan's corner kick brought his first goal for the senior side. Ryalls tried to collect the cross under the bar and could only turn the ball into his own net.

Brennan got a second later in the game when a shot from Mark Pearson rebounded off the 'keeper and straight into the Irishman's path. He made no mistake and United led 2–0. Five minutes from the end of that unforgettable night Alex Dawson scored the third. United had reached the quarter-finals of the FA Cup.

The crowd turned for home, their heads full of memories of that remarkable game, their hearts full of sadness as they realised the full extent of Munich. The new team had carried on where the Babes had left off . . . but they would never see their heroes again.

Two days after that cup-tie Duncan Edwards lost his fight to survive, and the sadness of Munich was rekindled.

Farewell to the flowers of Manchester

Manchester United had to continue and chairman Harold Hardman had made this clear in his message on the front cover of the Sheffield Wednesday programme:

United will go on . . . the club has a duty to the public and a duty to football. We shall carry on even if it means that we are heavily defeated.

Here is a tragedy which will sadden us for years to come, but in this we are not alone. An unprecedented blow to British football has touched the hearts of millions. Wherever football is played United is mourned.

The weeks following the tragedy revealed moving stories about the players who lost their lives.

Roger Byrne would have learned when he returned to Manchester that his wife Joy was expecting a child. Thirty-eight weeks after his death Roger had a son.

Geoff Bent treasured a picture of himself taking the ball off Tom Finney in one of the 12 First Division games he played, and the newspaper cutting was kept by his young wife Marion. His daughter Karen was a babe in arms when he died.

Eddie Colman, the 'cheekie chappie' from Salford, was just three months past his 21st birthday when he was killed.

Duncan Edwards, the youngest player to appear for England, was planning to get married to his fiancée, Molly. He had been a senior

Football returns to Old Trafford 15 days after the air crash. The programme for the fifth round FA Cup tie against Sheffield Wednesday bears the moving words of chairman Harold Hardman who told supporters 'United will go on'. Inside the United teamsheet was blank; even up to kick-off time no-one was certain who would be playing as the club searched for players

footballer for only four years, and was 22. Today, a stained glass window in St Francis's Church in his home town of Dudley remains as a tribute to a great player.

Mark Jones left a young wife, June, and a baby son, Gary. The ex-bricklayer was just 24 years of age. He doted on his black Labrador retriever, Rick. The dog pined away to its death shortly after the disaster.

David Pegg was only 22 and had edged himself into the England side at a time when Tom Finney and Stan Matthews were ending their international careers. His ambition was to be successful with United, and he had achieved that aim.

Tommy Taylor was also planning to marry and had told his fiancée, Carol, that he was looking forward to getting home from Belgrade for a pint of Guinness and to listen to his records with her.

Liam Whelan was a deeply religious boy, and Harry Gregg remembers clearly his last words as the aircraft accelerated down the runway: 'If the worst happens I am ready for death . . . I hope we all are.'

Eleven years later an official inquiry cleared Captain James Thain of any responsibility for the accident. The official cause was recorded as a build-up of melting snow on the runway which prevented the Elizabethan from reaching the required take-off speed.

Through the Munich Air Disaster a bond between Manchester United and its supporters was welded. Since that day, the club has been one of the best supported in Britain, and even though it never achieved the domination

The original Munich Memorial above the main entrance to Old Trafford. Due to extensive development at the stadium the club had a new memorial made and re-sited at the Warwick Road end of the ground. The tablet bears the names of the officials and players who died in the air crash. A plaque in memory of the journalists who died hangs in the press box

Old Trafford stands in silence on 6 February 1988 as players and supporters show their respect for those who died at Munich. The 30th anniversary of the disaster was marked with a 1−0 win over Coventry City. Liam O'Brien (fifth from left) was the scorer, the goal coming at four minutes past three, the time that the aircraft crashed

The stained glass window at St Francis in the Priory Church in Dudley, Worcestershire in memory of Duncan Edwards. Although only 21 when he died, Duncan played a total of 175 games for United and scored 21 times. He played for his country 18 times.

threatened by the potential of the Babes, since 1972-73 Old Trafford's attendances have been the highest in the Football League. Anyone who was a supporter at the time of Munich has remained loyal to the club. Those who came afterwards perhaps failed to understand the magnitude of the club's loss but have absorbed the meaning of Munich. It was the day a team died, but still plays on.

THE FLOWERS OF MANCHESTER

One cold and bitter Thursday in Munich
      Germany,
Eight great football stalwarts conceded victory,
Eight men will never play again who met
      destruction there,
The Flowers of British football, the Flowers of
      Manchester.

Matt Busby's boys were flying, returning from
      Belgrade,
This great United family, all masters of their
      trade,
The pilot of the aircraft, the skipper Captain
      Thain,
Three times they tried to take off and twice turned
      back again.

The third time down the runway disaster followed
      close,
There was slush upon that runway and the aircraft
      never rose,
It ploughed into the marshy ground, it broke, it
      overturned
And eight of the team were killed when the
      blazing wreckage burned.

Roger Byrne and Tommy Taylor who were
      capped for England's side
And Ireland's Billy Whelan and England's Geoff
      Bent died,
Mark Jones and Eddie Colman, and David Pegg
      also,
They lost their lives as it ploughed on through the
      snow.

Big Duncan he went too, with an injury to his
      frame,
And Ireland's brave Jack Blanchflower will never
      play again,
The great Matt Busby lay there, the father of his
      team,
Three long months passed by before he saw his
      team again.

The trainer, coach and secretary, and a member of
      the crew,
Also eight sporting journalists who with United
      flew,
And one of them Big Swifty, who we will ne'er
      forget,
The finest English 'keeper that ever graced the
      net.

Oh, England's finest football team its record truly
      great,
Its proud successes mocked by a cruel turn of fate.
Eight men will never play again, who met
      destruction there,
The Flowers of English football, the Flowers of
      Manchester.

'The Flowers of Manchester', words anon. Recorded by The Spinners on their album 'Black and White', Phillips International 6382 047.

The 1960s: Greatness and glory

The United squad immediately after Munich. Of the 12 only Bobby Harrop (extreme left back row) did not take part in the cup tie against Sheffield Wednesday
Back row: Bobby Harrop, Ian Greaves, Freddie Goodwin, Harry Gregg, Stan Crowther, Ron Cope, Shay Brennan and Bill Inglis. Front row: Jack Crompton, Alex Dawson, Mark Pearson, Bill Foulkes, Ernie Taylor and Colin Webster. Former goalkeeper Crompton had left United two years before Munich and joined Luton Town as their trainer. He came back to Manchester at the request of Jimmy Murphy as the club rebuilt

18 April 1958 and Matt Busby is home again. Seventy one days after the air crash the United manager arrives at his home in Kings Road, Chorlton, to be welcomed by a group of supporters. For the schoolboys of the fifties the effect of the Munich disaster was lasting: those who followed the club at that time would always remain loyal. They had lost their heroes and would find new ones under the leadership of Busby

Inset: Jimmy Murphy brings together two players of contrasting backgrounds who played an important part in the rebuilding of United. On the left is Bobby Charlton, who survived Munich to become one of the game's finest ambassadors With him is Ernie Taylor, signed from Blackpool as he was on the verge of joining Sunderland

The great side of the 1960s

Some men are born great, some achieve greatness and some have greatness thrust upon them. Jimmy Murphy came to appreciate what Shakespeare had in mind when Busby whispered to him: 'Keep the flag flying', and suddenly the responsibility for the survival of Manchester United was laid on his shoulders.

How do you continue playing a game against a background of death and destruction with so much suffering and grief? As Jimmy wrote in his book:

At first I felt as if I was going out of my mind, not knowing where to start. Previously Old Trafford had worked like a machine with Matt at the top presiding over all our efforts, sound in judgment and experience, with that incredible flair for public relations, always courteous, urbane and seemingly never forgetting anyone's face, so that he was always able to put people at their ease and talk to them.

But now I had to try and keep the club in business, without Matt's guidance and strength to fall back on, without dear Bert Whalley's unflagging energy and zeal for the club, without Tom Curry, the quiet-spoken yet highly professional team trainer, who also had a lifetime of football experience to draw on. On the administrative side we had lost the club secretary, Walter Crickmer, a man with a shrewd brain which worked with a computer-like efficiency.

Murphy's obvious problem was to get a side out for the next match, but he also had to attend to the survivors, help the bereaved and go to the funerals. He did all these things. Cometh the hour, cometh the man, and though he started in management as an assistant and retired in a similar capacity, during his time in command he brought order out of chaos and answered the call like a born leader.

Jimmy Murphy assembled the boys and his new signings to beat Sheffield Wednesday in the rearranged fifth round of the FA Cup. He took away his youngsters to prepare them for men's work in the comparative calm of the Norbreck Hydro Hotel at Blackpool. For the rest of that season he kept taking his squad to the Norbreck, so that many of the accompanying football writers will forever associate the smell of the chlorine from the indoor baths with those emotionally charged weeks in the aftermath of Munich.

Jimmy Murphy had been an integral part of the post-war success and the creation of the Busby Babes, but this was the time when the depth of the club was put to the test and the quality of the youngsters was not found wanting. Working with the reserves and juniors had always been the special preserve of Murphy. It was Jimmy who honed the young reserves ready for the final push into the League team. A great many players owe a lot to his perception and thoroughness, as even the greatest, like Bobby Charlton, will tell you.

Wilf McGuinness, another who graduated through the Murphy academy, simply says: 'Without Jimmy Murphy a lot of us would never have made it as footballers. At times we almost hated him because he drove us so hard. But it was always for our own good and we certainly respected him.'

In 1986 United's association of former players made Jimmy their first honorary life member in appreciation of his work. Despite retiring as assistant manager in 1971 when Sir Matt stepped down, he carried on scouting for the club part-time for many more years.

As a player Murphy, a fiery wing half capped by Wales, was with West Bromwich Albion from 1928 until the outbreak of the Second World War. The son of a Welsh mother and Irish father brought up in Wales, he was naturally musical, and as a young man when he wasn't playing football he played the organ in Treorchy Parish Church. He was the youngest player in the Welsh team when he was 21. In all he was capped 22 times and also captained his country.

Murphy finished the war as an NCO in charge of a Services Sports Centre at Bari in Italy. One day he was talking in his usual Welsh way to a group of soldiers. On the fringe listening and liking what he heard was Sergeant-Major Busby. At the end he came up to shake hands and said that if Jimmy fancied a job when he was demobbed then he should call in at Old Trafford. Jimmy Murphy became Busby's first signing, a shrewd one, too, as he proved in the vital early days and then when the chips were really down and he had to take over.

He fought back the tears after Munich to become the lifeline for the club's survival. Although always well respected at home, the way he coped brought him to the notice of the world and the following year he had offers to manage Brazil and Juventus. He turned them down. He had found his life's work at Old Trafford and he knew it.

Three days after United beat Wednesday in that emotional post-Munich Cup-tie they were plunged back into League football with 66,000 packed into Old Trafford to see a 1–1 draw with Nottingham Forest. The patched-up team won only one of the remaining 14 League fixtures after Munich, but they were never humiliated and they never lost heart. They picked up five draws which with the win at Sunderland saw them hang on for an extremely commendable ninth place.

United's really sterling efforts came in the FA Cup, of course. After beating Sheffield Wednesday – described in the previous chapter – they had to travel to West Bromwich for the sixth round. They ran themselves ragged to lead 2–1 with only four minutes to go, but then Harry Gregg was ruled to have carried a cross over his goal line. It didn't matter, as inspired again by the fervour of the Old Trafford crowd and the return to action of Bobby Charlton for the replay the Reds won 1–0. The winner came from Colin Webster after a last-minute run down the wing by Charlton.

Then it was back to the Midlands for a 2–2 draw in the semi-final at Villa Park with Fulham. The replay at Highbury, with Fulham enjoying almost a home tie, was a momentous match, won by United 5–3 with the help of a hat-trick from Alex Dawson, nicknamed the Black Prince. So United were through to Wembley for a final against Bolton. A telephone call from Munich saying that Matt Busby was no longer on the danger list somehow seemed to set the seal on a truly remarkable achievement.

Nat Lofthouse, the legendary 'Lion of Vienna' after his exploits for England in Austria, and the Bolton captain, recalls the final vividly:

Some of the fellows who died at Munich were among my pals. Barely a fortnight before the disaster I was having a drink with them at Old Trafford after they had thrashed us 7–2 in the League.

The thousands of neutrals at Wembley wanted United to beat us. Their incredible fight-back from Munich had captured the imagination of the world. We walked out of that tunnel into an incredibly emotional

atmosphere. But I would not be honest if I did not say that I was only interested in beating them. I was a professional who played for Bolton Wanderers. All that mattered was for Bolton to win the FA Cup.

The teams for the final were:

Bolton: Hopkinson, Hartle, Banks, Hennin, Higgins, Edwards, Birch, Stevens, Lofthouse, Parry, Holden.

Manchester United: Gregg, Foulkes, Greaves, Goodwin, Cope, Crowther, Dawson, Taylor, Charlton, Viollet, Webster.

Had United scored first, it is more than likely that the wave which had carried them to Wembley would have engulfed Bolton. But Lofthouse saw to it that whatever the Reds wanted they would have to fight for. Inside five minutes the old warhorse struck the first decisive blow. A corner from Holden was only half cleared and fell to the feet of Bryan Edwards. His centre towards the far post was met by Lofthouse, whose low drive gave Gregg no chance. It was as if in that moment the Red bubble had burst – as if the tragic events of the recent past had suddenly caught up with them.

Deflated, they fell apart. A terrific drive from Charlton did crash against the Bolton upright, and had that gone in the magic may have stirred them again. But within minutes Bolton scored again at the other end . . . although it was a goal which to this day the United lads claim should never have been allowed. Dennis Stevens hit a fierce shot from out on the left. Gregg, perhaps deceived by the pace of the shot, could only palm the ball into the air. As he jumped to catch it, the onrushing Lofthouse barged the ball and Gregg into the back of the net. Even Lofthouse could hardly believe his luck when referee Sherlock awarded a goal:

I am quite convinced that I did foul Gregg, but you could hardly expect me to argue when the referee gave a goal! Even so, I believed that we deserved to win. United never put us under pressure. We always seemed to have something in hand. It was an emotional occasion when the final whistle blew, but what really left me with a lump in my throat was when Matt Busby, supported by walking sticks and by Jimmy Murphy and physiotherapist Ted Dalton, limped into our dressing room after the match to congratulate us. What a magnificent gesture.

Harry Gregg was made of stern stuff. Like Bill Foulkes he escaped the crash without injury, and he stayed on the scene despite warnings to get clear for fear of an explosion. He helped dazed and injured survivors from the wreckage, including a baby.

Signed from Doncaster only a few weeks before the disaster for a then record fee for a goalkeeper of £23,500, Gregg became one of the firm foundations in the rebuilding. He emerged as one of the stars of the 1958 World Cup in Sweden as he helped Northern Ireland through to the quarter-finals.

He was angry about the Lofthouse incident!

Right: Harry Gregg gets the better of this challenge with Nat Lofthouse but couldn't prevent the Lion of Vienna scoring both goals to give Bolton Wanderers a 2–0 victory in the FA Cup final of 1958

Below: Jimmy Murphy and Bill Ridding (left) lead out their teams at Wembley for the 1958 FA Cup final. Matt Busby was there as a spectator on sticks, barely recovered from the Munich accident. United had battled on after the crash, carried on a tide of emotion through ties against Sheffield Wednesday, West Bromwich Albion and Fulham. Though the second goal by Nat Lofthouse when he knocked goalkeeper Harry Gregg into the back of the net was controversial, Bolton were worthy winners

'Nat blatantly barged me over the line,' he said. 'A goal should never have been awarded. I remember sitting seething in the bath at Wembley praying that Lofthouse wouldn't retire before I had had chance to get my own back. I'm happy to tell you that he didn't . . . and I did!'

The heroes of the post-Munich season

The following season might have been expected to come as an anti-climax. Certainly another Wembley trip was soon removed from the possibilities with a third round knock-out at Norwich, but in the League the Reds finished the 1958–59 season as runners-up behind Wolves.

That was really an incredible achievement and it was done without any dramatic rush into the transfer market. Dennis Viollet and Albert Scanlon returned to action after recovering from their injuries.

Warren Bradley, an England amateur international winger from Bishop Auckland was

signed midway through the season and Matt Busby had recovered sufficiently by the end of September to pay a then record £45,000 for Albert Quixall from Sheffield Wednesday. The rest of the team was made up of reserves suddenly given a new responsibility and, of course, the youngsters who had been in the pipeline. The success of the team spoke volumes for the quality of the juniors who had been working in the shadow of the Busby Babes.

The team took a few weeks to settle, but a run of 11 wins out of 12 games between November and February put them in the frame with the Wolverhampton team of Stan Cullis.

United was a team built for attack and they netted more than a hundred League goals with 29 from Charlton, the best scoring season of his career, 21 from Viollet, 16 from Scanlon and 12 from 24 appearances by Bradley. The team had emerged by the end of the season to line up:

Gregg, Greaves, Carolan, Goodwin, Foulkes (Cope), McGuinness, Bradley, Quixall, Viollet, Charlton, Scanlon.

Both inside-forward Ernie Taylor and wing-half Stan Crowther, the emergency signings after Munich, had departed, their brief but vital holding missions accomplished. They had helped give United a breathing space, Crowther bringing vigour to the team while Taylor used his vast experience to put his foot on the ball and direct operations. He had played only 30 League and Cup games for United, but the little general had been priceless. He was 33, with his great years of winning FA Cup medals with Newcastle and Blackpool well behind him. He was only 5ft 4in (1.63m), with tiny feet, but his reading of the game and his passing more than made up for the lack of inches. United let him move on to his home team of Sunderland and he still managed another 70 games before going into non-League football with Altrincham. He emigrated to New Zealand to do some coaching before returning to England to settle in the north-west again. He died in 1985. His short career at Old Trafford had been long enough to see others step forward to pick up the baton.

Bobby Charlton

None stepped forward so effectively as Bobby Charlton, who went into Munich a boy and came out of that season a man. He had of course already given ample notice of his prodigious talent in the youth team and as a young player beginning to nudge the original Busby Babes. His 14 appearances and 10 goals had brought him a championship medal in 1957 and he had won a first-team place again just before the crash.

Matt Busby, back on his feet after grievous injuries at Munich, gathers his forces around him for the start of the 1958–59 season, a mixture of survivors, new signings, a few old hands and youngsters suddenly thrust into the fray.
Front row: Jack Crompton (trainer), Ted Dalton (physiotherapist), Johnny Berry, Jimmy Murphy (assistant manager), Ernie Taylor, Ronnie Cope, Albert Scanlon, Stan Crowther, Matt Busby (manager), Bobby English, Shay Brennan, Bill Foulkes, Dennis Viollet, Ray Wood, Tommy Heron, Freddie Goodwin, Kenny Morgans, Wilf McGuinness, Warren Bradley, Bill Inglish (assistant trainer).
Back: Nobby Lawton, Barry Smith, Jimmy Elms, Reg Holland, Harold Bratt, David Gaskell, Mark Pearson, Alex Dawson, Bobby Harrop, Joe Carolan, Jimmy Shiels, Johnny Giles, Ian Greaves, Gordon Clayton

46

He says about those early days leading up to his League debut in a 4–2 win at Charlton Athletic in October 1956:

I thought I was never going to get into the team. I was scoring a lot of goals in the reserves and I kept thinking surely Matt Busby would play me now. Everyone kept telling me I would get a game soon, but it never seemed to happen. Ironically three weeks before my debut I sprained my ankle in a collision with Keith Marsden of Manchester City when playing for the reserves. Then just before the Charlton match, Sir Matt asked me if I was OK. Actually I wasn't, but I wasn't going to let my long awaited chance go by, so I crossed my fingers and said yes.

The Boss said good and that I would be playing the next day. I carried the leg a little, but it went well for me and I managed to score two goals, one from close in and one from outside the box. I was still dropped for the next game, which just shows you how severe the competition was that season. I had played in place of Tommy Taylor who had been injured and he was fit again so had to come back.

I got back into the team for the following match in place of the injured Dennis Viollet, and that's how it went for the rest of the season, in and out whenever Tommy, Dennis or Billy Whelan was injured. I didn't become a regular until the following season, about two months before the Munich accident. Then I was in off my own bat. In those days they didn't put you in until you were really ready.

For ages they just seemed to move the more experienced players around.

Bobby Charlton was such an outstanding figure at Old Trafford and played for such a long time that it is difficult to know at what point of the club's history a tribute to his service should be made. He had many fine moments in a distinguished career for both Manchester United and England, spanning 17 seasons of First Division football.

In terms of facts and figures, Charlton made 604 League appearances, scoring 198 goals, a club record on both counts which looks capable of standing for all time. In the FA Cup he played in 78 ties to score 20 goals. In European competition he made 45 appearances for a tally of 22 goals. He collected three championship medals, an FA Cup winner's medal in 1963 and of course the European Cup winner's medal in 1968, as well as helping to win the World Cup for England in 1966 in an international career of 106 appearances, during which he set a scoring record of 49 goals, another achievement likely to stand the test of time.

He was awarded the OBE in 1969, and the CBE in 1974. In 1966 he was voted Footballer of the Year in both England and Europe. But even the stream of honours and medals don't really do justice to his career, because there was both a warmth and a dignity about him which endeared him not just to Manchester United fans, but to followers of football all over the world.

The name of Bobby Charlton is universally known. It's possible to strike a chord of recognition with a foreigner, neither knowing a

Even as a young man Bobby Charlton was the Pied Piper of football. Back home in Beatrice Street, Ashington, Northumberland, he shows the local youngsters how it's done at Old Trafford. He is still teaching aspiring young players 30 years later at his world famous summer schools which now cover many other sports besides football

word of each other's language, based simply on mentioning Manchester and Bobby Charlton. Russian border guards on Checkpoint Charlie in Berlin, not known for their sense of fun, grinned hugely on the day Charlton passed through with United.

There was always a grace about his play which some have thought took football more into the realms of ballet than any other player's. He was loved for his thundering goals: not for him the tap-in, more the zoom of the rocket. His sporting attitude was impeccable. The only time he was booked somehow got lost from the record when everyone realised it had been a mistake of one kind or another. Not that there wasn't passion in his game. His desire to win never flagged, and he had the reputation among his team-mates as something of a moaner who used to nag at them if they were falling short of what he expected.

No-one could doubt Charlton's dedication to his sport, a quality which had him at considerable variance with George Best when the Irishman began to stray from the fold. Bobby brought the old Corinthian spirit into the modern game and served it well. He proved a

soccer idol without feet of clay, even moving smoothly into another successful career after a brief and not particularly encouraging essay into management. He found the ideal outlet to follow his playing career. He took up interests in the travel business, but soon concentrated on his summer soccer schools which now embrace nearly all sports. All his courses get the Charlton personal touch as he weaves his sporting magic with new generations of budding stars.

It was certainly a fitting move by the board of Manchester United when they asked him to become a director in 1986, an invitation which keeps alive great traditions of the past while introducing an able man who will contribute to the future.

But this is running on far ahead of our story. Bobby Charlton in 1959 was a fledgling. He had joined Old Trafford as a schoolboy from Ashington in Northumberland. He came from good footballing stock, his mother, Cissie, being from the well-known Milburn soccer family. Two uncles, Jim and George, played for Leeds. Uncle Stan played for Leicester. His cousin Jackie Milburn was Newcastle United's great centre-forward of the 1950s.

Bobby was an outstanding schoolboy prospect, playing in the same England team as

Bobby Charlton is the shoulder-high hero with (left to right) Matt Busby, Harry Gregg, Noel Cantwell, Pat Crerand, David Herd, Shay Brennan, Denis Law, Nobby Stiles and John Connelly

another Babe and future United manager, Wilf McGuinness, and he drew scouts like a magnet, including Joe Armstrong from Old Trafford. Joe, never a professional player himself, spent a lifetime in junior circles and was a scout for Manchester City when Matt Busby had played at Maine Road. Busby invited the man with a twinkling eye and cherubic, smiling face to Old Trafford and when Joe retired from the GPO made him his chief scout. One day in 1953 he was peering through the mist at a schoolboy match in the north-east, and noticed the talents of the young Charlton shining through the fog, and Jimmy Murphy says Joe couldn't get back quickly enough to report that he had seen a boy who he reckoned would become a world-beater.

Later, when he was ready to leave school and a host of clubs were knocking on his door, Bobby remembered that Joe Armstrong had been the first to take a real interest in him. He had liked 'Uncle Joe' and paid tribute to him when he was presented with his Footballer of the Year trophy in London many years later.

Bobby did not have an easy apprenticeship. Murphy reckons they had to work hard on him to improve his short-passing game and curb his tendency to hit speculative long balls all the time. Charlton well remembers the lessons. 'Jimmy used to play with us in practice matches and he used to come up behind me and kick me on the back of the legs. I think he was trying to toughen me up, and also perhaps to encourage me to pass the ball a bit quicker,' he says now.

Certainly Bobby proved a quick learner as he emerged after Munich as one of the key players round whom Manchester United could build. He missed two games immediately after the crash and then resumed playing with a heightened responsibility. By the start of the 1958–59 season he was in full flow. He scored a hat-trick in the opening game of the season at home to Chelsea and he bagged a couple more four days later at Nottingham Forest. He stormed through the season for his total of 29 League goals. When he and Dennis Viollet hit scoring form together, United were unstoppable. They each scored twice to finish with a 6–1 win against Blackburn Rovers, and later in the season Portsmouth also crashed 6–1 at Old Trafford with Charlton and Viollet again sharing four of the goals.

Charlton and Viollet scored a goal apiece to beat Wolves 2–1 at Old Trafford in the February, so that by April the two clubs were level on points at the top of the table. But Wolves had a couple of games in hand and they finished powerfully to take the title by six points. Really United had no right to finish runners-up after the grievous blow suffered at Munich just the previous season. Such a position was really beyond their wildest dreams and even Busby admitted that it had been far better than he had expected.

What made it so startling of course was that the club had been able to find so many players from within. Warren Bradley enjoyed great success after joining as an amateur. He was quickly launched into the England team and in fact won three caps to add to 11 amateur appearances. Born in Hyde, Cheshire, he was a school teacher and soon made himself at home among the professional stars. His intelligence and quiet confidence helped, qualities which later saw him become headmaster of a big Manchester comprehensive school, but he hardly ranked as a major signing, at least not as far as his fee was concerned, a modest donation to Bishop Auckland.

The only real concession United had made to the transfer market following the emergency signings of Taylor and Crowther was in recruiting inside-forward Albert Quixall from Hillsborough. The blond-haired Yorkshireman was bought in keeping with Busby's policy of putting players on to the Old Trafford stage who had personality and entertainment value as well as being able to do a job of work. Albert was the golden boy of his day. In his native Sheffield he had swept everything before him . . . captain of his school, his city, his county, his country and then playing for the full England team by the age of 18.

Quixall helped to maintain the Busby tradition for creative, skilful football in a difficult period. He had charisma, though he didn't make a fortune from football. Looking back he says: 'I suppose I was born 20 years too early. I remember an article on me at the time saying that my record transfer fee made me worth my weight in gold. Perhaps that was true, but it didn't do much for me personally. I don't harp on that though because you can't translate everything into money. I achieved a lot in my teens and had some great times in football. I'm not bitter by any means.'

You could hardly blame him if he was. Working after football for years in a scrap metal yard near Manchester where he settled, he was young enough to see near-contemporaries prosper out of all proportion with a fraction of his talent . . . yet he was too old to have caught the gravy train himself.

Dennis Viollet was another supremely gifted player who hit the heights just a little too soon to catch the explosion in football wages and finances. Dennis, a local youngster who grew up playing ball around Maine Road, was in fact a Manchester City fan like the rest of his family. Joe Armstrong and Jimmy Murphy persuaded him to come to Old Trafford and his career straddled the Munich disaster. He was one of the Busby Babes who survived the crash to play a vital role in the rebuilding period.

Viollet's best season came as United embarked on the 1959–60 season, hoping to build on their runners-up position of the previous season. That they finished only seventh was hardly the fault of Viollet, who broke Jack Rowley's club scoring record by notching 32 League goals.

He was a master craftsman, a sleek ghost of a player who scored his goals with stealth, skill and speed. He was not a typical robust centre-forward, but his rather frail-looking appearance belied his strength. He was resilient, and overall he scored 159 goals in 259 League appearances spread over ten seasons of first-team soccer.

He eventually left Old Trafford in 1962 to play for Stoke, and helped them win the Second Division Championship for Tony Waddington. He played in the States for a spell, then after winning an Irish FA Cup winners' medal with Linfield he settled in America, becoming involved in their football. His next visits to England were to accompany his talented tennis daughter on trips to play at Junior Wimbledon.

Viollet's record scoring season should have brought him more than two caps for England. There was, in fact, a case to be made out around 1960 for playing the entire United forward line at international level.

United again topped 100 League goals in that 1959–60 season, with Dennis's 32 being followed by 18 from Charlton, 13 from Quixall, and eight and seven from wingers Bradley and Scanlon. Alex Dawson, a centre-forward who also played on the wing, was also forcing his way into the team and grabbed a promising 15 from only 22 appearances. Johnny Giles and Mark Pearson, pilloried by Burnley's controversial and outspoken chairman Bob Lord as a Teddy Boy, played occasionally.

United were too erratic to win the title. One week they would score four, the next they would concede four. Things came to a head in January when the team went to Newcastle and lost 7–3. Busby suddenly swooped in the transfer market to pay £30,000 for wing-half Maurice Setters from West Bromwich Albion. He wanted the bandy-legged, tough-tackling Setters to stiffen the midfield. What a contrast he made with Quixall. Their styles were at the opposite ends of the football spectrum and there wasn't much love lost between them.

It was a period of retrenchment for United, with Busby taking the rebuilding in steady fashion. At the end of 1960 he bought again, paying £29,000 for the West Ham and Republic of Ireland left-back Noel Cantwell.

The intelligent and articulate Irishman became a sound influence and a splendid captain. But there was no instant success with United unable to improve on seventh in the League in the 1960–61 season, and making a fourth-round exit in the FA Cup.

The 1961–62 season did bring a run in the Cup, United reaching the semi-finals only to lose 3–1 against Spurs at Hillsborough. The League, however, saw them slip to 15th. Busby knew it was time for action. There were not enough talented youngsters coming through fast enough. Just before the start of the 1961–62 season he had bought centre-forward David Herd, son of his former team-mate Alex, from Arsenal for £32,000. Herd had obliged by scoring 14 goals, but the goal touch had deserted the others and Herd's tally was the best effort.

The arrival of Law and Crerand

So in the summer of 1962 Busby spent again and pulled off his best-ever transfer coup. He brought Denis Law home from Italy's Torino for a record £115,000.

United now had a twin strike force of Law and Herd, backed by Charlton and Quixall and a new youngster, Johnny Giles, with another home product, Nobby Stiles, occasionally forcing his way into the team at half-back.

Still it wasn't quite right. The attack looked full of goals, but they only clicked spasmodically. Busby decided that the service to the men up front wasn't good enough. So he went out to buy a player who could supply the right kind of ammunition for Law and Herd to fire. The result was the arrival, in February 1963 for £43,000 from Glasgow Celtic, of right-half Pat Crerand. Busby now had the right balance in the half-back line, Setters the ball-winner on the left and Crerand the distributor on the right.

It was too late to pull things round in the League and the Reds ended the 1962–63 season in 19th place, their lowest position under Busby's management. But the potential was there, and it showed in the FA Cup as the Reds sailed through every round without a replay, to beat Southampton 1–0 in the semi-final at Villa Park and face Leicester City at Wembley.

For a change, because of their League position, the Reds were the underdogs. Leicester had finished fourth in the First Division and had the reputation of being a side with an iron defence. So the stage was set for a clash between the irresistible force and the immovable object when the following teams took the field at Wembley on 25 May 1963:

Manchester United: Gaskell, Dunne, Cantwell, Crerand, Foulkes, Setters, Giles, Quixall, Herd, Law, Charlton.

THE FOOTBALL ASSOCIATION CHALLENGE CUP COMPETITION

THE FOOTBALL ASSOCIATION | CENTENARY YEAR

FINAL TIE

LEICESTER CITY
v
MANCHESTER UNITED

OFFICIAL PROGRAMME | ONE SHILLING

WEMBLEY
EMPIRE STADIUM

SATURDAY, MAY 25th   Kick-off 3 p.m.

Above: Once they were team-mates at Old Trafford but here a confrontation of like characters . . .the fiery Denis Law of United and the aggressive Maurice Setters in the white shirt of Stoke City

Left: Up for the Cup . . . and Manchester United's first success five years after the calamity of the Munich air crash

Below left: Noel Cantwell, captain of Manchester United, shakes hands with Leicester City skipper Colin Appleton under the watchful eye of referee Ken Aston at the start of the 1963 FA Cup final

Above right: Gordon Banks clears from Denis Law at Wembley in 1963, but the Leicester City and England goalkeeper couldn't stop United winning 3–1 to take the FA Cup. It was sweet relief for United who struggled all season in the League, looking relegation candidates at one stage, and finishing in 19th place, the low water mark in Matt Busby's management career

Right: Celebration time for Pat Crerand, Albert Quixall and David Herd after winning the FA Cup in 1963. The Sheffield-born Quixall, crowned with the Cup, was the golden boy of his era, playing international football at every level and costing then a record fee of £45,000 from Sheffield Wednesday

Leicester: Banks, Sjoberg, Norman, McLintock, King, Appleton, Riley, Cross, Keyworth, Gibson, Stringfellow.

From the first whistle it was obvious that the Reds had torn up the form book. Law, in particular, was in one of those moods when it would have taken a Centurion tank to stop him. The famous Leicester 'iron curtain' looked more like a torn curtain, as Law danced through at will.

Crerand, who had taken time to settle into the side, was also having a field day on Wembley's wide-open spaces, and it was one of those inch-perfect passes which enabled Law to swivel and drive home the first goal after 29 minutes. The longer the game went on, the more composed and confident United looked. In the 58th minute, they underlined their superiority when Herd rounded off a sweet move, involving Giles and Charlton, by sweeping the ball past Gordon Banks. The game was as good as won. In a late flurry Keyworth scored for Leicester, but Herd grabbed his second to make the final scoreline 3–1 to United.

The victory more than made up for the Reds' disappointing League form, and finally buried the memory of their two Wembley defeats in 1957 and 1958. More than that, it indicated that from the ashes of Munich, Busby was on the way towards building another side capable of taking English soccer by storm.

United had flexed their muscles and had given notice that they were back in business as a top team again. They looked forward to season 1963–64 in more confident mood, and used their Cup victory as a launching pad to go with more conviction for the big prizes. They didn't do too well in the European Cup Winners' Cup, squandering a first leg win of 4–1 against Sporting Lisbon by losing 5–0 in Portugal. It was United's most embarrassing defeat in their history and the story is told more fully in the chapter on Europe.

However, they reached the semi-finals of the FA Cup to play West Ham and finished runners-up in the League. Denis Law, the matador of Old Trafford, enjoyed his best scoring season in a year which was also significant for the debut in League football of a young, black-haired Irishman with flashing eyes.

Matt Busby gave George Best his first game on 14 September 1963, playing him at outside-right against West Bromwich Albion at Old Trafford. David Sadler, the young bank clerk from Maidstone, Kent, with whom he shared digs at Mrs Fullaway's in Davyhulme, scored in a 1–0 win.

Ian Moir replaced Best for the next League match, but Busby had noted his performance and called up the youngster to play against Burnley at Old Trafford in December. Busby was ringing the changes because two days previously, on Boxing Day, his team had gone down 6–1 at Turf Moor. Best came in for the return and scored in a sweet 5–1 revenge win.

The famous football litany of Charlton, Law and Best had now come together, though at this stage Best was very much the junior partner. The man at the height of his powers was Law, scoring a fantastic total of 46 goals in League and Cup. Thirty of them came from 30 League appearances, helping the Reds finish second to Liverpool, four points adrift. He scored ten in six FA Cup-ties and notched another eight in ten games in the European Cup Winners' Cup. There was the usual 20 from David Herd, while Bobby Charlton weighed in with nine, but Busby was still tinkering with the team.

He changed goalkeepers at one point, replacing Harry Gregg for a spell with David Gaskell. Halfway through he switched Tony Dunne to left-back in place of Noel Cantwell and brought in Shay Brennan at right-back. Inside-right was causing him problems with one of his youngsters, Phil Chisnall, dropped in favour of Graham Moore, the Welsh international. David Sadler was in and out, still searching for his best position, defender, midfield or striker. Nobby Stiles was brought in at left-half to take over from Maurice Setters, and give nothing away in terms of matching fire with fire. Ian Moir played half a season on the wing. There had probably been just a few too many changes to get the better of Liverpool, who proved their right to be champions by winning 1–0 at Old Trafford in November and then beating United 3–0 at Anfield on the run-in for the title. Those four points separated the two teams at the end of the season.

All-in-all, it was a marked improvement on the previous season's 19th position, and they had also fought some sterling battles in the FA Cup especially against Sunderland in the quarter-final. The fans had enjoyed a spectacular 3–3 game at Old Trafford and then admired a stout 2–2 draw after extra time at Roker Park. United proved to be the team with the stamina as Sunderland finally collapsed and went down 5–1 in the second replay at Huddersfield.

The semi-final took United to Hillsborough on an exceedingly wet day to meet West Ham and they didn't play well as they slid to a 3–1 defeat. Geoff Hurst scored the decisive third goal after a splendid run down the wing by Bobby Moore. The Hammers' theme tune of 'Forever Blowing Bubbles' had an appropriate twist as the London fans sang their heads off in the rain while United's followers trekked miserably back home across the Pennines. The Hillsborough hoodoo had struck again. But there was happier news on the Cup front at youth level as the club gathered momentum again. The kids won the FA Youth Cup after a seven-year gap, heralding the arrival of more promising youngsters.

George Best, Willie Anderson and David Sadler had already played in the first team. Other players from the successful youth team who went on to play in the League side were Jimmy Rimmer, the goalkeeper, full-back Bobby Noble, winger John Aston and wing-half John Fitzpatrick.

United were blooming again at all levels accompanied by imaginative development off the field. Plans were announced for the building of a new cantilever stand in readiness for Old Trafford as a venue for the 1966 World Cup in England. The bulk of the finance was to be raised by a football pool run by a Development Association on a scale not previously seen in soccer.

There was a buzz about the place again, though Busby knew he needed a more settled side than the one which had just chased Liverpool home, and despite his many changes he felt he needed a top-class winger. So during the summer of 1964 he bought the experienced John Connelly from Burnley for £60,000. The winger, equally at home on either flank, had already won League and FA Cup medals at Turf Moor and it proved to be an inspired signing.

Champions again

Connelly was the final piece in the jigsaw which turned a team of runners-up into champions. The whole thing fell into place as the Reds swept to success in season 1964–65, pipping Leeds United for the title. In the days when goal average, rather than difference, settled issues, United won by the narrow margin of 0.686 of a goal.

United still had a game in hand when they knew they had won the Championship, so the final game at Villa Park didn't matter all that much and it was duly lost. The significant aspect was that they were champions for the first time

Manchester United were champions for the first time after the Munich disaster in season 1964–65, no mean feat considering that they had virtually had an entire team destroyed.
Their medal-winning squad lined up:
Front Row: John Connelly, Bobby Charlton, David Herd, Denis Law and George Best. Middle: Jack Crompton (trainer), Shay Brennan, David Sadler, Bill Foulkes, John Aston, Noel Cantwell and Matt Busby (manager). Back: Nobby Stiles, Tony Dunne, David Gaskell, Pat Dunne, Pat Crerand and John Fitzpatrick

Denis Law and David Herd in the dark shirts watch eagerly as United storm to a 3–1 victory against Arsenal at Old Trafford, the match which brought them the 1965 championship. Law scored twice while George Best got the other goal

Autographs :

since Munich. Bobby Charlton and Bill Foulkes were the only crash survivors remaining in the team.

Connelly more than played his part, scoring 15 goals from outside-right while Best dazzled on the left to score ten. Charlton, now operating in a midfield role, scored ten as well, while Law led the scoring with 28, supported again by 20 from Herd. But while the forwards attracted the headlines, they owed a great deal to the defence. Bill Foulkes, the centre-half, and the two full-backs, Shay Brennan and Tony Dunne, were ever-presents. They conceded only 39 goals to help provide their personable new goalkeeper, Pat Dunne, with a championship medal. Pat was to flit quickly across the Old Trafford stage. A modest £10,000 signing from Shamrock Rovers, he spent less than three seasons at United. He seemed to come from nowhere and disappear almost as quickly, but he played his part.

The team's championship qualities had not

53

been immediately apparent when only one win had come in the opening six games, but they picked up thereafter, dropping only one point in their next 14 games. The highlight was a 7–0 thrashing of Aston Villa at Old Trafford with four of the goals down to Law.

They dropped a few points in mid-season, but put in another searing run of ten wins in 11 games to take the title.

United had an all-round strength now that also saw them do well in the other competitions. They were, in fact, chasing a treble for most of the season. They reached the semi-finals of the European Fairs Cup (later to become the UEFA Cup), and at the same time stormed through to the semi-finals of the FA Cup and an appointment with their deadly rivals from Elland Road. Leeds United were coming to the height of their powers under Don Revie, and not everyone admired their methods. Manchester United had more than an abrasive streak as well, so it was a volatile mix when the two teams met at Hillsborough.

League points had been shared, each side winning 1–0 on their own ground, and the atmosphere for the Cup-tie was hostile. The match was fierce and bad-tempered and could have done with stricter refereeing. There were no goals and the replay was staged at Nottingham Forest's ground. Referee Dick Windle, perhaps conscious of his leniency at Sheffield, tightened up considerably, and the players also held themselves in check better, knowing full well that one or two of them had been fortunate to stay on the field for the full 90 minutes in the first game. But it was still a mess of a match which constantly had to be stopped for fouls. It was reckoned that Manchester United had conceded more than 20 free-kicks in the original game, and almost as many in the replay. They finally paid the penalty for trying to play Leeds at their own game. With less than two minutes to go they gave away one free-kick too many and their former inside-forward, Johnny Giles, who had failed to hit it off with Busby after coming through the juniors, punished them. His cleverly flighted kick into the goalmouth was headed home by Billy Bremner, the Leeds ball of fire. So Leeds went to Wembley, leaving the Reds contemplating their third semi-final defeat in four years.

The other leg of the treble collapsed as well with semi-final defeat in the Fairs Cup after a play-off third game against Ferencvaros in Budapest long after the official end to the season. Nevertheless it had been a mighty year with many memorable games on the three fronts, and they had made their mark with the Championship trophy back at Old Trafford to show for their efforts. The team showed few changes with the medals going to:

Pat Dunne, Brennan, Tony Dunne, Crerand, Foulkes, Stiles, Connelly, Charlton, Herd, Law, Best.

It was a well balanced strong side.

Denis Law

Law was at his peak in that Championship season as the attacking star, yet when he had started his career in England with Huddersfield Town in 1955, Bill Shankly had said of him: 'He looked like a skinned rabbit.' But once Shankly had seen him play he knew that here was something special. After only 80 games, and with Huddersfield having slid into the Second Division, he was sold for £56,000 to First Division Manchester City.

City kept Law for a season and then made a handsome profit, selling him to Torino for £110,000, giving him what he describes as the worst 12 months of his life.

'It was like a prison' said Law. 'I am not one for the high life. All I wanted was to be treated like a human being. It wasn't long before I realised I had made a ghastly mistake. It all finally blew up when Torino refused me permission to play for Scotland. That was the end as far as I was concerned. I stormed out so quickly that I left all my clothes behind. I never saw them again.'

Torino threatened Law with all sorts of legal sanctions to try to get him back to Italy, but in the end they gave in. So on 12 July 1962, Denis Law signed for Manchester United for a record fee of £115,000. And what a marvellous deal it turned out to be. For a decade, the 'king' ruled over his Old Trafford empire. The United fans respected the skills of Bobby Charlton, they revelled at the sight of the genius which was George Best, but they worshipped Denis Law, the hero of the Stretford End.

'What I walked into from Italy was the finest football club in the world with the finest manager,' said Law. 'Matt Busby always stuck by me through thick and thin. Your problems at home, your illnesses, any little worries – they were all his business. That's what made him so different. That is why you gave everything for him on the field.'

Not that Law was always the apple of Busby's eye. Three times between 1963 and 1967, his fiery temperament landed him in trouble with referees. Twice he was suspended for 28 days. And that is not the type of record guaranteed to endear you to Matt Busby.

He had a head-on clash with Busby in 1966, when he grandly told the club in a letter that unless he was offered better terms he would ask for a transfer. Busby refused to be blackmailed, even by the jewel in his Old Trafford crown, called his bluff and transfer-listed him. A few days later, a sheepish Law made a public apology.

But the good times outweighed the bad. Law helped the Reds win the League title in 1964–65 and 1966–67, and collected an FA Cup winners' medal in 1963. He was also voted European Footballer of the Year in 1964. Sadly injury forced him to miss United's greatest triumph – the European Cup final victory in 1968. Perhaps because of this his fondest memory at Old Trafford remains the 1963 FA Cup final against

A well earned breather and a glass of refreshment for Denis Law as he relaxes alongside Noel Cantwell after clinching the League championship in 1965

Leicester: 'It was one of the greatest games I played for United. I can see Paddy Crerand now hitting me with a perfect ball from the left wing. I turned quickly and hit the ball into the net past Gordon Banks' right hand. It was the first goal, and one I had always dreamed of scoring at Wembley.'

The Demon King was electric near goal. When he jumped he seemed to have a personal sky hook, so long did he hang in the air above defenders.

His razor reflexes and courage brought him 171 goals from 305 League appearances in his ten years at Old Trafford. In the FA Cup he had an incredible return of 34 goals in 44 appearances, while European competition brought him the even more impressive scoring rate of 28 goals in 33 matches. The Stretford End took him to their heart: they perhaps loved not just his goals but the streak of villainy that also ran through his game.

In July 1973, after battling against a knee injury for two years, United allowed him to join Manchester City on a free transfer in recognition of his services. Perhaps the best way to illustrate the bond which existed between Law and Old Trafford, is to recall an incident in April 1974, when Law's back-heeled goal for Manchester City sent United plunging into the Second Division. This time there was no characteristic punching of the air in celebration. Law, head down, walked slowly back to the centre circle with the look of a man who had just stabbed his best friend in the back.

Law scored 30 goals in 55 international appearances for Scotland. His whole career brought him 217 League goals in 452 games. After retiring in 1974, at the end of his second spell with Manchester City, he virtually hung up his boots. His bravery had left him with a legacy of injuries which wouldn't really permit him to play any more. That was the price he paid for his storming career.

The other Championship winners

Just like Denis Law, there was something of the lost waif about George Best when he arrived at Old Trafford. He was a skinny 15-year-old from Belfast, desperately homesick at being away from home for the first time in his life. Indeed, after 24 hours, he and his young Irish companion from Belfast, Eric McMordie, fled back to Ireland. But Busby was quickly on the phone, and with the help of his father, George was persuaded to give it another go.

Best had been recommended by United's legendary Northern Ireland scout Bob Bishop, who sent this simple note to Busby: 'I think I have found a genius.' It wasn't long before Harry Gregg and his United team-mates found out that Bishop was not exaggerating. Gregg recalls:

I think the first time I ever saw George in action was when I volunteered to go to our training ground, The Cliff, one afternoon to help with the kids. There was a bit of a practice game planned and I went in goal on one side with George on the other. After a while he got the ball and raced clear of our defence. I had always prided myself on the fact that I could make forwards do what I wanted in these circumstances. But this slip of a boy shook his hips and had me diving at fresh air while the ball went in the other corner of the net.

I thought, right, you won't get away with that again. But blow me, a few minutes later he brought the ball up to me again . . . and did exactly the same thing. I knew in that moment that the club had a very rare talent on their hands.

Best brought his young genius to bear on the left wing, often roaming far for the ball, while the more orthodox Connelly supplied penetration on the right flank. Law and Herd fired in most of the ammunition, scoring nearly 50 goals between them.

Charlton and Crerand generated ideas and movement while the whole pattern was based on solid defence. Centre-half Bill Foulkes was rightly proud of his department's contribution and was the first to point up the increasingly effective role of the fast emerging Nobby Stiles. After winning the Championship he said:

The forwards are the glamour boys, especially the ones who score goals. But I would say we are stronger in defence now than we have ever been since I joined the club 17 years ago.

55

The career of Nobby Stiles is perhaps an example of how hard it is for a defender to steal the limelight. He must be one of the most under-rated players in the game. He is regarded by most people as a strong-tackling wing-half, a destroyer if you like, and indeed this is an important role in any team which he does exceptionally well for Manchester United.

But he also has skills which are often overlooked. For instance he is a fine reader of a game. He brings aggression to the team, and let's be honest, without some aggression in your team you might as well stop in the dressing room. Nobby will also supply hard work involving a lot of unselfish running.

He probably didn't help himself in his early days by getting into trouble. He is impetuous, though if you knew him off the field you would find it difficult to imagine. His nickname for instance at the club is 'Happy'.

I must admit that Happy has had his unhappy moments on the field of play, but I think he has improved. Fortunately Alf Ramsey has been able to see his real worth. He at least has a high regard for his skills or he would not be playing him as a link man at wing-half for England.

England need more players like him. It is all very well having a team full of highly skilled individualists, but not all of them are noted for hard work and someone has to supply the steam for the outfit to function.

If you had 11 Nobby Stiles in a team you would not need to worry about losing. He is a player in the real meaning of the world. I think he and I struck up a good understanding in our Championship season.

Our full backs, Tony Dunne and Shay Brennan, also played well together. What a contrast this pair make to the old-time defenders who were invariably big brawny fellows whose aim was to stop the wingers at any cost. Both Tony and Shay are strong and they don't lack courage, but they are not exactly bruisers. They fit into the modern concept which calls for defenders to have the skill of forwards with an eye for going up in attack whenever the situation calls for it.

Both of them rely on skill for getting the ball rather than brute strength, and they can speed along, especially Tony who must be one of the fastest backs in the business.

The tackling of Nobby Stiles improved when he began to wear contact lenses. He had worn glasses from a young age and naturally took them off for football. The situation left him short on visual judgement. As Bobby Charlton once said: 'Nobby doesn't so much tackle people as bump into them.' It's said that his eyesight was so defective that he once left a football banquet in a big hotel, returned, sat down and then realised he was at someone else's dinner.

Certainly there was a marked improvement in Stiles' timing when he started to wear contact

Above: Trouble and George Best went hand in hand towards the end of his career as his name went into referees' notebooks with increasing regularity

Top: Nobby Stiles was a terrier defender for both United and England as he clearly demonstrates here

Left: Alex Stepney, the United goalkeeper, is on the receiving end of a finger-wagging lecture from Nobby Stiles

lenses, and he went on to become one of England's heroes when they beat West Germany to win the World Cup at Wembley in the summer of 1966. Who can forget the merry jig he did round Wembley without his front teeth but with a grin that seemed to spread across his entire face? Stiles and Bobby Charlton reflected great credit on Manchester United with the way they performed for England on the World Cup stage.

Disciplinary problems

What did not reflect so well on Old Trafford around this period was the number of times United players were in trouble with referees.

Although Stiles improved his tackling with the advantage of being able to see, he still let his feelings run away with him with gestures of annoyance at referees.

Denis Law rarely finished a season without being sent off, Pat Crerand had his volatile moments and eventually George Best ran into trouble with referees.

In the 1963–64 season Noel Cantwell, David Herd, Denis Law and Pat Crerand were all sent off. Albert Quixall was dismissed while playing for the reserves and even Bobby Noble was sent off playing for the youth team.

In 1964–65, on the way to the Championship, Law received the second of his four-week bans after clashing at Blackpool with the ego of York referee Peter Rhodes, who was determined to make clear who had the last word in such matters. Cantwell and Harry Gregg were given early baths with the reserves and Stiles was fined £100 for totalling too many cautions.

Gregg and Crerand received marching orders in 1965–66. Another Championship year in 1966–67 saw Stiles sent off and later suspended for three weeks for accumulating too many bookings. Law survived the season but managed to get himself dismissed on a summer tour in Australia.

The European Cup triumph of 1967–68 was accompanied by a six-week ban for Law following a spectacular bust-up and very early bath with Ian Ure against Arsenal. John Fitzpatrick, Brian Kidd and Carlo Sartori were also sent off.

Needless to say, cautions were numerous and revealed an undisciplined trait in the make-up of an otherwise gloriously successful period. The black streak contrasted so vividly with the man at the helm, a manager who throughout his career represented all that was fair and best in the game of football. There is no simple explanation except to say that United were playing more games than most, matches of high tension, in this period, and that many of their offences were in retaliation. Crerand for one couldn't abide cheats, and if he felt an opponent was taking a liberty with him he was more inclined to take an immediate swing at him than wait in the time-honoured way to get his own back with a hard tackle when the chance arose.

Law was a highly strung character who reacted fiercely to provocation and Stiles was another impatient character who couldn't suffer fools, poor referees and poor linesmen gladly.

Busby never went in for the tactics of Don Revie at Leeds, but possibly, after the experience of Munich, he was prepared to turn a blind eye to some of the excesses of his players in his ambition to make Manchester United a power in the game again. As the years went by he was not getting any younger and he was a man in a hurry. In any case how did you control the emotions of a player like Denis Law, so explosive and so often kicked black and blue by opponents seeking to contain him?

The talented trinity of Denis Law, George Best and Bobby Charlton celebrate a goal for Manchester United against Wolves in March 1966. It was because of the entertainment value of players like this famous trio, coupled with success, that attendances at Old Trafford started to boom. An average League crowd of 53,984 watched the team in 1966–67. The following season a record was established with a League average at Old Trafford of 57,759, a figure never likely to be bettered on an English club ground in these days of stricter crowd control and reduced capacities

A second title in 1966–67

United launched into the 1965–66 season as champions determined to make an impression on three fronts and that is exactly what they did, even though they failed to land a trophy.

They were playing in their beloved European Cup again and produced some splendid football until stopped by Partizan Belgrade in the semi-finals. The Reds reached the semi-finals of the FA Cup as well after one or two scares. For instance in the fifth round at Wolves they were two goals down after only nine minutes, both from penalties, but recovered for Law (two), Best and Herd to give them a 4–2 win. They beat Preston in the sixth round after a replay at Old Trafford to reach the semi-finals for the fifth successive season. But a hectic season seemed to catch up with them when they played Everton at Burnden Park just three days after meeting Partizan Belgrade in the second leg of the European semi-final. Best was missing with a knee injury and his colleagues looked jaded in contrast to Everton, who had fielded virtually a reserve team the previous Saturday in order to rest their senior players. They were later fined £2,000, but that was little consolation for United, who fought stubbornly but without any spark on their way to a 1–0 defeat.

It seemed as if the two Cup runs had dissipated United's strength in the League, too. David Herd scored 24 League goals, Charlton got 16 and Law 15, but the Reds never strung more than three wins together on the trot. They were always among the leading group of clubs and put in a great finish, beating Blackburn 4–1 away and whipping Aston Villa 6–1 at Old Trafford, but they had to be content with fourth place while Liverpool took the title six points ahead of Leeds and Burnley and ten ahead of United.

Bobby Charlton and Nobby Stiles went off to play for England in the World Cup triumph and everybody reported back for the start of season 1966–67 determined to learn from the near-misses.

They didn't make a particularly good start, but Busby made a few changes. He had Bobby Noble and Johnny Aston ready after coming through with the team which had won the FA Youth Cup in 1964. Noble took over at left-back and Aston at outside-left, with Best switched to the right to replace the departed Connelly. David Sadler also won a regular place as an attacking midfield player.

Busby bought a new goalkeeper, paying Tommy Docherty at Chelsea £50,000 for Alex Stepney. At the end of the season the manager described the arrival of Stepney as the biggest single factor behind the winning of the 1966–67 Championship four points in front of Nottingham Forest. United were particularly strong in the second half of the season, perhaps helped by the fact that they were not in Europe and that they were knocked out of both the FA Cup and the League Cup in early rounds.

The Reds certainly clinched the title with a flourish, beating West Ham 6–1 in London to take the honours with a match to spare. It was the biggest away win of the season in the First Division. The team went through the season unbeaten at home, where they were watched by a League average crowd of 53,800. They were in relentless mood, even to the end. As Nobby Stiles said afterwards: 'Just after we had scored our sixth goal at West Ham I trotted over to Bill Foulkes and said: "Congratulations, Bill, on your fourth championship medal", but all he did was give me a rollicking and tell me to concentrate on the game.'

It was determination by Stiles that had started the scoring, though. The England wing-half thrust for goal and pressured the West Ham defence into trouble. The ball spun loose across the area for Bobby Charlton to streak through a gap between two players and hammer home a goal after only two minutes. Pat Crerand, Bill Foulkes and George Best added goals to put the Reds four up in the first 25 minutes. Denis Law scored twice in the second half, one from the penalty spot, for a swashbuckling finale.

It was a crashing climax to a season in which the Reds paced the title with a perfect sense of timing and produced a remorseless last lap that was too good for their opponents. For this was a Championship won on the classical formula of winning at home and drawing away. This was the pattern from Christmas as they turned for home into the second half of the season. The sequence started with a 1–0 win at Old Trafford against Spurs on 14 January. The following week at Maine Road the Reds drew 1–1 with Manchester City. And they never looked back as they marched on to a run of eight away draws backed by eight home victories. This was the solid base, consistent and relentless, from which they sprang to tear West Ham to pieces and take the title.

At the turn of the year United had been locked in a three-horse race, jockeying for top place with Liverpool, while Nottingham Forest were the dark horses rising swiftly after a long and powerful winning run. By mid-March United were still level pegging with Liverpool, though ahead on goal average, and Forest had dropped back a little. On 25 March came one of those decisive games, for on that day United, the challengers, took on Liverpool, the reigning champions, in the lion's den at Anfield.

The Reds had feared Liverpool all season, particularly after only drawing with them at Old Trafford in December. In fact Denis Law was having nightmares. He dreamed that he was playing at Anfield, took the ball up to Ron Yeats, beat him, scored a goal . . . and then fell into The Kop! As it turned out, no-one scored, but the point was a great result for United and a bad one for Bill Shankly's men, who slowly slid out of the picture after failing to close the gap that the match had offered.

Forest now turned out to be the greater danger. The Forest fire was spreading and they were breathing down United's neck. They got within a point at one stage, and the game that proved decisive for them was on 11 February when they came to play at Old Trafford.

There was a 62,727 attendance, with the gates locked. It took the Reds until five minutes from the end to crack Forest, but the scoring maestro, Law, then banged in the winner. That was the beginning of the end for the team, managed by old United maestro Johnny Carey, though no-one at Old Trafford will forget the first encounter of the season between the two clubs at Nottingham in October. The Reds crashed to their heaviest defeat of the season, beaten 4–1, and they slipped to eighth in the table, the low water mark of the campaign.

The 'Busby boobies' had been one football writer's description of that performance. Hardly that perhaps, but it was certainly a critical game, and a significant one for Bobby Noble, who along with Noel Cantwell was drafted into the team after the defeat. The choice of Noble meant that Matt Busby had once again turned to his fruitful youth in an hour of need. The youngster took his chance brilliantly until a car accident following his return from Sunderland robbed him of the last few games and his career.

Shay Brennan slipped quietly but effectively back into his place to keep the victory push going. A much more difficult problem was posed when David Herd broke his leg against Leicester City at Old Trafford on 18 March in the act of scoring his 16th League goal. It could easily have been Herd's best scoring season with United and it was with some anxiety that the manager waited to see whether the team could get by without any more goals from him.

No doubt he recalled the injury to George Best at a similar stage of the previous season. For when Best had injured his knee, leading to a cartilage operation, the whole team faded and they lost the FA Cup semi-final and the European Cup semi-final. But this time they stayed steady, and others came forward to help shoulder the scoring burden.

Law, of course, remained the leading spirit in United's sparkling attack. Charlton came back to his best in the second half of the season, and after Herd's injury stepped up his scoring rate, notably with a fine pair against Sheffield Wednesday at Hillsborough. The United manager also helped cover Herd's absence by switching Stiles into the attack to add more fire and bringing David Sadler, a most versatile performer, back from the forward line to form a fine double centre-half pairing with Foulkes.

59

Stiles, now wearing his dental plate for matches because he considered that his fierce toothless appearance as seen on television during the World Cup frightened referees and got him into trouble, finished the season in fine form. Although the attack dazzled in many games with George Best another brilliant ace in the pack, United's defence paved the way by holding on through some lean scoring spells and hard away games. Foulkes started the season with many people wondering whether the club should have bought a new centre-half; he gave the answer himself with some uncompromising displays.

Every player played his part, including Tony Dunne, brilliant at full-back and Irish Footballer of the Year; Pat Crerand, the architect of so much of United's midfield play; the young left-winger John Aston, who came through a critical spell superbly, and players who came in for brief but vital periods like Noel Cantwell, wing-half John Fitzpatrick and forward Jimmy Ryan.

And what wonderful support there was to urge them to the Championship. The Old Trafford crowd – over a million watched United's home League games, the highest since the war – and the fans who travelled to bring record gates at several away matches, also helped bring European football back to Old Trafford.

Matt Busby gave notice he would be there to lead the next campaign. 'I'm too young to retire,' said the longest serving club manager in the game.

It wasn't just winning the Championship that brought the crowds flocking to watch United home and away in such numbers: it was the quality of their football and the personalities packed into their team.

George Best

George Best had become a cult figure by this time. He took your breath away with his finesse on the field and he was worshipped off it, especially by the girls. He was a new breed of footballer, with a following more like that of a pop star.

It was the age of the Beatles and the swinging sixties and George, with his cute eyes and Beatle haircut was ready to swing with the best of them. Girls sobbed as they stared at him through the windows of the team coach. Writers flocked to his door to examine the magic not just of his play but of his appeal for beauty queens and actresses.

Busby had already declared: 'George has the lot. He's a world-class footballer.' Alf Ramsey was sighing: 'I wish he had been born in England.' Of course it all went wrong at the end, but in 1967 he was simply a brilliant player. His life style off the field was still regarded as a bit of a lark, certainly by the media.

After all, he was different. By early 1966 he had opened a men's boutique with a partner, Malcolm Mooney, in Cheshire. Later he moved

Right: George Best in full flight against Manchester City at Maine Road

Opposite: The bewitching George Best liked at times to taunt opponents, at least those who tried to kick him!

Below: Fame on the football field made George Best into a much sought after figure on the social scene, even meeting Prime Minister Harold Wilson at Downing Street . . . and no doubt hearing a few tales of Huddersfield Town!

Bottom: In the Swinging Sixties George Best, complete with the status symbol of a Jaguar car, set new trends for football by opening his own boutique

his shop into the centre of Manchester. Later still he had a night club. But at the beginning he simply swept everything before him, a prince of players who also planned to become the first British footballer millionaire.

It was already difficult to appreciate that this was the young boy who had come over from Belfast to join United aged 15 and almost immediately gone back to Ireland because he was homesick and didn't like it. Now he was so cool that he was always the last man into the dressing room to get changed for the match.

Defining what made him such a great player is difficult. Most simply, he could do virtually everything just a little better than almost everybody else. His balance was exquisite, helped by a natural grace of movement. He had a perfectly proportioned physique, and was much stronger than he appeared. He had the ability not only to take the ball past opponents but to get himself past as well, skipping neatly over flying boots and avoiding all the other physical attempts to stop him which his skill provoked.

Few succeeded in nailing him, and he was rarely injured, although often going into areas where players get hurt. He was just so nimble, a quality which also made him a very good ball-winner. He seemed able to go in for the ball and come out with it without even making contact with the man in possession.

He could run with the ball seemingly tied to his proverbial bootlaces. He could play one-twos off an opponent's legs; it would look like a lucky break the first time, and then you realised he was doing it deliberately. On reflection he didn't seem to score many headers, but it didn't matter because he could do so much with his feet; he was a true footballer.

The players all had their own ideas about how the team came to win the 1966–67 Championship. Bobby Charlton said: 'We won it because we believed right from the start that we could do it.'

Pat Crerand said: 'Being knocked out of the FA Cup so early was a blessing in disguise. Also the fact that we weren't competing in Europe. There were no Wednesday matches to worry about, no race against time to get players fit. By Saturday everybody was bursting to play. There was no pressure. In fact it was our easiest season.'

George Best reflected: 'If the Championship were decided on home games we would win it every season. This time our away games made the difference. We got into the right frame of mind.'

Tony Dunne added: 'We realised that teams without as much ability as us were giving more effort. Our great players in particular realised this and came through at just the right time.'

Noel Cantwell, no longer a regular, summed up: 'It's simply that Matt Busby has built another great team.'

So United celebrated the success which had given them another tilt at the European Cup after the disappointment of failing to do justice to themselves in foreign competition against Partizan Belgrade two years previously.

Busby, now in his 21st year as manager at Old Trafford, had only one cloud on his horizon. He needed another forward to take over from David Herd, who had broken his leg the previous season.

Herd knew all about scoring long before Busby had persuaded Arsenal to part with him in the summer of 1961 for £40,000. The previous season he had finished second to Jimmy Greaves as the Football League's top marksman. The United manager had played with his father, Alex Herd, at Manchester City and watched father and son achieve the rare distinction of playing in the same League team together at Stockport County.

The Manchester clubs had let Herd slip through their fingers as a youngster. His father still lived near the Edgeley Park ground when David travelled north to join an exciting era at Old Trafford. Because of players like Charlton, Law and Best, Herd often seemed to get second

billing, but his contribution should never be underestimated.

In his first season at Old Trafford, while still settling in, he scored 14 League goals, but then he reeled off a string of 19, 20, 20 and 24 before breaking his leg in March of the 1966–67 Championship season with his tally at 16. He was actually in the process of scoring against Leicester in a 5–2 win when the fracture occurred. It was a bad one and you could see his foot hanging at a broken angle.

'I was watching my shot on its way into goal when Graham Cross came sliding in and that was it,' he recalls now. 'I was getting a bit long in the tooth, and there were a few in the team in a similar position, so the following season I was transferred to Stoke. I had two good seasons there, but the broken leg was the end of the good times for me with Manchester United.'

After Stoke, and two years in management at Lincoln, he retired from football to concentrate on his motor car and garage business in Davy-hulme, near Manchester, and play cricket locally at Timperley and Brooklands. He has been a

Matt Busby leads his players round Old Trafford on a lap of honour after United won the championship again in 1966–67. Bill Foulkes holds the trophy aloft followed by Tony Dunne, Pat Crerand, Alex Stepney, Denis Law, George Best, John Aston, Bobby Charlton and Shay Brennan. The manager named Alex Stepney as the biggest single factor behind the title success after buying him from Chelsea for £50,000 early in the campaign. United went through the season unbeaten at home and clinched the title with a flourish, winning 6–1 at West Ham, the best away win of the season in the First Division

United season ticket holder for years and has seen a procession of strikers struggle to achieve what seemed to come so naturally to him and reach the target of 20 League goals in a season.

He says: 'I don't like harking back, but in my day 20 goals was quite commonplace, not just by me but by Denis Law, George Best and Bobby Charlton. When we won the Championship the first time in 1964–65 five of us were in double figures. The second time in 1966–67 there were four of us with at least ten apiece. United have had a lot of good players since those days, but because of the way the game is played now by so many teams it is more difficult to score. Actually I feel sorry for the strikers of today.'

United certainly found the right man to follow in David Herd's footsteps in 1967. Brian Kidd, born downtown in Collyhurst, went to St. Patrick's School, a place of soccer learning which had already produced Nobby Stiles and many more. His father was a bus driver on the route which went past Old Trafford; perhaps being held up in traffic jams on match days accounted for dad being a Manchester City fan, though he raised no objections to his son joining United when he left school. Busby took young Brian on tour to Australia in 1967, and deemed him ready.

Kidd was always solidly built and strong on the ball and Busby put him in the FA Charity Shield match against Spurs at the beginning of 1967–68, a match entertainingly drawn 3–3. He made his League debut in the opening match of the season, lost 3–1 at Everton. Still only 18, he stayed in the side for the rest of the season to score 15 goals in 38 appearances. After three months of senior football he was picked for the first of his England Under-23 caps, playing on the wing against Wales with team-mate David Sadler at centre-half.

The season saw yet another youngster from the juniors reach the first team. Francis Burns, who had captained the Scottish schoolboys, had also been on the tour of Australia, and after recovering from a close-season cartilage operation was brought in at left-back, with Tony Dunne switching sides to squeeze Shay Brennan out for lengthy spells. The shaggy haired John Fitzpatrick, a Scottish terrier of a wing-half also from the youth team, played quite a few games, but it was still basically the team of the previous season.

Despite losing the opening game, United went the next 11 without defeat and just after the turn of the year, the reigning champions held a five-point lead at the top of the table. They seemed on course to keep their title, and there were many who saw their FA Cup third-round exit in a replay against Spurs as confirmation that they would see success in the League again.

A poor spell which started in mid-February saw them lose their advantage. Five defeats in a run of eight games let Manchester City into the race. Losing to the Blues 3–1 at Old Trafford at this point didn't exactly help their cause.

The two Manchester clubs were level on points when they went into their final matches. With the second leg of their European Cup semi-final against Real Madrid in Spain only four days distant, United wavered and lost 2–1 at home to lowly Sunderland. Manchester City on the other hand finished with a flourish to beat Newcastle United 4–3 at St James's Park and so take the title by two points.

Blame certainly could not be laid at the feet of George Best, who played 41 League games and scored 28 goals, his best season as a marksman, which coupled with his feats in European competition saw him voted Footballer of the Year. In any case finishing second was not exactly failure, particularly when set against their achievement this season of winning the European Cup. The pursuit of the elusive trophy which had cost them so dearly in 1958 had become something of an obsession by this time, and as the quarter-finals approached in late February, their concentration was focusing more and more on Europe.

Law was missing in the last couple of championship games with a further recurrence of knee trouble which finally put him into hospital for an operation while his team were playing Benfica in the final of the European Cup. The Scot had been troubled for a long time by his knee, and at one point he was told that there was nothing physically wrong with it and that the problem was his imagination. Subsequently after an operation had removed some foreign bodies from the joint, he had them bottled in preservative and labelled: 'They said they were in my mind.'

No-one could really begrudge City their Championship. The partnership of Joe Mercer and Malcolm Allison had produced a fine team featuring players like Francis Lee, Colin Bell, Mike Summerbee, Tony Book, Mike Doyle and Alan Oakes.

The United fans had also seen some splendid matches and had responded to the achievements of the team, their colourful personalities and their entertaining brand of football in unbelievable numbers. The average League attendance at Old Trafford was 57,696, an all-time British record surpassing Newcastle United's crowds of the immediate post-war boom years. United's figures will probably never be beaten following the reduction of ground capacities in keeping with more stringent safety requirements.

The supporters had no time really to feel disappointment at seeing the Championship move across the city. As soon as the Sunderland match was over, the club were packing for Spain and a date with their old friends, the matadors of Madrid. Anticipation was at fever pitch, and after all, it was really a season which belonged to Europe. One only felt sorry for Manchester City, whose Championship achievement after so many long lean years was to be so soon overshadowed by their neighbours' triumph in the European Cup!

EUROPEAN CHAMPION CLUBS' CUP

BENFICA F.C.

MANCHESTER UNITED

FINAL

ORGANISED BY THE FOOTBALL
ASSOCIATION ON BEHALF OF THE

UNION DES ASSOCIATIONS
EUROPÉENNES DE FOOTBALL

WEDNESDAY MAY 29th 1968

Kick-off 7·45 p.m.

ONE SHILLING

OFFICIAL PROGRAMME

WEMBLEY

EMPIRE STADIUM

Europe! Europe! Europe!

Manchester United beat Benfica 4–1 in extra time at Wembley to win the European Cup . . . grasped firmly here at long last by Bobby Charlton, the captain

Manchester United travelled through a vale of tears to become the champions of Europe. It must have been a bittersweet moment indeed for Matt Busby when his club finally won the European Cup. How the memories must have flooded back that fine May evening at Wembley in 1968 when the Reds beat Benfica 4–1 in extra time to become the first English team to conquer the Continent.

It had been a long, hard journey, setting out in recriminations with the Football League and enduring the misery and woe of Munich before arriving at that golden triumph. So many Busby Babes had perished on the way.

'For a long time the responsibility of urging us down that road to Europe weighed heavily on my mind, but of course no-one knew the catastrophe that lay ahead. Like the rest of life we just have to do our best and do what seems right at the time,' explains Sir Matt Busby today.

Certainly there was sadness as well as joy when Busby and Bobby Charlton fell into each other's arms out on the pitch at Wembley. It was much more than the glow of victory as one of the surviving players of the Munich tragedy turned to the manager who had himself come back from the brink of death. It was the journey's end, the climax to a great adventure, which like life itself had contained sorrows and successes.

As Bill Foulkes, the other crash survivor who also shared a winning hug with Busby, reflects: 'I had come the whole way with the Boss trying to make Manchester United the champions of Europe. I thought the destruction of our team at Munich would have been the end of it, but he patiently put together another side. I'm proud to have been a part of it, and for those of us who lost our friends coming home from a European Cup-tie in 1958, our victory seemed the right tribute to their memory.'

Years of work fashioning a team capable of challenging the best in Europe had been destroyed on that fateful trip home from Belgrade.

Back in 1956, Busby and his chairman, Harold Hardman, had even defied the authority of the League for the right to pick up the gauntlet and compete in a championship of champions. Together they had changed the face of English football and Wembley saw Matt Busby fulfil his great dream. It was a triumph against adversity as well as a gladiatorial victory. Little wonder the tears flowed afresh, almost drowning the happiness of winners. You could see the emotion in the faces of the two Munich survivors, Bill Foulkes, who was making his 30th appearance in the European Cup, and Bobby Charlton, who had played in 20 of the ties. Both certainly knew what the occasion meant to Matt Busby.

Even the youngest, Brian Kidd, who celebrated his 19th birthday on the day of the final, was gripped by the significance of the game.

'I want us to win for the Boss', he kept saying.

Foulkes, who had scored the winning goal in the semi-final second leg in Real Madrid, was convinced that if they were good enough to beat their old Spanish rivals, they could account for Benfica. For although Benfica were still a fine side, packed with internationals, United had beaten them 5–1 in Lisbon at the quarter-final stage of the European Cup two years earlier, and with the advantage of playing the final in England at Wembley, defeat was simply never contemplated.

The team that played Benfica reflected the patience, planning and philosophy of Busby. For although money had played its part in rebuilding the club after the shattering tragedy of Munich the fact remained that only two men in the Wembley line-up had come to Old Trafford for big fees. It was basically a team fashioned from boys recruited when they left school and groomed in the distinctive environment of Old Trafford. With Denis Law watching the final from a hospital bed after a knee operation, only Alex Stepney and Pat Crerand had cost fees among the 12 men named for the big day.

The absence of Law, who had had an injury-haunted season anyway, United took in their stride. By now George Best had arrived in world class. He was at his peak. Matt Busby knew that the spirit of the team was right. During the sunny days at Egham he had described it: 'Their heart is right and this is the important thing.'

Best certainly needed heart as he ran up against the hard tackling of the Portuguese champions. He was tripped early by Cruz, and when his colleague Humberto joined in the harassing, the Portuguese player had his name taken by the referee. But with Benfica obsessed with the necessity for marking Best – no doubt they had vivid memories of their massacre at his hands two years previously – other players were left with more freedom. David Sadler, for instance, missed more than one opportunity of opening the scoring. Bobby Charlton saved his embarrassment when he leapt into the air to head a centre from Tony Dunne high into the far corner of the net. A Charlton header was a rarity, and this one was beautifully timed.

Perhaps sensing victory, John Aston began the first of many brilliant runs on the left wing and Best contributed a dazzling piece of football to help Sadler to another near-miss. Ten minutes from the end Benfica pulled themselves together and Jaime Graca hit an equaliser after

Below: A serious looking Manchester United walk out for the final of the European Cup in 1968 led by skipper Bobby Charlton followed by Alex Stepney, Brian Kidd and George Best. Italian referee Concetto Lo Bello (left) leads the two teams

Above: John Aston was an unlikely star in the final of the European Cup. He produced a sparkling display of fast, elusive running down the flank capped by threatening crosses. Late in the game he cut Benfica's right side to ribbons and was a key figure in the victory

Left: Best was tightly marked right from the start of the Wembley final. Henrique won this challenge, but the Irish imp was to have the last word

Top: Matt Busby said his team had great heart and that it was a quality which filled him with confidence as he prepared the players for the final of the European Cup. They certainly had to draw on something as they sank on to the Wembley turf with the score level 1–1 at the end of normal time. For five precious minutes Busby moved among them to inspire their will to fight and massage their spirit of heart which he knew in the end could be the winning factor . . . and how right he was proved

Torres, who up to this point had been well held by Bill Foulkes, had headed the ball down to him.

Now it was United's turn to wilt as Benfica surged forward and Eusebio, for once escaping Nobby Stiles, had victory at his feet. He burst through and hammered a tremendous shot which Stepney saved superbly with a sheer reflex action. Perhaps if Eusebio had been content to try and score modestly, he would have made it easily; but the Portuguese star hit the ball hard and his shot was too close to Stepney, whose reflexes were tested as he parried the ball away. It was the save of the match and Eusebio stayed behind to pat his opponent on the back and contribute his applause.

Stiles reckoned afterwards that if the game had gone on without a break for a few more minutes Benfica would have won.

'For me it was like the World Cup Final with England all over again when Germany pulled level just before the end,' he said. So normal time ended with the score 1–1 and Matt Busby strode on to the field to talk to his tired team for five precious minutes.

'I told them they were throwing the game away with careless passing instead of continuing with their confident football. I told them they must start to hold the ball and play again.' This was the Busby inspiration that roused the players and brought out the 'heart' he had spoken about before the match.

John Aston hit back at the fans who had booed him at Old Trafford earlier in the season with a tremendous display in extra time, cutting Benfica's right flank to pieces. Aston led the offensive, but in the first minute of extra time it was Stepney who kicked a long clearance which Kidd headed forward for Best. Watch-dog Cruz was tiring now and he failed to hold his opponent as Best tore away. Henrique came out of his goal to narrow the angle, but Best swerved to his left on a curve round the Benfica goalkeeper before clipping the ball into the net.

Benfica were on their knees as United came in for the kill. Kidd headed Charlton's corner kick at Henrique. The goalkeeper somehow beat out the ball but Kidd was there again to head in off the bar for a real birthday celebration. Charlton supplied the final touch with a typically graceful flourish as he flicked Kidd's right-wing centre high into the Benfica goal to hammer home a 4–1 win.

United's long quest was over, the European Championship was at Old Trafford at last. Best was voted Footballer of the Year by the English soccer writers, and a little later he was elected European Player of the Year, the youngest ever. Soon afterwards came the announcement that Matt Busby was to be knighted for his services to sport.

John Aston confessed to a great deal of personal satisfaction, to which he was entitled following a trying time in the League. United had worn blue in the final. 'Blue is a good colour for the Astons,' he said. 'My dad wore a blue shirt when he won an FA Cup winners' medal with United in 1948.'

David Sadler was also a relieved man: 'I was ready to shoulder the blame of losing after missing a couple of early chances.' But in any case he underestimated his contribution with spot-on passing and the way he had constantly turned defence into attack.

A lot of people had also underestimated Nobby Stiles after a press build-up suggesting he might try to kick the great Portuguese World Cup star Eusebio out of the game. He explained:

Left: Bobby Charlton is the first to admit that losing his hair at a relatively early age was not caused by too much heading of the ball. Thunderbolts from either foot were a speciality, but headed goals were rare . . . perhaps reserved for special occasions. Certainly his sense of occasion was immaculate when he headed this goal to open the scoring against Benfica in the final of the European Cup. It was a superb score as he leapt high into the air to flick a centre from full-back Tony Dunne into a corner of the net. The header, perhaps not unnaturally, seemed to take most of the Press photographers by surprise. Graham Collin of the *Oldham Evening Chronicle* was one of the few, perhaps the only, cameraman to catch the United captain in full flight just a fraction of a second after striking the ball

Left: George Best completed a hat-trick of European Players of the Year when he was voted top man by continental soccer writers in 1968. Bobby Charlton and Denis Law were previous holders of the Golden Ball award chosen by football reporters from 24 countries. George's European success followed his election as Footballer of the Year in England and at home in Northern Ireland. His *Le Ballon D'Or* came from 61 votes with Bobby Charlton second on 53 and Dragan Dzajic, the Yugoslav winger from Belgrade, third with 46 votes. Sir Matt Busby made the presentation at Old Trafford with Bobby Charlton and Denis Law out on the pitch to add their congratulations

Right: Victory parade as Alex Stepney, Bobby Charlton and Shay Brennan finally get their hands on the European Cup

'I was frightened before the game with all the ballyhoo about how I would mark Eusebio. People were suggesting I was a clogger. One newspaper said he had asked the referee for protection. I just don't believe he ever said that. I respect him and I find him all right. I have never gone out to kick him and I have played against him four times.'

Three of those games were for United and the other was for England and in all those matches the scoring star had managed only one goal, and that was from the penalty spot. That night Stiles again played him fairly with the emphasis on positioning rather than contact. Stiles does hasten to add, though: 'In the European final I have got Alex Stepney to thank for two great saves which kept my personal scoresheet clean.'

It was a good day for Tony Dunne, who not only completed a hat-trick of Cup medals,

adding a European medal to those he won in the English FA Cup and the Irish Cup, but backed the Derby winner as well.

Shay Brennan enjoyed a change of fortune: 'I lost my place just before United played in the final of the FA Cup in 1963. This time I came in on the last lap, so naturally it meant even more to me.'

Brennan had taken over from young Francis Burns two games before the end of the season, but Burns was not forgotten by the thoughtful Pat Crerand, already displaying his skills as a television panellist, who told guests at the civic reception: 'We have a squad of first-team players and I would like you to thank from us those who were not on the park against Benfica but who helped us reach the final.'

Bobby Charlton summed up: 'On the morning of the game I can remember thinking that we had come too far and had been through too

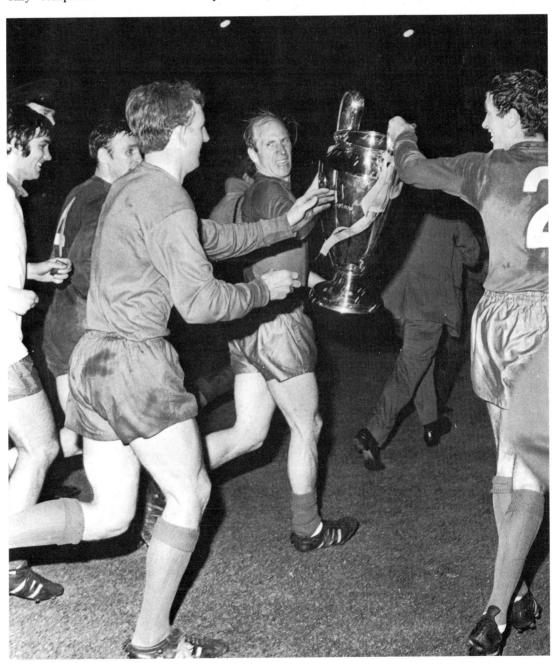

Above left and above:
Home in triumph outside
Manchester Town Hall with
the European Cup while
police link arms to keep
huge and enthusiastic
crowds at a safe distance

much for us to fail. When the final whistle had gone I remember feeling it was the ultimate achievement, not just for the individual players but for Matt Busby. It had been our duty. For some of us it had become a family thing. We had been together for so long, and while people recognised that we had had some great teams, there had been nothing in the European record book until 1968 to show for it.'

The teams for the final of the European Cup at Wembley on 29 May 1968 were:

Manchester United: Stepney, Brennan, A. Dunne, Crerand, Foulkes, Stiles, Best, Kidd, Charlton, Sadler, Aston. Sub: Rimmer.

Benfica: Henrique, Adolfo, Humberto, Jacinto, Cruz, Jaime Graca, Coluna, Jose Augusto, Torres, Eusebio, Simoes. Sub: Nascimento.

Referee: Concetto Lo Bello of Italy. Attendance: 100,000

United enter Europe despite League

Of course the story of Manchester United in Europe began a lot earlier than Wembley 1968, 12 years earlier to be precise, and the first battle was not out on the pitch but in the boardroom.

Modern European club competition began in the season 1955–56, originally the idea of a Frenchman and taken up again by the sporting magazine *L'Equipe*, who urged that the respective League champions of the member nations of the European Football Associations should compete for a European Championship. Representatives of clubs from 16 countries met in Paris in April of 1955 to draw up rules and a format for the new contest. Chelsea had been invited to attend, as champions of the Football League, but under pressure from the League declined. It was argued that they would have difficulty fulfilling their home commitments in League and Cup if they were involved in travelling all over Europe. It's done quite easily now of course, but in 1955 it was an entirely novel concept. Credit is due then to the Scottish authorities who had the imagination to see the possibilities and to allow Hibernian to enter.

FIFA gave its blessing to the idea and the first tournament was a great success, though in the usual insular way it was largely ignored in England. Hibernian reached the semi-finals, where they lost to Rheims, incidentally picking up around £20,000 for their trouble. At least England had a man in the final . . . Arthur Ellis refereed in Paris when Real Madrid beat Rheims 4–3.

The following season Manchester United were champions and accordingly were invited to participate. Busby was keen to take part. It seemed to him a logical progression for the best in England to put themselves up against the best from other countries. He had seen the standard of international football in England fail to move with the times. He had watched with alarm the pupils of other countries proving better than their teachers in Britain. He had marvelled as the Hungarians, who had come to Wembley in 1953 and won 6–3, demonstrated that it hadn't been an accident by beating England 7–1 in Budapest six months later. England had even been beaten by the United States of America.

Now here was a chance to show that at club level at any rate England were still powerful. He knew he had a good team backed with enough quality reserves to cope with injuries and a busy fixture programme. The League management committee again advised against entering and a letter duly arrived forbidding United to take part. But of course this was really a Football Association matter beyond the parish of the League competition, and Busby quietly had a word with Stanley Rous, then secretary of the FA, later to become president of FIFA. Rous already had a global view of football and Busby had a similar vision. Besides, it was an opportunity to earn more revenue and stimulate both players and fans.

Rous gave the nod, and Harold Hardman, the chairman of Manchester United, did not need much persuading. 'This is where the future of the game lies,' said Matt, and the chairman, a solicitor and game little man who never lost his enthusiasm for football, carried the board.

Johnny Berry was a key link between Matt Busby's first championship team of 1952 and the two title successes with the Busby Babes four years later. Busby signed him from Birmingham City in 1951 to fill the gap left by Jimmy Delaney at outside right. He was a tricky little winger who also won four England caps before the Munich accident ended his career with crippling injuries. He returned to his native Aldershot where he opened a sports shop business with his brother Peter, who also played League football, and later retired to continue living in the area

Hardman had been a full international player while an amateur winger at Everton, and was one of only three amateur players this century to win an FA Cup winners' medal. He also played for United, and was a director of the club for 50 years.

So United entered and were drawn in the preliminary round against Anderlecht, the champions of Belgium. The first leg was played in Brussels on 12 September 1956; it was a step into the unknown for United, who were disappointed that for their first competitive match on foreign soil they were going to be without the powerful Duncan Edwards.

In the event Jackie Blanchflower, who took his place, turned in a star performance. United had an early let-off when Mark Jones handled only for Jef Mermans, the Anderlecht captain, to hit the post. Bill Foulkes hastily cleared the rebound. Then Eddie Colman created a goal for Dennis Viollet and Tommy Taylor scored to give the Manchester men a 2–0 win.

The return leg was played a fortnight later at Maine Road – the Old Trafford floodlights weren't yet ready – and United were in a purposeful mood. No-one realised just how determined they were to make sure there was no slip-up. It turned out that 43,635 spectators that night were privileged to see one of the finest performances from one of the finest sides England has ever produced.

United would have beaten any club side in the world that night. The ball sped from man to man as though it were moved by some magical influence. Ten times in 90 minutes the Anderlecht keeper picked the ball out of his net. It would have made news if an English First Division side had beaten a Fourth Division side by that margin. But this was Anderlecht, one of the top sides in Europe. The poor keeper must have felt he was having a nightmare as the goals poured past him from Viollet (4), Tommy Taylor (3), Billy Whelan (2) and Johnny Berry. Busby, who before that night must have thought he had seen it all, could scarcely believe his eyes.

However, the cocky Busby boys were nearly shot out of the Cup in the next round when they took on West German champions Borrussia Dortmund. Thousands packed into Maine Road expecting another goal glut. It looked possible for 35 minutes as Viollet (2) and David Pegg put United in a commanding position. But the Red Devils took things too easily. Roger Byrne tried to put a ball back to goalkeeper Ray Wood only to hand a goal on a plate to Kapitulski. A few minutes later another silly mistake gave the Germans a second, to cut United's advantage to 3–2.

Now United had a real battle on their hands when they travelled to the Ruhr for the return. They were cheered on by 7,000 British servicemen and held the Germans to a goal-less draw with an uncharacteristic backs-to-the-wall defensive performance.

Six weeks later England's new soccer ambassadors took on Spanish champions Bilbao in the first leg of the quarter-finals. Bilbao had not been beaten on their own ground for three years. It looked as if the Babes were to learn their first bitter European lesson when they trooped off at half-time trailing 3–0. Amazingly, within eight minutes of the restart, they had pulled back to 3–2 with goals from Taylor and Viollet. But United slumped and Bilbao were coasting home again at 5–2. With five minutes to go the Reds were as good as out of the European Cup. Then Billy Whelan, the quiet boy from Dublin, picked up the ball in his own half. He started to dribble, dragging the ball through the mud, beating man after man in a wriggling 40-yard run before drawing keeper Carmelo and thumping the ball into the top left-hand corner.

The return at Maine Road was not a masterly display of football skill. Bilbao came with one thought in mind – they were two goals to the good and from the first whistle they brought everyone back in defence. But United were too fast, too eager. The crowd fell silent as chance after chance was missed. Busby, on the touchline, lost his usual composure. He wriggled and squirmed, smoking one cigarette after the other. As half-time approached he waved big Duncan

71

Edwards upfield to try to break the deadlock. A minute later Edwards struck – a stunning drive which was speeding towards the net until a defender stuck out a foot. The ball flew to the unmarked Viollet – and the Reds needed only two goals.

The game restarted even more feverishly. Within minutes the crowd were roaring again. Viollet had scored. No, he hadn't. German referee Albert Deutsch had whistled for offside. Now it was Tommy Taylor's big moment. He took the game by the scruff of the neck and shook it until victory was won. In the 70th minute he danced around Garay and cracked a left-foot drive against the post. Two minutes later he sailed around Garay again. This time there was no woodwork to help Bilbao.

The scores were level. The fans had screamed themselves hoarse and the Reds were whipped into a frenzy to get the extra goal which would give them absolute victory. Five minutes to go and still Bilbao hung on. Then Taylor again made a breathtaking dash along the right touchline. Little Johnny Berry, anticipating the move, had raced into the centre-forward position. Gently Taylor rolled the ball back. Berry's right foot did the rest.

That gay night in Manchester when Busby and his young braves celebrated a European Cup semi-final appearance, took place on 6 February 1957 . . . just 12 months precisely before the appalling disaster at Munich.

Real Madrid, United's opponents in the semi-final, were the greatest football team in the world. On a spying mission to Nice in the spring of 1957 Busby saw them in action for the first time. He saw the electrifying pace of Gento on the left wing, the class of Riall, the brilliance of Mateos, who goaded his opponents like a matador, Frenchman Kopa, who had the full range of skills, and above all the man who was one of the greatest footballers of all time – Alfredo di Stefano.

The United manager knew that his young team were going to need a slice of luck to win through but he had planned his assault on Real to the last detail when the party flew to Madrid for the first leg in April. The game at Real's magnificent Bernabeu Stadium was watched by a crowd of 120,000, and from the first whistle it was obvious what was Busby's trump card. The man he set to mark maestro di Stefano was not the powerful Duncan Edwards but the little man from Salford, Eddie Colman. Colman stuck to his man as though he was a long-lost brother.

Nevertheless Real's artistic, colourful football opened up a two-goal lead. The Reds pulled one back through Tommy Taylor, but the Spanish champions scored a third through Mateos late in the second half. United flew back to Britain and in the following weeks strode majestically on to win the League title again and reach the Cup Final. In between came the return with Real.

The game at Old Trafford, with floodlights now installed, illustrated once again the gap between top-class Continental soccer and the best in Britain. Real Madrid did not fall into the same defensive trap as Bilbao. For 20 minutes they absorbed everything that the Reds could throw at them and then struck with lightning speed. Gento opened up the United defence for Kopa to put Real ahead. Another burst from the flying left-winger created a goal for di Stefano. The 60,000 crowd were shocked into silence. It was all so easy, so artistic.

Sheer guts brought the Reds back into the game with a goal from Taylor and another from young Bobby Charlton. For once the Real defenders were glad to kick for safety but like true European champions they withstood the assault, and won the tie on a 5–3 aggregate.

Busby gave his verdict on the first season in Europe: 'The performance at the start of the competition when we beat Anderlecht so handsomely was the finest exhibition of teamwork I had ever seen from any side either at club or international level. At the end, when we met Real Madrid in the semi-final it was a contest between two great teams – a mature side and a young one, and of course experience told. But our time will come.'

The United manager had every right to fling out such a confident promise. He had built a team which had made a big impression in Europe as well as winning the First Division for the second year running and looking certain to win the FA Cup at Wembley as well.

The decision to brave the wrath of the insular Football League and enter Europe had been entirely vindicated. There had been a scare though. The team were close to being snowbound in northern Spain after the Bilbao match. The players actually helped to clear snow off the wings of their aircraft so that they could take off. You could see the dangers the League had in mind, but United had coped . . . and the football world was their oyster.

How the gods sometimes smash down the mighty. There is no knowing what Manchester United might have achieved in season 1957–58 and thereafter but for the awful calamity at Munich. They were in the European Cup again as champions, of course, and they opened their campaign in convincing manner with a 6–0 win over Shamrock Rovers in Dublin. Billy Whelan turned on the style for his visit home to score twice, and there were two goals from Tommy Taylor and one apiece from wingers Johnny Berry and David Pegg. United took the return leg at Old Trafford in rather casual mood, much to the delight of the Irishmen, who were delighted to score twice before going down 3–2 as Dennis Viollet struck a couple of times and Pegg scored again.

Dukla Prague presented stiffer opposition in the first round proper. The Czechs had a half-back line of internationals but they could not prevent the Reds from establishing a 3–0 lead from the first leg at Old Trafford. Colin Webster, Tommy Taylor and David Pegg were the scorers. United were more accustomed now to the niceties of two-legged ties and they adopted a careful approach in Prague. With the help of some sterling play from Eddie Colman at wing-half they restricted Dukla to a 1–0 win to sail through with an aggregate 3–1 victory.

United had another fright on the way back home, though. Their plane back to London couldn't take off from Prague because the airport in England was closed through fog. Busby knew that the League would come down on them like a ton of bricks if they were late for a domestic fixture. Hastily they made other arrangements. They caught a flight to Amsterdam and completed the journey by taking a boat from the Hook of Holland to Harwich and then travelling by train and coach to Manchester.

They arrived home weary on the Friday, a day later than planned. It was the experience in Prague that made the club take the first ill-fated decision to charter a plane for their next foreign trip . . . to play Red Star in Belgrade.

In the first leg at Old Trafford international goalkeeper Beara made a string of super saves to see the Yugoslavs take an interval lead through Tasic. With Duncan Edwards still in dominant mood and winning his battle with the skilled Sekularac, United finally got the goals they deserved through Eddie Colman and Bobby Charlton for a 2–1 win.

They hadn't had such a slender lead to take abroad before and everyone wondered whether it would be enough, but they were an increasingly powerful team as they had demonstrated in their classic 5–4 victory at Arsenal on the eve of departure for Belgrade.

We have dealt in detail with that fateful final match in Belgrade before the disaster. The club were jubilant at the end of the game, of course, because their 3–3 result for an aggregate 5–4 win had put them into the semi-finals of the European Cup for the second season running. As Jackie Blanchflower, a spectator at the game

and later severely injured at Munich, reflects now: 'It was the last match for so many, a long time ago now, but not so easy to forget for those of us still bearing the scars.'

Just as Manchester United had had to carry on in the FA Cup and the League, so they had to face up to their commitments in Europe. By the time the semi-finals came round it was May. This gave the team a breathing space, but by then the pressure of their do-or-die efforts in the FA Cup were beginning to catch up with them. Five days after losing to Bolton at Wembley they were facing up to AC Milan at Old Trafford.

It seemed that sentiment for United had run out in high places. England picked Bobby Charlton for a friendly against Portugal at Wembley, so that the Reds were unnecessarily deprived of one of their quality players, the kind needed for a match against a team like AC Milan. United also lost him to England for the second leg as he was chosen to play against Yugoslavia – in Belgrade of all places. Little wonder he had a poor game. What else could have been expected from a visit so soon to the scene of the last match before the crash? England didn't play Charlton at all during the World Cup in Sweden that summer, adding insult to injury so far as United were concerned.

So the patched-up Reds had to call up young Mark Pearson to add to the other youngsters who had already struggled manfully to fulfil the obligations of the club following the disaster. Their emergency signings, Ernie Taylor and Stan Crowther, were both in the team, along with Munich survivors Harry Gregg, Bill Foulkes, Dennis Viollet and Kenny Morgans.

They fought bravely in the first leg to win 2–1 with a penalty from Ernie Taylor and a goal from Viollet. But it was a slim lead to take to the San Siro Stadium for the second leg six days later. There was no great tide of emotion willing them on in Milan, just the usual massive, noisy crowd of Italians complete with fireworks and flares.

An 80,000 crowd bombarded the English players with cabbages and carrots, a quite new experience for most of the United team who slowly but surely slid to a 4–0 defeat. As Bill Foulkes puts it now: 'I think we had run out of emotional steam. By the time the European semi-finals had come round a lot of us were pretty well drained. The crowd certainly did not show us any sympathy. We held our own in the first half but they crushed us in the second. They had some good players of course. It was a sad end to a horrific season. I knew that afterwards I was just happy to rest and count my good fortune that I was at least playing football when so many of my old team-mates and friends had died.'

The team which lined up for both legs against the Milanese was:

Gregg, Foulkes, Greaves, Goodwin, Cope, Crowther, Morgans, Taylor, Webster, Viollet, Pearson.

Manchester United's first campaign in Europe ended with defeat in the semi-finals against Real Madrid. But it was defeat with honour, for the Reds had shocked a few people on their way to the last four in the European Cup and had reminded the Continent that the game in England was still alive and kicking despite disappointing international results. United lost the first leg 3–1 in Spain, but could only draw 2–2 at Old Trafford. Here Tommy Taylor goes for goal and indeed scored along with Bobby Charlton. But as Busby summed up: 'When we met Real Madrid it was a contest between two great teams – a mature side and a young one, and of course experience told.' He added: 'But our time will come,' as indeed it did

While Manchester United recuperated mentally as well as physically during the summer, the club received an invitation to play in the European Cup the following year, in addition to Wolves, the new English champions. It was a gesture born out of sympathy for the grievous blow they had suffered, and perhaps there was a practical motive in that another run in Europe would help the club survive by boosting their financial resources. The English Football Association initially gave their blessing, but it soon became apparent that the League still harboured resentment at the way United had flouted their authority to enter European competition in the first place. They seized the opportunity to write and say they could not give their consent.

The Old Trafford board were incensed at what they privately considered to be a petty decision. They promptly went to the board of appeal of the Football League who came down on United's side and said they *could* take part. The rules of the League say that decisions by the appeal board are final, but the League weren't finished yet. They referred the matter to the joint FA and League Consultative Committee, which decided that United were ineligible.

They instructed Stanley Rous, secretary of the FA, to write saying: 'The committee is of the opinion that, as by its name this is a competition of champion clubs, Manchester United does not qualify to take part in this season's competition. Consent is therefore refused.'

There was of course no denying the logic of the finding, but where was the spirit? United had no option but to bow out of Europe to concentrate on rebuilding and fighting their way back in the normal way. No more concessions for Munich.

The next European adventure

It took another six years for the club to qualify for a European tournament again, a period of struggle and rebuilding which is documented in the previous chapter. The gateway back to Europe came with the FA Cup success in 1963 to put the Reds into the European Cup Winners' Cup the following season.

Season 1963–64 was a good all-round effort by the Reds in that they reached the semi-finals of the FA Cup to play West Ham and they finished runners-up in the League behind Liverpool. They also opened their campaign in Europe convincingly enough, drawing 1–1 with a goal from David Herd against Willem II in Holland and then going to town on the Dutchmen in the second leg at Old Trafford. Denis Law grabbed a hat-trick while Bobby Charlton, Phil Chisnall and Maurice Setters also scored to complete a rousing 6–1 win to go through comfortably 7–2 on aggregate.

The next round brought the kind of opposition disliked in European football, a tie against fellow countrymen. On this occasion Spurs, as holders, were their opponents. The first leg was at White Hart Lane where Spurs registered a 2–0 win with goals from Dave Mackay and winger Terry Dyson. The stage was set for another close encounter in the return, with Tottenham confident they could turn their two-goal advantage into an aggregate win. But the second leg went sour for the Londoners. Mackay broke his leg in an accidental collision and they went down to a 4–1 defeat. David Herd and Bobby Charlton shared United's four goals.

The Reds were rampaging through everything on three fronts . . . contesting the League, sailing along in the FA Cup and in the next round of the Cup Winners' Cup running up a handsome 4–1 lead against Sporting Lisbon in the first leg at Old Trafford. It looked as if they were as good as through their European quarter-final as Denis Law helped himself to a hat-trick with the help of two penalties and Bobby Charlton hit the other.

Then a few cracks began to appear as Sunderland exhausted them in the FA Cup by taking them to three games in the sixth round on wet, muddy pitches before they were able to finish off the Roker Park club. This was followed by the sickening disappointment of losing their FA Cup semi-final against West Ham.

But no-one expected the collapse that occurred in the second leg of the Cup Winners' Cup against Sporting Lisbon in Portugal. The Reds squandered their three-goal advantage to lose by an incredible 5–0 and go out of their second major competition in five days.

It was the extent of their surrender which was so devastating, and to this day it remains their darkest hour in Europe, their only humiliation. Everything went wrong, and Pat Crerand still cannot really explain just why there was such a complete collapse:

We really did make a mess of it. It should have been easy. Perhaps assuming that we were as good as through was our big mistake. The first leg had certainly been easy. I remember thinking at the time what a poor side they were. What we didn't perhaps appreciate in those early years in Europe was how some foreign teams could present themselves so differently home and away. Over in Portugal I think our goalkeeper froze at the start, but I don't blame him for losing because the rest of us didn't get going either.

Lisbon hit United with two early goals and then repeated the punishment straight after the interval. Silva completed a hat-trick and they were never in any trouble. It just seemed as if the Manchester men were a spent force. They weren't though, as they showed on their return home by winning 3–2 at Tottenham with a top-class performance to keep their championship hopes alive.

But they had certainly made a mess of their ambitions in two Cup competitions. United were flabbergasted by the extent of their defeat in

Manchester United had just one season in the Inter Cities Fairs Cup before it was taken over to become the UEFA Cup. But they did well in the competition which was originally established as a football extension of trade fairs held around Europe in the big commercial centres. They reached the semi-finals when they went out after three tough games against Ferencvaros, losing 2–1 in the final game in Budapest. The semi-final against Racing Strasbourg produced one of their notable away leg performances, winning 5–0 in France. John Connelly scores one of the goals watched by Denis Law (number 10) who scored twice

Lisbon and Matt Busby was outraged. Bill Foulkes said that for the one and only time in his long career the manager slammed into them for their performance. Pat Crerand describes it by saying: 'Matt raged at us. He was normally dignified in defeat and even when he was angry he didn't lose his temper. But he did that night, and what was going to happen to us when we got back to Manchester was nobody's business. He told us our performance was an insult to the people of Manchester.'

In public Busby was more diplomatic, which of course was his way. He said: 'The boys left so much of themselves at home. The three matches against Sunderland took a lot out of them, and the semi-final at Hillsborough against West Ham on such a muddy pitch finally drained them mentally and physically. I am sure the heavy programme of matches pulled us down.'

The players didn't help themselves when they tried to drown their sorrows after the match. They stayed out late and several of them broke the team curfew. They got themselves off the hook by winning so well at White Hart Lane and Busby scrubbed the fines he had threatened them with for being late back to the team hotel in Lisbon.

The embarrassed team which would like to forget the nightmare in Lisbon lined up:

Gaskell, Brennan, A Dunne, Crerand, Foulkes, Setters, Herd, Chisnall, Charlton, Law, Best.

Full points at Tottenham kept United on the title trail, so all was not lost, though a run of three draws and a couple of defeats in the last nine games saw them lose their grip on the championship to finish second. Nevertheless a runners-up spot was good enough to qualify them for a place in the Fairs Cup the following season.

It was another incredibly exciting season all round in 1964–65, with the Reds once again chasing a treble until the very last stages. They went all the way in the League of course, taking the Championship at the expense of Leeds, and

they reached the semi-final of the FA Cup again, this time losing to Leeds in a replay. They were scoring goals galore, with Denis Law mean and magnificent, David Herd on target again, George Best accelerating into magic gear, and new signing John Connelly bringing flair and goals to the right wing. In defence they gave little away as Bill Foulkes and young Nobby Stiles struck the perfect partnership, allowing Pat Crerand and Bobby Charlton to create in midfield.

United operated like a well-oiled machine and nowhere was this more in evidence than in the Fairs Cup. Although they only drew 1–1 in the first leg of their opening round against Djurgaarden in Sweden, they went to town in the return to the tune of 6–1. Law got a hat-trick.

The Germans of Borussia Dortmund in the next round didn't know what had hit them. Charlton scored a hat trick in another 6–1 win in Dortmund, and narrowly missed repeating his three-goal salvo in the second leg 4–0 victory in Manchester.

The scoring slowed in the third round when United drew English opponents. Everton did well to hold them to a 1–1 draw in the first leg at Old Trafford, Connelly providing the lifeline for the Reds. Everton were favourites at Goodison Park for the return, but United pulled out all the stops and with goals from Connelly and Herd won 2–1.

The Reds were quickly back in form in the next round, banging in five against Racing Club in Strasbourg. They conserved their energies at Old Trafford with a goalless game to go through to the semi-finals.

United had been the new League Champions for a month by the time the first leg of the semi-final against Ferencvaros came round on 31 May 1965. This time, because of the competition's complicated format they had had time for a rest, but it didn't do them much good. Law got a penalty and Herd scored twice, but the men at the back didn't have their usual tight grip with the result that United, with a 3–2 win, had only a one-goal lead from the first leg at Old Trafford. The Hungarians' second goal was particularly unfortunate for the Reds, a long lob into the goalmouth from Rakosi so deceiving Pat Dunne that he allowed the ball to bounce in front of him and then sail gently over his head into the net. It was a gift for Ferencvaros, who were top of their League and boasted players like centre-forward Florian Albert.

It was with some misgiving that the Reds set off for the second leg, and their mood was not helped by the difficulties of the journey, with a strike delay at London Airport and a hold-up in Brussels. It was a trip when everything seemed to go wrong and misfortune spilled over into the match. Just before half-time Albert set Varga off running for goal. He was still some way out when he tried a speculative shot which Pat Dunne looked to have well covered. In fact the shot didn't reach him because the ball struck

Nobby Stiles on the shoulder and he promptly cleared. The referee amazingly awarded a penalty for hand-ball. Even allowing for the referee thinking it had hit him on the arm, the shot had come too quickly for it to be anything but accidental.

Novak scored with the penalty and United lost their cool. Pat Crerand was sent off along with Orosz when they finally turned on each other after a running battle. The goal was the only one of the match, levelling the tie. United were fortunate in that the rule counting away goals double in the event of an aggregate draw was not yet in force. But it still wasn't their lucky day, and Matt Busby returned grimly to the dressing room having lost the toss for choice of venue for the replay. Back to Budapest went

United, now a month into the close season with most other British footballers enjoying their summer holidays. It was a difficult trip again, and they even forgot the English sausages the British Embassy had asked them to bring out!

United, this time determined to wrap up the tie, went straight to the attack and dominated the first half hour. Unhappily Denis Law hesitated a fraction too long with a good chance, and Ferencvaros punished them just before the interval. Their right-winger cut inside Tony Dunne for just about the first time in the match and let fly with a swerving shot which dipped into the top corner of the goal. In the second half Ferencvaros' left-winger scored after a series of shots had been blocked. John Connelly pulled a goal back, but other chances went begging.

Charlton blasted over the top, Best nearly dribbled one in and Herd missed a sitter.

Bill Foulkes sadly remembers: 'We were playing long after the end of the normal season, and we were just not geared up for the occasion. The edge had gone off our play. After all our great efforts during the season, we had gone off the boil.'

Nobby Stiles recalls: 'The penalty against me for handling was harsh. I flung myself to block the shot and stopped it with my shoulder. We paralysed them in the third game but just couldn't get the ball in the net. I still look back proudly on that season though. I shall always remember it for some great football. It was a good team and at least we won the Championship.'

The team which played unchanged in all three matches against Ferencvaros was:

Pat Dunne, Brennan, Tony Dunne, Crerand, Foulkes, Stiles, Connelly, Charlton, Herd, Law, Best.

The Championship put the Reds back into the top competition, the European Cup, in 1965–66 and they produced another brave campaign on three fronts. They slipped to fourth in the League, but they again reached the semi-finals of the FA Cup and the semi-finals in Europe.

The European season will be remembered for an incredible performance at the quarter-final stage against Benfica in Lisbon which was inspired by George Best, who came home as El Beatle. Best destroyed the Portuguese champions with one of the finest individual displays ever seen in European football, or anywhere else for that matter. He must have had cotton wool in his ears when Matt Busby delivered his pre-match tactics, because the performance bore no relation to the script.

When that season opened Best was just making the English soccer fans sit up and take notice. He had established a regular place in Manchester United's side the season before, in which he only missed one game in helping the Reds pip Leeds United for the First Division title on goal average. However, glimpses of his future life-style were beginning to emerge. A string of late nights took the edge off his form and brought the first of many dressing-downs from Matt Busby. Then, after a miserable performance against Newcastle, he was dropped for three games, including the opening round of the European Cup against HJK Helsinki.

United won 3–2 in Finland without him, but he was restored for the second leg after turning in a brilliant performance for Northern Ireland against Scotland. The shock of losing his place had done the trick and George was back to his impudent best, running the Finns ragged in a 6–0 victory in which he scored twice.

The East Berlin army team Vorwaerts were beaten 2–0 away and 3–1 at home to give United a quarter-final tie against Benfica.

The Portuguese side, managed by the wily Bela Guttman, had taken over from Real Madrid as the masters of European soccer, winning the European Cup in 1961 and 1962 and losing the next final to Milan only after being hit by injuries during the game. Best can still vividly recall the first leg at Old Trafford on 2 February 1966: 'It was one of those nights when you could almost feel the crackle of the atmosphere. I recall best of all the fantastic pace at which the game was played and then thinking during the second half that our lead of 3–1 was ideal. Then Eusebio worked one of his tricks to get his side a valuable goal. He sent our defence the wrong way with a quick shuffle of his feet and curled in a centre for a goal which Torres scored with his knee.'

A fantastic victory in Lisbon

So the Reds were going to Lisbon with the slenderest of leads, and with bitter memories of their last visit two years earlier when they had surrendered a three-goal lead to Sporting Lisbon. The second leg was played at the Stadium of Light. This was how the Reds lined up:

Gregg, Brennan, A Dunne, Crerand, Foulkes, Stiles, Best, Law, Charlton, Herd, Connelly.

The atmosphere was electric, with all roads to the stadium jammed solid. Concetto Lo Bello, the Italian referee, was delayed, and Benfica added to the tension by presenting Eusebio with his Footballer of the Year award on the pitch. It worked the crowd up to a fever pitch and the game, scheduled to start at 9.45 pm, did not get under way until after 10 pm. George Best recalls:

We were all ready 20 minutes before the game was due to start. This was very unusual, for Pat Crerand didn't usually put his things on until the last minute. Some of the lads were kicking a ball about to while away the time and I saw it bounce across to Paddy. Like a man who couldn't control his emotions any longer, he smashed it against a full-length mirror on the wall. The mirror exploded into a thousand pieces. As soon as the slivers of glass stopped tinkling there was complete silence. Then Bobby Charlton said, 'Now just everyone forget that has happened.' Soon we were out before the noisiest crowd I have ever experienced. I felt superb. The atmosphere sent the blood coursing through my veins. It seemed to add power to my muscles, imagination to my brain.

Busby wanted United to hold Benfica for the first 20 minutes. But Best refused to be held in check. He simply took the game by the scruff of the neck and didn't let go until victory was assured.

He scored the first goal after only six minutes when he soared to head a free-kick from Tony Dunne past Costa Pereira. Then six minutes later he scored one of the finest ever seen in Lisbon when he weaved around three Benfica defenders before stroking the ball into the corner.

Matt Busby had the gift of commanding respect from his players without needing to rant and rave. It was a relationship akin to that of pupil and headmaster during schooldays. Yet he was not aloof and loved in his early days to get among his players on the training field. In later years golf was frequently the common meeting ground. Left to right on this occasion in 1966 are Pat Crerand, Bill Foulkes, Matt Busby and Noel Cantwell

Another tremendous burst brought a third goal for John Connelly as Benfica reeled, astounded at the way this brilliant broth-of-a-boy had led an all-out assault when what they had expected was grim defence. Shay Brennan put through his own net to bring Benfica back in the game, but the Reds struck again in the last quarter, Law laying on a goal for Crerand and Charlton waltzing through at the end for a 5–1 win (an incredible 8–3 on aggregate).

'The Lisbon fans had never seen their team so humiliated,' says Best. 'I remember counting our players during the match. Every time I looked up there seemed to be nothing but a United man to pass to. I couldn't go wrong.'

Best had convinced the sporting Benfica fans that they had just seen a future world star. A man rushed at him as he was leaving the field brandishing a knive . . . an alarming moment until he explained that he only wanted a lock of Best's hair. He walked off the plane back in England wearing a huge floppy sombrero which he had bought while souvenir hunting. The photographers snapped a picture which went around the sporting world. George Best had gone to Lisbon as one of the new boys in Manchester United's glittering array of stars. He came back a world star in his own right, never again to live in the shadows of men like Charlton and Law.

Matt Busby summed it all up simply by saying: 'This was our finest hour. The way they won gave me one of the greatest football moments of my life.'

The Lisbon newspaper, *Dario de Noticias*, wrote: 'Manchester United were fabulous in all that is most artistic, athletic, imaginative and pure in football.'

Italy's *Corriere dello Sport* declared: 'The myth of Benfica collapsed in fifteen minutes, destroyed by the powerful irresistible Manchester who showed themselves as the great stars of European soccer, worthy rivals to Internazionale of Milan for the European Cup.'

But fate was waiting round the corner for the team now hot favourites to win the European Cup. Just over a fortnight later in the sixth round of the FA Cup Best was brought down from behind. It wasn't a violent tackle but he fell awkwardly for once and twisted his right knee. It was a classic case of a torn cartilage, the occupational hazard of footballers, and it couldn't have occurred at a more critical stage of the season. Best was left out for the next two games. At this stage all the club were admitting was that their Irish star had strained ligaments. Behind the scenes they worked round the clock trying to get him fit for the first leg of the European semi-final against Partizan Belgrade in Yugoslavia. He was put back into the League team for a game against Leicester at Old Trafford as a test for the semi-final which was to follow just four days later. Twice he went down clutching the suspect knee as pain stabbed through it in certain overstretched positions.

The rest of the time he moved like the player of old. The fact that the team lost 2–1 at home seemed incidental. The big thing was that George had survived the test and the decision was taken to gamble with him in Belgrade.

Partizan were an ordinary side without much flair, but they did have one redeeming feature which had made them champions at home and brought them to the last four in Europe: they were as hard and unrelenting as the Partizans of the war whom their club was named after.

The Reds started as if capable of carrying on where they had left off in Lisbon. After only five minutes Best had wriggled through only to miss with a fair chance. Then he put Denis Law clear with a centre, but the Scot could only bounce the ball against the bar off his body as he tried to run it into the net. After that United faded. Hasanagic scored for Partizan and soon after Best began to feel the nagging pain in his knee return. Becejac made it a 2–0 win for the home team and Busby admitted: 'We played badly.'

Best had failed to produce his Lisbon fireworks, understandably so in the circumstances of his injury, but the gamble of playing him could hardly be called ill-conceived, because he had still managed to look the most effective player. It was a situation which spoke volumes for the display of the rest of the team! The Belgrade game was the last of the season for Best, who on the return home went straight into hospital for a cartilage operation.

Willie Anderson took Best's place for the second leg a week later but again United were below par. Partizan summoned up all their qualities of resistance and didn't crack until 15 minutes from the end, when an awkward centre from Nobby Stiles was helped into the net by a Yugoslav defender. United attacked all night but Partizan had bolted the door. The Old Trafford cause was not helped when Pat Crerand flared in response to a crunching tackle and was sent off. So Partizan held out, losing 1–0 on the night, but going through on a 2–1 aggregate, leaving Manchester United with the feeling that they had blown a great chance of reaching the final for the first time. Said Denis Law: 'By rights after the Benfica game we should have gone on to win the European Cup, but we played badly in the semi-finals against Partizan.'

The disappointed men in the second leg were: Gregg, Brennan, A Dunne, Crerand, Foulkes, Stiles, Anderson, Law, Charlton, Herd, Connelly.

Three days after bowing out of Europe, United lost their FA Cup semi-final against Everton at Burnden Park. Again it was only by the narrow margin of 1–0, but it seemed that when George Best had dropped out of action some of the magic had gone with him. The Championship challenge had also fizzled out with the result that they finished fourth in the League, not good enough for a place in Europe the following season. The big bonus from that was that in 1966–67, free of European commitments and knocked out early in both the FA Cup and the League Cup, United were left to concentrate on winning the League. For a change they had only one target and they made sure they didn't miss it. They emerged Champions of 1966–67 with four points to spare in front of Nottingham Forest to go forward for their big date with destiny in the European Cup.

The 1967–68 European Cup campaign

The 1967–68 campaign opened with an easy tie against the Hibernian part-timers of Malta, coached by a priest, Father Hilary Tagliaferro, who also doubled as a sports writer in a wide-ranging career. The Maltese were a little out of their depth. Indeed Father Hilary even lost one of his flock on the way to Manchester for the first leg. Francis Mifsud went to buy an ice cream in London and got lost. The 17-year-old remembered where he was due to play football though, so caught a train to Manchester to return to the fold and enable Scotland Yard to relax. United made rather hard work of the match until Denis Law and David Sadler scored two goals each for a 4–0 win. The happy Maltese were rather pleased to have kept the score so low, and all they wanted back on their George Cross island was an entertaining match.

United have always had an enthusiastic following in Malta with a well-appointed supporters' club and the whole island seemed to be at the airport to welcome the Reds for the return. They escorted the team to the Hilton Hotel in a cavalcade of cars, motor bikes and buses, horns and hooters blaring, so that one wondered who were the home team. The match itself was an anti-climax and ended in a goalless draw, with United too apprehensive on the rock-hard, sandy pitch to produce anything special.

The next round brought a much tougher draw in all meanings of the word tough. United's opponents were Sarajevo, kinsmen of the Partizan team which had dashed their hopes two years previously. Matt Busby, stifling memories of Munich, ordered a charter plane for the first time since to ease a long, difficult journey. The last 200 miles still had to be done by coach through the mountains to the ancient historical city of Sarajevo, where Archduke Ferdinand had been assassinated to trigger the First World War. Pat Crerand maintained that Ferdinand had opted for assassination rather than make the return journey along such a tortuously winding road! The welcome was warm, but hardly extended beyond the starting whistle.

George Best was repeatedly chopped down, Brian Kidd was heavily marked and Francis Burns was so violently brought down that Mirsad Fazlagic, the national Yugoslav captain, was booked. Trainer Jack Crompton was on and off the field, treating United players so often that Crerand reckoned that half the crowd

probably thought he was playing. But the Reds at least kept their heads and came home with a goalless draw, a good result in the circumstances. Sarajevo were just as hard at Old Trafford, so United were delighted when Best avoided the flying boots to reach Kidd's centre with a header which the goalkeeper could only palm out. John Aston whipped the ball back in for an 11th minute lead.

The Yugoslav tactics rebounded on them when they spotted Best taking a swing at their goalkeeper. The punch missed and was also missed by the referee. So an incensed Fahrudin Prljaca went looking for revenge on behalf of his keeper and kicked Best so blatantly that the referee had no option but to send him off. Down to ten men they had no chance. Best rammed home the fact by scoring in the 65th minute. Outside-right Salih Delalic headed a goal for Sarajevo, but too late to influence the game at three minutes from the end. So the Reds moved on with a 2–1 win to meet Gornik Zabrze in the quarter-finals, and feeling pretty pleased with themselves for winning through while Denis Law served a 28-day suspension.

The Poles themselves had performed well to beat the fancied Dynamo Kiev, who in turn had knocked out Glasgow Celtic, the European Cup holders. They had emerged as the dark horses of the competition.

The first leg in Manchester came as a refresher after the previous round and was a splendidly sporting affair. Henryk Latocha clung closely to Best, but played him very fairly – and well. But around the 60th minute the Irishman escaped to let fly with a rocket of a shot which Florenski could only help into his own goal. Kostka played well in the visitors' goal until Brian Kidd flicked a shot from Jimmy Ryan past him. A 2–0 win was fair enough, especially with Denis Law missing again, this time with the start of his knee problem. Jimmy Ryan had played well in his place, but was replaced by the more defensive John Fitzpatrick for the second leg to help protect the two-goal advantage.

It was bitterly cold and snowing when United arrived in Gornik, so much so that Matt Busby went looking for the referee with a view to seeking a postponement. But the familiar figure of the Italian, Concetto Lo Bello, couldn't be found with the result that the Reds had to go out to play on a snow-covered pitch with snow still falling. United, wilier now in the art of European football, played a mature game. Gornik scored 20 minutes from the end through their danger man, Lubanski, who had played for Poland at the age of 16. His goal gave the Poles a 1–0 victory but it was an aggregate defeat.

It had been a well disciplined away performance. As Charlton commented 'Surely now the myth that our team can only play it off the cuff and have no idea of working to a plan has been exploded. We played to certain tactics and they succeeded.'

79

The Gornik manager, Dr Geza Kalocsai, paid Best a generous compliment: 'If there is a better winger I haven't seen him. Best could have played at any time in any of the world's great teams.'

So Manchester United were in the semi-finals of the European Cup for the fourth time, and were drawn against their old friends and rivals, Real Madrid. The stage was set for what many fans would have preferred to see as the final. Certainly there couldn't have been a higher hurdle. Although they were not quite the power they had been in their hey-day, when they had won the trophy five times on the trot, Real were still more than capable of beating any club side in the world on their day.

United had the slight disadvantage of being drawn at home for the first leg, but this was balanced by the fact that Real would be without their best forward, Amancio, who was under suspension. Not another person could have been

squeezed into Old Trafford when the teams met for the first leg. The teams were:

United: Stepney, A Dunne, Burns, Crerand, Sadler, Stiles, Best, Kidd, Charlton, Law, Aston. Sub: Rimmer.

Real Madrid: Betancort, Gonzales, Sanchis, Pirri, Zunzunegui, Zoco, Peruz, Luis, Grosso, Velazquez, Gento. Sub: Araquistain.

The Spaniards, renowned for their attacking flair, surprisingly adopted an ultra-defensive policy. United, for their part, could never really break down the massed Real defence, due perhaps to the fact that Denis Law was a pale shadow of his usual self because of the knee injury which was to put him in hospital just a few days later. In the end United were thankful to take a one-goal lead to Madrid – scored by George Best – but that was a frighteningly slender advantage against a team like Real in front of their own fanatical supporters.

In between the two ties Busby flew to Lisbon to see the other semi-final between Benfica and Juventus, where he formed the opinion that whoever won the United–Real tie would go on to win the trophy. 'Obviously, the big one for us is the second leg against Real,' he said. 'If only we can survive that, I feel we have a good chance at Wembley.'

Foulkes the hero of Madrid

Twenty-one days after the Old Trafford tie the two teams met again in Madrid. For the most important game in the history of the club Busby decided not to risk Law, but recalled the ageing defender Bill Foulkes for his 29th European Cup tie. David Sadler kept his place as an extra attacker and Shay Brennan came in at full-back in place of Francis Burns.

On the morning of the match the tension was almost unbearable. Nobby Stiles and Pat Crerand decided that a visit to the local Catholic church would help to take their minds off things. When the collection plate was passed round, Nobby found himself stuck for loose change and had no option but to put a 100-peseta note on the plate. Crerand glanced up in amazement. 'Hey, Nobby, that's bribery,' he whispered. Obviously even the vastly experienced Stiles realised that the Reds were going to need all the help that was going.

At first it seemed that even Nobby's little 'bribe' was not going to save United. Real were the exact opposite of the team which had played at Old Trafford. The ball was whisked from man to man as if on an invisible string and with United defenders chasing shadows it came as no surprise when Pirri headed a free-kick past Stepney after half an hour.

An uncharacteristic error by Shay Brennan allowed Gento to make it 2–0 and although Zoco sliced Dunne's centre past his own keeper, Amancio quickly scored again after fooling two defenders to give Real a 3–1 interval lead. United, it seemed, were down and almost out.

Busby then pulled his master-stroke. As the United players slumped down wearily, waiting for the expected dressing-down, he told them: 'Go out there and enjoy yourselves. You have done well to get so far so don't worry. Let's go out and attack.'

John Aston recalls that dressing-room scene: 'Actually, I had never seen the boss look so old. Real had been running past us in that first half as if we didn't exist. In fact, if it hadn't been for Nobby Stiles they would have run up a rugby score. And yet here was Matt Busby, looking as if he was carrying the world's worries on his shoulders, telling us to go out and enjoy ourselves. The man was incredible.'

Busby's half-time pep-talk helped to change the players' outlook. But what gave them the heart to fight on was the sight of the Real players coming back for the start of the second half. Says Aston:

We were amazed. Some of them looked like it was an effort to drag one leg after the other. We looked at ourselves, and compared with Real we were as fresh as daisies. Obviously, their players had been told to come out and run us off our legs in the first half. To an extent that had worked. But the score was only 3–2 for them on aggregate and they had shot their bolt. I have never known a game in which the two halves were so different.

In the second period the Reds ran their opponents ragged. But the vital goal wouldn't come. Then Crerand lobbed the ball forward. A header by Foulkes fell between the Real goalkeeper and his defenders, and before anyone could move, Sadler had stolen in to glance the ball home. Now the scores were level with just under 15 minutes to go and the stage was set for one of the most memorable, emotional moments in United's various European games. Aston picks up the story:

The last few minutes are something I shall never forget. I can still see Paddy Crerand taking a throw-in on the right and finding George Best. George set off on a run which left two or three of their defenders kicking fresh air. At the same time big Bill Foulkes suddenly began to gallop out of defence. Just what got into him no one will ever know. I remember that people on the trainer's bench were screaming at him to get back but he ploughed on and on. I don't know if George saw him but he pulled the ball back right into his path. I thought, 'Oh, God, this is going to go over the stand,' because, even in training, Bill always blasted the ball. But this time Bill just calmly side-footed the ball into the corner of the net. I don't know who was the more surprised – Bill or the rest of us.

So Foulkes, the most unlikely goal-scoring hero of all time, a survivor of the other semi-final between the two clubs 11 years earlier, had booked a place in the final with his only European Cup goal. Foulkes insists:

I still don't know what possessed me to go forward and score the goal which won the tie for us. After so many games with no thought of scoring, it seems almost unbelievable as I look back. I was lucky even to be playing. I had missed the first leg against Real with a bad knee and I had played only two League games when the manager picked me for the return in Madrid. I think Matt went for the experience because I wasn't really fit. My knee was strapped up and I was hobbling really.

Leading up to the goal, I had called for the ball when Paddy Crerand took a throw-in. He threw it to George Best instead who shot off down the field. Perhaps it was with moving slightly forward to call for the throw-in which prompted me to keep running. Anyway I reached the corner of the box and found myself calling for the ball again. I thought George was going to shoot, but instead he cut back a beautiful pass to me. It was perfect and I just had to side-foot it in at the far side.

In the dressing-room after the match Bobby Charlton and Matt Busby were both unashamedly crying. 'I can't help it, I can't help it,' said Busby, over and over again as if the tension and heartache of striving for the trophy over the years had finally been released.

Aston felt very much the same, as though Real Madrid and not the other finalists – Benfica – were all that stood between Busby and the realisation of his dream. 'After that game in Madrid I really believed that we were somehow fated to win the European Cup,' he admits. 'The way Real ran out of steam, the way Bill Foulkes scored his goal . . . it was as if it had all been decided beforehand.'

Perhaps it had. Perhaps the hand which had plucked away those marvellous Busby Babes decided to do something to settle the score. Perhaps Nobby Stiles's little 'bribe' did the trick. Whatever the reasons, Manchester United went on to win the European Cup in a never-to-be-forgotten final at Wembley. But in many respects, the trophy had been won in Madrid 35 days earlier when the Reds met and conquered the most fabulous club side in the history of soccer.

The shabby matches with Estudiantes

Winning the European Cup brought two tilts in foreign football the following season. The immediate challenge was to play for the World Club Championship against Estudiantes, the South American champions . . . and what a bitter experience this turned out to be.

The series of world games between the northern and southern hemispheres had long been marred by violence, and the match between Glasgow Celtic and Racing Club of the previous year had been a particularly bad example, so the warm, hospitable welcome afforded United as they arrived in Buenos Aires for the first leg was pleasant and encouraging. There were parties, barbecues and even a specially arranged polo match for the entertainment of the visiting Englishmen. The first jarring note came when Matt Busby took his team to an official reception with the object of building goodwill with the opposition, only to find that Estudiantes had pulled out at the last minute. An angry Busby took his team back to their hotel. The United manager was none too pleased either to read in the local press an interview purporting to come from Otto Gloria, the Benfica manager, describing Nobby Stiles as 'an assassin'.

Estudiantes even carried an article in the match programme quoting Otto Gloria saying that Stiles was 'brutal, badly intentioned and a bad sportsman'. The Argentinians were still smarting, of course, from Alf Ramsey's description of their World Cup team in England two years previously as 'animals'. Stiles was in the 1966 tournament, so from the Argentinian point of view it was good retaliatory stuff. However, it was totally irresponsible of Estudiantes to put such remarks in their programme, of course, and it did nothing to cool an already hostile atmosphere.

The pre-match entertainment was bizarre. Out on the pitch pretty girls gave a display of folk dancing wearing colourful national costume, while on the running track behind the goals waited platoons of steel-helmeted riot police armed with staves and tear-gas guns. It showed the two faces of Argentina. One thing which soon became clear as the teams walked out into the highly charged arena was that the crowd, fuelled by the pre-match publicity, had cast Nobby as the villain of the piece.

Bobby Charlton in the dark shirt anxiously following the action in the second leg of the World Championship match with Estudiantes at Old Trafford.

The World Championship matches with Estudiantes widened Manchester United's horizons considerably. Although the fixture between the champions of Europe and South America had an unhappy history of violence, it hadn't really prepared United for the naked aggression and general hostility they met in Buenos Aires. As Matt Busby summed up: 'Holding the ball out there put you in danger of your life.'

United lost the first leg 1–0 and then drew 1–1 at Old Trafford in the return, with Willie Morgan their goal scorer. The interesting thing is that Busby's conclusion after the match was that given the chance of competing again he

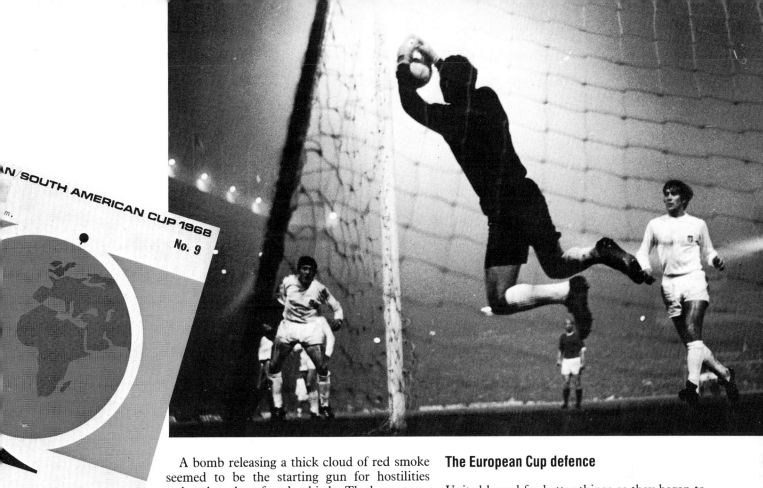

A bomb releasing a thick cloud of red smoke seemed to be the starting gun for hostilities rather than the referee's whistle. The home team laced into United with Bilardo, the manager of Argentina at the 1966 World Cup in Mexico, one of the most violent players. Busby said later: 'Holding the ball out there put you in danger of your life.'

It was hardly surprising that United never really got going. They fought mainly a rearguard action which was pierced only once. In the 28th minute the centre forward, Conigliario, headed in a corner from Veron.

It was inevitable that Stiles would get into trouble. Even the officials seemed to be gunning for him. At one point a linesman had called the referee over apparently to complain that he had been standing too close to Bilardo. Then he was sent off for angrily waving his arm at a linesman when he was flagged for offside. Considering he had been butted, punched and kicked, yet had walked calmly away without retaliating, it seemed a relatively minor offence. Yet it cost him his place in the return leg in Manchester through automatic suspension as United went out to face the South Americans a goal down.

United were confident they could pull back, but they were hit by Veron breaking through a badly guarded goalmouth to score after only five minutes. From then on they found it difficult to penetrate the well-drilled defence of the visitors. Denis Law had to go off with a badly cut leg, which brought on Carlo Sartori as substitute, and George Best got himself sent off after squaring up to Medina who was dismissed with him. Brian Kidd sent Willie Morgan through to score for a 1–1 draw on the night, but of course the Inter-Continental Cup went to Buenos Aires on the strength of their home victory.

The European Cup defence

United hoped for better things as they began to defend their precious European Cup. They went willingly to work on Waterford in the opening round, winning 3–1 in Ireland with a hat-trick from Denis Law and piling on the agony with a 7–1 win at Old Trafford. This time Law went one better and scored four.

George Best missed both legs against Anderlecht in the next round because of a two-match suspension stemming from his dismissal against Estudiantes. But Law was still in form near goal and scored twice in a 3–0 home win. There was nearly a hiccup in the away leg. United lost 3–1 in Belgium, but survived thanks to the goal scored by newcomer Carlo Sartori, another young lad from Collyhurst.

The Reds were back to their best for the quarter-final against Rapid Vienna, who arrived at Old Trafford for the first leg with the boost of having just knocked Real Madrid out of the tournament. They received short shrift from United in the second half, though, and were sent back home to Austria as 3–0 losers. Best made up for his absence in the previous round with a sparkling performance. He scored the first and third goals, with Willie Morgan, United's £100,000 summer signing from Burnley, marking his European debut by notching the other.

United conformed more now to European tactics and played carefully in Vienna for a 0–0 result. But Rudolf Vytacil, the Rapid manager, still felt moved to say: 'I was astounded at United's ability to attack away from home. United have a very good tactical approach and they are the tops of all Europe.'

With Best in the side the team's performance just could not be predicted; to a large extent it

was the secret of their European success, though they more than met their match when they came up against A C Milan in the semi-finals. The San Siro Stadium, scene of their European Cup defeat in the Munich season, was again a bedlam of rockets, smoke bombs and fanatical supporters waving huge banners. It was an atmosphere which called for nerves of steel, and though United had vast experience at this stage, their team had a high proportion of players who had passed their peak and under pressure were showing hairline cracks.

They certainly found Milan a tough nut to crack. Winners of the trophy in 1963, they had a magnificent defence which had conceded only 11 goals in 26 League games. Fabio 'The Spider' Cudicini, the keeper, had men who wove a nearly impenetrable web in front of his goal. The Reds failed to get through it as Best felt the full weight of the Italian marking system. A goal from Angelo Sormani in the 33rd minute and one from Kurt Hamrin just after the interval gave Milan a 2–0 win.

United were not without hope for the second leg. They approached the tie with every confidence, though Crerand had warned: 'Two goals down against any team is bad enough, but against Milan it's like being four down, they are so good at the back.' He proved a good judge. The Reds flung themselves forward but didn't break through until the 70th minute. It was a fine goal, created when Best at last eluded Anquilletti, and was scored fittingly enough by Bobby Charlton. It was United's 100th in European football. But it wasn't enough on the night. The fans thought their team had scrambled an equaliser 13 minutes from the end when Pat Crerand chipped a ball in. The players swore that the ball had crossed the line, but it wasn't given.

The unruly element in the Stretford End couldn't contain their disappointment at this decision. They started hurling all manner of rubbish and missiles on to the pitch with the result that Cudicini was hit by a piece of brick. The Italian goalkeeper might well have overdramatised, but the fact remained that he had been hit and play was held up for some considerable time while the referee sorted out the pandemonium which erupted. As it happened, the behaviour of the hooligans might well have cost their team their last chance of a replay, because when the game was finally resumed the momentum which the Reds had been building up was never picked up again. The team had lost their rhythm, and though they finished 1–0 winners on the night they went out of the European Cup 2–1 on aggregate.

It was a sad end for Matt Busby on his last game in Europe as team manager before going upstairs to become general manager. But he still found the sporting spirit to say: 'I was very proud of the team. They were magnificent. They gave everything and you cannot ask for more.'

An even sadder ending was the sequel to the missile throwing at Old Trafford and the wild scenes in Milan. Both clubs were warned by UEFA about the future conduct of their fans, and United were ordered to erect a screen behind their goals before playing in European competition again. There was no need to start work immediately, though, because their finishing place of 11th in the League and a sixth-round knock-out in the FA Cup meant there was no place for them in any of the Continental tournaments.

It was in fact eight years before United qualified for a European return, a completely different era with a new generation of players and staff.

The return to Europe under Docherty

Tommy Docherty was the manager who led the Reds back to the Continent, and he did not disguise either his excitement or the way he was going to try to uphold the tradition for fine football established by Sir Matt Busby. He declared:

Ever since I came here I've planned for the return of United to the team's natural element of European football. That is why we have played as many games as possible against European teams during my two years. I hang the pennants which are presented to us when we go abroad for friendly matches round my office and I mentally tick off each country visited. The pennants are piling up now and each one represents valuable European experience. Now we are back to try to recreate more of the old glories of Manchester United, and we shall endeavour to do it with style, playing adventurous football true to the traditions of Manchester United and striving to bring a smile back into European football.'

Sir Matt, now a director at Old Trafford, was clearly overjoyed to see the return. 'It is very gratifying to look back and consider what we started 20 years ago,' he said.

So the Doc led the charge back into Europe with a place in the 1976–77 UEFA Cup on the strength of third place in the League the previous season, and true to his promise they opened like the cavalry against Ajax in Holland's Olympic Stadium. They failed to score but went close several times. Indeed the players were convinced they had scored just after the interval when a fierce shot from Stewart Houston was fumbled by the goalkeeper. Piet Schrijvers turned sharply to scoop the ball away, with nearby players like Stuart Pearson convinced it had crossed the line. Lou Macari hit the post with a flick at goal from Gordon Hill's corner, and Ajax were involved in several other scrambles. Yet the Dutchmen survived to emerge 1–0 winners when Rudi Krol, their World Cup star and a survivor from the days when Ajax ruled the European roost, left his sweeper's post to jink through to slip the ball past Alex Stepney just before the interval.

United were disappointed to lose, but as Docherty chortled at the end to the Ajax president: 'Sorry, my friend, one goal won't be enough for you in Manchester.'

That's how it worked out, too, after Docherty had sent on his substitute, Steve Paterson, to allow Brian Greenhoff to move from centre-half into midfield. Greenhoff stepped up the tempo after Lou Macari had scored two minutes before the interval to make it 1–1 on aggregate. He powered down the right and with the help of Steve Coppell crossed for Sammy McIlroy to touch home the winner. United, lacking Stuart Pearson in the second leg through injury, had been short of penetration, but the tactical switch had made all the difference.

'It was one of those decisions which makes a manager look a fool or a hero, but thanks to the lads involved, particularly Brian Greenhoff, the best player on the pitch, it came off,' said Docherty.

But as United celebrated their return to Europe, Tomislav Ivic, the Yugoslav manager of Ajax, pointed out: 'United play beautiful football, but the Germans and the Italians have harder man-to-man marking and a more defensive attitude . . . and that will be the test.'

So it proved with round two bringing United up against Juventus, who had just knocked neighbouring Manchester City out of the competition. United won the first leg at Old Trafford 1–0 with a beautifully struck goal in the 31st minute from Gordon Hill to earn this compliment from the Juventus coach, Giovanni Trapattoni: 'Hill was superb, not just for his goal but for his skills. Sometimes there were three or four of my men on him but still he got through. A very clever player indeed.'

But the Reds had also been stunned by some of the ferocity of the Italians, especially early on. It was clear the Reds were in the big league this time, and if they had any doubts about the class of the opposition, they were soon dispelled in Turin. The Reds were without Martin Buchan again, a defender they needed more than ever in the Stadio Communale. Hill headed a cross from Coppell wide early on, and Alex Stepney made some brave saves, but it was only a matter of time. Roberto Boninsegna struck a brilliant goal after half an hour and another just after the hour. Romeo rubbed in the defeat with a goal five minutes from the end for 3–0 on the night.

Docherty summed up: 'We were babes in Europe, but I was glad that I had been able to bring back a taste of European action.'

In the second leg, in fact, it had been men against boys and it was clear United had a lot to learn, but as Sir Matt Busby had discovered 20 years previously, you don't conquer Europe in a season. It takes time, application and patience.

At least the club didn't have to wait long for another crack at Europe. For though dispatched very efficiently by Juventus in their European adventure, they had picked themselves up in splendid style in the FA Cup to beat Liverpool at Wembley and so qualify for the European Cup Winners' Cup in season 1977–78.

Trouble with the fans

By then they were under new management of course with Dave Sexton having replaced the sacked Tommy Docherty, and Sexton could hardly have had a more traumatic baptism when he took his team to France to play at St Etienne. For this was a tie fought on two fronts, on and off the field. Out on the pitch United performed well in a 1–1 draw. Gordon Hill smashed home a right-wing centre from Stuart Pearson in the 76th minute, with Christian Synaeghel scrambling in an equaliser just three minutes later.

But the real drama was happening on the terraces where the French club had ignored all United's appeals for segregation of the fans. Fighting broke out and the riot police swept in to charge at the English fans and lay about them indiscriminately.

Chairman Louis Edwards said at the time: 'I felt no shame for the United fans, only sorrow. I saw innocent people beaten down by police with batons. Their action was totally unprovoked. When the hooligan element we are unfortunately saddled with erupts I'm the first to condemn them, but this was not the case here. The United fans were unfortunately the victims of their reputation.'

The reaction of UEFA's disciplinary committee was simply to toss United out of the competition and award the tie to St Etienne. But United appealed and won the day in front of a tribunal in Zurich, producing a mass of evidence to show that they had warned the French club of the risks they were taking in neglecting segregation. The appeal commission ruled that the original sanction had been too severe and they said that the excellent behaviour of the Manchester United players had been taken into consideration as well. They allowed United to stay in the competition, but ordered them to pay a £7,500 fine and play the second leg at a neutral stadium at least 200 kilometres from Manchester.

Although reinstatement was a victory, the ban on playing at Old Trafford was a set-back for Dave Sexton in his first venture into Europe as manager of the Reds. But the club kept cool heads and after deciding to play at Plymouth won 2–0. They gambled with a semi-fit Stuart Pearson and he obliged with a 33rd minute goal before limping off with a recurrence of hamstring trouble. United clinched the tie when Steve Coppell turned inside to beat two men and Curkovic in goal with a firm shot.

Unfortunately for the second year running United came to grief in the next round. FC Porto proved far too good for them. The power, pace and precision of the Portuguese men o' war sank the Reds 4–0 in Portugal. It was like the Juventus away leg all over again, only this time United responded much better at home. In fact they came close to turning the tie upside down with a dazzling 5–2 victory at Old Trafford.

In this match, Steve Coppell led a superb assault all evening. He scored an early goal himself, forced Murca to put through his own goal and then after Jimmy Nicholl had rifled one in, shot the Reds into a 4–1 lead. Seninho broke away to score a second for Porto, so that although Pearson got a fifth for the Reds, it was an aggregate defeat. At least a 5–6 exit was splendid entertainment and it had been a fighting farewell. As Sexton summed up: 'I was proud of them. They did everything I asked, even to the point of scoring five goals.'

United missed a couple of seasons of European competition, but finishing runners-up in the Championship to Liverpool in 1979–80 saw them return to Europe for season 1980–81 in the UEFA Cup again.

This proved to be their shortest ever European run, as they failed at the first fence against Widzew Lodz. Unusually their undoing was at home in the first leg. Sammy McIlroy scored, but they allowed the Poles to leave with a 1–1 draw and it was simply not good enough. Over in Poland United fought gamely but without inspiration for a goalless draw. Widzew went through on the away goals rule which had been introduced into European matches, having scored at Old Trafford.

It was an undistinguished season all round, with the club finishing eighth in the League and going out of the FA Cup in the fourth round. It wasn't a huge surprise when Dave Sexton was asked to leave, with Europe's early exit one of the factors behind his departure.

Ron Atkinson took over; it was another blank season on the European front but Bryan Robson, Remi Moses, Frank Stapleton and Norman Whiteside were all introduced to help the club finish third in the Championship. This meant another run in the UEFA Cup for season 1982–83, though once again it was a short-lived campaign.

Valencia were the first-round opposition and what a stormy tie it proved to be. By the end everyone was calling them the villains of Valencia. Again United let themselves down in a home first leg. The Spaniards were tough and tactical, and the Reds were simply knocked out of their stride to finish with a 0–0 result. Later Valencia were severely reprimanded and fined £1,000 for what UEFA described as 'repeated misdemeanours'.

But the punishment was laughable compared with the result the Spanish side had achieved. Over in Spain United made a tremendous fight of it. Their opening was marvellous as Bryan Robson led a fierce assault only to have a goal disallowed for raising his foot too high in the scoring of it. A minute before half-time they scored a good goal, Robson sending Ray Wilkins away and then sprinting to the far post to head home the captain's pin-point cross.

United seemed set for a fine win, but a quarter of an hour from the end Kevin Moran tripped Ribes for Solsona to score with a penalty. Valencia were on the boil again and Roberto soon rammed the winner home.

The tie had really been lost in Manchester where Valencia owed a lot to their strong-arm tactics. Ron Atkinson declared afterwards: 'The time has come for UEFA to put a stop to those teams which seek to win European matches by consistently breaking every rule in the book. The only way is to kick the offenders out of the competition. Reprimands and fines are a small price to pay for ultimate victory.'

There was violence off the field as well, much of it prompted by the Spanish police who were responsible for some indiscriminate baton

Arthur Graham was signed by Ron Atkinson to replace injured winger Steve Coppell in 1983. He was squeezed out a year later by the arrival of Jesper Olsen and Gordon Strachan, but played his part in maintaining United's tradition for wing play. He had a good year in 1983–84 and scored in a 2–1 win against Spartak Varna in Bulgaria in the second round of the European Cup Winners Cup

That seemed to be the signal for United to reveal the best of their character, and they hit back to go in front with goals from Bryan Robson and Norman Whiteside. Dukla pulled level for 2–2 on the night and 3–3 overall, but United went through on the away goals rule.

Spartak Varna were gobbled up without too much trouble. Robson and Arthur Graham scored in a 2–1 win in Bulgaria and then the Reds won 2–0 in Manchester, Frank Stapleton netting both goals.

Then came a mighty tussle with Barcelona in the quarter-final. The first leg in the magnificent Nou Camp Stadium was lost 2–0. Graeme Hogg sliced through his own goal and the Spaniards nicked their second goal just before the end. United missed a lot of chances. In fact Bryan Robson, like a true captain, came home saying don't blame Graeme Hogg for the own-goal but himself for the opportunities he had failed to put away.

The great match with Barcelona

Robson seemed to take the second leg as a personal challenge and he led an incredible fight back which belongs in the top drawer of United's European achievements. There was a tremendous rapport from the 58,000 fans as United took the game to their opponents, at the same time keeping a wary eye on Diego Maradona.

They pulled back the first goal after 25 minutes, Hogg touching on a Wilkins corner for Robson to score with a diving header, bravely ignoring the flying boots. Robson smashed in number two after the Spanish goalkeeper had failed to hold a drive from Wilkins. Whiteside headed a ball down for Stapleton to score the winner. It was a nail-biting finish with Mark Hughes lucky to escape being penalised in the area for a foul on Alonso. Bobby Charlton, a hero in the old glory days and now a director, danced with delight on his seat.

Unhappily United were without the injured Robson and Arnold Muhren for the first leg of the semi-final against Juventus at Old Trafford, and to make matters worse Wilkins was serving a suspension. The Reds tried willingly enough but couldn't stop Paolo Rossi scoring with the help of a deflection off Hogg after 15 minutes. Substitute Alan Davies made it 1–1, but most fans feared the worst in Turin.

The Reds were still without Robson, and Whiteside was only fit enough to make the substitutes' bench. He came on late in the game to demonstrate his liking for the big occasion by scoring an equaliser after Boniek had given Juventus an early lead. It seemed likely to be enough to take the match into extra time, but with only a minute remaining, Rossi sped away to score a beautiful winner.

Juventus went on to win the Cup, beating Porto, to leave Ron Atkinson enthusing, even after he had left Old Trafford: 'I take great

charges at English supporters. United were so appalled that they announced that they no longer wanted their supporters to travel on to the Continent with them. David Smith, the chairman and organiser of the supporters' club, said that he would no longer be organising any tours abroad: 'I fear that if things are allowed to continue someone is going to lose his life and I cannot take that kind of responsibility.'

These were ominous rumblings and warning for crowd disasters that lay ahead, though sadly few realised it at the time, especially those in high places with UEFA.

After losing to Valencia, United went on to beat Brighton in the final of the FA Cup to earn a return to the European Cup Winners' Cup in season 1983–84. This time they put up a much better show to reach the semi-finals, a run that was more like the old days. The first-round draw against Dukla Prague also sent the minds of older fans racing down memory lane. The Czechs had given the old Busby Babes a good game and they certainly tested Ron Atkinson's men. In fact United only escaped defeat in the first leg at Old Trafford by a few minutes. Ray Wilkins got a late penalty for a 1–1 draw. Even so Dukla were optimistic about the return and things certainly did not look good for the Manchester men when Dukla took a 10th minute lead in Prague.

Above: After putting Barcelona to flight in the European Cup Winners Cup in 1983–84, the semi-final came as an anti-climax. The Reds drew the first leg 1–1 at Old Trafford against Juventus and then crashed to a 2–1 defeat in Italy

Above left, left and above right: The quarter-final against Barcelona in the European Cup Winners Cup in 1984 produced an epic, with a fight-back by Manchester United. United lost the first leg in Spain 2–0. The second leg at Old Trafford was a personal triumph for the captain who was mobbed and carried off shoulder high by fans at the end of United's inspiring 3–0 victory. The confrontation with Barcelona brought United up against world star Diego Maradona. In this European collision, Maradona was eclipsed by Robson who scored two of the goals

personal satisfaction from restoring the good old days to Manchester United, especially when we put Barcelona to flight. I doubt if anything will ever outshine that famous victory, which surpassed anything I have experienced in the game. It was even better than winning the FA Cup!'

United finished fourth in the League that season to give them their final run in Europe before the ban on English clubs which followed the tragedy at the European Cup final at the Heysel Stadium, Brussels, in 1985. They opened season 1984–85 in the UEFA Cup with a home first leg against Raba Gyor of Hungary and won comfortably 3–0 with goals from Robson, Hughes and Muhren. The Hungarians made more of a show in their own country but goals from Alan Brazil and Muhren, a penalty, provided the Reds with a 2–2 draw and safe passage through to meet PSV Eindhoven.

The Dutchmen provided two tight games, goalless in Holland and then 1–0 in United's favour at Old Trafford, the goal coming from a penalty by Gordon Strachan. Dundee United saw the Reds at their best. The Scots came to Old Trafford first and played well for a 2–2 draw. Robson scored and Strachan got another penalty, though he also let his countrymen off the hook by missing one as well. United played a storming game in Dundee with goals from Hughes and Muhren along with an own-goal seeing them safe with a 3–2 win.

Videoton, another Hungarian club, whom United played in the quarter-finals provided a huge anti-climax. United outplayed them over the two legs but couldn't finish them off. In the first leg in Manchester Frank Stapleton had two goals disallowed for offside before netting one that counted for a 1–0 win. It wasn't much of a lead but everyone was confident it would be enough because there had been nothing special about the Hungarians. But the goals wouldn't come in Hungary, either, despite United supplying most of the pressure, and Videoton sneaked a 1–0 win with the help of a deflection from a free kick. So it was all square, and extra time saw the teams still level. So for the first time in Europe United went into a penalty shoot-out . . . and lost 4–5. Frank Stapleton and Mark Hughes, the two strikers of all people, missed their penalties while the luckless Gary Bailey dived the wrong way for every one of Videoton's kicks!

It was a particularly disappointing finish for Bailey, who has since retired through injury and must now remember his last moments in European competition as picking penalties out of the back of the net. It was in fact a frustrating way for the whole of Manchester United to bow out of a scene which over a span of nearly 30 years has brought them glory and such excitement.

Like everyone else in England they wait now impatiently for a reprieve of the ban on English clubs which will see more chapters written for the grand European adventure.

NO. 15.—THE NEWTON HEATH TEAM.

CLEMENTS. ERRENTZ. COLVILL
MI
HENRYS. STEWART. FITZIMMONS.
PERRINS. DONALDSON,
COUPAR, HOOD.
TIMMONS (Trainer). FARMAN.

Birth of a legend

The men of Newton Heath who played in the club's first season in the Football League. Goalkeepers Warner and Davies are missing, otherwise the players are those who appeared regularly throughout the season. Some records show that on 7 January 1893 Newton Heath played with only ten men, with Stewart (third from right, centre row) in goal. Could this be the day when the photographer called?

To give George Stephenson, the railway engineer, a part to play in the Manchester United story might seem the work of an overstretched imagination, but the man who had a leading role in the development of rail transport did indeed make a contribution. He came to Manchester in the late 1820s to build the first passenger railway from the city, to Liverpool. He chose for the Manchester terminal the site of Castlefield, the flat area on the outskirts of the city where the Roman legions had settled on their way north to combat the Picts and Scots and where they had built a fortress named Mancunium, which developed into the city of Manchester. It was the perfect spot for Stephenson, offering no unmanageable gradients to his famous 'Rocket' when it began its journeys to and from Liverpool Road Station, the first railway station in the world.

Stephenson's first passenger railway was the Manchester and Liverpool Railway, and as time passed and it became clear that the project was a success, other lines opened. One of these was a line operating in the opposite direction, the Manchester and Leeds Railway, setting off from Oldham Road, Newton Heath, and terminating in the Leeds area where its lines met with those of the North Midland Railway. Eventually the two companies combined, and formed the Lancashire and Yorkshire Railway Company, which had a branch at one end of its line, in Newton Heath.

This was in 1847 when the game of football was still going through a complicated phase of its progress towards becoming a major part of the lives of British working people. There were plenty of centres where the game was played, but no uniformity in its rules. Schools, colleges and universities had football as part of their recreational activities, but the game played at Cambridge, for example, differed from that of Eton.

It was not until 1863 that a group of football enthusiasts from the London area met in the Freemason's Tavern in Great Queen Street, London, and formed the Football Association, and eventually after much arguing and a walk-out by certain representatives, drew up the first rules of association football.

In 1872 the Football Association introduced its first national competition. A trophy was bought for £20 and named the Football Association Cup, attracting entries from as far apart as the Queen's Park Club in Glasgow and Donnington in Lincolnshire, although the majority of teams were from the London area. Wanderers beat the Royal Engineers 1–0 at Kennington Oval in the first Cup final. Football had arrived as a public sport, with 2,000 having watched the game.

Six years later, when the railways of the country had grown into a gigantic network from the tiny acorn George Stephenson had planted in Manchester, the Dining Room Committee of the Lancashire and Yorkshire Railway Company responded to a request from men of the Carriage and Wagon Works for permission, and funds, to start their own football team.

The men chose the title 'Newton Heath LYR' for the team, (the LYR being Lancashire and Yorkshire Railway) their nearest rivals being the men from the company's Motive Power Division (the engine drivers and maintenance men) whose team was 'Newton Heath Loco'(motive). Newton Heath LYR were given a pitch on a stretch of land in North Road, close to the railway yard. It was a bumpy, stony patch in summer, a muddy, heavy swamp in the rainy months. But the men of Newton Heath LYR didn't really care – football was a means of enjoyment and the mud would wash off. At first games were mostly inter-departmental, or against other railway workers carried in along the lines from Middleton, Oldham, Earlestown and St Helens. The team grew in stature and reputation, and eventually found that it dominated most of the domestic competitions.

There were many other clubs in the area and a Manchester Cup competition had been launched, so Newton Heath LYR entered in 1885 and reached the final. The following year they again competed, and this time won. The game was attracting a great deal of interest, and the success of the side was looked upon as bringing prestige to the Lancashire and Yorkshire Railway Company by the executives, who were quite prepared to make allowances for men to take time off work in order to prepare for important fixtures.

In 1887 Newton Heath LYR again reached the final of the Manchester Cup, only to lose, but the club was now ready for a major step in its history, as football itself took a massive stride forward. Meetings had taken place several times amongst representatives of many of the northern clubs to discuss the formation of a combination of teams who would take part in a new competition. Small leagues were in existence in various parts of the country, but the plans under consideration were for a league of a much grander nature. In 1888 the Football League was formed, its twelve members having a strong northern domination, but with others from the Midlands also involved.

The original twelve were Preston North End, Aston Villa, Wolverhampton Wanderers, Blackburn Rovers, Bolton Wanderers, West Bromwich Albion, Accrington Stanley, Everton, Burnley, Derby County, Notts County and Stoke City. All were based in industrial towns or cities, and each linked to the other by the railways.

Familiar names? All but Accrington Stanley survived the first 100 years of the Football League, but by 1988 there were rumblings that the super-clubs, including United, Liverpool, Tottenham and Everton might form their own breakaway league.

In the first season Preston North End dominated the League, going through their 22 games without a single defeat, and for good measure they won the FA Cup as well, beating Wolves 3–0 at the Oval.

Newton Heath did not consider themselves strong enough to compete with the elite of the game, but they were growing in stature and it became obvious that the opposition being provided locally was not enough to test the mettle of the 'Heathens'. In 1888 they had the proud record of not losing a game at home until October, when a team of touring Canadians came to Manchester and beat them before 3,000 spectators in what was the first 'international' game played at North Road.

The programme for that game has survived the passage of time and reveals the Newton Heath line up for the game, even though two places are not filled:

Goal: T Hay; right-back, J Powell; left-back, A N Other; half-backs, T Bourke, J Davies, J Owen; right-wing, A N Other, R Doughty; centre, J Doughty; left-wing, J Gotheridge, J Gale

The missing players were most likely Mitchell and Tait, for added to the nine names printed in the programme, they formed the eleven who started the following season for the club. The referee that afternoon was Mr J J Bentley from Bolton who, a quarter of a century later, would become secretary-manager of Manchester United, the club not yet created.

The club join the Football Alliance

By that time the idea of League football played between towns rather than within local boundaries, was catching on and in 1889, Newton Heath joined other clubs on the verge of the Football League to form the Football Alliance.

In their first season Newton Heath finished eighth, having played the eleven companions in their new league: Sunderland, Darwen, Crewe Alexandra, Bootle, Grimsby Town, Birmingham St George's, Walsall Town Swifts, Sheffield Wednesday, Small Heath, Nottingham Forest and Long Eaton.

They also played in the first round of the FA Cup, and had the misfortune to be drawn against Preston North End, the holders, who beat them 6–1 at Deepdale, the only consolation for Newton Heath being that they had scored against the 'Invincibles', which is more than many of their Football League 'superiors' had done the previous season.

In 1890 another major step came for Newton Heath. They began to sever their links with the railway company. The letters 'LYR' were dropped from their title. The club appointed its first full-time official, the secretary A H Albut, who arrived from Aston Villa and set up office in a terraced cottage close to North Road, at 33 Oldham Road, Newton Heath.

There was still a strong connection with the railways, even though the club was no longer supported by the social committee of the Lancashire and Yorkshire Railway. Most of the players worked for the railways, and it was this which had made the club successful in the first place. A job on the railways was considered a job for life, and being able to offer a talented footballer work in the Manchester area allowed the club to attract men from all parts of the country. Also, because they were 'staff' the players had concessionary travel, and the team was able to get from game to game without the added burden of transport to pay for.

Professionalism in football had started three years before the formation of the Football League and some of Newton Heath's players earned money by playing for the club. But their reward was small, helping only to boost their wages from their normal employment, and hardly putting them with high wage-earners.

Newton Heath had attracted some players who were highly rated in the game, Welshmen like the Doughty brothers, Jack and Roger, who found work in the railway depot and whose football skills earned them international honours. There were others in the side who had sound reputations, like goalkeeper Tom Hay, who moved to the area from Staveley close to the railway town of Crewe, and Pat McDonnell, a craggy Scot whose search for work led to him walking from Glasgow to Manchester, where he was given a job at Newton Heath and won his place in the side.

Jack Powell, the full-back, had a remarkable rise to fame. He was new to the game when the Welsh club Druids, in Ruabon, signed him but it was obvious that he had a bright future. After just three games he was selected to play for his country against England in 1879. In 1887 he registered as a professional with Newton Heath. Mitchell, Davies, Owen, Tait and Sam Black, skipper before Powell's arrival, had all played a part in the growth of the club from a works team to one good enough to represent the city of Manchester against clubs from other areas.

Sam Black always remained an amateur. He refused payment while those around him accepted the few shillings a week they could earn from their football. Black played with Newton Heath for most of the 1880s before returning to his native Burton on Trent and turning to refereeing.

It was as a referee that Sam Black found his way into football history. During a game between Woolwich Arsenal and Burnley he refused to award the Londoners a goal, because the Burnley 'keeper had pointed out to him that the bladder inside the ball had burst out through the stitching on one of the panels, and its erratic flight had made it impossible to catch. Black's verdict was that he could not award a goal because the game has to be played with a 'ball', and as the object which had ended in the Burnley net did not constitute a ball in the true sense of the word, because it was not round, then it could not constitute a goal either!

At the end of the 1889–90 season Stoke City had finished bottom of the Football League, having won just three games in the entire season, and found life a struggle both on and off the field. They asked if they might stand down, and were replaced by Sunderland from the Alliance, who were highly successful. A link between the two leagues had been forged.

In their second season of Alliance football, Newton Heath did no better than in their first. They won seven games once again, five of them at North Road, their biggest victory being against Crewe, 6–3. Their biggest defeat was 8–2 at Nottingham Forest.

New players had been introduced as some of the older, long serving members retired or moved to other clubs. Slater had taken over in goal, Mitchell and McMillan were full-backs and the half-back line was Roger Doughty, Ramsey and Owen. Farman played right-wing, with Jack Doughty inside him and at centre-forward Evans. Milarvie and Sharpe played on the left for virtually the whole season, but there were changes in other positions. Stewart edged out Jack Doughty, who was in his last season with the club, and Clements arrived on the scene as a left full-back.

That summer Stoke City were allowed to re-enter the Football League, having proved too strong for the Alliance. The move was possible because the League's members decided that they would enlarge their numbers by two, and they also accepted Darwen. Now there were fourteen clubs, and Sunderland had proved their worth by finishing in seventh place, only six points away from the Champions, Everton.

Sunderland's strength was further illustrated the following season when they won the title, and it was also a season of great significance for Newton Heath. With Darwen now out of the Alliance and Stoke back in the higher reaches, two new clubs filled their places, Ardwick FC from Manchester, and Lincoln City.

Ardwick eventually became Manchester City, and the first time the two great Manchester rivals met under senior league conditions was on Saturday, 10 October 1891, when Newton Heath won 3–1 at North Road, thanks to goals from Farman (2) and Donaldson. Strangely, the two sides had met the previous week in an FA Cup qualifying round, when Newton Heath won 5–1, so they had started favourites for that first league 'derby' clash.

The Newton Heath team for the Alliance game was:

Slater, McFarlane, Clements, Sharpe, Stewart, Owen, Farman, Edge, Donaldson, Sneddon, Henrys.

The win marked another milestone for the club, as it was the first time since joining the Alliance that the team had celebrated three successive victories.

By the end of the season they were undefeated at North Road, and had lost just three times: at Burton on Trent to the Swifts, at Muntz Street in Birmingham where Small Heath beat them 3–2, and at the Town Ground in Nottingham, where Forest showed their strength in a 3–0 victory. Forest won the Alliance, Newton Heath were runners up.

Newton Heath became a First Division side

Then in 1892 the Football League again decided to enlarge. It divided into two divisions, the League becoming the First Division, and growing to 16 clubs, whilst a Second Division was formed by others from the Alliance and clubs such as Northwich Victoria, Rotherham and London's first professional club, Woolwich Arsenal.

Nottingham Forest and Newton Heath were invited to join the First Division. So the club which had struggled for those first two seasons had reached a pinnacle just at the right moment, and was now one of football's elite.

Elite by status, but not one of the rich clubs by a long way. Newton Heath seemed to stagger from financial problem to financial problem. Harry Renshaw, the first Newton Heath correspondent from the *Manchester Evening News*, wrote of the club's plight, and its operations from 33 Oldham Road:

The rent of the cottage was just six shillings a week [30 pence] and to increase the social side the club rented a schoolroom in Miles Platting as a place where supporters and players might meet. It was a place where they might spend time together in a common cause, and to add to the facilities a billiards table was purchased. But, sad to relate, the venture was not a success. Indeed at one meeting of directors the only light available was from three candles fixed in ginger beer bottles. The reason? The Corporation had cut off the gas supply, and served a summons on the club!

However, according to Renshaw's story, the summons was put to good use by the crafty Albut. He had his eye on a player with another club and knew that the man was unsettled and having problems getting his wages. So he met the player, lent him the summons and let him use it to threaten his club, telling them that he would 'serve it' if they didn't let him join Newton Heath. They did and his presence increased gate receipts by £10 for the next game.

The Heathens first season in the Football League was one of direct comparison with their performance off the field. They struggled, and yet survived.

The first game Newton Heath played in the First Division was against Blackburn Rovers, a formidable force from northern Lancashire. The town of Blackburn had provided football with its first 'super club'. In 1884 Rovers won the FA Cup, beating Queen's Park from Glasgow in the final. The following year they repeated the feat against the same final opponents and then in 1886 beat West Bromwich Albion in a replayed final and were awarded a special trophy for winning the Cup in three successive seasons. In 1890 Blackburn beat Sheffield Wednesday 6–1 in the final, and the next season won the cup for the fifth time in eight years by beating Notts County 3–1.

When the 1892–93 season began Newton Heath approached their first fixture against three-times Cup winners Rovers with some trepidation. The match was at Rovers' ground, and despite goals from Coupar, Donaldson and Farman, ended in a 4–3 defeat.

The men who carried the banner of Newton Heath into football's top section were:

Warner, Clements, Brown, Perrins, Stewart, Erentz, Farman, Coupar, Donaldson, Carson, Matthieson.

Seven days later Manchester witnessed its first Football League game with one change to that original line-up, Mitchell replacing Clements at right full-back and remaining in that position until the end of the season. The first home game ended in a 1–1 draw with Burnley, the Scot Robert Donaldson again scoring as he would do with regularity throughout that first season.

Newton Heath made a poor start, losing their next two games at Burnley and Everton, then followed this with a draw at West Bromich and defeat by the Throstles at North Road. The Heathens had played six games in the first Division without a win, but when victory did arrive it came in true style. The club's first

League win was in a game against Wolverhampton Wanderers, a club which would continue to be a rival until the days of the Busby Babes, and on Saturday 15 October 1892 Newton Heath won 10–1!

Nevertheless, the season was a long difficult road for the club, with victories few and far between, and when Blackburn knocked them out of the FA Cup in January 1893 it seemed a bleak journey for the 'Railwaymen'. When April came and the season ended with a 3–3 draw against Accrington Stanley, Newton Heath were 16th in the First Division, bottom of the table.

It is interesting to note here that in the 1986–87 season the League Management Committee caused a minor sensation when they introduced their proposals for end of season play-offs in an effort to trim down the First Division to twenty clubs. The bottom three clubs in the First Division were relegated, the top two from the Second Division promoted. The remaining place (in the first year the number of clubs was cut to 21, the final reduction being made in season 1987–88) was contested by a play-off series between the First Division club finishing fourth from the bottom, and the Second Division clubs in third, fourth and fifth places.

This 'new' method of securing or winning a position in the top division was a cause of great controversy. But it was not a new scheme – far from it.

The Football League in 1892 had decided that at the end of the season, the three bottom clubs in the new First Division would meet the first three of the Second Division for the right to play in the top section the following year.

	P		D	L	F	A	Pts
Sunderland	30	22	4	4	100	36	48
Preston North End	30	17	3	10	57	39	37
Everton	30	16	4	10	74	51	36
Aston Villa	30	16	3	11	73	62	35
Bolton Wanderers	30	13	6	11	56	55	32
Burnley	30	13	4	13	51	44	30
Stoke City	30	12	5	13	58	48	29
West Bromwich Albion	30	12	5	13	58	69	29
Blackburn Rovers	30	8	13	9	47	56	29
Nottingham Forest	30	10	8	12	48	52	28
Wolverhampton Wdrs.	30	12	4	14	47	68	28
Sheffield Wednesday	30	12	3	15	55	65	27
Derby County	30	9	9	12	52	64	27
Notts County	30	10	4	16	53	61	24
Accrington Stanley	30	6	11	13	57	81	23
Newton Heath	30	6	6	18	50	85	18

Small Heath – later to become Birmingham City – were top of the Second Division, so on 22 April 1893, two weeks after the season officially ended, the clubs met at Stoke for the deciding 'Test Match'. It ended 1–1, with Farman's goal earning Newton Heath the right to fight once again in a replay. A crowd of over 6,000, many of them railway workers from Manchester, crossed the Pennines to see Newton Heath win

Take your partners for a game of football! A lighthearted moment during a training session at Bank Street. In the background stands the club's 'twelfth man', the chimneys which were said to belch out acrid fumes if United were losing. This picture was taken about a year before the move to Old Trafford

the replay at Bramall Lane, Sheffield, 5–2. Three goals from Farman, plus one each from Cassidy and Coupar were enough to secure their place in the First Division for the 1893–94 season.

The club's ground at North Road had come in for heavy criticism during the season not only from defeated opponents but from the local supporters and Newton Heath's own players. Secretary Albut had a mission: to find a new playing area. In 1893 the club left the cloying mud of North Road, where on dry days stones and flints made life difficult for the players and on wet afternoons spectators had to squelch their way to and from the ground through ankle deep slime.

The new ground was in Bank Street, Clayton. Here the mud of North Road was replaced by the toxic fumes of a chemical works which ran alongside the pitch. There were those who claimed that if the Heathens were losing, the factory would belch out heavy smoke, on the premise that home players were accustomed to it, while it made life difficult for the visiting side. The registered office moved from Oldham Road to Bank Street, secretary Albut being quite prepared to share the wooden hut with the local newspaper which provided the telephone.

The move from North Road was partly because of the mud, and partly because of the cost of playing there. When Newton Heath was a railway team the Lancashire and Yorkshire Railway had been prepared to pay the rent for the use of the ground to the Manchester Cathedral authorities who owned the land. When Newton Heath broke their connections with the railway company, this arrangement ceased and the rent increased. While the move to Clayton meant a good walk for many of Newton Heath's supporters, the club at least had a ground to call its own, and paid rent directly to the Bradford (a district of Manchester) and

Clayton Recreative Committee, instead of being forced to hand over 'a very handsome rent' to the Lancashire and Yorkshire Railway, who were only paying a nominal amount to the church authorities.

So the second season of League Football began and this was to have a significant effect on the future of the club. They won their first game at the new ground, beating Burnley 3–2, and by 23 September 1893 could look back on four games which had seen them winning twice, drawing once and losing 3–1 at West Bromwich.

It was the return fixture against the Midlands club which was to lead to a strange turn of events, and seriously affect Newton Heath's financial position. Football had now become very popular and newspapers assigned correspondents to cover games – readers pored over their words as the only means of following their favourites' progress. The newspaper was the bearer of facts, the bringer of truth, and when West Bromwich were beaten 4–1 on 14 October, readers of the *Birmingham Daily Gazette*, published on the Monday after the game, were stunned to read the words of 'Observer':

It wasn't football, it was simply brutality and if these are the tactics Newton Heath are compelled to adopt to win their matches, the sooner the Football Association deal severely with them the better it will be for the game generally.

Newton Heath's officials were sent a cutting of the story, and were furious. This was criticism which they felt was unwarranted and decided to take the newspaper and its writer – William Jephcott – to court. They got the referee to back their claim, and he gave them ample support by writing to the *Manchester Guardian* that the game had not been the rough-house described in the Midlands newspaper, but had in his opinion been 'one of the best games he had ever controlled'. The referee, Mr. J R Strawson of Lincoln, wrote:

> Not once was any decision that I gave questioned, the play of both sides was a credit to their clubs and a credit to the game.

In March the following year, after a season of football that saw Newton Heath still fighting for survival, the Manchester Civil Court judge, Mr Justice Day, granted Newton Heath one farthing damages, and ordered both parties to pay their own costs. This was a body blow indeed for the club.

The first club to be relegated

From that game with West Bromwich, early in the season, until the last game of the 1893–94 campaign, only three League victories came Newton Heath's way, so it was no surprise to anyone when they found themselves involved in the play-off Test Match again.

Liverpool had topped the Second Division, eight points clear of Small Heath, and when Blackburn's ground at Ewood Park was chosen as the venue for the deciding game, Newton Heath felt that the odds were stacked against them. The game ended in a 2–0 defeat, Liverpool were promoted from the Second Division, and Newton Heath became the first club ever to be relegated. They stayed in the Second Division for the next twelve seasons, but during that time the club was transformed, and perhaps that court case and its crippling outcome was fate playing a hand in the growth of Manchester United.

Newton Heath ended their first season in the Second Division in third place, again qualifying for the play-offs, but this time losing to Stoke, whose season had ended with them third from bottom in the First Division. Ironically, Liverpool were the only club to be relegated after losing their Test Match to Bury.

The play-off system was changed the following season to a mini-league among the qualifying clubs, among whom were again Newton Heath, who finished in second place in the regular season. They first played Burnley, who were the bottom club of the First Division, then after winning and losing to them, faced Sunderland. They drew at Bank Street, then lost in the north-east and stayed down.

A season later the play-offs were abandoned in favour of automatic promotion and relegation of the top two and bottom two clubs. Burnley and Newcastle United moved up to replace Stoke and Blackburn, leaving the two Manchester clubs, City and Newton Heath in third and fourth places in the Second Division. By the turn of the century Newton Heath had missed promotion by two places for two successive seasons, and seen their financial position worsen. Players' demands were not high, but they did have the backing of the Players' Union, predecessor of the Professional Footballers Association, formed in 1898 in Manchester, at the Spread Eagle Hotel in Corporation Street.

Saved by a St Bernard

Fate was to to take a hand again. Newton Heath had ended the 1901 season in tenth place. Attendances for their Second Division games had dropped off, and the club needed cash. It was decided to organise a grand bazaar, in St James' Hall in Oxford Street, and here one man and his dog stepped into the creation of a legend. In his official history of 1948 Alf Clarke wrote:

A St Bernard dog, with a barrel fastened to its collar, was one of the attractions at the show. One night, after the place had closed (it was the third night of the four days of the bazaar) the dog apparently knocked over a part of a stall in the centre of the room. A hurried search revealed that the dog had broken loose and a fireman on duty in the hall saw two eyes staring at him in the darkness. He had no idea it was the dog and rushed out of the side entrance to the building. The St Bernard went out the same way.

Below: The pocket version of the club's history written by Alf Clarke of the *Manchester Evening Chronicle* and published in 1948. The booklet told some of the stories included in this history and was printed to coincide with the club's FA Cup achievements of that year. Alf Clarke was one of the journalists who died at Munich

Above: Perhaps one of the most important events in the history of Manchester United was the fund-raising bazaar of 1901. The efforts of Newton Heath to stay afloat in football's formative years led to the event being staged. It was from St James's Hall that Harry Stafford's dog strayed to find its way to J H Davies

John Henry Davies, first chairman of Manchester United and the man whose wealth created the club from the failing Newton Heath. Davies was managing director of Manchester Breweries and not only rescued the club from extinction when he became involved in 1901, but put up the £60,000 to build Old Trafford. The chance meeting of Davies and Harry Stafford was indeed a stroke of good fortune

What happened next has, over the years, become distorted somewhat, with parts added to give the story greater impact perhaps, but the *Manchester Evening News* of September 1906 (five years after the event, and 42 before Alf Clarke's recollections were published) told the story thus:

The animal was found by a friend of Mr James Taylor, and was seen by Mr J H Davies, who fancied it. The making of the bargain led to the meeting of Mr Davies and Stafford, and the latter, knowing the low water in which his club was in, asked Mr Davies for a contribution to its funds. This led to the club changing hands.

Harry Stafford was the club right-back and captain, and he and Taylor and Davies, a brewer, were to play a part in saving the club from extinction, so the role of the St Bernard can hardly be exaggerated.

Early in 1902 Newton Heath's creditors could wait no longer. The club had debts of £2,670 and was on the verge of bankruptcy, a fate which had already seen Bootle FC forced to quit the League and be replaced by Liverpool. Would Newton Heath also slip out of existence?

A creditors' meeting was held at New Islington Hall, but although secretary James West reported that there were no new tradesmen's debts outstanding since the date of the winding-up order, the club still needed £2,000 to make it solvent again. Harry Stafford then got to his feet and told the meeting that he knew where he could get hold of the money, massive amount though it was.

Stafford said he had met four businessmen who were each willing to invest £500, but who in turn would require a direct interest in running the club. The Newton Heath directors agreed, or were forced into agreement by the creditors, and the four men, J Brown of Denton, W Deakin of Manchester, together with James Taylor and John Henry Davies, eventually came forward with their proposals.

Manchester United is born

On 28 April 1902 Newton Heath FC was no more. It was replaced by Manchester United Football Club.

The selection of the new title was not straightforward, though. While the 'uniting' of Davies's group and Stafford's club might have seemed an obvious inspiration for the name, others were tabled. Manchester Central was one suggestion, but this was rejected because it sounded too much like a railway station. There was in fact a Central Station in Manchester (now the site of the G-MEX Exhibition Centre) which later served the Old Trafford area, and with Newton Heath's railway connections perhaps the name was not as ridiculous as it seems. Manchester Celtic was also put forward but turned down on the grounds that it might be felt that there was some link with Celtic organisations.

Eventually Louis Rocca, a man who would play a leading role on the club's scouting staff for the next 48 years, came forward with the name Manchester United and it was unanimously adopted. A new president was elected, Mr John Henry Davies, and Harry Stafford teamed up with James West to organise the day-to-day running of the club. Stafford was given the licence for one of Davies's public houses, and the St Bernard settled into its new home with the brewer's daughter! The curtain came down on Newton Heath as the club finished just four places from the foot of the Second Division.

The following season, as Manchester United, new spirit and new players took them to fifth from the top, but they were forced to look on with some envy as their rivals Manchester City were promoted.

Ernest Mangnall

The 1903–04 season began with a home draw against Bristol City, and defeats at the hands of Burnley and Port Vale, a start which led to a call for action from the supporters. Then in late September 1903 there arrived on the scene a man who was to play as important a part in the building of the Manchester United of today as any other . . . Ernest Mangnall.

Mangnall was the club's first *real* manager and a man who knew how to use the media to promote football, and to a certain extent himself. He was a well-known sportsman with a love of cycling. So strong in fact was his affection for life in the saddle, that he rode from his home town of Bolton to Land's End, then to John O'Groats and back, before his career took him into football.

Ernest Mangnall's cycling activities saw him heavily involved with the National Cyclists Union, and Bolton Cycling Club and Bolton Harriers Athletic Club. He was involved at the turn of the century with the opening of Burnden Park, which was used for cycling and athletics as well as football, and eventually he was elected to Bolton Wanderers board of directors. In March 1900 he moved into management, taking over at Burnley from Harry Bradshaw, who moved south to manage Woolwich Arsenal. A football manager in the early years of the game was referred to as the club 'secretary' but he was responsible for selecting the team, deciding on the tactics to use, and conducting training sessions.

Mangnall was later to go on record as saying that he felt players should not use a ball too much during practice sessions, but should build up their physical fitness. 'A ball should only be used one day a week', he said, a true sign of the times.

In a series of articles for the *Manchester Evening News* he wrote:

A great, intricate, almost delicate, and to the vast majority of the public an incomprehensible piece of machinery is the modern, up to date, football club. It is a creation peculiarly by itself. There is nothing like it and it is only when one takes an active and practical part in the manipulation of the strings that work such an organisation that one realises in the fullest sense what it all means.

The veriest layman need not be told that the greatest and first essential to success is the selection of a capable team, but it requires a deep rooted and special knowledge to know and to obtain the right stamp of men. How many clubs have lamentably failed and steered perilously near the rocks of irretrievable adversity by starting out with men with reputations; 'stars' as they are popularly called?

They are fickle, difficult to manage, and most times too supremely conscious of their own importance. 'Balloon headedness' is a disease which has ruined more promising players and brought greater disaster to clubs than anything else I know of.

There must be a judicious blending of the young and old. A team may carry three or four men of small stature, but too many wee men, no matter how clever and artistic, will not do, for the reason that the strain of First Division football becomes more severe every season.

As they say in the world of fisticuffs, 'Nothing beats a good little'un like a good big'un!'

Ernest Mangnall's approach to football was the direct route, he knew where he was going

and woe betide anyone who stood in his path. Manchester United was to be a successful club and he would see to that. At the end of his first season as manager United were third in the Second Division table, two places ahead of his old club Burnley. Manchester City were runners-up in the First Division. No fewer than 28 players had appeared in first team games that season as Mangnall searched for the right blend.

The 1904–05 season began well, in fact it took on record-breaking proportions, when after drawing with Port Vale in the opening fixture, then beating Bristol City a week later, United lost to Bolton on 17 September 1904, and then went on a run of games which saw them not lose another game until February 1905. Eighteen games without defeat, 16 of them wins.

The season had started with a set-back for the club, or at least for Harry Stafford, now a director, and former secretary James West. Stafford as a publican had held the licence to sell alcohol at Bank Street for several years. As he was leaving his public house, and as James West was a licensee, West made an official application to Manchester City Magistrates to take over the sale of alcohol at the ground, and was turned down.

Not being able to sell drink inside the ground meant a loss of revenue to United, but taken in the light of modern developments it is remarkable to read the report of the court case in September 1904:

Mr Fred Brocklehurst, appearing for the club, said that the decision would govern some 33 to 34 Saturdays during the season. The application was solely on the grounds of public requirement. It was only during the quarter of an hour's interval in the game that it became of serious moment to the spectators to have facilities for refreshments. Probably from 25,000 to 30,000 spectators were there every Saturday and they included a large number of visitors.

There were three ways in which they might obtain refreshments. They might bring bottles containing drink into the ground, and he believed a great many would do so. Such a practice could not conduce to temperance. Whereas previously people had perhaps one small glass of whisky during the interval, they would probably take more upon the ground and consume it there. He believed that last Saturday, after a licence had been refused, there had been more drunkenness after the match than for the whole of the previous twelve months.

There was a danger too that this taking bottles into the ground could be dangerous. People might use them as missiles if they did not agree with the decision of the referee (laughter).

The Chairman: 'The spectators don't carry shooters with them like the Americans do?'

Mr Brocklehurst: 'They don't, if they did we might have to put up notices saying "Don't

The club's influential captain Charlie Roberts, who appeared on the scene in 1904 and played until the outbreak of the First World War in 1914. Roberts played three times for England in 1905 and skippered United to all their major successes in the early 1900s. Roberts caused a minor sensation by insisting on playing in shorts which were above knee length

There had recently been alterations to the ground and the bar was situated such as there was no temptation for people who did not want to drink to go to it. Mr Brocklehurst said it would really be in the interests of temperance to grant the licence.

Mr Johnston: 'Do you seriously suggest that more people went to public houses after the match?'

Mr Brocklehurst: 'Yes, they went to show that if they could not get one drink on the ground they could get three drinks off it!'

Mr J E Mangnall, secretary of the United Football Club, said a large number of empty bottles were found on the ground after the match on Saturday.

Mr Johnston: 'Did you see any bottles that had contained lemonade or milk?'

Mr Mangnall: 'No, I didn't see any of that kind.' (laughter)

The application was refused.

There was worse to come for secretary West and Harry Stafford. West had resigned to make way for Ernest Mangnall, but they were both later suspended from football by the FA for making illegal payments to players, something which was commonplace in the early years of the game.

Stafford later said: 'I have been the Lord High Everything for the club since it came under its present proprietorship. Everything I have done has been done under the best interests of the club.'

Stafford claimed he had been questioned and found guilty of only one misdemeanour and that was that after obtaining a player from Scotland, he had paid him his wages in advance before he had been registered as a 'fully accredited member' of the club.

Under Ernest Mangnall, United finished their second season in third place, missing promotion for the second year by one position. But the backbone of United's first successful side was being created by the manager. Jack Picken was signed from Plymouth Argyle, Harry Moger, the goalkeeper, from Southampton and Charlie Roberts from Grimsby Town. His fee of £400 was considered a bargain the year before Alf Common became the first ever £1,000 player when he left Sunderland to join neighbouring Middlesbrough. Roberts was to captain the side from his position at centre-half and was a revolutionary in that he wore shorts at a time when players were encouraged to keep their knees covered.

In 1905–06, Ernest Mangnall's third full season in charge, United won promotion, finishing second, four points behind Bristol City, the pair changing places with Nottingham Forest and Wolves. Manchester United were a First Division team.

That year, too, they reached the quarter-finals of the FA Cup, stepping into unknown territory after victories over Staple Hill, Norwich City and Aston Villa. They were then beaten by

shoot the referee he's doing his best!" ' (renewed laughter).

Continuing, Mr Brocklehurst said it was suggested that pass-out checks could be issued but with so many people in the ground this would be impossible. The third alternative was to obtain an occasional licence. That there had been proper supervision and control in the past was shown by the fact that there had, in the past, been no complaint at all. Every Saturday fifteen policemen and fifteen other attendants were present to maintain order.

WELSH ASS? CUP,   FIRST LEAGUE CHAMP CUP,
MANCHESTER CUP,   FOOTBALL ASS? CHAM SHIELD,
ENGLISH CUP,   INTERNATIONAL CAPS & MEDALS,

A man and his footballing achievements. Billy Meredith's playing career spanned almost 30 years in which he played for Chirk, where he helped them win the Welsh FA Cup; Northwich Victoria; Manchester City, with whom he won his first English FA Cup winners' medal in 1904 and United. After joining United he helped to win that trophy once again in 1909 and collected championship medals in 1908 and 1911. Meredith played 48 times for Wales, and eventually rejoined City in 1921

Woolwich Arsenal 3–2. It was obvious to the thousands following the team that real success was sure to come soon.

In 1904, when Manchester City had finished runners-up to Sheffield Wednesday in the First Division, they had thrilled the people of Manchester (or at least half of them) by reaching the FA Cup final. In 1900 Bury had shown the way for local football by bringing the Cup to the area for the first time, beating Southampton 4–0, and three years later they did it again, this time thrashing Derby County by the final's biggest

winning margin to date, 6–0. The 1904 final saw City winning 1–0 at Crystal Palace in a local 'derby' final against Bolton Wanderers.

It was the backbone of that City side which was to turn United into a footballing power after a shrewd piece of negotiation by Ernest Mangnall.

A year after that great victory one of City's star players, the legendary winger Billy Meredith, was suspended from the game for three years, firstly for trying to bribe an Aston Villa player to throw a game, and then for illegally trying to obtain payment from City while under suspension – when his punishment included a ban on even going to the ground. Even though the suspension prevented Meredith from playing until April 1908, in May 1906 Mangnall signed him for £500. It would turn out to be money well spent.

United started their first term in the First Division well enough, winning at Bristol City, drawing with Derby and Notts County, then beating Sheffield United at Bramall Lane, but Mangnall was constantly on the look-out for new players in an effort to compete with their rivals from across Manchester.

Mangnall buys City players

Then a bombshell, which proved disaster to City and boom-time for United, hit the game. A Football Association inquiry, which had been investigating the activities of many clubs, discovered that Manchester City had been making illegal payments to their players. There was an uproar and five City directors were forced to resign. That was perhaps the lesser of the two 'sentences' heaped upon the club by the FA for in the other, 17 players – the backbone of the Cup-winning side – were banned from playing for City for life. In a move unheard of before or since, City had to sell most of their playing staff or the club would not be allowed to continue in the Football League.

The news was greeted with disguised delight by other clubs. The vultures would swoop to pick the bones of the successful City side and improve their own chances.

With Meredith having already been signed by United, the spotlight turned on Herbert Burgess, thought to be the best full-back in the game. Everton, Newcastle United, Bolton, Celtic and Chelsea all wanted him but it was Ernest Mangnall who beat them to the punch.

The FA's sentence on the City players also suspended them from playing football at all until January 1907, and two months before the punishment was due to end, City announced a meeting at the Queens Hotel, in Manchester's Piccadilly. Clubs interested in their players were invited to attend . . . it was an auction of footballers!

Ernest Mangnall had no intentions of competing against rival clubs, many much richer than United, so he made arrangements to approach the players he wanted before the meeting started. The other clubs did not like it at all, and Everton made an official complaint to the FA about their loss of Burgess to United – who also signed inside-forward Alec 'Sandy' Turnbull and Jimmy Bannister, another striker.

Everton claimed that on 8 November 1906 they had agreed to exchange Percy Hill with City for Burgess, placing a valuation of £600 on their player. City had given them a transfer form which was completed in every way except for Burgess's signature, but they had not been able

to find the player to get him to sign. The reason for this was obvious. He was with Ernest Mangnall, who was persuading him to join United, and as a Manchester man he didn't need much persuasion!

The *Manchester Evening Chronicle* of December 1906 told how Burgess had sent a telegram to City, saying he would not sign for Everton, and they had allowed United officially to approach him. The story also told of the distribution of the City players:

On inquiry at the Football Association offices in High Holborn today, our London correspondent learned that the following transfers of the suspended Manchester City players have been officially sanctioned and the registrations formally made.

A Turnbull to Manchester United; T Hynds to Woolwich Arsenal; F Booth to Bury; J McMahon to Bury; James Bannister to Manchester United; J H Edmonson to Bolton Wanderers; G T Livingstone to Glasgow Rangers; H Burgess to Manchester United.

So far as the Football Association is concerned with the transfer of Burgess, he is a Manchester United player.

Meredith's suspension was adjusted to end along with his former City colleagues and on 1 January 1907 a crowd of over 40,000 turned up at Bank Street to see United's new quartet in action against Aston Villa. They weren't disappointed. Sandy Turnbull got the only goal of the game, and United went on to end the season in eighth place in the First Division.

Champions . . . and bother abroad

There were greater things on the horizon. The following season, 1907–08, Manchester United won the League Championship for the first time, a feat even the great City team had failed to achieve. They won in fine style, nine points ahead of Aston Villa and City, winning 23 of their 38 games and only letting their form slip away after the title had been secured.

That summer Manchester United played in Europe. The club decided to take its players on a summer tour to Hungary and Austria and were one of the first northern sides to play abroad. As English champions they were a great attraction, but even in 1908 there were signs of a disease which would spread into the game in later years. Earlier that season United's players had been pelted with mud and stones after they left Bradford City's ground, and there had been reports of similar outbreaks of hooliganism at Sheffield Wednesday. In Hungary their 'friendly' was anything but amicable.

The *Manchester Evening News* report of the game tells how:

It was by no means football weather when Manchester United arrived in Budapest from Vienna, for the sun had left its bronze impress even upon the face of Charlie Roberts.

Having seen their side score twice against United, even though losing 6–2, the Hungarians came to the second match hoping to see at least a draw, for the Ferenczvaros Torna Club are the leaders of the local league, and only one goal has been scored against them all season.

Alas, such are the vagaries of the game, that before the local lads knew where they were, little Jimmy Bannister had opened the account, and Meredith added a second. A moment from the second kick-off Meredith caught the ball on his toe and running fully half the length of the field at top speed, scored another brilliant goal. There were now fully 11,000 spectators and the applause was deafening.

From this point the attitude of the crowd changed. The weakness of the local lads was apparent at every point, and, what was more painful, all could see it. Then followed a series of incidents which augmented the chagrin all Hungarians felt. Up to this point the referee had been passable, then the hostility of the crowd led to a series of adverse and pitiable decisions against the United. One cause of discontent was the removal of men who were stationed beside each goal as additional referees to inform the referee proper what happened on the line. These men shouted 'offside', 'touch' or 'goal' repeatedly, until play near goal became impossible. Finally they were removed.

On renewing the game, Wall broke away on the left and scored with a great shot. Five minutes later he was badly fouled by one of the opposing half-backs and after a lengthy appeal, awarded a penalty. This was taken by Moger (the United goalkeeper) who easily beat the Hungarian. By this act of one goalkeeper shooting at the other, the feelings of the crowd were again intensified and trouble brewed all round the ground.

Soon after the change of ends Picken got away and put in a beautiful ground shot which swerved into the net out of the reach of the custodian, 6–0. It was not long after this that a regrettable incident occurred.

Thomson was pulled up for fouling and he protested loudly against the decision. The game was stopped. Thompson thereupon – unable to speak the language – caught hold of the referee's hand to direct him to the spot to demonstrate how and what really had happened. This act was misunderstood by Gabrilovitch, the referee, and his hand rose threateningly. The referee being a very tall man, Duckworth rushed up to aid the centre-half. Nobody understood each other and were ordered off. Both refused to go, and rightly so. For fully fifteen minutes arguments and gesticulation prevailed. Interpreters were requisitioned and eventually after an apology, the game was renewed, and Wall added another goal, the end coming in partial darkness with the score 7–0.

It was what happened next that made Ernest Mangnall vow: 'We will never go to Budapest again'. As the team left the field they were

attacked by the crowd. Harry Renshaw, the *Manchester Evening News* reporter, wrote:

Everybody made for the gateway through which the players must pass on their way to the dressing room . . . Harry Moger was struck across the shoulders by one of these [rioters] with a stick. Stacey was spat upon, Picken and Charlie Roberts struck, in fact nearly all the team were given a reminder. Then the police charged the rioters, and fully twenty were arrested and dragged into one of the club rooms which was utilised as a police station. Even in the dressing room the team were not safe and a shower of heavy stones let in more air and daylight.

The menu from a celebration dinner signed by some of the guests. The signatures include those of entertainer George Robey, a close friend of Ernest Mangnall (whose autograph is below Robey's), and players Alex Bell, Dick Duckworth, Harry Moger, and Billy Meredith together with others who took part in the successful campaigns between 1908 and 1911

The players left the ground under police escort and were on their way back to their hotel in a row of coaches when the rioters attacked again:

Particular attention was paid to the last carriage and a huge stone knocked me down and cut my head. Then Alec Bell was hit behind the ear, and Picken received another. I was then hit on the head again. It was so sudden that the players had no time to raise the hoods of the carriages. Mr Mangnall was hit and Thomson caught it badly in the neck, with Wall and several others. Many arrests were made and the police were compelled to draw their swords.

United were glad to get back to England again and although the Hungarian incident made headline news for several weeks, it was quickly forgotten as rumour strengthened that the club was about to move from Bank Street to a new ground. As early as August 1907 'Wanderer' had written in the *Manchester Evening Chronicle*:

The club is sure to remain at Clayton another season, but the intention is to move to a new ground as soon as possible, and it is just about a thousand to one that the home chosen will be at Old Trafford and that when erected it will compare with any ground in the kingdom.

There can be no better site than Old Trafford where the City and Salford cars [trams] meet, the Sale and Altrincham service is tapped, and the cricket ground station would be available. The air would be purer for both the crowd and the players, and everything seems in favour of such a change and choice.

'Wanderer' also tipped United to do well that season, and, as noted, they obliged with the First Division title. The following 1908–09 season was not quite so successful in the League, but the FA Cup was a different story.

Part one of a photographic mystery. The players of 1908-09 pose with the English Cup after their victory at Crystal Palace. However a virtually identical picture appears on page 110 showing the same players with the League Championship trophy of 1911. Both photographs have been published as authentic records of each event since 1909 but only one can have been taken at the exact time of the successes

Manchester United, 1908-9

(Reserve) (Reserve)   MOGER   HAYES   BELL
MEREDITH DUCKWORTH   ROBERTS   J. TURNBULL   A. TURNBULL   STACEY
(Reserve)   (Reserve)   HALSE   WALL

United up for the Cup

The Cup campaign began at Bank Street with a game against Brighton and Hove Albion who had little consolation for their long journey north. Facing a team determined to restore the faith of their supporters after a disappointing lapse of four defeats in their eight games before the first round of the Cup, Brighton had to defend in depth and United won by the only goal of the game.

The second round was played on 6 February, when Everton, who were to finish second in the League, came to Clayton, and again it was a one-goal victory. In the third round Blackburn Rovers, who ended the season in fourth place in the League, were thrashed 6–1 when the third successive tie was played at Bank Street.

Then came the decisive game of the victorious run, when fate played a hand. United were drawn away to Burnley and were losing one-nil when the game was abandoned because of a blinding snowstorm, casually described in the *Weekly Dispatch* as 'conditions of a most rigorous character'. Four days later, on 10 March 1909, United won the replayed game 3–2 and Ernest Mangnall was able to leave the ground of his former club with a feeling of satisfaction.

The semi-final was played at Bramall Lane with Newcastle United as the opposition. The Geordies were on their way to the League Championship, and many felt that they would win both competitions. But it was the year of United – Manchester United – and they reached the final for the first time, thanks to another one-goal success.

So to the final at Crystal Palace: Manchester United versus Bristol City, and United taking their first step into the last stage of the competition which had captured the imagination of the football following public, more so even than the Championship. Here, for one day, London belonged to the people of the north and the west. Trains carried supporters to the capital and a huge crowd gathered at the ground.

Before the final Ernest Mangnall had taken his players away from the distractions of Manchester, where supporters had caught 'Cup fever' for the first time. The Royal Forest Hotel at Chingford housed the players before their trip to the stadium, and they prepared for the game with training sessions, strolls in the nearby woodlands and games of golf.

With both United and Bristol being teams who played in red jerseys and white shorts, the Football Association made them select neutral colours. Bristol chose blue and white, while United proudly announced that they would play in 'an all white costume relieved with a thin red line at the neck and wrists, and with the red rose of Lancashire on the breast'. In order to obtain the best possible publicity for their Cup final build-up Ernest Mangnall arranged for music hall star George Robey to present the kit to the players – with the press on hand.

In the smart all-white strip, with its red V dropping from the shoulders to the centre of the chest United no doubt had the same effect on both spectators and opposition as did the first glimpse of Real Madrid almost 50 years later, when they earned themselves the title of 'the

Action from the 1909 English Cup Final as United put pressure on the Bristol City goal. Sandy Turnbull scored the only goal of the game to thrill the Manchester fans who travelled to London for the Crystal Palace final. The shirts worn by Turnbull and Meredith are on permanent display in the club's museum

Louis Rocca suggested the name Manchester United as Newton Heath was wound up, and there is no doubting his loyalty to the club. In 1909 he rode in style to Manchester Central Station to join the official welcoming party for the first United cup homecoming. His decorated carriage was the centre of attraction. Twenty years later Rocca was appointed assistant manager as the club again struggled to survive

Spanish ghosts'. The spectres of Manchester certainly haunted Bristol City on the afternoon of Saturday, 24 April 1909.

The almost annual visit of northerners to the capital was something the London press appeared to enjoy. They wrote of the Lancashire supporter with his voice which seemed deeper than that of his southern counterpart as supplying a 'pulsating drone note in the fantasia of enthusiasm'. One paragraph ran:

The northern contingent pay great attention to the matter of commissariat. They bring stone jars of strong ale and sandwiches an inch thick, packed in little wicker baskets which are also used for conveying carrier pigeons.

Yes, Manchester was once again 'Up f' t' Cup' but this time it was the red and white of United taking over from the sky blue of City.

Like so many finals since, and probably some before, the game did not live up to its pre-match expectations. Sandy Turnbull scored the only goal and man of the match was Billy Meredith, adding another Cup winners' medal to the one he won with City in 1904.

Meredith was indeed an outstanding player noted for his casual approach to the game and his insistence on playing with a toothpick in his mouth. When play was in an area of the field

away from him, Meredith would talk to the crowd, or put the toothpick to work, and he drew this description from Don Davies, the *Manchester Guardian* columnist 'Old International':

Meredith was the Lloyd George of Welsh football. The parallel is by no means perfect, but it was curious how many points of resemblance could be traced. Both men had a following not far short of the entire Welsh nation; both were hailed by friends as the highest product of Welsh genius and by opponents as the lowest form of Welsh cunning. Both found it necessary to leave Wales to find adequate scope for their talents, yet both returned repeatedly in their hey-day to pay off debts in their heart-felt gratitude.

Round 1894 when Meredith was a youth, the newly formed Manchester City Football Club sent a deputation to Chirk, North Wales, with orders to bring him back. This mission was fulfilled but not without some hair-raising experiences. The angry townsfolk, roused by the thought of a local genius being sold for alien gold, seized one of the deputation and threw him into a nearby horse-trough. It is safe to assume that the sight of the stripling for whom he had suffered, did little to warm this gentleman's damp spirits on the journey home in the train! The Manchester United team in the final was: Moger, Stacey, Hayes, Duckworth, Roberts, Bell, Meredith, Halse, J Turnbull, A Turnbull, Wall.

The triumphant team returned home with the English Cup. Ernest Mangnall was the proudest man in the city as he strode from Central Station carrying the trophy in his right hand, grey jacket unbuttoned to reveal his waistcoat and watch-chain. His bowler hat was cocked slightly but his face was expressionless as he watched his players board a horse-drawn open-topped bus for the journey through the streets, three days after that memorable game.

Manchester turned out in its masses. Cloth caps filled the streets in a woollen ocean stretching as far as the players were able to see . . .

The *Manchester Evening News* of Tuesday, 27 April 1909 described the 'wild scenes greeting United's homecoming':

An hour before the time the train was due to arrive at Central Station large crowds of people assembled outside the station and behind the barricades of the approach leading to the platform at which the London train usually comes in. The great majority wore the United colours, and an ice cream merchant attracted considerable attention with his huge red and white umbrella and his similarly coloured barrow. Gutter merchants who did a good business with 'memory cards' of Bristol City came in for a good deal of good

humoured badinage, while the United favours attached to a cardboard representation of the English Cup sold like hot cakes.

Five waggonettes, gaily decorated with red and white bannerettes and ribbon, were waiting, two containing members of the St Joseph's Industrial School Band. The arrival of Rocca's Brigade, gaudily dressed in the colours of the United Club, was the signal for an outburst of cheering.

The London train hove in sight, and amid a scene of wild enthusiasm Mr Mangnall emerged carrying the cup on high, followed by the players, their wives, and other people who had travelled from the Metropolis.

The band struck up 'See the Conquering Hero Comes' and there was a great scramble by the crowd, which had been permitted to enter the platform, to reach the players.

Some were carried shoulder high, and ultimately were comfortably seated in the third waggonette. Sticks were waved and hats were thrown in the air and the enthusiasm was unbounded when Roberts, carrying the trophy, came into view.

So the conquering heroes made their journey to Manchester Town Hall in Albert Square, scene of so many homecomings in recent years, but this was United's first.

United had ended the 1908-09 season 13th in the League, but the Cup win meant success for Mangnall's men for the second time. Before the start of the next season football went through a major change, and the men of Manchester were largely responsible for it.

Charlie Roberts proudly holds the English Cup, predecessor of the FA Cup, as he stands with the United party on their arrival back in Manchester from the 1909 Cup Final. Chairman J H Davies is on his right, and next to him Ernest Mangnall, the club's secretary-manager. The players rode in carriages from Central Station to the town hall for a civic reception

The team become outcasts

Although the Union of Professional Footballers had been formed in 1898 at that meeting in the Spread Eagle Hotel, ten years later players were still having difficulty in getting their employers to recognise their rights as trade unionists. There were constant battles for wage increases in smaller clubs, and with amateur and part-time players available, the role of the full-time professional was not as secure or as rewarding as it might later, in some cases, become.

In 1908 United had played a game against Newcastle United to raise funds for their union, and they did it against the wishes of both the League and the Football Association. For the next twelve months the Players' Union sought affiliation to the Federation of Trades Unions and just before the 1909–10 season was due to start matters reached crisis point. The football authorities feared that, as Federation members, footballers might be drawn into arguments which were far removed from the game. If miners, cotton workers or railwaymen demanded a change in working conditions, would they ask for the support of other trade unionists? If they did, could they force the players to strike?

On 27 August 1909, five days before the start of the new season, representatives of the League clubs met in Birmingham and decided that any player admitting to being a member of the union should be suspended, have his wages stopped, and be banned from taking part in any game.

The move by the League and the Football Association was to try to prevent a strike. It almost caused one. Instead of persuading players that being part of a union would not be of any help to them, it convinced footballers all over the country that the only way for them to achieve their aims of better pay and conditions was to be part of such a body.

The next day Ernest Mangnall and the United board called the players to a mass meeting. Twenty-seven turned up, the exceptions being Harry Moger, who was attending a family funeral, and Jimmy Turnbull.

The players were told about the League directive, and under a headline 'Manchester United's Grave Position', the *Manchester Evening News* reported:

The various speakers pointed out to the men the very serious position the club was in, having three matches to play in the opening six days of the season.

Some discussion followed and the players said they would like it to be thoroughly understood that they had no grievance whatever with the club, but they were fighting for what they believed to be a just principle, and therefore they intended to retain their membership of the Players' Union.

After the players left the room the committee held a meeting and it was decided to wire the Bradford City club immediately, so as to cause no inconvenience, to the effect that, owing to the Manchester United players having determined to remain members of the Players' Union, the club had no players, and consequently the League fixture which should be played with Bradford City, at Clayton, on

The United squad and Coleman of Everton form the 'Outcasts' line-up after being suspended for standing firm for their union rights. Only 24 hours before the 1909–10 season was about to start, the threatened strike by members of the Players' Union was called off

H. MOGER, J. PICKEN, W. CORBETT, R. HOLDEN, H. BURGESS, J. CLOUGH, W. MEREDITH, G. BOSWELL
G. WALL, A. TURNBULL, C. ROBERTS (Captain), T. COLEMAN, R. DUCKWORTH.

Wednesday next, could not be proceeded with.

The decision of the United players will certainly cause a sensation in the football world, and looked at from any point of view the men cannot but be admired for the fight they have made. In the history of trade unionism there has never been a situation like the present one. By their loyalty to a cause which they believe to be a just one, twelve of the players have already forfeited £28 each, and by their attitude today they have incurred even further risks. Every player in the League who remains a member of the trade union will at once be suspended.

Two days before the new season, most clubs were claiming to have signed enough amateurs to get fixtures under way, but not United. The players joked about being the 'Outcasts' posing for a now famous photograph, but they stood firmly by their beliefs.

On 31 August, the eve of the new season, the authorities had a change of heart, and gave in. The Players' Union was recognised, the suspensions were removed, and the arrears of pay were allowed. In the eyes of many, this was one of Manchester United's most important victories. Had they not stayed together their cause would have been lost.

It would have been a tragedy if the strike had gone ahead because United were on the verge of moving to their new ground. Immediately after the Cup final success John Henry Davies had once again shown that his heart, and his wealth, were deeply embedded in the club he had taken over by chance. He pledged to lend the massive

sum of £60,000, which even from the head of a company like Manchester Breweries Ltd was a gigantic amount, worth millions by today's standards. The move to Old Trafford was finalised.

The strike threat over, work was able to continue, and the days at Bank Street were numbered. A large crowd turned up to see the game against Bradford City and gave the 'Outcasts' a warm reception. They replied with a 1–0 win.

The season went reasonably well, and always there was the move to the new ground to look forward to. On 22 January 1910, United played their last game at Bank Street in front of a modest 7,000 or so loyal supporters. They won 5–0, a fine way to say goodbye to a ground which held many memories for the players and the club's followers. Charlie Roberts scored twice, Connor and Hooper added two more, and Billy Meredith brought down the curtain. A week before that last League game at Bank Street, Burnley had taken revenge for the Cup defeat the previous season by knocking United out of the competition in the first round. United buckled down to a Championship attempt.

The move to Old Trafford

The move to Old Trafford took place in midseason, and preparations were made for the opening game against Liverpool, on 19 February 1910. A week before the event invitations were sent out to local dignitaries:

The President (Mr J H Davies) and Directors of the Manchester United Football Club ask your acceptance of enclosed, and extend a cordial invitation to attend the opening match on Saturday next.

The ground is situated at Old Trafford near the County Cricket Ground, and can be reached by three tram routes: Deansgate, Piccadilly and St Peter's Square.

The ground when completed will hold over 100,000 people. The present Stand will accommodate 12,000 people seated.

The formal opening of the ground took place during the week before the first match, after equipment had been moved into the new offices from the old ground at Clayton. And just in time. Two days before the Liverpool game fierce gales struck the Manchester area and the old wooden grandstand at Bank Street was blown down, wreckage spilling across into the roadway and badly damaging houses opposited. Had this happened during a game it would have been a terrible disaster. As it was no-one was injured.

So Old Trafford became the home of Manchester United and for the first game thousands walked the road in from Salford, others packed tramcars and carriages. The crowd inside looked in awe at the huge grandstand as it filled with well-known local faces, and tried to catch a glimpse of the celebrities present, including Ernest Mangnall's friend George Robey.

Manchester United Football Club, Ltd.,

WINNERS OF THE LEAGUE CHAMPIONSHIP, 1907-8.
WINNERS OF THE MANCHESTER CUP, 1908.
WINNERS OF THE FOOTBALL ASSOCIATION CHARITY SHIELD, 1908.
WINNERS OF THE ENGLISH CUP, 1909.

TELEPHONE 68, OPENSHAW.
TELEGRAMS:
"MANGNALL, CLAYTON, MANCHESTER."
SECRETARY:
J. E. MANGNALL.

BANK STREET, CLAYTON
MANCHESTER,
February 15th, 1910.

OPENING OF NEW GROUND,

Manchester United v. Liverpool,

FEBRUARY 19th, 1910.

Dear Sir,

The President (Mr. J. H. Davies) and Directors of the Manchester United Club ask your acceptance of enclosed, and extend a cordial invitation to attend the opening Match on Saturday next.

The ground is situate at Old Trafford near the County Cricket Ground, and can be reached by three tram routes—Deansgate, Piccadilly and St. Peter's Square.

The ground when completed will hold over 100,000 people. The present Stand will accomodate 12,000 people seated.

An early reply will greatly oblige.

Yours truly,

J. E. MANGNALL,
Secretary.

Left: Guests of the club received this invitation to the official opening of Old Trafford and were thrilled by what they saw. The ground never reached its predicted capacity of 100,000 but has a record of 76,962 achieved at the 1939 FA Cup semi-final. Today 25,500 seats form just under 50 per cent of the stadium's safety limit

Right: The Manchester County Football Asociation Cup, the first trophy to be won by Newton Heath. It was success in this competition which persuaded the club to reach for more distant horizons and which eventually led to League status. The trophy was unearthed in recent times and now stands in the club museum after many years in a bank vault

Below: The English Cup winners medal presented to Dick Duckworth in 1909 as United continued the successful run started a season earlier with their first Championship

United had injury problems. Alan Bell was missing at left-half, Blott taking his place alongside Charlie Roberts, with Dick Duckworth in his familiar position at right-half. George Stacey and Vince Hayes were the fullbacks in front of Harry Moger in goal, and the forward line was Meredith, Harold Halse, Homer, Sandy Turnbull and George Wall.

Sandy Turnbull scored the first of United's three goals, latching on to a centre from Meredith, but Liverpool were always in contention, closing the score to 2–1 before George Wall got United's third, then levelling at 3–3 through Goddard and Stewart, before the latter got his

second of the afternoon. So the Merseysiders spoiled the celebrations by winning 4–3.

But United were now able to compete in the status league as well as on the football field and Old Trafford became a showpiece ground, eventually staging the 1915 FA Cup final. In 1911 the replay between Bradford and Newcastle was played there, then in 1915 Sheffield United beat Chelsea 3–0 in Manchester.

The 1909–10 season ended with United in fifth place but a year later they were champions once more. Under Ernest Mangnall's direction they had won the League Championship of 1907–08; became the first winners of the FA

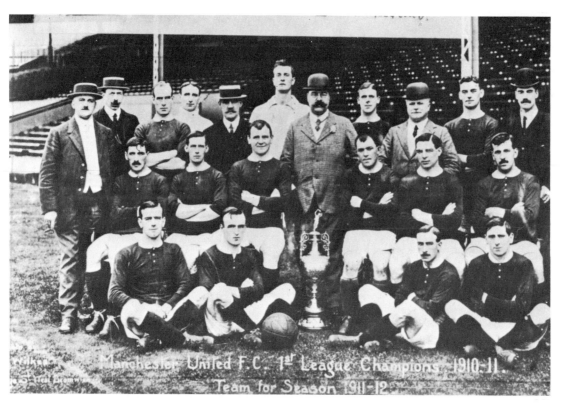

Manchester United F.C. 1st League Champions 1910-11. Team for Season 1911-12.

At the start of the 1911–12 season the Manchester United players, secretary-manager Ernest Mangnall (left) and chairman John H Davies (centre), gathered at Old Trafford for a photo-session. The outcome of this has since puzzled many football historians. This picture shows the team with the League Championship trophy they won in 1910–11, but an identical picture of the same men in the same positions with the officials wearing the same clothes was also taken with the English FA Cup, which the club won in 1909 (see page 103). On this second photograph Charlie Roberts (seated third from left) is holding the ball, the only difference apart from the trophy. So did United borrow the Cup from holders Bradford City, or was this the work of a clever photo-artist in later years?

Charity Shield which was introduced in 1908, and the Manchester Cup the same year; then won the FA Cup in 1909. The Championship of 1910–11 would be their final peak under the man whose role in Manchester football is one of unquestionable importance.

New players came, familiar faces left Old Trafford, and the team that took the title by just one point from Aston Villa was quite different from the one which earned the title three years earlier.

Enoch 'Knocker' West had been bought from Nottingham Forest. He was a centre-forward with a reputation for goal-scoring and lived up to it by netting 19 in the League campaign. Other new faces were goalkeeper Edmonds, who played for the latter half of the season when Moger was out, Arthur Donnelly, who filled in both full-back positions, and Hoften, a right-back.

The season reached an exciting climax on the last Saturday, 29 April 1911, when Aston Villa, leading the table by one point, were away to Liverpool, and United were at home to Sunderland.

So fickle is the football supporter that, with the Championship a possibility, only 10,000 made the journey to Old Trafford for what turned out to be a decisive game. A week earlier United had lost 4–2 at Villa Park and that, it seemed, was that. But on that last day of the season Liverpool, lying in the lower half of the table, pulled off a remarkable victory, beating Villa 3–1, while United thrashed Sunderland 5–1, two goals from Harold Halse and one each from Turnbull and West, plus an own goal, giving them the title.

It would be 41 years before the League Championship would return to the club, and

United's victory once again in the FA Charity Shield of 1911, when they beat Southern League Swindon Town 8–4, marked the end of a great era for the club.

In August 1912, after a season in which United had finished 13th in the First Division, and lost to Blackburn in the fourth round of the FA Cup, they also lost Ernest Mangnall. The manager who had been at their helm throughout their successful years left to join Manchester City.

The *Manchester Evening Chronicle* of 21 August 1912 reported under a single column headline that the United maestro had moved to Hyde Road, home of the Old Trafford club's biggest rivals:

The City directors did not come to a decision without long and anxious consideration, and among the names before them were those of Mr J J Bentley and Mr H C Broomfield. At the last moment there seemed a possibility of the negotiations breaking down, but late last night the directors interviewed Mr Mangnall after a three hours' discussion, and an hour later the announcement was made that he had been appointed.

Mr W H Wilkinson (chairman) welcomed the new manager and wished him every success. Mr Mangnall, in reply, said he hoped to see the Hyde Road club soon take the position which Manchester City ought to take. Nothing that he could do to attain that end should be left undone.

Ernest Mangnall's place as secretary-manager was taken by J J Bentley, and under his guidance United reached fourth place in the League in the 1912–13 season. But the great names were drifting out of the game, and those who had been part of those championship-winning sides were now reaching the end of their playing days. Had Ernest Mangnall seen what the future held for the club when he decided to leave?

By the end of the 1913–14 season only Stacey, Duckworth, Meredith, Turnbull, West and Wall were left, and by the end of the following season crowds had dropped to below an average of 15,000, and United escaped relegation by just one point.

To make matters worse Mangnall's Manchester City ended the last season before the First World War, 1914–15, in fifth place, their highest since his departure from Old Trafford. The United side which began the season was almost unrecognisable:

Beale, Hodge, Stacey, Hunter, O'Connell, Knowles, Meredith, Anderson, Travers, West, Wall.

Although Ernest Mangnall had often been referred to in newspaper reports as United's 'manager', his actual title was secretary, and it wasn't until 1914 that the first official football manager of the club was appointed. John Robson, who arrived from Brighton and Hove Albion in December 1914, worked under secretary Bentley and took charge of playing arrangements. He stayed in the post until 1921.

The First World War brought football to a standstill and had a crippling effect on United, who were faced with massive overheads for the running of Old Trafford.

The club also lost a lot of its charisma with the departure of Mangnall, who was a great publicist and who took his gift to City.

The war also robbed United of one of its stars. Sandy Turnbull was killed in France, and when life returned to normal in 1919 and football resumed there was a very different line-up for the first game against Derby County:

Mew, Moore, Silcock, Montgomery, Hilditch, Whalley, Hodge, Woodcock, Spence, Potts, Hopkin.

Attendances rose following the turmoil of war, and by the end of the 1919–20 season crowds of over 40,000 were commonplace, but the League position of 12th place did little to inspire. A season later John Chapman replaced John Robson as manager, and also filled the secretarial role, but once more Ernest Mangnall stole the Manchester spotlight when his club

Football began again after the First World War, with United finishing in 12th place in Division One. This line-up includes goalkeeper George Mew who played in all 42 games that season, full-backs Charlie Moore (left) and John Silcock on either side of him, and in the centre of the front row Billy Meredith bridging the gap between the early 1900s and the twenties

opened its new ground at Maine Road. Mangnall was clearly leaving his mark on Manchester football.

Relegation and promotion

Then, in 1922, came the final blow for United. They were relegated, after winning just eight of their 42 games (the First Division had been increased to 22 clubs immediately after the war, when plans were also being made for the introduction of a Third Division).

Billy Meredith had left United in 1921 to re-sign for Ernest Mangnall, and by the time United played their first game in the Second Division for 16 years, none of the great stars of the successful pre-war years remained. They finished fourth in the table, having had hopes of winning promotion until defeats at Blackpool in late March and at home to Leicester in April had seen them slip out of contention.

A season later, 1923–24, they were 14th in the Second Division, but then came a breath of fresh air in the 1924–25 season. It began with a showpiece game at Maine Road, where a combined City and United side played Everton and Liverpool as a testimonial for Ernest Mangnall, now ready to retire from football management and take up a career in journalism. It ended with United winning promotion, finishing second to Leicester City, and a season later in 1925–26 the improvement was maintained with a respectable ninth place in the top flight.

Fate this year twisted the tail of Manchester City. The two Manchester clubs met in the semi-final of the FA Cup with City winning 3–0 at Bramall Lane, but then the Sky-blues not only lost the final 1–0 to Bolton Wanderers, but were relegated to the Second Division.

New stars had begun to emerge for United: Joe Spence, an outside-right who played a record 510 League and Cup games in his 14 years' service; Frank Barson, a towering centre-half who had been a blacksmith before turning to football; and Clarrie Hilditch, a wing-half who became player-manager in 1926–27 as the club looked for a new man to succeed John Chapman.

In 1927 John Henry Davies died. The man who had saved the club from slipping out of existence in 1902, and who had played such an important part in the creation of Manchester United, could no longer be turned to at difficult times. He was replaced by G H Lawton, who bridged the gap between two major benefactors.

A new manager was appointed. Herbert Bamlett's pedigree for football management was strange and somewhat unorthodox. Bamlett was a former referee – in fact he had gone down in the record books as the youngest to take charge of an FA Cup final when he officiated in 1914 when only 32. He had then moved into management and had been in charge at Oldham Athletic, the now defunct Wigan Borough and Middlesbrough.

In 1924 Manchester showed its appreciation of Ernest Mangnall's contribution to football with a testimonial game at Maine Road. Under Mangnall's leadership United won the championship in 1908 and 1911 and the Cup in 1909. He was not only influential in the building of Old Trafford, but of Maine Road too after moving to City as their secretary-manager

One of Bamlett's most unusual connections with United was that it was he who had been in charge of the controversial FA Cup quarter-final at Turf Moor in 1909 when the game was stopped by a blizzard. So bad was the weather that afternoon that young Mr Bamlett had been too cold to blow his whistle when he decided to abandon the match and had handed it to United's captain Charlie Roberts to call a halt to proceedings, much to the amusement of the Manchester supporters and the dismay of the locals.

Under Bamlett, whose assistant was Louis Rocca, the man who had been general 'dogs-body' at Newton Heath, and who had acted as a scout for the club during its successful years, United slipped slowly down the First Division: 15th in 1926–27; 18th in 1927–28; 12th in 1928–29; 17th in 1929–30; and then, in 1931, relegation as bottom club.

What a terrible season that was. As Tommy Docherty might have described it: 'They started off badly, then deteriorated.'

They lost their first game of the season, at home to Aston, and followed this with eleven more successive defeats, so that by October 1930 their record read:

P	W	D	L	F	A	Pts
12	0	0	12	14	49	0

Something had to be done, but what? United had massive debts and could not afford new players, but even so they plunged recklessly into the transfer market, only adding to their own downfall. By the end of that season they had scored 53 goals in their 42 games, and conceded a massive 115, winning only six times at Old Trafford. No wonder they went down.

Another financial rescue

So began the 1931–32 season, which was to have a lasting effect on the club, or at least, events which occurred during the period were. In the Second Division United again found themselves fighting for their lives. They lost their first two games, to Bradford City in Yorkshire and to Southampton at Old Trafford, before low attendances. Only 3,507 loyal souls turned up to watch the opening game of the season. The United supporters were voting with their feet, and the board of directors got the message.

Herbert Bamlett had lost his job in April 1931, and the manager's role was filled temporarily by Walter Crickmer, the club's secretary since 1926. His assistant was Louis Rocca, still dedicated to the club he had followed since the Newton Heath days. But times were getting harder. By December 1931 Manchester United was on the rocks. Deeply in debt, unable to pay off instalments on the loan made to the club to build Old Trafford, with no chance of paying for players they had obtained from other clubs, they faced bankruptcy. Another saviour was needed, but could Manchester produce another John Henry Davies?

Crisis came in Christmas week when the players went to pick up their wages and were told there was no money available. Stacey Lintott, a sportswriter, picked up the story, but before he wrote it he went to see a contact of his, James W Gibson, whose company was a major garment producer, specialising in army uniforms.

Gibson had a love of sport, and was persuaded to help the club. He met United's directors, laid down his terms and agreed to help out on the understanding that he would become chairman and be able to elect his own colleagues on the board. The directors had no choice – they either went to the wall with their club, or agreed to Gibson's proposals. So the club was once again saved from extinction.

James Gibson invested over £30,000 of his own money in the club – half the original cost of Old Trafford – paid the players' wages, settled outstanding accounts and began to put the ship back on an even keel again.

A new manager was found: Scott Duncan, who had risen to fame as a footballer with Glasgow Rangers and Newcastle United. This time United had an ex-player at the helm, an idea that had worked with other clubs, a former professional knowing how to approach the game in a professional manner. Scott Duncan spent money on new players as he tried to build a strong side, but whether he spent wisely is debatable.

In the season in which they had almost faded to obscurity United finished 12th in the Second Division, a year later they were sixth, and then in 1933–34 not even Gibson's money could prevent them from sliding to the lowest ebb in the club's history, just one point away from the Third Division.

In fact the future of the club in the Second Division hung by a slender thread as late as the final day of the season. The date, 5 May 1934 is significant in the club's history for on that day, and for the previous week since drawing with Swansea, the club was last but one in the table. Never since the days those railway workers started their team had the club been in such a lowly position.

Lincoln were bottom, and nothing could stop them from being relegated. United were above them, seven points better off, and one point behind Millwall, who filled the 20th position. On 5 May United were away to Millwall, and knew that they had their own fate in their hands.

New signing Hacking was in goal, playing his tenth game since his transfer from Oldham, and in front of him were full-backs Griffiths and Jones. The half-back line of Robertson, Vose and McKay supported a forward line which read: Cape, McLenahan, Ball, Hine and Manley. The last-named normally played wing-half but was brought in to play outside-left so that he would add his defensive qualities if things got tough.

United played their hearts out. Manley scored first, Cape added a second and United won 2–0 . . . but what might have happened to this great club had that result been reversed and Manchester United had begun 1934–35 as a Third Division side? Incidentally, the week that United spent in that lowest point in their history, began the day that Manchester City, with Matt Busby in the side, won the FA Cup.

The new season began with Scott Duncan's new players in the line-up and ended with United fifth from the top, a much improved performance and one which brought the crowds back to Old Trafford, especially those who had been embarrassed by the failure of the Red Devils while Manchester City had lifted the Cup. A season later and United had something to celebrate. Not since Ernest Mangnall's team had won the Championship and the FA Charity Shield in 1911, had Old Trafford's trophy room been blessed with a major piece of silverware. The club had got used to playing second fiddle to Manchester City, but times at last were beginning to change. In 1935–36 they won the Second Division title, not perhaps the most coveted award the game has to offer, but certainly better than facing relegation, and a big improvement on their achievements over the previous quarter of a century.

Scott Duncan's team had achieved this with a tremendous run-in to the end of the season, stringing together 19 games without defeat and clinching promotion with a 3–2 win over Bury at Gigg Lane, where two goals from Tom Manley and another from George Mutch brought the 31,562 fans spilling onto the pitch. It is interesting to note that in 1987, when United were drawn against Bury in the Littlewoods Cup, the game was switched from Gigg Lane to Old Trafford because the ground safety limit at Bury is now restricted to 8,000.

United's only defeat after the beginning of the year, apart from a 2–0 exit from the FA Cup at Stoke, had been to lose by the only goal of the game at Bradford City on 4 January, and even though Charlton Athletic tried to close the gap United won promotion by a single point after both clubs had each won 22 of their 42 games.

They had started the 1935–36 season with Hall pushing Breedon out of the goalkeeper's spot after just one game and they had the good fortune to have several players who were virtually ever-presents throughout the season. Tom Curry was responsible for the fitness of the players, and he must have been proud of their response. Of the full-backs, Griffiths and Porter, only John Griffiths missed a single game of the 42, right-half Jim Brown missed just two, one of them a defeat at Blackpool, and centre-half George Vose was absent only for the 4–0 win at home to Burnley. Of the others, George

Mutch was an ever-present, playing either at inside-right or centre-forward and scoring 21 goals in the League, and Henry Rowley scored just two fewer despite missing five matches.

Constantly being able to field a virtually unchanged side, Scott Duncan knew that he had a chance of success, and the players he had brought into the club from a variety of backgrounds took United back into the First Division for the first time since the start of the decade. Their stay, however was short. If ever the expression 'after the Lord Mayor's Show comes the dustcart' could be applied to football, here surely was the perfect example as 1936–37 followed the celebrations of 1935–36.

There were changes in the line-up at the start of the season: John, Redwood, Porter, Brown, Vose, McKay, Bryant, Mutch, Bamford, Rowley and Manley starting the campaign. A young man named Walter Winterbottom made his League debut for the club at Elland Road, Leeds, as they slipped to their ninth defeat in 16 games, with only three victories to their name. Winterbottom was never renowned as a player, but became manager of England from 1946 to 1963.

By the end of the season United had won only ten games, eight of them at Old Trafford, and a season after celebrating their return from the Second Division, they were back there.

Scott Duncan resigned and went to manage non-league Ipswich Town, and top-scorer

The players who won the Second Division Championship of 1935–36 gather at Old Trafford before the start of the following season, when they were relegated once again! On the extreme right is James Gibson, the chairman whose generosity saved the club from extinction. Standing second from the left is Tom Curry, and on the ground (front right) Bert Whalley, who remained with the club until both were killed in the Munich air disaster 22 years later

George Mutch took the road to Preston and a place in the game's Hall of Fame. Mutch had scored 46 goals in his 112 League games for United and three more in his eight FA Cup appearances, but it was for one goal he scored for the club which bought him from United for £5,000 that he is remembered. It was in the 1938 FA Cup final at Wembley, when Preston met Huddersfield and the scores were level 0–0 in the dying minutes of extra-time. George Mutch ran into the penalty area with the ball and was tripped. A penalty, and the last kick of the game. Mutch took it and hit the ball with a powerful shot, which struck the underside of the square crossbar, bounced down over the line and spun into the back of the net. George Mutch had made footballing history, but it is worth noting that had Mutch not taken the kick himself, the man who would have gone into the record books in his place was Preston's second-string penalty taker, Bill Shankly.

Back for 36 years at the top

United were not too disappointed at the success of their ex-player, for as the FA Cup came back to the north-west, United also had something to celebrate. Their big-dipper ride through football was back at the top, after plunging to the depths a season earlier. They ended the 1937–38 season as runners-up in the Second division to Aston Villa.

United won promotion by the skin of their teeth. Hot on their heels were Sheffield United, who in their 42 games scored 73 goals against 56, giving them a goal average of 1.738. United, with exactly the same record, 22 wins and nine draws, netted 82 goals against 50, an average of 1.952 – they went up, Sheffield stayed down. Coventry were only a point behind.

The season had seen new players once again take their places in the line-up. Walter Crickmer had been given the reins for another spell as temporary manager, and with Tom Curry and Louis Rocca remaining in the backroom, United tried out a blend of youth and experience.

Rocca, on one of his visits to Ireland, had spotted a young forward, Johnny Carey, and after bringing him to Manchester was delighted with his progress into the first team. Carey made his debut on 25 September 1937, against Southampton, and played just one more game before a ten-match break. He returned in Christmas week to score in the 3–2 win over Nottingham Forest, the club he would later manage after a career with United which saw him recognised as one of the best full-backs the game had produced.

A month before Duncan had resigned he had bought Jack Rowley from Bournemouth. Rowley was a prolific goal-scorer, making his debut as an outside-left in a home win over Sheffield Wednesday on 23 October 1937. He arrived on the scene at the right time. United had started the season badly, and as it followed their year of

relegation, crowds fell off. To make matters worse Manchester City had won the League Championship in 1936–37 and had been the major crowd pullers in the city as the Red fans stayed silent and at home.

Another new player to win his way into the side was Stan Pearson, a Salford-born lad who made his debut in a game which was the turning point of the season. From August until 6 November, three days before Scott Duncan resigned, United had won only five of their 14 matches. The side which started the season was Breen, Griffiths, Roughton, Gladwin, Vose, McKay, Bryant, Murray, Bamford, Baird and Manley. On 13 November, after Duncan had gone, the line-up looked different to say the least. Jack Breedon was in goal, Bert Redwood at right-back, Roughton at left. Right-half was Jim Brown, Vose remained at centre-half, and Bert Whalley played left-half. Bill Bryant stayed at outside-right with Baird inside him and Tommy Bamford centre-forward. Young Stan Pearson played inside-left, with Tom Manley outside him, a team of experience blending with young enthusiasm, and Chesterfield, the opposition, never knew what hit them.

Bamford scored four times, and Baird, Bryant and Manley scored to make it a 7–1 win. United lost just five more matches in the remainder of the season and were promoted. If some seasons have been of more importance to the history of Manchester United than others, that 1937–38 season must rank highly, even though the club failed to win any major trophies. Promotion to the First Division at such a time, with war impending, can only be looked upon as an act of good fortune. In that same season Manchester City were relegated along with West Bromwich Albion, and both failed to return a season later. United ended the 1938–39 campaign in 14th place in the First Division, but it was events outside football which would have a long-lasting effect on the club.

At the outbreak of the Second World War football was suspended. From 1939 until 1946–47 there was to be no League competition, and while United played no serious football during the period of the war, when the game began again after years of friendlies and make-shift matches, they would start again in the First Divison.

A major historical event had once again played an important role in the Manchester United story. Because of the Second World War the club found itself bracketed with the elite and was to remain in the upper section for 36 years. In that time United would achieve successes never dreamt of by Harry Stafford, reach peaks beyond the far-seeing imagination of Ernest Mangnall, and develop its stadium beyond the riches of men like John Henry Davies and James Gibson. It would also find itself a manager to reign longer than any who had gone before him, and that man would step into the breach after the war. His name . . . Matt Busby.

Manchester United at the start of the 1968–69 season proudly displaying the European Cup they had won the previous May. Back row: Bill Foulkes, John Aston, Jimmy Rimmer, Alex Stepney, Alan Gowling, David Herd. Middle: David Sadler, Tony Dunne, Shay Brennan, Pat Crerand, George Best, Francis Burns, Jack Crompton (trainer). Front: Jimmy Ryan, Nobby Stiles, Denis Law, Matt Busby (manager), Bobby Charlton, Brian Kidd, John Fitzpatrick. But despite the European triumph, the team had peaked. It was a side growing old gracefully and lacking the edge to keep them competing for fresh honours. Matt Busby was preparing to retire and a few of his stars were of like mind. They finished 11th that season and they never finished higher than eighth before relegation arrived six years after winning the European Cup

Beyond Busby: Search for a successor

So we come to the point where we started our story . . . the Matt Busby era, the most successful in the history of Manchester United and, of course, the most tragic.

We broke into history and make no apology for opening our book with the Busby Babes, the drama of European competition and the Munich catastrophe. It was a renaissance period for the whole of football as folk flocked back to the game after the grim days of the Second World War.

Under the guidance of Busby, Manchester United emerged a giant, surviving the most terrible of blows to conquer Europe. But even Sir Matt Busby couldn't go on for ever, nor could his great team of 1968, and so we pick up our tale again as the great man looks for a new commander to take his beloved club into the 1970s.

Even as they were winning the European Cup in 1968 and finishing runners-up for the Championship it was clear that some of the players were no longer in their prime and that changes would have to be made. Some of the decisions were going to be difficult, both in terms of judgement and feeling, and Busby thought long and hard about whether he wanted to be the manager to close one book and open yet another.

He opened the 1968–69 season in charge and there was little inkling that he was ready to step back from the day-to-day running of the team. In any case Busby was not the kind of man to bow out in a blaze of glory after winning the European Championship.

There were matters in hand such as the world confrontation with Estudiantes and, of course, a defence of their European crown, but the League soon revealed cracks in the team.

Three games were lost in the opening month of August. A 3–1 defeat at West Bromwich raised few eyebrows, but going down 4–0 at home to Chelsea was not the kind of result the fans expected. Then there was the entertaining but curious 5–4 defeat at Sheffield Wednesday. Busby tried to bolster the team by buying winger Willie Morgan, a Scottish international, for £110,000 from Burnley, but in September,

October and November they managed to win only three games. The most frequent result was a draw.

Denis Law and George Best manfully shouldered the burden, but by the end of the season their goal figures were down on previous seasons. Law scored 19 and Best 14, and Bobby Charlton was reduced to five. Morgan managed six, and the slump was eventually reflected in a League placing of 11th. Three defeats in succession around Christmas gave Sir Matt food for thought and by January he had reached a decision . . . he would 'go upstairs' to become general manager and leave a new man to run the team. The club issued a statement which read:

Sir Matt has informed the board that he wishes to relinquish the position of team manager at the end of the present season.

The chairman and directors have tried to persuade him to carry on and it was only with great reluctance that his request has been accepted. The board fully appreciates the reason for his decision and it was unanimously agreed that Sir Matt be appointed general manager of the club which he is very happy to accept.

Chairman Louis Edwards went on to explain: 'Of course we knew that it had to come but this does not mean that Sir Matt will be any less involved with Manchester United. In fact the post of general manager carries even wider responsibilities and my board are well content to think that in future they can call upon Sir Matt's unique football experience in both home and international fields.'

Behind the scenes the chairman and directors had tried hard to persuade Busby to carry on, but his mind was made up. The clue to his thinking lay in a few words he had uttered spontaneously during the glow of European victory. 'Let us hope this is not the end, just the beginning,' he had said just the day after making United the champions of Europe.

No doubt as he pondered that instinctive feeling, he explored how the task was to be accomplished and whether he really wanted to start all over again. He knew that it was the end

of another era and that after 23 years at the helm it was a job for a younger man. He had built three great teams and now a fourth was required. His mind must have gone back to the time he had started out, young and ambitious and that that was what was required all over again.

In a way Busby was paying a price for his own success, because he had made the club so big that it was becoming increasingly more difficult for one man to control. As he put it himself at the time:

Manchester United are not just a football club any longer but a kind of institution. The demands are such that I was neglecting the all-important thing . . . the team. So many things need attention that I feel my move to general manager is a step in the right direction. I feel it is time for someone in a tracksuit to take over the players again out on the training pitch. The heaven and hell of winning and losing matches should be falling on younger shoulders, too.

The reorganisation was announced in the January to take effect at the end of the season and so give the club due time to find the right man to look after the team.

The press had a field day searching out likely candidates. The names of Don Revie, Johnny Carey, Ron Greenwood, Jimmy Adamson and Brian Clough were freely mentioned, but few questioned whether such experienced managers would be willing to take up an appointment which was going to be under the general management of Sir Matt Busby.

Wilf McGuinness

The club solved the problem by looking within and deciding to promote one of their junior staff to take charge of the players with a title of chief

coach. Wilf McGuinness, the 31-year-old trainer with the reserves, was the man chosen to follow in the great man's footsteps.

The appointment of McGuinness came with the announcement in April 1969, saying:

The board has given further consideration to the changes which will occur at the end of the season and has decided to appoint a chief coach who will be responsible for team selection, coaching, training and tactics.

Mr Wilf McGuinness has been selected for this position and will take up his duties as from 1 June and in these circumstances it is not necessary to advertise for applications as was first intended.

Sir Matt will be responsible for all other matters affecting the club and players and will continue as club spokesman.

Busby revealed his relief when he said:

My trouble is that it is almost impossible to forget football for a minute of my waking life. I have it for breakfast, dinner and supper. Driving the car I'm thinking of it. If I go out socially, everybody wants to talk football. The only time I get a break is on the golf course. I'd like to read but I don't get the time. Really it's football all the way, other people's football, too. Sometimes I go to another match and they start speculating who I have come to see. But I haven't come to see anybody. I've just come to look and listen and enjoy a match and know what's going on.

If he needed any reminders of the pressures, his experience between the announcement of his semi-retirement in the January and the end of the season provided ample evidence of the wisdom of his decision. The team ran riot with an 8–1 win against Queen's Park Rangers at Old Trafford, including a hat-trick from Willie Morgan, but there were other less convincing performances.

Following the drama of the games against Estudiantes with all the off-field tensions, came the volatile ties against AC Milan in the European Cup with crowd trouble at Old Trafford. It was a young man's game all right.

Wilf McGuinness was Busby's recommendation and the appointment had the advantage of keeping the management within the family of Old Trafford; it did however beg the question of total control, and was in marked contrast to the conditions insisted upon by Busby when he was brought to the club as a young man.

McGuinness had the additional problem of being asked to take charge of players who were his contemporaries, but these thoughts were only clouds on a distant horizon when the enthusiastic Wilf assembled his players for pre-season training in the summer of 1969. Wilf was certainly steeped in the tradition of the club and had always possessed qualities of leadership. As a schoolboy he captained not only Manchester Boys, but Lancashire and England as well. In fact he quite enjoys pointing out that a certain Bobby Charlton played under his command at schoolboy level!

Wilf McGuinness had the unenviable task of taking over from Sir Matt Busby as manager of Manchester United. United had the idea of keeping the appointment in the club family with the result that they called him up from his job as reserve team trainer to make him first-team coach. Later he was promoted to team manager, but though he did well enough by ordinary standards, it wasn't quite good enough for Old Trafford. He was in charge for 20 months, starting in April 1969, and then being offered his old job back in December 1970

United's chief scout Joe Armstrong was one of the first to note his capacity to take charge:

The first thing you noticed about Wilf as a youngster was that he was an aggressive little footballer always belting his way forward. We watched him progress from local area teams right through to England, and nothing summed him up better than when he captained England against Wales at Wembley in 1963.

England were two goals down, but you could see young McGuinness roll up his sleeves and simply drive his team back into the game and they came out with a creditable 3–3 draw.

Naturally Wilf had a number of clubs tracking him by that time, and he was eventually signed by United in the back of a car outside Manchester's fruit market where his father worked, but it wasn't as easy as some schoolboy signings. Jimmy Murphy remembers:

It took us some time to sign him. Joe Armstrong met his parents and eventually I did as well, but we didn't seem to be getting anywhere. So much so that my patience became a little exhausted and I finally put it to him bluntly: 'Are you joining us – yes or no?' And as we sat in the back of the car I also asked him if he thought he was Duncan Edwards.

Even in those days Wilf was a youngster who knew his own mind and was capable of expressing himself quite determinedly.

When he eventually arrived we had a tremendous amount of work to do on him. My late friend, Bert Whalley, did a heck of a job with him. He developed into a player who was a prodigious worker. He was a good listener. He never missed a trick, and even at the age of 15 was always seeking guidance and advice.

It stood him in good stead and he overcame what appeared to be his non-physical attributes in no uncertain manner. As a lad it would be difficult to imagine a more ungainly looking player. On his own admission he was flat-footed, knock-kneed, and he ran with his knees up in a peculiar style. He reminded me somewhat of a young colt put out to grass for the first time.

Yet despite these natural disadvantages, he became a most successful footballer who went all the way to play for England. All credit to him for overcoming his natural disadvantages.

Big names never bothered him. His approach to football was always right, as time proved. He also showed tremendous spirit and guts after breaking a leg.

As a junior McGuinness was one of the Busby Babes and played in three of the FA Youth Cup winning teams in the 1950s. He made his League debut against Wolves in October 1955, and remembers it vividly:

I can still hear Jimmy Murphy winding me up for the game and urging me to remember everything I had been taught. He said we hate Wolves and everything in black and gold, and I kept dutifully saying yes Jimmy. He told me I would be up against Peter Broadbent and that he would be doing his best to take my win bonus out of my pocket and then I wouldn't have any money to take my mother a box of chocolates after the match. He had me so wound up that when we went out for the kick-off and Peter Broadbent came across like the gentleman he is to wish me as a youngster good luck on my debut, I just shouted at him: 'Shove off, you thieving beggar.'

United won 4–3, but the young McGuinness made only three League appearances that season. His problem was that he was a left-half, and the great Duncan Edwards played in that position. His best season didn't come until after Munich. Then in 1958–59 he made 39 League appearances. Sadly, in the middle of the following season, he broke his leg playing for the reserves against Stoke. It was a bad break, and though he attempted a come-back it was impossible and he was forced to retire at the age of 22. But at least he had his qualities of leadership and United had no hesitation recruiting him as assistant trainer to Jack Crompton in charge of the reserve team.

Before long the Football Association made him the England youth team coach and in 1968 he was appointed their manager after helping Sir Alf Ramsey as a training assistant during preparations for the 1966 World Cup.

So the youthful McGuinness was not without management experience when he was handed command of the Busby empire. Yet, looking back, was there a veiled doubt in the minds of the board?

There was a definite probationary ring about the title they gave him. Chief coach was not even team manager, the phrase used originally when it was announced that Sir Matt would become general manager. Sir Matt explained:

This is a sort of preliminary. All the great names in the game started this way. He has a bit of experience to pick up yet in management and it's a question of starting this way. I think he will have enough to bite on with responsibility for the team without taking on other things which could come later. The question of team manager could come probably in a year or so. We hope it will.

Obviously everyone hoped that, but did the qualified authority communicate to the players that here was a new boss who had yet to convince the club that he could do the job? Bobby Charlton, senior player, captain, distinguished international and a pal, wrote, perhaps significantly, in a foreword to a club book:

No-one can be sure just how this change-over will work out. After all Sir Matt has been at the helm of Manchester United for 23 years. He has been the boss in every sense of the word . . . manager, tactician, coach, adviser, disciplinarian, simply everything. Even though he will be there in the background still, we are bound to miss him.

Wilf McGuinness coaching the England youth side for the international tournament in Leipzig in 1969. He was made the England youth coach in 1968. A broken leg finished his playing career at the age of 22, but he had already made his mark as a leader of men and Manchester United did not hesitate to take him on to their staff following unsuccessful attempts to play again. The Football Association were also impressed by him and he was called by Sir Alf Ramsey to help as a junior coach to prepare the England team for the World Cup in 1966

Bobby did go on to say that United could not have chosen a better man to follow in his footsteps and that after six years on the club training staff Wilf was no stranger to putting the rest of them through the hoop. He still added, though, with a touch of foresight: 'It may not be easy, there will be problems.'

On the pitch at least the difficulties soon manifested themselves. The opening game of the 1969–70 season, away to Crystal Palace, was drawn 2–2, a fair start in the circumstances, but then came three successive defeats, including losing 2–0 to Everton at Old Trafford and then going down at home again 4–1 to Southampton. This was followed by a 3–0 defeat at Everton and the fans were starting to worry.

United bought a new centre-half to replace the veteran Bill Foulkes, who had been given quite a chasing by centre-forward Ron Davies in the Southampton game. They bought Ian Ure from Arsenal for £80,000. It later transpired that Ure was not McGuinness's choice but Busby's, underlining at a very early stage the difficulties of dividing responsibility for running a team. McGuinness would later claim that he didn't want Ure, while the players he did want to buy,

like Malcolm Macdonald and Mick Mills, were refused him.

At the same time the arrival of Ure did steady the defence down, and once he was at centre-half, using his craggy height, the team played the next eight League games without losing.

The new coach was unlucky in that for most of the season he was without Nobby Stiles, recovering from a cartilage operation and problems with his knee. He could have done with a fighter like him in the ranks, though John Fitzpatrick did his best to supply a fair amount of aggression. The team continued to hold their own, but in terms of winning the Championship it was becoming clear that new blood was required. The goal scoring was shared mainly by George Best again with 15, a welcome increase to 12 by Bobby Charlton and a useful 12 from Brian Kidd. Willie Morgan scored seven. There were lapses like a 4–0 beating at Manchester City and a 5–1 crash at Newcastle, immediately avenged by a 7–0 win against West Bromwich at Old Trafford in the next match.

The team were still capable of turning it on, as they demonstrated whenever they played in Cup competition. They did Wilf McGuinness proud

Alex Stepney makes a brave save at the feet of Joe Royle the Everton centre forward. Stepney, who joined United from Chelsea after starting his career with Millwall, is one of the few Londoners to have settled at Old Trafford. In fact he took to life in the north so well that after leaving United to play in the United States he returned to make the Manchester area his home again. He played more than 500 League and Cup games for the Reds

George Best battles against Leeds United in the mud of Hillsborough in the semi-final of the 1970 FA Cup. The game ended goalless and it was a similar result in the replay at Villa Park before Billy Bremner scored for a 1–0 victory for Leeds at Burnden Park. So near yet so far was the theme for Manchester United in Cup football in 1970. They reached the semi-finals in both the FA Cup and League Cup, only to have their dreams of Wembley shattered in both competitions

suspension, he was in trouble just two months later after another tantrum with a referee. This time he was playing for Northern Ireland against Scotland at Windsor Park and was sent off for dissent. Eric Jennings, the FA Cup final referee, claimed that he was spat at and that mud was thrown at him.

Manchester United feared the worst, but the Irish FA discovered a FIFA rule which allowed them to deal with the dismissal and they decided that the sending off had been sufficient punishment. They did this with all due speed, with the result that Best was able to play against England and score a fabulous goal just four days later. The English League secretary Alan Hardaker accused the Irish FA of 'wangling' the rules, but United didn't complain too much!

Back in the FA Cup, Best behaved and helped knock Middlesbrough out of the competition 2–1 at Old Trafford, following a 1–1 draw at Ayresome Park. This gave the Reds a semi-final against the old enemy from Elland Road and it took three encounters with Leeds before a goal was scored. After the sides had battled vainly to score at Hillsborough and Villa Park, the tie moved to Burnden Park. It was won by a solitary goal scored by Billy Bremner after eight minutes. A centre from Peter Lorimer was headed across goal by Allan Clarke. It hit Mick Jones on the knees and ran out to the edge of the box for Bremner to beat Alex Stepney with a rocket of a drive. Bremner, the man who had knocked United out of the FA Cup in 1965 with a lone goal, had done it again.

It was a record semi-final with 173,500 spectators paying £155,478 for the three games, and they had had good value for their money. Wilf McGuinness had every right to feel pleased with his management, especially as it was his second semi-final of the season. His team had also put together a good run in the League Cup. In the opening rounds they won a home tie against Middlesbrough 1–0 and knocked out Wrexham 2–0 at Old Trafford. Burnley put up more resistance, drawing 0–0 at Turf Moor only to lose 1–0 in Manchester. Derby were beaten in two attempts in the same scoring pattern to bring a two-legged semi-final against Manchester City.

The City fans were oozing confidence after watching their team thrash the Reds 4–0 in the League at Maine Road. Their high expectations seemed fully justified when Colin Bell shot the Blues ahead at Maine Road to round off a thrusting run from Francis Lee, always a derby danger to United in this period. In the second half United raised their game. Bobby Charlton scored a 66th minute equaliser and George Best cut loose after a quiet start. Nobby Stiles, playing in only his second game of the season following a cartilage operation, was an inspiration as United rallied, but they couldn't prevent City having the last word with a late penalty which gave them a 2–1 advantage to take to Old Trafford.

reaching the semi-finals in both the FA Cup and the League Cup. In the FA Cup they opened modestly with the help of an own-goal for a 1–0 win at Ipswich. They cut loose in the next round at Old Trafford, beating Manchester City 3–0, and then really let rip at Northampton to smash the home side 8–2.

This game belonged to George Best, who had missed the previous round through suspension. He had been given a four-week ban for knocking the ball out of referee Jack Taylor's hands as the Wolverhampton official was leaving the field at the end of the League Cup semi-final against Manchester City at Maine Road. Best returned to action for the Northampton Cup-tie and in typical fashion scored six goals. Kim Book, the Northampton goalkeeper and brother of Manchester City's Tony, described it:

> Best was brilliant, fantastic, fabulous. I don't think any of us knew where to look for him. The space he found was amazing. It got to the stage where I thought he was going to score every time he had the ball, and six times I was right. He is so fast, so cool, so devastating.

It was also true to say that his temperament was beginning to fray. Despite his lengthy

Best played in the second leg, although he had knocked the ball out of referee Jack Taylor's hands following the disputed penalty as the players left the pitch. It was a rash moment which subsequently brought him a month's suspension, but he was still in action for the return with City a fortnight later. It was not one of Alex Stepney's happiest nights. The United goalkeeper allowed a powerful drive from Francis Lee to jump out of his arms for Ian Bowyer to score. Then he ignored the fact that a free-kick from Lee was indirect and parried the shot instead of safely letting it into his goal. Mike Summerbee slipped the rebound in to give the Blues a 2–2 draw on the night.

United's goals came from Denis Law, following a shot from Best, and from Paul Edwards who came up from full-back to finish off a masterly pass from Pat Crerand. The Reds had fought hard and had had a goal from Best disallowed for offside. Still, they had to bow out 4–3 on aggregate. Just as in their FA Cup semi-final, they hadn't really enjoyed many breaks, with the result that Wilf McGuinness had just fallen short of cementing his appointment with the glory and razzmatazz of a trip to Wembley. Nevertheless, to reach the last four in two Cup competitions in his first season was a creditable achievement . . . or so most people would think, but in reality getting so near without actually playing in a final seemed to prompt more critical questions than acknowledgements for a good first effort. The final League position of eighth was an improvement of three places, but again, so many people were wanting more. The fact that the McGuinness team beat Watford 2–0 at Highbury in a match for third place between the losing FA Cup semi-finalists brought in revenue, but it counted for little when measured against United's ambitions.

For the third season in succession, more than a million spectators had packed Old Trafford, but behind the scenes there were rumblings. No-one knew better than McGuinness that despite two semi-finals, changes were needed, and at the end of the season came reorganisation and a clear-out.

Bill Foulkes retired after a glorious career spanning 18 seasons of First Division football. Denis Law was put up for sale at £60,000, Don Givens was listed at £15,000 and nine other players were given free transfers, including Shay Brennan, who had joined the club with Wilf McGuinness 16 years previously. The two of them were great pals. Each was best man at the

Wilf McGuinness talks to his troops . . . a pep talk at the training ground at the Cliff for the playing staff during pre-season preparation for the new season in 1969. McGuinness's own career ended prematurely through injury. He was only 32 when asked to take charge of a squad which contained a high proportion of contemporaries, and some even older men

other's wedding and it must have been difficult when Wilf had to break the news to his friend.

It was an equally bitter pill for Law to swallow, though he admitted:

I was not surprised when United decided to put me on the transfer list. I had been unfit for a year, in and out of the team and not exactly hitting the headlines when I was playing. The 1969–70 season was undoubtedly the worst in my career. I made only ten League appearances and scored just two goals. That's not the Denis Law I like to think about and I am sure it fell far short of Old Trafford standards.

The club were looking ahead, promoting McGuinness from chief coach to team manager. John Aston, associated with United for 30 years as player and coach, was made chief scout to take over from the long-serving Joe Armstrong, who was retained in an advisory capacity in recognition of his 25 years' star-spotting. Bill Foulkes was put in charge of the coaching and training of the young players. Laurie Brown succeeded Ted Dalton as physiotherapist, Ken Merrett was made assistant secretary to Les Olive, and Ken Ramsden was appointed ticket office manager.

But there was still the feeling that the youthful

McGuinness was heading for a crisis out on the pitch as season 1970–71 began. Another slow start posed questions. Two defeats and a goalless home draw in the opening three games had the alarm bells ringing. Jimmy Rimmer took over from Alex Stepney in goal, but other than go into the transfer market, there was not a lot McGuinness could do. The stalwarts were still there, and though some of them might have been slowing up slightly, there was no-one better at the club to take their place.

The defence was built round Ian Ure with Nobby Stiles and Tony Dunne battling gamely. Paul Edwards, later to play at centre-half, had come in at right-back and John Fitzpatrick was a regular in midfield, wearing Pat Crerand's number four shirt. Bobby Charlton, Denis Law, George Best, Brian Kidd and David Sadler were all in the side with the likes of Willie Morgan, John Aston, Alan Gowling and Carlo Sartori challenging for regular places in the attack.

On paper United still had a top-class team, and indeed despite the disastrous start they did pick up for a spell. One of the problems was that while individually the older players still had a lot of football left in them, collectively as a team they were a bit long in the tooth. On their day they were still capable of producing winning performances, as they showed once again by reaching the semi-final of the League Cup. They sailed through their first round with a 3–1 win at Aldershot, and then with the help of successive home draws, knocked out Portsmouth 1–0, Chelsea 2–1 and Crystal Palace 4–2. But they struggled in the first leg of their semi-final against Aston Villa at Old Trafford. Perhaps demoralised by a 4–1 home defeat against Manchester City four days before, they couldn't master their Third Division opponents.

Andy Lochhead blazed Villa into the lead just before the interval. Brian Kidd immediately equalised with a spectacular goal from Carlo Sartori's cross, but even that failed to rouse United and Villa went home feeling proud of their 1–1 draw.

Hammered again in the League, losing 3–1 at home to Arsenal, United went to Villa Park in jittery mood. The flaws of the first half of the season were mirrored as they slid to a 2–1 defeat and exit from the competition. Kidd scored another fine goal after quarter of an hour, but Andy Lochhead beat Ian Ure in the air to equalise and Pat McMahon headed the winner.

United had done well to reach the semi-finals of course, but to lose yet again just one step short of Wembley, and this time to a Third Division team, was a bitter blow to the fans who thought they had a good Cup-fighting team, even if it was a side with problems sustaining an effort in the League. Certainly the defeat was the death warrant for the management career of Wilf McGuinness at Old Trafford, and after a 4–4 draw at Derby County three days later on Boxing Day, he was relieved of his first-team duties. Sir Matt announced in a statement:

The directors had a special meeting last night to discuss the performances of the team and decided to release Wilf McGuinness from his duties as team manager. As he did not wish to leave the club, and as the club felt he still had a part to play, he was offered his former position as trainer of the Central League side, which he has accepted. The board have asked me to take over team matters for the time being and until a new appointment is made in the close season.

Sir Matt, grim-faced and upset, explained:

I did not want to take charge of the team again, but my directors asked me to. At my age, I feel I have had enough of managerial worries at team level. It means becoming involved with players again. I shall be at their training sessions again. It's something I think I am capable of doing for a while, though I would have preferred we were not in this situation. It is unfortunate that things have not worked out. I feel very sorry for Wilf, who was appointed on my recommendation. He might have been a wee bit raw.

Later Sir Matt told his protégé where he thought he had gone wrong. 'You failed to get the players with you,' he said.

This was an apt summing up – whether the fault lay in McGuinness or the players is a moot point. Certainly at least two of the senior men had been to see Sir Matt behind the manager's back, perhaps in a genuine concern for the club's plight, though hardly a move calculated to help the manager's authority.

One player was reported anonymously in the *Sunday Times* as saying:

The problem for Wilf McGuinness was he had no personality. He did not understand that the team he was controlling needed handling in a special way. I am not saying we were special, but after all, we had won the European Cup and we were being told what to do by a man who had never been anywhere. People go on about us buying our way out of trouble, but I believe we would have been screwed even if Wilf had had a million quid to spend.

A more responsible note was struck by David Sadler, who questioned the attitude of his team-mates saying:

Not everyone, sadly, would play for Wilf. The side as a whole did not give a hundred per cent effort for him. As soon as Sir Matt returned to the scene it changed at once.

Ian Ure, left in the dark shirt, jumps high with team-mate John Aston during a troubled season. Ure was Wilf McGuinness's first signing as the new manager rushed to plug a leak early in season 1969-70. The Scot was bought from Arsenal after three heavy defeats in the four opening fixtures

This raises the role played by Sir Matt. McGuinness is the first to make it clear that his old boss did not directly interfere, but did his very presence cast a shadow over the new man?

The outspoken Brian Clough with his feel for the underdog expressed his sympathy for McGuinness. He wrote:

It is a long time since we stopped offering sacrificial lambs in this country, but McGuinness was virtually one. From the day he took over he never had a chance. He had to deal with established professionals who were used to Sir Matt, who is such a part of Old Trafford that automatically he is the first person you look for whenever you set foot inside the place. For all the wonderful service he had given Manchester United, Sir Matt could have had a crowning moment of brilliance if he had gone gracefully out. In his 20 or 30 years of vast experience, he had tasted every single aspect and emotion of the game, except of course, having to give it up.

The issue, of course, was never as simple as that. Sir Matt was striving for continuity when he promoted McGuinness from the ranks. His attitude, from grooming his own players to making staff appointments, had always been to emphasise the family. Liverpool more recently have had great success finding managers from inside the club, and no-one has questioned Kenny Dalglish's ability to exercise authority over players who were once team-mates. The truth is that the fading glory boys of 1968 were always going to pose problems . . . whoever the manager.

Sir Matt himself could still control them, as he showed when he picked up the reins again. Although bundled out of the FA Cup in a third-round replay on a frozen pitch at Middlesbrough, he took the team to Chelsea for a 2–1 win and a five-match unbeaten run with only one point dropped. When they beat Spurs 2–1 at Old Trafford it was the first home win for over three months. The team clawed their way back up the table to finish eighth again, while McGuinness went back to running the reserves. Not for long though. After two months he decided to quit the club he loves, saying:

I did not leave immediately because I had a lot of things to sort out. It was one of the most difficult decisions of my life. For 18 years I have been devoted to United. I grew up with them. It has been my life, but now I realise I must make a future for myself away from Old Trafford.

He agonised over what had gone wrong and concluded:

I thought I had time. I was on a contract which still had 18 months to run, but the simple truth is that the results went badly for me. We have been in three Cup semi-finals, something that cannot be claimed by any other club, and yet each time we fell short of reaching the final. If we had made it in any one of those competitions, things might have been so different.

The extent of the turmoil within McGuinness can be judged by the fact that soon afterwards, as he attempted to rebuild his career in Greece, his hair fell out almost overnight and what little grew again was white. After three years as manager of Aris Salonika, Wilf managed York City and in more recent years settled as a coach and physiotherapist with Bury. Even after the passing of many years his failure at Old Trafford still hurts. In 1987 he went back with Bury to play at Manchester United in a Littlewoods Cup defeat, an emotional journey which revived old memories. He said:

I have no ill-feelings. I'm still a fan despite what happened to me. The good things of growing up at United as a teenager with Duncan Edwards and the rest still outweigh the bad.

But the sack was still far worse than my broken leg. It left me heartbroken and angry. They didn't give me time to do the job.

My son Paul was at United for two years and when I go back for meetings of the old boys' association, I am friendly with Sir Matt and Jimmy Murphy, but there is something in my head that says they didn't give me the support I should have had when I needed it.

I didn't mind players going behind my back to Matt. What I did mind was that he accepted their side of the story rather than mine.

With hindsight it seems the board were more concerned with persuading Matt Busby to stay on as manager than in properly preparing a successor. Perhaps Wilf McGuinness would have made it if he had been brought on to the first-team scene a year earlier, so that he could have flexed his managerial muscles as a senior trainer instead of being thrust right into the spotlight from working backstage.

The experience certainly did nothing for the image of Manchester United who were right back to square one with few, if any, of their problems solved. It had been the worst playing record since the Second World War, for although the club had finished lower in the League on occasions there had invariably been a good FA Cup run to soften the blow.

It was a poor silver jubilee for Sir Matt after 25 years at Old Trafford, though this did not prevent the directors from marking the occasion with the presentation of a silver tea service. He also earned a vote of thanks from chairman Louis Edwards, who said:

I have nothing but admiration for Sir Matt, particularly for the way he helped the club at a vital time. It was an act of great courage to return to take control of the team again. He really did not want to be saddled with this onerous burden again after handing over 18 months previously, and the board could not have asked him to take a bigger step. It was a fine gesture because after his achievements in the game he had nothing to gain for himself, but quite a lot to lose. This did not concern

Bobby Charlton's 100th international cap. In honour of the occasion he was made captain. Bobby Moore (left) follows as the skipper walks out with Northern Ireland captain Terry Neill for the match at Wembley in April 1970. Charlton made a record 106 appearances for England and scored a record 49 goals

him. He did it for the club and in my view he is the great man of football. We were heading for the Second Division until he took over again. He rescued us brilliantly.

Nevertheless there were still enormous difficulties waiting to be resolved. The fans were demanding new blood. United hadn't bought anyone for two years, with Ian Ure their last signing. In fact they had bought only three players in six years – Ure, Willie Morgan and Alex Stepney. The team which played at Newcastle in October 1970, had cost just £5,000 in the transfer market, and that was a modest thankyou to Shelbourne for full-back Tony Dunne. The team which lined up for that 1–0 defeat was:

Rimmer, Edwards, Dunne, Fitzpatrick, James, Sadler, Burns, Best, Charlton, Kidd, Aston. Sub: Watson.

Mind you, Law was out injured and it was quite an expensive reserve side containing players like Crerand, Stepney, Morgan and Ure.

Sir Matt restored most of those players to get the team out of trouble, but they weren't getting any younger and even Bobby Charlton was wondering if he had played his last game for England following the 1970 World Cup in Mexico. The new players were finding it hard to win the crowd over. Alan Gowling, a local boy from Stockport School, was studying for an economics degree when United recruited him part-time. He played for the British Olympic team, and as a university man earned the nickname of Bamber after Gascoigne from the television quiz programme. Some of the fans had less complimentary names for him, his gangling build and loping stride reminding one writer of 'a startled ostrich on wildly telescopic legs'. More locally he was called the 'Galloping Chip'. He made it in the end but once admitted: 'Whenever I get a chance in the first team it is in place of one of the crowd's favourites. I come in when Denis Law, the player the fans made their king, or Brian Kidd, another hero on the terraces, is injured. It has been hard work getting myself accepted.'

Alan in fact made 64 League appearances for United, but it wasn't until he had moved on to Newcastle to strike a great partnership with Malcolm Macdonald that he hit his best form, and at the same time emerged an outstanding chairman of the Professional Footballers' Association. Alan's fight to establish himself at Old Trafford reflected the difficulties of this transitional period.

The behaviour of George Best did not help much either. Although he was top scorer with 18 League goals, he was becoming increasingly difficult to manage. Apart from periodic petulance on the field, usually involving referees, the first outward sign that all was not well came on Christmas Day. He simply failed to turn up for training, the only player to shirk an obviously unpopular chore. McGuinness was considerably annoyed because the player had no real excuse,

beyond perhaps a sore head after Christmas Eve celebrations. It was agreed that he should be sent home when he reported the next day for the match at Derby County. Then came second thoughts. They fined him £50 instead and played him. Of course he scored to help achieve a 4–4 draw. But should expediency have come before discipline?

United received a poor reward for their leniency. Less than a fortnight later the player was due to meet Busby at Piccadilly Station to catch a train to London for a personal appearance in front of the FA disciplinary committee to answer for three bookings. He failed to turn up, and Sir Matt had to travel down on his own and then use all his eloquence to placate the commission whose members were in no mood to indulge a young man who could not even arrive on time for his disciplinary hearing. The hearing was put back until later in the day so that Best, who had pleaded feeling unwell when his housekeeper had arrived at his home in Bramhall first thing in the morning, could catch a later train. When he eventually arrived at Euston Station he was mobbed by photographers, reporters, television cameras and girls. George Best was a show on his own. It took him 10 minutes to fight his way through in his smart blue suit, pink shirt and white tie.

He was given a suspended six-week suspension, but just five days later he missed another train. This time he failed to report for morning training before the team set off for London in readiness for a match at Chelsea the following day. Sir Matt expected him at the station, but he was still missing. John Aston was sent for as a replacement and Busby announced that Best need not bother coming at all. The player travelled to London anyway and went to ground hiding in the flat of his latest girl friend. Busby expected him to report to the ground on Monday, but he was still in London beseiged by the media. He was suspended by the club for a fortnight and it took the combined efforts of his agent, Ken Stanley, and business partner, Malcolm Mooney, to bring him back to face the music.

Busby saw him on Tuesday and Best, now in salmon pink trousers with black sweater, apologised and said he had had personal problems. Busby said: 'We have settled it amicably and we start from scratch again.' Best said: 'I want to stay with Manchester United until I finish my football. I am going to try as hard as I can to get back to my best.'

The suspension still stood and the Irishman went off home to Belfast to stay with his parents while the big debate raged as to what had gone wrong with the golden boy. Pat Crerand, his team-mate and a friend, said on television:

If he keeps going the way he is, he won't last much longer than another two or three years. He's not got the same respect for football. He's a little bit slack. He's got to be willing to buckle down to it, especially at the pace he is

It was a troubled season, not made any easier by the disciplinary troubles encountered by the fiery Fitzpatrick. A product of the winning Youth Cup side of 1964, he twice won a first-team place only to lose it on each occasion through suspension. He was caught in the classic vicious circle for a player of his type: his aggression was one of his main qualities, but it was also his weakness. His heaviest punishment came in 1969 when he was handed an eight-week suspension after collecting three cautions in quick succession. Nearly all his offences were for late tackles, as he tried to make up for his lightweight nine stone (57 kg) with endeavour.

Fitzpatrick's best seasons came under the command of Wilf McGuinness. It was sad that not long after he had succeeded in tempering his play slightly he suffered a severe knee injury. Although he tried to pick up his career again back in his native Scotland it was a struggle and he moved into the wine importing business in Aberdeen.

The season also brought an end to the career of Nobby Stiles at Old Trafford. He had also fought a losing battle with a knee injury and in the February the club let it be known that they were willing to listen to offers. Three months later he was transferred to Middlesbrough for a modest £20,000, still only 29, but with a total of 363 League and Cup appearances to his credit, not to mention a reputation as one of the club's most popular players.

Nobby, or Norbert to give him his Sunday best name, subsequently played for Preston under Bobby Charlton and he also became manager at Deepdale for a spell. He linked up with his brother-in-law, Johnny Giles, the former United inside-forward, at West Bromwich Albion, at one point managing them before settling as their youth coach.

Sir Matt always said that Nobby played every match as if it were a matter of life or death, which is no doubt why the supporters took to him so readily, and why fans abroad loved to hate him. In Madrid he was hit on the head by a bottle, in Italy he was spat on and hissed, in South America he was described as an assassin! His father was an undertaker and proud of his son, but he took great exception to the English reporter who once described Nobby as a player looking as if he was trying to create business for the family firm!

Nobby's first-team career at Old Trafford was brought to a close with the development of David Sadler in his role as cover alongside the centre-half, the position to become known as centre-back. Paul Edwards and Steve James competed for the centre-half berth, which dumped Ian Ure in the reserves for a long spell.

It all added up to a most difficult period of change which had proved too much for the youthful Wilf McGuinness, and though Sir Matt had galloped to the rescue to secure relief, the problems were still there as the board looked for someone to follow the legendary manager.

Left: John Fitzpatrick played in the F A Youth Cup winning team of 1964 and made his League debut the following year.
He was always a fiery player, too much so for some referees with the result that he served some substantial suspensions along with Denis Law, a fellow Aberdonian.
A badly broken leg in 1971 ended his playing career at the age of 26.
Since then he has become a wine importer back in Aberdeen

living. Maybe George gets his head turned a little bit. He is not as fit as as he should or could be. He's got this terrific talent and it's going to waste, and that's the shame about it.

It emerged later that it wasn't just his playboy streak that turned him into the runaway soccer star. He had also grown somewhat disillusioned with the decline of the team, and he felt, probably rightly too, that too much was being expected of him. He once remarked: 'Everyone makes mistakes – mine just seem to get more publicity than other people's.'

That was certainly true, just as it was true that he had presented Wilf McGuinness with a stack of problems which even the experienced Busby found difficult enough. For a young man in his first big job it must have seemed like a nightmare. What should he have done for instance when he caught a girl in the player's room a few hours before a semi-final? Drop his best player in the interests of discipline, or let him get away with it and let the rest of the team rumble about one rule for George Best and another for the others?

A more summery Manchester United line up for a charity cricket match.
Back row: George Best, Shay Brennan, Alan Gowling, Jack Crompton, Alex Stepney, Bobby Charlton.
Front: Wilf McGuinness, David Sadler, Nobby Stiles, David Herd, Pat Crerand

Frank O'Farrell takes over

Jock Stein and Dave Sexton were among the names discussed by the directors. Brian Clough was talked about by the fans as a suitable successor, but the controversial Nottingham Forest boss did not have even a starting price inside Old Trafford following his outspoken suggestion that Busby had made Wilf McGuinness into a sacrificial lamb.

The club were looking for an experienced manager this time after gambling unsuccessfully with their own youngster, and they finally settled on Frank O'Farrell, who had a good, solid record of achievement. He was to bring with him from Leicester City his partner at Filbert Street, Malcolm Musgrove, a coach who like his boss had grown up as a player in the think-tank era of West Ham with the likes of Malcolm Allison, Dave Sexton, Noel Cantwell, John Bond and Ken Brown.

The parallels with Sir Matt were strong, even down to strong convictions as Roman Catholics. They had both started from modest family backgrounds. Frank's first ambition was to follow in his father's footsteps and drive the express trains from Cork to Dublin. He did indeed start his working life shovelling coal on the Irish Railways. He also impressed playing for his local team Cork Hibernian which brought him into English football at West Ham. He became a stylish wing-half and captain before joining Preston where he again became captain to reveal his powers of leadership. He was capped nine times for the Republic of Ireland, playing in the 1958 World Cup.

O'Farrell started on the ground floor of management as player-coach with Weymouth and made club history by taking the Southern League team to the fourth round of the FA Cup. When injury ended his career he stayed on as manager and steered the club to their first Championship. This brought him an invitation to manage Torquay and in his first season he brought them up from the Fourth Division to the Third. He followed Matt Gillies as manager of Leicester in December 1968, and failed to save them from dropping into the Second

Division, but he did enjoy a run to Wembley in the FA Cup, where they lost to Manchester City. After two seasons he brought Leicester back to the First Division as Champions and it was his steady progress in management through all levels which attracted United. He had used the transfer market shrewdly and economically, and when handling the public relations of a big club, he had proved forthright in his utterances without being sensational or irresponsible.

O'Farrell looked an eminently sound choice and he accepted the invitation to come to Old Trafford proffered in the chairman's car parked on a lonely side road at Mackworth just outside Derby, and he said about his contract: 'It's long enough to achieve what I hope to achieve.'

Stung by criticism that his presence as general manager had not given McGuinness a fair chance, Sir Matt voluntarily gave up his paid post and joined the board as a director. He said:

> The idea seemed to build up that if I stayed as general manager I would want to interfere. It was a wrong impression, but it was splashed about and I admit the talk influenced me. Frank O'Farrell did not make an issue of it, in fact he said he hoped his coming was not the reason and he didn't mind whether I stayed on as general manager or director.

So O'Farrell had a clear field and he voiced firm ideas for the future, in keeping with the Busby traditions:

> I have no preconceived ideas. I don't prejudge any situation or individual. I just want to see for myself and make up my own mind. The entertaining image must be maintained, but at the same time if modications in style are necessary to make the team a more efficient unit, then they must be made. In principle a team needs a sound defence. That is the basis, but it doesn't mean that I have to be defensive minded.

O'Farrell's remarks about the defence suggested he had already studied the First Division table, which revealed that while his new team had finished third highest scorers, the goals-against was their worst for eight years.

Malcolm Musgrove, who followed Jimmy Hill as chairman of the Professional Footballers' Association, believed United had made the right appointment. He said:

> 'Frank O'Farrell is one of the few people who could have come to Old Trafford. The job is so big it's hardly true. Yet Frank will measure up. He is the ideal choice. His greatest quality is his honesty, yet you don't pull the wool over his eyes. I think we make a good partnership and I hope it will show for Manchester United.'

That partnership was going to be sorely tried and tested in the next 18 months, both on and off the pitch, but there were no such fears as the new management team got off to a brilliant start. Although they drew 2–2 at Derby on the opening day, they won the next three and only lost one of their first 14 games. By early October they were at the top of the First Division, and as

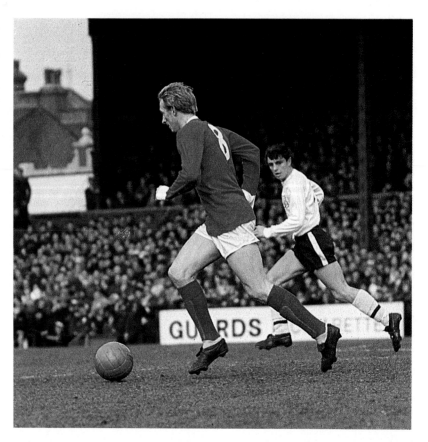

Christmas approached they were into a five-point lead, with only one other defeat.

With the help of a hat-trick at Southampton, Best was bowling along with 14 League goals in 19 games. Law had also rocketed into scoring form again after his injury problems, with a dozen goals in the first half of the season. The successful gambit seemed to have been the conversion of Gowling and Morgan to midfield. The team had also taken in their stride the closure of Old Trafford for a fortnight at the start of the season because of a knife thrown on to the pitch the previous winter. This had meant playing the home game against Arsenal at Liverpool and meeting West Bromwich at Stoke. Both games had been won 3–1 and it seemed the Reds could do nothing wrong as far as their results were concerned.

But not everyone was convinced that United had a team capable of staying at the top. Malcolm Allison and Brian Clough both said the Reds were in a false position, though it is doubtful if either realised how dramatically they were going to be proved right.

The first signs of cracking came in the League Cup in November with a fourth-round defeat against Stoke in a second replay. Then, after three successive draws in December, came seven successive defeats. United skidded down the table just about as fast as they had gone up it. The biggest crash came towards the end of that dreadful run when they lost 5–1 at Leeds to prompt scathing criticism from centre-half Jack Charlton. Perhaps tinged with envy after years somewhat in the shadow of brother Bobby, he let rip in a newspaper article to say:

Denis Law was the king as far as United fans were concerned. They liked the streak of villainy which ran through his play as well as his excellence as a goal scorer. Not a big man by any means, but as quick as lightning in front of goal, he spent 11 seasons at Old Trafford, scoring a remarkable 236 goals in 393 appearances in League, domestic cup and European competition. Born in Aberdeen, he came into English football with Huddersfield Town, moved to Manchester City and then went abroad to play for Torino in Italy. Matt Busby rescued him from a miserable time in Italian football by paying a then record £115,000. He rejoined Manchester City and scored his final League goal with a back-flick which sent United into the Second Division and left Law looking as if he had stabbed his best friend in the back!

Martin Buchan

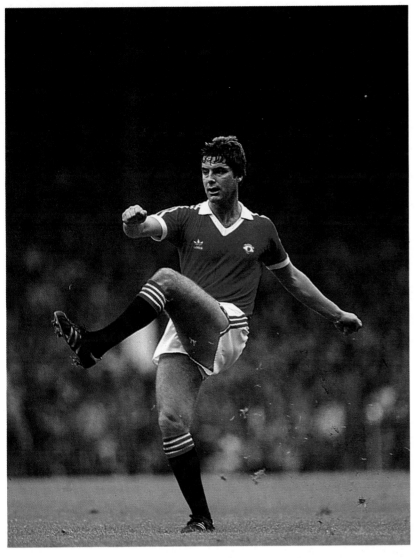

Martin Buchan was the most valuable legacy of Frank O'Farrell's management. The United manager signed the Scot from Aberdeen for £125,000 in March 1972, and he played at Old Trafford for 12 seasons. He was a remarkable defender, a man who knew his own mind and an obvious captain. In 1977 he captained United to victory in the FA Cup against Liverpool to become the first player to skipper both English and Scottish Cup-winning teams. He subsequently played for Oldham and was briefly a manager at Burnley before returning to his native Aberdeen

Buchan at 23 was a super signing, who went on to play 455 League and Cup games for United, becoming their captain and a remarkable character. Already a Scottish international, he was the exception from Scotland who proved the rule, adjusting immediately to the pace of English football. His debut was marked by a 2–0 defeat at Spurs, but his influence on those around him was very evident and he quickly slowed the rate of descent down the League table. United lost only four of their last 12 games with Buchan in the side. Tommy Docherty, then the manager of Scotland, said: 'He will be better than Bobby Moore. He has more pace and does not take Moore's chances. Buchan is always safe.'

The player arrived with the reputation of being something of a loner. Certainly he was different. His short back and sides contrasted strangely with the flowing locks of Best and Morgan. He could speak Spanish and French and said he was interested in learning German. He played the guitar and declined to join the usual football card schools. It's also true to say that he enjoyed being different from the usual run of professional footballer, which didn't always endear him to his team-mates. He was, though, so dedicated and good at his job, that he was always respected. He didn't suffer fools gladly, and you had to stay alert in conversation with him, as the reporters and a succession of managers were to discover. The football writer who asked him for a quick word was met with the reply: 'How about velocity?'

In the age-old game among players of goading managers he was an artist. He was still too new to try anything on with O'Farrell, but later both Tommy Docherty and Ron Atkinson suffered.

Docherty was left spitting blood on a pre-season tour in Denmark. The Doc had given permission for everyone to wear casual gear for a short flight to a match, and with the weather hot, everyone was in T-shirts and even shorts. Buchan turned up in white collar and tie, smartly pressed slacks and club blazer. He was immaculate and looked at least the chairman of the club, while the Doc, the manager was left looking like a holiday-maker.

The skipper didn't exactly endear himself to Ron Atkinson when he was manager on another foreign tour and pleasantly asked Martin if he had ever played on this particular ground. 'Yes,' said Martin. 'I captained Scotland here once while you were playing in the Fourth Division.' You had to keep awake when you had dealings with Martin Buchan!

He was the first and only player to refuse to hand over his passport to the club on the grounds that he wasn't a schoolboy and perfectly capable of looking after his own property.

When he moved from United to Oldham, joker Andy Goram put Wintergreen oil in his underpants while he was out training. He went red in the face when he got dressed but didn't

Some of the players Manchester United have got just don't realise how lucky they are. They have at Old Trafford something we don't have at Elland Road. It irritates me. We are perhaps the second best crowd pullers away from home, but come what may, Manchester United are still first. That is what I mean about Manchester United players being lucky. They have this much going for them from the moment they come into the team.

Put it down to the legend or the habit of years. Why this massive public appeal isn't enough on its own to light a fire under every Manchester United player I don't know. But it doesn't happen. Not as often as I think it ought. It's part of their trouble.

The inspiration of a new manager and the fresh coaching techniques of Malcolm Musgrove had fired some of the old skill and enthusiasm in the first half of the season, but it all vanished in the seven-match burn-out. O'Farrell knew it was time to turn to the transfer market, and he made two excellent signings in the space of a fortnight. First he moved to Aberdeen with £125,000 for Martin Buchan and then paid £200,000 for Ian Storey-Moore from Nottingham Forest.

say a word. The next day, though, the Oldham goalkeeper found his shoes nailed to the floor.

But Oldham will also remember his principles. For when he moved from United to Boundary Park he was given a contract awarding him a £3,000 bonus after two years, but after suffering a succession of injuries he tore the contract up; he felt he had not played enough games to justify taking the money.

That was Martin Buchan, a man of honour who served United well for 12 seasons. Most United fans will best remember him for the unusual sight in one match at Old Trafford of seeing him box the ears of one of his own players. The embarrassed recipient of the captain's displeasure was Gordon Hill, a winger who was apt to neglect his defensive duties, and on this occasion he got a smart cuff on the head to remind him that he was expected to come back and help his colleagues at the back.

Though a great captain, Martin Buchan was never cut out to be a manager. He once confessed when he was still playing that he doubted whether he would make it in management. 'I don't think I could put up with trying to handle awkward beggars like me,' he said. And so it proved after a brief and inevitable clash on principle at Burnley. Soon after, he went back home to Aberdeen where he enrolled for a degree at the university. That didn't last long either because he couldn't stand what he considered to be the juvenile antics of all the students!

Signing Buchan in Februrary 1972 was Frank O'Farrell's best day's work and a handsome legacy long after he had departed. O'Farrell's second signing, a week later, was also a good buy, but Ian Moore eventually ran into bad luck with injuries.

United thought at one point after agreeing terms with Forest that they had lost the player to Derby County. O'Farrell broke off discussing terms with the player so that Moore could fulfil a promise and speak to Brian Clough the Derby manager. Clough swept Moore away and actually got the player's signature on a transfer form. On the strength of that he paraded him round the Baseball Ground as Derby's new signing. Happily for Old Trafford the document didn't carry Forest's signature, so that it was meaningless, and United were able to complete the transfer for the player to make his debut against Huddersfield and score in a 2–0 win. Moore played the last 11 games and scored five goals, a splendid start, and with Buchan steadying the ship at the back United recovered to finish eighth in the League again.

Moore was 27 and in 250 League games for Forest he had scored 120 goals, a good return for a winger and a welcome boost for United's scoring potential. For although Best finished as top scorer with 18 League goals he had got most of them in the first half of the season, and Law was down to 13 and Kidd 10.

Best's disappearing act

The question marks against Best were mounting. During the summer the player went missing again, this time failing to report for duty with Northern Ireland, and the episode ended with him threatening to retire from football. He had been a source of worry for the new manager right from the start of the season. In only the second League game he was sent off against Chelsea at Stamford Bridge by Norman Burtenshaw for abusive language. An FA disciplinary commission cleared him after accepting his plea that his swearing had been directed at team-mate Willie Morgan and not at the referee.

Morgan backed up the player, who was well represented by Cliff Lloyd, the secretary of the Professional Footballers' Association who outshone Perry Mason on the day. United were very worried because if Best had been found guilty a six-week suspended ban would have come in to operation as well as any other further punishment. A lot of people thought Best lucky to escape, and O'Farrell privately indicated which version he believed.

At least Best behaved for a while and in fact enjoyed fabulous form again, but in January he failed to turn up for training, and just when the team needed him. O'Farrell immediately dropped him, fined him two weeks' pay, ordered him to train in the afternoons as well as the mornings and cancelled his days off for five weeks to make up for the week's training he had skipped.

Then at the end of the season, after signing off with a goal in a 3–0 win against Stoke, the team which had knocked United out of the FA Cup in the sixth round, Best disappeared on the eve of the British Championships. The day after he should have joined the Northern Ireland squad he turned up at a luxury hotel in Marbella on the Spanish coast. Against a background of jet-set living and champagne by the side of a sun-soaked swimming pool, he announced that he had had his fill of football, Manchester United and the Irish international team. The day after announcing his retirement he celebrated his 26th birthday. Frank O'Farrell said:

I know he has been drinking a lot and has been going out with a lot of girl friends and keeping late hours. These things and pressures from outside the game have wrecked him.

He is, like all other geniuses, difficult to understand. I don't think he can cope with his own problems. And there is nobody he can really lean on for help. He is like a boy lost. He needs someone to help him. We at Old Trafford have done everything possible to help him. He acknowledges this, but the plain fact is he finds it extremely difficult to communicate his problems to other people and I feel we have not really reached him.

Best was expected to link up with his club in Tel Aviv for the final game of their summer tour, but he didn't make that either and was posted absent without leave. A few days later he crept back into Manchester and at a secret meeting with O'Farrell said it was all a big mistake and that he wanted to play again after all.

Best certainly hadn't made Frank O'Farrell's first season in charge at Old Trafford any easier. His behaviour had been a big distraction, as if there weren't enough problems already. Yet how could any manager turn his back on a player still only 26 who was still capable of turning on incomparable football. For all his troubles and truancy he had missed only two League games, and he was still the top scorer. He simply had to be forgiven and welcomed back into the fold.

On the brighter side another boy from Belfast made a significant entrance on to the Old Trafford stage. Sammy McIlroy, sent over from Ireland by Bob Bishop, the scout who had nurtured Best as a boy, was given his League debut at the age of 17 against Manchester City at Maine Road. He scored an exciting goal in a 3–3 draw to win a bottle of champagne from Best, and in fact scored in each of his first four League games. He made such an impact that he played for Northern Ireland within three months of his League debut, still only 17. The team towards the end of Frank's first season read:

Stepney, O'Neill, Dunne, Buchan, James, Sadler, Best, Kidd or McIlroy, Charlton, Law, Moore.

Pat Crerand hadn't played, though still retained as a player and he had been put in charge of the youth team while Bill Foulkes looked after the reserves.

The slide in the second half of the season after doing so well up to Christmas had been disappointing, but the arrival of two new players and the debut of the teenage McIlroy had offered hope for the next season. There was a lot still to accomplish, as Frank O'Farrell readily admitted, but few could have anticipated the disasters lying in wait as season 1972–73 got under way.

The team opened with a terrible string of results. They lost the first three games, drew the next four and then lost two more. Those first nine games saw them score only three goals. The alarm bells were ringing for Frank and he turned urgently to the transfer market.

There was never any doubt about the ability of George Best to score as spectacularly off the field as he did on it. Actress Susan George certainly seems pleased with life with George when she was 19 and on holiday in Palma Nova

George Best in action for United against Colin Harvey of Everton

He bought Wyn Davies from Manchester City for £60,000, and the Welshman scored on his debut against Derby at Old Trafford to help notch the first win of the season. But by now the Reds had gone to the bottom like a lead weight. A week later Frank swooped again to land Ted MacDougall from Third Division Bournemouth for £200,000. MacDougall scored on his second appearance for a 1–0 win against Birmingham, but pressure was building up. Losing 4–1 at home to Spurs didn't help; nor did a morale-sapping derby defeat at Maine Road.

The departures of O'Farrell and Best

Ironically United won their next two games, but the board were already making plans for a new manager. The *Manchester Evening News* carried a story with the headline 'Be Fair to Frank', urging the club to give the manager time, but that only succeeded in getting the joint author of this history, David Meek, banned from travelling on the team coach.

Ted MacDougall signing for Frank O'Farrell. Although he had been playing in the Third Division, MacDougall had always scored a lot of goals and indeed he got five in his first 12 games for United. The transfer turned sour. Later he complained that senior players had resented his arrival and he had an unhappy time under Tommy Docherty after O'Farrell's departure

United were sinking fast and had won only five League games when they crashed 5–0 at Crystal Palace on 16 December in 1972. Denis Law is in the thick of the action with Wyn Davies on the floor as the Reds struggle vainly for a goal. This was the game which hammered the final nail into the managerial coffin of Frank O'Farrell. The heavy defeat was the last straw as far as Sir Matt Busby and his directors were concerned. One of the spectators at Selhurst Park was Tommy Docherty, the manager of Scotland, and United moved quickly to ask him if he was interested in taking over at Old Trafford. The Doc needed asking only once!

The final blow for O'Farrell came on 16 December at Crystal Palace where his team crashed 5–0. Significantly Tommy Docherty, then manager of Scotland, was watching the match.

After the game Sir Matt Busby seized the opportunity to ask him if he was interested in coming to Old Trafford. The Doc indicated that he was; he could do little else since it had been his ambition to manage Manchester United for 25 years!

First had to come the night of the long knives, an evening of wining, dining and dancing to celebrate the finale of Bobby Charlton's testimonial. Frank O'Farrell, Malcolm Musgrove and John Aston were all at the banquet and ball which went on into the early hours. There could have been little sleep for the directors before they met at the offices of chairman Louis Edwards and the decision was taken to sack the management team. The statement issued on Tuesday, 19 December 1972, read:

In view of the poor position in the League, it was unanimously decided that Mr O'Farrell, Malcolm Musgrove and John Aston be relieved of their duties forthwith.

Side by side with the sacking of the manager almost inevitably ran another chapter in the saga of George Best. Once again the Irishman was in crisis and gave notice that he was quitting in a letter to the board. He wrote:

. . . therefore I have decided not to play football again, and this time no-one will change my mind. I would like to wish the club the best of luck for the remainder of the season and for the future. Because even though I personally have tarnished the club's name in recent times, to me and thousands of others, Manchester United still means something special.

It was clearly the end of the road, at least as far as Manchester United were concerned. O'Farrell had been patient. He had in fact improved Best's contract to make him, in keeping with his drawing power, the best paid player at the club. He had even contemplated making him captain to make him feel he was receiving the respect his ability deserved. On one occasion he flew to Belfast to talk to his parents. The player was missing at the time and had left word that he had gone home to see his mother and father. When Frank got there he discovered that Mr and Mrs Best had not seen the runaway star.

Best had of course upset quite a few players, Bobby Charlton in particular, who considered it wrong for a player to be so indulged. Bobby, now a director of the club, tells funny stories these days about the difficulties of life with George Best, but at one point he threatened to quit if the player was reinstated after disappearing. It took Frank's powers of persuasion to get his captain to see that it was wrong to make the manager choose between two players.

The club were at some pains at the end to make it clear that they had in fact 'sacked' George Best as well as the manager before the player's letter of resignation had reached them. The statement announcing the sacking of Frank O'Farrell also said:

Furthermore, George Best will remain on the transfer list and will not be selected again for Manchester United as it is felt it is in the best interest of the club and the player that he leaves Old Trafford.

The above statement was prepared after the meeting of directors this morning. In the afternoon a letter addressed to the board was received from George Best stating that he had decided he was unable to continue and would

It's crisis time again for Manchester United as chairman Louis Edwards runs the gauntlet of waiting television cameras on his way to a meeting at the Cliff training ground. It was the prelude to the sack for Frank O'Farrell, who had lasted 18 months as manager in succession to Wilf McGuinness. By Christmas 1971, in his first season, he had the Reds runaway leaders five points in the lead at the top of the First Division. But the bubble burst and they slipped back to finish in eighth place. The slide continued the next season and he was sacked at Christmas

not play football again. This letter was opened at the board meeting at 4.15pm when members of the staff were informed of these decisions.

So it turned out the board had beaten the player to the punch by a few hours, though it is difficult to see how it mattered, except perhaps to Frank O'Farrell, who might well have wished for that kind of backing from the directors a little earlier in the whole protracted drama with the player. Frank left the club with great bitterness, a feeling which persisted for many years, and perhaps will for the rest of his life. His departure certainly ended his career in football as a top manager, though he did return in an advisory capacity with Torquay for a while.

He had had enormous problems to sort out at Old Trafford, and such was the status of the senior players, the answers could not be found overnight. Like Wilf McGuinness before him he felt he had not been given enough time. Soon after his arrival he told friends that the players he had inherited could never be his team. They belonged to Sir Matt, but they couldn't simply be cleared out all in one go. Frank planned to build round Martin Buchan, Ian Storey-Moore and Ted MacDougall. 'They are my players, most of the others belong to Sir Matt, and until they have all gone I shan't have my team,' he said.

He ran out of time, and the old and the new didn't gel either. Storey-Moore, signed by O'Farrell soon after the big slide had started, summed it all up when he said:

It was a terrible time to be with United. It was a transitional period. The older players resented the newer ones. There were a lot of cliques and it wasn't a friendly atmosphere, which was probably reflected in our performances out on the field.

Manchester United are a great club of course and I was happy to join them – I was just disappointed that I was not there for the good times. I hit the club at the wrong period. I damaged my ankle soon after Frank O'Farrell left and hardly played again. I was only 27 or 28.

Storey-Moore made only 39 League appearances for United before his flying wing displays were halted by injury, but he will be remembered for his 11 goals, and his bizarre signing.

The senior players, from their point of view, saw Frank O'Farrell as someone distant and remote. Denis Law, for instance, once quipped: 'Frank O'Farrell – who's he?' He later summed up: 'Mr O'Farrell came as a stranger and went as a stranger.'

Whether the reason for this gulf and lack of communication was the fault of the manager or the senior players, it certainly didn't produce a recipe for success on the field.

From where Frank stood, other teams had left United behind in terms of effort and team-work. He considered that players who had enjoyed

success under the old regime resented his new methods. He likened Old Trafford to Sleepy Valley. The old stars were going out. Even that most dedicated and conscientious of players, Bobby Charlton, was on the brink of retirement. And all the time there had been the divisive problem of the wandering Best. Willie Morgan didn't pull any punches when he said:

George thought he was the James Bond of soccer. He had everything he wanted and he pleased himself. He had money, girls and tremendous publicity. He lived from day to day. Until right at the end, he got away with it when he missed training or ran away. So he didn't care. People made excuses for him; he didn't even have to bother to make them himself.

People talked about pressures and depressions. It was rubbish. He just hadn't any responsibilities, nothing to worry about at all. All kinds of people covered up for him, even the press, and he was lucky to get away with it for so long.

More sympathetically, Bill Foulkes said:
Looking back I feel guilty. George was a youngster when he came into a great side, and

Ian Storey-Moore was a brilliant signing for United, a fast flying winger with an eye for scoring goals. He got five in 11 appearances after signing for Frank O'Farrell in March 1972, from Nottingham Forest. Unfortunately for both player and manager he seriously injured his ankle midway through the following season and it was virtually the end of his career. He also complained later about the dissension and cliques at Old Trafford which made things so difficult for O'Farrell.

I don't think we senior players took enough interest in him. Older players influenced me a great deal when I was young, but we failed to influence George Best. We all went our separate ways and I wish now we had involved him more away from the ground.

The Irishman's letter of resignation was not quite the end of his association with Manchester United. He continued to flirt with the game, but with Slack Alice, the night club and disco he opened, claiming most of his attention it was not long before the aptly named Alice finally got her man.

Certainly there was need for a dynamic personality and bold leadership when the United directors looked round for Frank O'Farrell's successor, and of course in Tommy Docherty they found just the man.

But though things were bad on the field, there was still a lot going for the club. The ground itself, for instance, was looking better than ever. There was an elegant new stand at the scoreboard end complete with more private boxes, which made a superb sweep of cantilever round from Trafford Park. The development of the ground had been a particular ambition of chairman Louis Edwards, who had put great energy and business acumen into creating revenue off the field.

The flagship for raising finance was the Development Association, a pools operation launched in 1961 by Bill Burke, who had set up a similar project at Edgbaston for Warwickshire County Cricket Club. The pool, starting from nothing, had quickly become the biggest of its kind in the country, with some 200,000 members served by an army of agents. The prize money had steadily risen and in its first ten years it had provided more than £500,000 for the development of the ground. The Association had contributed substantially to the cantilever stand that was built for the World Cup in 1966 and they had paid for the new scoreboard cantilever.

Manchester United have since gone into many other money-making activities, with sponsorship now a major source of revenue, but the pool is bigger than ever and was the forerunner for the creation of a business empire.

Far right: Manchester United now run their own souvenir shop. Initially it was leased to Sir Matt Busby on his retirement as a gesture of appreciation for his sterling work at Old Trafford. Recently they bought out the remainder of the lease and have plans to expand the Red Devils business arm of their commercial empire

Below: A view of one of the stands at the famous Old Trafford football ground

The club were very healthy from the financial point of view, regularly making a gross profit of six figures, and the fans were coming by bus, boat and train from places far removed from Manchester. A chef regularly flew in from Jersey, his loyalty inspired on the day Sir Matt had visited his orphanage in Didsbury. 'I was only eight, but I remember vividly Sir Matt giving all us kids five bob each. I thought the best way I could show my appreciation would be to watch his team play. So I went to the next game and have been a supporter ever since,' he explained.

The manager of Tottenham Hotspur's souvenir shop at White Hart Lane was revealed one day as the vice-chairman of United's supporters club branch in London. The Fan Club reported hundreds of new members, many of them from overseas. The supporters in Malta had their own club headquarters on the island. The enthusiasm for the club was boundless, as was shown on the night Glasgow Celtic came to Old Trafford to play a testimonial in honour of Bobby Charlton.

Left: He broke all records and won everything possible, but remained completely unspoiled . . . so wrote Sir Matt Busby in a tribute to the long-serving Bobby Charlton

Right: Bobby Charlton made his debut for Manchester United in October 1956, scoring twice in a 4–2 win against Charlton Athletic at Old Trafford. He retired at the end of the season 1972–73 after a club record 604 League appearances. This is his farewell appearance at Old Trafford in the last but one match of the season with a guard of honour from the players of Manchester United and Sheffield United as he goes out for a presentation

Left: United scored a first when they set up a museum at Old Trafford in 1987 to house and display all their memorabilia. They have developed a vast range of trophies, medals, shirts, boots and many treasured items which have been given or loaned by former players

Tribute to Charlton

The date was 18 September 1972. The team had yet to win a League game that season, but the fans put that behind them to pay tribute to one of their favourites who had graced the game for 20 years. There were 60,538 people packed into Old Trafford probably feeling a little like Sir Matt Busby when he wrote in the testimonial programme:

When Bobby first came to Old Trafford he was a very shy lad, but it never showed on the field of play. I remember the goals he scored when he was only 18. I have vividly implanted in my mind the sight of him volleying David Pegg's centre home in the FA Cup semi-final against Birmingham at Hillsborough. It was a tremendously hit shot and he repeated it in his first international, playing for England against Scotland at Hampden Park when he half-volleyed the ball into the back of the net.

I cannot begin to describe all the other wonderful goals he has scored or list his proud international career, except to say what a marvellous contribution he made in the World Cup of 1966 with his valuable goals.

Could I also ever forget his header in the final of the European Cup, a goal that set us on the path towards the victory that had been our aim for so long.

He has broken all records and won everything possible that there is to win. Yet he has remained completely unspoiled, still prepared to do more than his fair share for the cause of Manchester United. The shy boy has blossomed now into a man with a great sense of assurance, confidence and responsibility.

It was a night of nostalgia, which to a certain extent had been the problem for Frank O'Farrell. Manchester United had become a club living on its past. The giant was slumbering again . . . but not for long as Manchester braced itself for the arrival of Tommy Docherty, larger than life and the terror of the transfer market.

The Doc reckoned he had the right prescription for an ailing club.

The 1970s: Docherty and Sexton

In the 48 hours between Frank O'Farrell's dismissal and the announcement of the new appointment, Pat Crerand and Bill Foulkes, now both on the coaching staff, took charge of training, but on the Friday of the most traumatic week the club had experienced for years, the Doc arrived and made it clear that he was the boss:

This is the greatest club in the world, and I am so proud to be part of it. I've always wanted to get to the top in football management and being at the best club must be just that. Now I want to get United back on its feet, we are in a bad position, but it isn't impossible, we've got to get down to winning some games, we seem to have forgotten how to do that. But if we win, we'll get it right again, it's as simple as that.

Docherty's 'wind of change' was a hurricane. It swept through Old Trafford, whipping up clouds of dust which for years had hidden the harsh truth from not only those in charge, but from the thousands who followed the team. Docherty could look at the situation from the position of the outsider, he had no axe to grind, neither had he any reason to feel that his actions would offend. It was no time to be sentimental, his target was success, and if it meant that his decisions might upset the normal pattern, he would make them nevertheless.

In his book 'Call the Doc' (Hamlyn 1981) he wrote about his impressions when he first took over the manager's job:

It seemed to me that Denis Law was at a stage of his career when he wasn't worried about how he played. All he was concerned with was how long he could go on playing. He had stopped trying. I felt there were others who had been great but could no longer contribute their best and amongst these I'd include Tony Dunne, David Sadler and to a certain extent Brian Kidd.

Those players, together with goalkeeper Alex Stepney, his deputy Jimmy Rimmer, Bobby Charlton and John Fitzpatrick were the only remaining members of the 1968 squad still on the playing staff. George Best had announced his

retirement, Bill Foulkes and Pat Crerand were on the coaching staff and the rest had either retired or moved to other clubs.

It was Docherty's job to build another great side, but to do so he felt that he had also to make sure that players were not being given a red shirt to wear on a Saturday afternoon simply on past performances. 'Reputations are amazing things in football,' he said. 'I have come across players who have good and bad reputations, and found them to be the exact opposite when I have had them under me. Reputations should really count for nothing. It's performances that matter, and if a player can no longer perform then it is time for him to go.'

Docherty's brusque manner suited some, and upset others, but it was obvious from the start that the Doc had a purpose in life and woe betide anyone who stood in his way. The first game under Docherty was on Saturday 23 December 1972, at a time of year when attendances at football matches drop to their lowest. That Saturday 46,382 turned up to see United play Leeds, an increase of 13,000 on the 'bleak Saturday' of the previous two seasons and only 7,000 fewer than had watched United beat Liverpool 2–0 early in November. It was perhaps too much to expect that Docherty's arrival would transform a struggling side into one which would beat Don Revie's powerful team, but there was at least hope. Docherty was given a rapturous welcome by the supporters before the game, and had already indicated that he was a 'man of the people' by his willingness to stop and chat with fans as he made his way to the stadium. They had seen his face on television, heard his words on radio, and he had filled the sports pages of every newspaper since his appointment.

That first game had the build-up of a major theatrical event and it attracted the curious and the hopeful. Could the Doc find a cure for United's ailments? They wondered and they wished.

The noise inside Old Trafford was deafening when Ted MacDougall fired United in front. It was his fifth goal since his arrival and one which released a wave of relief. United were back! But there was disappointment when Allan Clarke scored an equaliser in the dying minutes and it ended 1–1. United were in 21st place and only Leicester City were below them. Could it be that the clubs which had fought for glory in the FA Cup final of 1963 would now share another moment of football history – relegation? Not if Tommy Docherty had anything to do with it.

'At least I know what's wanted of me,' he joked in typical Docherty style, 'we can only go up. If we get any lower we'll fall off the pools coupons!'

Here was another reason the supporters felt that Docherty was on their side – he was on the same wavelength as the fans, able to stand up to the best of them in an argument and hit back with the sharpest wisecracks.

The re-building had to start quickly, and having been in charge of the Scottish side it was obvious where the new manager would turn. George Graham, from Arsenal's recent double-winning side, was bought for £120,000, a considerable increase on the £6,000 Docherty had paid for him when he signed him from Aston Villa in 1964 while manager of Chelsea. The story had hardly made the sports pages when another Scot was bought. Alex Forsyth, a sturdy full-back from Partick Thistle, signed for £100,000. Two days later Docherty added to his backroom staff by bringing Tommy Cavanagh from Hull City, where he left Terry Neill's coaching team.

Cavanagh's explosive approach was designed to bring discipline into the squad, and the Liverpudlian was keen to make a success of his new post. His and Docherty's paths had crossed briefly at Preston North End when Cavanagh had been signed as a young player while Docherty was already playing for the first team. While Tommy Docherty continued in the First Division, his friend went on to play for Stockport County, Huddersfield Town, Doncaster Rovers, Bristol City and Carlisle United before going into coaching. They had never played in the same League side but knew each other's methods.

Cavanagh had been successful with Nottingham Forest before his move to Boothferry Park, and his appointment at Old Trafford was an indication of his ability. He had great respect for Docherty:

Working with Tommy Docherty was a great thrill. He knew exactly what he wanted and how he would achieve it. He was a man who knew the way to get the best out of his players, yet he would stand for no nonsense. Tommy always had great enthusiasm for the game and this rubbed off on everyone who came into contact with him, he had an effect right through the club from the youngest little supporter right up to the chairman Louis Edwards.

Docherty's threat that he would not allow players to 'perform on their reputations' became

The building of Docherty's 'tartan army' began when Alex Forsyth joined the club from Partick Thistle, a second signing and a second Scot bought by the new manager. The solidly built defender played 99 League games for United, won a second Division championship medal in 1975 and was in the cup final side of 1976. He moved to Glasgow Rangers after losing his place to Jimmy Nicholl whose own career took him to Ibrox some years later

apparent early in his reign as manager. 'There are players here who are not up to Manchester United standard,' he had said.

On 30 December United were due to play Everton at Old Trafford but the game was called off because of bad weather. It gave Tommy Docherty a little more breathing space. He needed time to get new players and to assess those already in his squad. As he said:

I had other players in mind, but it was getting hold of them. I had already drawn up a list of who I would like to get and the chairman was

Tommy Cavanagh, the man Docherty brought to Old Trafford to help rebuild a crumbling side. Cavanagh had previously been with Nottingham Forest and Hull City, and his reputation as a coach was excellent. But his strict disciplinary code brought opposition from some players. 'They're just ships that pass in the night', Cavanagh would say. Eventually his ship left the Old Trafford moorings on the termination of Dave Sexton's contract

fantastic, he just let me get on with it, he didn't want to see United in trouble and neither did I.

The first game under Docherty's direct influence was at Arsenal and the side was a mixture of the remnants of the Busby side of the 1960s, players brought in by O'Farrell and the Doc's new boys:

Stepney, Young, Forsyth, Graham, Sadler, Buchan, Morgan, Kidd, Charlton, Law, Storey-Moore.

A big blow to the club had occurred three days before the game when Sammy McIlroy, one of the promising youngsters being considered by Docherty for his first extended run of senior football, was badly injured in a car accident. It was feared at the time that McIlroy might never play again.

Also missing were Ted MacDougall and Wyn Davies, veteran full-back Tony Dunne, and youngster Tommy O'Neill, who had been Dunne's partner for most of the season.

The changes did little to stop United slipping into further trouble and they lost 3–1. United had gone in the direction Docherty feared – instead of moving up the table they were now bottom.

The Scottish take-over

The rebuilding had to continue and the sports pages that weekend gave a clue as to who might be next on the Docherty shopping list. From Scotland came the news that Lou Macari had asked Glasgow Celtic for a transfer. Macari was one of Docherty's Scottish squad, and there was widespread speculation that he would move south to either Old Trafford or Anfield.

With United knocked out of the FA Cup 1–0 by Wolves, it was time to buy again, and Jim Holton a big, solid centre-half, was bought from Shrewsbury to increase the Docherty clan of Scots. Five days after the Cup defeat the club paid £200,000 for Macari, a record to a Scottish club at the time, and snatched him away from the grasp of Bill Shankly at Anfield.

Mick Martin, a Republic of Ireland midfield player, was bought from the Irish League club Bohemians, and was waiting in the wings as United played West Ham at Old Trafford, and the Stretford End became the tartan army. Alex Stepney, full-back Tony Young and Bobby Charlton were the only Englishmen in the side, Wyn Davies, the substitute, represented Wales, and the rest were Scottish.

There were 50,878 in Old Trafford to see goals from Bobby Charlton and Lou Macari, but still United could not take maximum points, and had to settle for a draw.

The crowd hoped for success for United and were perhaps disappointed that they had not seen a victory, but they certainly were not totally disheartened, because four days later just under 59,000 turned up for the re-arranged game with Everton, hoping that United could avenge the 2–0 defeat they had suffered at Goodison in the third game (and the third defeat) of the season. Everton were in mid-table, United bottom, and even though the game ended goal-less it gave the United fans hope that the revival had started.

Only three players had survived from the side which lost at Goodison; Stepney, Morgan and Buchan, and Docherty's line-up was:

Stepney, Young, Forsyth, Martin, Holton, Buchan, Morgan, MacDougall, Charlton, Macari, Graham. Sub: Kidd.

Since the sacking of Frank O'Farrell and the appointment of Tommy Docherty, United had hardly been out of the headlines and the Everton game produced another as Ted MacDougall stormed away from Old Trafford before the game ended, after being brought off and replaced by Kidd.

Docherty had made no secret of his opinion of MacDougall – he felt he was over-rated, yet MacDougall had a pedigree which totally contradicted this view. He had started his career with Liverpool but had failed to make the grade and, after working as a compositor with a local newspaper in Widnes, where he had been raised when his family moved south from Scotland, he had been signed by York City. Later he moved to Bournemouth where he took a step into the record books by scoring an incredible nine goals during an FA Cup tie against Margate. He had shown this was no fluke by scoring 42 League goals in Bournemouth's promotion season of 1970–71, and then 35 the following year in the Third Division.

But Tommy Docherty had made it clear in newspaper and radio interviews that MacDougall did not fit into his long-term planning, and so far as the player was concerned, being substituted was regarded as a public demonstration of this fact.

Docherty's first win was on 10 February 1973, when once again a crowd of over 50,000 packed the stadium for the visit of Wolves.

The Wolverhampton players must have noticed a difference to the United side they had beaten a month earlier, not just from the new faces in the side, but from its vigorous approach. Bobby Charlton scored both goals in a victory which brought relief, and as it came the week after Jim Holton had earned a point by scoring in a 1–1 draw with Coventry, United rose to 18th position, almost as high in the table as they had been at any time that season.

Joy was shortlived. A week later at Ipswich they lost 4–1 to Bobby Robson's side, and again the threat of relegation loomed large. United were 21st in the division with just twelve fixtures remaining. True they were improving, but would they have enough games left to survive? Having won just six out of 30 matches, it seemed unlikely that they could turn into a side which could now win half of the games left.

The game at Ipswich turned out to be Ted MacDougall's last for the club. A week later he was sold to West Ham for £150,000.

Other players, whose links with Old Trafford had been forged long before MacDougall came on the scene, also looked as if they could soon depart. Denis Law was offered a move to Hearts but turned it down, Bobby Charlton hinted that he might retire at the end of the season, and the imminent end of these careers, coupled with the enforced retirement of John Fitzpatrick because of an arthritic condition, did nothing for morale. United were tipped as one of the relegation favourites by the bookmakers.

They held their fate in their own hands. The fixture list was more like the script of a thriller. They were due to play clubs which could also be relegated, and the winner could stay out of the dreaded bottom two. The first of these was West Bromwich Albion, and a 2–1 win for United at the Hawthorns, thanks to goals from Kidd and Macari, plunged the Midlands club to the foot of the table.

It was not an altogether happy match for United, however. Alex Stepney broke two fingers making a brave save and was ruled out of the game for at least three weeks. Jimmy Rimmer was plunged into the cauldron of survival for his first League game of the season, and with Jim Holton out through suspension, United could not hold out against Birmingham City at St Andrews and lost 3–1. They were in 19th place with ten fixtures remaining.

Charlton retires and Law is transferred

Against all odds, United now had their best run of the season, and wins over Newcastle and Southampton sandwiching a draw at Tottenham kept three clubs below them in the table – West Brom, Norwich and Crystal Palace. They played Norwich next, and won 1–0 thanks to a Mick Martin goal. Four days later they beat Crystal Palace, and then they drew 2–2 at Stoke to ease themselves up into 16th place. Surely they were safe now.

Bobby Charlton took the opportunity to tell Tommy Docherty that he was retiring. The player who had been Britain's best ambassador for football had decided that he would go out at the top: 'I have had a wonderful life in the greatest game in the world, and I always said that only I would know when I would want to retire. That time has come, and I'll leave the game with some marvellous memories.'

Ironically the game which would make United totally safe was against Manchester City, on 21 April 1973, and it came at the end of seven matches without defeat. Bobby Charlton's last derby game attracted a crowd of 61,676, but though it ended goal-less the United fans could celebrate survival. They spilled on to the pitch in the dying seconds, and some of the City officials wondered if the game might have to be replayed, as it was forced to end short of 90 minutes. But the result stood.

It was high spirits and the opportunity to celebrate their success which had taken the

United supporters on to the field . . . a season later the same fixture would end very differently.

Eighteenth place was the reward for United's run, and Crystal Palace and West Bromwich Albion were relegated. But although the campaign was over United were still in the news. Denis Law and Tony Dunne were given free transfers as Tommy Docherty prepared his squad for the following season, and the move was not seen as a compliment by Law.

In his autobiography 'Alex Stepney' (Arthur Barker, 1978), the United goalkeeper told how his colleague learned about the decision:

He was in a bar in Aberdeen watching television with a group of friends when suddenly he saw a head and shoulders picture of himself on the screen. 'Denis Law has been given a free transfer by Manchester United, along with Eire international Tony Dunne,' said the announcer.

Denis is a fiercely proud man and that was a bitter shock to him. For one of the greatest names the game has produced to find out that he had been sacked – for that is what it amounted to – in that way, was a great injustice and an insult. Denis never forgave Tommy Docherty for that.

Controversy and Tommy Docherty were once again walking hand in hand. But the United manager was looking to the future, and he illustrated this on the afternoon when Bobby Charlton played his final competitive game, in the unusual setting of Verona Football Club's stadium in Italy. As Charlton signed off with two powerfully hit goals, a young Irish midfielder made his debut, and delighted all those who watched. Gerry Daly had his first taste of top level football in the Anglo-Italian Tourna-

ment and played a vital role in his club's 4–1 win. As Daly arrived on the scene Bobby Charlton bowed gracefully out of Old Trafford to take over as manager of the club which had given Tommy Docherty his first opportunity in England, Preston North End.

During the summer of 1973 there was much speculation about the future make-up of the League. The League Secretary, Alan Hardaker, had put forward a revolutionary scheme in which he proposed a reduction in the number of clubs in the First Division. He advocated a top section of 20 clubs with three, instead of two, relegation and promotion places. While the scheme as a whole was not considered by the League's Annual Meeting, the three up and three down idea was accepted for the following 1973–74 season.

Before this started Frank Blunstone was appointed youth team manager. He had been one of Tommy Docherty's players when he was manager of Chelsea, and gave up his job as manager of Brentford to move north. His task was to produce young players for the club, and continue the work of his predecessors, who had maintained a constant flow since the days of the Babes. However, as United started their first full season under Docherty they had just two players in their line-up who had come through the club's apprenticeship scheme: Tony Young, an Urmston-born full-back and Steve James, from Yorkshire, who played alongside Holton in the back four. Another young player was substitute for the first game at Arsenal – Sammy McIlroy, who had fought his way back to fitness after recovering from his road accident.

United lost to Arsenal, but then beat Stoke City and QPR at Old Trafford to give the supporters some hope, but it turned out to be false. They went through a spell which was even worse than the previous season, going from September to the New Year with only three wins. By 12 January 1974 they were in 21st position – one place higher than at the same time a year earlier.

Docherty promised the supporters that the future was bright: 'We have some good young players coming through. Boys like Sammy McIlroy, Brian Greenhoff and Gerry Daly are all going to make it to the top. All they need is time.'

But did Docherty have time? His critics were swift to point out that Denis Law, who had signed for Manchester City during the close season, still had his golden touch, and had scored twice on his debut against Birmingham City. Could Law still have offered United something had he been allowed to stay?

Ironically, no sooner had Law and Charlton left Old Trafford than the third member of the trinity which had achieved greatness, George Best, decided to return. George left behind the sunshine of Spain and told his club that he would like to play again. The prodigal son was allowed the opportunity.

Then nobody realised the extent of Best's drink problem, and it was only later that it became apparent that it was one reason for George's waywardness. He reappeared on 20 October 1973, not fully match fit, yet capable of demonstrating that his skills had not deserted him in a 1–0 win over Birmingham City. Mick Martin replaced him when his tiredness showed.

The only goal of that game was scored not by Best, but by Alex Stepney, the goalkeeper. It was his second goal of the season, the first being against Leicester at Old Trafford, when United were awarded a penalty. He had filled the role in pre-season friendlies, and Docherty had handed him the task when the new campaign began.

'I thought the Doc was joking at first,' he said after his first success, 'it was all right taking penalties in friendlies, but in a First Division game? I could hear the crowd gasp when I ran upfield, but I have got to be honest, I never thought of anything but scoring. If I had wondered what would happen if I hit the woodwork, or the goalkeeper saved the shot and booted the ball downfield it might have been different. It was only afterwards when people pointed this out to me that I realised the risks we were taking.'

Was Stepney's penalty-taking pure Docherty bravado, with the United manager cocking a snook at tradition, or was it a reflection of his feelings for the ability of other members of his team? Whatever the thinking behind the move, it brought a modicum of spice to a season which was once more offering little joy to United followers. However, by New Year Best had gone again, and Alex Stepney's reign as penalty-taker had ended.

With Alex Forsyth still out of the side, Tommy Docherty signed another full-back, this time a recognised left-sided player, Stewart Houston, from Frank Blunstone's former club, Brentford. Docherty had come across the player briefly during his last months as manager of Chelsea, and the tall, strong Scot held his place in the side for the remainder of the season.

After defeats at Queen's Park Rangers and West Ham, the side drew with Arsenal at Old Trafford on 19 January then in February completed their second month of the New Year without a single League victory, losing to Coventry and Leeds, then drawing with Derby County and Wolves. So sad was their progress that in the seven opening games of 1974, only four goals were scored, and two of them came in the 2–2 draw at Derby.

Fracas at Maine Road

By early March, when United travelled to Bramall Lane to face Sheffield United, only one side had a worse record than them in the First Division and that was Norwich City, who added a twist to the story by signing none other than Ted MacDougall from West Ham in an effort to

The sixth of September 1973 and George Best is back at Old Trafford. The bearded wanderer agreed to play again after retiring from football but his stay with United was both turbulent and short and after 12 appearances and two goals Best had gone again. 'It is one of the tragedies of life that we never saw the full potential of George,' said Tommy Docherty

That game did nothing to enhance United's reputation. Since Docherty took over they had been criticised for being over-physical, and fingers were once again pointed after this incident, which led to both Macari and Doyle being suspended and fined by the Football Association.

The game had ended in a 0–0 draw and the point taken from City did little to help the plight of United. By the end of March they still stared relegation in the face and it seemed impossible for them to survive, especially as the change in the system meant that they had to reach the haven of 19th, and not 20th place.

Another Scot was bought, Jim McCalliog from Wolves, and another member of the European Cupwinning side played his final game for the club: Brian Kidd's last game was the 3–1 win at Chelsea which once more gave hope that Docherty could again play Houdini.

United were living from day to day, hanging on to the First Division by the tips of their fingers. Then they won three successive games – at Norwich then at home to Newcastle and Everton – with McCalliog scoring three times in two appearances. But the drama of the season came on Saturday 27 April, four days after a painful 1–0 defeat at Everton, when Mick Lyons scored a crucial goal.

stay in the top flight. United won at Sheffield thanks to a Lou Macari goal. Then, eleven days later came a remarkable game, the clash with Manchester City.

It was a cold, damp night and a crowd of 51,331 turned up at Maine Road. For the City fans it was a game of lesser importance than for those who followed United, but here, they felt, was an opportunity to avenge a defeat which had stayed in the memory. In 1963, as United struggled and City slumped, a draw at Maine Road had made United safe and relegated City, Albert Quixall scoring for United after Denis Law had been fouled. Now with City safe in mid-table and with United standing with one foot in the grave, it was time for revenge.

The tension was higher than that of a normal derby and it reached boiling point when suddenly the diminutive Macari and City's rugged defender Mike Doyle began throwing punches at one another, close to the touchline in front of the main grandstand. The boxing mismatch was quickly over as players from both sides intervened, but referee Clive Thomas had his hands full to prevent a battle as the staff from both benches ran on to the field. The linesmen raced to help, and the Welsh referee ordered Macari and Doyle off.

They refused to go.

With the crowd howling, and outbreaks of fighting amongst supporters, Thomas marched both sets of players off the field, and it seemed at first as if he had abandoned the game, only for both teams to return minutes later without the two offenders.

City and Law send United down

United had two games remaining and, their rivals in relegation were ending the season that afternoon. Norwich City were bottom with 29 points, United above them with 32. Occupying the new relegation position of 20th place were Southampton on 34 points, one behind the club above them, Birmingham City. United's lifeline was thin but it was still there. If Birmingham were to lose – and they were at home to Norwich – and United could win their two remaining fixtures, the Midlands club would be relegated and United would survive. Southampton were away to Everton, and United at home to . . . Manchester City!

The 57,000 crowd was hushed at half-time when the electronic scoreboard at Old Trafford printed out the scores from the other games . . . Everton 0 Southampton 2, Birmingham 2 Norwich 1. The derby game was goal-less, but still there was hope. If United could win, and Norwich fight back . . .

Then, with eight minutes remaining, the death blow was struck. Through a ruck of players the ball bobbled and rebounded. The scrambling Alex Stepney was helpless as it passed out of his reach. A City player had his back to the goal, only feet away from the line. He back-heeled the ball over the line, and turned slowly upfield as his supporters and team-mates leapt in celebration. Denis Law had relegated the club that rejected him, but he felt no sweet taste of revenge, only a bitter sadness.

The goading began. Chanting taunts from the City section of the crowd announced the harsh truth to the United followers. United were going down.

The more reckless in the Stretford End could take it no longer, and in their hundreds and then thousands they climbed the short wooden picket fencing and spilled on to the pitch. This was no end of season celebration, this was an invasion to stop the game, and it led to steel fences being erected before the next season. The United supporters filled the playing area and the riot ended the game. But the result stood and United were relegated.

As it happened, Birmingham won their game, so no matter what the outcome of the derby United could not have stayed in the top Division that they had occupied since before the Second World War. Docherty wept in the dressing room, but bravely faced the media only minutes after the game was called off. He said: 'Words can't describe how sick I feel at the moment. I can't believe that this has happened, but I know it has. All I can say is that we have gone down with the makings of a good side, and that hopefully that side will bring us back again as quickly as possible.'

Manchester United were in the Second Division: after the glory years of the 1960s, the brilliance of the 1950s and the building of the 1940s, the unbelievable had become a reality.

Tommy Docherty's team had been improving but he knew that there were areas which needed to be strengthened, and he was quick to move. In cloak and dagger style Stuart Pearson was signed from Cavanagh's former club Hull City. The transfer – £200,000 cash plus the lanky Peter Fletcher – went through on the eve of the Liverpool–Newcastle FA Cup final, and was lost in the deluge of publicity previewing the Wembley game.

United bounce straight back

United stepped into the unknown the following season, 1974–75, at London's Brisbane Road, Orient's ground having the claim to stage the first Manchester United Second Division game since 7 May 1938. United won 2–0 with goals from Stewart Houston and Willie Morgan. Their stay in the Second Division would be short. In that opening game the 4-3-3 line-up was:

Stepney, Forsyth, Holton, Buchan, Houston, Greenhoff, Daly, McCalliog, Morgan, Pearson, Macari. Sub: McIlroy.

United won their first four games to top the division, and stayed at the top for the whole season.

Defeat came for the first time at Carrow Road, Norwich, where the vast army of United supporters blackened the club's name yet again when they ran riot. The social problem of hooliganism caused a major headache for the club. Because it had the biggest following of any side in the League, it also appeared to have the biggest percentage of unruly supporters.

Attendances at all games had risen, and at Old Trafford huge audiences witnessed the revival. When Sunderland, lying second, came to Manchester the biggest Second Division crowd in United's history turned out to watch the game: 60,585. The home supporters were stunned when Sunderland took a 2–1 lead through two goals from Billy Hughes, but such was the confidence of United that they fought back and goals from Morgan and McIlroy pushed them to a 3–2 win. Pearson had scored the first. It was a victory in the style the long-serving supporters had come to associate with United.

A week later, however, there was major upset in another thrilling game. Jim Holton, by now well established as a Scottish international, broke his leg in a 4–4 draw at Sheffield Wednesday's Hillsborough. It turned out to be Holton's last senior game for the club.

Holton, the centre-back, was hit by a terrible run of bad luck. He fought back to fitness by the start of the following season, then in a freak accident was injured again. United were playing Red Star Belgrade in a pre-season friendly at Old Trafford, and had just taken the field when Holton slipped on a loose ball while trying to get out of the way of a fierce drive from Alex Forsyth. He badly twisted his knee and was carried off before the game had started. A few weeks later he turned out in a reserve game as he

once more attempted a come-back, and broke his leg for a second time. Holton never made it back into the first team, and was transferred to Sunderland to pick up the pieces of a shattered career.

The cricketing Arnie Sidebottom and Steve James filled the gap left by the big man and took United into the New Year still ahead of the pack, but Docherty was not yet satisfied. He sold McCalliog to Southampton and used the £40,000 he received to buy university graduate Steve Coppell from Tranmere Rovers. Coppell had played for the Wirral club while completing his studies at Liverpool University, and came on as substitute for United in the 4–0 victory over Cardiff City at Old Trafford, replacing Willie Morgan.

Coppell's arrival signalled the end for Morgan, who played just four more games before leaving to join his former club Burnley during the summer of 1975. Morgan's departure was not amicable. He left after a series of much publicised incidents, and then a television condemnation of Tommy Docherty led to him being sued by his former manager for libel. The case was heard in 1978 and this in turn led to Docherty being charged with perjury after withdrawing from the first battle. Docherty appeared at the Old Bailey in 1981 and was found not guilty.

With Coppell firmly established in the side, nothing could stop United from winning promotion, and a Macari goal at the Dell put United back in the First Division on 5 April 1975. A fortnight later they were confirmed as Second Division Champions after drawing 2–2 with

Notts County. Docherty had brought success back to Old Trafford. He said:

They always reckon that the Second Division trophy is the one that nobody really wants to win. It means that at some time you have to have failed to be competing for it, unless you have come up from the Fourth Division. I don't really take that view. We have won against tough opposition and now we are back at the top. And we haven't finished yet.

United's start to the 1975–76 season was remarkable. They won five of their first six games, three of them away from home. By mid-September they had been top of the First Division for five weeks. Tommy Jackson, an

Left: 'Six foot two, eyes of blue, big Jim Holton's after you!' sang the United supporters and the brown-eyed Scot forgave the artistic licence. Holton was a popular character but injury led to a tragic end to his days at Old Trafford. The strong centre-back broke his leg twice, first in a League game at Hillsborough, then as he fought his way towards fitness in a reserve game. The injuries forced him away from the club and in 1976 he joined Sunderland.

experienced midfield player with Everton and Nottingham Forest, had been added to the side, and by November, after a loss of form had seen the side slump to fifth place, Docherty paid out £70,000 for another bright young player, Millwall winger Gordon Hill.

'I think the Doc bought me to make the other players laugh,' Hill joked after his arrival. The slimly built Cockney, with a turn of speed to match his powerful shooting, had a reputation of being a jester, and he certainly gave the supporters something to smile about.

United continued to challenge for the Championship, but a bleak spell early in the New Year saw Liverpool and Queen's Park Rangers forge ahead of them, and they finished the season in third place. United had qualified for the UEFA Cup, but they had their eyes on another trophy.

Cup Final disappointment

While League form had slipped, United had a great run in the FA Cup, reaching the final. Home wins over Oxford and Peterborough, and a 2–1 away victory at Leicester, had seen them tipped to do well in the competition. Having reached the quarter-finals it looked as if their hopes had been dashed when they could only manage a draw with Wolves at Old Trafford on 6

March. But three days later they pulled off a remarkable victory at Molineux, taking the game 3–2 in extra time.

Their opponents in the semi-final were Derby County, one of the challengers for the League Championship, but neither side, each at one time chasing the 'double' were to win any honours. Gordon Hill's two goals took United to Wembley where they were to lose to

Southampton.

The final was an anti-climax to a successful season, but perhaps the bitterest pill for Tommy Docherty to swallow was that the Second Division Southampton side won through a goal created by Jim McCalliog, with Alex Stepney beaten by an unfortunate bounce which increased the power of a Bobby Stokes' shot. The day after the final tens of thousands turned out to welcome back the defeated players. 'If this is what they do when we come back without the Cup, what's it going to look like next year?' said Tommy Docherty.

He was not the only member of the party to predict a Wembley return. Martin Buchan, in a near silent dressing room immediately after the game, said: 'I don't think that we have failed. There are a lot of other clubs who would like to have taken our place this afternoon. To reach a Cup final is a great achievement, and we'll be back. We'll be back next year to win.'

By the time the 1976-77 season started only Alex Stepney and Martin Buchan were left of the players brought to the club by managers before Tommy Docherty. The Doc had built his team, and young hopefuls were emerging from Blunstone's efforts with the youth teams. Jimmy Nicholl was able to force the right full-back's role away from Alex Forsyth, Arthur Albiston proved himself to be a player of promise, and David McCreery was on the edge of the team being used regularly as substitute.

Yet another link with the European Cup side of 1968 had left the club. Pat Crerand, who had been appointed Docherty's assistant, left to move into full management. There were rumours of clashes between the two Scots and Docherty was later to reveal his feelings in his book:

I dislike Pat Crerand, but my reasons for appointing him my number two were twofold. I did it because at the time I thought that he could do a good job, and I also thought that it was what Sir Matt Busby wanted.

The United manager claimed that Crerand left the club bearing a grudge against Docherty because he had not recommended him for the post of assistant manager at Glasgow Celtic:

He must have been very disappointed to have left United at his own request, only to see us reach two successive Cup finals.

United reached that second final after a slump in League form of alarming proportions. At one stage they led the First Division, then went eight games without a victory and slumped to 17th. Out came the Docherty cheque book

Left: Laurie Brown sits between Tommy Docherty and Tommy Cavanagh on the United bench. Brown was unaware that behind his back Docherty and his wife Mary were having an affair. When the matter came into the open Brown kept his job as physiotherapist, Docherty lost his, and Cavanagh stayed on as assistant to Dave Sexton

again and Jimmy Greenhoff, older brother of Brian, was bought from Stoke City. Greenhoff arrived at a time when United were out of the UEFA Cup having lost to Juventus, but still in the League Cup and optimistic of reaching Wembley by that route. 'I felt something was missing' said Docherty. 'I had switched Sammy McIlroy back into midfield to take over from Gerry Daly and things started to happen for us again. When Jimmy came the balance was right again.'

The elder Greenhoff began to pay back his transfer fee with his first goal in a 4–0 victory over Everton on 27 December 1976, a result which brought some consolation after the Merseysiders had ended United's League Cup hopes with a 3–0 win at Old Trafford. There followed a successful run from mid-January to April which pushed them back up the table, but with Liverpool well in front the Championship seemed unreachable.

However, in the FA Cup United did well. After beating Walsall 1–0 in the third round, they were drawn against Dave Sexton's QPR at Old Trafford. It was in this game that Docherty recognised: 'You need a bit of luck to win cups and we had our share today.' Dave Sexton agreed:

I remember the game vividly. The pitch was half frozen – one long strip was perfect, the other three quarters of the ground was bone hard. It meant that on the good ground players could keep their feet, on the bad they ran stiff-legged. United broke down their left flank on the good surface, and David Webb moved across to challenge, but he lost his footing on the frozen area, fell flat on his back and missed the cross. Lou Macari, who had been totally unaffected by the conditions, got on the end of it and scored the only goal.

Luck had taken United through to round five and the draw for that part of the competition made the headlines: 'United to meet Saints – play it again Reds'.

Southampton versus Manchester United, a repeat of the 1976 final, and at the Dell. Had United's luck run out? No home advantage, and facing a side that had already beaten them, they had to be second favourites.

It ended in a 2–2 draw. Lou Macari scored first and David Peach levelled from the penalty spot. Then Gordon Hill put United in front again, but before half-time Peach got a second equaliser. For the second 45 minutes the cut and thrust went on, but there were no further goals. Now Southampton had to come to Old Trafford, and the scales had tipped against them.

In the United squad that afternoon was a 17-year-old youngster from Accrington taken along for the experience: Mike Duxbury. He said 'I didn't really think that I had any chance of playing, but it was a great thrill to be part of the first team set-up, and what a game to watch, it was amazing.'

Duxbury had yet to make his senior debut,

but playing for the opposition both in the game at the Dell and in the Old Trafford replay, was Ted MacDougall, returning once again to haunt Docherty. Three days before the replay United beat City 3–1 at Old Trafford, and were now seven points behind Liverpool, the leaders, but had two games in hand. Was it going to be another year when the 'double' beckoned?

Two Jimmy Greenhoff goals saw United into the sixth round with a 2–1 win, David Peach again scoring for Southampton to nurse the unhappy memory of having netted three times and ending on the losing side.

The quarter-final draw gave United home advantage against Aston Villa, and Houston and Macari scored in a 2–1 win in front of the fourth successive crowd of over 57,000 in games at Old Trafford. The biggest of those attendances had been for the League game with Leeds United, when 60,612 filled the ground . . . and it was Leeds who provided the semi-final opposition.

In the other semi-final Liverpool and Everton met at Maine Road, while United travelled into Yorkshire to face Leeds at Hillsborough.

Wembley again

Within a quarter of an hour United had booked their ticket to Wembley. They played with confidence as Leeds seemed to be overcome by the occasion. First Jimmy Greenhoff – once a Leeds player before his move to Stoke – scored, then Steve Coppell, and United's lively forwardline continued to cause problems for the Leeds defence all through the match. Gordon McQueen was Leeds' centre-half – later he was to join United. At the other end Joe Jordan, another future United player, was always a threat, and late in the game Leeds scored from the penalty spot, Allan Clarke taking the kick. But it was too late, and United were through.

The scenes in the dressing room were even wilder than the previous year. Tommy Cavanagh danced and shouted 'We're back, we're back!' as if trying to convince anyone within earshot. There was a quiet confidence about the players as they gathered their thoughts, and Tommy Docherty proclaimed: 'We've got a second chance, and we won't make any mistakes this time – by the way, who do we play?'

The Merseyside semi-final had ended in a draw and it was four days later before Liverpool won through in a second game at Maine Road, watched by most of the United players.

In the build-up to the 1976 final there had been bad publicity for the players when a row broke out between representatives of their Cup final 'pool' and the local media. The players wanted the newspapers, radio and television companies, who interviewed them regularly throughout the season, to contribute to a central fund. The majority of the companies refused on the grounds that such contributions, while being traditional, should be voluntary and not demanded. The story was published and did nothing

Left: The shot from Southampton's Bobby Stokes flashes past the outstretched Alex Stepney for the only goal of the 1976 FA Cup Final and the favourites are beaten by the Second Division side. In later years Tommy Docherty argued that recordings of the game showed that the referee should have blown for offside, but Martin Buchan, who skippered the side, said on the day: 'We lost because we didn't play well . . . but we'll be back next year and we won't get it wrong then'. A year later United won the cup

for morale. Some players were willing to help the media without payment, others refused, and there was a division amongst the squad. Eventually the matter was settled, but the damage had been done.

As soon as they reached the 1977 final the 'pool' representatives announced that they would not be making any demands, but that if any organisation wished to contribute they would be welcomed, but anyone not wishing to do so would have no restrictions placed upon them. The response was one hundred per cent.

All hopes of the Championship vanished in the days after the semi-final, as the team picked up only one point in four games. Then 18 days before Wembley, United lost to Liverpool at Anfield and Tommy Docherty amazed everyone by saying: 'We have learned something tonight. We can beat Liverpool at Wembley.'

Had they discovered the Achilles heel of Paisley's side? There were many who watched the 1–0 defeat who felt that United had been the better team, but had given away an unlucky goal to the side which was aiming for an incredible treble of League, FA Cup and European Cup. Kevin Keegan had scored in what, amazingly, was to be Liverpool's last win of the League campaign. They drew three out of their last four fixtures and lost the last, yet still won the Championship.

As for United's run-in to Wembley, they were hit by a devastating blow in a rough-house of a game at Bristol City when Stewart Houston was stretchered off with a broken ankle. Wembley was just a fortnight away when Arthur Albiston, a 19-year-old Scot, was called into the side. He played three full games before the final.

United and Docherty win the Cup

United spent Cup final week at the Selsdon Park Hotel in Croydon, arriving there after losing 2–1 to West Ham at Upton Park on the Monday before the big game. Liverpool had also been in action at Bristol, and they too lost by the same margin. A week of media coverage followed, with television cameras following the players, journalists arranging interviews, and microphones being held under the noses of anyone willing to talk. Tommy Docherty loved every minute and the build-up was positive.

There were injury doubts kept secret, however, despite the constant presence of the nation's sporting journalists, and on the Thursday evening a curtain came down on everything except pre-arranged contact with the players. By Saturday morning all was ready and United rode to Wembley in style, with television viewers able to watch their progress thanks to a camera on the team coach.

Liverpool were favourites to win. As League Champions and European Cup finalists their pedigree far outweighed Docherty's Dynamos, but it was United who rose to the occasion. The final was played at a hectic pace, Liverpool

pressurising young Albiston, who showed that he had a bright future ahead of him as he handled the foraging of McDermott, and the speed of Heighway who switched wings to cause confusion.

United held out till half-time, and realised as the second half started that they were not playing an invincible side. With five minutes gone Jimmy Greenhoff broke downfield and found Pearson with a precision pass. The striker ran forward, brushing aside a challenge and fired a low shot towards the right-hand post. Clemence in the Liverpool goal seemed late to move to cover it and the ball passed his outstretched left arm before he could extend his dive fully. United were ahead!

Back came Liverpool and a Joey Jones cross from the left was hit firmly by Case into the roof of Alex Stepney's net – two goals within three minutes and the cheers of the United fans choked by the sudden upsurge from Liverpool.

Another three minutes and United were ahead again thanks to a remarkable goal, and a strike which had a certain amount of luck attached to it. Tommy Smith and Jimmy Greenhoff tangled, Smith blocking a scoring chance from the United forward. The ball ran off to Macari who fired at goal, but the shot was well off target, and Clemence moved to his left to cover. The shot hit Greenhoff who was still between Macari and Smith, and deflected from his chest, over his right shoulder and into the net well beyond Clemence, for the winning goal.

A year after vowing that they would be back, the team celebrated as the FA Cup was passed around the dressing room. There were wild scenes as champagne was poured into the trophy, there were smiles and songs from players and Docherty's backroom team, and the tears of sadness from the previous year were replaced by tremendous joy. Sammy McIlroy perhaps summed up the occasion when he said:

It's the dream of every footballer to come to Wembley and play in the FA Cup final, and it's a great thrill to take part in such a game. But there is no feeling like winning. When we lost last year we were gutted, and we know how the Liverpool players feel right now. They have our sympathy, because we know what it's like.

The celebrations went on into the night. An official banquet at the Royal Lancaster Hotel was followed by a private party for the players and officials, their wives and friends at the Royal Garden Hotel where they were staying.

Martin Buchan ordered a trolley full of champagne and the joy of winning the cup was apparent . . . but Tommy Docherty had left the group to walk in Hyde Park, alone with his thoughts. He spent most of the night strolling in the silence of the park, making what for him was an important personal decision. Docherty was deciding how to break the news, before the media discovered it and splashed it, that he was leaving his wife to set up permanent home with

Right: Some of the most amazing scenes ever witnessed at a Wembley homecoming greeted the players as they arrived back in Manchester after winning the FA Cup in 1977. Tommy Docherty led his players into Manchester Town Hall for a civic reception but the celebrations hid the secret which was to rock Old Trafford and ended his days as manager. Within a month Tommy Docherty had lost his job, but those who worshipped the team he built still think of the Docherty era as one of excitement and success

Right: Stuart Pearson and Gordon Hill hold the FA Cup aloft after their 1977 2–1 win over Liverpool, but before the next visit to Wembley both had ended their playing days at Old Trafford. Hill was bought by Docherty after he was appointed manager of Derby County later in 1978 and Pearson stayed on before injury led to him being left out of the side and his announcement on the morning of the 1979 Cup final that he wouldn't play for United again

another woman. That the woman was Mary Brown, wife of the club physiotherapist Laurie, made the situation more difficult than if she had no connections with United.

The team returned to Manchester to a sensational welcome. It was perhaps the biggest homecoming the city had seen since 1968, when the European Cup was shown to English fans for the first time. Certainly it was greater than the turn out the previous year when the Cup-less team had returned. The speeches were short, and the civic reception was perhaps the last thing many of the players wanted. They had

been away from home for a week, had just taken part in football's showpiece, and had wined and dined since the final whistle. All that most of them wanted was to go home.

United were back in Europe, and after winning their first major trophy since 1968, there was talk of being able to wrest the Championship from Liverpool's grip. Could United take the title in 1978? If they could, it would be without Docherty's driving force.

Docherty forced to go

News of the love affair became public. Accusing fingers were pointed at the club, and at the couple who had been forced to make the heartbreaking decision of ending two marriages in order that they could share their lives together. 'The Mary Brown Affair' was headline news for weeks and eventually, even though he claimed that he was given an assurance that his private life would not affect his position as manager, Tommy Docherty was called before the board.

The meeting was held in Louis Edwards' home in Alderley Edge. The directors met the man who had taken their club to Wembley 44 days earlier and asked for his resignation. He refused, and was dismissed.

Docherty was driven quickly away from the luxury detached house, and club secretary Les Olive leaned through a groundfloor window to read a short statement saying that Tommy Docherty was no longer manager of Manchester United.

'I found it hard to believe', said Docherty

later. 'These days marriages break up every day. But people don't lose their jobs because they fall in love with someone.'

Ten years after their private lives had become public, Tommy Docherty and Mary Brown were free to marry and did so.

Dave Sexton arrives

Just ten days after Docherty's dismissal, Dave Sexton was appointed manager, following in the Scot's footsteps for the third time in his career. Sexton succeeded Docherty at Chelsea, and Docherty had briefly been manager of Queen's Park Rangers before Sexton.

Having left Loftus Road Sexton realised the size of the task which lay ahead of him at Old Trafford. He was following the most successful manager the club had seen since Busby, and a man who was extremely popular with the supporters. The extrovert Docherty was a com-

plete contrast to the introvert Sexton and Sexton would find him a hard act to follow.

With Tommy Cavanagh staying as his assistant manager, Sexton moved into his office, shocking many by having one of the walls painted bright blue – at Old Trafford! He got ready for the new season and had the unique honour of leading his players out at Wembley for his first game in charge – the 1977 FA Charity Shield against champions Liverpool. The stadium was full for the spectacle but the game did not live up to expectations. Neither side managed to score and Liverpool debutant Kenny Dalglish, signed from Celtic for a record £440,000 to replace Kevin Keegan, who had joined SV Hamburg, could do nothing to break the deadlock.

There was one moment in the game which proved later to have serious repercussions. Jimmy Greenhoff was badly hurt as he was challenged by goalkeeper Ray Clemence on the

Above: United are back. Lou Macari scores his 16th goal of the 1974–75 season to clinch promotion one year and 21 days after the sadness of relegation. The 1–0 win at Southampton was followed by victory over Fulham at Old Trafford and a draw at Notts County secured the Second Division championship by three points from rivals Aston Villa

edge of the area. Greenhoff was felled and the injury affected the United striker for the remainder of his career. Because of it he missed the start of the 1977-78 season, his place going to McCreery, with Ashley Grimes, a gangling Irish midfielder, taking over McCreery's regular number 12 shirt.

The 1977–78 season could have had no better start for Sexton, Lou Macari scoring a hat-trick in a 4–1 home victory over Birmingham City – but this was the team Docherty had built and the supporters were quick to remind the new manager of this fact, chanting the Doc's name regularly.

It was these same supporters who involved the club in one of the most embarrassing moments in its history when the first season under Sexton was just a month old. Crowd trouble in St Etienne resulted in United at first being banned from the Cup Winners' Cup, then reinstated and ordered to play the second leg of their tie with the French club at a ground 300 kilometres from Manchester. They chose Home Park, Plymouth.

United lost their first games of the new season at Maine Road on 10 September, then at home to Chelsea a week later, on the day Tommy Docherty was appointed manager of Derby County.

By November, United had slumped to 15th in the table and Sexton made his first significant change to the side, dropping goalkeeper Alex Stepney and calling in Paddy Roche who had been in the wings for the past three seasons. Roche had almost got his chance under Docherty, and was about to start the 1975–76 season, but his father had died in the week leading up to the game and Alex Stepney had stayed in goal.

Even with a new goalkeeper Sexton's side was inconsistent. Two results clearly illustrate this. On 17 December they lost 4–0 at home to Nottingham Forest, then in the next game, on Boxing Day away to Everton, they won 6–2. In this game Sexton brought in teenage striker Andy Ritchie for his debut, and while the youngster failed to score, he did enough to stay in the side for four games.

Sexton made his first major move in the transfer market on 6 January 1978 when he signed Joe Jordan from Leeds United for £350,000, but the big striker did not play for

almost a month because he was 'Cup-tied' and under suspension. During his enforced absence United were knocked out of the FA Cup after scraping through the third round with a replay victory over Carlisle.

This again was seen as an illustration of United's inability to string together a series of good results. They lost at home to Birmingham City, then beat Ipswich at Portman Road, while between these games having to fight for a draw in the FA Cup at Carlisle. In this game Brian Greenhoff was sent off after deliberately handling the ball, but victory in the replay was consolation for this disappointment.

After appearing to struggle against lesser opponents United suddenly raised their game when Tommy Docherty brought his new club to Old Trafford and the 4–0 victory over Derby must have given Dave Sexton some satisfaction. But if his predecessor was disappointed after his first visit to Old Trafford since his dismissal, it was Sexton's turn in the next game when United met their doom in the Cup. There were signs that it would be hard when it took a last-minute Steve Coppell equaliser to earn a draw at Old Trafford against a revived West Bromwich Albion, whose new manager had been in charge for just a fortnight. His name was to become familiar at Old Trafford: Ron Atkinson.

Right: Joe Jordan between chairman Louis Edwards and Dave Sexton at his signing for United. He cost Sexton £350,000 in January 1978, a sharp contrast to the £15,000 Leeds United paid when they bought him from Morton eight years earlier. A strong centre-forward, he joined his great friend Gordon McQueen as a popular figure with United's followers. In 1981, following the departure of Dave Sexton, he was swift to sign for AC Milan for £175,000

The replay at the Hawthorns went into extra time, and there were memories of the game at Wolverhampton two season before when United won through. It was not to be this time, and although there were arguments that an equaliser had been prevented by the outstretched hand of Derek Statham, the Albion full-back, United lost 3–2. So with three months of the season left, they had only pride to play for.

On 9 February, Sexton bought again, bringing centre-half Gordon McQueen from Leeds for £495,000 to join his best friend Joe Jordan. Jordan had made his debut on 8 February, and McQueen made his first appearance at Anfield 17 days later. Even so, it was 8 April before United won a game with both their costly signings in the side.

A series of draws during March kept United in mid-table, and then in April the supporters were stunned when Gordon Hill, one of the most popular players in the side, was sold for £250,000. The buyer? Tommy Docherty.

Immediately there were claims and counter-claims that there had been a vendetta against Hill by his team-mates. 'They didn't like me and didn't want me to do well', said Hill, and an incident during one game when Martin Buchan had slapped his face was used as an illustration. 'He was a selfish player', was the response from Sexton.

Four victories, against QPR, Norwich, West Ham and Bristol, gave United the chance to end the season on a high note, but tenth in the table was not looked on as a sign of success by the fans and it was obvious that Dave Sexton would have to bring them trophies if his popularity was to match Docherty's.

The following season, 1978–79, saw the visit of Real Madrid for the club's centenary game with Dave Sexton proud to be in charge at such a time:

No club has captured the imagination like Manchester United, and it is a great thrill for me to be here. But rather than looking back over what has happened before, I'd like to look ahead.

I feel that in the next ten years there will be changes. Football is a family game and I would like to see stadiums providing areas for family seating.

Sponsorship is another aspect of the game which can be developed and I wouldn't be surprised to see players wearing shirts bearing a sponsor's name before long.

We must also get ready to accept foreign players into our game, as well as some of our players going abroad. The only snag in this area, as far as I can see it, is our taxation system does not make a move to this country as attractive as one abroad.

United won the centenary game 4–0, and ten days after Sexton had spoken about his views on the future of the game, his forecast of foreign players coming into the Football League was made fact, when Ipswich Town signed Arnold

Muhren from Dutch club Ajax.

United had opened the new season with Roche in goal and despite winning only five games by November, were in the top six. They had been knocked out of the League Cup in a surprising game, Third Division Watford scoring twice through Luther Blissett, a self-confessed United supporter. This bringing a comment from his chairman Elton John, which would no doubt be outweighed by other games in the future:

This has been the greatest moment of my time in football. To come to a place like Old Trafford and beat Manchester United is an incredible feeling – now I'd like to see us use all this enthusiasm to get into the Second Division.

On 11 October 1978 United were away to Birmingham City and lost 5–1. Immediately Sexton moved for the chequebook and agreed to buy Coventry City goalkeeper Jim Blyth. He

Below: Gordon McQueen lost a large percentage of his playing career through injury, but still became a popular figure at Old Trafford. The tall centre-half scored 26 goals in his 228 appearances, many of them spectacular headers from corner kicks and his determination won the hearts of the supporters. A cruel stroke of bad luck robbed him of a place in Scotland's World Cup side of 1978, when he slid into a goal-post, damaging his knee, during an international in Scotland

Above: Pirri the Real Madrid captain exchanges pennants with Martin Buchan before the start of United's centenary game on 7 August 1978. The game illustrated the relationship between the two clubs, built during the late 1950s when Real dominated European football and strengthened after the Munich air disaster when the Spanish club offered help as United struggled to survive. The centenary game ended in a 4–0 win for United

said that Roche's confidence had been shattered, not just by the Birmingham scoreline, but by the lack of support he was getting from the fans, who felt that Stepney was being wasted in the Central League side. Blyth arrived at Old Trafford to face the bright lights of television crews who had been told of the signing. The media gathered for interviews and photographs, but then the news came through that the deal was off. Blyth had not passed the insurance medical.

Sexton was in a difficult position. Stepney had not played any first team games, Roche had already been told by the move to sign Blyth that he was no longer being considered as first choice goalkeeper, and United were 48 hours away from their next game. So on 18 November the name of Gary Bailey was written on the team sheet for the first time, and the tall young blond faced Ipswich Town, the side from his Suffolk birthplace.

Bailey had arrived at Old Trafford after playing university football in South Africa, where he had lived since his family emigrated there when he was four years old. Goalkeeping was in Bailey's blood, as his father Roy had kept goal for Ipswich from 1955 to 1964, and had been a member of the 1962 Championship-winning side.

Young Gary Bailey had a steady debut in a 2–0 victory, and stayed in the side for the rest of the season.

In the League United continued their indifferent performances of the previous season. New players were introduced. Mickey Thomas was bought from Wrexham to replace Hill on the left

of the attack, and Ritchie had a run of nine games at centre-forward when Jordan was injured.

Stuart Pearson was out of the side through injury and was not to play another League game for United. He came back into the reckoning for the FA Cup and played well in the third-round win over Chelsea.

Bad weather hit football at the start of 1979, wiping out the whole of the club's January League programme, and the only other fixture proved to be Stuart Pearson's last game for United. It was the fourth-round Cup-tie at Craven Cottage, put back to 31 January by the freeze, and Pearson was badly injured in a terrible tackle which put him out of the reckoning for the remainder of the season.

The game ended in a 1–1 draw and United won the replay 12 days later after the freeze once more delayed matters. In the fifth round they were again drawn away to opposition from a lower division, this time Colchester United. Bad weather forced the clubs to switch the game to midweek and on a freezing night the Third Division side did their best to upset the form book, but United won 1–0 thanks to a Jimmy Greenhoff goal.

The possibility of a Wembley return ended all rumblings about poor League form, but luck was again against the team when the sixth-round draw paired them with Tottenham at White Hart Lane. When a solid, professional performance earned them a replay at Old Trafford, the scent of Wembley was really in their nostrils. In the second game goals from McIlroy and Jordan powered United through to their third FA Cup semi-final in four years, but once more it was Liverpool who stood in their way.

The semi-final was at Maine Road and it was Liverpool who struck the first blow, Kenny Dalglish putting them ahead, but Jordan restored the balance. There was a moment of panic when Liverpool were awarded a hotly disputed penalty, but when McDermott missed United rallied, and Brian Greenhoff followed his brother's example by scoring a vital Cup goal to put them ahead. Six minutes from the end Hansen equalised, forcing United into their eighth game of the Cup campaign.

Four nights later, at Goodison Park, the elder Greenhoff scored yet another crucial goal, and although Liverpool at times laid siege in the United half of the field they were beaten. United were back at Wembley, and Dave Sexton had the chance of emulating Docherty and finally erasing all the disadvantageous comparisons.

The 'five-minute' final

In the build-up to Wembley Brian Greenhoff was injured, but felt he would be fit for the final. There was competition for places even as the side relaxed at Selsdon Park again, their 'lucky' hotel. Would Grimes edge out the nervous Thomas? Would young Ritchie's strength earn him a place? Sexton named his side. The eleven who had beaten Liverpool would start the final against Arsenal:

Bailey, Nicholl, Albiston, McIlroy, McQueen, Buchan, Coppell, Jimmy Greenhoff, Jordon, Macari, Thomas.

For the massive United contingent amongst the supporters the final was a dull affair. The yellow and blue banners of Arsenal were held high as first Talbot, and then Frank Stapleton scored before half-time. Sexton's side seemed to offer little resistance and all United had won was the toss of the coin to decide who would wear their normal red on the big day.

Then, with five minutes remaining United found hope. Gordon McQueen, lunging forward, scored. The United chants at last were louder than those of the Londoners. Suddenly supporters who had been preparing to make an unhappy exit from the stadium stopped gathering their belongings to turn their attention to the game again. Journalists who had already written the story of United's defeat began to scribble new words on their notepads, and when Sammy McIlroy danced through the tiring Arsenal defence and slid the ball into the net for a second goal, the game took on a whole new life.

The scores were level with seconds rather than minutes left. United had earned extra time and, looking the fresher team were looking forward to the whistle and the extra half-hour.

Instead, Liam Brady ran forward for Arsenal, crossing into the United half unchallenged. Macari went after him, but Brady's pass out to the left found Graham Rix. He ran forward again evading his opponents and sent over a high cross. Bailey appeared to hesitate, expecting his defence to cover, and Alan Sunderland forced the ball home. Arsenal had won what became known as 'the five-minute final' 3–2.

'It was the worst feeling ever,' Gary Bailey recalls. 'To be out of a game for so long and then suddenly be back in with a chance, only to have your hopes dashed that way, was sickening. I'll never forget that day.'

Nor will Dave Sexton: 'I think that too many of our players were looking ahead to extra time, and lost concentration.'

Before the final, Stuart Pearson had announced his future intentions: 'I will never play for Manchester United again', he said. On 7 August 1979 he joined West Ham. Being left out of the side had hurt.

Seven days later Dave Sexton continued the building of a side which he could call his own, and bought Ray Wilkins from Chelsea for a massive £777,777, as two more of Docherty's players were sold. The first of these was David McCreery, bought by the new Queen's Park Rangers manager Tommy Docherty. He had joined the relegated London club on the eve of United's Cup final. The next player sold was Brian Greenhoff, reversing his brother's move by joining Leeds for £350,000. The side which began the 1979–80 season contained five players introduced by Sexton.

The start to the new campaign was one of the best for several years, four wins and two draws taking United to the top of the table by mid-September, and there was optimism that the 13-year gap since the last Championship win might be bridged. By the turn of the year the lowest position United had filled was third, and this followed their first defeat away to Wolves. At home they were unbeaten, but they were out of the League Cup, having lost at Norwich.

Remarkably Norwich's visit to Old Trafford brought about a total reversal of the 4–1 cup upset at Carrow Road. United won 5–0, their biggest victory of the season, and the two points took them to the top once again. From the Norwich game, on 24 November, until they lost to Wolves for a second time in front of a 51,000 crowd at Old Trafford on 9 February, United lost only two games. The first was in the League, to fellow contenders Liverpool, the next, their first home defeat, to Spurs in the FA Cup.

It was the sixth Cup-tie between the two clubs in two seasons. United had beaten the Londoners on their way to Wembley in 1978–79, and knocked them out of the League Cup thanks to a 4–3 aggregate win, and now found themselves drawn against Spurs again in the FA competition four months later. United thought they were in with a chance when they forced Spurs to travel to Old Trafford for a third-round replay, but in a frantic second game Spurs won. They did so with Glenn Hoddle in goal after Aleksic had been hospitalised by a collision with Joe Jordan, grabbing the winner in extra time from the head of Ardiles.

Criticism of fans and chairman

However, it was events away from the field which made the headlines. First, two Middlesbrough fans were killed when a wall collapsed on spectators as they left Ayrsome Park, and accusing fingers were pointed at United's rowdy supporters. Then a television programme accused the club of operating outside the rules.

Granada Television's 'World in Action' produced by Geoffrey Seed, a United supporter, accused chairman Louis Edwards of instigating payments to young players as a method of persuading them to join the club. It claimed that United operated a secret cash fund to use for matters such as this, and also accused the chairman of irregular share dealings. Louis Edwards strongly denied the accusations, which became the subject of a joint inquiry by the Football League and the Football Association, and said: 'I have never done anything at Manchester United that I am ashamed of. I have always been proud to be chairman of this great club, and anything I have done has been in its best interests.'

A month after the allegations Louis Edwards died of a heart attack, to be succeeded by his son Martin as chairman of the club.

The 'Five Minute final' and United celebrate as Sammy McIlroy (rising on one knee, right) scores an incredible equaliser. United trailed 2–0 with five minutes to go, then Gordon McQueen put them back in the game before McIlroy's goal. Joy was shortlived as straight from the kick-off Arsenal scored another to win the 1979 FA Cup

The battle for the Championship continued between Liverpool and United but an amazing scoreline on 1 March caused concern: Ipswich Town 6 United 0. And that match included two penalties saved by Bailey!

Since his arrival, Ray Wilkins had missed only two games. The first was the home defeat by Wolves, the second the trouncing at Ipswich in a game which Sir Matt Busby, the club's president-elect described thus:

It was not the sort of result to make you feel confident of winning the Championship, but I remember that one player was outstanding. Arnold Muhren, the Dutch mid-fielder was brilliant – his part in the victory for his side was one of great importance, and he linked up well with his fellow countryman Frans Thijssen.

Was Sexton's premonition about the influx of foreign players coming true? Perhaps it was, because United's substitute that afternoon was Nikola Jovanovic, the Yugoslav defender, signed from Red Star Belgrade.

From the Ipswich disgrace to the end of the season only three more games were lost, the final result deciding the destiny of the title. The first of these upsets came at Nottingham's City Ground, where in an ill-tempered game Sammy McIlroy was ordered off by Clive Thomas after disputing a penalty from which John Robertson put the home side in front. Forest won 2–0, with Garry Birtles scoring the second.

Three days later United and Liverpool began their run-in to the end of the season when they met at Old Trafford, and a 2–1 win for United narrowed the gap to four points with six games remaining. The game also saw Jimmy Greenhoff playing his first full match of the season – and scoring the winner.

During what turned out to be the club's most successful season since 1968, as far as League position was concerned, United were accused by the media of lacking warmth. Under a headline of 'Cold Trafford', Dave Sexton's weakness in handling day-to-day press inquiries was exposed. The article alleged that Sexton was so unlike his predecessor that journalists who specialised in reporting the club's affairs were having difficulty in going about their work.

'I'm not here to help people fly kites', Sexton said. 'I will be the first to speak if there is something to speak about, but it is not my job just to fill the pages of newspapers.'

His approach was directly opposite to that of Docherty, who was never out of the news, eager to talk about anything whether it involved his club or not. Yet, as the Championship battle reached its end, Sexton was willing to give his views: 'We are in with a definite chance. If we can do well in the last six fixtures then we can win the title, but we are also hoping for mistakes from Liverpool.'

Five successive wins following the Liverpool game was the players' response to the challenge, but it was to no avail. On the last afternoon of the season United lost 2–0 at Leeds, Liverpool won 4–1 at Anfield against Aston Villa, and the race was lost by two points.

Brian Greenhoff, rejected by Sexton, was in the Leeds line-up for that last game, and recalls:

I remember it was impossible for United really. They had to win by a cricket score to have any chance of taking the title. Liverpool's goal difference was far superior, and they had a game in hand. United were still in with a chance at half-time, as Liverpool and Aston Villa were drawing 1–1, but we were in front 1–0. Derek Parlane got our first and when Kevin Hird got the second from the penalty spot it was all over.

I felt sorry for my brother and all my pals in the United team, but Liverpool won, so there was nothing they could've done.

Liverpool lost their final game of the season and the top of the First Division ended:

	P	W	D	L	F	A	Pts
Liverpool	42	25	10	7	81	30	60
Manchester United	42	24	10	8	65	35	58

So Dave Sexton could look forward to another season in charge of United, and was confident of doing well: 'We have the players, and the ability to go one better in 1980–81, and that is our aim'.

During the summer of 1980 Sexton tried unsuccessfully to buy Republic of Ireland star Liam Brady from Arsenal. Brady was at the end of his contract and free to negotiate with any club. Arsenal had put a fee of £1.5 million on the player and Sexton made it clear that United would be willing to find the money if Brady agreed to the move. They talked, and there was strong speculation that Sexton had persuaded the player to move north, but he announced that he would be joining Italian giants Juventus, adding weight to Sexton's 1978 prediction that players would go abroad because they could earn more under foreign taxation.

The move, incidentally, proved costly for Arsenal, because United would have met their asking price, but when Brady went to Italy the fee was fixed at the European maximum of £600,000.

So there was no Brady when the new season started and an injury jinx which had hit the club during pre-season training continued. Just after the players had reported back from their summer break, which followed a tour of America, Gordon McQueen fell awkwardly over a hurdle, and Ray Wilkins pulled up with a groin strain. Both missed the opening game against Middlesbrough, where Kevin Moran deputised for McQueen as he had done on eight occasions the previous year.

Injuries sink Sexton

Injuries became a millstone around Dave Sexton's neck. Slowly they pulled him down, causing him to use 16 players in the first three fixtures. Nothing went right for United. In the first game Jordan limped off with a knee injury. Gary Bailey was able to disguise the fact that he had dislocated a finger making a save towards the end of the game, but he too was ruled out for the next two matches.

In the second game Grimes was hurt, and in the third Moran's bravery cost him dearly. He lunged at Birmingham's Keith Bertschin as the striker went for goal, and badly twisted his ankle, to be replaced by League debutant Mike Duxbury.

'We are in a desperate position as far as injuries go,' Sexton said after the game, 'but we aren't too worried. There's a long way to go in the season and I'm sure we'll get things right once we have our full squad back again.' And as for Moran's injury: 'This is the sort of thing we can expect from a player like Kevin, he is very brave and strong. He'd run through brick walls if you asked him, and he never thinks about personal safety.'

Moran, who had joined United from Pegasus, was missing for the next five League games and

the two-legged League Cup clash with Coventry City. These League Cup-ties saw United out of the competition by early September, losing 1–0 at Old Trafford, and by the same scoreline at Highfield Road, with spurned goalkeeper Jim Blyth adding irony to the event by playing in both games for Coventry without conceding a goal.

Scoring goals was proving a problem and the club went six games with only one successful strike and that came from central defender Jovanovic in a 1–1 draw with Sunderland. By 13 September 1980 United had won just one game in the League, and drawn three of their four other First Division games. Sexton had tried Andy Ritchie at striker, alongside the rejuvenated Jimmy Greenhoff, who was fighting through the pain of a pelvic injury, and elsewhere gambled with young players. He was even forced to recall Chris McGrath from the reserve pool for his first game in three years. McGrath played one game, against Birmingham at St Andrews, and that was his last appearance for the club.

Ritchie also played his last game for United early that season in the 0–0 draw at Tottenham, which came four days after the League Cup exit. Injuries and the continuing poor results were increasing the pressure on Sexton to pull the club out of its misery.

Incredibly, with a side made up of eight of Docherty's players, and without Sexton's expensive signings Jordan, McQueen and Wilkins, the club had its second, and biggest, win of the season. The goal famine ended when Leicester City were thrashed 5–0 with goals from Jovanovic (2), Coppell, Grimes and Macari, who was replaced by 17-year-old Glasgow-born Scott McGarvey, another debutant, in the second half.

By mid-October the murmurings of discontent were growing louder, as the injury list grew longer. Buchan had been added to the ever-growing numbers unfit to play, and McQueen aggravated his injury again when he tried a return in the derby game at Old Trafford which ended in another predictable draw. After 12 League games there had been one defeat, but only three wins and the eight drawn games were the subject of most contention.

The unhappy Ritchie was sold to Brighton, and the £500,000 paid for the teenager was used to balance the books when Sexton plunged for Garry Birtles of Nottingham Forest, a prolific score who had netted 32 times in his 87 League games under Brian Clough. This, it was felt, was a better pedigree than young Ritchie's 13 goals in 26 full appearances. Ritchie was, however, still a month away from his 20th birthday, and revealed after the move that he felt he had been the target of too much criticism from assistant manager Tommy Cavanagh, and this contributed to his eagerness to leave.

Birtles cost United a massive £1,250,000, the largest amount up to that time (October 1980) that the club had paid for any player. His inclusion in the side brought two successive

victories, although Birtles himself failed to score.

Those wins at Stoke and at home to Everton proved merely to be an oasis in a desert of drawn games, and a 1–0 defeat at Crystal Palace on 1 November served as a harsh reminder that Sexton's ship was not sailing on a steady course. He could claim that half the crew was missing, but the storm clouds were beginning to build up and United's hopes of winning the Championship were sinking fast. Half the season had gone and United's two defeats were swamped by 13 drawn matches and only six victories as ahead lay the busy Christmas period.

McQueen was still out, Wilkins had tried to return but aggravated his injury in training, and Buchan, who had missed fewer than 30 games since his arrival in Aberdeen in 1972, had been absent for 12 of the first 21 matches. The management refused to respond to media suggestions that there was a crisis, but all was certainly not right.

After defeats at Arsenal and to Ron Atkinson's West Brom, United stepped into 1981 with three games against Ritchie's club Brighton. Such is the irony of football that the clubs were paired against each other in the third round of the FA Cup a week before their League meeting at Old Trafford.

Ritchie was given a rapturous welcome by the Old Trafford crowd as Birtles returned for his first game in a month after he, too, had joined the ranks of the walking wounded with an ankle injury early in December. Those same supporters joined the travelling fans from Brighton to sing the praises of their former favourite as he headed his new club into a two-goal lead at half-time. The headlines were already being written when United staged a fightback to draw 2–2 and earn a replay at Brighton four days later.

United won 2–0 and Garry Birtles scored his first goal since his expensive move. Wilkins played in both matches although it was obvious that he was below full fitness.

Again fate played its part in the outcome of the season. Having beaten Brighton in the Cup, United were drawn at Nottingham Forest, meaning a return for Birtles. However, unlike Ritchie, Birtles was unable to score against his old club and Forest won 1–0. With 15 matches left there was only the Championship to aim for and there was speculation that Dave Sexton's future lay in the balance.

Would the selling of Ritchie, a player who had cost the club nothing, prove to be an expensive mistake by Sexton? Certainly Birtles had not shown anything like the goalscoring he had produced for Clough, and the result was a slump from the end of January until mid-March, when the club went without a win.

The solidarity given to the defence by the presence of McQueen had been a vital factor missing from the side. He had been out for all but four League games by the time that a revival began.

United were in mid-table and had lost four out of five games, one of these at home to Leeds United, when a lacklustre performance had the crowd shouting for Sexton's head. Was this the type of result to get a manager the sack? Sexton's response was a cold stare, and a reluctant reply: 'That's not the sort of question I can answer. We have had terrible injury problems this season, and everyone knows it.'

His players' response after the fourth of those defeats was to stage a late rally of nine games without losing, and after McQueen's return, seven successive victories, which was the best run by the team since the days of Busby in 1964. But it was too late and on 30 April 1980, five days after the closing victory over Norwich was watched by an Old Trafford crowd of 12,000 fewer than that of the previous season, Dave Sexton lost his job.

He was stunned by the news, but refused to criticise the club. He had taken United higher than anyone since Busby yet had failed, but he remained the gentleman to the end, saying only in private: 'There can be few managers who have lost their job after seven consecutive victories . . .'

The 1980s: Atkinson and Ferguson

Republic of Ireland striker Frank Stapleton eludes Mark Lawrenson of Liverpool, one of his international colleagues. Only a decision to move to Anfield rather than Old Trafford prevented the two playing together at club level. Stapleton was bought by Atkinson in the summer of 1981 in a move which caused ill-feeling between United and the directors of Arsenal the club which reluctantly sold him

Success, it would seem, is not the sole criteria by which the manager of Manchester United is judged. He can achieve success on the field yet still fail in the eyes of his employers, or the majority of supporters, or both. It is not the success but how it is achieved which matters most, and the narrowness of the line between pleasing board and fans or leaving them cold illustrates the fragility of the manager's position.

The man walking the tightrope may well be able to cross from end to end without a fall, but if he does so with no excitement for his audience, no hint that he might slip, then what is the point of him being up there in the first place?

Docherty walked the tightrope with a touch of flair and showmanship, yet still stumbled. Sexton was sure-footed but lost his balance when the audience failed to respond to his obvious talents. Whoever was to follow these two would need to be a combination of them both.

Such is the enormity of the managerial task it could be beyond the grasp of a man who simply knows how to select a winning side. He needs to be able to project the right image, mingle with both grass-root supporter and distinguished guest and not seem out of place with either, and have the gift of man managment as well as a steady hand when dealing with large cash transactions. All this in one man?

Immediately after the decision to terminate the contracts of both Sexton and his assistant Tommy Cavanagh, United began the search for a replacement. As in the past, the name of Brian Clough was mentioned, and reasons were given by the newspaper speculators as to why, and why not, the Nottingham Forest manager could be approached.

Lawrie McMenemy, who had taken Southampton from obscurity to success, was said to be the name at the top of the club's short list. McMenemy had the right public image to prove popular with the fans, had the obvious ability to manage, and if he could achieve such heights at a club as small as Southampton, then what would he do with a giant like United? McMenemy had been the man who had brought England's

biggest star since George Best back to the Football League after he had earned his fortune in West Germany, and if he could persuade Kevin Keegan to play for him, could he get other world stars to respond in the same way?

McMenemy had his own views on management which seemed so close to the unwritten guidelines of the club: 'You don't have to win trophies to be successful. The biggest thing is getting the best out of what you have got, and giving the public what it wants.'

But, when given the chance, McMenemy turned down the opportunity to give Manchester United's public what it wanted.

Ron Atkinson gets the job

Bobby Robson's name was also linked with the vacancy, before eventually, in June 1981, the new man was chosen. He was a Liverpudlian, whose managerial rise had been swift. From the parochial surroundings of Kettering Town to the awe-inspiring heights of Old Trafford was the route for Ronald Frederick Atkinson.

Ron Atkinson had shown at West Bromwich Albion that he was capable of producing a first-class team with limited resources, and the step he took from the Hawthorns to Manchester United was perhaps for him not such a giant stride as had been his moving to West Bromwich from his first League club after Kettering, Cambridge United. His credentials were based on his previous successful managership. Ron Atkinson had been a hero of Oxford United in his playing days, taking part in their drive from Southern League to Second Division, but it was not his playing background which had seen him recognised as the right material to lead Manchester United back to greatness.

A larger-than-life character, his arrival at Old Trafford brought swift changes. In came Atkinson, and out went coaches Harry Gregg and Jack Crompton, youth coach Syd Owen, and physiotherapist Laurie Brown. The new broom was indeed making a clean sweep as Atkinson brought in his own backroom staff to replace those with links to the past. Crompton and

Gregg had ties with the great sides of the three decades after the Second World War, but Ron Atkinson wanted his own men in the backroom.

Mick Brown, his right-hand man at West Brom, was appointed assistant manager. Brian Whitehouse, another from the Hawthorns, became chief coach, and Eric Harrison took charge of the youth team after leaving Everton's staff. The man who replaced Laurie Brown was Jim Headridge, physiotherapist at Bolton Wanderers, but tragedy struck before the new season was under way when, during a training session, he collapsed and died at the Cliff Training Ground. The man described by Atkinson as 'the best physio in the business' was eventually replaced by Jim McGregor, a popular choice, who had been at Goodison Park with Harrison, and before that at Oldham Athletic.

The first gap Atkinson had to fill on the field was that left by Joe Jordan who, as soon as his contract allowed him, had signed for Italian giants AC Milan, adding more weight to the predictions of Sexton in 1978. The new manager bought Frank Stapleton from Arsenal, who unlike Brady, his fellow countryman, decided to seek his fortune in Manchester rather than follow him abroad when his contract also ended. But his move north caused some ill feeling between the two clubs.

Arsenal wanted close on £2 million for their striker, while United reckoned him to be worth £750,000. In the end a League Tribunal fixed the price at £900,000, and this upset Arsenal. Their directors refused to dine with United's the next time the clubs met and it took several months before the matter was settled – but Arsenal got a cheque for only £900,000. United need not have paid anything for the tall, dark-haired Irishman as, together with David O'Leary, he had trained in Manchester as a 15-year-old on a summer scheme. Neither boy had been seen as a potential player and both were allowed to slip through the net.

Atkinson's next buy was John Gidman, the Everton right-back whose move from Goodison included the sale of Mickey Thomas to the Merseyside club. Both new players arrived too late to take part in a pre-season tournament in Scotland where United lost to Southampton and West Ham and clearly showed their recently appointed manager that there was a need for change. The man in charge of the host club was also one day to be connected to United . . . Alex Ferguson of Aberdeen.

Dave Sexton meanwhile had been appointed manager of Coventry City, and the first fixture of the season had a hint of inevitability about it – Coventry City versus Manchester United.

Both Stapleton and Gidman played in that opening game, but the problems of the previous season were still apparent, and although a Lou Macari goal gave United some hope, it was Coventry City – and Dave Sexton – who celebrated the first win of the season. Sexton's new side had beaten his old one 2–1.

Atkinson knew exactly what was expected from him. In his book 'United to Win' (Sidgwick and Jackson, 1984) he wrote:

From the moment I stepped through the door at Old Trafford I was under no illusions about the size of the task which confronted me. Although the club and its fans claimed they were the greatest in the world the argument did not hold water in the terms of recent achievements. The brutal truth is that Manchester United and its supporters were living in a fools' paradise, and had been doing so for some considerable time.

The late victories at the end of the previous season had helped to gloss over the fact that things were coming apart at the seams. Manchester United was simply not good enough to contemplate a tilt at any of the major prizes in the game.

Atkinson had been unsuccessful in his attempts to bring several players he wanted to Old Trafford before the season began. Glenn Hoddle decided to stay at White Hart Lane, despite an attractive offer from United's new manager. Mark Lawrenson said he would join Liverpool when a deal which would have taken Jimmy Nicholl and Ashley Grimes to Brighton in a cash-plus-player move fell through, and Frank Worthington slipped through Atkinson's fingers when he made the move from Birmingham to Leeds. Even though Worthington was over 30 the United manager felt that his flair and entertaining skills would have filled a void at the club which had not been done since the days of Denis Law.

Another player who attracted Atkinson was

The summer of 1981 and Ron Atkinson faces the media after being appointed manager of United. Atkinson outlines his plans for the future of the club under the watchful eye of chairman Martin Edwards, but like all those who succeeded Matt Busby, the championship eluded him and the ghosts of the 1960s were forever around him

Forest's Trevor Francis, but the £1 million fee quoted by Brian Clough was too high, and when Middlesbrough asked for £600,000 for David Armstrong, Atkinson decided that he would return to his old club for the talent needed to transform United.

Atkinson signs Bryan Robson

In a deal worth more than £2 million West Brom agreed to sell Bryan Robson and Remi Moses to United. This fee, together with the £70,000 compensation for the loss of their manager certainly made the Midlands club richer financially, if poorer in the playing area. While the haggling over the total cost of both players went on Moses was allowed to move north to his home town. He had been raised in Manchester's Moss Side, and he made his debut by coming on as substitute in the side's first win of the new season against Swansea City at Old Trafford.

That game also marked another milestone. Garry Birtles scored his first League goal, after 29 previous games without success. Was this to be the turning point Atkinson hoped for?

Robson was eventually signed too late to make his debut against Wolves on 3 October 1981, but he was paraded before a crowd of close on 47,000 and his presence, after the spectacle of an on-the-pitch signing, seemed to rub off on his new colleagues. The carnival atmosphere created by the event probably contributed to United running in their biggest win of the season, overwhelming struggling Wolves 5–0. Sammy McIlroy, sensing that his days in midfield might now be numbered, hit a hat-trick,

and Birtles and Stapleton scored the other goals.

Robson's fee had finally been settled at £1.5 million, making him the costliest player in Britain at that time, and he eventually made his league debut in the perfect setting of the derby game at Maine Road, in front of 52,037 supporters, who saw him give a solid performance in a 0–0 draw.

Gordon McQueen was plagued by injury for most of Atkinson's first season, allowing Kevin Moran to establish himself further. Only Ray Wilkins and Albiston played in every League game, with Robson making 32 out of a possible 33 appearances as the side showed distinct signs of improvement and finished third in the table behind Liverpool and Ipswich Town.

United failed in the two domestic cup competitions, however, losing 1–0 at Watford in the FA Cup and by the same scoreline in both legs of their League Cup-ties against Tottenham Hotspur, where Bryan Robson made his club debut. But as third-placed club in the First Division they qualified for the UEFA Cup in Atkinson's second season.

Whiteside makes his debut

Towards the end of that first term, when the Championship had slipped out of reach, the new manager had tried some of his younger players, and after using him once as substitute against Brighton, gave Norman Whiteside his first taste of a full League game. The raw-boned, strong Irish lad was only 17 years and eight days old when he made that full debut, and the future certainly looked brighter than Atkinson had first

Ron Atkinson adds his name to the contract already signed by Bryan Robson the player he groomed in his days as manager of West Brom. A huge crowd filled Old Trafford to witness the signing and the biggest win of the season – 5–0 against Wolves – with Sammy McIlroy, the player about to lose his place to Robson, scoring a hat-trick. Watching the on-the-pitch proceedings are chairman Martin Edwards and secretary Leslie Olive (standing)

painted it when he showed his flair for scoring goals in a 2–0 win over Stoke City.

Watching Whiteside with a certain amount of pride from the heart of the opposing midfield was Sammy McIlroy, who had been transferred that February for £350,000, ending his links with the club he had joined as a schoolboy. He said:

I'd known Norman since he was a young lad. He must have been about 13 when he first came to Old Trafford and whenever the kids from Northern Ireland came over I always made sure that I had a chat with them, and because I was in the international side I suppose it meant a lot to them.

I knew Norman was going to be something special, because he was a man well before his time. We used to joke that he was nine when he was born!

He was big and strong and difficult to knock off the ball, and he had a lot of good control for a big player.

It's always a special feeling when a youngster you have known makes it to the top and the Big Man's stayed a close friend and we have played together many times for Northern Ireland.

Whiteside in fact got his international break just weeks after making his full League debut, when he was flown out to Spain with the Northern Ireland squad for the 1982 World Cup. He played in all his country's games, helping them to reach the second phase of the competition before being knocked out by France, and found his own place in the record books as the youngest player up that time to have played in the finals. The previous holder of that title was none other than Pelé.

As for Sammy McIlroy, he was given a testimonial by the club, and for the game brought Tommy Docherty back to Old Trafford along with his stars of 1977, and the reunited squad showed Ron Atkinson that they still had plenty of skill left in them.

Whiteside had emerged from Eric Harrison's Youth Team, which for the first time since 1964 – when George Best was in the side – reached the final of the FA Youth Cup. Also playing in the team was Mark Hughes.

In the summer of 1982 Atkinson again moved into the transfer market and took advantage of the end of Arnold Muhren's contract with Ipswich to sign the Dutch star.

Then he brought Peter Beardsley back into English football after he had played in the North American Soccer League with Vancouver Whitecaps, the side which had signed Jimmy Nicholl six months earlier, thereby taking him back to his Canadian birthplace. The 21-year-old Beardsley had been watched by United when he was with Carlisle, but had not been signed. Atkinson felt that the player might fit into his plans but he played only part of one game before being allowed to move away, and eventually he signed for Newcastle United.

In 1987 Beardsley was transferred from Newcastle to Liverpool for a record fee of £1.9 million.

Atkinson's plans of building his side around the goalscoring skills of Garry Birtles had been scrapped by the time the 1982–83 season got under way, and the player who cost a million was sold back to Nottingham Forest for just £300,000.

It was difficult for the supporters to understand why the club appeared to be losing money. A sponsorship deal with Japanese electronics company Sharp had brought in revenue, and attendances had averaged 44,571 during the 1981–82 season, yet the accounts showed that transfer purchases had run up a massive debt of over £2,200,000.

The Sharp sponsorship included the introduction of a new design of shirt bearing the words 'Sharp Electronics' but these could only be worn for games which were not shown on television, a ruling which was later dropped. There was some adverse comment that United should associate itself with a foreign based company, but there were some strong connections between the electronics giant and the football club – not simply because Sharp employed many supporters in their Manchester workforce.

The Sharp depot at Newton Heath is virtually the site of the railway yards where the workers of the Lancashire and Yorkshire Railway formed their football team. It is certainly close enough to feel that those men of 1878 must have walked through it on their way to and from their work. Reason enough for the link, although Martin Edwards would go a step further: 'Sharp are the leaders of their particular field and I would like to think that we as a football club are leaders of ours. Like Manchester United the name of Sharp is known throughout the world, and any sponsor we were to get involved with had to be a company of this stature.'

Certainly the team looked 'sharp' in their opening games of the new season, beating Birmingham City, then Nottingham Forest by three goals to nil, before a defeat at West Brom, where Bryan Robson scored against his old club, was followed by three more wins. By late September United were top of the First Division.

However, once again it was not to be their year in the Championship race, although in the cup competitions it was a different story.

In the Milk Cup – the Milk Marketing Board had introduced their own trophy for the 1982 final after becoming sponsors of the League Cup – United beat Bournemouth in the first round. However, in the second leg of the tie Ray Wilkins was badly injured and taken to hospital with a fractured cheekbone.

The injury was a major turning point in his career. While out of the game for virtually the whole of the following four months he lost the captaincy of both United and England to Bryan Robson and his absence must have made some contribution to later moves by Atkinson.

The Dutch master, Arnold Muhren whose move to Old Trafford came when his contract at Ipswich Town ended. Muhren later returned to the Netherlands to continue his career with Ajax and in 1988 was in the Dutch side which won the European Championships in West Germany

More problems with supporters

Meanwhile, in Europe United had fallen at the first hurdle, going out of the UEFA Cup to Valencia, and the second leg of that clash had serious repercussions on supporters.

Before the season started chairman Edwards had warned United followers about behaviour abroad. During the summer of 1982 there had been outbreaks of violence in Switzerland and Norway, involving England supporters. In Belgium, rioting by Aston Villa followers had also turned the spotlight on the 'English disease', and Edwards said: 'I hope our fans will behave as well off the field as our team do on it. I feel certain that UEFA officials will clamp down very heavily on any misbehaviour.'

As it turned out it was the Spanish supporters who bore the brunt of the blame for a major outbreak of crowd violence in Valencia. Many United followers claimed that they were the innocent parties when their coaches were stoned and individuals were beaten up by Spanish thugs, but fingers were once more pointed at Britons abroad. In the match programme following the 2–1 defeat Atkinson wrote:

I hope our Spanish experience will give us an extra incentive, and while the inquests have been quite detailed I cannot let our short dramatic entry in the UEFA Cup go by without paying tribute to both our players and our supporters.

Our lads were bitterly disaopinted, and they tackled the tie with the kind of attitude and composure that I expect from the team, but it was always going to be difficult and we were playing a very provocative team. Our supporters were given a rough ride by the Valencia supporters and even suffered violence from the Spanish police, which was quite appalling. It is not easy to be a fan abroad these days and while we must never cease trying to make sure our own behaviour is impeccable the United following was subjected to a great deal of harassment.

The club's official approach to the increasing problem was to state that there would no longer be any organised trips for supporters abroad and to ask that in future supporters did not travel to foreign away games.

Football itself was on the verge of a major debate about its future. In October 1982 there were discussions about the possible change of the game's financial structure with proposals that clubs might keep their own match day takings for home fixtures rather than give the visiting side a percentage share. Other suggestions being tabled by various chairmen included the formation of a 'Super League' made up of the larger clubs – but was this not what former League Secretary Alan Hardaker had mooted in the 1970s?

On the field United's progress in the Milk Cup took them to Bradford City's Valley Parade, where 15,568 crammed into a stadium which was to be the scene of a terrible fire tragedy in 1985. The game ended in a 0–0 draw as, for the first time, the United teamsheet included the name of Paul McGrath, a tall central defender who had been born in London, yet raised in Dublin, and who spoke with a soft Irish accent. He had recovered from a cartilage operation which had halted his progress but he did well enough to stay in the side for the League game with Tottenham three days later, when Arnie Muhren scored his first goal for the club in a 1–0 win.

McGrath had replaced the injured Kevin Moran, but Moran returned in time for the replay with Bradford City and scored one of the four goals which took United through to the fourth round. The opponents this time were Laurie McMenemy's Southampton, and Gordon McQueen and Norman Whiteside scored the two goals which took United to the next stage. Confidence was high at the turn of the year but Steve Coppell was having problems with a knee injury picked up while on duty for England, and with him sidelined, Ray Wilkins came back for the last game of 1982, a 3–0 defeat at Coventry.

United were third in the table at the start of 1983 but Liverpool were ten points clear at the top. After beating West Ham 2–0 in the third round of the FA Cup, United thrashed a Birtles-less Nottingham Forest 4–0 to reach the Milk Cup semi-final. Wembley seemed a distinct possibility but Ron Atkinson refused to make any predictions: 'That isn't our style. Of course we want to win things, but let's win them first and talk about them later.'

However, the feeling inside the United camp was one of optimism that while they might not be able to catch Liverpool in the League they stood a good chance in both cups. This optim-

Right: Bryan Robson scores his second goal against France in the 1982 World Cup finals in Spain. Robson found his way into the record books earlier in the game when he put England in front after only 27 seconds. This is the fastest goal scored in the finals and is yet to be surpassed

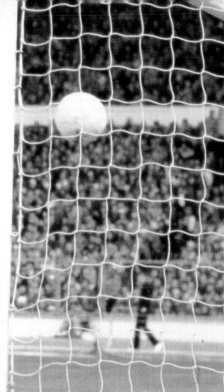

ism turned out to be well founded, and after United beat Arsenal in an opening leg of the Milk Cup semi-final, Wembley was just a game away.

That first leg was played at Highbury and at one stage United led 4–0, and only two late goals by the home side gave them any hope of success at Old Trafford. As it turned out United won the second leg 2–1 to reach Wembley with an impressive 6–3 aggregate. In the other semi-final Liverpool had beaten Burnley, so once more it was the 'old enemy' standing in the way of a major trophy.

United were also progressing in the FA Cup, and by the time the Milk Cup Final was played on 26 March 1983, had reached the semi-final of that competition. Two visits to Wembley in one season? There was a chance.

Unlucky Milk Cup defeat at Wembley

The team to face Liverpool was selected from the fit players Atkinson had at his disposal. Gidman had been out all season, Macari had earned himself the nickname of 'the Judge' (having appeared on the bench more times than any other player in the squad) and just before the final Bryan Robson was hurt. It was the first time since his arrival from West Bromwich Albion that United had to play without their new skipper for more than one game. He had badly torn ankle ligaments in the game against Arsenal, so Wilkins came back just in time. With Martin Buchan now a forgotten man in the reserves the line up was:

Bailey, Duxbury, Albiston, Moses, Moran, McQueen, Wilkins, Muhren, Stapleton, Whiteside, Coppell. Sub: Macari.

The final brought bitter disappointment for Ron Atkinson and his players. Norman Whiteside scored a great goal after only 12 minutes, but then United's problems started. Kevin Moran was badly hurt in a tackle and

forced to limp off, making way for the tiny Macari to come on to the field, then Gordon McQueen tore a hamstring. Macari was switched to right full-back, and his striker colleague Frank Stapleton pulled back into the defence to take over from the hobbling McQueen, who tried his best to complete the game.

Inevitably Liverpool equalised when a long range shot from full-back Alan Kennedy beat Bailey, and it looked as if it was all over. Somehow United held out until the whistle for the end of normal time and had to play a further half-hour of extra time with their crippled resources. Ron Atkinson recalls:

Our only hope was to hold out for that final 30 minutes, but Liverpool won when Ronnie Whelan scored a spectacular goal ten minutes into the first period of extra time. He ran down our right flank and I thought he was looking up to pass inside, but then he hit a powerful curling shot into the roof of our net. Gary Bailey had no chance with that one, but I should imagine that the first goal will haunt him for the rest of his life. I'm sure he knows he should have stopped it.

There was one major moment of controversy in the game, and it involved the Liverpool goalkeeper, Bruce Grobbelaar. At one stage he left his area and brought down the injured Gordon McQueen as he limped down the right wing with the ball. It seemed to many that he should have been sent off, but he escaped, and so apparently did Liverpool.

With the Milk Cup handed to Bob Paisley who was retiring as Liverpool's manager, United had now to concentrate on a return to Wembley in the FA Cup. In that competition they had followed their third-round win over West Ham with a 2–0 victory at Luton. Then came Derby County at the Baseball Ground and a 1–0 win through another Norman Whiteside goal.

In the sixth round United were paired with

Crippled by injuries and with Lou Macari playing full-back as Frank Stapleton found himself in the back four, United were hoping to hold on until extra-time against Liverpool in the 1983 Milk Cup final. Ronnie Whelan had other ideas, he hit a long range curling shot which beat Gary Bailey and took the trophy to Anfield

Everton at Old Trafford, and it provided one of the most amazing spectacles of Atkinson's spell in charge. United were still third in the League and the Everton tie was just seven days after a 2–1 victory at Maine Road. The crowds were flocking to watch United. In four fixtures, the Arsenal Milk Cup-tie at Old Trafford, a 1–1 home draw with Liverpool, the City game, and the Everton Cup-tie, they had attracted a total of 217,630 spectators, the largest number, 58,198, packing Old Trafford for the Everton clash.

The Everton side was captained by Mark Higgins, and Ray Wilkins led United in Robson's absence. Also missing from the Merseysiders' line-up was Peter Reid, who remembers the game vividly:

It was a real Cup tie; high-speed football played right from the kick-off with both sides coming close to scoring several times. If anything I would have felt that Everton had perhaps done enough to deserve a draw, and we were just getting ready for the final whistle, and the announcement of the replay details, when Ron Atkinson played his trump card.

That trump card was Lou Macari. Atkinson remembers:

I was looking for a player to pull off so that I could get Louie into the game. I shouted to the nearest player to me, I think it was Arthur Albiston, but he didn't hear me, although Mike Duxbury looked across towards the bench. I signalled for him to come off the field and pushed little Louie out . . . at that point

I'd have pulled Gary Bailey off if he had looked my way! Play was down the left flank, Louie jumped up to knock down a high ball, I think it was only the second touch he had – he'd only been on the field for a few moments – and Frank Stapleton hit a shot at goal. Jim Arnold had no chance, the ball bent round his arm and into the net. The Judge had done it again!

The shrewd use of the substitute paid off, and United were in a semi-final for the second time that season. Of the three clubs left in the competition United drew what many felt was the toughest opponent for the last hurdle before Wembley, Arsenal, while in the other game Sheffield Wednesday and Brighton battled for the right to face the winners.

Wembley again

Villa Park staged the United–Arsenal encounter, and it seemed at one point as if the Londoners would get revenge for the Milk Cup defeat when Tony Woodcock put them ahead with a crisp stab ten minutes before half-time. But in the second half United began firing on all cylinders, and Ashley Grimes picked out the now fit Robson with a perfectly flighted cross from the left flank and watched as his skipper blasted the ball past George Wood, the Arsenal goalkeeper.

United's football matched the sunshine of Birmingham, and Norman Whiteside's winning goal was the brightest moment of the afternoon.

It was a goal from Norman Whiteside which took United to Wembley for a second time in 1983. The youngster scored from long range as the Reds fought back from behind in the semi-final against Arsenal at Villa Park. Bryan Robson scored United's equaliser from a precise cross from Ashley Grimes and after the disappointment of the Milk Cup defeat United booked their return ticket

He remembers it:

> Arthur Albiston took the ball on a run down the left, and I could see an opening. As his pass reached me I went for the volley and I knew I had hit a sweet shot. The ball flew into the net, and there was no way anyone was going to stop us after that moment.

Lowly Brighton were winners of the other semi-final, beating their Second Division opponents 2–1 and finding themselves in the rare position of being destined for relegation as bottom club while still in with a chance of winning a major honour.

The build-up to Wembley saw both finalists being hit by bad luck. Steve Foster, the Brighton captain, was booked during a game at Notts County and automatically suspended from the final, and three days later at Highbury, disaster struck Remi Moses.

Having twice beaten the London side in vital games the League match was understandably a clash of high tension which exploded in the second half with an incident described by Ron Atkinson in his book:

> We were without Frank Stapleton, Arnold Muhren, Bryan Robson, Steve Coppell and Arthur Albiston, through injuries, and not surprisingly were losing the match 3–0. Some of the Arsenal players had not been too happy with Remi Moses since his all-action performances against them in two semi-finals. Moses clashed with Arsenal's Peter Nicholas and was sent off by the referee, Eric Reid, for allegedly butting the Highbury player. I had a perfectly clear view of the entire incident and to this day remain absolutely convinced that Moses, if not the cruel victim of outrageous gamesmanship, was unlucky that the referee was unsighted at the crucial moment.

Atkinson felt that the linesman closest to the United bench had seen the incident, and he shouted to him to tell the referee what had happened. The linesman ignored him, but as Moses left the field referee Reid lectured Atkinson for leaving the bench. The United manager swore at the official and was later censured for 'bringing the game into disrepute'. The following day Atkinson was quoted in the sports pages of several national newspapers:

> Last week at the Wembley international I was in conversation with an Arsenal player who told me they were out to get Moses. That is what happened. Moses stood still and the Arsenal player went down. He could not have fallen harder if he'd been hit by a steam hammer. I think it's a sad day when players attempt to get other members of their own profession booked or sent off.

Moses was out of the final and so was Foster. The Brighton player took his suspension to the High Court, claiming that he was being deprived of his rights to play football by the ruling, but the case was dismissed.

United were also without the stricken Steve Coppell, and at one stage it seemed as if Laurie Cunningham would make a sensational return to big-time English football. Cunningham had been transferred from West Brom to Real Madrid in 1978, but after being hailed as a hero by the Spanish crowds he was injured, and slipped out of the spotlight. Ron Atkinson offered him the chance to pick up the pieces of a shattered career and took him on loan in March 1983, bringing him on as substitute for the game at Everton which United lost 2–0. Four days later Cunningham replaced full-back Albiston during the home game against Watford, and scored the only goal of his short stay at the club. But he was not to play in the Cup final.

During the build-up Gary Bailey was injured and replaced by Jeff Wealands, who had moved to Old Trafford from Birmingham City, and there were other scares as McQueen was again hurt, and Arthur Albiston was still having treatment. By the time the final arrived United found themselves firm favourites. Having finished third in the Championship behind Liverpool and Watford, they knew that they had a last and outstanding chance of glory at Wembley.

Brighton made history by arriving at the stadium by helicopter, but it was a story of a different kind which made the headlines. After just two League games United had called up an unknown youngster, Alan Davies, a Manchester-born player who claimed a loyalty to Wales because his grandparents came from there. Davies wore the number 11 shirt vacated by Steve Coppell and soon got involved 'I remember that I was quite nervous at the start and I wanted to make sure that I got into the game quickly. The other lads were great to me, Ray Wilkins and Arnold Muhren gave me plenty of encouragement and it was a tremendous moment for me.'

There were fears in the United camp that the game might go the same way as the 1976 final, when underdogs Southampton had beaten the favourites, and when Brighton scored first and still led at the interval Ron Atkinson had to lift his players. Ten minutes into the second period Mike Duxbury broke down the right, overlapping with Davies, and crossed the ball towards the edge of the penalty area. Whiteside flicked on across the face of the Brighton goal, and Frank Stapleton was there at the far post to force the ball home. Brighton's goalkeeper, Graham Moseley (a Manchester-born player) had no chance, and even less with United's second.

Ray Wilkins had scored few goals during his time at Old Trafford, but in the 74th minute he set Wembley alight with a bending long-range shot which curled around Moseley and into the net. Sixteen minutes remained and United led 2–1. It seemed as if the Cup was destined for Old Trafford until three minutes before the end of the game. Brighton's Gary Stevens then fired home a shot which beat Gary Bailey. The goal had started with a corner taken by Jimmy Case, scorer of Liverpool's equaliser against United in 1977. Was this to be his revenge for that defeat

six years before?

The game went into extra time and in one last desperate surge Brighton almost stole the Cup. Michael Robinson, whose career had seen him at one time playing in Manchester with City, pulled a cross over to the feet of Gordon Smith, scorer of the afternoon's first goal. Smith ran into the six-yard box, but Bailey, possibly remembering the last moments of his previous FA Cup final, threw himself bravely at the Brighton player, blocking the shot completely.

The game ended in deadlock, with a replay five days later. United fielded the same team:

Bailey, Duxbury, Albiston, Wilkins, Moran, McQueen, Robson, Muhren, Stapleton, Whiteside, Davies.

Cup winners again

Brighton had the suspended Foster back, but Moses' two-match suspension meant that he also missed the replay. However, he was there to celebrate as United ran Brighton into the ground.

Davies was magnificent and his performance caught the eye of the Welsh FA, who called him up for their summer internationals.

It was Davies who combined with Arthur Albiston to lay on the first of two first-half goals which destroyed the Brighton challenge. Robson scored from the final pass and then two minutes

later Davies tipped on a corner from Arnie Muhren and Norman Whiteside scored to add another line to his pedigree. In a year when he had played his first full season, and with a World Cup behind him, he had scored in both Wembley finals of 1983.

Brighton hit back and Case came close to scoring, but Bailey made a good save as the ball seemed to be passing over his head. Then, almost on half time, Robson scored his second, running on to a Stapleton header. Three goals in front at the break, United were out of Brighton's reach. There was only one additional goal in the second half, scored from the penalty spot by Arnie Muhren after Robson had been pulled back by Gary Stevens, and the Cup was on its way back to Manchester.

Ironically the official welcome for the team had been the day following the original final, when the players rode on an open-top bus from Dunham Massey, near Altrincham, into the city centre. The Cup-less heroes had been hailed by their supporters along the seven-mile route, but after they won the trophy there was no civic reception. Instead the team travelled home by train to be greeted by several thousand supporters at the Manchester end of the line, then the squad split up, with the internationals joining their various groups in preparation for the home nations clashes.

The Cup did go on a tour of the area, three

Below: For Brighton's Manchester-born goalkeeper Graham Moseley the 1983 FA Cup final was an occasion to forget. He became the first 'keeper in post-war finals to concede a total of six goals, two in the original match and four in the replay. Here he grasps at fresh air as Ray Wilkins runs in to challenge, before Norman Whiteside grabs United's second

Left: Bryan Robson scores his second goal in the 1983 FA Cup final as the Brighton defence reels under United pressure. The 4–0 victory took the Cup back to Old Trafford after a gap of six years and it was the first time that United had been involved in a replay in the last stage of the game's most prestigious tournament

Below: The dreams of Brighton are shattered as Arnold Muhren scores United's fourth goal in the 1983 FA Cup final replay. Brighton had their moments of glory in the 2–2 draw five days earlier, but they found United in a ruthless mood for the second game and goals from Robson (2) and Whiteside paved the way for a memorable victory before Muhren hammered in the last nail

days after the final, when it was carried on the same open-topped bus by Gary Bailey, as the vehicle headed a field of almost 10,000 runners taking part in the Piccadilly Radio Marathon – perhaps the most unusual 'homecoming' there has ever been, and certainly one of the longest.

During the summer of 1983 Atkinson again turned his attention to the transfer market and was ready to make another major signing. The spotlight in Scotland had fallen on Charlie Nicholas of Celtic who had been in terrific form throughout the previous season. Atkinson and chairman Martin Edwards drove to London for talks with the player who was in the Scottish squad which was preparing for the game against England at Wembley. They spoke, and were under the impression that Nicholas was ready to agree to join United.

Nicholas was also fancied by Liverpool and Arsenal. After meeting Atkinson he told reporters: 'Atkinson talked more about himself than he did about Manchester United and me. He came on far too strong, and by the time the meeting was half way through I knew my dreams of playing for United had ended. Ron and I would not have got on.' It was obvious that he was not going to sign for Atkinson. Instead Nicholas joined Arsenal for £750,000, and Atkinson later wrote:

I was disturbed not so much by the words as by the sentiments in the article. If my behaviour had been as described I wasn't aware of it. I asked the chairman if I had come across that way in the meeting and I was assured that Nicholas' words in no way reflected the facts of the matter.

Atkinson later said he did not regret not signing Nicholas.

He did buy Arthur Graham from Leeds United for £45,000 as cover for Steve Coppell, who was still recovering from surgery when the new season was about to start. United spent some of the close season in Swaziland together with Tottenham Hotspur as the clubs played in a series of competitive exhibition games, and this once again led to speculation that Ron Atkinson was about to sign Glenn Hoddle. However, the club was linked with many players during the summer of 1983. Gary Lineker of Leicester City, Steve Archibald, Hoddle's colleague at

Right: The jubilant players celebrate victory in the replay of the 1983 FA Cup final. It was a case of third time lucky for United that season, having lost to Liverpool in the Milk Cup, then drawn with Brighton five days before the replay, their next trip to Wembley brought success

Below right: The Martin Buchan Testimonial brought Alex Ferguson to Old Trafford as manager of the successful Aberdeen – Buchan's first club. Buchan linked together five of the managers who followed Sir Matt Busby. He was bought by Frank O'Farrell, played on under Docherty, Sexton and finally Atkinson, and then for his final appearance before moving on to Oldham Athletic, was able to introduce Ferguson to the club he would take charge of in 1986

Tottenham, and Paul Walsh of Luton Town were said to be Atkinson's targets but no signs of deals materialised.

The sports pages also carried reports that Bryan Robson and Norman Whiteside were wanted by Italian giants AC Milan, and that Arsenal were ready to negotiate for an exchange deal which would take Ray Wilkins to Highbury, as Alan Sunderland moved north. Former City winger Peter Barnes was also linked to United by speculation.

Players did leave Old Trafford. Three days before the new season began with the Charity Shield at Wembley, Martin Buchan's testimonial game was played, with Alex Ferguson bringing his successful Aberdeen side to Manchester. Buchan had begun his playing career at Pittodrie, and the game served as a fitting tribute to a player who up to that time was the only man to have captained sides which had won the Scottish and the English FA Cups.

Aberdeen's appearance at Old Trafford gave Ron Atkinson the opportunity of having a close look at Gordon Strachan, a right-sided midfield player who seemed perfect to fill the gap left by Coppell, although he was still optimistic that the injured player would return.

The obvious replacement, Alan Davies, was the victim of a cruel stroke of bad luck just as he was about to become a regular in the side. The hero of the Cup final had played for Wales in their games against Northern Ireland and Brazil in the weeks after Wembley then, just as the new season was about to start, he broke a leg. He was playing for the reserve side in a friendly at Stamford in Lincolnshire, and before half-time found himself in hospital. The injury wrecked

MARTIN BUCHAN TESTIMONIAL
Manchester United v. **Aberdeen**
F.A. Cup Winners 1983   European Cup Winners' Cup and Scottish F.A. Cup Winners 1983
OLD TRAFFORD, WEDNESDAY; 17th AUGUST, 1983 KICK-OFF 7·30 p.m.
Donation **50p**

his career at Old Trafford. Although he managed to return before the end of the 1983–84 season, the opportunity to establish himself had vanished.

Martin Buchan moved to Oldham Athletic four days after his testimonial, and 24 hours later Ashley Grimes was sold to Coventry City.

Buchan's move came the day after United had beaten Liverpool in the Charity Shield, their fourth visit to Wembley in a year, their second victory. Once again Bryan Robson was the hero, scoring both goals.

Coppell's retirement

Arthur Graham made his debut for the club in the Charity Shield, and by the time it was announced that Steve Coppell was being forced into premature retirement because of his knee injury, the Scot had established himself as a member of the squad.

Coppell was shattered by the decision that he must give up:

I always felt that I would recover from the injury, but as time went on after the operation I knew that I wouldn't be able to play again. It is a terrible thing to face. We all know that when we get into our 30s our playing days will terminate, but I was only 28. I didn't know what to do. Obviously I had academic qualifications, having been to university, but I was a footballer, and I wanted to stay in the game.

After leaving the club Steve became the youngest manager in the Football League when he took charge of Crystal Palace.

United began the 1983–84 season with a 3–1 win over Queen's Park Rangers, but after leading 1–0 at half-time, lost to Nottingham Forest in the second successive home fixture.

The side began by playing attractive football, and eight wins and just two defeats in the eleven games to the end of October saw them sitting on top of the First Division, and there were signs that the future might be even brighter as a young striker emerged from the youth team.

Mark Hughes was beginning to cause a minor sensation in the lower teams. In a pre-season friendly against Port Vale he scored five times in a 10–0 win, and when United were paired with the Potteries club in the Milk Cup, Hughes came on as substitute in a 3–0 aggregate win.

Hughes eventually made his full debut at Oxford's Manor Ground in the fourth round of the Milk Cup, and scored in a 1–1 draw, but the tie proved to be the end of United in the competition that season. The replay at Old Trafford ended 1–1 after extra time and in the third game United were beaten 2–1 by an extra-time goal on a night when Gary Bailey was missing through injury, and Bryan Robson limped off before the end.

The defence of the FA Cup was no luckier and Ron Atkinson's fury after his players were beaten 2–0 by Third Division Bournemouth was only matched by that of the supporters, who chanted 'Atkinson out!' And this to a manager whose team had won the FA Cup and Charity Shield the previous season and which was currently lying second in the table to Liverpool.

If Atkinson's turn on the Old Trafford tightrope was not providing the supporters with thrills then they were hard to please, and by March, when Hughes was brought back into the

side and played at Barcelona in the third round of the Cup-winners' Cup the excitement reached fever pitch. This was the brilliant tie in which, after losing 2–0 at Nou Camp Stadium, United won 3–0 before 58,547 at Old Trafford, beating Barcelona and Maradona 3–2 on aggregate.

Once toppled from the top of the League table, United were constantly in the shadow of Liverpool, yet beat them at Old Trafford and drew at Anfield after leading for most of the game. Liverpool finished Champions, United fourth. During the season Graeme Hogg was introduced to the side, replacing McQueen, who was again injured at the start of 1984.

Alan Davies had a short but illustrious spell in the United side. Brought in to fill the gap left by the injury to Steve Coppell towards the end of the 1983 season, he had an outstanding FA Cup final and replay. Then after he had played for Wales, birthplace of his grandparents, he broke his leg before he had the opportunity to establish himself in the First division. Eventually he left the club to join Newcastle

Wilkins goes to Italy

However, it was the transfer of a player away from the club which made the biggest impact. Ray Wilkins was sold to AC Milan for £1.4 million. Wilkins was a popular player, especially with the younger supporters, and had been a great ambassador for the club, always willing to talk to fans, in a patient, well-mannered and understanding way. Wilkins left sadly, despite the financial attractions of his new life abroad. He said later: 'I never wanted to leave, but it was obvious that there was no place for me in future plans, so when the deal was drawn up between Milan and United that was that.'

There was also a question mark over the future of Norman Whiteside. Although the young striker had proved himself at every level, he lost his place to Hughes at the close of the 1983–84 campaign, and during the summer Atkinson's efforts in the transfer market finalised the purchases of Strachan from Aberdeen, Jesper Olsen, the Danish winger who was playing for Dutch club Ajax, and Alan Brazil from Tottenham, a player Atkinson had pursued for over a year.

The 1984–85 season started with Whiteside pushed out of the side by the arrival of the new players. He was named as substitute for the first

Right: Distant horizons for Ray Wilkins brought an end to his days at Old Trafford. The player who lost both the England and United captaincy to his close friend Bryan Robson, reluctantly moved on to play in Italy with AC Milan. Wilkins began his career at Chelsea where his obvious flair for leadership led to him being appointed the youngest captain in the history of the London club

Far right: Quick talking, quick witted and quick off the mark Gordon Strachan found himself playing under Alex Ferguson for a second time when United replaced Ron Atkinson in 1986. Strachan, a creative midfield player with immense skill and control, was bought by Atkinson under the noses of German club FC Cologne to add width and penetration to the side. The manager who sold him – Alex Ferguson when in charge at Aberdeen

The slightly built Jesper Olsen was brought to Old Trafford six months before he became a United player. The Dane was out of the game through injury when he agreed to move to English football from Dutch club Ajax. This gave Ron Atkinson the opportunity to introduce Olsen to his future colleagues before the transfer was finalised. Olsen was one of two United players to be included in the Danish squad for the 1986 World Cup, the other was full-back John Sivebaek

game at home to Watford, and a massive 53,668 turned up to see United thwarted by a Nigel Callaghan goal which earned his side a draw in the last minute.

Whiteside came on as a substitute for Brazil and won back his place in the fourth game of the season when the new striker was injured. Brazil was missing for five games, and by the time he returned Hughes had scored six times, Strachan had netted four goals, three of them as the newly elected penalty taker, and Whiteside had helped to justify his place with two goals in a 3–0 win at Coventry.

After four draws to start the season the side began to win, beating Newcastle 5–0, then

moving through to the second round of the UEFA Cup, and the third round of the Milk Cup, but they were inconsistent. They lost to Aston Villa 3–0 in Birmingham in a game which saw Didier Six playing English football for the first time, and the French star created the first of his new club's goals, laying on the cross for Peter Withe.

In the next League game United beat West Ham 5–1, then after beating Spurs 1–0 at Old Trafford, went down 5–0 at Goodison Park to an Everton side which ran them ragged. Atkinson's response to suggestions that his team did not show the consistency required to win the Championship was to defend them angrily:

This is the heaviest defeat I have ever had as a manager at any level, non-league included. No side has ever beaten one of my teams by five clear goals and I can tell you it hurts. But nothing has gone wrong. We were not happy with the way that we played, but there was little we could do about it. Everton played very well and that was that. We will get down to some serious training again on Monday morning and we will sort it out.

The next game was again against Everton, this time in the third round of the Milk Cup and it turned out to be a disastrous night for John Gidman, who headed the winner for Everton, past his own goalkeeper Gary Bailey. Gidman had returned to the side following an injury to Mike Duxbury and continued at right-back for most of the remaining games. Duxbury had risen from obscurity to top-level football and took the England full-back shirt away from Nottingham Forest's Viv Anderson, only to lose it back to him during a seven-match absence up to late November 1984.

By this time the team had risen to third place in the First Division, behind Everton and Tottenham, and had done so by using a

175

backbone of 13 players. The side which had started the season was:

Bailey, Duxbury, Albiston, Moses, Moran, Hogg, Robson, Strachan, Hughes, Brazil, Olsen.

Added to these 11 players were Whiteside and Gidman.

Frank Stapleton missed the start of the season through injury but began to edge his way back into the side in December 1984 when the boisterous Hughes suffered a two-match suspension after being sent off at Roker Park, Sunderland, in a game which United lost 3–2.

Injuries had started to take their toll once more. Moran was out for 14 games, and Hogg joined him in the treatment room with a pelvic strain which eventually required surgery. He missed 13 successive matches as Gordon McQueen stepped back into the side, and Billy Garton, a young defender from Salford, made his League debut in a 3–2 win at Leicester.

Strachan and Hughes were fighting a private battle to see who would end the season as top scorer and at the turn of the year the Welsh youngster was one goal ahead on 14, and was catching the eye of many experts who were hailing him as a great find. Strachan was the penalty king, eight of his first 13 goals coming from spot kicks, but he began to lose his confidence after misses in a UEFA Cup game against Dundee United, and in the New Year's Day game with Sheffield Wednesday, which ended in defeat. He said:

I never really gave any thought to things like pressure when I was taking a penalty, but people began asking me about how I felt, and

if I was 'under any pressure' and before I knew where I was, I began to worry. After I had missed my fifth I didn't feel much like taking spot kicks, even though I had scored from eight of them.

By mid-January 1985 United were still in third place, but eight points adrift of League leaders Everton, and six behind second placed Tottenham. It looked once more as if the Championship would prove too difficult for Ron Atkinson's players, but in the FA Cup there were signs of encouragement.

In the third round they were drawn at home to Bournemouth and handed out an emphatic three-goal revenge for the previous season's embarrassment, with Strachan, Stapleton and McQueen scoring.

Robson's injury problems

Seven days later came a game which will not so much be remembered for its scoreline, as for its effect on England's World Cup chances over a year later. Coventry were the visitors for a League game in which Bryan Robson chased a high ball as it dropped towards his opponents' goal. The ball was out of the United captain's reach, and he was running at top speed as he passed the upright on the main grandstand side of the Stretford End goal. His momentum carried him down the sloping edge of the pitch beyond the goal-line and he was still running as he crossed the narrow red shale track between the playing area and the steel perimeter fencing.

Robson stuck out his left leg, aiming to use an advertising hoarding as a brake. His foot caught the smooth, brightly painted surface, and his studs skidded off immediately, throwing him head first behind the board. He fell heavily, and lay in obvious pain as assistance was called by players from both sides who had run off the field to help him.

There were fears that he had collided with one of the large steel transformers which had been erected at intervals behind each goal as electrical under-soil heating was installed by the club, but afterwards he said: 'No, I missed the box but I fell very heavily on my right elbow and that did the damage. My shoulder was dislocated, and the pain was tremendous. I remember very little about the incident. Jim McGregor ran to me and I think he gave me a pain-killing injection. I was wheeled away on a stretcher and taken to hospital.'

It was the first of four dislocations for Robson which ended in despair for him in the 1986 World Cup finals when he fell heavily during a game with Morocco and took no further part in the tournament. After the competition the England manager Bobby Robson said: 'With a fully fit Bryan Robson we would have won the World Cup.'

Back in 1985 few thought that the injury against Coventry would have such a long term

Mark Hughes was the second influential player to emerge from the youth team of the 1980s, the first being Norman Whiteside. Hughes made his debut in a Milk Cup tie at Oxford and scored – an action he was to repeat when he played his first senior League game and his first international for Wales

His right arm clasped to his chest, Bryan Robson is assisted off the field in Monterrey after dislocating his shoulder. The injury sparked off a row between England manager Bobby Robson and the United hierarchy, Robson claiming that had the United player undergone surgery before the World Cup it would have improved England's chances of success. Manager Robson went on record, saying 'With a fully fit Bryan Robson, we would have won the World Cup'

effect, although the game was to leave a lasting impression on United's season. It was their second successive home defeat of the New Year, Terry Gibson scoring Coventry's goal, and hopes of staying in the Championship race were dashed.

A week after the League game, Coventry returned for the fourth round of the FA Cup and Hughes and Paul McGrath – who had started an extended run in the side over the Christmas period – scored the goals which gave United their passage into the next stage of the competition.

The draw for the fifth round took United to Ewood Park, Blackburn, scene of so many historical clashes between the two clubs, and with Rovers having a promotion-chasing season in the Second Division it seemed a tough tie for the Reds.

The pitch was bone-hard, the streets surrounding the ground covered in snow, yet close

Despair in the England dressing room during the 1986 World Cup game against Morocco. Ray Wilkins glances across to his captain Bryan Robson who is still in pain after dislocating his shoulder. Wilkins himself was sent off for the first time in his career as England drew 0–0 with the competition's outsiders

on 23,000 braved the conditions, many of them hoping to see United toppled. But it was United's superior skill, allied to the conditions, which led to the first goal when Blackburn defender Mick Rathbone failed to control the ball on the frozen surface, and Strachan nipped in to chip over Terry Gennoe in the home goal, after just seven minutes.

Blackburn launched a flurry of attacks, but in the 88th minute a brave run through the defence by Paul McGrath, in which he held off three strong challenges led him to getting a second goal and United were through.

However, the injury jinx once again struck. Near the end of the game Remi Moses went down in pain, his ankle badly hurt. He limped off and was out of football not just for the remainder of the season, but for all but four games of the following campaign, and it was not until the 1986–87 season that he returned with anything like regularity, and that only after surgery. He even clashed with Atkinson and the club by going abroad for treatment in a frantic effort to get himself back into the game.

Fate had dealt Moses a second stunning blow. After missing the 1983 FA Cup Final because of suspension, he was again sidelined as his colleagues proceeded towards Wembley once more.

With Robson's influence missing, United were expected to slide, but remarkably they went nine games without defeat during his absence. For half of these McGrath played in midfield, with Hogg and Moran teaming up again in the back four, and then when Moran was hurt, McGrath took his place and Duxbury wore the shirt of Moses.

Atkinson played Strachan wide on the right and Olsen on the left, with Whiteside dropping deeper into midfield as Hughes and Stapleton led the attack, and United looked a competent machine, even though they were operating without two crucial parts.

Injuries were a problem, but Atkinson appeared to have strength in reserve and this was clearly illustrated when Gary Bailey was hurt and young goalkeeper Stephen Pears was drafted in for the games against Coventry in the League and the FA Cup, then for the the home clashes with West Brom and Newcastle. Pears was on the losing side just once, but eventually he was allowed to leave the club to go to his native north-east, first on loan and then signed permanently by Middlesbrough.

Pears had won the hearts of the Old Trafford crowd when he saved a Terry Gibson penalty during the FA Cup game, but Bailey was back in goal by the Blackburn tie and stayed there for all but one of the remaining fixtures.

United were drawn at home to West Ham for the quarter-final, and the game came three days after what was to turn out to be an historic game for the Manchester supporters. United had beaten Videoton, the Hungarian side, in the UEFA Cup and Frank Stapleton's lone goal was the last to be scored at the ground in a European competition before English clubs were banned in the summer of 1985.

West Ham were seven places from the foot of the table and 17 points behind United, but in a thriller of a game they threatened to cause a major upset, until Norman Whiteside took the game by the scruff of the neck.

Twenty minutes of the game had gone when United scored their first, but it came after three anxious moments in their own penalty area. As early as the opening minute Paul Goddard had shot over the bar, then the Londoners appealed for a penalty when Hogg appeared to handle in the 13th minute, and 60 seconds later Alan Dickens fired a shot wide after running at Bailey's goal. So when Gidman took a throw for United on the right and picked out Hughes, there were cheers of celebration and relief as the Welsh youngster hit the back of the net with a fierce left-foot shot which beat Tom McAllister as the West Ham goal-keeper dived to his right.

Back came the Hammers and Bailey was forced to make two good saves, before a cross from the right was turned into his own net by Hogg. The 47,000 crowd erupted as Whiteside put United back in front after a Strachan corner was headed down by McGrath, and at half time it was 2–1.

After the break, in a frantic battle for supremacy, United pressed forward but West Ham held out until the 74th minute when Hogg made amends for his earlier error by chipping a free-kick into the path of Whiteside, and the 19-year-old blasted the ball home. At 3–1 it seemed all over, but West Ham fought back and seven minutes from the end Paul Allen scored. One more for a replay, and the Hammers felt they could do it.

United, however, had other ideas and a super run by Strachan took him into the West Ham penalty area and he seemed certain to score when he was tripped. Referee Trelford Mills pointed to the spot, and the home crowd held its breath. With penalty misses against Dundee United, QPR, Sheffield Wednesday, Blackburn Rovers, and a week earlier against Everton, Gordon Strachan had lost his crown as the penalty 'king'. But Whiteside stepped up, completed his hat-trick and put United through to the semi-finals for the second time in three seasons.

United were still in the Championship race, which was being led by Everton, and beat second-placed Spurs 2–1 at White Hart Lane three days after the Cup-tie. Spurs, who were just behind Everton, were away to Liverpool, who were breathing down the necks of third-placed United, in their next game.

Three nights after the Tottenham victory United were again back in London, facing West Ham for the second time in six days, on this occasion in a First Division clash. West Ham wanted revenge for the Cup defeat, and threw themselves at United. Hogg handled to give away a penalty which Ray Stewart converted,

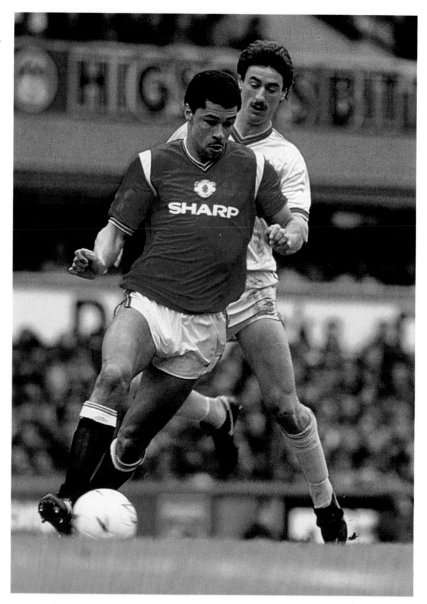

but five minutes later Frank Stapleton scored his fifth goal of the season from a Gidman free kick and it was 1–1.

Then United gave away their second own goal inside a week when Duxbury dived to try to head clear a cross, only to turn the ball into his own net. Ron Atkinson had just one ace left in his hand, and in the 61st minute of the game he played it. Off came Whiteside and on went Robson, back for the first time since 12 January, ten games earlier. Six minutes later the United captain threw himself at a corner and in true schoolboy-hero style headed the equaliser.

Mark Hughes makes his mark

United's chances of winning the League and Cup double were realistic, even though Everton were well ahead in the title race, and after beating Aston Villa 4–0 at Old Trafford, Atkinson was being tipped as the man to emulate Busby as a creator of champions. Hughes scored a hat-trick in this match and his performances in his first full season earned him

Paul McGrath holds off a challenge from Liverpool's Ian Rush as another attempt to score against United fails. Despite his remarkable record, Rush never scored against United during his time at Anfield

the 'Young Footballer of the Year' award, given to him through the votes of his fellow professionals in the PFA.

When the club's hopes of European honours vanished in the Hungarian mud as Videoton won a UEFA Cup penalty 'shoot-out', it became clear where United's interests lay.

In the FA Cup they were drawn once more against Liverpool, and faced them at Anfield on 31 March 1985 in a League game, a fortnight before their semi-final date. United won 1–0 through a Frank Stapleton goal, and then went on to beat Leicester 2–1, and Stoke 5–0. Was this going to be the year of the Championship which had eluded the club since 1967?

Three days after the devastation of Stoke Atkinson's hopes were dashed at Hillsborough when Lee Chapman pushed the ball over the line after Stephen Pears, playing his last senior game for United, failed to hold a Shirtliff shot from a Brian Marwood cross, and Wednesday won 1–0.

The gap between United and leaders Everton had been narrowed to just four points but this defeat, and Everton's victory in their next game, gave the Merseysiders a seven-point lead with seven games remaining. Everton seemed to be in an invincible position.

So it was the FA Cup which became the main target and supporters began to look forward to the possibility of a sixth Wembley final within a decade. United met Liverpool at Goodison Park, while Everton faced Luton Town in the other semi-final at Villa Park. The prospect of an all-Merseyside final had caught the imagination of the sporting press and the build-up to the games helped to create an amazing atmosphere, especially at the Everton ground.

United had no intention of sitting at home watching Liverpool play Everton in the final on television, and set about their task with great spirit. They forced a stream of corner kicks, held out when Rush broke through but shot over the bar, then took the lead.

The first goal came after a first half in which Hogg had been booked for a foul on Rush, Whiteside had been floored by Whelan and had clashed with Sammy Lee, and Gidman had created a scoring chance from a free-kick.

It was in the 69th minute when Hughes struck, ramming the ball home after a Robson shot had been blocked. The game seemed over until Ronnie Whelan tried a shot from outside the box four minutes from time and levelled the scores. Once more a Liverpool-United game went into extra time, and eight minutes into the first period Frank Stapleton's shot was deflected to make it 2–1.

Surely this time United were through? But no, back came Liverpool, and in the final

The Liverpool defence tries to cover a United scoring attempt in the first of the two FA Cup semi-finals of 1985. United led twice in the game only for Liverpool to fight back and force a replay. The first game was played at Goodison Park, home of Liverpool's closest rivals, Everton, the replay was at Maine Road, Manchester City's ground

minute referee George Courtney ignored a linesman's flag and allowed a Paul Walsh goal to stand. It was a bitter blow for Atkinson: 'We had the game won, we did everything that we had to do this afternoon and still we haven't got to Wembley.'

The game was replayed at Maine Road four nights later and the own-goal jinx once again struck United. In the 39th minute Paul McGrath tried to head a cross over his own bar, and instead beat Bailey to put Liverpool in front. United were stunned, but having had the better of the play up to that time, were in confident mood and came back immediately the second half had started.

Bryan Robson ran at the Liverpool defence and unleashed a powerful shot which Grobbelaar

could not reach and it was 1–1. Twelve minutes later the dynamic Hughes forced himself through the Liverpool back four as he chased a Strachan pass and hit the winner.

Everton, the League leaders, provided the opposition for the Wembley final on 18 May. Before that United saw their Championship hopes disappear completely as they drew with Southampton and Sunderland at Old Trafford, and even though they had victories at Luton and Norwich on each side of those games the four points lost were vital. A 3–1 win at QPR was followed by a debacle at Vicarage Road, Watford, where the Hornets beat United 5–1 in the last League game, but the players' minds by then were on the Cup final which was five days away.

Agony of Moran

The players spent that time in Windsor, at a Thames-side hideaway hotel far removed from the pressures of Wembley, and it was perfect preparation for the big game. They trained at nearby Bisham Abbey, and relaxed on the lawns of the hotel in tranquil surroundings as Ron

Atkinson wrestled with a problem. He had to select the side he hoped would beat Everton, but he had doubts about the fitness of certain key players.

Graeme Hogg had played regularly since the start of the year while Kevin Moran had been out for a 13-game spell, returning just before the season ended. Hogg had a pelvic problem and Atkinson knew this only too well, so he decided on the eve of the final to play Moran. It proved a crucial decision but not for obvious reasons.

Alan Brazil was the other unlucky player. He had taken over from the injured Hughes in the closing games, but even though he had scored 12 times in just 20 outings, he could not even win the substitute's shirt for the final. This went to Mike Duxbury. The United line up was:

Bailey, Gidman, Albiston, Whiteside, McGrath, Moran, Robson, Strachan, Hughes, Stapleton, Olsen. Sub: Duxbury.

Everton, by now champions, were favourites to win the final, but it was a game remembered not so much for its football as for a moment during the second half when Kevin Moran carved an unwanted niche in the history of the game.

It happened when Peter Reid, that dynamo of a midfielder, was running at full speed towards the United penalty area. The Everton player had picked up the ball from a moment of hesitation by McGrath and was clear of the Reds' defence. Moran threw himself feet first at Reid, his right foot pushing the ball away, his left catching the Everton player. Reid's momentum carried him into the air and he dramatically rolled over several times. Referee Peter Willis blew for a foul and called Moran to him.

The United player seemed angry that his challenge should be thought unfair by the

Right: FA Cup final 1985: Everton goalkeeper Neville Southall flings himself across goal in a vain attempt to stop Norman Whiteside's cup-winning shot from the far edge of the penalty area. The goal came in extra-time as United, reduced to ten men after having Kevin Moran sent off, staged a gallant fight against the odds

Left: The final whistle is blown in the FA Cup semi-final replay at Maine Road and United are back at Wembley. Ron Atkinson celebrates the win as he leaps from the trainer's bench with Liverpool beaten 2–1. The victory took United to their third Wembley final in as many seasons and avenged the 1983 Milk Cup final defeat

Below: Drama in the 1985 FA Cup Final at Wembley as Kevin Moran becomes the first player to be sent off in football's showpiece. Referee Peter Willis points to the touchline and stands his ground as Moran pleads for leniency. Gordon Strachan tries to console Moran as Bryan Robson and Mark Hughes join their colleague. 'I almost hit the referee' Moran said afterwards

Above: Whiteside turns after scoring and the United players begin to converge on the young Irishman as the expressions on the faces of the Everton defenders sum up their feelings

Right: United 1 Everton 0 and the ten men are only minutes away from causing a major upset

referee, but said nothing, turning his back to the official so that Willis could note his number. Moran began to walk away after the caution and was then shocked to learn that he had been sent off. He was the first player ever to be dismissed in an FA Cup final.

Moran was stunned. He grabbed referee Willis in a vain attempt to plead his innocence. Willis stood firm, pointing to the touchline and growing angry at the player's attitude. Moran was incensed and had to be pulled away from the official by his team-mate at both club and international level, Frank Stapleton.

Bryan Robson pleaded with Willis and was ignored. The Everton players joined in, and Reid walked alongside Moran as he was led from the field by Jim McGregor, holding back tears and swaying as if about to faint.

Millions of television viewers were at that very moment being shown an action replay of the incident which clearly illustrated the intention of Moran's challenge. He had pushed the ball away from Reid with his right foot before making contact with the player, but the referee did not have the same opinion as the television commentary team, nor did he have the advantage of being able to see the incident from several different angles.

Moran had to sit on the United bench as the game went into extra time. He said afterwards:

It was the worst moment of my life. I couldn't believe what had happened to me, I honestly didn't think that I'd fouled Peter, but even if I did I didn't think it warranted a sending off. I went crazy, I didn't know what was happening, except that here was a man sending me off for something I thought I hadn't done. I asked for mercy and got none.

No goals had come in the first 90 minutes, but in extra time the ten men from Manchester found the inspiration to create just one vital opportunity, and it fell to Norman Whiteside.

Hughes, in his own half, pushed the ball forward beyond the Everton midfield. Whiteside ran after it, lengthening his stride as he found extra strength. Strachan raced alongside in support, and van den Hauwe the Everton left-back came to challenge. Whiteside turned inwards, the full-back stumbled and Whiteside hit a left-foot shot goalwards as van den Hauwe fell, obscuring the ball momentarily from the view of Southall in the Everton goal. The ball was level with the goalkeeper when he became aware of the danger, throwing himself outwards in an effort to block its path, but the ball was round him and into the net. United had won the FA Cup again.

The players went to collect their medals. Moran accompanied them and was told by an FA official that his was being withheld. A player sent off at Wembley does not qualify for a medal, winner or loser. However, such was the public outcry, backed by the television evidence, that several weeks later Moran was rewarded with his medal.

181

The sending-off had turned an ordinary final into one of major significance, and the interest created by Moran's misfortune transformed him into a folk hero.

When United returned with the Cup the following day there were wild scenes as the team travelled once more on their open-topped bus to Manchester Town Hall, and when Moran demonstrated his eloquence with political-style oratory the tens of thousands gathered in Albert Square and listening on radio took him to their hearts. 'We won the Cup for the supporters of Manchester United, because they are the best. You are the greatest in the world', he said, emphasising each word with a punch of his fist, the rest of his speech being drowned in deafening cheers.

United had won another major trophy. They ended their First Division campaign by once again occupying fourth place.

The 1985–86 season began by United losing to Everton in the Charity Shield, Graeme Hogg replacing Moran who was suspended, and the new campaign proved to be one of great importance for Ron Atkinson.

Since his arrival his side had not ended a season outside the top four, had qualified for Europe and won the FA Cup twice, but he had still been unable totally to convince the majority of supporters that he was the right man for the managerial seat at Old Trafford. His record proved he was successful, but the supporters' comments, and their acceptance of Atkinson the man, showed that he was walking the tightrope without winning over his audience.

He was accepted by the media as a man who was easy to work with unless angered. He had dealt with a difficult personal problem in a way which caused not the slightest embarrassment to the club when he had called a 'press conference' to announce that he had left his wife to set up home with another woman, thus preventing any sensational exposures in the tabloid newspapers. He had a circle of close friends with whom he could confide, yet that vital relationship with the grass-roots supporter was missing.

Brilliant start to 1985–86 season

However, anyone with any doubts about his managerial capabilities had little evidence to use against him as United began their 1985–86 season by setting a new club record for successive victories.

After the Charity Shield they beat Aston Villa, Ipswich, Arsenal, West Ham, Nottingham Forest, Newcastle, Oxford, Manchester City, West Brom and Southampton in the League. Ten games, ten wins, and naturally top of the First Division.

The victories had a price. John Gidman broke his leg in the second game at Ipswich, Jesper Olsen was hurt before the West Ham match, allowing Peter Barnes, signed during that summer, to make an impressive debut, and

United's match against West Ham was fraught with incident after the referee disallowed a goal from Mark Ward, despite Ward's protestations. United went on to beat West Ham 1−0.

Mark Higgins tussles with Frank McAvennie in the FA Cup fifth-round replay against West Ham at Old Trafford in March 1986. Mark seemed finished in football when he quit at Everton with a bad back injury, but Manchester United gave him a second life by repaying his insurance money to take him back into the Football League.

He fought his way back into first-team football although he failed to win a regular place with United, his career was launched again and he moved on to play successfully for Bury.

Gordon Strachan dislocated his shoulder scoring at West Brom.

United invested in a new goalkeeper, Chris Turner from Sunderland, who at £250,000 was the most costly number one the club had ever bought. But he was sidelined by the outstanding performances of Bailey in the record-breaking run.

United had qualified for Europe but there were no foreign competitions that season following the Heysel Stadium tragedy, when rioting at the Liverpool-Juventus European Cup final had led to the deaths of 39 Italian supporters. Instead a new competition was introduced, while at the same time the Football League decided to trim the First Division to 20 clubs by the 1988−89 season. The Super Cup became the target of those clubs prevented from playing in Europe by the UEFA ban, and it was eventually won by Liverpool.

United's run of victories ended with a draw at Luton but it was November before they lost their first League game, going down 1−0 to Sheffield Wednesday at Hillsborough. Injuries had forced Atkinson to use no fewer than 18 players up to that fixture, only one of them, goalkeeper Turner, not having competed in the League.

Colin Gibson was bought from Aston Villa as Ron Atkinson decided that he wanted to strengthen his left full-back options and early in the new year a second Gibson, Terry from Coventry City, moved to Old Trafford in a player-plus-cash deal which took Alan Brazil to Highfield Road.

After the tremendous start things began to go wrong. After the Sheffield Wednesday defeat United were knocked out of the Milk Cup at Anfield, and got just two points from three further League games.

Injuries still plagued the club. Playing for England, Bryan Robson limped off at Wembley after chasing a ball behind the goal and tearing a hamstring. He returned for the game at Sheffield Wednesday and repeated the injury which kept him out until the New Year. Robson missed the remainder of the Milk Cup games after taking part in the two-legged second round against Crystal Palace – Steve Coppell's club – as goals from Peter Barnes and Norman Whiteside gave United a 1−0 win in each match.

In the third round there was controversy as United beat West Ham 1−0 at Old Trafford. Norman Whiteside scored what turned out to be the only goal of the game, converting an Olsen pass from the goal-line in the 76th minute, but it was a 'goal' that was not a goal which caused a stir. Mark Ward fired a 25-yard free-kick into Gary Bailey's net but as referee Frank Roberts had indicated that it was indirect there was no goal. Ward argued that Bailey had touched the ball in his efforts to make a save, although Bailey denied it.

By December United were still top of the League, but their form slipped dramatically.

Just one win in five games was followed by a 3−1 win at Villa Park. Then, when the first home defeat of the season occurred against Arsenal on 21 December a small section of the supporters demonstrated against the manager. 'What do they think they're talking about?' was Atkinson's retort. 'They seem to forget I've brought them the Cup twice – and would Bryan Robson be playing here if it wasn't for me? They have very short memories.'

Defeat at Goodison Park followed, and only bad weather prevented what might have been a tragic run of defeats as the long trip to Newcastle on 28 December was postponed.

Mark Hughes' form had also taken a significant slide. In his opening 13 games he had scored ten goals, then in the next 13 League fixtures he managed just two. The period bridged the start of the New Year and the start of the FA Cup campaign.

This opened with a tie against Rochdale, switched to Old Trafford because Spotland could not cater for the numbers who might attend, and United won 2−0. The tie saw the return to football of Mark Higgins, who had been forced to retire from the game after a bad injury. The former Everton captain had turned to Atkinson for a chance to try again and after training with United joined them, repaying the insurance claim he had received when he quit.

Robson returned for the next round of the Cup, against Sunderland at Roker Park. The game ended goal-less, but the talking point was a clash between Robson and Barry Venison. Both players fell to the ground, Robson got up first and tried to step over the Sunderland player, catching him on the head with his boot. The linesman closest to the incident saw it as a deliberate kick, and Robson was sent off for the first time in his career.

United won the replay 3−0 with Robson in the side, but by the time his two-match suspension started he was injured again. Four days after the second Sunderland game the England captain limped off at Upton Park after twisting his ankle during a 2−1 League defeat, as United found themselves knocked off the top of the table.

Meanwhile the news had leaked out that Mark Hughes was set to join Barcelona at the end of the season. This angered United's supporters when they read of the speculation.

Tear-gas at Anfield

In February 1986 a second Dane was added to the squad as international full-back John Sivebaek joined Jesper Olsen, and was plunged into an amazing debut game against Liverpool at Anfield. Feelings were high among supporters and when the United coach arrived at Anfield, a brick struck the window close to where Mark Hughes was sitting. Then, as the players entered the ground, they were sprayed with tear gas and several children, caught in the cloud, had to be taken to hospital for treatment. The United party went on to the pitch to clear their eyes and lungs and an angry gesture towards the Kop by Ron Atkinson was wrongly interpreted. Worst affected in the United party was youngster Clayton Blackmore:

I didn't know what had happened. We just stepped off the coach and someone sprayed something at us. My eyes poured with tears and I couldn't breathe. Whatever it was I caught most of it straight in the face. The Boss got us out on to the pitch immediately, but it was a bit frightening – we could've been sprayed with anything.

Blackmore did not play in the game, which ended in a 1–1 draw. Colin Gibson scored the first goal but John Wark got Liverpool's equaliser just before half-time.

The incidents before the game plus attacks on coachloads of United supporters, led to concerted efforts by both clubs to eliminate ill-feeling in future clashes. In 1986–87 directors of both clubs met representatives of the media in Manchester and Liverpool (including the present co-authors Tom Tyrrell and David Meek) and drew up a peace plan. This included rival mascots leading out the teams, representatives of each club travelling on the opposition coach, and joint functions for supporters.

A month after the Liverpool game United again played West Ham. They had been drawn against them in the fifth round of the FA Cup and the game had serious consequences for England's World Cup hopes. In the summer of 1986 England were due to go to Mexico for the competition, but when Bryan Robson fell on his elbow and repeated the shoulder dislocation of the previous year, there were major doubts about the player's long-term fitness. West Ham won the tie after a replay to end United's Cup hopes for the season.

Atkinson bought Peter Davenport, a prolific goalscorer with Nottingham Forest, as it became clear that Mark Hughes was going to Spain. Davenport was no stranger to Old Trafford, having been a United supporter since he was a small boy. 'I used to stand at the Stretford End with my dad and my brother, and never missed a game for a long time. Considering we lived on the Wirral that wasn't a bad claim', he said after signing.

However, like Garry Birtles, who had been bought by Dave Sexton as a goal-scorer, Davenport found it difficult to adjust to United's methods and ended the season with just one goal in eleven games, and that was scored from the penalty spot in the final home fixture.

In a season wrecked by injuries United ended the campaign in fourth place in the Championship, filling that spot for the third successive year. They ended the season with Terry Gibson on crutches with torn knee ligaments, Gordon Strachan out with a pelvic strain, Graeme Hogg recovering from surgery for a similar injury, Remi Moses undergoing treatment on his ankle,

and Peter Barnes, Colin Gibson and Kevin Moran all sidelined through muscle strains. As well as this Gary Bailey was in hospital having an operation on a knee injury sustained while on England duty, and Bryan Robson was wearing a shoulder harness in an effort to play in Mexico without having surgery.

Hughes had gone to Spain in a £1.8 million transfer deal by the time the next season started, having ended his United career at Watford by scoring a spectacular goal in a 1–1 draw in the last match of the 1985–86 season. He explained his departure as follows:

I have got to say that I am looking forward to going to Barcelona, but I'm leaving behind a lot of friends at Old Trafford. It's by my own choice that I'm going. It was an offer that was too good to miss, and I want to clear up the matter of reports that I've been forced away from the club. This isn't true. The reports have come about because I had been told to deny any links with Barcelona, and some people got the wrong idea. I'm looking forward to going, and I know that the fans over there will give me a great reception and that's something to look forward to, but we all know how fickle fans can be and I know I've got to produce the goods in Spain.

When the 1986–87 season began Robson was still recovering from the surgery required to repair the damage to his shoulder after two more dislocations, one in the build-up to Mexico and the other in a World Cup match in Monterrey, and Gary Bailey was back in hospital for a further operation on his troublesome knee. United began the campaign with Chris Turner in goal, Duxbury, McGrath, Moran and Albiston as the back four, Strachan, Blackmore, Whiteside and Olsen in midfield and Stapleton and Davenport up front. They lost the first three games, two of them at home.

Sivebaek was brought in for a drawn game at Leicester as United found themselves at the bottom of the table. In the next game United recovered some of their pride by beating Southampton 5–1 at Old Trafford, then lost three more League games by the end of September. Robson had returned for the Southampton win and showed signs that he was not too far away from his normal level when he scored in the defeat at Everton and the draw at Nottingham Forest.

A 7–2 aggregate win in the Littlewoods Cup (a change of sponsor for the League Cup) gave some hope, but the opposition was Port Vale, who could not provide the challenge United would face in the next round against Southampton. By the time this game came round United had played 12 League games, won three and drawn three, and their six defeats had sent them plunging to the foot of the table.

United drew 0–0 with Southampton at Old Trafford, then on 1 November drew at home to Coventry City in front of a dissatisfied crowd of 36,946, many of them making their feelings felt with comments aimed at the director's box as

Alex Ferguson rises from the bench during a game at Old Trafford. The United manager said at the end of the 1986–87 season that he felt that he needed five players to create a side capable of challenging Liverpool for the championship. He was able to buy just two before the new campaign began, Viv Anderson and Brian McClair

they left the ground before the final whistle.

Atkinson is sacked

On Tuesday, 4 November 1986, United played their final game under Ron Atkinson. It was the replay against Southampton at the Dell, and a game which increased the injury burden which had weighed Atkinson down. Colin Gibson tore his hamstring again after just two partial outings at the start of the season, and Norman Whiteside limped off with a knee ligament injury before half-time. He was replaced by Nicky Wood, who had ended his studies at Manchester University to concentrate on his playing career. Moran was on instead of Gibson. A minute before half-time Southampton scored, and in the second half took control, winning 4–1.

The United manager was far from happy:

Up to half-time I thought that we were the better team, I honestly believed that we would get into the game in the second half and make something of it, but George Lawrence ran riot. It's seldom that you can find any consolation in defeat, but we had problems with injuries again and I thought that the players battled terribly well considering those. Jimmy Case ran the show though, and there was nothing we could do about it.

Jimmy Case, tormentor of Manchester United, had contributed to the end of Ron Atkinson's spell on the Old Trafford tightrope.

The next day the club's directors met informally to discuss the situation, and 24 hours later at 10.30 am on 6 November, Martin Edwards summoned Ron Atkinson and Mick Brown to his office at Old Trafford.

An hour later a statement was issued which said that the contracts of both men had been terminated. Atkinson was no longer manager.

The men and women of the media gathered outside the normally open gates of the Cliff training ground hoping for an opportunity to see the man who had been forced to stand down from his post, and shortly before noon were allowed into the courtyard where Atkinson held his final audience:

Obviously I'm disappointed. I'd go on record as saying that I have been at the club for five and a half years. Five of them have been very good years which I have enjoyed immensely, but this year things went against us and you have seen the outcome today. I actually had no indication of what was going to happen. I came down here today expecting to have a nice five-a-side and some training, but the chairman sent for me and told me reluctantly – I felt reluctantly – that they had decided to dispense with my services, because of the results over the last few months, and I accept that totally. I don't feel bitter about it, I don't hold any bitterness against the club.

I honestly feel that we had just started to turn the corner with our recent run of results but I never expected this to happen. I don't think if you are a positive person you ever look on the black side, you look on the positive side. I came here this morning knowing that we are playing Oxford on Saturday and to get a side capable of winning there. Now someone else has got that responsibility, and whoever it is I sincerely hope they do well.

I've no axe to grind at all. I've worked for a chairman who I consider to be as good as any chairman in the game, and I don't think that this job is any harder than being manager of any other club. True this is the biggest club in the country and the manager has his problems, but I don't think the manager of Rochdale would feel that his problems were any smaller than mine have been, or any bigger.

You are always aware that these things might happen but you must never look at it in that light. But I am sure that there are good times ahead for the club, once whoever takes over gets all the key players fit again.

Alex Ferguson is appointed

Atkinson bowed out and drowned his sorrows that night with a party at his Rochdale home, but by then he knew who would succeed him, for Martin Edwards was swift to appoint a new man. Three hours after sacking Ron Atkinson, the United chairman flew to Scotland where he had been given permission to talk to Aberdeen's manager, Alex Ferguson. The man who was to succeed Atkinson remembers the day clearly:

It was a beautiful sunny morning and I drove back to Pittodrie from a training session and I saw the chairman's car there. And I thought to myself 'the old yen's here early today' – it was about a quarter to twelve. I went into my office and he was sitting at my desk, and he had his hand on the telephone. I said hello to him and told him he was in early, and he threw me a piece of paper. 'I've been asked to phone this gentleman,' he said. On the paper was Martin Edwards' name and phone number.

He said 'Do you want me to 'phone him?' and I said that I did, and I went out of the room because I didn't want to be there. I just asked if he would tell me what had happened after the call.

I went back after going down to the dressing rooms and he said that he had spoken to Mr Edwards and that he was flying up straight away and would go to my house. He said that his son would collect the United chairman from the airport and take him there. I said it was quick, and he said 'If you want the job there's nothing we can do to stop you.'

There was nothing else I could do, so I went home and told my wife and sons, and right away they were against the idea. I think they were just shocked at the thought of leaving Aberdeen, because it's a lovely city and the boys were settled in at school. We had good players and a good club, but we sat down and my wife said that I was right, I had to take the job.

The boys went off to school and were sworn to secrecy not to tell a soul, and when they came back I think that they began to realise how big a prospect it was and how I had to accept.

The following morning Alex Ferguson arrived at the Cliff, met his new players and immediately was impressed:

This is luxury for me, because at Aberdeen we didn't have our own training ground, we used school pitches. But I've got to put these things to good use and get down to picking a winning side. I know the club's had injury problems and my sympathy goes to Ron Atkinson in that sense. You need luck in football and he didn't have any.

The new manager was an optimist:

We aren't in a desperate position, the League can still be won. It's no use me coming here and *not* thinking that every game we play we can win, that's the only way that we can attack things. That's the attitude I had at Aberdeen – there's a game to be played and we must go out and win it. Tomorrow we have to win, simply that.

As for his new chairman, Martin Edwards was swift to back up Ferguson's optimism:

I am sure that we have made a wise choice. We had to move quickly – once we had decided to get rid of Ron we wanted to replace him as quickly as possible.

When we had the meeting to decide that we wanted to make the change we decided that Alex Ferguson was the man that we wanted to replace Ron Atkinson.

It was also evident that the United chairman knew what he expected from his new manager:

We are looking to be the premier club in England and obviously to be that we have to win the First Division Championship. That was our aim throughout Ron Atkinson's reign and will continue to be our main priority. It would be very rash to call Ron Atkinson a failure because he didn't win the title. In the five full seasons he was here he never finished outside the top four, he won us the FA Cup twice and got us to the final of the Milk Cup, plus the semi-final of the European Cup Winners Cup, so I don't think under any circumstances you could class Ron Atkinson a failure. The only thing is that he didn't achieve the First Division Championship.

If Ron Atkinson had not failed, why then had he lost his job? Others both before and after Busby had aimed for the League Championship and as Tommy Docherty once had said:

There are 92 clubs in the Football League, but there can only be one which finishes at the top of the First Division. They have succeeded, but it doesn't mean that the others have failed. If winning the Championship was the only yardstick, 91 managers would get the sack every season.

Atkinson had brought some success to the club, and had sold two players, Wilkins and Hughes, for record amounts, but his judgment on the buying side was questionable. He had allowed Beardsley to pass through the club to become a world star and had missed the opportunity to buy Gary Lineker before he moved from Leicester City to Everton. He had been let down in his purchase of Alan Brazil, who never really lived up to his reputation, although it became clear in later years that the player had been seriously hindered by injury. In buying Robson, Moses, Strachan, Olsen, Gidman and Gibson he had spent wisely, in persuading Muhren to move to Old Trafford he had shown great guile. Yet still he was replaced.

The supporters of Manchester are the final judges. Ron Atkinson had given them a successful team, but had failed to win their hearts.

An immediate question mark hung over the squad inherited by Alex Ferguson, but chairman Edwards was quick to dismiss speculation that Bryan Robson and Remi Moses might not figure in the new manager's plans:

Remi has been fighting to get back after his injury and is winning that battle. Bryan is the captain of England. I cannot think that there is any danger that Alex Ferguson would want to discard either of them, just because they were Ron Atkinson's players at West Brom before coming to Old Trafford.

The new manager will need time. He has to assess his new players as well as the opposition in the English League, which is new to him but not unknown. He's got a lot to do, and a lot to learn in the next few weeks.

I don't think that we can expect miracles overnight – but Alex Ferguson will, he's that type of man!

The new manager selected his side for his first game, away to Oxford, where Ron Atkinson was thought of as a hero. For his first team talk he used heroes as a theme, telling his new squad:

You players have got the chance to be the ones who win the Championship for Manchester United for the first time in 20 years. To do so you have to take over from men like Law and Best and Charlton, or you'll always walk with their ghosts. It could be your greatest triumph, for you, and for your supporters, if you can emulate those heroes.

On the day Atkinson lost his job he had telephoned the training ground immediately after his meeting with the chairman and informed Brian Whitehouse, the coach. Whitehouse then had the unhappy task of informing the players that their manager had been sacked. His first job under Ferguson was to help select the side to face Oxford.

With Bailey still unfit Chris Turner was the automatic choice in goal, Duxbury was at right-back, having shared that position for most of the season with Sivebaek, whose arrival at the club had led to John Gidman being left out of

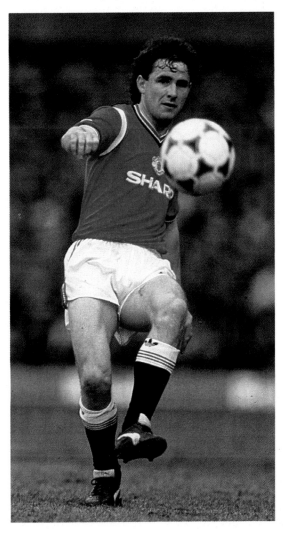

Arthur Albiston made his debut for the club in 1977 and gave an impressive display in the FA Cup final that year as United beat Liverpool to win the cup. The Scottish left full-back won three FA Cup winning medals with United, the only player ever to achieve this feat. In 1988 Albiston was granted a testimonial and given a free transfer. 'In view of his fine record with the club it would not have been right for us to ask for a fee,' said Alex Ferguson

the squad and consequently joining Manchester City. Arthur Albiston was at left-back. He was a player Ferguson knew, and had been a member of the Scottish World Cup squad in Mexico, managed by the new man in charge of United. Ferguson had taken the international reins following the death of Jock Stein.

Hogg and Moran played at the centre of the defence, McGrath moving into midfield together with Moses, Blackmore and Barnes as Davenport and Stapleton led the attack. Olsen was substitute, having started just six League games that season, and it seemed just a matter of time before the Dane would be leaving the club.

The Moses-Olsen incident

Olsen was obviously unhappy. He had been hailed a hero on his arrival from Ajax, but had fallen out of favour, and the purchase of Barnes did not help matters. He was also the unfortunate victim of an incident which must have contributed to the demise of Atkinson. It happened a month before the Oxford game when Olsen was led away from the training ground with blood streaming from a huge gash around the eye. He was taken to hospital and within minutes Atkinson described the incident:

I think it's typical of the way things can go for you sometimes. Jesper and Remi Moses clashed heads in a training accident this morning. He's split his eye and had to have stitches, consequently he'll miss the Littlewoods Cup game tomorrow at Port Vale.

Atkinson's words were printed on the sports pages of the national newspapers, but there was another version of the story. Watching the training session had been two Danish journalists, a reporter and a photographer, and they claimed that Moses had struck Olsen while reacting to a tackle from the player.

For two days the story made headline news. Olsen was quoted, saying: 'There is no doubt about it, Moses hit me – it was no accident.' His mother, in Denmark told reporters that her son was very upset by the incident and wanted to get away from United as quickly as possible. The whole affair did little for morale and four days after the incident, when Atkinson again gave his version of the story, those outside the club were left to decide for themselves who they believed. Atkinson said:

I gave my version on Monday ten minutes after it happened. I was probably the nearest person to the accident, where the two lads clashed heads. Now all of a sudden because of something which has appeared in a Danish newspaper, the dirt's flying everywhere.

I can tell you it was simply and purely a training accident, a bit of a freak one maybe, but it was still an accident.

It took place about 70 or 80 yards away from the nearest spectator – our training sessions are open to the public. There were two or three players round the ball, so I wouldn't think that anyone would have had a particularly good view of it. The photographer who took a picture took it minutes after it happened. We are talking about Danish journalists who have obviously come over here to get a sensational story, that's what they're paid for. There happened to be English journalists there who saw nothing untoward at all. I won't be taking any action about the matter, because there is no action to take.

It was an impossible situation to deal with satisfactorily. Olsen's version, eventually printed in English newspapers, totally contradicted that of his manager. From the club's point of view whoever was right or wrong mattered less than United's dirty linen being aired in public. It did Ron Atkinson no favours.

United lost their first game under Ferguson 2–0, with Olsen playing for the last 15 minutes. His bravery against Wimbledon three games later earned Olsen a place in the side for the next 16 League and Cup games, and Barnes was sold to Manchester City, his original club.

Ferguson brought Archie Knox, his assistant at Aberdeen, to be his right-hand man at Old Trafford, and the Scots injected new spirit into the club. Training became longer and harder and players responded to the new methods. Bryan Robson said after a few weeks:

There's no doubt about it, things have changed, and the players seem to like the way things are being done. I've got to be honest and say that I've never felt stronger in my legs than I do now. I have had a lot of trouble with my hamstring, but the manager has got me doing different routines to strengthen my legs and they seem to be working.

On the pitch the new methods showed. United became a side which used fitness as well as skill to compete, and their willingness to run led to victory over Liverpool at Anfield – their only away win of the whole First Division campaign – as Ferguson tested his squad.

He used no fewer than 23 players during his first season, amongst them Terry Gibson, who had almost joined Watford in the week Atkinson was replaced, but who was eventually transferred to Wimbledon after waiting almost a year for his home debut. Gibson was given a chance by Ferguson, playing 12 First Division games and taking part in both FA Cup ties played that season.

The first was against Manchester City at Old Trafford, when a crowd of 54,295 witnessed Norman Whiteside scoring the only goal of the afternoon in the 67th minute. But the state of the pitch was poor, and pointed the way to the trouble that would come to a head in the fourth round.

Media criticism and regular comments from supporters had led to the club installing an undersoil heating system, but, as if to back up comments previously made by chairman Edwards, it had proved unsatisfactory.

Although costing over £80,000, sections of it had failed and consequently, when there was a hard frost, parts of the ground were frozen while others were perfect for play. Before the City tie, hot air machines were placed around the frozen sections pumping warmth under large blankets borrowed from the nearby cricket ground. The scheme worked and the pitch was perfect.

It was different for the next round, however, when United were again drawn at home, to Coventry City. Alex Ferguson took the players away to the Lake District to prepare for the game. Five wins and four draws had lifted them away from the relegation zone and the prospect of a good Cup run justified such preparations. On the morning of the game the manager was stunned when he arrived at Old Trafford. The pitch was bone hard, a sudden frost having caught out the groundstaff. The game was turned into a lottery, and United were the losers. Keith Houchen scored for Coventry with a 20th minute shot after the ball bobbled away from Turner on the slippery surface. Coventry went on to win the FA Cup and United replaced their undersoil heating during the summer of 1987.

After their Cup hopes ended United spent the remainder of the season in mid-table, ending the

Gary Walsh got into football through the government's YTS project and eventually signed professional forms with United. In December 1986 he made his debut against Aston Villa and became first choice 'keeper by the start of the 1987–88 season. However, after being concussed in the game against Sheffield Wednesday in October 1987 he lost his place, and a further head injury during the club's visit to Bermuda kept him out for the remainder of the season

Obviously I am very sad to be giving up the game, when I could have another ten years or more at the top. But I am leaving with some tremendous memories and I feel honoured to have played for a club as great as Manchester United.

During the summer of 1987 Frank Stapleton was transferred to the Dutch team Ajax, where his former club-mate Arnie Muhren was extending his career, and John Sivebaek was sold to St Etienne of France.

Viv Anderson and Brian McClair arrive

In their places came Ferguson's first signings, England full-back Viv Anderson, and Scotland's Brian McClair.

Anderson had been a trialist with United as a boy, but had not been taken on and had eventually become a player with his home town club Nottingham Forest. He was then transferred to Arsenal after winning major honours with Forest, including the European Cup and the First Division Championship, and was a regular in the England side.

Anderson and McClair signed together on 1 July and both players had their transfer fees finalised by the Football League's independent tribunal. United paid £250,000 for Anderson, but McClair, scorer of 35 goals in his final season with Celtic, cost over three times as much. Celtic valued the player at £2 million, United offered well below that, and eventually a cheque was signed for £850,000.

For Ferguson it was the first step towards success:

When I first arrived at this club I felt that I had to give myself time to look at the players I had taken over. I knew that I would eventually make changes, and I have gone on record as saying that I think I need to strengthen as many as five positions. It may be that I have the players for those positions already, it's up to them to show me that, but if not then I will find them elsewhere.

By the time the first full season under his management was about to commence Alex Ferguson had stamped out a clear message of intent to his players. He selected his strongest side from the squad and this shocked some.

Young Walsh was again in goal, although Turner had played in some pre-season matches, Anderson was at right-back, and Mike Duxbury on the left, in preference to the left-footed Albiston. Gibson was one of several players who had been informed that they might be made available for transfer should there be any enquiries, the others being Hogg and goalkeeper Turner. Peter Davenport was linked to other clubs, but began the season as one of the two substitutes allowed in all games after a change in the rules during the summer.

For the opening game at Southampton McGrath and Moran formed the centre of the defence, Moses, Strachan, Robson and Olsen

Above: Viv Anderson and Brian McClair become United players at a joint signing ceremony staged for the media in the club trophy room. Left to right are: Mike Edelson (director), Viv Anderson, Alex Ferguson, Martin Edwards (chairman), Brian McClair, Maurice Watkins (director)

Right: England right full-back Viv Anderson already had a string of honours to his name when he joined United. He was a member of Brian Clough's successful Nottingham Forest side before moving to Arsenal. However when his contract ended he was keen to join United, a club he had trained with as a schoolboy

campaign in 11th place, their lowest position since the relegation season of 1973–74. But there were signs that the 1987–88 season would have more to offer.

During the months of Ferguson's management Gary Walsh, an 18-year-old goalkeeper, was drafted into the squad, and his presence led to Chris Turner asking for a transfer. Gary Bailey came back from injury and played in five games before announcing that he was being forced into retirement by a knee problem identical to that which had led to the end of Steve Coppell's playing days.

Bailey returned to his parents' home in South Africa to continue the university studies he had abandoned to take up his footballing career, after a hastily arranged testimonial. He said:

were in midfield and Whiteside returned to his role of attacker alongside McClair.

The Scot quickly began to repay his transfer fee, and by Christmas had scored 14 goals, more even than Hughes in his first full term, and Alex Ferguson added fuel to the flames of speculation by hinting that the prospect of McClair and the Welsh striker playing together was not simply wishful thinking.

Hughes was finding that life with Barcelona was not what he had expected. He had flown home early in 1987 after being de-registered by the Spanish giants, which made him unable to play for them under the two-foreign-players rule, and he was immediately linked with his old club.

He played in the Gary Bailey Testimonial and scored four spectacular goals. Afterwards he said:

I am still a Barcelona player and can do nothing unless my club wants me to do it. I have always said that if ever I came back to English football then there is only one club I would want to play for and that's United. I have a lot of friends here and get on well with the supporters.

Unofficially Hughes had hinted that he was ready to return, and this led to Alex Ferguson flying to Barcelona for talks with the player and his manager Terry Venables. After his trip he said:

I want to bring Mark back to United, but at present the main problem is with the Inland Revenue. Mark has to stay abroad until after

GARY BAILEY TESTIMONIAL
MANCHESTER UNITED
v
ENGLAND XI
at Old Trafford

Sunday 10th May 1987   Official Souvenir Programme 50p

Mexico v England — Azteca 1985

Left: When injury cut short the career of goalkeeper Gary Bailey, he was swift to return to his parents' home in South Africa and extend his education at Witt's University. Within a month of the announcement that his playing days were to end his testimonial game was staged at Old Trafford. United met an England eleven

April 1988 otherwise he would be liable for taxation on the money he has earned since he left this country. We can do nothing until then, but I promise that I will do my best to get him playing for United again.

An injury to Paul McGrath forced Ferguson into the transfer market again in December 1987 and the target this time was Steve Bruce of Norwich City. The club was on the verge of paying £1 million to Glasgow Rangers for their England international centre-back Terry Butcher, but 24 hours before the deal would have become public knowledge, the player broke his leg. United had revealed their hand and when they turned to Norwich City for Bruce, after being rejected by Middlesbrough in a bid for Gary Pallister, they found the club difficult to deal with.

During the summer Alex Ferguson had failed to persuade Norwich to part with striker Kevin Drinkell, whom he saw as a likely partner for McClair, and when negotiations for Bruce opened he was told that the price was £1 million – the fee he had been ready to pay for Butcher. The clubs seemed to have reached agreement on a fee of £800,000 some 48 hours before United were due to play Oxford at Old Trafford on 12 December 1987. Nothing happened; the player had his bags packed ready to move north but was told that he was not being allowed to go. By 5 pm on Friday 11 December Bruce was still a Norwich player, and it took another six days before he was signed.

At first Norwich said they wanted to sign a replacement, then, after John O'Neill from QPR joined them, they said Bruce would not be released until a second player had been bought.

The sweet life he expected in Barcelona turned sour for Mark Hughes who in 1987 was once more linked with United as he found himself no longer wanted by the Spanish giants. Hughes was forced to play on loan in Germany with Bayern Munich after his registration was cancelled by Barcelona, and this sparked off speculation in Britain that he was ready to return to Old Trafford. When sold by United he brought a club record £2.2 million; in June 1988 he re-signed for a fee of £1.5 million to join Brian McClair in United's forward line

Steve Bruce joined United in December 1987 after a fortnight of negotiations with Norwich City. In the end he cost £800,000 and made his debut at Fratton Park, Portsmouth, on 19 December. Bruce's commitment made him a popular player immediately with the supporters and took him to the verge of full international honours in his first season at Old Trafford

Eventually Alex Ferguson called the deal off on 17 December, after Norwich chairman Robert Chase apparently attempted to increase the fee. Finally the Norfolk club had a change of heart and Bruce signed later that day.

Bruce made his debut in a game at Portsmouth which saw the almost rejected Turner playing in goal for his third successive game, all of them victories. Turner had won back his place after Walsh was concussed for the second time that season. The first injury was in the victory over Sheffield Wednesday at Hillsborough, the first time United had taken maximum points since the Yorkshire club's return to the First Division in 1984. The second came during a trip to Bermuda which caused a sensation for another reason, and also revealed Ferguson's strength as a man capable of dealing with a difficult situation.

The trip was arranged to coincide with United's 'blank Saturday', the fate befalling each First Division club during the 1987–88 season, when there were 21 teams competing. United played two games on the island, but it was not their football which made headline news.

Clayton Blackmore was arrested and held by police while investigations were carried out regarding a serious accusation being made against him by a young American woman. The police eventually released him after the Bermudan Attorney General ruled that there was no case to answer, but the woman told newspapers her version of the alleged incident.

News reporters beseiged the airport as the team returned, but Blackmore had travelled back a day ahead of his colleagues with club solicitor Maurice Watkins. United found themselves the centre of media attention, but Alex Ferguson remained calm. He allowed sports journalists into the training ground, and as the team were about to leave for the game at QPR called Blackmore into his Friday press conference, where he answered questions from the same newspaper representatives who regularly gathered information from the club. By the weekend the spotlight had burnt itself out and the matter was closed.

Discipline was mentioned by Alex Ferguson when he faced shareholders at the club's annual meeting, and he told them that he had his own methods of dealing with such matters, but he added that these were not being discussed in such a public place as the packed Europa Suite, part of the club's lavish restaurant complex. As he looked out on the supporters gathered before him Alex Ferguson must have felt that he was amongst friends. He was the new man on the tightrope, but in his short time in charge he had shown that his heart was as much in the club as theirs. He was taking his first steps with caution, but with style. He had won over the staff under him, from the laundry ladies with whom he and Archie Knox share a daily cup of tea at 8.00 am to the chairman and his board of directors.

His natural gift for dealing with people from every walk of life was self-evident and he was filling the role of public relations officer as well as team manager. Small things mattered to Alex Ferguson. Requests for autographs became important and these were organised to coincide with Friday training sessions, when his players were faced with the week's demands for signed books, photographs and footballs, used to raise money for charity.

Pre-match preparation was re-organised. Instead of meeting at the ground and travelling to a city centre hotel for a Saturday morning meal the players were told to report to Old Trafford, where they would eat in the grill room, then relax in their lounge, or mingle with supporters.

Ferguson's influence led to the appointment of a new groundsman, the building of new dressing rooms, and a general awareness amongst his players and the administrative staff that all were responsible for the success of Manchester United.

The future for United

In 1987 the club introduced its own membership scheme to fall in line with government measures to curb football hooliganism. The United scheme was designed to give those who joined something in return for their entry fee. The club gave discount for all home games, and for goods bought at the souvenir shop. Members were sent badges and year books, and given free admission to all reserve games as well as a complimentary ticket for the club museum.

The scheme came in for some criticism in its early stages but by the end of 1987 over 40,000 supporters had joined. The idea had developed from suggestions put to the club by Bobby Charlton, and it was he, speaking at the 1987 annual meeting, who outlined his hopes for the future of Manchester United:

I have been to Barcelona and seen the way that their membership scheme works. It enables them to raise huge amounts of capital at the start of every season, and that is one of the ways that they are able to compete with the best in Europe. It may take several years before this club can stand alongside them from a financial point of view, but we have started to take a step in that direction.

Financial security is important, and in order to be successful on the field you have to be successful off it.

As far as I, and my fellow directors are concerned, we have in Alex Ferguson the perfect man to lead us to success. Even in the short time he has been here he has shown us that he is doing things the right way. I can see no reason why Alex should not be here for the next 30 years, and I wish him every success for the future . . . the future of Manchester United.

United entered 1988 with optimism. Victory over reigning champions Everton at Old Trafford had restored them to fourth place in the

table, and although slim, the chance of Alex Ferguson taking the club to its first championship win for 21 years remained.

Liverpool stood in their way, leading the First Division and unbeaten in the League by the turn of the year. It seemed that nothing could prevent the First Division title from once more returning to Anfield, and when United drew with lowly Charlton Athletic on New Year's Day it became obvious that the fight was not only uphill, but virtually impossible.

Defeat in the Littlewoods Cup quarter-final at Oxford was soul-destroying: 'We were hoping for success in one of the domestic cup competitions,' Alex Ferguson said after losing 2–0 at the Manor Ground, 'now we have only the FA Cup to aim for.' He called for a positive response from his players, but newspaper speculation that he would stage a wholesale clear-out at the end of the season did nothing to boost morale.

There was a glimmer of hope as the Oxford game was followed by a 2–1 televised win at Highbury, then victory over Chelsea before the biggest crowd of the season at Old Trafford as 50,700 witnessed a 2–0 win which took United through to the fifth round of the FA Cup and another visit to Arsenal's ground. This was a game which could have devastated the side for the rest of the season. After trailing 2–0 at half-time Brian McClair scored to put United back in the game. Confidence was restored and the pendulum swung United's way. After being totally dominated for the first 45 minutes they took the upper hand and pressurised Arsenal who were lucky to clear several chances away from their besieged goal, then Norman Whiteside was tripped with three minutes remaining and United were awarded a penalty, which McClair failed to convert.

It was an incident which would have left a lasting impression on many players, but McClair faced the media immediately after the game,

claiming: 'When you score you are ready to take the bouquets, so you also have got to be prepared to stand up and take the criticism when you miss.' He also stepped forward to take the next penalty when the opportunity arose weeks later at Oxford. However, Alex Ferguson had removed this responsibility from his leading scorer who would have left Highbury with 21 goals to his name that season had his penalty been converted.

The media used the defeat to emphasise that United's season had ended even though February had not. Crowds began to fall and a League defeat at Norwich had Alex Ferguson demanding that his players 'show me that they want to play for Manchester United'. Many responded but Norman Whiteside and Paul McGrath reacted unexpectedly. Both said that they were unhappy at Old Trafford and asked for transfers in highly publicised moves which stunned United's followers. 'I have had some great years at Old Trafford,' said Whiteside, 'but I feel that the time has come for a change. I want to play abroad, I would not consider playing for another English club except United, but I would like to try my hand on the continent.'

McGrath's demand for a move came a short time after Whiteside's, although there had been newspaper speculation that all was not well between the player and the club following a much publicised motoring accident which led to McGrath being injured and later fined and banned from driving on a drinks charge. 'I feel that I have gone stale,' he said, 'and I would like a new challenge.' The Republic of Ireland defender had been out of action for five months when Alex Ferguson decided that he was fit to play again but the supporters showed whose side they were on when McGrath was booed by the home fans during the game against Luton, and Whiteside was the target of chants of 'You only want the money!' as he sat on the substitute's

Above right: Gordon Strachan turns after scoring United's third goal at Anfield to earn a point against Liverpool. United took an early lead but slipped to 3–1 down before their fightback

Left: A fee of £750,000 brought Scotland's goalkeeper Jim Leighton to Old Trafford

Below: A moving moment for Arthur Albiston as, with his sons Ross (left) and Ryan, he runs a lap of honour around Old Trafford to end his career with the club following his testimonial game. He later joined Ron Atkinson at West Bromwich Albion

bench during the same game.

There was cause for celebration during the fixture, however, when Brian McClair scored his twentieth League goal of the season, the first United player to reach this mark since George Best 20 years earlier and an unbeaten run since the reversal at Norwich had taken them into second place.

Liverpool were champions elect, and the rivalry between the two clubs reached boiling point on Easter Monday – a week before the Luton game – when United held the Merseysiders to a 3–3 draw at Anfield in an inspired performance. United led as early as the second minute through a Bryan Robson goal, but Liverpool fought back and by the first minute of the second half were 3–1 ahead. To add to their problems United had Colin Gibson sent off for a second bookable offence but the ten men played inspired football, Robson got a second with a deflected shot and Gordon Strachan levelled the scores in the 77th minute.

It was probably the frustration of seeing his team lose their lead and the chance of securing the title within one more game which led to Liverpool manager Kenny Dalglish triggering off a clash with Alex Ferguson after the game. The incident made headline news but was dealt with quietly by the Football Association. Both managers were told to be more careful about their behaviour in the future.

A month later Liverpool were champions and United had secured second place just nine points behind them, closing a 17-point lead to just a three-game difference. Nottingham Forest were third, eight points adrift and Everton, who had been favourites to finish runners-up, ended their season 11 points behind United and 20 behind their neighbours Liverpool.

United collected 81 points, their biggest tally since the three-points-a-win system was introduced and there was much cause for optimism as

the season ended: 'I know that we are not very far away from having a side which can take the championship. During the coming weeks I shall make every effort to strengthen areas of the team which I feel should be improved, and I know that we will challenge the best in our next campaign,' said Alex Ferguson at the end of his first full season as manager.

In May 1988 he bought Aberdeen's Scottish international goalkeeper Jim Leighton for a record £750,000 as his plans for rebuilding were put into action, but only one player was told that his services would no longer be required at the club . . . Arthur Albiston was given a free transfer as a career spanning 11 years of League football with the club came to a close with a testimonial game against Manchester City. 'I have some wonderful memories of my time here, and I know that the club is going to reach the top once again very soon. While I'm sad to be leaving I can look back on some great times and I am proud to have shared in the successes which have come our way while I have been here,' said Albiston, the only United player ever to have won three FA Cup winners' medals with the club, having played in the finals of 1977, 1983 and 1985.

So Alex Ferguson was able to look towards the future with the words of his chairman echoing the thoughts of every United supporter: 'Time alone will tell but I am sure that Alex Ferguson will lead us to greater success than we have enjoyed in recent years. The fruits of his labours in rebuilding a vigorous youth policy, completely overhauling our scouting system and instilling a feeling of pride in everyone who wears a United shirt will I am positive be clear for all to see before very long . . . and I look forward to the future of Manchester United.'

Manchester United match-by-match statistical record

Abbreviations

P: games played
W: wins
D: draws
L: defeats (losses)
F: goals scored
A: goals conceded

Pts: points
Appearances (goals) refer to League games only
Figures shown as ² etc refer to goals scored by individual players
Players' names in final column, from 1965–66 onwards, are substitutes
* own-goal

SEASON 1889–1890
FOOTBALL ALLIANCE

21 Sep	Sunderland A	H	W	4–1
23 Sep	Bootle	A	L	1–4
28 Sep	Crewe Alex	A	D	2–2
19 Oct	Walsall T Swifts	A	L	0–4
26 Oct	Birmingham St G	A	L	1–5
9 Nov	Long Eaton R	H	W	3–0
30 Nov	Sheffield Wed	A	L	1–3
7 Dec	Bootle	H	W	3–0
28 Dec	Darwen	A	L	1–4
25 Jan	Sunderland	A	L	0–2
8 Feb	Grimsby T	A	L	0–7
15 Feb	Nottingham F	A	W	3–1
1 Mar	Crewe Alex	H	L	1–2
15 Mar	Small Heath	A	D	1–1
22 Mar	Long Eaton R	A	W	3–1
29 Mar	Darwen	H	W	2–1
5 Apr	Nottingham F	H	L	0–1
7 Apr	Small Heath	H	W	9–1
14 Apr	Grimsby T	H	L	0–1
19 Apr	Birmingham St G	H	W	2–1
21 Apr	Walsall T Swifts	H	W	2–1
26 Apr	Sheffield Wed	H	L	1–2

FA Cup

18 Jan	Preston N E (1)	A	L	1–6

Football Alliance

	P	W	D	L	F:A	Pts	
Newton Heath	22	9	2	11	40:45	20	8th

SEASON 1890–1891
FOOTBALL ALLIANCE

6 Sep	Darwen	H	W	4–2
13 Sep	Grimsby T	A	L	1–3
20 Sep	Nottingham F	H	D	1–1
27 Sep	Stoke C	A	L	1–2
11 Oct	Bootle	A	L	0–5
18 Oct	Grimsby T	H	W	3–1
1 Nov	Crewe Alex	H	W	6–3
8 Nov	Walsall T Swifts	A	L	1–2
22 Nov	Nottingham F	A	L	2–8
29 Nov	Sunderland	H	L	1–5
13 Dec	Small Heath	H	W	3–1
27 Dec	Bootle	H	W	2–1
5 Jan	Stoke C	H	L	0–1
10 Jan	Birmingham St G	A	L	1–6
17 Jan	Walsall T Swifts	H	D	3–3
24 Jan	Sheffield Wed	A	W	2–1
14 Feb	Crewe Alex	A	W	1–0
21 Feb	Sheffield Wed	H	D	1–1
7 Mar	Small Heath	A	L	1–2
14 Mar	Birmingham St G	H	L	1–3
28 Mar	Darwen	A	L	1–2
11 Apr	Sunderland	A	L	1–2

FA Cup

4 Oct	Higher Walton (Q1) (tie switched to Manchester)	H	W	2–0
25 Oct	Bootle Res (Q2)	A	L	0–1

Football Alliance

	P	W	D	L	F:A	Pts	
Newton Heath	22	7	3	12	37:55	17	9th

SEASON 1891–1892
FOOTBALL ALLIANCE

12 Sep	Burton Swifts	A	L	2–3
19 Sep	Bootle	H	W	4–0
26 Sep	Birmingham St G	A	W	3–1
10 Oct	Ardwick	H	W	3–1
17 Oct	Grimsby T	A	D	2–2
31 Oct	Burton Swifts	H	W	3–1
7 Nov	Crewe Alex	A	W	2–0
21 Nov	Lincoln C	H	W	10–1
28 Nov	Walsall T Swifts	A	W	4–1
12 Dec	Sheffield Wed	A	W	4–2
19 Dec	Ardwick	A	D	2–2
26 Dec	Small Heath	H	D	3–3
1 Jan	Nottingham F	H	D	1–1
9 Jan	Bootle	A	D	1–1
30 Jan	Crewe Alex	H	W	5–3
20 Feb	Sheffield Wed	H	D	1–1
27 Feb	Small Heath	A	L	2–3
5 Mar	Walsall T Swifts	H	W	5–0
19 Mar	Nottingham F	A	L	0–3
26 Mar	Grimsby T	H	D	3–3
2 Apr	Lincoln C	A	W	6–1
9 Apr	Birmingham St G	H	W	3–0

FA Cup

3 Oct	Ardwick (Q1)	H	W	5–1
24 Oct	Heywood (Q2) (scratched)	H	W	W–0
14 Nov	South Shore (Q3)	A	W	2–0
5 Dec	Blackpool (Q4)	H	L	3–4

Football Alliance

	P	W	D	L	F:A	Pts	
Newton Heath	22	12	7	3	69:33	31	2nd

SEASON 1892–1893
FOOTBALL LEAGUE (DIVISION 1)

3 Sep	Blackburn R	A	L	3–4
10 Sep	Burnley	H	D	1–1
17 Sep	Burnley	A	L	1–4
24 Sep	Everton	A	L	0–6
1 Oct	W B A	A	D	0–0
8 Oct	W B A	H	L	2–4
15 Oct	Wolverhampton W	H	W	10–1
19 Oct	Everton	H	L	3–4
22 Oct	Sheffield Wed	A	L	0–1
29 Oct	Nottingham F	A	D	1–1
5 Nov	Blackburn R	H	D	4–4
12 Nov	Notts Co	H	L	1–3
19 Nov	Aston Villa	H	W	2–0
26 Nov	Accrington S	A	D	2–2
3 Dec	Bolton W	A	L	1–4
10 Dec	Bolton W	H	W	1–0
17 Dec	Wolverhampton W	A	L	0–2
24 Dec	Sheffield Wed	H	L	1–5
26 Dec	Preston NE	A	L	1–2
31 Dec	Derby Co	H	W	7–1
7 Jan	Stoke C	A	L	1–7
14 Jan	Nottingham F	H	L	1–3
26 Jan	Notts Co	A	L	0–4
11 Feb	Derby Co	A	L	1–5
4 Mar	Sunderland	H	L	0–5
6 Mar	Aston Villa	A	L	0–2
31 Mar	Stoke C	H	W	1–0
1 Apr	Preston NE	H	W	2–1
4 Apr	Sunderland	A	L	0–6
8 Apr	Accrington S	H	D	3–3

Test Match

22 Apr	Small Heath (At Stoke)		D	1–1

Replay

27 Apr	Small Heath		W	5–2

Newton Heath kept First Division status

FA Cup

21 Jan	Blackburn R (1)	A	L	0–4

Football League

	P	W	D	L	F:A	Pts	
Newton Heath	30	6	6	18	50:85	18	16th

SEASON 1893–1894
FOOTBALL LEAGUE (DIVISION 1)

2 Sep	Burnley	H	W	3–2
9 Sep	W B A	A	L	1–3
16 Sep	Sheffield Wed	A	W	1–0
23 Sep	Nottingham F	H	D	1–1
30 Sep	Darwen	A	L	0–1
7 Oct	Derby Co	A	L	0–2
14 Oct	W B A	H	W	4–1
21 Oct	Burnley	A	L	1–4
28 Oct	Wolverhampton W	A	L	0–2
4 Nov	Darwen	H	L	0–1
11 Nov	Wolverhampton W	H	W	1–0
25 Nov	Sheffield U	A	L	1–3
2 Dec	Everton	H	L	0–3
6 Dec	Sunderland	A	L	1–4
9 Dec	Bolton W	A	L	0–2
16 Dec	Aston Villa	H	L	1–3
23 Dec	Preston NE	A	L	0–2
6 Jan	Everton	A	L	0–2
13 Jan	Sheffield Wed	H	L	1–2
3 Feb	Aston Villa	A	L	1–5
3 Mar	Sunderland	H	L	2–4
10 Mar	Sheffield U	H	L	0–2
12 Mar	Blackburn R	H	W	5–1
17 Mar	Derby Co	H	L	2–6
23 Mar	Stoke C	H	W	6–2
24 Mar	Bolton W	H	D	2–2
26 Mar	Blackburn R	A	L	0–4
31 Mar	Stoke C	A	L	1–3
7 Apr	Nottingham F	A	L	0–2
14 Apr	Preston NE	H	L	1–3

Test Match

28 Apr	Liverpool (At Ewood Park)		L	0–2

Newton Heath were relegated to Division Two

FA Cup

27 Jan	Middlesbrough (1)	H	W	4–0
10 Feb	Blackburn R (2)*	H	D	0–0
17 Feb	Blackburn R (2R)	A	L	1–5

*after extra time

Football League

	P	W	D	L	F:A	Pts	
Newton Heath	30	6	2	22	36:72	14	16th

SEASON 1894–1895
FOOTBALL LEAGUE (DIVISION 2)

8 Sep	Burton W	A	L	0–1
15 Sep	Crewe Alex	H	W	6–1
22 Sep	Leicester Fosse	A	W	3–2
6 Oct	Darwen	A	D	1–1
13 Oct	Arsenal	H	D	3–3
20 Oct	Burton Swifts	A	W	2–1
27 Oct	Leicester Fosse	H	D	2–2
3 Nov	Manchester C	A	W	5–2
10 Nov	Rotherham T	H	W	3–2
17 Nov	Grimsby T	A	L	1–2
24 Nov	Darwen	H	D	1–1
1 Dec	Crewe Alex	A	W	2–0
8 Dec	Burton Swifts	H	W	5–1
15 Dec	Notts Co	A	D	1–1
22 Dec	Lincoln C	H	W	3–0
24 Dec	Port Vale	A	W	5–2
26 Dec	Walsall	A	W	2–1
29 Dec	Lincoln C	A	L	0–3
1 Jan	Port Vale	H	W	3–0
5 Jan	Manchester C	H	W	4–1
12 Jan	Rotherham T	A	L	1–2
2 Mar	Burton W	H	D	1–1
23 Mar	Grimsby T	H	W	2–0
30 Mar	Arsenal	A	L	2–3
3 Apr	Walsall	H	W	9–0
6 Apr	Newcastle U	H	W	5–1
12 Apr	Bury	H	D	2–2
13 Apr	Newcastle U	A	L	0–3
15 Apr	Bury	A	L	1–2
20 Apr	Notts Co	H	D	3–3

Test Match

27 Apr	Stoke C (at Burslem)		L	0–3

Newton Heath stayed in Division 2

FA Cup

2 Feb	Stoke C (1)	H	L	2–3

Football League

	P	W	D	L	F:A	Pts	
Newton Heath	30	15	8	7	78:44	38	3rd

SEASON 1895–1896
FOOTBALL LEAGUE (DIVISION 2)

7 Sep	Crewe Alex	H	W	5–0
14 Sep	Loughborough T	A	D	3–3
21 Sep	Burton Swifts	H	W	5–0
28 Sep	Crewe Alex	A	W	2–0
5 Oct	Manchester C	H	D	1–1
12 Oct	Liverpool	A	L	1–7
19 Oct	Newcastle U	H	W	2–1
26 Oct	Newcastle U	A	L	1–2
2 Nov	Liverpool	H	W	5–2
9 Nov	Arsenal	A	L	1–2
16 Nov	Lincoln C	H	D	5–5
23 Nov	Notts Co	A	W	2–0
30 Nov	Arsenal	H	W	5–1
7 Dec	Manchester C	A	L	1–2
14 Dec	Notts Co	H	W	3–0
21 Dec	Darwen	A	L	0–3
1 Jan	Grimsby T	H	W	3–2
4 Jan	Leicester Fosse	A	L	0–3
11 Jan	Rotherham T	H	W	3–0
3 Feb	Leicester Fosse	H	W	2–0
8 Feb	Burton Swifts	A	L	1–4
29 Feb	Burton W	H	L	1–2
7 Mar	Rotherham T	A	W	3–2
14 Mar	Grimsby T	A	L	2–4
18 Mar	Burton W	A	L	1–5
23 Mar	Port Vale	A	L	0–3
3 Apr	Darwen	H	W	4–0
4 Apr	Loughborough T	H	W	2–0
6 Apr	Port Vale	H	W	2–1
11 Apr	Lincoln C	A	L	0–2

FA Cup

1 Feb	Kettering (1)	H	W	2–1
15 Feb	Derby Co (2)	H	D	1–1
19 Feb	Derby Co (2R)	A	L	1–5

Football League

	P	W	D	L	F:A	Pts	
Newton Heath	30	15	3	12	66:57	33	6th

SEASON 1896–1897
FOOTBALL LEAGUE (DIVISION 2)

1 Sep	Gainsborough T	H	W	2–0
5 Sep	Burton Swifts	A	W	5–3
7 Sep	Walsall	H	W	2–0
12 Sep	Lincoln C	H	W	3–1
19 Sep	Grimsby T	A	L	0–2
21 Sep	Walsall	A	W	3–2
26 Sep	Newcastle U	H	W	4–0
3 Oct	Manchester C	A	D	0–0
10 Oct	Small Heath	H	D	1–1
17 Oct	Blackpool	A	L	2–4
21 Oct	Gainsborough T	A	L	0–2
24 Oct	Burton W	H	W	3–0
7 Nov	Grimsby T	H	W	4–2
28 Nov	Small Heath	A	L	0–1
19 Dec	Notts Co	A	L	0–3
25 Dec	Manchester C	H	W	2–1
26 Dec	Blackpool	H	W	2–0
28 Dec	Leicester Fosse	A	L	0–1
1 Jan	Newcastle U	A	L	0–2
9 Jan	Burton Swifts	H	D	1–1
6 Feb	Loughborough T	H	W	6–0
20 Feb	Leicester Fosse	H	W	2–1
2 Mar	Darwen	H	W	3–1
13 Mar	Darwen	A	W	2–0
20 Mar	Burton W	A	W	2–1
22 Mar	Arsenal	H	D	1–1
27 Mar	Notts Co	H	D	1–1
1 Apr	Lincoln C	A	W	3–1
3 Apr	Arsenal	A	W	2–0
10 Apr	Loughborough T	A	L	0–2

Test Match

19 Apr	Burnley	A	L	0–2
21 Apr	Burnley	H	W	2–0
24 Apr	Sunderland	H	D	1–1
26 Apr	Sunderland	A	L	0–2

Newton Heath stayed in Division 2

FA Cup

12 Dec	West Manchester (Q1)	H	W	7–0
2 Jan	Nelson (Q2)	H	W	3–0
16 Jan	Blackpool (Q3)	H	D	2–2
20 Jan	Blackpool (Q3R)	A	W	2–1
30 Jan	Kettering (1)	H	W	5–1
13 Feb	Southampton (2)	A	D	1–1
17 Feb	Southampton (2R)	H	W	3–1
27 Feb	Derby Co (3)	A	L	0–2

Football League

	P	W	D	L	F:A	Pts	
Newton Heath	30	17	5	8	56:34	39	2nd

SEASON 1897–1898
FOOTBALL LEAGUE (DIVISION 2)

4 Sep	Lincoln C	H	W	5–0
11 Sep	Burton Swifts	A	W	4–0
18 Sep	Luton T	A	L	1–2
25 Sep	Blackpool	H	W	1–0
2 Oct	Leicester Fosse	H	W	2–0
9 Oct	Newcastle U	A	L	0–2
16 Oct	Manchester C	H	D	1–1
23 Oct	Small Heath	A	L	1–2
30 Oct	Walsall	H	W	6–0
6 Nov	Lincoln C	A	L	0–1
13 Nov	Newcastle U	H	L	0–1
20 Nov	Leicester Fosse	A	D	1–1
27 Nov	Grimsby T	H	W	2–1
11 Dec	Walsall	A	D	1–1
25 Dec	Manchester C	A	W	1–0
27 Dec	Gainsborough T	A	L	1–2
1 Jan	Burton Swifts	H	W	4–0
8 Jan	Arsenal	A	L	1–5
12 Jan	Burnley	H	D	0–0
15 Jan	Blackpool	H	W	4–0
26 Feb	Arsenal	H	W	5–1
7 Mar	Burnley	A	L	3–6
19 Mar	Darwen	A	W	3–2
21 Mar	Luton T	A	D	2–2
29 Mar	Loughborough T	H	W	5–1
2 Apr	Grimsby T	A	W	3–1
8 Apr	Gainsborough T	H	W	1–0
9 Apr	Small Heath	H	W	3–1
16 Apr	Loughborough T	A	D	0–0
23 Apr	Darwen	H	W	3–2

FA Cup

29 Jan	Walsall(1)	H	W	1–0
12 Feb	Liverpool (2)	H	D	0–0
16 Feb	Liverpool (2R)	A	L	1–2

Football League

	P	W	D	L	F:A	Pts	
Newton Heath	30	16	6	8	64:35	38	5th

SEASON 1898–1899
FOOTBALL LEAGUE (DIVISION 2)

3 Sep	Gainsborough T	A	W	2–0
10 Sep	Manchester C	H	W	3–0
17 Sep	Glossop	A	W	2–1
24 Sep	Walsall	H	W	1–0
1 Oct	Burton Swifts	A	L	1–5
8 Oct	Port Vale	H	W	2–1
15 Oct	Small Heath	A	L	1–4
22 Oct	Loughborough T	H	W	6–1
5 Nov	Grimsby T	H	W	3–2
12 Nov	Barnsley	H	D	0–0
19 Nov	New Brighton	A	W	3–0
26 Nov	Lincoln C	H	W	1–0
3 Dec	Arsenal	A	L	1–5
10 Dec	Blackpool	H	W	3–1
17 Dec	Leicester Fosse	A	L	0–1
24 Dec	Darwen	H	W	9–0
26 Dec	Manchester C	A	L	0–4
31 Dec	Gainsborough T	H	W	6–1
2 Jan	Burton Swifts	H	D	2–2
14 Jan	Glossop	H	W	3–0
21 Jan	Walsall	A	L	0–2
4 Feb	Port Vale	A	L	0–1
18 Feb	Loughborough T	A	W	1–0
25 Feb	Small Heath	H	W	2–0
4 Mar	Grimsby T	A	L	0–3
18 Mar	New Brighton	H	L	1–2
25 Mar	Lincoln C	A	L	0–2
1 Apr	Arsenal	H	D	2–2
3 Apr	Blackpool	A	W	1–0
4 Apr	Barnsley	A	W	2–0
8 Apr	Luton T	A	W	1–0
12 Apr	Luton T	H	W	5–0
15 Apr	Leicester Fosse	H	D	2–2
22 Apr	Darwen	A	D	1–1

FA Cup

28 Jan	Tottenham H (1)	A	D	1–1
1 Feb	Tottenham H (1R)	H	L	3–5

Football League

	P	W	D	L	F:A	Pts	
Newton Heath	34	19	5	10	67:43	43	4th

SEASON 1899–1900
FOOTBALL LEAGUE (DIVISION 2)

2 Sep	Gainsborough T	H	D	2–2
9 Sep	Bolton W	A	L	1–2
16 Sep	Loughborough T	H	W	4–0
23 Sep	Burton Swifts	A	D	0–0
30 Sep	Sheffield Wed	A	L	1–2
7 Oct	Lincoln C	H	W	1–0
14 Oct	Small Heath	A	L	0–1
21 Oct	New Brighton	H	W	2–1
4 Nov	Arsenal	H	W	2–0
11 Nov	Barnsley	A	D	0–0
25 Nov	Luton T	A	W	1–0
2 Dec	Port Vale	H	W	3–0
16 Dec	Middlesbrough	H	W	2–1
23 Dec	Chesterfield	A	L	1–2
26 Dec	Grimsby T	A	W	7–0
30 Dec	Gainsborough T	A	W	1–0
6 Jan	Bolton W	H	L	1–2
13 Jan	Loughborough T	A	W	2–0
20 Jan	Burton Swifts	H	W	4–0
3 Feb	Sheffield Wed	H	W	1–0
10 Feb	Lincoln C	A	L	0–1
17 Feb	Small Heath	H	W	3–2
24 Feb	New Brighton	A	W	4–1
3 Mar	Grimsby T	H	W	1–0
10 Mar	Arsenal	A	L	1–2
17 Mar	Barnsley	H	W	3–0
24 Mar	Leicester Fosse	A	L	0–2
31 Mar	Luton T	H	W	5–0
7 Apr	Port Vale	A	L	0–1
13 Apr	Leicester Fosse	H	W	3–2
14 Apr	Walsall	H	W	5–0
17 Apr	Walsall	A	D	0–0
21 Apr	Middlesbrough	A	L	0–2
28 Apr	Chesterfield	H	W	2–1

FA Cup

28 Oct	South Shore (Q1)	A	L	1–3

Football League

	P	W	D	L	F:A	Pts	
Newton Heath	34	20	4	10	63:27	44	4th

SEASON 1900–1901 FOOTBALL LEAGUE (DIVISION 2)

1 Sep	Glossop	A	L	0–1
8 Sep	Middlesbrough	H	W	4–0
15 Sep	Burnley	A	L	0–1
22 Sep	Port Vale	H	W	4–0
29 Sep	Leicester Fosse	A	L	0–1
6 Oct	New Brighton	H	W	1–0
13 Oct	Gainsborough T	A	W	1–0
20 Oct	Walsall	H	D	1–1
27 Oct	Burton Swifts	A	L	1–3
10 Nov	Arsenal	A	L	1–2
24 Nov	Stockport Co	A	L	0–1
1 Dec	Small Heath	H	L	0–1
8 Dec	Grimsby T	A	L	0–2
15 Dec	Lincoln C	H	W	4–1
22 Dec	Chesterfield	A	L	1–2
26 Dec	Blackpool	H	W	4–0
29 Dec	Glossop	H	W	3–0
1 Jan	Middlesbrough	A	W	1–2
12 Jan	Burnley	H	L	0–1
19 Jan	Port Vale	A	L	0–2
16 Feb	Gainsborough T	H	D	0–0
19 Feb	New Brighton	A	L	0–2
25 Feb	Walsall	A	D	1–1
2 Mar	Burton Swifts	H	D	1–1
13 Mar	Barnsley	H	W	1–0
16 Mar	Arsenal	H	W	1–0
20 Mar	Leicester Fosse	H	L	0–1
23 Mar	Blackpool	A	W	2–1
30 Mar	Stockport Co	H	W	3–1
5 Apr	Lincoln C	A	L	0–2
6 Apr	Small Heath	A	L	0–1
9 Apr	Barnsley	A	L	2–6
13 Apr	Grimsby T	H	W	1–0
27 Apr	Chesterfield	H	W	1–0
	FA Cup			
5 Jan	Portsmouth (S)	H	W	3–0
9 Feb	Burnley (1)	H	D	0–0
13 Feb	Burnley (1R)	A	L	1–7

Football League

	P	W	D	L	F:A	Pts	
Newton Heath	34	14	4	16	42:38	32	10th

SEASON 1901–1902 FOOTBALL LEAGUE (DIVISION 2)

7 Sep	Gainsborough T	H	W	3–0
14 Sep	Middlesbrough	A	L	0–5
21 Sep	Bristol C	H	W	1–0
28 Sep	Blackpool	A	W	4–2
5 Oct	Stockport Co	H	D	3–3
12 Oct	Burton U	A	D	0–0
19 Oct	Glossop	A	D	0–0
26 Oct	Doncaster R	H	W	6–0
9 Nov	W B A	H	L	1–2
16 Nov	Arsenal	A	L	0–2
23 Nov	Barnsley	H	W	1–0
30 Nov	Leicester Fosse	A	L	2–3
7 Dec	Preston NE	A	L	1–5
21 Dec	Port Vale	H	W	1–0
25 Dec	Lincoln C	A	L	0–2
1 Jan	Preston NE	H	L	0–2
4 Jan	Gainsborough T	A	D	1–1
18 Jan	Bristol C	A	L	0–4
25 Jan	Blackpool	H	L	0–1
1 Feb	Stockport Co	A	L	0–1
11 Feb	Burnley	H	W	2–0
15 Feb	Glossop	H	W	1–0
22 Feb	Doncaster R	A	L	0–4
1 Mar	Lincoln C	H	D	0–0
8 Mar	W B A	A	L	0–4
15 Mar	Arsenal	H	L	0–1
17 Mar	Chesterfield	A	L	0–3
22 Mar	Barnsley	A	L	2–3
28 Mar	Burnley	A	L	0–1
29 Mar	Leicester Fosse	H	W	2–0
7 Apr	Middlesbrough	H	L	1–2
19 Apr	Port Vale	A	D	1–1
21 Apr	Burton U	H	W	3–1
23 Apr	Chesterfield	H	W	2–0
	FA Cup			
14 Dec	Lincoln C (IR)	H	L	1–2

Football League

	P	W	D	L	F:A	Pts	
Newton Heath	34	11	6	17	38:53	28	15th

SEASON 1902–1903 FOOTBALL LEAGUE (DIVISION 2)

6 Sep	Gainsborough T	A	W	1–0	Whitehouse	Stafford	Read	Morgan	Griffiths	Cartwright	Richards[1]	Pegg	Peddie	Williams	Hurst
13 Sep	Burton U	H	W	1–0	..	..	..	..	..	..	Schofield AJ	..	..	..	..[1]
20 Sep	Bristol C	A	L	1–3	..	..	..	..	..	..	..	..	..	..	..[1]
27 Sep	Glossop	H	D	1–1	..	..	..	..	..	..	..	..	..	..	..[1]
4 Oct	Chesterfield	H	W	2–1	..	Bunce	..	Cartwright	Hayes	Banks	Pegg	Richards	..	Preston[2]	..
11 Oct	Stockport Co	A	L	1–2	..	..	..	..	..	..	..[1]	..	..	..	..
25 Oct	Arsenal	A	W	1–0	Birchenough	Rothwell	..	Morgan	Griffiths	..	..	..	Beadsworth[1]	Williams	..
8 Nov	Lincoln C	A	W	3–1	..	..	..	..	Ball	..	..	Beadsworth	Peddie[2]	..	..[1]
15 Nov	Small Heath	H	L	0–1	..	Stafford	Rothwell	..	..	..	..	..	..	..	..
22 Nov	Leicester F	A	D	1–1	..	..	..	..	Downie[1]	..	..	..	..	Smith	Williams
6 Dec	Burnley	A	W	*2–0	..	Read	..	Downie	Griffiths	..	Schofield AJ	Peddie	Pegg[1]	Richards	Hurst
20 Dec	Port Vale	A	D	1–1	..	Rothwell	Read	..	..	Cartwright	..	Richards	..	Peddie[1]	Lappin
25 Dec	Manchester C	H	D	1–1	..	..	..	..	..	..	..	Morrison	..[1]	..	Beadsworth
26 Dec	Blackpool	H	D	2–2	Whitehouse	..	..	..[1]	..	..	Morrison[1]	Beadsworth	..	..	Lappin
27 Dec	Barnsley	H	W	2–1	Saunders	Stafford	..	..	..	Morgan	..	Richards	..	..[1]	..[1]
3 Jan	Gainsborough T	H	W	3–1	Birchenough	Rothwell	..	Morgan	Downie[1]	Ball	..	Preston	..[1]	..[1]	..
10 Jan	Burton U	A	L	1–3	..	..	..	..	Beadsworth	Cartwright	Schofield AJ	Morrison	Downie	..[1]	..
17 Jan	Bristol C	H	L	1–2	..	..	..	..	Downie	..	Morrison	Richards	Preston[1]	..	Hurst
24 Jan	Glossop	A	W	3–1	..	..	..	Downie[1]	Griffiths[1]	Banks	..[1]	Peddie	Pegg	Bell	..
31 Jan	Chesterfield	A	L	0–2	..	Stafford	Rothwell	..	..	..	..	Pegg	Bell	Peddie	..
14 Feb	Blackpool	A	L	0–2	..	..	..	Griffiths	Downie	..	Bell	Morrison	Arkesden	..	..
28 Feb	Doncaster R	A	D	2–2	Cartwright	Christie	Read	Downie	Griffiths	..	Morrison[2]	Pegg	Peddie	Arkesden	Smith
7 Mar	Lincoln C	H	L	1–2	Birchenough	Stafford	Rothwell	..[1]	..	Cartwright	..	Street	..	..	Hurst
9 Mar	Arsenal	H	W	3–0	..	Marshall	Read	Ball	..	..	Schofield AJ	Morrison	Pegg[1]	Peddie[1]	Arkesden[1]
21 Mar	Leicester F	H	W	5–1	..	..	Rothwell	Fitchett[1]	..[1]	..	..	..[1]	..[1]	..	Smith[1]
23 Mar	Stockport Co	H	D	0–0	..	..	..	..	..	..	..	..	..	..	..
30 Mar	Preston NE	H	L	0–1	..	..	Read	Downie	..	..	..	..	Fitchett	..	Hurst
4 Apr	Burnley	H	W	4–0	..	Rothwell	..	..	..[1]	..	..	..[1]	Cleaver	..[2]	Smith
10 Apr	Manchester C	A	W	2–0	..	..	..	..	..	..	..[1]	..	Pegg	..[1]	Arkesden
11 Apr	Preston NE	A	L	1–3	..	Marshall	..	..	..	Fitchett	Morrison	Pegg[1]	Arkesden	..	Rothwell
13 Apr	Doncaster R	H	W	4–0	..	..	..	..	..[1]	Cartwright	Pegg	Morrison[1]	Bell[1]	Arkesden[1]	Smith
18 Apr	Port Vale	H	W	2–1	..	Rothwell	..	..	..	Smith	Morrison	Pegg	Arkesden	Cartwright	Schofield[2]
20 Apr	Small Heath	A	L	1–2	..	..	..	..	Bell	Banks	Schofield AJ	Peddie[1]	Pegg	Beadsworth	Smith
25 Apr	Barnsley	A	D	0–0	..	Fitchett	..	..	Griffiths	..	..	Pegg	Arkesden	Cartwright	Beadsworth
	FA Cup														
1 Nov	Accrington S. (3Q)	H	W	7–0	Whitehouse	Stafford	Read	Morgan[1]	Griffiths	Banks	Pegg	Richards[1]	Peddie[1]	Williams[3]	Hurst
13 Nov	Oswaldtwistle R (4Q)	H	W	3–2	Saunders	Rothwell	..	..	..	..	Schofield AJ	Pegg[1]	Turner	Beadsworth[1]	Williams[1]
29 Nov	Southport Cent. (5Q)	H	W	4–1	Birchenough	..	..	Downie	..	..[1]	..	Richards	Pegg[3]	..	Peddie
13 Dec	Burton U (Int)	H	D	1–1	..	..	..	..	..[1]	Cartwright	..	..	..	Peddie	Hurst
17 Dec	Burton U (R)†	H	W	3–1	..	..	..	..	..	..	..[1]	Beadsworth	..[1]	..[1]	..
7 Feb	Liverpool (1)	H	W	2–1	..	Stafford	Rothwell	..	..	..	Street	Pegg	Peddie[2]	Smith	..
21 Feb	Everton (2)	A	L	1–3	..	Rothwell	Read	..	..[1]	..	..	..	..	..	..

†away tie switched to Manchester (Bank Street)

Appearances (goals)

Arkesden 9 (2) · Ball 4 · Banks 13 · Beadsworth 9 (1) · Bell 5 (1) · Birchenough 25 · Bunce 2 · Cartwright 22 · Christie 1 · Cleaver 1 · Downie 22 (5) · Fitchett 5 (1) · Griffiths 25 (4) · Hayes 2 · Hurst 16 (4) · Lappin 5 (1) · Marshall 6 · Morgan 12 · Morrison 20 (7) · Peddie 30 (11) · Pegg 28 (7) · Preston 4 (3) · Read 27 · Richards 8 (1) · Rothwell 22 · Saunders 1 · Schofield AJ 16 (3) · Smith 8 (1) · Stafford 10 · Street 1 · Whitehouse 7 · Williams 8 · Own goals 1 · Total 32 players (53)

Football League

	P	W	D	L	F:A	Pts	
Manchester C	34	25	4	5	95:29	54	1st
Manchester U	34	15	8	11	53:38	38	5th

SEASON 1903–1904 FOOTBALL LEAGUE (DIVISION 2)

5 Sep	Bristol C	H	D	2–2	Sutcliffe	Bonthron	Read	Downie	Griffiths[2]	Robertson A	Gaudie	Robertson T	Arkesden	Robertson A	McCartney
7 Sep	Burnley	A	L	0–2	..	..	..	..	..	Cartwright	..	McCartney	Robertson A	Arkesden	Robertson T
12 Sep	Port Vale	A	L	0–1	..	..	..	..	..	..	..	Schofield AJ	..	..	..
19 Sep	Glossop	A	W	5–0	..	..	..	..[1]	..[2]	Hayes	Schofield AJ	Gaudie	Arkesden[1]	Bell	Robertson A[1]
26 Sep	Bradford C	H	W	3–1	..	..	..	..	..	Cartwright	Gaudie	Schofield AJ	Pegg[3]	Arkesden	..
3 Oct	Arsenal	A	L	0–4	..	..	Blackstock	..	..	..	Hayes	Grassam	..	..	Morrison
10 Oct	Barnsley	H	W	4–0	Moger	..	..	..	..[1]	..	Schofield AJ	..	..[2]	..	Robertson A[1]
17 Oct	Lincoln C	A	D	0–0	Sutcliffe	..	..	..	..	..	..	..	..	..	..
24 Oct	Stockport Co	H	W	3–1	..	..	..	..	..	Robertson A	..[1]	..[1]	..	..[1]	..
7 Nov	Bolton W	H	D	0–0	..	..	..	..	..	Cartwright	..	Morrison	..	..	..
21 Nov	Preston NE	H	L	0–2	..	..	..	..	..	Robertson A	..	..	..	..	..
19 Dec	Gainsborough T	H	W	4–2	..	Blackstock	Robertson A	Duckworth[1]	..	Cartwright	..	Pegg	Grassam[1]	..[1]	..[1]
25 Dec	Chesterfield	H	W	3–1	..	Bonthron	Read	Gaudie	..	Robertson A	Pegg	McCartney	..	..[2]	..[1]
26 Dec	Burton U	A	D	2–2	Moger	..	Hayes	..	..	..	..	..	..	..[2]	Wilkinson
2 Jan	Bristol C	A	D	1–1	Sutcliffe	..	..	Bell ..	McCartney	Griffiths[1]	Arkesden	Robertson A	..	Robertson A	..
9 Jan	Port Vale	H	W	2–0	..	..	Read	Robertson A	Griffiths	Robertson A	McCartney	Grassam[1]	Robertson A	Arkesden[1]	..
16 Jan	Glossop	H	W	3–1	..	..	..	..	..	Downie[1]	..	Morrison	Grassam	..[2]	..
23 Jan	Bradford C	A	D	3–3	Moger	..	Hayes	Downie	..[2]	..[1]	Schofield AJ	..	..	..	..
30 Jan	Arsenal	H	W	1–0	Sutcliffe	..	..	..[1]	..	Robertson A	..	..	..	..	Robertson A[1]
13 Feb	Lincoln C	H	W	2–0	..	..	..	..	..[1]	Morrison	..	Pegg	Bell	..	..
9 Mar	Blackpool	A	L	1–2	..	..	..	..	..	Robertson A	..	Grassam[1]	Kerr	..	Wilkinson
12 Mar	Burnley	H	W	3–1	..	..	..	..	..[1]	..	..	Morrison	Grassam[2]	..	..
19 Mar	Preston NE	A	D	1–1	..	..	..	..	..	..	..	..	..	..[1]	..
26 Mar	Grimsby T	H	W	2–0	..	..	..	..	..	..	..	Hall	Kerr	Robertson A[2]	Schofield J
28 Mar	Stockport Co	A	W	3–0	Moger	..	..	..	..	..	..[1]	..[1]	Pegg[1]	Schofield AJ	Robertson A
1 Apr	Chesterfield	A	W	2–0	..	..	..	..	Bell[1]	Cartwright	..	..[1]	Grassam	McCartney	..
2 Apr	Leicester F	A	W	1–0	..	..	..	..	..	Robertson A	..	..	..	..[1]	..
5 Apr	Barnsley	A	W	2–0	..	..	..	..	Griffiths	..	..[1]	McCartney	..[1]	Hall	..
9 Apr	Blackpool	H	W	3–1	..	..	..	..	..	..	..[1]	Hall	..[2]	McCartney	..
12 Apr	Grimsby T	A	L	1–3	..	..	..	..	..	..	..	..	..[1]	..	..
16 Apr	Gainsborough T	A	W	1–0	..	..	..	..	..	..	..	..	..	..	..[1]
23 Apr	Burton U	H	W	2–0	..	..	..	..	Lyons	..	..	Hartwell	..[1]	Arkesden	..[1]
25 Apr	Bolton W	A	D	0–0	..	..	..	..	..	..	..	..	..	Robertson A	Arkesden
30 Apr	Leicester	H	W	5–2	..	..[1]	..	..	Griffiths[1]	..	..[2]	Pegg	Robertson A[1]	Arkesden	Hartwell
	FA Cup														
12 Dec	Small Heath (Int)	H	D	1–1	Sutcliffe	Bonthron	Blackstock	Downie	Griffiths	Cartwright	Schofield AJ[1]	Morrison	Grassam	Pegg	Robertson A
16 Dec	Small Heath (IntR)†	A	D	1–1	..	..	..	..	..	..	..	..	..	Arkesden[1]	..
21 Dec	Small Heath (IntR)† (at Bramall Lane)	N	D	1–1	..	..	..	Cartwright	..	Gaudie	Robertson A	Arkesden	..	Morrison	Schofield AJ[1]
11 Jan	Small Heath (IntR) (at Hyde Road, Manchester)	N	W	3–1	..	..	Read	Downie	..	Cartwright	Schofield AJ	Morrison	..[1]	Arkesden[2]	Wilkinson
6 Feb	Notts Co (1)	A	D	3–3	..	..	Hayes	..[1]	..	Robertson A	..[1]	..	..	..[1]	Robertson A
10 Feb	Notts Co (1R)	H	W	2–1	..	..	..	..	..	Cartwright	..	..[1]	Pegg[1]	..	..
20 Feb	Sheffield Wed (2)	A	L	0–6	..	..	..	..	..	..	..	..	..	..	..

†after extra time

Appearances (goals)

Arkesden 26 (11) · Bell 6 (1) · Blackstock 7 · Bonthron 33 (1) · Cartwright 9 · Downie 29 (4) · Duckworth 1 (1) · Gaudie 7 · Grassam 23 (11) · Griffiths 30 (11) · Hall 8 (2) · Hartwell 1 · Hayes 21 · Kerr 2 · Lyons 2 · McCartney 13 (1) · Moger 13 · Morrison 9 · Pegg 13 (6) · Read 8 · Roberts 2 · Robertson A 24 · Robertson A 27 (10) · Robertson T 3 · Schofield AJ 26 (6) · Schofield J 2 · Sutcliffe 21 · Wilkinson 8 · Total 28 players (65)

Football League

	P	W	D	L	F:A	Pts	
Preston NE	34	20	10	4	62:24	50	1st
Manchester U	34	20	8	6	65:33	48	3rd

SEASON 1904–1905 FOOTBALL LEAGUE (DIVISION 2)

Date	Opponent			Score												
3 Sep	Port Vale	A	D	2–2	Moger	Bonthron	Hayes	Downie	Roberts	Robertson A	Schofield A [1]	Allan [2]	Mackie	Peddie [1]	Arkesden
10 Sep	Bristol C	H	W	4–1											Williams [1]
17 Sep	Bolton W	H	L	1–2										[1]	
24 Sep	Glossop	A	W	2–1					[1]	Bell		[1]			
8 Oct	Bradford C	A	D	1–1					Bell	Robertson A			Peddie	Arkesden [1]	Robertson A
15 Oct	Lincoln C	H	W	2–0					Roberts	Bell	[1]		[1]	[1]	Williams
22 Oct	Liecester F	A	W	3–0				Duckworth			[1]				
29 Oct	Barnsley	H	W	4–0				Downie [1]	Bell	Robertson A	[1]	[1] [1]			
5 Nov	W B A	A	W	2–0					Roberts					[1]	[1]
12 Nov	Burnley	H	W	1–0										[1]	
19 Nov	Grimsby T	A	W	1–0						Bell [1]			[1]		
3 Dec	Doncaster R	A	W	1–0											
10 Dec	Gainsborough T	H	W	3–1								[1]		[2]	
17 Dec	Burton U	A	W	3–2									[3]		Hartwell
24 Dec	Liverpool	H	W	3–1					[1]					[1]	Williams [1]
26 Dec	Chesterfield	H	W	3–0		[1]					Grassam	[2]			
31 Dec	Port Vale	H	W	6–1					[1]		Schofield A	[3]		[1]	
2 Jan	Bradford C	H	W	*7–0					[2]			[1]		[2]	Hartwell
3 Jan	Bolton W	A	W	4–2								[2]	[1]		Williams [1]
7 Jan	Bristol C	A	D	1–1			Blackstock					Grassam		[1]	
21 Jan	Glossop	H	W	4–1			Hayes		Fitchett			[1]	Mackie [2]	[1]	
11 Feb	Lincoln C	A	L	0–3					Roberts			Allan	Peddie		
18 Feb	Leicester F	H	W	4–1								[1]	[3]		
25 Feb	Barnsley	A	D	0–0		Fitchett	Blackstock		Griffiths		Beddow				
4 Mar	W B A	H	W	2–0		Bonthron	Fitchett		Roberts				[1]		[1]
11 Mar	Burnley	A	L	0–2					Griffiths						
18 Mar	Grimsby T	H	W	2–1					Roberts			[1]	Duckworth [1]		Wombwell
25 Mar	Blackpool	A	W	1–0								Grassam [1]		Peddie	
1 Apr	Doncaster R	H	W	6–0					Bell	Robertson A	[1]		[3]	[1]	[1]
8 Apr	Gainsborough T	A	D	0–0					Roberts	Bell					
15 Apr	Burton U	H	W	5–0								Duckworth [2]	Peddie [2]	Arkesden [1]	
21 Apr	Chesterfield	A	L	0–2								Allan			
22 Apr	Liverpool	A	L	0–4							Schofield A	Duckworth			
24 Apr	Blackpool	H	W	3–1	Valentine	Holden	Blackstock	Duckworth				Allan [1]	[1]	[1]	

FA Cup

Date	Opponent			Score											
14 Jan	Fulham (Int)	H	D	2–2	Moger	Bonthron	Hayes	Downie	Bell	Robertson A	Schofield A	Grassam	Mackie [1]	Arkesden [1]	Williams
18 Jan	Fulham (IntR)†	A	D	0–0					Fitchett	Bell		Lyons	Grassam		
23 Jan	Fulham (IntR)	N	L	0–1								Grassam	Mackie		Hartwell
	(at Villa Park)														
	† after extra time														

Appearances (goals)

Allan 27 (16) · Arkesden 28 (15) · Beddow 9 (1) · Bell 29 (1) · Blackstock 3 · Bonthron 32 · Downie 32 (1) · Duckworth 8 (6) · Fitchett 11 · Grassam 6 · Griffiths 2 · Hartwell 2 · Hayes 22 (1) · Holden 1 · Mackie 5 (3) · Moger 33 · Peddie 32 (17) · Roberts 28 (2) · Robertson A 8 (1) · Robertson A 1 · Schofield A 24 (4) · Valentine 1 · Williams 22 (6) · Wombwell 8 (1) · Own goals 1 · Total 24 players (80)

Football League

	P	W	D	L	F:A	Pts	
Liverpool	34	27	4	3	93:25	58	1st
Manchester U	34	24	5	5	81:30	53	3rd

SEASON 1905–1906 FOOTBALL LEAGUE (DIVISION 2)

Date	Opponent			Score												
2 Sep	Bristol C	H	W	5–1	Moger	Bonthron	Blackstock	Downie	Roberts	Bell	Beddow [1]	Picken [1]	Sagar [3]	Peddie [2]	Arkesden
4 Sep	Blackpool	H	W	2–1									[1]		Wombwell
9 Sep	Grimsby T	A	W	1–0											
16 Sep	Glossop	A	W	2–1	Montgomery					[1]	[1]		Peddie	Arkesden	
23 Sep	Stockport C	H	W	3–1									Sagar [1]	Peddie [2]	
30 Sep	Blackpool	A	W	1–0					[1]				Peddie	Arkesden	
7 Oct	Bradford C	H	D	0–0	Valentine								Sagar	Peddie	Arkesden
14 Oct	W B A	A	L	0–1								Lyons	Dyer		Wombwell
21 Oct	Leicester	H	W	3–2							Schofield A	Picken	Sagar [1]	[2]	
25 Oct	Gainsborough T	A	D	2–2			[2]								
28 Oct	Hull C	A	W	1–0		Holden							Peddie	Arkesden	
4 Nov	Lincoln C	H	W	2–1					[1]			Donaghey	Sagar	Picken [1]	
11 Nov	Chesterfield	A	L	0–1		Bonthron							Peddie		
18 Nov	Port Vale	H	W	*3–0	Moger	Holden		Duckworth				Peddie [1]	Beddow [1]		Williams
25 Nov	Barnsley	A	W	*3–0									[1]	[1]	
2 Dec	Clapton O	H	W	4–0								[2]		[2]	
9 Dec	Burnley	A	W	3–1		Bonthron	Holden					[1]	[1]	[1]	
23 Dec	Burton U	A	W	2–0				Downie			[2]		Sagar		
25 Dec	Chelsea	H	D	0–0											Wombwell
30 Dec	Bristol C	A	D	1–1					[1]				Picken [1]	Williams	
6 Jan	Grimsby T	H	W	5–0								Allan	[3]	[2]	
15 Jan	Leeds C	H	L	0–3		Holden	Blackstock								
20 Jan	Glossop	H	W	5–2		Duckworth	Holden			Robertson		Peddie [1]	[1]	[2]	[1]
27 Jan	Stockport C	A	W	1–0		Bonthron				Bell		[1]			
10 Feb	Bradford C	A	W	5–1							[1]		[2]		Wombwell [1]
17 Feb	W B A	H	D	0–0											
3 Mar	Hull C	H	W	5–1							[1]	[1]	Sagar [1]	[2]	
17 Mar	Chesterfield	H	W	4–1									[1]	[3]	
24 Mar	Port Vale	A	L	0–1							Lyons				
29 Mar	Leicester C	A	W	5–2						[1]	Schofield A	[3]	[1]	[1]	
31 Mar	Barnsley	H	W	5–1									[3]	[1]	
7 Apr	Clapton O	A	W	1–0							Wombwell		[1]		Wall [1]
13 Apr	Chelsea	A	D	1–1		Blew			Bell	Duckworth			[1]		
14 Apr	Burnley	H	W	1–0		Bonthron							[1]		
16 Apr	Gainsborough T	H	W	2–0	Valentine	Holden	Blackstock				Schofield A		Allan [2]		Wombwell
21 Apr	Leeds C	A	W	3–1	Moger				Roberts	Bell	Womwell [1]	[1]		Sagar	Wall
25 Apr	Lincoln C	A	W	3–2					Bell	Duckworth		Donaghey	[2]	Arkesden	[1]
28 Apr	Burton U	H	W	6–0					Roberts			Peddie [1]	Sagar [2]	Picken [2]	[1]

FA Cup

Date	Opponent			Score											
13 Jan	Staple Hill (1)	H	W	7–2	Moger	Bonthron	Holden	Downie	Roberts	Bell	Schofield A	Allan [1]	Beddow [3]	Picken [2]	Williams [1]
3 Feb	Norwich (2)	H	W	3–0				[1]				Peddie [1]	Sagar [1]		
24 Feb	Aston Villa (3)	H	W	5–1									[2]	[3]	Wombwell
10 Mar	Arsenal (4)	H	L	2–3									[1]		

Appearances (goals)

Allan 5 (5) · Arkesden 7 · Beddow 21 (11) · Bell 36 (2) · Blackstock 21 · Blew 1 · Bonthron 26 (2) · Donaghey 3 · Downie 34 · Duckworth 10 · Dyer 1 · Holden 27 · Lyons 2 · Moger 27 · Montgomery 3 · Peddie 34 (18) · Picken 33 (20) · Roberts 34 (4) · Robertson A 1 · Sagar 20 (16) · Schofield A 23 (4) · Valentine 8 · Wall 6 (3) · Williams 10 (1) · Wombwell 25 (2) · Own goals 2 · Total 25 players (88)

Football League

	P	W	D	L	F:A	Pts	
Bristol C	38	30	6	2	83:28	66	1st
Manchester U	38	28	6	4	90:28	62	2nd

SEASON 1906–1907 FOOTBALL LEAGUE (DIVISION 1)

Date	Opponent		Res	Score	1	2	3	4	5	6	7	8	9	10	11
1 Sep	Bristol C	A	W	2–1	Moger	Bonthron	Holden	Downie	Roberts[1]	Bell	Schofield A[2]	Peddie	Sagar	Picken[1]	Wall
3 Sep	Derby Co	A	D	2–2	..	..	..	..	..	..	..	..	..	..	..
8 Sep	Notts Co	H	D	0–0	..	..	..	..	..	..	..	..	..	..	..
15 Sep	Sheffield U	A	W	2–0	..	..	..	..[1]	..	..[1]	Beddow	Yates	Wombwell	..	..
22 Sep	Bolton W	H	L	1–2	..	..	..	..	..	..[1]	Wombwell	Peddie[1]	..	..	..
29 Sep	Derby Co	H	D	1–1	..	..	Buckley	..	..	..[1]	Schofield A	Peddie	Alan	..	..
6 Oct	Stoke C	A	W	2–1	..	..	Blackstock	..	..	..	Duckworth[2]	..	..	..	..
13 Oct	Blackburn R	H	D	1–1	..	..	Holden	..	Bell	Duckworth	Schofield A	..	Wombwell	..	..[1]
20 Oct	Sunderland	A	L	1–4	..	..	..	..	Roberts	Bell	Duckworth	..[1]	Picken	..	..
27 Oct	Birmingham	H	W	2–1	..	..	..	..	..	..	Young	Wombwell	Peddie[1]	Picken	..
3 Nov	Everton	A	L	0–3	..	..	..	..	..	..	..	..	..	Yates	..
10 Nov	Arsenal	H	W	1–0	..	..	..	..[1]	Duckworth	..	Schofield A	..	..	Picken	..
17 Nov	Sheffield Wed	A	L	2–5	..	..	..	..	..	..	Berry	..	Menzies[1]	Peddie[1]	..
24 Nov	Bury	H	L	2–4	..	..	Blackstock	..	Roberts	..	..	..	..	..[1]	..[1]
1 Dec	Manchester C	A	L	0–3	..	..	Duckworth	..	..	..	Beddow	..	..	Picken	..
8 Dec	Middlesbrough	H	W	3–1	..	..	Holden	Duckworth	..	..	Schofield A	..	Sagar[1]	..	..[2]
15 Dec	Preston NE	A	L	0–2	..	..	..	..	..	..	..	..	..	..	..
22 Dec	Newcastle U	H	L	1–3	..	..	..	..	..	..	..	Peddie	Menzies[1]	..	..
25 Dec	Liverpool	H	D	0–0	..	Holden	Blackstock	..	..	..	Berry	..	..	..	..
26 Dec	Aston Villa	A	L	0–2	..	Duckworth	Holden	Downie	..	Wombwell	Berry	Peddie	..	..	..
29 Dec	Bristol C	H	D	0–0	..	Bonthron	..	..	..	Duckworth	Wombwell	Berry	..	..	..
1 Jan	Aston Villa	H	W	1–0	..	..	Burgess	Duckworth	..	Bell	Meredith	Bannister	..	Turnbull A[1]	..
5 Jan	Notts Co	A	L	0–3	..	..	..	..	Buckley	..	..	..	..	..	..
19 Jan	Sheffield U	H	W	2–0	..	..	..	..	Holden	..	..	Peddie	Beddow	..[1]	..[1]
26 Jan	Bolton W	A	W	1–0	..	..	..	..	Roberts	..	..	Picken	Berry	..[1]	..
2 Feb	Newcastle U	A	L	0–5	..	Holden	..	..	..	..	..	Menzies	..	Picken	..
9 Feb	Stoke C	H	W	*4–1	..	..	..	..	..	..	..[1]	Picken[2]	..	Menzies	..
16 Feb	Blackburn R	A	W	4–2	..	..	..	..	..	..	..[2]	..	Sagar[1]	Turnbull A[1]	..[2]
23 Feb	Preston NE	H	W	3–0	..	..	..	..	..	..	Berry	..	Sagar[1]	..	..
2 Mar	Birmingham	A	D	1–1	..	..	..	..	Buckley	..	Meredith	..	Menzies[1]	..	..
16 Mar	Arsenal	A	L	0–4	..	Bonthron	..	..	Holden	..	..	Bannister	..	..	..
25 Mar	Sunderland	H	W	2–0	..	Holden	..	..	Roberts	..	..	Williams[1]	..	..[1]	..
30 Mar	Bury	A	W	2–1	..	..	..	..	..	..	..	..[1]	..	..[1]	..
1 Apr	Liverpool	A	W	1–0	..	Bonthron	..	..	..	..	..	..	..	..	..
6 Apr	Manchester C	H	D	1–1	..	..	..	Downie	..[1]	..	..	Picken	..	..	..
10 Apr	Sheffield Wed	H	W	5–0	..	..	..	Duckworth	..	Downie	..	..[1]	Sagar[1]	..	..[3]
13 Apr	Middlesbrough	A	L	0–2	..	..	..	..	..	Bell	..	..[1]	..	..	..
22 Apr	Everton	H	W	3–0	..	Holden	..	..	..	..	..	Bannister[1]	..	..[1]	..

FA Cup

Date	Opponent		Res	Score	1	2	3	4	5	6	7	8	9	10	11
12 Jan	Portsmouth (1)	A	D	2–2	Moger	Holden	Blackstock	Duckworth	Roberts	Bell	Meredith	Wombwell	Menzies	Picken[1]	Wall[1]
16 Jan	Portsmouth (1R)	H	L	1–2	..	Bonthron	Holden	Downie	Duckworth	..	..	..	..	..	..[1]

Appearances (goals)

Allan 3 · Bannister 4 (1) · Beddow 3 · Bell 35 (2) · Berry 9 · Blackstock 3 · Bonthron 28 · Buckley 3 · Burgess 17 · Downie 19 (2) · Duckworth 28 (2) · Holden 27 · Menzies 17 (4) · Meredith 16 (5) · Moger 38 · Peddie 16 (6) · Picken 26 (4) · Roberts 31 (2) · Sagar 10 (4) · Schofield A 10 (2) · Turnbull A 15 (6) · Wall 38 (11) · Williams 3 (1) · Wombwell 14 · Yates 3 · Young 2 · Own goals 1 · Total 26 players (52)

Football League

	P	W	D	L	F:A	Pts	
Newcastle U	38	22	7	9	74:46	51	1st
Manchester U	38	17	8	13	53:56	42	8th

SEASON 1907–1908 FOOTBALL LEAGUE (DIVISION 1)

Date	Opponent		Res	Score	1	2	3	4	5	6	7	8	9	10	11
2 Sep	Aston Villa	A	W	4–1	Moger	Holden	Burgess	Duckworth	Roberts	Bell	Meredith	Bannister[1]	Menzies	Turnbull A	Wall[1]
7 Sep	Liverpool	H	W	4–0	..	..	..	..	..	..	..	..	..[3]	..[2]	..[1]
9 Sep	Middlesbrough	H	W	2–1	..	..	..	..	..	..	..	..	..	..	..
14 Sep	Middlesbrough	A	L	1–2	..	..	..	..	..	Thomson	..	..[1]	..	..	..
21 Sep	Sheffield U	H	W	2–1	..	..	..	..	..	Bell	..	..	..	..[2]	..
28 Sep	Chelsea	A	W	4–1	..	..	..	..	..	..	..[2]	..[1]	Turnbull J[1]	..[1]	..
5 Oct	Nottingham F	H	W	*4–0	..	..	..	..	..[1]	..	..[1]	..[1]	..	..	..[2]
12 Oct	Newcastle U	A	W	6–1	..	..	Stacey	..	..	..	..	..[1]	..	..[1]	..[1]
19 Oct	Blackburn R	A	W	5–1	..	..	Burgess	..	..	..	..	..[2]	..	..[3]	..
26 Oct	Bolton W	H	W	2–1	..	..	..	..	..	..	..[2]	..[1]	..	..	..
2 Nov	Birmingham	A	W	4–3	..	..	..	..	..	..	..[1]	..	Picken	..	..[1]
9 Nov	Everton	H	W	4–3	..	..	..	..	..	..	..[1]	..	Turnbull A[2]	..	..[2]
16 Nov	Sunderland	A	W	2–1	..	..	..	..	..	..	..	..	..	..	..
23 Nov	Arsenal	H	W	4–2	..	..	..	..	..	..	..	..	..[4]	Williams	Wall
30 Nov	Sheffield Wed	A	L	0–2	..	..	..	..	..	..	..	..	..	..	..[2]
7 Dec	Bristol C	H	W	2–1	..	..	Stacey	..	..	..	..	..	..	..	..
14 Dec	Notts Co	A	D	1–1	..	..	Burgess	..	..	..	..	..[1]	..	..[2]	..[1]
21 Dec	Manchester C	H	W	3–1	..	..	..	..	..	..	..	..[2]	..[1]	..	..
25 Dec	Bury	H	W	2–1	..	..	Stacey	..	..	..	..	..	..	..	..[1]
28 Dec	Preston NE	A	D	0–0	..	..	..	..	..	..	..	..	..	..	..
1 Jan	Bury	A	W	1–0	..	..	..	..	..	..	..	..	..	..	..
18 Jan	Sheffield U	A	L	0–2	..	..	Burgess	Whiteside	McGillivray	..	..	..	Picken	..	..
25 Jan	Chelsea	H	W	1–0	..	..	..	Downie	Roberts	..	..	Picken	Menzies	..[1]	..
8 Feb	Newcastle U	H	D	1–1	..	..	..	Duckworth	Downie	..	..	Bannister	..[1]	Turnbull A	..
15 Feb	Blackburn R	H	L	1–2	..	..	..	..	Roberts	..	..	..	..[1]	Wilson	Wall
29 Feb	Birmingham	H	W	1–0	..	..	Stacey	..	..	..	..[1]	..	..	..	..
14 Mar	Sunderland	H	W	3–0	..	Stacey	Burgess	..	..	..	..	Berry[1]	Picken	..	..
21 Mar	Arsenal	A	L	0–1	Broomfield	..	..	..	..	Downie	..	Turnbull J[1]	..	..	..
25 Mar	Liverpool	A	L	4–7	Moger	..	Dalton	..	..	Downie	..	Turnbull J[1]	..	Turnbull A[1]	..[2]
28 Mar	Sheffield Wed	H	W	4–1	Broomfield	..	Burgess	..	Downie	Bell	..	Halse[1]	..	Turnbull A[1]	..[1]
4 Apr	Bristol C	A	D	1–1	..	..	..	..	Roberts	Downie	..	..	..[1]	..	..[1]
8 Apr	Everton	A	W	3–1	..	..	..	..	..	Bell	Berry	Turnbull J	..	..	..
11 Apr	Notts Co	H	L	0–1	..	..	..	..	Downie	..	Meredith	Halse	..	..	..
17 Apr	Nottingham F	A	L	0–2	..	..	..	Stacey	Roberts	Downie	..	Bannister	..	..	..
18 Apr	Manchester C	A	D	0–0	..	Duckworth	Stacey	Downie	..	..	..	..	Picken[1]	Turnbull J	..[2]
20 Apr	Aston Villa	H	L	1–2	..	..	..	..[1]	..	Thomson	..	Halse[1]	Picken	..	..
22 Apr	Bolton W	A	D	2–2	..	..	..	..	..	..	..	..	..	..	..
25 Apr	Preston NE	H	W	*2–1	Moger	Stacey	Hulme	..	..	..	..	..[1]	..	..	..

FA Cup

Date	Opponent		Res	Score	1	2	3	4	5	6	7	8	9	10	11
11 Jan	Blackpool (1)	H	W	3–1	Moger	Holden	Stacey	Duckworth	McGillivray	Bell	Meredith	Bannister[1]	Turnbull J	Turnbull A[1]	Wall[2]
1 Feb	Chelsea (2)	H	W	1–0	..	..	Burgess	..	Roberts	..	..	..	..	..[1]	..
22 Feb	Aston Villa (3)	A	W	2–0	..	Stacey	Holden	Burgess	..	..	..	Berry	..	..[1]	..[1]
7 Mar	Fulham (4)	A	L	1–2	..	..	Burgess	Duckworth	..	..	..	Turnbull J[1]	..	..	..

Appearances (goals)

Bannister 36 (5) · Bell 35 (1) · Berry 3 (1) · Broomfield 9 · Burgess 27 · Dalton 1 · Downie 10 · Duckworth 35 · Halse 6 (4) · Hulme 1 · McGillivray 1 · Menzies 6 · Meredith 37 (10) · Moger 29 · Picken 8 (1) · Roberts 32 (2) · Stacey 18 (1) · Thomson 3 · Turnbull A 30 (25) · Turnbull J 26 (10) · Wall 36 (19) · Whiteside 1 · Williams 1 · Wilson 1 · Own goals 2 · Total 25 players (79)

Football League

	P	W	D	L	F:A	Pts	
Manchester U	38	23	6	9	81:48	52	1st

SEASON 1908–1909 FOOTBALL LEAGUE (DIVISION 1)

Date	Opponent		Res	Score	1	2	3	4	5	6	7	8	9	10	11
5 Sep	Preston NE	A	W	3–0	Moger	Stacey	Burgess	Duckworth	Roberts	Bell	Meredith	Halse[1]	Turnbull J[2]	Picken	Wall
7 Sep	Bury	H	W	2–1	..	..	..	..	..	..	..	.. [2]	Christie	..	..[1]
12 Sep	Middlesbrough	H	W	6–3	..	..	..	..	..	..	..	Bannister[4]	Halse[1]	..	..[1]
19 Sep	Manchester C	A	W	2–1	..	Duckworth	Stacey	Bannister	..	Downie	..	Hardman[1]	Halse[1]	..	..
26 Sep	Liverpool	H	W	3–2	..	..	..	Downie	..	Bell	..	Halse[2]	..	Turnbull A	..
3 Oct	Bury	A	D	2–2	..	Hulme	..	Duckworth	..	..	..	..	..	..	..[1]
10 Oct	Sheffield U	H	W	2–1	..	..	..	..	..	..[2]	..	Bannister	..	..	..
17 Oct	Aston Villa	A	L	1–3	..	..	..	..	..	..	..	..	Halse[1]	..	..
24 Oct	Nottingham F	H	D	2–2	Wilcox	Linkson	..	..	..	Downie	..	Halse	Turnbull J	..[2]	..
31 Oct	Sunderland	A	L	1–6	Moger	Stacey	Burgess	..	Downie	Thomson	..	Bannister	Halse	..[1]	..
7 Nov	Chelsea	H	L	0–1	..	..	Hayes	..	Picken	Bell	..	Bannister	Halse	..	..
14 Nov	Blackburn R	A	W	3–1	..	..	..	..	Bell	Downie	..	Halse[1]	Turnbull J[1]	Wall[1]	Hardman
21 Nov	Bradford C	H	W	2–0	..	..	..	..	Curry	..	..	..[1]	Picken[1]	Wall[1]	
28 Nov	Sheffield Wed	H	W	3–1	..	..	..	..	Roberts	..	..	..[1]	..[1]	..[1]	..
5 Dec	Everton	A	L	2–3	..	..	..	..	..	Bell	..	Bannister[1]	Halse[1]	Wall	Hardman
12 Dec	Leicester F	H	W	4–2	..	Linkson	..	..	Curry	Downie	..	Halse	Picken[1]	..[3]	..
19 Dec	Arsenal	A	W	1–0	..	..	..	..	Roberts	..	..	Bannister	Halse[1]	Picken	Wall
25 Dec	Newcastle U	A	L	1–2	..	Stacey	..	..	..	Bell	..	..	..	Turnbull A	..[1]
26 Dec	Newcastle U	H	W	1–0	..	..	..	..	..	..	..	..	..[1]	..	..
1 Jan	Notts Co	H	W	4–3	..	..	..	..	..	..[1]	..	..	..[2]	..	..[1]
2 Jan	Preston NE	H	L	0–2	..	..	..	..	..	..	..	Picken	..	..	..
9 Jan	Middlesbrough	A	L	0–5	..	..	..	..	..	..	..	Berry	..	..	..
23 Jan	Manchester C	H	W	3–1	..	..	..	..	..	Downie	..	Livingstone[2]	Halse	..	..[1]
30 Jan	Liverpool	A	L	1–3	..	..	..	..	..	..	..	..	..[1]	..	..
13 Feb	Sheffield U	A	D	0–0	..	..	..	Downie	Curry	Bell	Halse	..	Turnbull J	..	..
27 Feb	Nottingham F	A	L	0–2	..	..	..	..	..	..	Payne	Bannister	..	Picken	..
13 Mar	Chelsea	A	D	1–1	Moger	..	..	Duckworth	Roberts	Downie	Meredith	Halse	..	Turnbull A	..[1]
15 Mar	Sunderland	H	D	2–2	..	Donnelly	..	Downie	..	Bell	Payne[1]	Livingstone	..	..[1]	..
20 Mar	Blackburn R	H	L	0–3	..	Holden	Linkson	Duckworth	Curry	Downie	Halse	..	..	Picken	..
31 Mar	Aston Villa	H	L	0–2	..	..	Hayes	..	McGillivray	..	Meredith	Bannister	Livingstone	..	Ford
3 Apr	Sheffield Wed	A	L	0–2	Wilcox	Linkson	Stacey	Curry	Roberts	McGillivray	..	..	Quinn	Livingstone	..
9 Apr	Bristol C	H	L	0–1	Moger	Hayes	..	Duckworth	..	Downie	..	Halse	..	..	Wall
10 Apr	Everton	H	D	2–2	..	Stacey	Hayes	..	Curry	..	..	Halse	Turnbull J[2]	Picken	Ford
12 Apr	Bristol C	A	D	0–0	..	..	Linkson	..	Roberts	..	..	Livingstone	..	..	Wall
13 Apr	Notts Co	H	W	1–0	..	..	..	..	..	..	..[1]	Halse	..	..	Ford
17 Apr	Leicester F	A	L	2–3	..	Linkson	Hayes	Downie	Curry	Bell	..	..	Turnbull J[1]	Christie	Wall[1]
27 Apr	Arsenal	H	L	1–4	..	Stacey	Linkson	Duckworth	Roberts	..	Halse	..	..	Turnbull A	..
29 Apr	Bradford C	A	L	0–1	..	..	..	..	..	..	..	..	..	..	..

FA Cup

Date	Opponent		Res	Score	1	2	3	4	5	6	7	8	9	10	11
16 Jan	Brighton (1)	H	W	1–0	Moger	Stacey	Hayes	Duckworth	Roberts	Bell	Meredith	Halse[1]	Turnbull J	Turnbull A	Wall
6 Feb	Everton (2)	H	W	1–0	..	..	..	..	..	..	..	Halse[1]	Livingstone	..	..
20 Feb	Blackburn R (3)	H	W	6–1	..	..	..	..	..	..	..	..[3]	..	..[3]	..
5 Mar	Burnley (4)	A	*		..	..	..	..	..	..	Meredith	Halse	..	..	..
10 Mar	Burnley (4)	A	W	3–2	..	..	..	..	..	..	..	..[1]	..	..	..
27 Mar	Newcastle U (SF)	N	W	1–0	..	..	..	..	..	..	..	..[1]	..	..	..
	(at Bramall Lane)														
24 Apr	Bristol C (F)	N	W	1–0	..	..	..	..	..	..	..	..	..[1]	..[1]	..
	(at Crystal Palace)														

*match abandoned after 72 minutes because of snow. Score Burnley 1 United 0

Appearances (goals)

Bannister 16 (1) · Bell 16 (1) · Berry 1 · Burgess 3 · Christie 2 · Curry 8 · Donnelly 1 · Downie 22 · Duckworth 33 · Ford 4 · Halse 29 (14) · Hardman 4 · Hayes 22 · Holden 2 · Hulme 3 · Linkson 10 · Livingstone 11 (3) · McGillivray 2 · Meredith 34 · Moger 36 · Payne 2 (1) · Picken 13 (3) · Quinn 1 · Roberts 27 (1) · Stacey 32 · Thomson 1 · Turnbull A 19 (5) · Turnbull J 22 (17) · Wall 34 (11) · Wilcox 2 · Total 30 players (58)

Football League

	P	W	D	L	F:A	Pts	
Newcastle U	38	24	5	9	65:41	53	1st
Manchester U	38	15	7	16	58:68	37	13th

SEASON 1909–1910 FOOTBALL LEAGUE (DIVISION 1)

Date	Opponent		Res	Score	1	2	3	4	5	6	7	8	9	10	11
1 Sep	Bradford C	H	W	1–0	Moger	Stacey	Hayes	Duckworth	Roberts	Bell	Halse	Blott	Bannister	Turnbull A	Wall
4 Sep	Bury	H	W	2–0	..	..	..	..	..	..	Livingstone	Turnbull J[2]	..	..[1]	..
6 Sep	Notts Co	H	W	2–1	..	..	..	..	..	..	..	..[1]	Picken	..	..[1]
11 Sep	Tottenham H	A	D	2–2	..	..	..	..	.. [1]	Downie	Blott	Halse	..[1]	Turnbull A	..[1]
18 Sep	Preston NE	H	D	1–1	..	..	..	..	..	..	Meredith	..	..	..	..
25 Sep	Notts Co	A	L	2–3	..	..	..	Downie	..	Blott	..	..	..	..[2]	..
2 Oct	Newcastle U	H	D	1–1	..	..	..	Duckworth	..	Bell	..	..	..	..	..[1]
9 Oct	Liverpool	A	L	2–3	Rounds	..	..	..	..	..	..	..	..	..[2]	Ford
16 Oct	Aston Villa	H	W	2–0	Moger	..	..	..	..	..	..	..[1]	..	..[1]	Wall
23 Oct	Sheffield U	A	W	1–0	..	..	..	..	..	..	..	..	..	..	..[1]
30 Oct	Arsenal	H	W	1–0	..	..	..	..	..	Blott	Livingstone	Homer	..	..	..[1]
6 Nov	Bolton W	A	W	3–2	..	..	..	..	..	Bell	Halse[1]	..[2]	..	..[1]	..[1]
13 Nov	Chelsea	H	W	2–0	..	..	..	..	..	..	Picken	..[2]	..	..[1]	..[1]
20 Nov	Blackburn R	A	L	2–3	..	Holden	Stacey	..	..	..	Picken	..[2]	..	..	..
27 Nov	Nottingham F	H	L	2–6	..	Stacey	Hayes	..	..	..	Halse[1]	..	Picken	..	..[1]
4 Dec	Sunderland	A	L	0–3	..	Holden	..	..	..	..	Livingstone	..	Turnbull A	..	..
18 Dec	Middlesbrough	A	W	2–1	..	..	Burgess	..	..	..	Homer[1]	Turnbull J	..[1]	..	..
25 Dec	Sheffield Wed	H	L	0–3	..	..	Stacey	Donnelly	Blott	Whalley	..	..	Wall[1]	Homer	Picken	Connor
27 Dec	Sheffield Wed	A	L	1–4	..	Stacey	Hayes	Livingstone	..	..	Quinn	Picken	Turnbull A[1]	Wall[1]	
1 Jan	Bradford C	A	W	2–0	..	..	Hayes	Livingstone	..	..	Picken	..	Turnbull A[1]	Wall[1]	
8 Jan	Bury	A	D	1–1	..	..	..	..	Roberts[2]	Blott	Meredith	..[1]	Hooper[1]	..	Connor
22 Jan	Tottenham H	H	W	5–0	..	..	..	..	..	Blott	Halse	..	Hooper[1]	..	..[1]
5 Feb	Preston NE	A	L	0–1	..	..	..	..	..	..	Picken	Halse	..	..	Wall
12 Feb	Newcastle U	A	W	4–3	..	..	Holden	..	..	..	..	Halse	Homer[1]	Turnbull A[2]	..[1]
19 Feb	Liverpool	H	L	3–4	..	..	..	Duckworth	..	Bell	Halse	Homer[1]	..	..[1]	Connor
26 Feb	Aston Villa	A	L	1–7	..	..	Holden	..	..	..	..	..	Turnbull J	Picken[1]	Connor
5 Mar	Sheffield U	H	W	1–0	..	..	Hayes	..	Livingstone	..	Connor	..	Turnbull J	Picken[1]	Wall
12 Mar	Arsenal	A	D	0–0	..	..	..	..	Whalley	Meredith	..	..	..	..	..
19 Mar	Bolton W	H	W	5–0	..	Duckworth	Stacey	Livingstone	Roberts	..	..[1]	..[1]	..[1]	..[1]	..[1]
25 Mar	Bristol C	H	W	2–1	..	Hayes	..	Duckworth	Whalley	..	..[1]	..[1]	Turnbull A	..
26 Mar	Chelsea	A	D	1–1	..	Stacey	Hayes	..	..	..	..[1]	..	Turnbull A	Picken
28 Mar	Bristol C	A	L	1–2	..	Duckworth	Blott	..	..	..	..	..[2]	Picken	..
2 Apr	Blackburn R	H	W	2–0	..	Stacey	Duckworth	Livingstone	..	..	..	..[2]	..	Connor
6 Apr	Everton	H	W	3–2	..	..	..	..	..	..	..	..[2]	..	Wall
9 Apr	Nottingham F	A	L	0–2	..	..	..	Livingstone	Roberts	Bell	Picken	Halse	Turnbull A	..[1]
16 Apr	Sunderland	H	W	2–0	..	..	Donnelly	..	..	..	..[1]	Homer	..[1]	..[1]
23 Apr	Everton	A	D	3–3	..	Holden	..	Duckworth	..	..	Connor	..[4]	..	Connor
30 Apr	Middlesbrough	H	W	4–1	..	..	..	..	Livingstone	Meredith	..[4]	..	Connor

FA Cup

Date	Opponent		Res	Score	1	2	3	4	5	6	7	8	9	10	11
15 Jan	Burnley (1)	A	L	0–2	Moger	Stacey	Hayes	Duckworth	Roberts	Curry	Meredith	Picken	Halse	Turnbull A	Wall

Appearances (goals)

Bannister 1 · Bell 27 · Blott 10 (1) · Burgess 1 · Connor 8 (1) · Donnelly 4 · Downie 3 · Duckworth 29 · Ford 1 · Halse 27 (6) · Hayes 30 · Holden 7 · Homer 17 (8) · Hooper 2 (1) · Livingstone 16 · Meredith 31 (5) · Moger 37 · Picken 19 (7) · Quinn 1 · Roberts 28 (4) · Rounds 1 · Stacey 32 · Turnbull A 26 (1) · Turnbull J 19 (9) · Wall 32 (14) · Whalley 9 · Total 26 players (69)

Football League

	P	W	D	L	F:A	Pts	
Aston Villa	38	23	7	8	84:42	53	1st
Manchester U	38	19	7	12	69:61	45	5th

SEASON 1910–1911 FOOTBALL LEAGUE (DIVISION 1)

Date	Opponent			Score											
1 Sep	Arsenal	A	W	2–1	Moger	Holden	Stacey	Duckworth	Roberts	Bell	Meredith[1]	Halse[1]	West[1]	Turnbull A	Wall
3 Sep	Blackburn R	H	W	3–2	..	..	..	..	..	..	..	..	..	..	[1]
10 Sep	Nottingham F	A	L	1–2	..	Stacey	Hayes	..	..	..	..	..	..	[1]	
17 Sep	Manchester C	H	W	2–1	..	Linkson	Stacey	..	..	..	..	..	[1]	[1]	
24 Sep	Everton	A	W	1–0	..	Holden	..	..	..	..	..	..	[1]		.. [2]
1 Oct	Sheffield Wed	H	W	3–2	..	..	..	..	..	..	..	[1]			
8 Oct	Bristol C	A	W	1–0	..	..	..	Livingstone	..	..	..	[1]		Picken	
15 Oct	Newcastle U	H	W	2–0	..	..	..	Duckworth	..	Livingstone	..		[2]	Turnbull A[1]	
22 Oct	Tottenham H	A	D	2–2	..	..	..	..	..	..	..			[1]	Connor
29 Oct	Middlesbrough	H	L	1–2	..	Linkson	..	..	..	..	..		[1]		[1]
5 Nov	Preston NE	A	W	2–0	..	..	..	..	..	Curry	..				Wall
12 Nov	Notts Co	H	D	0–0	..	..	..	..	..	..	..		..	[2]	[1]
19 Nov	Oldham	A	W	3–1	..	..	..	Livingstone	.. [1]	..	..		Hooper		[1]
26 Nov	Liverpool	A	L	2–3	..	..	..	..	..	..	Picken	Homer[2]			[1]
3 Dec	Bury	H	W	3–2	..	Holden	..	..	..	Whalley	..				
10 Dec	Sheffield U	A	L	0–2	..	Donnelly	..	Whalley	..	Bell	..		West[1]		[1]
17 Dec	Aston Villa	H	W	2–0	..	..	..	..	..	..	[1]	[2]	[2]		[1]
24 Dec	Sunderland	A	W	2–1	..	..	..	..	..	..	[1]				
26 Dec	Arsenal	H	W	5–0	..	..	..	..	..	Livingstone	Sheldon				
27 Dec	Bradford C	A	L	0–1	..	..	..	..	..	Bell					
31 Dec	Blackburn R	A	L	0–1	..	..	..	Livingstone	Whalley		Meredith[1]		Homer[1]	West	[1]
2 Jan	Bradford C	H	W	*1–0	..	..	..	Whalley	Roberts				West	Turnbull A[1]	[1]
7 Jan	Nottingham F	H	W	4–2	..	..	..	Duckworth	.. [1]		Halse	West			
21 Jan	Manchester C	A	D	1–1	..	..	..	..	..	Sheldon					
28 Jan	Everton	H	D	2–2	..	..	..	..	..	Meredith	Homer[1]	.. [1]	Picken[1]		
11 Feb	Bristol C	H	W	3–1	Edmonds	..	..	..	..		Halse[1]		Turnbull A		
18 Feb	Newcastle U	A	W	1–0	Moger	Hofton	Donnelly	..	Whalley		Homer	[1]			
4 Mar	Middlesbrough	A	D	2–2	Edmonds	Donnelly	Stacey	.. [1]	Roberts		Picken	[2]		[1]	Connor[1]
11 Mar	Preston NE	H	W	5–0	..	Hofton	..	..	.. [1]			[1]		[1]	
15 Mar	Tottenham H	H	W	3–2	..	..	..	..	..						
18 Mar	Notts Co	A	L	0–1	..	Donnelly	..	..	..		Sheldon				Wall
25 Mar	Oldham	H	D	0–0	..	Hofton	..	..	..		Halse	.. [2]			Sheldon
1 Apr	Liverpool	H	W	2–0	..	..	..	Whalley	.. [1]		[1]	Homer[2]			Wall
8 Apr	Bury	A	W	3–0	..	..	..	.. [1]							West[1]
15 Apr	Sheffield U	H	D	1–1	..	..	Donnelly	Hodge Jas	Bell	Whalley		Hooper			Wall
17 Apr	Sheffield Wed	A	D	0–0	..	..	..	Duckworth	Whalley	Bell		[2]	West		Connor
22 Apr	Aston Villa	A	L	2–4	..	..	..	..	..	Hodge Jas		[2]	.. [1]		[1]
29 Apr	Sunderland	H	W	*5–1	..	Donnelly	..	..	..						Blott

FA Cup

Date	Opponent			Score											
14 Jan	Blackpool (1)	A	W	2–1	Moger	Donnelly	Stacey	Duckworth	Roberts	Bell	Meredith	Picken[1]	West[1]	Turnbull A	Wall
4 Feb	Aston Villa(2)	H	W	2–1	..	..	..	..	..	..	..	Halse[1]	..		[1]
25 Feb	West Ham (3)	A	L	1–2	Edmonds	..	..	..	..	..	..	..	..	[1]	

Appearances (goals)

Bell 27 · Blott 1 · Connor 7 (1) · Curry 5 · Donnelly 15 · Duckworth 22 (2) · Edmonds 12 · Halse 23 (9) · Hayes 1 · Hodge Jas 2 · Hofton 9 · Holden 8 · Hooper 2 · Homer 7 (6) · Linkson 7 · Livingstone 10 · Meredith 35 (5) · Moger 26 · Picken 14 (4) · Roberts 33 (1) · Sheldon 5 · Stacey 36 · Turnbull A 35 (18) · Wall 27 (5) · West 34 (19) · Whalley 15 · Own goals 2 · Total 26 players (72)

Football League

	P	W	D	L	F:A	Pts	
Manchester U	38	22	8	8	72:40	52	1st

SEASON 1911–1912 FOOTBALL LEAGUE (DIVISION 1)

Date	Opponent			Score											
2 Sep	Manchester C	A	D	0–0	Edmonds	Hofton	Stacey	Duckworth	Roberts	Bell	Meredith	Halse	Homer	Turnbull A	Wall
9 Sep	Everton	H	W	2–1	..	..	..	..	..	..	..	[1]	Anderson	[1]	..
16 Sep	W B A	A	L	0–1	..	..	..	..	..	..	..	Hamill	Halse	..	..
23 Sep	Sunderland	H	D	2–2	..	..	.. [2]	..	..	..	..	..	..	..	..
30 Sep	Blackburn R	A	D	2–2	..	..	..	..	..	..	Sheldon	Halse	West[2]	..	..
7 Oct	Sheffield Wed	H	W	3–1	..	..	..	..	..	..	Meredith	[2]	[1]	..	..
14 Oct	Bury	A	W	1–0	..	..	..	..	..	..	..			[1]	..
21 Oct	Middlesbrough	H	L	3–4	..	Holden	..	..	..	..	..	[1]	[1]	[1]	..
28 Oct	Notts C	A	W	1–0	..	Donnelly	..	Whalley	..	..	..	[1]		[1]	Blott
4 Nov	Tottenham H	H	L	1–2	..	..	..	Duckworth	..	..	..	..			Wall
11 Nov	Preston NE	H	D	0–0	..	..	..	..	.. [1]	..	..	..			Blott
18 Nov	Liverpool	A	L	2–3	..	..	..	..	.. [1]	..	..		[2]		
25 Nov	Aston Villa	H	W	3–1	Moger	Linkson	..	..	..	..	..	[1]	[2]	..	Wall
2 Dec	Newcastle U	A	W	3–2	Edmonds	..	..	..	..	..	..	[1]	..	..	
9 Dec	Sheffield U	H	W	1–0	..	..	..	..	..	..	..	[1]		[1]	
16 Dec	Oldham	A	D	2–2	..	..	..	..	..	..	..	[1]			
23 Dec	Bolton W	H	W	2–0	..	..	..	..	..	..	..	..			
25 Dec	Bradford C	H	L	0–1	Moger	..	..	..	..	..	..		[1]		
26 Dec	Bradford C	A	W	1–0	Edmonds	..	..	..	..	Whalley	Hamill		[1]		
30 Dec	Manchester C	H	D	0–0	..	..	..	..	..	Bell	.. [1]				
1 Jan	Arsenal	H	W	2–0	..	..	..	..	..	..				Blott	.. [1]
6 Jan	Everton	A	L	0–4	..	Holden	Donnelly	..	..	..	Halse	McCarthy	Turnbull A		
20 Jan	W B A	H	L	1–2	..	..	Stacey	..	..	..	Hamill	Whalley			
27 Jan	Sunderland	A	L	0–5	..	..	..	..	..	..	Sheldon	West			
10 Feb	Sheffield Wed	A	L	0–3	..	..	..	Blott	Whalley	..	Halse				
17 Feb	Bury	H	D	0–0	..	..	..	Livingstone	Bell	Hodge Jas	.. [2]				
2 Mar	Notts C	H	W	2–0	..	Linkson	..	Duckworth	Roberts	..	Sheldon		Hamill		
16 Mar	Preston NE	A	D	0–0	..	..	Donnelly	..	..	..	Meredith	Hamill	Nuttall[1]		Capper
23 Mar	Liverpool	H	D	1–1	Royals	..	..	..	..	..	..	Halse	Turnbull A		Blott
30 Mar	Aston Villa	A	L	0–6	..	..	..	..	Knowles	..	..	Hamill		[1]	Wall
5 Apr	Arsenal	A	L	1–2	Edmonds	..	..	Halse	..	Bell	..				.. [1]
6 Apr	Newcastle	H	L	0–2	Moger	..	..	Hodge Jas	..	Bell	..				
9 Apr	Tottenham H	A	D	1–1	Edmonds	..	..	..	Roberts	..	Sheldon		Nuttall[1]		
13 Apr	Sheffield U	A	L	1–6	..	..	..	..	..	..	Meredith				.. [1]
17 Apr	Middlesbrough	A	L	0–3	Moger	..	..	..	..	..	Hamill	[2]			
20 Apr	Oldham	H	W	3–1	..	..	Stacey	Knowles	..	..	Meredith[1]	Hamill	[2]		
27 Apr	Bolton W	A	D	1–1	..	..	..	..	..	..	.. [1]	[1]	[1]		
29 Apr	Blackburn R	H	W	3–1	..	..	..	..	..	..					

FA Cup

Date	Opponent			Score											
13 Jan	Huddersfield T (1)	H	W	3–1	Edmonds	Holden	Stacey	Duckworth	Roberts	Bell	Meredith	Halse[1]	West[2]	Turnbull A	Wall
3 Feb	Coventry C (2)	A	W	5–1	..	..	..	..	Whalley	..	..	[2]	[1]	[1]	[1]
24 Feb	Reading (3)	A	D	1–1	..	Linkson	..	..	Roberts	..	..	..	[1]	..	..
29 Feb	Reading (3R)	H	W	3–0	..	..	..	..	..	..	..	[1]		[2]	
9 Mar	Blackburn R (4)	H	D	*1–1	..	..	..	..	..	..	..		[2]		
14 Mar	Blackburn R (4R)†	A	L	2–4	..	..	..	..	..	..	..				
	†after extra time														

Appearances (goals)

Anderson 1 · Bell 32 · Blott 6 · Capper 1 · Donnelly 13 · Duckworth 26 · Edmonds 29 · Halse 24 (8) · Hamill 16 (1) · Hodge Jas 10 · Hofton 7 · Holden 6 · Homer 1 · Knowles 7 · Linkson 21 · Livingstone 1 · McCarthy 1 · Meredith 35 (3) · Moger 7 · Nuttall 6 (2) · Roberts 32 (2) · Royals 2 · Sheldon 5 · Stacey 29 (2) · Turnbull A 30 (7) · Wall 33 (3) · West 32 (17) · Whalley 5 · Total 28 players (45)

Football League

	P	W	D	L	F:A	Pts	
Blackburn R	38	20	9	9	60:43	49	1st
Manchester U	38	13	11	14	45:60	37	13th

SEASON 1912–1913 FOOTBALL LEAGUE (DIVISION 1)

Date	Opponents	V	R	Score	Beale	Linkson	Stacey	Duckworth	Roberts	Bell	Meredith	Hamill	West	Turnbull A	Wall
2 Sep	Arsenal	A	D	0–0	Beale	Linkson	Stacey	Duckworth	Roberts	Bell	Meredith	Hamill	West	Turnbull A	Wall
7 Sep	Manchester C	H	L	0–1	..	..	..	..	..	..	..	..	..	..	..
14 Sep	W B A	A	W	2–1	..	Holden	..	Whalley	..	..	..	Livingstone[1]	..	..	[1]
21 Sep	Everton	H	W	2–0	..	Duckworth	..	..	..	..	..	Nuttall	[2]	..	..
28 Sep	Sheffield Wed	A	D	3–3	..	Linkson	..	Duckworth	Whalley	Roberts	..	..	[2]	..	[1]
5 Oct	Blackburn R	H	D	1–1	..	..	Duckworth	Whalley	Roberts	..	..	..	..	..	[1]
12 Oct	Derby C	A	L	1–2	..	..	Donnelly	Duckworth	..	..	..	..	..	..	[1]
19 Oct	Tottenham H	H	W	2–0	..	..	Stacey	Whalley	..	..	Hodge Jas	..	..	[2]	..
26 Oct	Middlesbrough	A	L	2–3	..	..	..	Duckworth	..	..	..	..	..	[2]	..
2 Nov	Notts Co	H	W	2–1	..	..	..	..	..	Bell	..	..	Anderson[1]	West[1]	..
9 Nov	Sunderland	A	L	1–3	..	Holden	..	Whalley	..	..	Hodge Jas	Anderson	West[1]	..	..
16 Nov	Aston Villa	A	L	2–4	..	Linkson	..	Duckworth	..	Bell	Sheldon	..	..	..	[1]
23 Nov	Liverpool	H	W	3–1	..	Duckworth	..	Knowles	..	..	Meredith	Nuttall	Anderson[2]	West	[1]
30 Nov	Bolton W	A	L	1–2	..	..	..	..	Whalley	..	..	..	..	..	[1]
7 Dec	Sheffield U	H	W	4–0	..	Linkson	..	Duckworth	Roberts	..	..	Turnbull A[1]	[1]	[1]	[1]
14 Dec	Newcastle U	A	W	3–1	..	..	..	Whalley	Duckworth	..	Sheldon	..	..	[3]	..
21 Dec	Oldham	H	D	0–0	..	..	..	Duckworth	Roberts	..	..	..	..	..	..
25 Dec	Chelsea	A	W	4–1	..	..	..	..	Gipps	Whalley[1]	..	..	[1]	[2]	..
26 Dec	Chelsea	H	W	4–2	..	..	..	..	Hamill	Whalley	Gipps	..	[1]	[2]	..
28 Dec	Manchester C	A	W	2–0	..	Hodge Jas	..	Duckworth	Roberts	Whalley	Meredith	..	..	[2]	..
1 Jan	Bradford C	H	W	2–0	..	..	..	..	..	..	Sheldon	..	..	[2]	..
4 Jan	W B A	H	D	1–1	..	..	..	..	[1]	..	Meredith	..	..	..	..
18 Jan	Everton	A	L	1–4	..	..	..	..	Whalley	Bell	Sheldon	Nuttall	..	Hamill[1]	..
25 Jan	Sheffield Wed	H	W	2–0	..	..	..	..	Roberts	Whalley[1]	Meredith	Hamill	Anderson	West[2]	..
8 Feb	Blackburn R	A	D	0–0	..	..	..	..	..	..	..	Turnbull A	..	..	..
15 Feb	Derby C	H	W	4–0	..	..	..	..	..	..	..	[1]	..	[1]	Blott
1 Mar	Middlesbrough	H	L	2–3	Mew	..	..	..	Whalley[1]	Bell	..	[1]	West	Hamill	Wall
8 Mar	Notts Co	A	W	2–1	Beale	..	..	..	Roberts	..	Sheldon	[1]	Anderson[1]	West	..
15 Mar	Sunderland	H	L	1–3	..	Linkson	..	Livingstone	Roberts	Hamill	..	..	[1]	..	..
21 Mar	Arsenal	H	W	2–0	..	..	[1]	Roberts[1]	..	Hamill	..	..	..	..	..
22 Mar	Aston Villa	H	W	4–0	..	..	Hamill	..	Bell	..	[1]	..	..	[1]	[1]
25 Mar	Bradford C	A	L	0–1	Hodge Jas	..	..	..	..	..	..	..	..	..	[1]
29 Mar	Liverpool	A	W	2–0	..	..	..	..	..	..	..	Hunter	..	[1]	..
31 Mar	Tottenham H	A	D	1–1	..	..	..	..	..	..	..	Anderson	[1]	..	Blott[1]
5 Apr	Bolton W	H	W	2–1	..	..	..	..	..	..	..	..	..	..	Wall[1]
12 Apr	Sheffield U	A	L	1–2	..	..	..	Roberts	..	..	..	..	..	..	..
19 Apr	Newcastle U	H	W	3–0	..	..	..	..	..	..	Meredith	Hunter[2]	..	[1]	..
26 Apr	Oldham	A	D	0–0	..	..	..	..	..	..	..	..	..	..	..

FA Cup

Date	Opponents	V	R	Score	Beale	Hodge	Stacey	Duckworth	Roberts	Whalley	Meredith	Turnbull A	Anderson	West	Wall
11 Jan	Coventry (1)	H	D	1–1	Beale	Hodge	Stacey	Duckworth	Roberts[1]	Whalley	Meredith	Turnbull A	Anderson	West	Wall[1]
16 Jan	Coventry (1R)	A	W	2–1	..	..	..	..	..	..	..	..	Anderson[1]	..	..
1 Feb	Plymouth A (2)	A	W	2–0	..	..	..	..	..	..	..	..	[1]	Hamill	..
22 Feb	Oldham (3)	A	D	0–0	..	..	..	..	..	..	..	Hamill	..	West	..
26 Feb	Oldham (3R)	H	L	1–2	..	..	..	..	..	..	..	Turnbull A	..	West[1]	..

Appearances (goals)

Anderson 24 (12) · Beale 37 · Bell 26 · Blott 2 (1) · Donnelly 1 · Duckworth 24 · Gipps 2 · Hamill 15 (1) · Hodge Jas 19 · Holden 2 · Hunter 3 (2) · Knowles 2 · Linkson 17 · Livingstone 2 (1) · Meredith 22 (2) · Mew 1 · Nuttall 10 (2) · Roberts 24 (1) · Sheldon 16 (1) · Stacey 36 (1) · Turnbull A 35 (10) · Wall 36 (10) · West 36 (21) · Whalley 26 (4) · Total 24 players (69)

Football League

	P	W	D	L	F:A	Pts	
Sunderland	38	25	4	9	86:43	54	1st
Manchester U	38	19	8	11	69:43	46	4th

SEASON 1913–1914 FOOTBALL LEAGUE (DIVISION 1)

Date	Opponents	V	R	Score	Beale	Hodge Jas	Stacey	Duckworth	Whalley	Hamill	Meredith	Turnbull A	Anderson	West	Wall
6 Sep	Sheffield Wed	A	W	3–1	Beale	Hodge Jas	Stacey	Duckworth	Whalley[1]	Hamill	Meredith	Turnbull A[1]	Anderson[1]	West[1]	Wall
8 Sep	Sunderland	H	W	3–1	..	..	..	..	..	Knowles	..	Cashmore	..	..	..
13 Sep	Bolton W	H	L	0–1	..	..	..	..	..	Knowles	..	Cashmore	..	..	..
20 Sep	Chelsea	A	W	2–0	..	..	..	..	..	Hamill	..	Turnbull A	..	[1]	[1]
27 Sep	Oldham	H	W	4–1	..	..	..	..	..	..	..	..	[1]	[2]	[1]
4 Oct	Tottenham H	H	W	3–1	..	..	..	[1]	..	[1]	..	Hooper	..	..	[1]
11 Oct	Burnley	A	W	2–1	..	Chorlton	..	..	..	..	..	Turnbull A	[2]	..	..
18 Oct	Preston NE	H	W	3–0	..	Hodge Jas	..	..	..	..	..	..	[3]	..	..
25 Oct	Newcastle U	A	W	1–0	..	..	..	Gipps	..	Knowles	..	..	..	[1]	..
1 Nov	Liverpool	H	W	3–0	..	..	..	..	..	Hamill	..	Woodcock	..	[1]	[2]
8 Nov	Aston Villa	A	L	1–3	..	..	..	..	..	..	..	..	..	..	..
15 Nov	Middlesbrough	H	L	0–1	..	..	..	Duckworth	..	..	..	Turnbull A	Hooper	West	Wall
22 Nov	Sheffield U	A	L	0–2	Mew	..	..	Gipps	..	Haywood	..	..	West	Wall	..
29 Nov	Derby Co	H	D	3–3	..	..	..	..	..	..	[1]	[2]	Cashmore	West	..
6 Dec	Manchester C	A	W	2–0	Beale	..	..	Knowles	..	Hamill	..	..	[2]	West	..
13 Dec	Bradford C	H	D	1–1	..	..	..	Haywood	Knowles[1]	..	..	..	..	..	Thomson
20 Dec	Blackburn R	A	W	*1–0	..	..	..	..	opponents	..	..	..	..	..	Wall
25 Dec	Everton	H	L	0–1	..	..	..	Knowles	Whalley	..	..	..	..	..	..
26 Dec	Everton	A	L	0–5	..	..	..	..	..	..	[1]	Potts	West	Turnbull A	..
27 Dec	Sheffield Wed	H	W	2–1	..	Roberts	Hodge Jas	..	Hodge J	..	..	Woodcock	Hooper	..	[1]
1 Jan	W B A	H	W	1–0	..	Hodge Jas	Stacey	Gipps	Hamill	Haywood	..	..	Anderson	Woodcock	..
3 Jan	Bolton W	A	L	1–6	..	Roberts	Hodge Jas	..	Knowles	..	..	Turnbull A	..	West[1]	..
17 Jan	Chelsea	H	L	1–5	..	Hodge Jas	Stacey	Knowles	Whalley	Hamill	..	Potts	Woodcock	..	..
24 Jan	Oldham	A	D	2–2	..	..	..	..	Livingstone	Hudson	..	Woodcock[1]	West	Wall[1]	Norton
7 Feb	Tottenham H	A	L	1–1	..	..	..	Hudson	..	Hamill	..	Travers	..	Turnbull A	Wall[1]
14 Feb	Burnley	H	L	0–1	..	..	..	Haywood	West	Wall	..	Woodcock	Anderson	Travers	Norton
21 Feb	Middlesbrough	A	L	1–3	..	Chorlton	..	..	Knowles	Hamill	..	..	[1]	West	Wall
28 Feb	Newcastle U	H	D	2–2	..	..	..	..	Hodge J	..	Norton	Potts[1]	..	Travers	..
5 Mar	Preston NE	A	L	2–4	..	Rowe	..	..	..	..	..	..	..	..	[1]
14 Mar	Aston Villa	H	L	0–6	..	Chorlton	..	Livingstone	Hunter	Haywood	Meredith	Woodcock	..	West	..
4 Apr	Derby Co	A	L	2–4	..	Hodge J	..	Haywood	..	Hamill	..	Travers[1]	[1]	West	Norton
10 Apr	Sunderland	A	L	0–2	Royals	Hodge Jas	Hudson	Gipps	..	Haywood	Norton	..	..	..	Thomson
11 Apr	Manchester C	H	L	0–1	..	Hudson	Stacey	Knowles	..	Gipps	Meredith	..	..	..	..
13 Apr	W B A	A	L	1–2	..	..	..	..	..	..	..	[1]	West	Woodcock	..
15 Apr	Liverpool	A	W	2–1	..	..	..	..	..	Hamill	..	[1]	Anderson	..	Wall[1]
18 Apr	Bradford C	A	D	1–1	..	..	..	..	..	..	..	..	Cashmore	Anderson	Thomson[1]
22 Apr	Sheffield U	H	W	2–1	Beale	..	..	Hodge Jas	Knowles	Gipps	..	..	Anderson[2]	West	Norton
25 Apr	Blackburn R	H	D	0–0	..	..	..	Hodge Jas	Haywood	Hamill	Norton	..	..	..	Thomson

FA Cup

Date	Opponents	V	R	Score	Beale	Hodge	Stacey	Knowles	Livingstone	Whalley	Meredith	Turnbull A	Woodcock	West	Wall
10 Jan	Swindon T (1)	A	L	0–1	Beale	Hodge	Stacey	Knowles	Livingstone	Whalley	Meredith	Turnbull A	Woodcock	West	Wall

Appearances (goals)

Anderson 32 (15) · Beale 31 · Cashmore 3 · Chorlton 4 · Duckworth 9 · Gipps 11 · Hamill 26 · Haywood 14 · Hodge Jas 28 · Hodge J 4 · Hooper 3 · Hudson 9 · Hunter 7 · Knowles 18 (1) · Livingstone 3 · Meredith 34 (2) · Mew 2 · Norton 8 · Potts 6 (1) · Roberts 2 · Rowe 1 · Royals 5 · Stacey 34 (1) · Thomson 6 (1) · Travers 13 (4) · Turnbull A 17 (4) · Wall 29 (1) · West 30 (6) · Whalley 18 (2) · Woodcock 11 (2) · Own goals 2 · Total 30 players (52)

Football League

	P	W	D	L	F:A	Pts	
Blackburn R	38	20	11	7	78:42	51	1st
Manchester U	38	15	6	17	52:62	36	14th

1914–1915

SEASON 1914–1915 FOOTBALL LEAGUE (DIVISION 1)

Date	Opponent	H/A	Res	Score	Team / notes
2 Sep	Oldham	H	L	1–3	Beale · Hodge J · Stacey · Hunter · O'Connell[1] · Knowles · Meredith · Anderson · Travers · West[2] · Wall
5 Sep	Manchester C	H	D	0–0	Travers · West · Woodcock
12 Sep	Bolton W	A	L	0–3	Norton
19 Sep	Blackburn R	H	W	2–0	Gipps · Hunter · Meredith · Turnbull A · Anderson · West[2]
26 Sep	Notts Co	A	L	2–4	Norton
3 Oct	Sunderland	H	W	3–0	O'Connell · Hunter · O'Connell · Travers
10 Oct	Sheffield Wed	A	L	0–1	Gipps · Woodcock · Potts
17 Oct	W B A	H	D	0–0	Gipps · Woodcock · Wall[1] · Travers
24 Oct	Everton	A	L	2–4	Hudson · O'Connell · Whalley
31 Oct	Chelsea	H	D	2–2	Stacey · Gipps · Hunter[1] · Turnbull A · West[2]
7 Nov	Bradford C	A	L	2–4	O'Connell
14 Nov	Burnley	H	L	0–2	Mew · Meredith · Turnbull A · Travers · Woodcock · Wall
21 Nov	Tottenham H	A	L	0–2	Beale · Stacey · Hudson · Hodge Jas · Hunter · Wall · Anderson · West
28 Nov	Newcastle U	H	W	1–0	Hodge J · Stacey · Hunter · Knowles
5 Dec	Middlesbrough	A	D	1–1	
12 Dec	Sheffield U	H	L	1–2	
19 Dec	Aston Villa	A	D	3–3	Gipps · Meredith · Potts
26 Dec	Liverpool	A	D	1–1	Cookson · O'Connell
1 Jan	Bradford	H	L	1–2	Gipps · Cookson
2 Jan	Manchester C	A	D	1–1	
16 Jan	Bolton W	H	W	4–1	Knowles · Woodcock[1] · Cookson
23 Jan	Blackburn R	A	D	*3–3	Cookson · Woodcock[2]
30 Jan	Notts Co	H	D	2–2	
6 Feb	Sunderland	A	L	0–1	Spratt · Haywood
13 Feb	Sheffield Wed	H	W	2–0	Allman · Spratt · Travers
20 Feb	W B A	A	D	0–0	Spratt · Wall
27 Feb	Everton	H	L	1–2	Gipps · Meredith · Prince
13 Mar	Bradford C	H	W	1–0	Montgomery · Cookson · Norton · West · Wall
20 Mar	Burnley	A	L	0–3	
27 Mar	Tottenham H	H	D	1–1	Haywood · Meredith
2 Apr	Liverpool	H	W	2–0	Hodge J · Anderson[2] · Norton
3 Apr	Newcastle	A	L	0–2	
5 Apr	Bradford	A	L	0–5	Allman
6 Apr	Oldham	A	L	0–1	Knowles · Cookson · Turnbull A · Anderson · Hodge Jas
10 Apr	Middlesbrough	H	D	2–2	Stacey · Spratt · Haywood · Woodcock · Turnbull A[1]
17 Apr	Sheffield U	A	L	1–3	West[1] · Woodcock
19 Apr	Chelsea	A	W	3–1	Hodge J · Woodcock[1] · Anderson · West[1] · Norton[1]
26 Apr	Aston Villa	H	W	1–0	

FA Cup
Date	Opponent	H/A	Res	Score	Team
9 Jan	Sheffield Wed(1)	A	L	0–1	Beale · Hodge J · Stacey · Hunter · O'Connell · Cookson · Meredith · Fox · Anderson · West · Wall

Appearances (goals)

Allman 12 · Anderson 23 (10) · Beale 37 · Cookson 12 · Gipps 10 · Haywood 12 · Hodge J 26 · Hodge Jas 4 · Hudson 2 · Hunter 15 (2) · Knowles 19 · Meredith 26 · Mew 1 · Montgomery 11 · Norton 29 (3) · O'Connell 34 (2) · Potts 17 (4) · Prince 1 · Spratt 12 · Stacey 24 (4) · Travers 8 · Turnbull A 13 (2) · Wall 17 (2) · West 33 (9) · Whalley 1 · Woodcock 19 (7) · Own goals 1 · Total 26 players (46)

Football League

	P	W	D	L	F:A	Pts	
Everton	38	19	8	11	76:47	46	1st
Manchester U	38	9	12	17	46:62	30	18th

SEASON 1915–1916

Lancs Principal Tournament

Date	Opponent	H/A	Res	Score
4 Sep	Oldham A	A	L	2–3
11 Sep	Everton	H	L	2–4
18 Sep	Bolton W	A	W	5–3
25 Sep	Manchester C	H	D	1–1
2 Oct	Stoke C	A	D	0–0
9 Oct	Burnley	H	L	3–7
16 Oct	Preston NE	A	D	0–0
23 Oct	Stockport Co	H	W	3–0
30 Oct	Liverpool	A	W	2–0
6 Nov	Bury	H	D	1–1
13 Nov	Rochdale	H	W	2–0
20 Nov	Blackpool	A	L	1–5
27 Nov	Southport	H	D	0–0
4 Dec	Oldham	H	W	2–0
11 Dec	Everton	A	L	0–2
18 Dec	Bolton W	H	W	1–0
25 Dec	Manchester C	A	L	1–2
1 Jan	Stoke C	H	L	1–2
8 Jan	Burnley	A	L	4–7
15 Jan	Preston NE	H	W	4–0
22 Jan	Stockport Co	A	L	1–3
29 Jan	Liverpool	H	D	1–1
5 Feb	Bury	A	L	1–2
12 Feb	Rochdale	A	D	2–2
19 Feb	Blackpool	H	D	1–1
26 Feb	Southport	A	L	0–5

	P	W	D	L	F:A	Pts	
Manchester U	26	7	8	13	41:51	22	11th

Lancs Subsidiary Tournament

Date	Opponent	H/A	Res	Score
4 Mar	Everton	H	L	0–2
11 Mar	Oldham	A	L	0–1
18 Mar	Liverpool	H	D	0–0
25 Mar	Manchester C	H	L	0–2
1 Apr	Stockport Co	A	L	3–5
8 Apr	Everton	A	L	1–3
15 Apr	Oldham	H	W	3–0
21 Apr	Stockport Co	H	W	3–2
22 Apr	Liverpool	A	L	1–7
29 Apr	Manchester C	A	L	1–2

	P	W	D	L	F:A	Pts	
Manchester U	10	2	1	7	12:24	5	6th

SEASON 1916–1917

Lancs Principal Tournament

Date	Opponent	H/A	Res	Score
2 Sep	Port Vale	H	D	2–2
9 Sep	Oldham	A	W	2–0
16 Sep	Preston NE	H	W	2–1
23 Sep	Burnley	A	L	1–1
30 Sep	Blackpool	A	D	2–2
7 Oct	Liverpool	H	D	0–0
14 Oct	Stockport Co	A	L	0–1
21 Oct	Bury	H	W	3–1
28 Oct	Stoke C	A	L	0–3
4 Nov	Southport	H	W	1–0
11 Nov	Blackburn R	A	W	2–1
18 Nov	Manchester C	H	W	2–1
25 Nov	Everton	A	L	2–3
2 Dec	Rochdale	H	D	1–1
9 Dec	Bolton W	A	L	1–5
23 Dec	Oldham	H	W	3–2
30 Dec	Preston NE	A	L	2–3
6 Jan	Burnley	H	W	3–1
13 Jan	Blackpool	H	W	3–2
20 Jan	Liverpool	A	D	3–3
27 Jan	Stockport Co	H	L	0–1
3 Feb	Bury	A	D	1–1
10 Feb	Stoke C	H	W	4–2
17 Feb	Southport	A	W	1–0
24 Feb	Blackburn R	H	W	1–0
3 Mar	Manchester C	A	L	0–1
10 Mar	Everton	H	L	0–2
17 Mar	Rochdale	A	L	0–2
24 Mar	Bolton W	H	L	0–2
6 Apr	Port Vale	A	L	0–3

	P	W	D	L	F:A	Pts	
Manchester U	30	13	6	11	48:54	33	7th

Lancs Subsidiary Tournament

Date	Opponent	H/A	Res	Score
31 Mar	Stoke C	A	L	1–2
7 Apr	Manchester C	H	W	5–1
9 Apr	Port Vale	H	W	5–1
14 Apr	Stoke C	H	W	1–0
21 Apr	Manchester C	A	W	1–0
28 Apr	Port Vale	A	L	2–5

	P	W	D	L	F:A	Pts	
Manchester U	6	4	0	2	15:9	8	4th

SEASON 1917–1918

Lancs Principal Tournament

Date	Opponent	H/A	Res	Score
1 Sep	Blackburn R	A	W	5–0
8 Sep	Blackburn R	H	W	6–1
15 Sep	Rochdale	A	L	0–3
22 Sep	Rochdale	H	D	1–1
29 Sep	Manchester C	A	L	1–3
6 Oct	Manchester C	H	D	1–1
13 Oct	Everton	A	L	0–3
20 Oct	Everton	H	D	0–0
27 Oct	Port Vale	H	D	3–3
3 Nov	Port Vale	A	D	2–2
10 Nov	Bolton W	H	L	1–3
17 Nov	Bolton W	A	L	2–4
24 Nov	Preston NE	H	W	2–1
1 Dec	Preston NE	A	D	0–0
8 Dec	Blackpool	H	W	1–0
15 Dec	Blackpool	A	W	3–2
22 Dec	Burnley	A	W	5–0
29 Dec	Burnley	H	W	1–0
5 Jan	Southport	A	L	0–3
12 Jan	Southport	H	D	0–0
19 Jan	Liverpool	A	L	1–5
26 Jan	Liverpool	H	L	0–2
2 Feb	Stoke C	A	L	1–5
9 Feb	Stoke C	H	W	2–1
16 Feb	Bury	H	D	0–0
23 Feb	Bury	A	W	2–1
2 Mar	Oldham	H	W	2–1
9 Mar	Oldham	A	L	0–2
16 Mar	Stockport Co	H	W	2–0
23 Mar	Stockport Co	A	L	1–2

	P	W	D	L	F:A	Pts	
Manchester U	30	11	8	11	45:49	30	8th

Lancs Subsidiary Tournament

Date	Opponent	H/A	Res	Score
29 Mar	Manchester C	A	L	0–3
30 Mar	Stoke C	H	W	2–1
1 Apr	Manchester C	H	W	2–0
6 Apr	Stoke C	A	D	0–0
13 Apr	Port Vale	H	W	2–0
20 Apr	Port Vale	A	L	0–3

	P	W	D	L	F:A	Pts	
Manchester U	6	3	1	2	6:7	7	8th

SEASON 1918–1919

Lancs Principal Tournament

Date	Opponent	H/A	Res	Score
7 Sep	Oldham	H	L	1–4
14 Sep	Oldham	A	W	2–0
21 Sep	Blackburn R	H	W	1–0
28 Sep	Blackburn R	A	D	1–1
5 Oct	Manchester C	H	L	0–2
12 Oct	Manchester C	A	D	0–0
19 Oct	Everton	H	D	1–1
26 Oct	Everton	A	L	2–6
2 Nov	Rochdale	H	W	3–1
9 Nov	Rochdale	A	L	0–1
16 Nov	Preston NE	A	L	2–4
23 Nov	Preston NE	H	L	1–2
30 Nov	Bolton W	A	L	1–3
7 Dec	Bolton W	H	W	1–0
14 Dec	Port Vale	A	L	1–3
21 Dec	Port Vale	H	W	5–1
28 Dec	Blackpool	A	D	2–2
11 Jan	Stockport Co	A	L	1–2
18 Jan	Stockport Co	H	L	0–2
25 Jan	Liverpool	A	D	1–1
1 Feb	Liverpool	H	L	0–1
8 Feb	Southport V	A	L	1–2
15 Feb	Southport V	H	L	1–3
22 Feb	Burnley	A	L	2–4
1 Mar	Burnley	H	W	4–0
8 Mar	Stoke C	A	W	2–1
15 Mar	Stoke C	H	W	3–1
22 Mar	Bury	A	W	2–0
29 Mar	Bury	H	W	5–1

	P	W	D	L	F:A	Pts	
Manchester U	30	11	5	14	51:50	27	9th

Lancs Subsidiary Tournament (Sec 'C')

Date	Opponent	H/A	Res	Score
5 Apr	Port Vale	A	W	3–1
12 Apr	Port Vale	H	W	2–1
18 Apr	Manchester C	A	L	0–3
19 Apr	Stoke C	H	L	0–1
21 Apr	Manchester C	H	L	2–4
26 Apr	Stoke C	A	L	2–4
30 Apr	Blackpool	H	W	5–1

	P	W	D	L	F:A	Pts	
Manchester U	6	2	0	4	9:14	4	3rd

SEASON 1919–1920 FOOTBALL LEAGUE (DIVISION 1)

Date	Opponent			Score											
30 Aug	Derby Co	A	D	1–1	Mew	Moore	Silcock	Montgomery	Hilditch	Whalley	Hodge JA	Woodcock[1]	Spence	Potts	Hopkin
1 Sep	Sheffield Wed	H	D	0–0	..	..	..	..	..	..	..	Meehan	..	Woodcock	..
6 Sep	Derby Co	H	L	0–2	..	..	..	..	..	..	..	Woodcock	..	Meehan	..
8 Sep	Sheffield Wed	A	W	3–1	..	..	..	..	..	..	..	..	..	..	..
13 Sep	Preston NE	A	W	3–2	..	..	..	..	..	..	..	..	..[1]	..	..
20 Sep	Preston NE	H	W	5–1	..	..	..	..	..[1]	..	..	..[2]	..[2]	..[1]	..
27 Sep	Middlesbrough	A	D	1–1	..	..	..	..	..	..	..	..[1]	..	..	..
4 Oct	Middlesbrough	H	D	1–1	..	..	..	Meehan	..	..	..	..[1]	..	Toms	..
11 Oct	Manchester C	A	D	3–3	..	..	..	Whalley	Grimwood	Meehan	..[1]	..	..[1]	..	..[1]
18 Oct	Manchester C	H	W	1–0	..	..	..	Meehan	Hilditch	Whalley	..	Hodges	..	Woodcock	..
25 Oct	Sheffield U	A	D	2–2	..	..	..	..	..	..	..	..	..	..[1]	..[1]
1 Nov	Sheffield U	H	W	3–0	..	..	..	..	..	..	Hodges[1]	Potts	..[1]	..[1]	..
8 Nov	Burnley	A	L	1–2	..	..	..	..	..	Forster	Hodge JA[1]	Hodges	..	..	..
15 Nov	Burnley	H	L	0–1	..	..	..	..	..	..	Bissett	..	..	..	..
22 Nov	Oldham	A	W	3–0	..	..	..	..	..	Whalley	..	..[1]	..	Hodge JA	..[1]
6 Dec	Aston Villa	A	L	0–2	..	..	..	..	..	..	..	Hodge JA	..	Toms	..
13 Dec	Aston Villa	H	L	1–2	..	..	..	..	..[1]	Montgomery	Hodge JA	Hodges	..	..	..
20 Dec	Newcastle U	H	W	2–1	..	..	..	Grimwood	..	Whalley	Hodges[1]	Hodge JA	..[1]	Meehan	..
26 Dec	Liverpool	H	D	0–0	..	..	..	..	..	..	Meredith	Hodges	..	..	..
27 Dec	Newcastle U	A	L	1–2	..	..	..	..	..[1]	..	Bissett	..	..	..	..
1 Jan	Liverpool	A	D	0–0	..	..	..	..	..	..	Meredith	..	..	Woodcock	..
3 Jan	Chelsea	H	L	0–2	..	..	..	..	..	..	..	..	..	..	Robinson
17 Jan	Chelsea	A	L	0–1	..	..	..	..	..	..	..	Meehan	..	..	Hopkin
24 Jan	W B A	A	L	1–2	..	..	..	..	..	..	..	Potts	Woodcock[1]	Toms	..
7 Feb	Sunderland	A	L	0–3	..	..	..	..	..	Meehan	..	Bissett	Spence	Woodcock	..
11 Feb	Oldham	H	D	1–1	..	..	..	..	..	..	..	..[1]	Toms	..	..
14 Feb	Sunderland	H	W	2–0	..	Barlow	..	..	Harris[1]	Hilditch	Bissett	Hodges[1]	Spence	Meehan	..
21 Feb	Arsenal	A	W	3–0	..	..	..	..	..	..	..	..	..[2]	..	..[1]
25 Feb	W B A	H	L	1–2	..	..	..	..	..	..	..	..	..[1]	..	..
28 Feb	Arsenal	H	L	0–1	..	Moore	Spratt	..	..	..	..	..	..	..	..
6 Mar	Everton	H	W	1–0	..	..	Silcock	..	Hilditch	Meehan	Meredith	Bissett	Harris	Woodcock	..
13 Mar	Everton	A	D	0–0	..	..	..	..	..	..	..	..	Spence	..	..
20 Mar	Bradford C	H	D	0–0	..	..	Barlow	..	..	..	..	..	..	..	..
27 Mar	Bradford C	A	L	1–2	..	..	Silcock	..	Harris	Whalley	..	..[1]	Woodcock	Potts	..
2 Apr	Bradford P A	H	L	0–1	..	..	..	..	..	Meehan	..	..	Spence	Hodges	Prentice
3 Apr	Bolton W	H	D	1–1	..	Barlow	..	..	Montgomery	..	..	Woodcock	Toms[1]	Bissett	Hopkin
6 Apr	Bradford P A	A	W	4–1	..	..	..	..[1]	..	..	..	..[1]	..[1]	..[1]	..
10 Apr	Bolton W	A	W	5–3	..	Moore	..	..	..	..	..[1]	..[1]	..[1]	..[2]	..[1]
17 Apr	Blackburn R	H	D	1–1	..	..	..	Williamson	..	..	..	..	..	..	..[1]
24 Apr	Blackburn R	A	L	0–5	..	..	..	..	..	Forster	..	Hodges	..	..	..
26 Apr	Notts Co	H	D	0–0	..	Barlow	..	Forster	Whalley	Meehan	..	Bissett	..	Sapsford	Robinson
1 May	Notts Co	A	W	2–0	..	Moore	..	..	Montgomery	..	..	..[1]	Spence[1]	..	Hopkin

FA Cup

Date	Opponent			Score											
10 Jan	Port Vale (1)	A	W	1–0	Mew	Moore	Silcock	Grimwood	Hilditch	Whalley	Meredith	Meehan	Toms[1]	Woodcock	Hopkin
31 Jan	Aston Villa (2)	H	L	1–2	..	..	Spratt	..	..	..	..	Potts	Woodcock[1]	Meehan	..

Appearances (goals)

Barlow 7 · Bissett 22 (6) · Forster 5 · Grimwood 22 (1) · Harris 7 (1) · Hilditch 32 (2) · Hodge JA 16 (2) · Hodges 18 (4) · Hopkin 39 (5) · Meehan 36 (2) · Meredith 19 (2) · Mew 42 · Montgomery 14 (1) · Moore 36 · Potts 4 · Prentice 1 · Robinson 2 · Sapsford 2 · Silcock 40 · Spence 32 (14) · Spratt 1 · Toms 12 (3) · Whalley 23 · Williamson 2 · Woodcock 28 (11) · Total 25 players (54)

Football League

	P	W	D	L	F:A	Pts	
W B A	42	28	4	10	104:47	60	1st
Manchester U	42	13	14	15	54:50	40	12th

SEASON 1920–1921 FOOTBALL LEAGUE (DIVISION 1)

Date	Opponent			Score											
28 Aug	Bolton W	H	L	2–3	Mew	Moore	Silcock	Meehan[1]	Grimwood	Hilditch	Meredith	Bissett	Goodwin	Sapsford	Hopkin[1]
30 Aug	Arsenal	A	L	0–2	..	Hofton	..	Harris	Hilditch	Meehan	..	Spence	Toms	..	..
4 Sep	Bolton W	A	D	1–1	..	Barlow	..	Grimwood	..	..	Schofield P	Myerscough	Spence	..[1]	..
6 Sep	Arsenal	H	D	1–1	..	..	..	..	..	..	Spence[1]	Bissett	Myerscough	..	..
11 Sep	Chelsea	H	W	3–1	..	..	..	Harris	..	..[2]	Meredith	Hodges	Leonard[1]	..	..
18 Sep	Chelsea	A	W	2–1	..	..	..	..	..	..	..	Spence	..[2]	..	..
25 Sep	Tottenham H	H	L	0–1	..	Moore	Barlow	..	..	..	..	Miller	..	..	..
2 Oct	Tottenham H	A	L	1–4	..	..	..	..	Montgomery	..	Bissett	..	..	Spence[1]	Sapsford
9 Oct	Oldham	H	W	4–1	..	..	Barlow	Silcock	..	Hilditch	Forster	Meehan[1]	..[1]	Spence	Sapsford[2]	Partridge
16 Oct	Oldham	A	D	*2–2	..	..	..	..	..	..	..	..	..[1]	..	..
23 Oct	Preston NE	H	W	1–0	Steward	..	..	..	..	Meehan	Harrison	Hodges	Miller[1]	..	..
30 Oct	Preston NE	A	D	0–0	Mew	..	..	..	..	..	..	Miller	Leonard	..	Hopkin
6 Nov	Sheffield U	H	W	2–1	..	..	..	..	..	Forster	..	..	..[2]	Partridge	..
13 Nov	Sheffield U	A	D	0–0	..	Moore	..	..	..	Meehan	..	..	..	..	..
20 Nov	Manchester C	H	D	1–1	..	..	..	Forster	Harris	..	..	..[1]	..	Sapsford	..
27 Nov	Manchester C	A	L	0–3	..	..	..	Harris	Hilditch	..	..	..	..	Spence	..
4 Dec	Bradford	H	W	5–1	..	..	..	..	Grimwood	Forster	..	Myerscough[2]	Miller[2]	Partridge[1]	..
11 Dec	Bradford	A	W	4–2	..	..	..	..	..	..	..	..[2]	..[1]	..[1]	..
18 Dec	Newcastle	H	W	2–0	..	..	..	..	..	..	..	..	..[1]	..	..[1]
25 Dec	Aston Villa	A	W	4–3	..	..	..	..	..[2]	..	..	..[1]	..	..[1]	..
27 Dec	Aston Villa	H	L	1–3	..	..	..	..	..	..	..	..[1]	..	..	..
1 Jan	Newcastle U	A	L	3–6	..	..	..	..[1]	..	Hilditch	..	..	Spence	..[1]	..[1]
15 Jan	W B A	H	L	1–4	..	Barlow	..	..	..	Forster	..	Bissett	Miller	..[1]	..
22 Jan	W B A	A	W	2–0	..	Silcock	Barlow	Hilditch	..	..	..	Myerscough[1]	..	..[1]	..
5 Feb	Liverpool	H	D	1–1	..	Barlow	Silcock	..	..	..[1]	..	..	Spence	..	..
9 Feb	Liverpool	A	L	0–2	..	..	..	..	..	..	Meredith	..	Spence	..	..
12 Feb	Everton	H	L	1–2	..	..	..	..	..	..	..[1]	..	Miller	..	..
20 Feb	Sunderland	H	W	3–0	..	Moore	..	..[1]	..	..	Harrison[1]	Partridge	Goodwin	Sapsford	Robinson[1]
5 Mar	Sunderland	A	W	3–2	..	..	..	..	..	..	..	..	..[1]	..[2]	..
9 Mar	Everton	A	L	0–2	..	..	Barlow	..	..	Harris	..	..	..	..	..
12 Mar	Bradford C	H	D	1–1	Steward	..	..	..	..	Forster	..	Miller	..	..[1]	..
19 Mar	Bradford C	A	D	1–1	Mew	..	Silcock	..	Montgomery	..	..	Myerscough	Sapsford[1]	Partridge	..
25 Mar	Burnley	A	L	0–1	..	..	..	Harris	Hilditch	..	..	Spence	Miller	..	Hopkin
26 Mar	Huddersfield T	A	L	2–5	..	..	..	..	..	..	Meredith	..	..	..[1]	..
28 Mar	Burnley	H	L	0–3	..	..	..	Hilditch	Harris	..	Harrison	Bissett	Leonard	Sapsford	Partridge
2 Apr	Huddersfield T	H	W	2–0	..	..	..	..	Grimwood	..[1]	Meredith	..[2]	Miller	Partridge	Robinson
9 Apr	Middlesbrough	A	W	4–2	..	..	Barlow	..	..	..	..[1]	Spence[2]	..	..	Hopkin
16 Apr	Middlesbrough	H	L	0–1	..	..	Silcock	..	..	..	..	..	..	..	..
23 Apr	Blackburn R	A	L	0–2	..	..	..	..	..	Harris	Harrison	..	Miller	..	..
30 Apr	Blackburn R	H	L	0–1	..	..	..	..	..	..	Meredith	..[1]	..	..	..
2 May	Derby Co	A	D	1–1	..	..	..	..	..	Forster	..	..	Hopkin	Sapsford	Robinson
7 May	Derby Co	H	W	3–0	..	Radford	..	..	..	..	..	..	Spence[2]	..[1]	Hopkin

FA Cup

Date	Opponent			Score											
8 Jan	Liverpool (1)	A	D	1–1	Mew	Barlow	Silcock	Harris	Grimwood	Forster	Harrison	Bissett	Miller[1]	Partridge	Hopkin
12 Jan	Liverpool (1R)	H	L	1–2	..	Hofton	..	..	..	Albinson	..	..	..	..	..

Appearances (goals)

Barlow 19 · Bissett 12 (4) · Forster 26 · Goodwin 5 (1) · Grimwood 25 (4) · Harris 26 (1) · Harrison 23 (3) · Hilditch 34 (1) · Hodges 2 · Hofton 1 · Hopkin 31 (3) · Leonard 10 (5) · Meehan 15 (4) · Meredith 14 (1) · Mew 40 · Miller 25 (7) · Montgomery 2 · Moore 26 · Myerscough 13 (5) · Partridge 28 (7) · Radford 1 · Robinson 7 (2) · Sapsford 21 (7) · Schofield P 1 · Silcock 37 (1) · Spence 15 (7) · Steward 2 · Toms 1 · Own goals 1 · Total 28 players (64)

Football League

	P	W	D	L	F:A	Pts	
Burnley	42	23	13	6	79:36	59	1st
Manchester U	42	15	10	17	64:68	40	13th

SEASON 1921–1922 FOOTBALL LEAGUE (DIVISION 1)

Date	Opponent			Score	1	2	3	4	5	6	7	8	9	10	11
27 Aug	Everton	A	L	0–5	Mew	Brett	Silcock	Bennion	Grimwood	Scott	Gibson	Myerscough	Lochhead	Sapsford	Partridge
29 Aug	W B A	H	L	2–3	..	..	..	Harris	..	..	Harrison[1]	Spence[1]	Goodwin	Partridge[1]	Robinson[1]
3 Sep	Everton	H	W	2–1	..	..	..	..	..	..	..	Bissett	Spence	Sapsford	..
7 Sep	W B A	A	D	0–0	..	..	..	..	..	..	..	Bissett	Spence	Sapsford	..
10 Sep	Chelsea	A	D	0–0	..	..	..	..	..	..	..	..	..	..	..
17 Sep	Chelsea	H	D	0–0	..	..	..	..	Hilditch	..	..	Spence	Lochhead	..	..
24 Sep	Preston NE	A	L	2–3	..	Radford	..	..	..	..	..	..	..	Partridge[1]	Partridge
1 Oct	Preston NE	H	D	1–1	..	..	..	Brett	Bennion	Hilditch	..	..	..	Schofield P	Partridge
8 Oct	Tottenham H	A	D	2–2	..	..	Silcock	..	..	..	Bissett	Lochhead	Spence[1]	Sapsford[1]	..
15 Oct	Tottenham H	H	W	2–1	..	..	..	..	..	..	..	..	..	..	..
22 Oct	Manchester C	A	L	1–4	..	..	..	Brett	..	..	..	..	..	..	..
29 Oct	Manchester C	H	W	3–1	..	..	..	Silcock	Forster	..	Harrison	..	..	..	..
5 Nov	Middlesbrough	H	L	3–5	..	..	..	..	..	..	Gibson	..	..	..	..
12 Nov	Middlesbrough	A	L	0–2	..	..	..	..	..	..	Gibson	Bissett	..	..	..
19 Nov	Aston Villa	A	L	1–3	..	..	..	Barlow	Grimwood	Harris	Bissett	..	..	..	..
26 Nov	Aston Villa	H	W	1–0	..	..	..	Silcock	Harris	McBain	Harrison	Spence[1]	Henderson[1]	..	..
3 Dec	Bradford C	A	L	1–2	..	Brett	..	..	..	..	Lochhead	..	..	..	..
10 Dec	Bradford C	H	D	1–1	..	Radford	Scott	Hilditch	..	Harris	Gibson	..	..	..	..
17 Dec	Liverpool	A	L	1–2	..	Scott	Silcock	..	..	Grimwood	..	Myerscough	Spence	Partridge	Robinson
24 Dec	Liverpool	H	D	0–0	..	..	..	..	..	Harris	..	Lochhead	Henderson	..	..
26 Dec	Burnley	H	L	0–1	..	..	..	..	..	Harris	..	..	..	..	..
27 Dec	Burnley	A	L	2–4	..	..	..	..	..	..	..	..	..	Sapsford[1]	Partridge
31 Dec	Newcastle U	A	L	0–3	..	Radford	..	..	Grimwood	Scott	..	..	..	Spence	..
2 Jan	Sheffield U	A	L	0–3	Steward	Howarth	Radford	..	Harris	Forster	Taylor W	..	..	..	..
14 Jan	Newcastle U	H	L	0–1	Mew	Radford	Silcock	..	McBain	Grimwood	Gibson	Spence	Henderson	Sapsford	..
21 Jan	Sunderland	A	L	1–2	..	..	..	..	..	..	Spence[1]	..	..	..	Robinson
28 Jan	Sunderland	H	W	3–1	..	..	..	..	..	..	..	..	..	..	..
11 Feb	Huddersfield T	H	D	1–1	..	..	..	..	..	..	..	..	..	..	..
18 Feb	Birmingham	A	W	1–0	..	..	..	..	Bennion	..	Robinson	..	Spence[1]	..	Partridge
25 Feb	Birmingham	H	D	1–1	..	..	..	..	..	Haslam	McBain	Harrison	..	..	..
27 Feb	Huddersfield T	A	D	1–1	..	Barlow	..	..	..	Grimwood	..	..	..	..	..
11 Mar	Arsenal	H	W	1–0	..	Radford	..	..	..	..	..	..	..	..	..
18 Mar	Blackburn R	H	L	0–1	..	..	..	..	..	..	..	..	..	..	..
25 Mar	Blackburn R	A	L	0–3	..	..	..	..	..	..	Gibson	Hilditch	..	..	..
1 Apr	Bolton W	H	L	0–1	..	Barlow	..	..	Hilditch	..	Spence	Gibson	Grimwood	..	..
5 Apr	Arsenal	A	L	1–3	..	Brett	..	..	..	Grimwood	Harrison	Myerscough	Spence	Lochead[1]	..
8 Apr	Bolton W	A	L	0–1	..	Howarth	..	..	..	..	..	..	..	Sapsford	..
15 Apr	Oldham	H	L	0–3	..	..	..	..	..	McBain	..	..	..	..	..
17 Apr	Sheffield U	H	W	3–2	..	..	..	..	Hilditch	McBain	..	Lochhead[1]	Radford	Partridge[1]	Robinson
22 Apr	Oldham	A	D	1–1	..	Radford	..	..	..	..	..	Myerscough	Lochhead[1]	..	Thomas
29 Apr	Cardiff C	H	D	1–1	..	..	Pugh	..	Harris	..	..	..	..	..	..
6 May	Cardiff C	A	L	1–3	..	..	Silcock	..	..	..	..	..	..	..	..

FA Cup

Date	Opponent			Score	1	2	3	4	5	6	7	8	9	10	11
7 Jan	Cardiff C (1)	H	L	1–4	Mew	Radford	Scott	Hilditch	McBain	Harris	Gibson	Lochhead	Spence	Sapsford[1]	Partridge

Appearances (goals)

Barlow 3 · Bennion 15 · Bissett 6 · Brett 10 · Forster 4 · Gibson 11 · Goodwin 2 · Grimwood 28 · Harris 13 · Harrison 21 (2) · Haslam 1 · Henderson 10 (2) · Hilditch 29 · Howarth 4 · Lochhead 31 (8) · McBain 21 · Mew 41 · Myerscough 7 · Partridge 37 (4) · Pugh 1 · Radford 26 · Robinson 12 (1) · Sapsford 29 (9) · Schofield P 1 · Scott 23 · Silcock 36 · Spence 35 (15) · Steward 1 · Taylor W 1 · Thomas 3 · Total 30 players (41)

Football League

	P	W	D	L	F:A	Pts	
Liverpool	42	22	13	7	63:36	57	1st
Manchester U	42	8	12	22	41:73	28	22nd

SEASON 1922–1923 FOOTBALL LEAGUE (DIVISION 2)

Date	Opponent			Score	1	2	3	4	5	6	7	8	9	10	11
26 Aug	Crystal Palace	H	W	2–1	Mew	Radford	Silcock	Hilditch	McBain	Grimwood	Wood[1]	Lochhead	Spence[1]	Partridge	Thomas
28 Aug	Sheffield Wed	A	L	0–1	..	..	..	..	..	..	..	..	..[2]	Williams	..
2 Sep	Crystal Palace	A	W	3–2	..	Moore	..	..	..	..	..	..	..[1]	..	..
4 Sep	Sheffield Wed	H	W	1–0	..	..	..	..	..	..	..	..	..	..[1]	..
9 Sep	Wolverhampton W	A	W	1–0	..	..	..	..	Barson	McBain	..	..	..[1]	Partridge	..
16 Sep	Wolverhampton W	H	W	1–0	..	..	..	..	..	..	..	..	..	Partridge	..
23 Sep	Coventry C	A	L	0–2	..	..	..	..	..	..	Lyner	Sarvis	..	..	..
30 Sep	Coventry C	H	W	2–1	..	..	..	..	..	..	..	Lochhead	..[1]	Henderson[1]	..
7 Oct	Port Vale	H	L	1–2	..	..	..	..	..	..	..	..	..	Partridge	..
14 Oct	Port Vale	A	L	0–1	..	Radford	..	..	..	..	Wood	Bain	Myerscough[1]	Lochhead	Partridge
21 Oct	Fulham	H	D	1–1	..	..	Pugh	..	..	Grimwood	..	..	Lochhead	Williams	Partridge
28 Oct	Fulham	A	D	0–0	..	..	Silcock	..	..	..	..	..	..	McBain	..
4 Nov	Clapton O	H	D	0–0	..	..	..	..	..	..	..	..	..	..	..
11 Nov	Clapton O	A	D	1–1	..	..	..	..	..	..	Spence	..	Goldthorpe[1]	..	..
18 Nov	Bury	A	D	2–2	..	..	..	..	..	..	Spence	..	Goldthorpe[2]	..	..
25 Nov	Bury	H	L	0–1	..	..	..	..	..	..	..	..	..	..	..
2 Dec	Rotherham U	H	W	3–0	..	..	..	..	..	..	Wood	Spence[1]	Goldthorpe[1]	Lochhead[1]	..
9 Dec	Rotherham U	A	D	1–1	..	..	Moore	..	..	..	..	..	Goldthorpe[1]	Lochhead	..
16 Dec	Stockport Co	H	W	1–0	..	..	Silcock	..	..	..	Cartman	..	..	McBain[1]	..
23 Dec	Stockport Co	A	L	0–1	..	..	..	..	..	..	..	..	..	..	..
25 Dec	West Ham U	H	L	1–2	..	..	..	..	McBain	..	..	..	..	Lochhead[1]	..
26 Dec	West Ham U	A	W	2–0	..	..	..	..	Bennion	McBain	Wood	..	..	..[2]	..
30 Dec	Hull C	A	L	1–2	..	..	..	..	..	..	..	..	..	..[1]	..
1 Jan	Barnsley	H	W	1–0	..	..	..	Moore	Hilditch	Barson	..	Spence	Myerscough	..[1]	..
6 Jan	Hull C	H	W	*3–2	..	..	..	..	..	..	..	Wood	Barber	..[1]	..
20 Jan	Leeds U	H	D	0–0	..	Moore	Silcock	..	..	..	Lievesley	..	..	..	..
27 Jan	Leeds U	A	W	1–0	..	Radford	..	..	..	..	..	Myerscough[2]	..[4]	..	..
10 Feb	Notts Co	A	W	6–1	..	..	..	..	Bennion	..	Thomas	..	..	..[1]	..
17 Feb	Derby Co	H	D	0–0	..	..	..	..	..	..	..	..	..	..	..
21 Feb	Notts Co	H	D	1–1	..	..	..	..	..	..	Spence	..	..	..[1]	..
3 Mar	Southampton	H	L	1–2	..	..	..	..	Hilditch	..	..	..	Macdonald[1]	..	..
14 Mar	Derby Co	A	D	1–1	..	..	..	..	Bennion	..	..	..	..	..	..
17 Mar	Bradford C	A	D	1–1	..	..	..	..	..	..	..	Mann	Goldthorpe[1]	..	..
21 Mar	Bradford C	H	D	1–1	..	..	Moore	..	..	..	..[1]	..	..[2]	..	Thomas
30 Mar	South Shields	H	W	3–0	..	..	Silcock	Hilditch	..	..	..	..	..	..	Thomas
31 Mar	Blackpool	A	L	0–1	..	..	..	..	Bennion	Hilditch[1]	..	..	..	..[1]	..
2 Apr	South Shields	A	W	3–0	..	..	..	..	..	..	..[1]	..	..	..	..
7 Apr	Blackpool	H	W	2–1	..	..	..	..	..	..	..	Bain[1]	..	..	..
11 Apr	Southampton	A	D	0–0	..	..	..	..	..	..	..	..	..	..	Partridge
14 Apr	Leicester C	A	W	1–0	Steward	..	..	..	..	..	..	..	..	..	..
21 Apr	Leicester C	H	L	0–2	Mew	..	..	..	..	Barson	Mann	Broome	Spence[1]	..	Thomas
28 Apr	Barnsley	A	D	2–2	..	..	..	..	..	..	..	..	..	..	Thomas

FA Cup

Date	Opponent			Score	1	2	3	4	5	6	7	8	9	10	11
13 Jan	Bradford C (1)	A	D	1–1	Mew	Radford	Silcock	Hilditch	Barson	Grimwood	Wood	Lochhead	Spence	Goldthorpe[1]	Partridge[1]
17 Jan	Bradford C (1R)	H	W	2–0	..	..	..	..	..	..	Barber[1]	..	Lievesley	Myerscough	..
3 Feb	Tottenham H (2)	A	L	0–4	..	..	..	..	..	..	..	..	..	..	..

Appearances (goals)

Bain 4 (1) · Barber 2 · Barson 31 · Bennion 14 · Broome 1 · Cartman 3 · Goldthorpe 22 (13) · Grimwood 36 · Henderson 2 (1) · Hilditch 32 (1) · Lievesley 2 · Lochhead 34 (13) · Lyner 3 · McBain 21 (2) · Macdonald 2 (1) · Mann 10 · Mew 41 · Moore 12 · Myerscough 13 (3) · Partridge 30 · Pugh 1 · Radford 34 (1) · Sarvis 1 · Silcock 37 · Spence 35 (11) · Steward 1 · Thomas 18 · Williams 5 (2) · Wood 15 (1) · Own goals 1 · Total 29 players (51)

Football League

	P	W	D	L	F:A	Pts	
Notts Co	42	23	7	12	46:34	53	1st
Manchester U	42	17	14	11	51:36	48	4th

SEASON 1923–1924 FOOTBALL LEAGUE (DIVISION 2)

Date	Opponent	H/A	Res	Score											
25 Aug	Bristol C	A	W	2–1	Mew	Radford	Moore	Bennion	Barson	Hilditch	Ellis	Goldthorpe[1]	Macdonald[1]	Lochhead[1]	McPherson
27 Aug	Southampton	H	W	1–0	..	..	..	..	..	..	..	..	..	..	..
1 Sep	Bristol C	H	W	2–1	..	..	..	..	..	..	..	Spence[1]	..	..	1	..
3 Sep	Southampton	A	D	0–0	..	..	..	..	..	..	..	..	..	..	..
8 Sep	Bury	A	L	0–2	..	..	..	..	..	..	..	..	..	..	..
15 Sep	Bury	H	L	0–1	Steward	..	..	Hilditch	..	Grimwood	..	Mann	Goldthorpe	..	..
22 Sep	South Shields	A	L	0–1	Mew	..	..	..	..	..	..		Spence	..	..
29 Sep	South Shields	H	D	1–1	..	..	..	..	..	..	..	Goldthorpe	Macdonald	..	..
6 Oct	Oldham	A	L	*2–3	..	..	..	Bennion	Hilditch	..	Spence	Lochhead	..	Kennedy	..
13 Oct	Oldham	H	W	2–0	Steward	Moore	Dennis	..	Haslam	Hilditch	..	Mann[2]	Bain[2]	Lochhead	..
20 Oct	Stockport Co	H	W	3–0	..	..	..	..	..	..	..			1	..
27 Oct	Stockport Co	A	L	2–3	..	..	..	..	..	..	..	Barber[1]	..	1	..
3 Nov	Leicester C	A	D	2–2	..	..	Radford	..	..	..	..	Mann	..	2	..
10 Nov	Leicester C	H	W	3–0	..	Tyler	Moore	..	Grimwood	..	..	1	..	1	..
17 Nov	Coventry C	A	D	*1–1	..	Radford	..	..	..	..	..	1	..	..	..
1 Dec	Leeds U	A	D	0–0	..	..	..	..	Barson	..	..	..	..	..	..
8 Dec	Leeds U	H	W	3–1	..	..	..	..	Grimwood[1]	..	1	..	..	2	..
15 Dec	Port Vale	A	W	1–0	..	..	..	..	..	..	..	1	..	..	Thomas
22 Dec	Port Vale	H	W	5–0	..	..	..	..	..	..	..		3	1	McPherson
25 Dec	Barnsley	H	L	1–2	..	..	..	Hilditch	..	1	Bennion	..	..	..	..
26 Dec	Barnsley	A	L	0–1	..	..	..	..	..	..	..	..	..	..	..
29 Dec	Bradford C	A	D	0–0	..	..	..	Bennion	Barson	Hilditch	..	..	..	..	..
2 Jan	Coventry C	H	L	1–2	..	..	..	..	..	..	..	..	1	..	..
5 Jan	Bradford C	H	W	3–0	..	..	..	..	..	..	..	..	1	1	1
19 Jan	Fulham	A	L	1–3	..	..	..	..	..	..	..	Smith T	..	1	..
26 Jan	Fulham	H	D	0–0	..	..	..	..	..	..	..	Mann	Smith T	..	..
6 Feb	Blackpool	A	L	0–1	..	..	..	..	..	..	..	Kennedy	Bain	Partridge	Thomas
9 Feb	Blackpool	H	D	0–0	..	..	..	..	..	..	..	..	..	Lochhead	McPherson
16 Feb	Derby Co	A	L	0–3	..	..	..	..	..	Grimwood	Ellis	Mann	Spence	..	..
23 Feb	Derby Co	H	D	0–0	..	..	..	..	Grimwood	Hilditch	..	Lochhead	..	Kennedy	Partridge
1 Mar	Nelson	A	W	2–0	..	..	..	..	..	..	..	Mann	1	..	McPherson
8 Mar	Nelson	H	L	0–1	..	..	..	..	..	..	Spence	..	Lochhead	..	..
15 Mar	Hull C	H	D	1–1	Mew	..	..	..	..	..	..	Smith T	1	Miller	Thomas
22 Mar	Hull C	A	D	1–1	..	..	..	..	..	..	..	..	..	1	..
29 Mar	Stoke C	H	D	2–2	..	Moore	Silcock	..	..	..	..	2	..	..	McPherson
5 Apr	Stoke C	A	L	0–3	..	..	..	..	..	..	..	..	..	..	..
12 Apr	Crystal Palace	H	W	5–1	Steward	..	..	Mann	..	..	Evans	1	Spence[4]	Lochhead	Partridge
18 Apr	Clapton O	A	L	0–1	..	..	..	..	..	..	..	..	..	..	..
19 Apr	Crystal Palace	A	D	1–1	..	..	..	..	..	..	..	..	1	..	..
21 Apr	Clapton O	H	D	2–2	..	..	..	Bennion	Haslam	..	2	..	..	..	McPherson
26 Apr	Sheffield Wed	H	W	2–0	..	..	..	Mann	..	..	..	1	McPherson	1	Thomas
3 May	Sheffield Wed	A	L	0–2	..	..	..	..	..	..	..	..	..	..	..

FA Cup

Date	Opponent	H/A	Res	Score											
12 Jan	Plymouth A (1)	H	W	1–0	Steward	Radford	Moore	Bennion	Barson	Hilditch	Mann	Bain	Spence	Lochhead	McPherson[1]
2 Feb	Huddersfield (2)	H	L	0–3	..	Silcock	..	..	..	..	..	Henderson	..	..	..

Appearances (goals)

Bain 18 (8) · Barber 1 (1) · Barson 17 · Bennion 34 · Dennis 3 · Ellis 11 · Evans 6 (2) · Goldthorpe 4 (1) · Grimwood 22 (2) · Haslam 7 · Hilditch 41 · Kennedy 6 (1) · Lochhead 40 (14) · Macdonald 7 (1) · McPherson 34 (1) · Mann 25 (3) · Mew 12 · Miller 4 (1) · Moore 42 · Partridge 5 · Radford 30 · Silcock 8 · Smith T 12 (4) · Spence 36 (10) · Steward 30 · Thomas 6 · Tyler 1 · Own goals 3 · Total 27 players (52)

Football League

	P	W	D	L	F:A	Pts	
Leeds U	42	21	12	9	61:35	54	1st
Manchester U	42	13	14	15	52:44	40	14th

SEASON 1924–1925 FOOTBALL LEAGUE (DIVISION 2)

Date	Opponent	H/A	Res	Score											
30 Aug	Leicester C	H	W	1–0	Steward	Moore	Silcock	Bennion	Barson	Hilditch	Spence	Smith T	Goldthorpe[1]	Lochhead	McPherson
1 Sep	Stockport Co	A	L	1–2	..	..	..	..	..	..	..	..	Henderson	1	..
6 Sep	Stoke C	A	D	0–0	..	..	..	Mann	..	..	..	..	..	..	..
8 Sep	Barnsley	H	W	1–0	..	..	..	..	Grimwood	..	..	..	1	..	..
13 Sep	Coventry C	H	W	5–1	..	..	..	..	Barson	Grimwood	1	..	2	1	1
20 Sep	Oldham	A	W	3–0	..	..	..	..	..	..	..	..	3	..	..
27 Sep	Sheffield Wed	H	W	2–0	..	..	..	..	..	..	..	1	..	..	.1
4 Oct	Clapton O	A	W	1–0	..	..	..	..	..	..	..	..	..	1	..
11 Oct	Crystal Palace	H	W	1–0	..	..	..	..	..	..	..	..	..	1	..
18 Oct	Southampton	A	W	2–0	..	..	..	..	..	..	..	..	..	2	..
25 Oct	Wolverhampton W	A	D	0–0	..	..	..	..	..	..	..	..	..	..	..
1 Nov	Fulham	H	W	2–0	..	..	..	..	..	..	..	..	1	1	..
8 Nov	Portsmouth	A	D	1–1	..	..	Jones T	..	..	..	..	1	..	..	Thomas
15 Nov	Hull C	H	W	2–0	..	..	Silcock	..	..	..	..	..	Hanson[1]	..	McPherson[1]
22 Nov	Blackpool	A	D	1–1	..	..	..	..	..	..	..	..	1	..	..
29 Nov	Derby Co	H	D	1–1	..	..	..	..	..	..	..	..	..	..	..
6 Dec	South Shields	A	W	2–1	..	..	..	..	..	..	..	..	Henderson[1]	..	1
13 Dec	Bradford C	H	W	3–0	..	Jones T	..	..	..	..	..	..	2	..	1
20 Dec	Port Vale	A	L	1–2	..	..	..	..	..	..	..	..	..	1	..
25 Dec	Middlesbrough	A	D	1–1	..	Moore	..	..	..	..	..	..	1	Kennedy	..
26 Dec	Middlesbrough	H	W	2–0	..	..	..	..	..	..	..	1	..	1	..
27 Dec	Leicester C	A	L	0–3	..	..	..	..	..	..	..	..	..	..	..
1 Jan	Chelsea	A	L	0–1	..	..	..	..	..	1	..	..	..	..	..
3 Jan	Stoke C	H	W	2–0	..	..	..	..	..	..	..	Lochhead	2	..	..
17 Jan	Coventry C	A	L	0–1	..	..	..	..	Haslam	..	..	Taylor C	..	Lochhead	..
24 Jan	Oldham	H	L	0–1	..	..	..	..	Barson	..	..	Smith T	..	Kennedy	..
7 Feb	Clapton O	H	W	4–2	..	..	..	Bennion	Grimwood	Bain	..	Lochhead	Pape[1]	2	1
14 Feb	Crystal Palace	A	L	1–2	..	..	..	..	..	Mann	..	1	..	..	..
23 Feb	Sheffield Wed	A	D	1–1	..	..	..	..	..	..	..	..	1	..	..
28 Feb	Wolverhampton W	H	W	3–0	..	..	Jones T	..	..	..	2	..	..	1	Partridge
7 Mar	Fulham	A	L	0–1	..	..	..	..	..	..	..	..	..	..	McPherson
14 Mar	Portsmouth	H	W	2–0	..	..	..	..	..	..	1	Rennox	..	Lochhead[1]	..
21 Mar	Hull C	A	W	1–0	..	..	..	..	..	..	..	..	..	1	..
28 Mar	Blackpool	H	D	0–0	..	..	..	..	..	..	..	..	..	..	..
4 Apr	Derby Co	A	L	0–1	..	..	..	Mann	Barson	Grimwood	..	..	..	..	Thomas
10 Apr	Stockport Co	H	W	2–0	..	..	..	Bennion	..	..	..	Smith T	2	..	..
11 Apr	South Shields	H	W	1–0	..	..	Silcock	..	..	..	..	..	..	1	McPherson
13 Apr	Chelsea	A	D	0–0	..	..	Jones T	..	..	..	..	..	..	..	..
18 Apr	Bradford C	A	W	1–0	..	..	..	..	..	..	..	..	1	..	..
22 Apr	Southampton	H	D	1–1	..	..	..	..	..	..	..	..	1	..	..
25 Apr	Port Vale	H	W	4–0	..	..	..	..	..	..	1	..	1	1	1
2 May	Barnsley	A	D	0–0	..	..	..	..	..	..	..	..	..	..	..

FA Cup

Date	Opponent	H/A	Res	Score											
10 Jan	Sheffield Wed (1)	A	L	0–2	Steward	Moore	Jones T	Mann	Grimwood	Hilditch	Spence	Smith T	Henderson	Kennedy	McPherson

Appearances (goals)

Bain 1 · Barson 32 · Bennion 17 · Goldthorpe 1 (1) · Grimwood 39 (1) · Hanson 3 (3) · Haslam 1 · Henderson 22 (14) · Hilditch 4 · Jones T 15 · Kennedy 11 (3) · Lochhead 37 (13) · McPherson 38 (7) · Mann 32 · Moore 40 · Pape 16 (5) · Partridge 1 · Rennox 4 · Silcock 29 · Smith T 31 (5) · Spence 42 (5) · Steward 42 · Taylor C 1 · Thomas 3 · Total 24 players (57)

Football League

	P	W	D	L	F:A	Pts	
Leicester C	42	24	11	7	90:32	59	1st
Manchester U	42	23	11	8	57:23	57	2nd

SEASON 1925–1926 FOOTBALL LEAGUE (DIVISION 1)

Date	Opponent	V	R	Score											
29 Aug	West Ham U	A	L	0–1	Steward	Moore	Silcock	Bennion	Barson	Bain	Spence[1]	Smith T	Iddon	Lochhead	McPherson
2 Sep	Aston Villa	H	W	3–0	..	..	..	Mann	.. [1]	Hilditch	.. [1]	..	Pape	.. [1]	..
5 Sep	Arsenal	H	L	0–1	..										
9 Sep	Aston Villa	A	D	2–2	..	..	..	Bennion	..	Mann	..	..	Hanson[1]	Rennox[1]	.. [1]
12 Sep	Manchester C	A	D	1–1	..	..	..	..	..	..	..	..	Lochhead[1]	.. [2]	
16 Sep	Leicester C	H	W	3–2	..										
19 Sep	Liverpool	A	L	0–5	..	..	..	Hilditch	.. [1]	..	..	..	..		
26 Sep	Burnley	H	W	6–1	..	..	..	.. [1]	..	Grimwood	..	.. [1]	Hanson[1]	.. [3]	Thomas
3 Oct	Leeds U	A	L	0–2	..	..								.. [1]	.. [1]
10 Oct	Newcastle U	H	W	2–1	..										
17 Oct	Tottenham H	H	D	0–0	..										
24 Oct	Cardiff C	A	W	2–0	..							Hanson	McPherson[2]	..	.. [1]
31 Oct	Huddersfield T	H	D	1–1	..										
7 Nov	Everton	A	W	3–1	..				Haslam	Mann	.. [1]	Smith T	.. [1]	.. [1]	.. [1]
14 Nov	Birmingham	H	W	3–1	..				Barson[1]	..	.. [1]	..	.. [2]		
21 Nov	Bury	A	W	3–1	..								.. [1]	.. [1]	.. [1]
28 Nov	Blackburn R	H	W	2–0	..								Hanson	.. [1]	
5 Dec	Sunderland	A	L	1–2	..				Haslam				Hanson	.. [1]	
12 Dec	Sheffield U	H	L	1–2	..				Barson				McPherson[1]		
19 Dec	W B A	A	L	1–5	..			Bennion	Haslam	Hilditch	..	Taylor C	.. [1]		
25 Dec	Bolton W	H	W	2–1	..			Hilditch	Barson	Mann	.. [1]	Hanson[1]			
28 Dec	Leicester C	A	W	3–1	..			Mann	Hilditch	Thomas	..	..	.. [3]		Hannaford
2 Jan	West Ham U	H	W	2–1	..			Hilditch	Grimwood	McCrae	.. [1]	..	.. [1]	.. [2]	Thomas
16 Jan	Arsenal	A	L	2–3	..	..	Jones T	Mann	Hilditch	McCrae	.. [1]	..	.. [1]		
23 Jan	Manchester C	H	L	1–6	..			Bennion	..	Mann	..	Taylor C	.. [1]		
6 Feb	Burnley	A	W	1–0	Mew	Moore		McCrae	Haslam	..	Hall	Smith T	.. [1]		Hannaford
13 Feb	Leeds U	H	W	2–1	..			..	..	..	..	Hanson	.. [1]	Sweeney[1]	
27 Feb	Tottenham H	A	W	1–0	..		Jones T					Smith T[1]	Rennox		Thomas
10 Mar	Liverpool	H	D	3–3	..		Silcock	Bain	Barson	..	Spence[1]		Hanson[1]	.. [1]	Partridge
13 Mar	Huddersfield T	A	L	0–5	..		Jones T	Bennion							
17 Mar	Bolton W	A	L	1–3	..		Astley	Haslam					McPherson[1]		Thomas
20 Mar	Everton	H	D	0–0	Steward	Inglis	Jones T	McCrae						Hanson	..
2 Apr	Notts Co	A	W	3–0	..	Moore	Silcock	Mann		McCrae	..		.. [1]	Rennox[2]	..
3 Apr	Bury	H	L	0–1	..								Hanson		
5 Apr	Notts Co	H	L	0–1	..		Jones T	Hanson	McCrae	Mann	..	Smith T			
10 Apr	Blackburn R	A	L	0–7	..		Silcock	Hilditch	Barson	..	..	Taylor C		Hanson	Hannaford
14 Apr	Newcastle U	A	L	1–4	..	Inglis	Jones T	..	McCrae	..	..	Smith T	Rennox	Rennox[1]	Thomas
19 Apr	Birmingham	A	L	1–2	..			..	Haslam				Hanson		.. [1]
21 Apr	Sunderland	H	W	5–1	..			..	Barson			.. [1]	Taylor C[3]	..	
24 Apr	Sheffield U	A	L	0–2	..			..	Haslam						
28 Apr	Cardiff C	H	W	1–0	..	.. [1]	Silcock		Barson				Hanson	Sweeney	
1 May	W B A	H	W	3–2	Richardson	..	..	..	..	..	..	Hanson	Taylor C[3]		Partridge

FA Cup

Date	Opponent	V	R	Score											
9 Jan	Port Vale (3)	A	W	3–2	Steward	Moore	Silcock	Mann	Hilditch	Grimwood	Spence[2]	Smith[2]	McPherson[1]	Rennox	Thomas [1]
30 Jan	Tottenham (4)	A	D	2–2	Mew	..	..	Hilditch	Haslam	Mann	.. [1]	Hanson	..	.. [1]	
3 Feb	Tottenham (4R)	H	W	2–0	..										
20 Feb	Sunderland (5)	A	D	3–3	..			McCrae	Barson	..	..	Smith	.. [1]		
24 Feb	Sunderland (5R)	H	W	2–1	..			..	..	..	..	..	.. [1]		
6 Mar	Fulham (6)	A	W	2–1	..			..	..	..	..	..	..		Hannaford
21 Mar	Manchester C (SF) (at Bramall Lane)	N	L	0–3	Steward	..	..	..	..	..	..	..	..		Thomas

Appearances (goals)

Astley 1 · Bain 2 · Barson 28 (3) · Bennion 7 · Grimwood 7 · Hall 3 · Hannaford 4 · Hanson 24 (5) · Haslam 9 · Hilditch 28 (1) · Iddon 9 · Inglis 7 (1) · Jones T 10 · Lochhead 5 (2) · McCrae 9 · McPherson 29 (16) · Mann 34 · Mew 6 · Moore 33 · Pape 2 · Partridge 3 · Rennox 34 (17) · Richardson 1 · Silcock 33 · Smith T 30 (3) · Spence 39 (7) · Steward 35 · Sweeney 3 (1) · Taylor C 6 (6) · Thomas 29 (5) · Total 30 players (66)

Football League

	P	W	D	L	F:A	Pts	
Huddersfield T	42	23	11	8	92:60	57	1st
Manchester U	42	19	6	17	66:73	44	9th

SEASON 1926–1927 FOOTBALL LEAGUE (DIVISION 1)

Date	Opponent	V	R	Score											
28 Aug	Liverpool	A	L	2–4	Steward	Inglis	Silcock	Hilditch	Barson	Mann	Spence	Smith T	McPherson[2]	Haworth	Thomas
30 Aug	Sheffield U	A	D	2–2	..			Bennion	Haslam	..	..	Hanson	.. [2]	Wilson	Partridge
4 Sep	Leeds U	H	D	2–2	..			..	Barson			.. [1]	.. [1]	Rennox	
11 Sep	Newcastle U	A	L	2–4	..			..	..	..	.. [1]	..	..		
15 Sep	Arsenal	H	D	2–2	..		Jones T	..	..			..	..		
18 Sep	Burnley	H	W	2–1	..			..	Grimwood		Chapman		Spence[2]		McPherson
25 Sep	Cardiff C	A	W	2–0	..	Jones T	Silcock	..	Barson [1]	Wilson	..	.. [1]	.. [1]		Hannaford
2 Oct	Aston Villa	H	W	2–1	..			..	..						
9 Oct	Bolton W	A	L	0–4	..			..	Haslam				McPherson		McPherson [1]
16 Oct	Bury	A	W	3–0	..			..	Grimwood			Sweeney	Spence[2]		
23 Oct	Birmingham	H	L	0–1	..			..	Barson						
30 Oct	West Ham U	A	L	0–4	..	Moore	Jones T	Hilditch	..	Mann	Spence	Harris	McPherson		Thomas
6 Nov	Sheffield Wed	H	D	0–0	..			..	Bennion		Wilson	Chapman	Smith T	Spence		McPherson
13 Nov	Leicester C	A	W	3–2	..			..	Grimwood		Spence		McPherson[2]	.. [1]	Thomas
20 Nov	Everton	H	W	2–1	..			..	..			.. [1]	.. [2]		
27 Nov	Blackburn R	A	L	1–2	..			..	..						
4 Dec	Huddersfield T	H	D	0–0	..			..	..						
11 Dec	Sunderland	A	L	0–6	..			..	..						
18 Dec	W B A	H	W	2–0	..		Silcock	..	..			.. [1]		Sweeney[2]	
25 Dec	Tottenham H	A	D	1–1	..			..	Barson			Mann	..	.. [2]	Partridge
27 Dec	Tottenham H	H	W	2–1	..			..	..			Rennox	..	Mann	
28 Dec	Arsenal	A	L	0–1	..	Jones T		..	Grimwood			..	Sweeney[1]		
1 Jan	Sheffield U	H	W	5–0	..	Moore		..	Barson[1]	Hilditch	.. [1]	..	.. [2]		
15 Jan	Liverpool	H	L	0–1	..		Jones T	..	Grimwood	Mann	..	Hanson			
22 Jan	Leeds U	A	W	3–2	..			..	..	Hilditch	.. [1]	Rennox[1]	Smith A		McPherson[1]
5 Feb	Burnley	A	L	0–1	..			..	Barson			Iddon			
9 Feb	Newcastle U	H	W	3–1	..		Silcock	Mann	Grimwood		.. [1]	Harris[1]	Hanson[1]		
12 Feb	Cardiff C	H	D	1–1	..			..	..					Rennox	Thomas
19 Feb	Aston Villa	A	L	0–2	..			Bennion	Barson	Mann					
26 Feb	Bolton W	H	D	0–0	..			..	Grimwood	Hilditch	Chapman	Smith T	McPherson		Hannaford
5 Mar	Bury	H	L	1–2	..		Jones T	..	Haslam			Spence	Smith A[1]	McPherson	Partridge
12 Mar	Birmingham	A	L	0–4	..			..							Hannaford
19 Mar	West Ham U	H	L	0–3	..		Silcock	..	Barson	Wilson	Spence	Hanson	McPherson	Sweeney	
26 Mar	Sheffield Wed	A	L	0–2	..			..	Grimwood			Smith T	Hanson	Rennox	
2 Apr	Leicester C	H	W	1–0	..			..	Barson	Hilditch	Chapman	Hanson	Spence[1]	Partridge	McPherson
9 Apr	Everton	A	D	0–0	..			..	..				.. [2]		Thomas
15 Apr	Derby Co	H	D	2–2	..			..	..			.. [1]		Wilson	McPherson
16 Apr	Blackburn R	H	W	2–0	..			..	..				.. [1]	Partridge	Thomas
18 Apr	Derby Co	A	D	2–2	..			..	Grimwood				.. [2]		
23 Apr	Huddersfield T	A	D	0–0	..			Mann	Barson			Sweeney			
30 Apr	Sunderland	H	D	0–0	..		Astley	Bennion		Wilson	Smith A	Hanson	..		
7 May	W B A	A	D	2–2	..		Jones T	..	Grimwood		Chapman	.. [1]	.. [1]		

FA Cup

Date	Opponent	V	R	Score											
8 Jan	Reading (3)	A	D	1–1	Steward	Moore	Silcock	Bennion[1]	Hilditch	Barson	Spence	Smith T	McPherson	Sweeney [1]	Partridge
12 Jan	Reading (3R)†	H	D	2–2	..			..	..	..	.. [1]	Hanson	..		
17 Jan	Reading (3R) (at Villa Park) †after extra time	N	L	1–2	..			..	..	..	..	Rennox	.. [1]		

Appearances (goals)

Astley 1 · Barson 21 (2) · Bennion 37 · Chapman 17 · Grimwood 17 · Hannaford 7 · Hanson 21 (5) · Harris 4 (1) · Haslam 4 · Haworth 2 · Hilditch 16 · Iddon 1 · Inglis 6 · Jones T 21 · McPherson 32 (15) · Mann 14 · Moore 30 · Partridge 16 · Rennox 22 (7) · Silcock 26 · Smith A 5 (1) · Smith T 10 · Spence 40 (18) · Steward 42 · Sweeney 13 (3) · Thomas 16 · Wilson 21 · Total 27 players (52)

Football League

	P	W	D	L	F:A	Pts	
Newcastle U	42	25	6	11	96:58	56	1st
Manchester U	42	13	14	15	52:64	40	15th

SEASON 1927–1928 FOOTBALL LEAGUE (DIVISION 1)

Date	Opponent	V	R	Score											
27 Aug	Middlesbrough	H	W	3–0	Steward	Moore	Silcock	Bennion	Barson	Wilson	Chapman	Hanson[1]	Spence[2]	Partridge	McPherson
29 Aug	Sheffield Wed	A	W	2–0	..	..	..	..	Hilditch	..	..	..	..	..	..
3 Sep	Birmingham	A	D	0–0	..	Jones T	..	..	Barson	..	..	..	..	..	..
7 Sep	Sheffield Wed	H	D	1–1	..	..	..	..	..	..	..	..	..	..	..[1]
10 Sep	Newcastle U	H	L	1–7	..	Moore	..	..	Hilditch	..	..	..	..[1]	..	Thomas
17 Sep	Huddersfield T	A	L	2–4	..	..	..	..	Haslam	Hilditch	..	..	..[2]	..	..
19 Sep	Blackburn R	A	L	0–3	..	..	..	..	..	Bain	..	..	..	..	..
24 Sep	Tottenham H	H	W	3–0	Richardson	..	..	..	..	Mann Wilson	Ramsden	..[2]	..	..	McPherson
1 Oct	Leicester C	A	L	0–1	..	..	..	..	Mann	Wilson	..	Sweeney	..	..	..
8 Oct	Everton	A	L	2–5	..	..	..	..[1]	Hilditch	..	Williams	Hanson	..[1]	..	..
15 Oct	Cardiff C	H	D	2–2	..	Jones T	..	..	Barson	..	..	Sweeney[1]	..[3]	Johnston[1]	..[1]
22 Oct	Derby Co	H	W	5–0	..	Jones T	..	..	..	..	..	Hanson	..	..	..[1]
29 Oct	West Ham U	A	W	*2–1	..	..	..	Mann	..	..	..	Hanson	..	..	..[1]
5 Nov	Portsmouth	H	W	*2–0	..	..	..	Bennion	..	..	..	..	..[1]	..	..
12 Nov	Sunderland	A	L	1–4	..	..	..	..	..	..	..	..	..[1]	..	..
19 Nov	Aston Villa	H	W	5–1	..	Moore	Jones T	..	..	..	..	Partridge[2]	..[1]	.. [1]	.. [1]
26 Nov	Burnley	A	L	0–4	..	..	..	..	..	..	..	..	..	..	..
3 Dec	Bury	H	L	0–1	..	Jones T	Silcock	..	Hilditch	..	..	..	..	..	Thomas
10 Dec	Sheffield U	A	L	1–2	..	Moore	Jones T	..	Mann	..	..	..	..[1]	..	Thomas
17 Dec	Arsenal	H	W	4–1	..	..	..	..	..	..	Spence[1]	..[1]	Hanson[1]	..	McPherson[1]
24 Dec	Liverpool	A	L	0–2	..	..	..	..	..	..	..	..[1]	..	..	..
26 Dec	Blackburn R	H	D	1–1	..	..	..	..	..	..	..	..	..	..	..
31 Dec	Middlesbrough	A	W	2–1	..	..	..	..	..	..	..	Taylor	..[1]	.. [1]	Partridge
7 Jan	Birmingham	H	D	1–1	..	..	..	..	..	..	..	..	..[1]	..	McPherson
21 Jan	Newcastle U	A	L	1–4	..	Jones T	Silcock	..	..	..	..	Partridge[1]	..	..	Partridge
4 Feb	Tottenham H	A	L	1–4	..	..	..	McLenahan	..	..	Chapman	Hanson	Spence	.. [1]	Partridge
11 Feb	Leicester C	H	W	5–2	..	Moore	Jones T	Bennion	..	..	Spence[2]	..[1]	Nicol[2]	Sweeney	Partridge
25 Feb	Cardiff C	A	L	0–2	..	Jones T	Silcock	..	..	..	..	..	..	Johnston	..
7 Mar	Huddersfield T	H	D	0–0	..	..	..	..	..	..	..	Partridge	Hanson	..	McPherson
10 Mar	West Ham U	H	D	1–1	..	Moore	Jones T	..	..	..	Chapman	..	..	.. [1]	..
14 Mar	Everton	H	W	1–0	..	..	..	..	..	..	Spence	Hanson	Rawlings[1]	..	..
17 Mar	Portsmouth	A	L	0–1	..	..	..	..	Barson	..	..	..	..	..	Thomas
28 Mar	Derby Co	A	L	0–5	..	Jones T	Silcock	..	Mann	..	..	..	..	..	..
31 Mar	Aston Villa	A	L	1–3	..	Moore	Jones T	..	..	McLenahan	..[1]	Rawlings[1]	Nicol	..	McPherson Thomas[1]
6 Apr	Bolton W	A	L	2–3	..	..	..	..	..	..	..	..	..	..	Thomas[1]
7 Apr	Burnley	H	W	4–3	..	Jones T	Silcock	..	..	..	Williams[1]	Ferguson	Rawlings[3]	.. [1]	..
9 Apr	Bolton W	H	W	2–1	..	..	..	Hanson	..	..	..[1]	..[1]	..	.. [1]	McPherson[1]
14 Apr	Bury	A	L	3–4	..	..	..	Bennion	..	..	Spence	..	..	.. [1]	Thomas[1]
21 Apr	Sheffield U	H	L	2–3	..	..	..	..	..	..	..	..	.. [1]	..	..
25 Apr	Sunderland	H	W	2–1	Steward	..	..	McLenahan	..	Wilson	..	Hanson[1]	..	..	..
28 Apr	Arsenal	A	W	1–0	..	Moore	Jones T	..	..	..	..	.. [3]	.. [1]	.. [1] [2]	..
5 May	Liverpool	H	W	6–1	..	..	..	..	..	..	..	..	..	..	..

FA Cup

Date	Opponent	V	R	Score											
14 Jan	Brentford (3)	H	W	7–1	Richardson	Jones T	Silcock	Bennion	Mann	Wilson	Spence[1]	Hanson[4]	McPherson[1]	Johnston[1]	Partridge
28 Jan	Bury (4)	A	D	1–1	..	..	..	..	..	..	.. [1]	..	..	.. [1]	Williams
1 Feb	Bury (4R)	H	W	1–0	..	..	..	..	..	..	..	..	..	..	..
18 Feb	Birmingham (5)	H	W	1–0	Steward	..	..	..	..	..	..	..	Nicol	.. [1]	Partridge
3 Mar	Blackburn (6)	A	L	0–2	Richardson	Moore	Jones T	..	..	..	..	..	Williams	..	..

Appearances (goals)

Bain 1 · Barson 11 · Bennion 36 (1) · Chapman 9 · Ferguson 4 · Hanson 30 (10) · Haslam 3 · Hilditch 5 · Johnston 31 (8) · Jones T 33 · McLenahan 10 (1) · McPherson 26 (6) · Mann 26 · Moore 25 · Nicol 4 (2) · Partridge 23 (5) · Ramsden 2 · Rawlings 12 (10) · Richardson 32 · Silcock 26 · Spence 38 (22) · Steward 10 · Sweeney 4 (1) · Taylor 2 · Thomas 13 (2) · Williams 13 (2) · Wilson 33 · Own goals 2 · Total 27 players (72)

Football League

	P	W	D	L	F:A	Pts	
Everton	42	20	13	9	102:66	53	1st
Manchester U	42	16	7	19	72:80	39	18th

SEASON 1928–1929 FOOTBALL LEAGUE (DIVISION 1)

Date	Opponent	V	R	Score											
25 Aug	Leicester C	H	D	1–1	Steward	Dale	Silcock	Bennion	Mann	Wilson	Spence	Hanson	Rawlings[1]	Johnston	Williams
27 Aug	Aston Villa	A	D	0–0	..	Moore	..	McLenahan	..	..	..	..	..	..	..
1 Sep	Manchester C	A	D	2–2	..	..	..	Bennion	..	..[1]	..	..[1]	..	.. [1]	..
8 Sep	Leeds U	A	L	2–3	..	..	.. [1]	..	..	..	.. [1]	..	..	..	..
15 Sep	Liverpool	H	D	2–2	..	..	..	..	Spencer	..	..	..	.. [1]	..	..
22 Sep	West Ham U	A	L	1–3	..	..	..	Mann	..	..	Hanson	Taylor C	.. [1]	..	..
29 Sep	Newcastle U	H	W	5–0	..	..	..	Bennion	..	..	Spence[1] [2]	Hanson[2]	.. [2]	.. [1]	..
6 Oct	Burnley	A	W	4–3	..	..	..	..	..	..	..	..	.. [1]	..	..
13 Oct	Cardiff C	H	D	1–1	..	..	..	..	..	..	..	..	..	.. [1]	..
20 Oct	Birmingham	H	W	1–0	..	..	..	..	..	..	.. [1]	..	.. [1]	..	Thomas
27 Oct	Huddersfield T	A	W	2–1	..	..	..	Mann	..	..	..	.. [1]	..	Rowley	Thomas
3 Nov	Bolton W	H	D	1–1	..	..	..	Bennion	..	..	..	.. [1]	..	..	Williams
10 Nov	Sheffield Wed	A	L	1–2	..	..	..	..	..	..	..	.. [1]	..	..	..
17 Nov	Derby Co	H	L	0–1	..	..	..	Hilditch	..	..	..	..	..	..	Thomas
24 Nov	Sunderland	A	L	1–5	..	..	..	Bennion	Mann	Hilditch	Ramsden[1]	..	Spence	.. [1]	Williams
1 Dec	Blackburn R	H	L	1–4	..	..	..	..	Spencer	..	Hanson[1]	Taylor C	Rawlings	..	..
8 Dec	Arsenal	A	L	1–3	..	..	Dale	..	Spencer	Wilson	Spence	Hanson[1]	Nicol	Sweeney	Partridge Thomas
15 Dec	Everton	H	D	1–1	Richardson	..	..	Hilditch	..	Wilson	Spence	Hanson[1]	Nicol	Sweeney	Partridge
22 Dec	Portsmouth	A	L	0–3	..	..	..	..	..	..	..	..	..	Johnston	Thomas Partridge
25 Dec	Sheffield U	H	D	1–1	..	Dale	Silcock	Bennion	..	..	Ramsden[1]	..	Rawlings	Johnston	..
26 Dec	Sheffield U	A	L	1–6	..	Inglis	Dale	..	..	Hilditch	..	..	..	Sweeney	..
29 Dec	Leicester C	A	L	1–2	..	Dale	Silcock	..	..	.. [1]	Spence	Sweeney	Hanson[1]	Johnston	..
1 Jan	Aston Villa	H	D	2–2	Steward	Moore	..	..	..	..	..	Hanson	Rawlings[1]	Rowley[1]	Williams
5 Jan	Manchester C	H	L	1–2	..	..	..	Mann	..	Wilson	..	Taylor C	Hanson	Sweeney[1]	Williams
19 Jan	Leeds U	H	L	1–2	..	..	..	Hilditch	..	..	..	Hanson	Reid[1]	Rowley[1]	Thomas
2 Feb	West Ham U	H	L	2–3	..	Dale	..	Bennion	Mann	Mann	..	..	.. [2]	..	..
9 Feb	Newcastle U	A	L	0–5	..	Moore	..	..	..	..	..	..	..	..	.. [1]
13 Feb	Liverpool	A	W	3–2	..	..	..	..	..	..	..	..	.. [2]	..	..
16 Feb	Burnley	H	W	1–0	..	..	Dale	..	..	..	..	.. [1]	.. [1]	..	..
23 Feb	Cardiff C	A	D	2–2	..	..	..	..	..	..	.. [1]	.. [1]	..	..	..
2 Mar	Birmingham	A	D	1–1	..	..	..	..	..	..	.. [1]	..	..	..	..
9 Mar	Huddersfield T	H	W	1–0	..	..	..	..	..	..	.. [1]	..	..	..	..
16 Mar	Bolton W	A	D	1–1	..	..	..	..	..	..	.. [1]	..	..	..	..
23 Mar	Sheffield Wed	H	W	2–1	..	..	Silcock	..	..	..	.. [1]	..	.. [1]	.. [1]	..
29 Mar	Bury	A	W	3–1	..	..	..	..	..	..	.. [1]	..	.. [2]	..	.. [1]
30 Mar	Derby Co	A	L	1–6	..	..	..	..	..	..	..	..	..	Boyle	Williams
1 Apr	Bury	H	W	1–0	..	..	Dale	..	..	.. [1]	..	..	.. [1]	Rowley	Thomas[1]
6 Apr	Sunderland	H	W	3–0	..	..	..	..	..	..	..	..	.. [2]	..	..
13 Apr	Blackburn R	A	W	3–0	..	..	..	..	..	..	Ramsden[1]	..	.. [2]	..	..
20 Apr	Arsenal	H	W	4–1	..	..	..	..	..	..	Spence	.. [1]	.. [2]	..	.. [1]
27 Apr	Everton	A	W	4–2	..	..	..	..	..	..	..	.. [2]	.. [2]	..	..
4 May	Portsmouth	H	D	0–0	..	..	..	..	..	..	..	..	..	..	..

FA Cup

Date	Opponent	V	R	Score											
12 Jan	Port Vale (3)	A	W	3–0	Steward	Moore	Silcock	Spencer	Mann	Wilson	Spence[1]	Hanson	Williams	Sweeney	Taylor C[1]
26 Jan	Bury (4)	H	L	0–1	..	..	..	..	..	..	..	Rawlings	Thomas	..	Thomson

Appearances (goals)

Bennion 34 · Boyle 1 · Dale 19 · Hanson 42 (19) · Hilditch 11 (1) · Inglis 1 · Johnston 12 (5) · McLenahan 1 · Mann 25 (1) · Moore 37 · Nicol 2 · Partridge 5 · Ramsden 5 (3) · Rawlings 19 (6) · Reid 17 (14) · Richardson 5 · Rowley 25 (5) · Silcock 27 (1) · Spence 36 (5) · Spencer 36 · Steward 37 · Sweeney 6 (1) · Taylor C 3 · Thomas 19 (4) · Williams 18 · Wilson 19 (1) · Total 26 players (66)

Football League

	P	W	D	L	F:A	Pts	
Sheffield Wed	42	21	10	11	86:62	52	1st
Manchester U	42	14	13	15	66:76	41	12th

1929–1930

Date	Opponent		Res	Score										
31 Aug	Newcastle U	A	L	1–4	Steward	Moore	Dale	Bennion	Spencer	Mann	Spence[1]	Hanson	Reid	Rowley	Thomas
2 Sep	Leicester C	A	L	1–4						1				1	
7 Sep	Blackburn R	H	W	1–0			Silcock				1				
11 Sep	Leicester C	H	W	2–1									Ball[1]		
14 Sep	Middlesbrough	A	W	3–2			Dale				1		Rawlings[3]		
21 Sep	Liverpool	H	L	1–2							1				
28 Sep	West Ham U	A	L	1–2					Mann	Wilson					
5 Oct	Manchester C	H	L	1–3			Silcock		Spencer	Mann			Reid		1
7 Oct	Sheffield U	A	L	1–3								Boyle[1]	Rawlings	Sweeney	
12 Oct	Grimsby T	H	L	2–5			Dale	Hilditch	Taylor C	McLenahan			Ball[1]	Rowley[1]	
19 Oct	Portsmouth	A	L	0–3				Bennion		Mann			Reid		
26 Oct	Arsenal	H	W	1–0				Taylor C	Spencer			Hanson	Ball[1]		
2 Nov	Aston Villa	A	L	0–1											
9 Nov	Derby Co	H	W	3–2				Bennion	Taylor C			1	1	1	
16 Nov	Sheffield Wed	A	L	2–7								1	1	1	
23 Nov	Burnley	H	W	1–0						Wilson	2	1	1		
30 Nov	Sunderland	A	W	4–2				Hilditch					1		
7 Dec	Bolton W	H	D	1–1									1		
14 Dec	Everton	A	D	0–0											
21 Dec	Leeds U	H	W	3–1			Jones T					1	2		McLachlan
25 Dec	Birmingham	H	D	0–0										1	
26 Dec	Birmingham	A	W	1–0								Boyle		1	1
28 Dec	Newcastle U	H	W	5–0	Chesters						1	2		1	
4 Jan	Blackburn R	A	L	4–5	Steward							2	1	1	
18 Jan	Middlesbrough	H	L	0–3											
25 Jan	Liverpool	A	L	0–1			Dale	Silcock	Bennion	Hilditch	4		Reid		
1 Feb	West Ham U	H	W	4–2									1		
8 Feb	Manchester C	A	W	1–0		Jones T							1	1	
15 Feb	Grimsby T	A	D	2–2		Moore							2		
22 Feb	Portsmouth	H	W	3–0								1	1		
1 Mar	Bolton W	A	L	1–4								Warburton[1]			1
8 Mar	Aston Villa	H	L	2–3		Dale					1		Ball[1]	McLachlan	Thomas
12 Mar	Arsenal	A	L	2–4								Boyle		Rowley[1]	McLachlan
15 Mar	Derby Co	A	D	1–1	Chesters	Jones T		McLenahan							
29 Mar	Burnley	A	L	0–4								McLenahan[2]			
5 Apr	Sunderland	H	W	2–1	Steward			Bennion					1 Reid	1	
14 Apr	Sheffield Wed	H	D	2–2									1 McLachlan	1	Thomas
18 Apr	Huddersfield T	H	W	1–0							1		1 Thomson	1	McLachlan
19 Apr	Everton	H	D	3–3						1			1 Ball		
22 Apr	Huddersfield T	A	D	2–2							1				
26 Apr	Leeds U	A	L	1–3										1	
3 May	Sheffield U	H	L	1–5											
	FA Cup														
11 Jan	Swindon (3)	H	L	0–2	Steward	Moore	Jones T	Taylor C	Hilditch	Wilson	Spence	Ball	McLachlan	Rowley	Boyle

Appearances (goals)

Ball 23 (11) · Bennion 28 · Boyle 15 (6) · Chesters 3 · Dale 19 · Hanson 18 (5) · Hilditch 27 (1) · Jones T 16 · McLachlan 23 (2) · McLenahan 10 (6) · Mann 14 (1) · Moore 28 · Rawlings 4 (3) · Reid 13 (5) · Rowley 40 (12) · Silcock 21 · Spence 42 (12) · Spencer 10 · Steward 39 · Sweeney 1 · Taylor C 16 · Thomas 21 (1) · Thomson 1 · Warburton 2 (1) · Wilson 28 (1) · Total 25 players (67)

Football League

	P	W	D	L	F:A	Pts	
Sheffield Wed	42	26	8	8	105:57	60	1st
Manchester U	42	15	8	19	67:88	38	17th

1930–1931

Date	Opponent		Res	Score										
30 Aug	Aston Villa	H	L	3–4	Steward	Jones T	Silcock	Bennion	McLenahan	Wilson	Spence	Warburton[1]	Reid[1]	Rowley[1]	McLachlan
3 Sep	Middlesbrough	A	L	1–3	Chesters	Dale					Ramsden		1		1
6 Sep	Chelsea	A	L	2–6						Hilditch	Spence[1]				
10 Sep	Huddersfield T	H	L	0–6					Hilditch	McLenahan			3		
13 Sep	Newcastle U	H	L	4–7				Williams		Dale				1	
15 Sep	Huddersfield T	A	L	0–3	Steward	Mellor				Dale			Bullock		
20 Sep	Sheffield Wed	A	L	0–3								Reid			
27 Sep	Grimsby T	H	L	0–2		Jones T		Bennion				Warburton	Reid		
4 Oct	Manchester C	A	L	1–4				Hilditch	McLenahan	Wilson	1	Gallimore	1		
11 Oct	West Ham U	A	L	1–5		Mellor	Dale	Bennion	Parker						1
18 Oct	Arsenal	H	L	1–2			Silcock							1	
25 Oct	Portsmouth	A	L	1–4								1	Bullock	1	
1 Nov	Birmingham	H	W	2–0									3		1
8 Nov	Leicester C	A	L	4–5			Dale					1			
15 Nov	Blackpool	H	D	0–0								1			
22 Nov	Sheffield U	A	L	1–3			Silcock				Ramsden	1			
29 Nov	Sunderland	H	D	1–1						McLenahan				1	
6 Dec	Blackburn R	A	L	1–4					McLenahan	Wilson	Spence[1]		Reid[1]		
13 Dec	Derby Co	H	W	2–1											
20 Dec	Leeds U	A	L	0–5						Lydon				Wilson	
25 Dec	Bolton W	A	L	1–3					Hilditch	Wilson	Ramsden		1	Rowley	
26 Dec	Bolton W	H	D	1–1			Dale						1		
27 Dec	Aston Villa	A	L	0–7											
1 Jan	Leeds U	H	D	0–0								Warburton[1]		Gallimore	
3 Jan	Chelsea	H	W	1–0								2	1		Hopkinson
17 Jan	Newcastle U	A	L	3–4			Silcock		McLachlan	Spence	1	1		Rowley	1
28 Jan	Sheffield Wed	H	W	4–1			Dale					1	1		
31 Jan	Grimsby T	A	L	1–2							1		Gallimore		
7 Feb	Manchester C	H	L	1–3								Thomson	1		
14 Feb	West Ham U	H	W	1–0								1	Bullock		
21 Feb	Arsenal	A	L	1–4								Warburton			
7 Mar	Birmingham	A	D	0–0									Reid		
16 Mar	Portsmouth	H	L	0–1											1
21 Mar	Blackpool	A	L	1–5		Jones T							Gallimore	Rowley	
25 Mar	Leicester C	H	D	0–0		Dale	McLenahan						Wilson	Gallimore	1
28 Mar	Sheffield U	H	L	1–2								McLenahan		Rowley	
3 Apr	Liverpool	A	D	1–1			Silcock	Bennion					Reid[1]	Gallimore	1
4 Apr	Sunderland	A	W	2–1								1	2	Rowley[1]	
6 Apr	Liverpool	H	W	4–1											
11 Apr	Blackburn R	H	L	0–1								1		Gallimore	
18 Apr	Derby Co	A	L	1–6									2	1	
2 May	Middlesbrough	H	D	4–4			Jones T	1							
	FA Cup														
10 Jan	Stoke C (3)	A	D	3–3	Steward	Mellor	Dale	Bennion	Hilditch	Wilson	Ramsden	Warburton	Reid[3]	Gallimore	McLachlan
14 Jan	Stoke C (3R)†	H	D	0–0									Thomson		1
19 Jan	Stoke C (3R) (at Anfield)	N	W	4–2						McLachlan	Spence[1]				Hopkinson[2]
24 Jan	Grimsby (4) †after extra time	A	L	0–1									Reid		

Appearances (goals)

Bennion 36 (1) · Bullock 10 (3) · Chesters 4 · Dale 22 · Gallimore 28 (5) · Hilditch 25 · Hopkinson 17 (4) · Jones T 5 · Lydon 1 · McLachlan 42 (2) · McLenahan 21 (1) · Mellor 35 · Parker 9 · Ramsden 7 · Reid 30 (17) · Rowley 29 (7) · Silcock 25 · Spence 35 (6) · Steward 38 · Thomson 2 (1) · Warburton 18 (5) · Williams 3 · Wilson 20 (1) · Total 23 players (53)

Football League

	P	W	D	L	F:A	Pts	
Arsenal	42	28	10	4	127:59	66	1st
Manchester U	42	7	8	27	53:115	22	22nd

SEASON 1931–1932 FOOTBALL LEAGUE (DIVISION 2)

Date	Opponent			Score											
29 Aug	Bradford	A	L	1–3	Steward	Mellor	Silcock	Bennion	Parker	McLachlan	Ferguson	Warburton	Reid[1]	Johnston	Mann
2 Sep	Southampton	H	L	2–3	..	..	..	..	..	McLenahan	..[1]	Spence	..[1]	..[1]	McLachlan
5 Sep	Swansea	H	W	2–1	..	..	..	McLenahan	..	McLachlan	..	Spence	..	..	Hopkinson[1]
7 Sep	Stoke C	A	L	0–3	..	..	..	..	..	..	Spence	Johnston	..	Rowley	..
12 Sep	Tottenham H	H	D	1–1	..	..	..	Bennion	Hilditch	Wilson	Ferguson	Gallimore	Spence	Johnston[1]	..
16 Sep	Stoke C	H	D	1–1	..	..	..	..	..	..	..	..[1]	Reid	..	Mann
19 Sep	Nottingham F	A	L	1–2	..	Jones T	..	..	Parker	..	..	Warburton[2]	Dean	..	Hopkinson
26 Sep	Chesterfield	H	W	3–1	..	..	..	..	Hilditch	..	..	..	..	..[1]	Robinson
3 Oct	Burnley	A	L	0–2	..	..	..	..	..	McLachlan	Mann	Gallimore[1]	Spence[1]	..	..
10 Oct	Preston NE	H	W	3–2	..	Mellor	..	..	..	..	..	..	..	..[1]	..
17 Oct	Barnsley	A	D	0–0	..	..	..	..	..	Wilson	..[1]	..[1]	..[1]	..	..
24 Oct	Notts Co	H	D	3–3	..	..	..	..	Wilson	McLachlan	..	..	..	..[1]	..
31 Oct	Plymouth A	A	L	1–3	..	..	..	..	Hilditch	..	..[1]	..	..[2]	..[2]	..
7 Nov	Leeds U	H	L	2–5	..	..	Dale	..	Parker	McLachlan	..[1]	..	..[1]	..	..
14 Nov	Oldham	A	W	5–1	..	..	..	..	Hilditch	..	..	..	..[1]	..	..
21 Nov	Bury	H	L	1–2	..	..	..	..	..	..	Johnston	..[2]	Robinson	Gallimore	
28 Nov	Port Vale	A	W	2–1	..	..	..	Lydon	..	Manley	..	..[1]	Reid	..[1]	
5 Dec	Millwall	H	W	2–0	..	..	Silcock	Bennion	..	..	..	..[1]	..	..	
12 Dec	Bradford C	A	L	3–4	Chesters	..	..	Bennion	..	..	..	..[1]	..[1]		
19 Dec	Bristol C	H	L	0–1	Steward	..	..	..	..	McLachlan	Hopkinson[1]	Ridding	..[1]	Johnston	
25 Dec	Wolverhampton W	H	W	3–2	..	..	..	..	..	..	..	..	Reid		
26 Dec	Wolverhampton W	A	L	0–7	..	..	..	..	Parker	..	Spence	Warburton[1]	Reid	Johnston	Whittle
2 Jan	Bradford	H	L	0–2	..	..	..	..	..	Hilditch	..	Ridding	..	Gallimore	Hopkinson
16 Jan	Swansea	A	L	1–3	..	..	Jones T	..	Vincent	..	..[1]	Warburton[3]	Ridding	..	
23 Jan	Tottenham H	A	L	1–4	..	Jones T	Silcock	..	..	..	..	Ridding[2]	..	Johnston[2]	
30 Jan	Nottingham F	H	W	3–2	..	..	..	McLenahan	..	..	..	Warburton	Reid	Gallimore	
6 Feb	Chesterfield	A	W	3–1	..	..	..	..	..	..	..	Gallimore[1]	..	Johnston	2
17 Feb	Burnley	H	W	5–1	..	Mellor	Jones T	Wilson	..	..	2	Ridding[1]	1	..	1
20 Feb	Preston NE	A	D	0–0	..	..	Silcock	Lievesley	..	..	..	..	2	Gallimore	Page
27 Feb	Barnsley	H	W	3–0	..	Jones T	..	..	..	..	1	..	3	Page	Fitton[1]
5 Mar	Notts Co	A	W	2–1	Moody	Mellor	..	Bennion	..	..	..	Page	..[1]	Johnston	
12 Mar	Plymouth A	H	W	2–1	..	..	..	..	..	..	..	Ridding	..[1]	Page	
19 Mar	Leeds U	A	W	4–1	..	..	..	Hopkinson	..	..	..	McDonald	Black	..	..[1]
25 Mar	Charlton A	H	L	0–2	..	..	..	Bennion	..	..	..	Page	..[1]	Reid	
26 Mar	Oldham	H	W	5–1	..	..	..	Hopkinson	..	..	..	McDonald	..[1]	Page	..
28 Mar	Charlton A	A	L	0–1	..	Mellor	..								

FA Cup

Date	Opponent			Score											
9 Jan	Plymouth A (3)	A	L	1–4	Steward	Mellor	Silcock	Bennion	McLenahan	Hilditch	Spence	Johnston	Ridding	Reid	McLachlan

Appearances (goals)

Bennion 28 · Black 3 (2) · Chesters 2 · Dale 4 · Dean 2 · Ferguson 8 (1) · Fitton 8 (2) · Gallimore 25 (6) · Hilditch 17 · Hopkinson 19 (5) · Johnston 28 (11) · Jones T 12 · Lievesley 2 · Lydon 2 · McDonald 2 · McLachlan 28 · McLenahan 11 · Manley 3 · Mann 13 (2) · Mellor 33 · Moody 8 · Page 9 · Parker 8 · Reid 25 · Ridding 14 (3) · Robinson 10 · Rowley 1 · Silcock 35 · Spence 37 (19) · Steward 32 · Vincent 16 · Warburton 7 (3) · Whittle 1 · Wilson 9 · Total 34 players (71)

Football League

	P	W	D	L	F:A	Pts	
Wolverhampton W	42	24	8	10	115:49	56	1st
Manchester U	42	17	8	17	71:72	42	12th

SEASON 1932–1933 FOOTBALL LEAGUE (DIVISION 2)

Date	Opponent			Score											
27 Aug	Stoke C	H	L	0–2	Moody	Mellor	Silcock	McLenahan	Vincent	McLachlan	Spence	Ridding	Black	McDonald	Page
29 Aug	Charlton A	A	W	1–0	..	..	..	..	..	..	..[1]	Warburton	Reid	..	Fitton
3 Sep	Southampton	A	L	*2–4	..	..	..	..	..	..	..	..	..[1]	..	Hopkinson
7 Sep	Charlton A	H	D	1–1	..	..	..	..[1]	..	..	..	McDonald	..	Page	..
10 Sep	Tottenham H	A	L	1–6	..	..	..	Hopkinson	McLenahan	..	..	..	Ridding[1]	Gallimore	Fitton
17 Sep	Grimsby T	H	D	1–1	..	..	..	Manley	..	..	Brown[1]	..	Spence[1]	Page	..
24 Sep	Oldham	A	D	1–1	..	..	..	..	Vincent	..	..	McLenahan	..	Gallimore	Hopkinson
1 Oct	Preston NE	H	D	0–0	..	..	..	Vincent	Frame	McLachlan	Spence	Chalmers	Reid	..	Brown
8 Oct	Burnley	A	W	3–2	..	..	..	..	..	..	..[1]	..	..	..[1]	..[1]
15 Oct	Bradford	H	W	2–1	..	..	..	..	..	..	..	..	..[2]	..	..
22 Oct	Millwall	H	W	7–1	..	..	..	..	..	..	..[1]	..	..[3]	..[1]	..[2]
29 Oct	Port Vale	A	D	3–3	..	Manley	..	..	..	..	..	Ridding[2]	..[1]	..	..[1]
5 Nov	Notts Co	H	W	2–0	..	..	..	..	..	..	..	..[1]	..	..	..
12 Nov	Bury	A	D	2–2	..	Silcock	..	..	..	..	Brown[1]	Warburton	..[1]	McDonald	Fitton
19 Nov	Fulham	H	W	4–3	..	Jones T	..	..	..	..	..[1]	Chalmers	..	Gallimore[2]	Stewart
26 Nov	Chesterfield	A	D	1–1	..	..	..	..	..	..	..	..	..[1]	..	..
3 Dec	Bradford C	H	L	0–1	..	..	..	..	..	..	..	..	..	McDonald	..
10 Dec	West Ham U	A	L	1–3	..	..	Silcock	..	..	..	..	..	..	..	..
17 Dec	Lincoln C	H	W	*4–1	..	..	..	..	..	..	..	Ridding	Reid[3]	Chalmers	..
24 Dec	Swansea	A	L	1–2	..	..	..	..	..	Manley	Spence[2]	..	..[1]	..	..
26 Dec	Plymouth A	A	W	3–2	..	Jones T	..	..	..	..	..	..	..	..	..
31 Dec	Stoke C	A	D	0–0	..	Mellor	..	..	McLenahan	..	..[1]	McDonald	Ridding[2]	..	McLachlan
2 Jan	Plymouth A	H	W	4–0	..	Jones T	..	..	..	..	..[1]	..[1]	..[2]	..	Stewart
7 Jan	Southampton	H	L	1–2	..	Mellor	..	Manley	Vincent	..	..	..	..	McDonald[1]	..
21 Jan	Tottenham H	H	W	2–1	..	..	Jones T	Vincent	Frame[1]	Manley	Brown	Chalmers	..	..	..[1]
31 Jan	Grimsby T	A	D	1–1	..	..	..	..	..	..	..	Spence	..	..[1]	..[1]
4 Feb	Oldham	H	W	2–0	..	..	..	..	..	..	Hopkinson[1]	Hine	..[1]	..	..[1]
11 Feb	Preston NE	A	D	3–3	..	..	..	..	..	Manley	Warburton[1]	..	Dewar[1]	..[1]	..
22 Feb	Burnley	H	W	2–1	..	..	Silcock	..	..	McLachlan	Manley	Ridding	..	Hine[1]	..
4 Mar	Millwall	A	L	0–2	..	..	Jones T	..	..	McLenahan	Mitchell	Hine	..	McDonald	..
11 Mar	Port Vale	H	D	1–1	..	..	..	..	..	McLachlan	Ridding	Ridding	..	..	..
18 Mar	Notts Co	A	L	0–1	..	..	Silcock	..	..	McLenahan	Spence	Ridding	..[1]	McDonald	..
25 Mar	Bury	H	L	1–3	..	..	..	McLenahan[1]	Vincent	McLachlan	..	..	..	Gallimore	..
1 Apr	Fulham	A	L	1–3	..	..	..	Vincent	Frame	..	Brown	..	..[1]	Hine	..
5 Apr	Bradford	A	D	1–1	..	..	Topping	..[1]	..	..	..	Chalmers	..	Gallimore	..
8 Apr	Chesterfield	H	W	2–1	..	..	..	..	..[1]	Manley	..[1]	..	..[1]	Hine	McLachlan
14 Apr	Nottingham F	A	L	2–3	..	..	..	..	..	..	..[1]	Hine[1]	..	McDonald	..
15 Apr	Bradford C	A	W	2–1	..	..	Silcock	..	..	..	..	..	..	..	..
17 Apr	Nottingham F	H	W	2–1	..	..	..	..	..	..	..[1]	..[1]	..	..	Hopkinson
22 Apr	West Ham U	H	L	1–2	..	..	Topping	..	..	..	..[1]	..[1]	..	..	..
29 Apr	Lincoln C	A	L	2–3	..	..	Silcock	..	..	..	Heywood	..[1]	..	Chalmers	Brown
6 May	Swansea	H	D	1–1	..	..	Topping	..	..	..	Heywood	..[1]	..	Chalmers	Brown

FA Cup

Date	Opponent			Score											
14 Jan	Middlesbrough (3)	H	L	1–4	Moody	Mellor	Silcock	Vincent	Frame	McLenahan	Spence[1]	Chalmers	Ridding	Reid	Stewart

Appearances (goals)

Black 1 · Brown 25 (10) · Chalmers 22 (1) · Dewar 15 (6) · Fitton 4 · Frame 33 (2) · Gallimore 12 (5) · Heywood 1 · Hine 14 (5) · Hopkinson 6 (1) · Jones T 10 · McDonald 21 (4) · McLachlan 17 · McLenahan 24 (2) · Manley 19 · Mellor 40 · Mitchell 1 · Moody 42 · Page 3 · Reid 11 (10) · Ridding 23 (11) · Silcock 27 · Spence 19 (7) · Stewart 21 (3) · Topping 5 · Vincent 40 (1) · Warburton 6 (1) · Own goals 2 · Total 27 players (71)

Football League

	P	W	D	L	F:A	Pts	
Stoke C	42	25	6	11	78:39	56	1st
Manchester U	42	15	13	14	71:68	43	6th

1933–1934

SEASON 1933–1934 FOOTBALL LEAGUE (DIVISION 2)

Date	Opponent			Score											
26 Aug	Plymouth A	A	L	0–4	Hillam	Mellor	Jones T	McLenahan	Vose	Manley	McGillivray	Hine	Dewar	Green	Stewart
30 Aug	Nottingham F	H	L	0–1	..	..	..	..	..	..	..	..	..	..	..
2 Sep	Lincoln C	H	D	1–1	..	..	..	Vincent	Frame	McLenahan	..	..	..	..(1)	..(1)
6 Sep	Nottingham F	A	D	1–1	..	..	..	Vose	..	..	..	..	..	Chalmers	..(1)
9 Sep	Bolton W	H	L	1–5	..	..	..	Vincent	..	..	..	..	..	Hine(1)	..
16 Sep	Brentford	A	W	4–3	..	Jones T	Silcock	Frame(1)	McMillen	Manley	Brown(2)	Warburton	..	Hine(1)	..
23 Sep	Burnley	H	W	5–2	..	..	..	Vose	..	..	..(1)	Frame	..(4)	..	..
30 Sep	Oldham	A	L	0–2	Hall	..	..	..	..	..	..	..	..	..	..
7 Oct	Preston NE	H	W	1–0	..	..	..	..	..	..	..	Chalmers	..	..(1)	Hopkinson
14 Oct	Bradford	A	L	1–6	..	..	McLenahan	..	Vincent	..	..	Ridding	..	..(1)	..
21 Oct	Bury	A	L	1–2	..	..	Silcock	McLenahan	McMillen	..	Warburton	Dewar	Byrne(1)	..	Stewart
28 Oct	Hull C	H	W	4–1	..	..	..	..	..	..	Heywood(2)	Hine(1)	Dewar	Green(1)	..(1)
4 Nov	Fulham	A	W	2–0	..	..	..	..	..	..	..(1)	..	..	..	..
11 Nov	Southampton	H	W	*1–0	..	..	..	..	..	..	Brown(1)	..	..	..	..
18 Nov	Blackpool	A	L	1–3	..	..	..	..	..	..	..(1)	Ridding	..	Hine	Black
25 Nov	Bradford C	H	W	*2–1	..	..	..	Vincent	Vose	..	..	..	..(1)	..	..(1)
2 Dec	Port Vale	A	W	3–2	..	Topping	..	..	..	..	..(1)	..	..	..	..
9 Dec	Notts Co	H	L	1–2	..	Silcock	..	..	..	McLenahan	..	Chalmers	..(1)	..	..
16 Dec	Swansea	A	L	1–2	..	..	McLenahan	McMillen	..	Manley	..	..	..	..	Hopkinson
23 Dec	Millwall	H	D	1–1	..	..	Frame	..	McMillen	..	Byrne	Hine	..	..	Stewart
25 Dec	Grimsby T	H	L	1–3	..	..	..	Vose(1)	..	..	McGillivray	McDonald	Byrne(2)	Chalmers	..
26 Dec	Grimsby T	A	L	3–7	..	Frame(1)	Topping	..	..	..	Byrne	Hine	Ball	..	..
30 Dec	Plymouth A	H	L	0–3	..	..	Jones T	..	..	..	Brown(1)	McGillivray	..	McLenahan	..
6 Jan	Lincoln C	A	L	1–5	..	Nevin	Topping	Frame	..	..	McGillivray	Hine	..(1)	McDonald	..
20 Jan	Bolton W	A	L	1–3	..	..	Silcock	..	..	..	Cape	..	..	..	..(1)
27 Jan	Brentford	H	L	1–3	..	Jones T	..	McLenahan	..	..	..(2)	McLenahan	..	Green(1)	..
3 Feb	Burnley	A	W	4–1	..	..	Nevin	Mann	Newton	..	..(1)	..	..	..(1)	..
10 Feb	Oldham	H	L	2–3	..	..	..	..	..	..	..	Chalmers	..	Gallimore(2)	..
21 Feb	Preston NE	A	L	2–3	..	..	Topping	McLenahan	Frame	..	..	Hine	..	..	..
24 Feb	Bradford	H	L	0–4	..	..	..	..	..	..	..	..	..	..	..
3 Mar	Bury	H	W	2–1	Behan	..	Silcock	..	Vose	Hopkinson	Ainsworth	..(1)	..	..	..
10 Mar	Hull C	A	L	1–4	Hillam	..	..	McMillen	..	..	McDonald	..(1)	..	..	..
17 Mar	Fulham	H	W	1–0	Hacking	Griffiths	Jones T	Robertson	Frame	McKay	Ainsworth	..(1)	..	..	Hopkinson
24 Mar	Southampton	A	L	0–1	..	..	..	..	..	..	Ridding	..	..	..	Manley
30 Mar	West Ham U	H	L	0–1	..	..	..	..	..	..	..(1)	McMillen	..	Hine	Gallimore
31 Mar	Blackpool	H	W	2–0	..	..	..	..	..	..	..(1)	Chalmers	..	..(1)	Manley
2 Apr	West Ham U	A	L	1–2	..	..	..	..	McMillen	..	..(1)	..	..	..	Brown
7 Apr	Bradford C	A	D	1–1	..	..	..	..	..	..	..	..	..	..	Hopkinson
14 Apr	Port Vale	H	W	2–0	..	..	..	..	Vincent	..	McMillen(1)	Brown(1)	..	..	..
21 Apr	Notts Co	A	D	0–0	..	..	..	..	..	..	..	..	..	..	..
28 Apr	Swansea	H	D	1–1	..	..	..	McMillen	Hopkinson	..	McKay	Ball	..	..	Topping(1)
5 May	Millwall	A	W	2–0	..	..	..	Vose	McKay	..	McLenahan(1)	..	..	..	Manley(1)

FA Cup

Date	Opponent			Score											
13 Jan	Portsmouth (3)	H	D	1–1	Hall	Jones T	Silcock	Vose	McMillen	Manley	Hine	McGillivray	Ball	McLenahan(1)	Stewart
17 Jan	Portsmouth (3R)	A	L	1–4	..	..	Nevin	..	..	..	Brown	Hine	..(1)	..	..

Appearances (goals)

Ainsworth 2 · Ball 18 (5) · Behan 1 · Black 4 (1) · Brown 15 (7) · Byrne 4 (3) · Cape 17 (7) · Chalmers 12 · Dewar 21 (8) · Frame 18 (2) · Gallimore 7 (3) · Green 9 (4) · Griffiths 10 · Hacking 10 · Hall 23 · Heywood 3 (2) · Hillam 8 · Hine 33 (6) · Hopkinson 9 · Jones T 39 · McDonald 4 · McGillivray 8 · McKay 10 · McLenahan 22 · McMillen 23 (1) · Manley 30 (2) · Mann 2 · Mellor 5 · Nevin 4 · Newton 2 · Ridding 5 · Robertson 10 · Silcock 16 · Stewart 25 (4) · Topping 6 (1) · Vincent 8 · Vose 17 (1) · Warburton 2 · Own goals 2 · Total 38 players (59)

Football League

	P	W	D	L	F:A	Pts	
Grimsby T	42	27	5	10	103:59	59	1st
Manchester U	42	14	6	22	59:85	34	20th

1934–1935

SEASON 1934–1935 FOOTBALL LEAGUE (DIVISION 2)

Date	Opponent			Score											
25 Aug	Bradford C	H	W	2–0	Hacking	Griffiths	Jones T	Robertson	Vose	McKay	Cape	Mutch	Ball(1)	Jones T J	Manley(2)
1 Sep	Sheffield U	A	L	2–3	..	..	..	..	..	..	..	..	..	..	..(1)
3 Sep	Bolton W	A	L	*1–3	..	..	..	..	..	..	..	..(3)	..	..	..
8 Sep	Barnsley	H	W	4–1	..	..	..	McLenahan	..	..	..	..	..	..	..
12 Sep	Bolton W	H	L	0–3	..	..	..	..	..	..	..	..(1)	..	..	..
15 Sep	Port Vale	A	L	2–3	..	Jones T	Topping	..	..	..	..	..(1)	..	Hine	Jones T J(1)
22 Sep	Norwich C	H	W	5–0	Langford	Mellor	Jones T	Robertson	..	..	Jones T J(1)	..	Cape(1)	McLenahan(1)	Owen(1)
29 Sep	Swansea	H	W	3–1	..	Griffiths	..	..	..	Manley(1)	..(2)	..	..(1)	McKay	..
6 Oct	Burnley	A	W	2–1	Hacking	..	..	..	..	..	..(2)	..	..	..	..
13 Oct	Oldham	H	W	4–0	..	..	..	..	..	..	..	..(1)	Hine	..(1)	..
20 Oct	Newcastle U	A	W	1–0	..	..	..	..	..	..	..	..	Bamford(1)	..(1)	..
27 Oct	West Ham U	H	W	3–1	..	..	..	..	..	..	..	..(2)	..	..(1)	Jones T J
3 Nov	Blackpool	A	W	2–1	..	..	..	..	..	..	Bryant	..(1)	..	..(1)	..
10 Nov	Bury	H	W	1–0	..	..	..	..	..	..	..	..	..	..(2)	Owen
17 Nov	Hull C	A	L	2–3	..	..	..	..	..	..	..	..(2)	..	Hine(1)	McLenahan
24 Nov	Nottingham F	H	W	3–2	..	..	..	..	..	..	..	McKay	..(1)	..	..
1 Dec	Brenford	A	L	1–3	..	..	..	..	..	..	..	Mutch	..	Rowley	Manley
8 Dec	Fulham	H	W	1–0	..	..	..	McLenahan	McKay	..	Mutch(1)	..	..	..	..(1)
15 Dec	Bradford	A	W	2–1	..	..	..	Robertson	..	..	..	..(1)	..	..(1)	..
22 Dec	Plymouth A	H	W	3–1	..	..	..	..	..	..	..	..(1)	..	..(1)	..(1)
25 Dec	Notts Co	H	W	2–1	..	..	..	..	..	..	..	..	..	..	Owen
26 Dec	Notts Co	A	L	0–1	..	..	..	McMillen	..	..	..	..	..	..	..
29 Dec	Bradford C	A	L	0–2	Langford	..	..	Vose	..	..	..	Cape(2)	..	..(1)	Manley
1 Jan	Southampton	H	W	3–0	Hall	..	..	..	..	..	..(1)	..	..	..(1)	..
5 Jan	Sheffield U	H	D	3–3	..	..	..	..	..	..	..	..(1)	Bamford	..(1)	Jones T J(1)
19 Jan	Barnsley	A	W	2–0	Hacking	..	Porter	..	..	..	Jones T J	Cape	..	..(1)	Manley(1)
2 Feb	Norwich C	A	L	2–3	..	..	Jones T	..	..	..	..	..	..	..(1)	Jones T J(1)
6 Feb	Port Vale	H	W	2–1	Hall	..	..	McKay	Robertson	Manley	Bryant	..	Boyd	..	..
9 Feb	Swansea	A	L	0–1	..	..	Porter	Robertson	McLenahan	McKay	..	..	..	..	..
23 Feb	Oldham	A	W	1–3	..	..	..	McKay	Vose	Manley	..	..	..(1)	..	Manley
2 Mar	Newcastle U	H	L	0–1	Langford	..	..	Robertson	..	McKay	Cape	..	..	..	..
9 Mar	West Ham U	A	D	0–0	..	..	..	..	..	..	..	..	..	..	..
16 Mar	Blackpool	H	W	3–2	..	..	..	..	..	Manley	Bryant	..(1)	Bamford(1)	..(1)	McMillen
23 Mar	Bury	A	W	1–0	..	..	..	..	..	..	Cape(1)	..	Boyd(1)	..	..
27 Mar	Burnley	H	L	3–4	..	..	..	McKay	..	..	..(1)	..	..(3)	McKay	Rowley
30 Mar	Hull C	H	W	3–0	..	..	..	Robertson	..	Owen	Bryant(2)	..	Cape	..	Owen
6 Apr	Nottingham F	A	D	2–2	..	..	..	..	..	..	..	..	..	Rowley	Owen
13 Apr	Brentford	H	D	0–0	..	..	..	..	..	McKay	..	..	..	McKay	Jones T J
20 Apr	Fulham	A	L	1–3	..	..	..	..	..	McLenahan	..	..	Bamford(1)	McKay	Rowley
22 Apr	Southampton	A	L	0–1	Hall	..	..	..	..(1)	..	..	..	..	..	Rowley
27 Apr	Bradford	H	W	2–0	..	..	..	..	..	Manley	..	McKay	..(1)	Rowley(1)	Owen
4 May	Plymouth A	A	W	2–0	..	..	..	..	..	..	..	Mutch	..	..	..

FA Cup

Date	Opponent			Score											
12 Jan	Bristol R (3)	A	W	3–1	Hall	Griffiths	Jones T	Robertson	Vose	McKay	Bryant	Mutch(1)	Bamford(2)	Rowley	Manley
26 Jan	Nottingham F (4)	A	D	0–0	Hacking	..	Porter	..	..	..	Cape	..	..	..	Jones T J
30 Jan	Nottingham F (4R)	H	L	0–3	..	..	Jones T	..	..	..	Bryant	..	..	..	..

Appearances (goals)

Ball 6 (1) · Bamford 19 (9) · Boyd 6 (4) · Bryant 24 (6) · Cape 21 (8) · Griffiths 40 · Hacking 22 · Hall 8 · Hine 4 (1) · Jones T 27 · Jones T J 20 (4) · Langford 12 · McLenahan 10 (1) · McKay 38 (3) · McMillen 4 (1) · Manley 30 (9) · Mellor 1 · Mutch 40 (18) · Owen 15 (1) · Porter 15 · Robertson 36 (1) · Rowley 24 (8) · Topping 1 · Vose 39 · Own goals 1 · Total 24 players (76)

Football League

	P	W	D	L	F:A	Pts	
Brentford	42	26	9	7	93:48	61	1st
Manchester U	42	23	4	15	76:55	50	5th

SEASON 1935–1936 FOOTBALL LEAGUE (DIVISION 2)

Date	Opponent		Res	Score											
31 Aug	Plymouth A	A	L	1–3	Breedon	Griffiths	Porter	Brown	Vose	McKay	Bryant	Mutch	Bamford[1]	Rowley	Chester[1]
4 Sep	Charlton A	H	W	3–0	Hall						Cape[1]		[1]	Ferrier	
9 Sep	Bradford C	H	W	3–1									[2]		
11 Sep	Charlton A	A	D	0–0											
14 Sep	Newcastle U	A	W	2–0						Manley			[1]	Rowley[1]	
18 Sep	Hull C	H	W	2–0							Bryant		[2]		
21 Sep	Tottenham H	H	D	0–0	Breedon	Redwood				McKay				Manley	
28 Sep	Southampton	A	L	1–2	Hall	Griffiths					Robbie			Rowley[1]	
5 Oct	Port Vale	A	W	3–0							Cape	[2]	[1]		[1]
12 Oct	Fulham	H	W	1–0											[1]
19 Oct	Sheffield U	H	W	3–1							[1]	[1]			
26 Oct	Bradford	A	L	0–1											
2 Nov	Leicester C	H	L	0–1											Owen
9 Nov	Swansea	A	L	1–2						Manley	Wassall		[1]		
16 Nov	West Ham U	H	L	2–3						McKay			Morton	[2]	Chester
23 Nov	Norwich C	A	W	5–3	Langford			Whalley			Cape		Bamford	[3]	Manley[2]
30 Nov	Doncaster R	H	D	0–0				Whalley							
7 Dec	Blackpool	A	L	1–4				Robertson				[1]			
14 Dec	Nottingham F	H	W	5–0	Hall			Brown				[1]	[2]	[1]	[1]
26 Dec	Barnsley	H	D	1–1								[1]			
28 Dec	Plymouth A	H	W	3–2								Gardner	Mutch[2]		[1]
1 Jan	Barnsley	A	W	3–0								[1]	[1]		[1]
4 Jan	Bradford C	A	L	0–1											
18 Jan	Newcastle U	H	W	3–1							Bamford		[2]	[1]	
1 Feb	Southampton	H	W	4–0							Bryant[1]			Ferrier	[2]
5 Feb	Tottenham H	A	D	0–0								Ferrier		Rowley	
8 Feb	Port Vale	H	W	7–2								Gardner	[1]	[2]	[4]
22 Feb	Sheffield U	A	D	1–1											[1]
29 Feb	Blackpool	H	W	3–2							[1]		[1]		
7 Mar	West Ham U	A	W	2–1							[1]		[1]		
14 Mar	Swansea	H	W	3–0									[1]	[1]	
21 Mar	Leicester C	A	D	1–1							[1]				
28 Mar	Norwich C	H	W	2–1								Ferrier		[2]	
1 Apr	Fulham	A	D	2–2				[1]			[1]				
4 Apr	Doncaster R	A	D	0–0								Gardner			
10 Apr	Burnley	A	D	2–2								Mutch	Bamford[2]		
11 Apr	Bradford	H	W	4–0	Breedon					Manley	[1]	[2]	[1]		Lang
13 Apr	Burnley	H	W	4–0	Hall			Whalley	Brown		[2]			[2]	
18 Apr	Nottingham F	A	D	1–1				Brown	Vose				[1]		
25 Apr	Bury	H	W	2–1										[1]	[1]
29 Apr	Bury	A	W	3–2						McKay		[1]			Manley[2]
2 May	Hull C	A	D	1–1									[1]		

FA Cup

Date	Opponent		Res	Score											
11 Jan	Reading (3)	A	W	3–1	Hall	Griffiths	Porter	Brown	Vose	McKay	Bamford	Gardner	Mutch[2]	Rowley	Manley[1]
25 Jan	Stoke C (4)	A	D	0–0							Bryant	Rowley		Ferrier	
29 Jan	Stoke C (4R)	H	L	0–2										Ferrier	

Appearances (goals)

Bamford 27 (16) · Breedon 3 · Brown 40 · Bryant 21 (8) · Cape 17 (2) · Chester 13 (1) · Ferrier 7 · Gardner 12 (1) · Griffiths 41 (1) · Hall 36 · Lang 4 (1) · Langford 3 · McKay 35 · Manley 31 (14) · Morton 1 · Mutch 42 (21) · Owen 2 · Porter 42 · Redwood 1 · Robbie 1 · Robertson 1 · Rowley 37 (19) · Vose 41 · Wassall 2 · Whalley 2 · Own goals 1 · Total 25 players (85)

Football League

	P	W	D	L	F:A	Pts	
Manchester U	42	22	12	8	85:43	56	1st

SEASON 1936–1937 FOOTBALL LEAGUE (DIVISION 1)

Date	Opponent		Res	Score											
29 Aug	Wolverhampton W	H	D	1–1	John	Redwood	Porter	Brown	Vose	McKay	Bryant	Mutch	Bamford[1]	Rowley	Manley
2 Sep	Huddersfield T	A	L	1–3			McLenahan					McClelland			[1]
5 Sep	Derby Co	A	L	4–5								Wassall[1]	[3]	Ferrier	
9 Sep	Huddersfield T	H	W	3–1			Mellor				[1]		[1]	Mutch[1]	
12 Sep	Manchester C	H	W	3–2			Roughton						[1]		[1]
19 Sep	Sheffield Wed	H	D	1–1									[1]		
26 Sep	Preston NE	A	L	1–3							[1]		[1]	Ferrier	
3 Oct	Arsenal	H	W	2–0								Mutch		Rowley[1]	
10 Oct	Brentford	A	L	0–4											
17 Oct	Portsmouth	A	L	1–2		Griffiths						Wassall			[1]
24 Oct	Chelsea	H	D	0–0						Whalley		Mutch			
31 Oct	Stoke C	A	L	0–3						McKay					
7 Nov	Charlton A	H	D	0–0										Ferrier	
14 Nov	Grimsby T	A	L	2–6			Mellor					[1]			
21 Nov	Liverpool	H	L	2–5			Roughton		McLenahan			[1]	Thompson[1]		[1]
28 Nov	Leeds U	A	L	1–2	Breen	Roughton	Porter	Winterbottom	Brown				Bamford	Thompson	
5 Dec	Birmingham	H	L	1–2		Redwood	Roughton		Vose			[1]		Rowley	
12 Dec	Middlesbrough	A	L	2–3					Brown	Manley[1]		Wassall	Mutch		Halton[1]
19 Dec	West Brom A	H	D	2–2								Mutch[1]	Bamford	McKay[1]	
25 Dec	Bolton W	H	W	1–0				Brown	Winterbottom					[1]	
26 Dec	Wolverhampton W	A	L	1–3										[1]	Lang
28 Dec	Bolton W	A	W	4–0						Whalley	[2]			[2]	
											[1]	[1]			
1 Jan	Sunderland	H	W	2–1											
2 Jan	Derby Co	H	D	2–2	Breedon						Cape		Rowley[2]		
9 Jan	Manchester C	A	L	0–1	Breen						Bryant	Vose			
23 Jan	Sheffield Wed	A	L	0–1								Mutch	Bamford	Baird	Wrigglesworth
3 Feb	Preston NE	H	D	1–1								Baird	Rowley	McKay	[1]
6 Feb	Arsenal	A	D	1–1		Griffiths	Winterbottom	Whalley	Vose	Manley		[1]			Lang
13 Feb	Brentford	H	L	1–3											
20 Feb	Portsmouth	H	L	0–1			Roughton	Winterbottom		Whalley		Mutch		Baird	Manley
27 Feb	Chelsea	A	L	2–4								Gladwin[1]	Bamford[1]		Wrigglesworth
6 Mar	Stoke C	H	W	2–1				Whalley	Winterbottom	McKay		McClelland[1]		[1]	
13 Mar	Charlton A	A	L	0–3								Mutch			
20 Mar	Grimsby T	H	D	1–1				Brown		Whalley	Cape[1]	Gladwin	Rowley		Bryant
26 Mar	Everton	H	W	2–1									Mutch[1]	[1]	Manley
27 Mar	Liverpool	A	L	0–2											
29 Mar	Everton	A	W	3–2					Vose	Manley	Bryant[1]	Baird	[1]	Ferrier[1]	Lang
3 Apr	Leeds U	H	D	0–0										Rowley	
10 Apr	Birmingham	A	D	2–2			Jones T	Gladwin		Whalley	Wrigglesworth	Gardner	Bamford[2]	McClelland	Manley
17 Apr	Middlesbrough	H	W	2–1			Redwood				Bryant[1]				Wrigglesworth
21 Apr	Sunderland	A	D	1–1			Roughton			McKay			[1]		Manley
24 Apr	WBA	A	L	0–1										Baird	

FA Cup

Date	Opponent		Res	Score											
16 Jan	Reading (3)	H	W	1–0	Breen	Vose	Roughton	Brown	Winterbottom	Whalley	Bryant	Mutch	Bamford[1]	McKay	Lang
30 Jan	Arsenal (4)	A	L	0–5		Redwood									Wrigglesworth

Appearances (goals)

Baird 14 (3) · Bamford 29 (14) · Breedon 1 · Breen 26 · Brown 31 · Bryant 37 (10) · Cape 4 (1) · Ferrier 6 (1) · Gardner 4 · Gladwin 8 (1) · Griffiths 21 · Halton 4 (1) · John 15 · Jones T 1 · Lang 8 · McClelland 5 (1) · McLenahan 3 · McKay 29 (4) · Manley 31 (5) · Mellor 2 · Mutch 28 (7) · Porter 2 · Redwood 21 · Roughton 33 · Rowley 17 (4) · Thompson 2 (1) · Vose 26 · Wassall 7 (1) · Whalley 19 · Winterbottom 21 · Wrigglesworth 7 (1) · Total 31 players (55)

Football League

	P	W	D	L	F:A	Pts	
Manchester C	42	22	13	7	107:61	57	1st
Manchester U	42	10	12	20	55:78	32	21st

1937–1938

SEASON 1937–1938 FOOTBALL LEAGUE (DIVISION 2)

Date	Opponent				1	2	3	4	5	6	7	8	9	10	11
28 Aug	Newcastle U	H	W	3–0	Breen	Griffiths	Roughton	Gladwin	Vose	McKay	Bryant[1]	Murray	Bamford	Baird	Manley[2]
30 Aug	Coventry C	A	L	0–1	..	..	..	..	..	..	..	..	..	..	..
4 Sep	Luton T	A	L	0–1	..	..	..	..	..	..	..[1]	Wassall	Mutch Bamford[1]	..	..[1]
8 Sep	Coventry C	H	D	2–2	..	..	..	..	..	..	..	..	..[3]	Ferrier[2]	
11 Sep	Barnsley	H	W	4–1	..	..	..	Brown	Winterbottom	..	..	..	..	..	..
13 Sep	Bury	A	W	2–1	..	..	..	..	..	..	..	..	..	..	..
18 Sep	Stockport Co	A	L	0–1	..	..	..	..	..	..	..	Mutch	..	..	..
25 Sep	Southampton	H	L	1–2	..	..	..	..	..	..	..	Gladwin	Thompson	Carey	..[1]
2 Oct	Sheffield U	H	L	0–1	..	..	..	..	Vose	..	..	Carey	Baird	Baird	..
9 Oct	Tottenham H	A	W	1–0	..	..	..	..	..	..	..	Wassall	Ferrier Bamford[1]	..	..[1]
16 Oct	Blackburn R	A	D	1–1	..	..	..	..	..	..	..	..	..	..	Wrigglesworth Rowley
23 Oct	Sheffield Wed	H	W	1–0	Breedon	..	..	..	..	..	..	Murray	..	Ferrier[1]	Rowley
30 Oct	Fulham	A	L	0–1	Breen	..	..	..	..	..	Wrigglesworth	Wassall	..	Whalley	Manley
6 Nov	Plymouth A	H	D	0–0	..	Redwood	..	..	..	Whalley	..	..	..	McKay	
13 Nov	Chesterfield	A	W	7–1	Breedon	..	..	..	..	..	Bryant[1]	Baird[1]	..[4]	Pearson[1]	..[1]
20 Nov	Aston Villa	A	W	3–1	..	..	..	..	..	McKay	..[1]	..[1]	..[1]	..[1]	
27 Nov	Norwich C	A	W	3–2	..	..	..	..	..	..	..[1]	..	..	..	Rowley[4]
4 Dec	Swansea	H	W	5–1	..	..	..	Whalley	..	..	..	..	..	..	
11 Dec	Bradford	A	L	0–4	..	..	..	..	Jones D	..	..	..	..	..	
27 Dec	Nottingham F	H	W	4–3	..	..	..	..	Vose	..[1]	Wrigglesworth[1]	..[2]	..	Carey[1]	..[1]
28 Dec	Nottingham F	A	W	3–2	..	..	..	Griffiths	..	..	Bryant[1]	..	..[1]	..	..
1 Jan	Newcastle U	A	D	2–2	..	..	..	Savage	Griffiths	..[1]	..[1]	..	..[1]	..[1]	..[1]
15 Jan	Luton T	H	W	4–2	Breen	..	..	..	Vose	..[1]	..[1]	..	..[1]	..	
29 Jan	Stockport Co	H	W	3–1	..	Griffiths	Redwood	..	..	Porter	..	..	Smith[1]	..	..[1]
2 Feb	Barnsley	A	D	2–2	..	..	..	..	..	..	..	..[1]	..	..	
5 Feb	Southampton	A	D	3–3	..	..	..[2]	Brown	..	..	..[1]	..	..[1]	..[1]	
17 Feb	Sheffield U	A	W	2–1	..	Redwood	Roughton	..	..	Manley	..	..	..	..	Manley
19 Feb	Tottenham H	H	L	0–1	..	..	..	..	..	McKay	..	..	..[1]	..	Rowley
23 Feb	West Ham U	H	W	4–0	..	..	..	..	Manley	..	Wassall[1]	..	Baird[2]	..	
26 Feb	Blackburn R	H	W	2–1	..	..	..	..[1]	..	..	..[1]	..	..	Carey	..[1]
5 Mar	Sheffield Wed	A	W	3–1	..	..	..	..	Vose	..	..	Baird[1]	..	..	
12 Mar	Fulham	H	W	1–0	..	..	..	..	..	..	..	..[1]	..	..	..[1]
19 Mar	Plymouth A	A	D	1–1	..	..	..	..	..	..	..[1]	..	Bamford Smith[2]	..	
26 Mar	Chesterfield	H	W	4–1	..	..	..	..	..	..	..	..	..	..,	
2 Apr	Aston Villa	A	L	0–3	..	..	..	..	..	..	..	..	..	..	
9 Apr	Norwich C	H	D	0–0	..	..	..	..	..	..	..	..	..	..	
15 Apr	Burnley	A	L	0–1	..	..	..	..	..	..	..	..	..	Pearson	
16 Apr	Swansea	A	D	2–2	..	..	..	Gladwin	..	Manley	..[1]	..[1]	Bamford	Smith[1]	..[1]
18 Apr	Burnley	H	W	4–0	..	..	..	Brown	..	McKay[2]	..[1]	..[1]	Smith	Pearson	..
23 Apr	Bradford	H	W	3–1	..	..	..	..	..	..[1]	..	..[1]	..	..	
30 Apr	West Ham U	A	L	0–1	..	..	..	Gladwin	..	..	..[1]	..	..	..	
7 May	Bury	H	W	2–0	..	..	..	Brown	Manley	..	..	..[1]	..	..	

FA Cup

Date	Opponent														
8 Jan	Yeovil (3)	H	W	3–0	Breen	Redwood	Roughton	Brown	Vose	McKay	Bryant	Baird[1]	Bamford[1]	Pearson[1]	Rowley
22 Jan	Barnsley (4)	A	D	2–2	..	..	..	..	..	..	..[1]	..	..	Carey[1]	
26 Jan	Barnsley (4R)	H	W	1–0	..	..	..	Savage	..	..	..	..[1]	..	..	
12 Feb	Brentford (5)	A	L	0–2	..	..	..	Brown	..	..	..	..	..	..	

Appearances (goals)

Baird 35 (12) · Bamford 23 (14) · Breedon 9 · Breen 33 · Brown 28 (1) · Bryant 39 (12) · Carey 16 (3) · Ferrier 5 (3) · Gladwin 7 · Griffiths 18 · Jones D 1 · McKay 37 (7) · Manley 21 (7) · Murray 4 · Mutch 2 · Pearson 11 (2) · Porter 2 · Redwood 29 (2) · Roughton 39 · Rowley 25 (9) · Savage 4 · Smith 17 (8) · Thompson 1 · Vose 33 · Wassall 9 (1) · Whalley 6 · Winterbottom 4 · Wrigglesworth 4 (1) · Total 28 players (82)

Football League

	P	W	D	L	F:A	Pts	
Aston Villa	42	25	7	10	73:35	57	1st
Manchester U	42	22	9	11	82:50	53	2nd

1938–1939

SEASON 1938–1939 FOOTBALL LEAGUE (DIVISION 1)

Date	Opponent				1	2	3	4	5	6	7	8	9	10	11
27 Aug	Middlesbrough	A	L	1–3	Breen	Redwood	Roughton	Gladwin	Vose	McKay	Bryant	Wassall	Smith[1]	Craven	Rowley
31 Aug	Bolton W	H	D	*2–2	Breedon	..	..	..	..	..	..	Craven[1]	..[1]	Pearson	..
3 Sep	Birmingham	H	W	4–1	..	Griffiths	Redwood	..	..	Manley	..[1]	..[1]	..[2]	..	..
7 Sep	Liverpool	A	L	0–1	..	..	..	..	..	..	..	..	..	..	..
10 Sep	Grimsby T	A	L	0–1	..	..	..	..	..	..	..	..	..	Carey	..
17 Sep	Stoke C	A	D	1–1	..	Redwood	Roughton	..	..	..[1]	..	..	..[1]	..[1]	..[1]
24 Sep	Chelsea	H	W	5–1	..	..[1]	Griffiths	..	..	..	..[1]	..	..	..	..
1 Oct	Preston NE	A	D	1–1	..	..	..	..	..	..	..[1]	..	..	..	..
8 Oct	Charlton A	H	L	0–2	..	..	..	..	..	..	..	..	..	..	..
15 Oct	Blackpool	H	D	0–0	..	..	..	..	..	Wrigglesworth	Wassall	..[1]	..	..	
22 Oct	Derby Co	A	L	1–5	..	Griffiths	Roughton	..	..	..	..	..	..	..	
29 Oct	Sunderland	H	L	0–1	..	Redwood	..	Brown	Manley	McKay	Bryant Rowley[1]	Carey	..	Pearson	Wrigglesworth
5 Nov	Aston Villa	A	W	2–0	Breen	..	Griffiths	Warner	Vose	..	..[1]	..	..	..	..[1]
12 Nov	Wolverhampton W	H	L	1–3	Breedon	..	..	..	..	..	..	..	..	..	
19 Nov	Everton	A	L	0–3	..	..	Roughton	..	Manley	Whalley	..	Gladwin	..	Carey	..
26 Nov	Huddersfield T	H	D	1–1	..	..	Griffiths	..	Vose	Manley	Bryant	Wassall	Hanlon[1]	Craven	Rowley
3 Dec	Portsmouth	A	D	0–0	..	..	..	..	..	..	Wrigglesworth	..	..	..	
10 Dec	Arsenal	H	W	1–0	..	..	..	..	..	..[1]	Bryant[1]	..	..[2]	Carey	..[1]
17 Dec	Brentford	A	W	5–2	..	..	..	..	..	..	..	..[1]	..	..	..
24 Dec	Middlesbrough	H	D	1–1	..	..	..	..	..	McKay	..	..	..	..	
26 Dec	Leicester C	H	W	3–0	Tapken	..	..	..	..	Brown	Wrigglesworth[2]	..	..[1]	..[1]	
27 Dec	Leicester C	A	D	1–1	..	..	..	..	..	..	..	..	..	..	
31 Dec	Birmingham	A	D	3–3	..	..	..	..	..	McKay[1]	Wassall	Carey	..[1]	Pearson[1]	Wrigglesworth
14 Jan	Grimsby T	H	W	3–1	..	..	..	..	..	..	Bryant	Wassall[1]	..	Carey	Rowley[2]
21 Jan	Stoke C	H	L	0–1	..	..	..	..	..	..	..	..	..	..	
28 Jan	Chelsea	A	W	1–0	..	..	..	..	..	..	..	..	..	Bradbury[1] Carey	..[1]
4 Feb	Preston NE	H	D	1–1	..	..	..	..	..	..	..	..	..[1]	Bradbury	
11 Feb	Charlton A	A	L	1–7	..	..	..	..	..	..	..[1]	..	..[3]	Carey[1]	
18 Feb	Blackpool	A	W	5–3	..	..	..	..	..	..	..	..	..	..	
25 Feb	Derby Co	H	D	1–1	..	..	..	..	..	..	..	..	..	..	
4 Mar	Sunderland	A	L	2–5	..	..	..	..	..	..	Rowley[1]	..	..[1]	..	Manley[1]
11 Mar	Aston Villa	H	D	1–1	Breen	..	..	..	..	Manley	Smith	..	..	..	Rowley
18 Mar	Wolverhampton W	A	L	0–3	..	..	..	..	..	..	..	..	..	Pearson	..
29 Mar	Everton	H	L	0–2	..	..	..	..	..	..	Dougan	..	..	..	..[1]
1 Apr	Huddersfield T	A	D	1–1	..	Griffiths	Roughton	..	..	..	..	Smith	..	Carey	..
7 Apr	Leeds U	H	D	0–0	Tapken	..	..	..	..	..	..	Wassall	..	..	..[1]
8 Apr	Portsmouth	H	D	1–1	..	..	..	..	..	..	..	Smith	..	..[1]	
10 Apr	Leeds U	A	L	1–3	..	..	..	Whalley	Manley	McKay	Bryant	Wassall	..[1]	..[1]	
15 Apr	Arsenal	A	L	1–2	Breedon	..	..	Warner	Vose	..	..[1]	..	..	..	Wrigglesworth
22 Apr	Brentford	H	W	3–0	..	..	..	..	..	..	..	..[1]	..	..	
29 Apr	Bolton W	A	D	0–0	..	Redwood	..	..	..	..	..	..	..[2]	..	Rowley
6 May	Liverpool	H	W	2–0	..	..	..	..	..	..	..	..	..	..	

FA Cup

Date	Opponent														
7 Jan	W B A (3)	A	D	0–0	Tapken	Redwood	Griffiths	Warner	Vose	McKay	Wrigglesworth	Wassall	Hanlon	Carey	Rowley
11 Jan	W B A (3R)	H	L	1–5	..	..[1]	..	..	Gladwin	..	..	..	..	..	Smith

Appearances (goals)

Bradbury 2 (1) · Breedon 22 · Breen 6 · Brown 3 · Bryant 27 (6) · Carey 32 (6) · Craven 11 (2) · Dougan 4 · Gladwin 12 · Griffiths 35 · Hanlon 27 (12) · McKay 20 (1) · Manley 23 (6) · Pearson 9 (1) · Redwood 35 (1) · Roughton 14 · Rowley 38 (10) · Smith 19 (6) · Tapken 14 · Vose 39 · Warner · Wassall 27 (4) · Whalley 2 · Wrigglesworth 12 (3) · Own goals 1 · Total 24 players (57)

Football League

	P	W	D	L	F:A	Pts	
Everton	42	27	5	10	88:52	59	1st
Manchester U	42	11	16	15	57:65	38	14th

SEASON 1939–1940 ALL MATCHES

Western Division Wartime Regional League

21 Oct	Manchester C	H	L	0–4
28 Oct	Chester	A	W	4–0
11 Nov	Crewe Alex	H	W	5–1
18 Nov	Liverpool	A	L	0–1
25 Nov	Port Vale	H	W	8–1
2 Dec	Tranmere R	A	W	4–2
9 Dec	Stockport Co	A	W	7–4
23 Dec	Wrexham	H	W	5–1
6 Jan	Everton	A	L	2–3
20 Jan	Stoke C	H	W	4–3
10 Feb	Manchester C	A	L	0–1
24 Feb	Chester	H	W	5–1
9 Mar	Crewe Alex	A	W	4–1
16 Mar	Liverpool	H	W	1–0
23 Mar	Port Vale	A	W	3–1
30 Mar	Tranmere R	H	W	6–1
6 Apr	Stockport Co	H	W	6–1
6 May	New Brighton	H	W	6–0
13 May	Wrexham	A	L	2–3
18 May	New Brighton	H	L	0–6
25 May	Stoke C	A	L	2–3
1 Jun	Everton	H	L	0–3

	P	W	D	L	F:A	Pts	
Manchester U	22	14	0	8	74:41	28	4th

Football League War Cup

20 Apr	Manchester C (1st leg)	H	L	0–1
27 Apr	Manchester C (2nd leg)	A	W	2–0
4 May	Blackburn R (1st leg)	A	W	2–1
11 May	Blackburn R (2nd leg)	A	L	1–3

SEASON 1940–1941

North Regional League

31 Aug	Rochdale	A	W	3–1
7 Sep	Bury	H	D	0–0
14 Sep	Oldham	A	L	1–2
21 Sep	Oldham	H	L	2–3
28 Sep	Manchester C	A	L	1–4
5 Oct	Manchester C	H	L	0–2
12 Oct	Burnley	A	W	1–0
19 Oct	Preston NE	H	W	4–1
26 Oct	Preston NE	A	L	1–3
2 Nov	Burnley	H	W	4–1
9 Nov	Everton	A	L	2–5
16 Nov	Everton	H	D	0–0
23 Nov	Liverpool	A	D	2–2
30 Nov	Liverpool	H	W	2–0
7 Dec	Blackburn R	A	D	5–5
14 Dec	Rochdale	H	L	3–4
21 Dec	Bury	A	L	1–4
25 Dec	Stockport Co	A	W	3–1
28 Dec	Blackburn R	H	W	9–0
4 Jan	Blackburn R	A	W	2–0
11 Jan	Blackburn R	H	D	0–0
18 Jan	Bolton W	A	L	2–3
25 Jan	Bolton W	H	W	4–1
1 Mar	Chesterfield	A	D	1–1
8 Mar	Bury	H	W	7–3
22 Mar	Oldham	A	W	1–0
29 Mar	Blackpool	A	L	0–2
5 Apr	Blackpool	H	L	2–3
12 Apr	Everton	A	W	2–1
14 Apr	Manchester C	A	W	7–1
19 Apr	Chester	A	W	6–4
26 Apr	Liverpool	A	L	1–2
3 May	Liverpool	H	D	1–1
10 May	Bury	A	L	1–5
17 May	Burnley	H	W	1–0

	P	W	D	L	F:A	Pts	
Manchester U	35	15	7	13	82:65	37	7th*

*Positions according to goal average not points

Football League War Cup

15 Feb	Everton (1st leg)	H	D	2–2
22 Feb	Everton (2nd leg)	A	L	1–2

SEASON 1941–1942 ALL MATCHES

30 Aug	New Brighton	H	W	13–1
6 Sep	New Brighton	A	D	3–3
13 Sep	Stockport Co	A	W	5–1
20 Sep	Stockport Co	H	W	7–1
27 Sep	Everton	H	L	2–3
4 Oct	Everton	A	W	3–1
11 Oct	Chester	A	W	7–0
18 Oct	Chester	H	W	8–1
25 Oct	Stoke C	A	D	1–1
1 Nov	Stoke C	H	W	3–0
8 Nov	Tranmere R	H	W	6–1
15 Nov	Tranmere R	A	D	1–1
22 Nov	Liverpool	A	D	1–1
29 Nov	Liverpool	H	D	2–2
6 Dec	Wrexham	H	W	10–3
13 Dec	Wrexham	A	W	4–3
20 Dec	Manchester C	A	L	1–2
25 Dec	Manchester C	H	D	2–2

Football League North Region: First Championship

	P	W	D	L	F:A	Pts	
Manchester U	18	10	6	2	79:27	26	4th

27 Dec	Bolton W (Cup Q)	H	W	3–1
3 Jan	Bolton W (Cup Q)	A	D	2–2
10 Jan	Oldham (Cup Q)	H	D	1–1
17 Jan	Oldham (Cup Q)	A	W	3–1
31 Jan	Southport (Cup Q)	A	W	3–1
14 Feb	Sheffield U (Cup Q)	A	W	2–0
21 Feb	Preston NE (Cup Q)	H	L	0–2
28 Feb	Preston NE (Cup Q)	A	W	3–1
21 Mar	Sheffield U (Cup Q)	H	D	2–2
28 Mar	Southport (Cup Q)	H	W	4–2
4 Apr	Blackburn R (Cup KO)	A	W	2–1
6 Apr	Blackburn R (Cup KO)	H	W	3–1
11 Apr	Wolverhampton W (Cup KO)	H	W	5–4
18 Apr	Wolverhampton W (Cup KO)†	A	L	0–2
25 Apr	Oldham A (Lancs Cup)	H	W	5–1
2 May	Oldham A (Lancs Cup)	A	W	2–1
9 May	Blackburn R (Lancs Cup)	A	D	1–1
16 May	Blackburn R (Lancs Cup)	H	L	0–1
23 May	Manchester C	A	W	3–1

†after extra time

League & Cup games were played as part of the **North Region Second Championship** (Results counted for each competition)

Football League North Region: Second Championship

	P	W	D	L	F:A	Pts	
Manchester U	19	12	4	3	44:25	28	1st

SEASON 1942–1943 ALL MATCHES

29 Aug	Everton	A	D	2–2
5 Sep	Everton	H	W	2–1
12 Sep	Chester	H	L	0–2
19 Sep	Chester	A	D	2–2
26 Sep	Blackburn R	A	L	2–4
3 Oct	Blackburn R	H	W	5–2
10 Oct	Liverpool	H	L	3–4
17 Oct	Liverpool	A	L	1–2
24 Oct	Stockport Co	A	W	4–1
31 Oct	Stockport Co	H	W	3–1
11 Nov	Manchester C	H	W	2–1
14 Nov	Manchester C	A	W	5–0
21 Nov	Tranmere R	A	W	5–0
28 Nov	Tranmere R	H	W	5–1
5 Dec	Wrexham	H	W	6–1
12 Dec	Wrexham	A	W	5–2
19 Dec	Bolton W	A	W	2–0
25 Dec	Bolton W	H	W	4–0

Football League North Region: First Championship

	P	W	D	L	F:A	Pts	
Manchester U	18	12	2	4	58:26	26	4th

26 Dec	Chester (Cup Q)	H	W	3–0
2 Jan	Chester (Cup Q)	A	L	1–4
9 Jan	Blackpool (Cup Q)	A	D	1–1
16 Jan	Blackpool (Cup Q)	H	W	5–3
23 Jan	Everton (Cup Q)	H	L	1–4
30 Jan	Everton (Cup Q)	A	W	5–0
6 Feb	Manchester C (Cup Q)	A	D	0–0
13 Feb	Manchester C (Cup Q)	H	D	1–1
20 Feb	Crewe A (Cup Q)	H	W	7–0
27 Feb	Crewe A (Cup Q)	A	W	3–2
6 Mar	Manchester C (Cup KO)	H	L	0–1
13 Mar	Manchester C (Cup KO)	A	L	0–2
20 Mar	Bury (Lancs Cup)	H	W	4–1
27 Mar	Bury (Lancs Cup)	A	W	5–3
3 Apr	Crewe A (Lancs Cup)	H	W	4–1
10 Apr	Crewe A (Lancs Cup)	A	W	6–0
17 Apr	Oldham (Lancs Cup)	H	W	3–0
24 Apr	Oldham (Lancs Cup)	A	L	1–3
1 May	Sheffield U	H	W	2–0
8 May	Liverpool (Lancs Cup F)	A	W	3–1
15 May	Liverpool (Lancs Cup F)	H	D	3–3

Games played between 26 Dec and 1 May (inc) formed the **North Region Second Championship**

Football League North Region: Second Championship

	P	W	D	L	F:A	Pts	
Manchester U	19	11	3	5	52:26	25	6th

SEASON 1943–1944 ALL MATCHES

28 Aug	Stockport Co	H	W	6–0
4 Sep	Stockport Co	A	D	3–3
11 Sep	Everton	H	W	4–1
18 Sep	Everton	A	L	1–6
25 Sep	Blackburn R	H	W	2–1
2 Oct	Blackburn R	A	L	1–2
9 Oct	Chester	H	W	3–1
16 Oct	Chester	A	L	4–5
23 Oct	Liverpool	A	W	4–3
30 Oct	Liverpool	H	W	1–0
6 Nov	Manchester C	A	D	2–2
13 Nov	Manchester C	H	W	3–0
20 Nov	Tranmere R	H	W	6–3
27 Nov	Tranmere R	A	W	1–0
4 Dec	Wrexham	A	W	4–1
11 Dec	Wrexham	H	W	5–0
18 Dec	Bolton W	H	W	3–1
25 Dec	Bolton W	A	W	3–1

Football League North Region: First Championship

	P	W	D	L	F:A	Pts	
Manchester U	18	13	2	3	56:30	28	2nd

27 Dec	Halifax T (Cup Q)	H	W	6–2
1 Jan	Halifax T (Cup Q)	A	D	1–1
8 Jan	Stockport Co (Cup Q)	A	W	3–2
15 Jan	Stockport Co (Cup Q)	H	W	4–2
22 Jan	Manchester C (Cup Q)	H	L	1–3
29 Jan	Manchester C (Cup Q)	A	W	3–2
5 Feb	Bury (Cup Q)	A	W	3–0
12 Feb	Bury (Cup Q)	H	D	3–3
19 Feb	Oldham (Cup Q)	H	W	3–2
26 Feb	Oldham (Cup Q)	A	D	1–1
4 Mar	Wrexham (Cup KO)	A	W	4–1
11 Mar	Wrexham (Cup KO)	H	D	2–2
18 Mar	Birmingham (Cup KO)	A	L	1–3
25 Mar	Birmingham (Cup KO)	H	D	1–1
1 Apr	Bolton W	A	L	0–3
8 Apr	Bolton W	H	W	3–2
10 Apr	Manchester C	A	L	1–4
15 Apr	Burnley	H	W	9–0
22 Apr	Burnley	A	D	3–3
29 Apr	Oldham	H	D	0–0
6 May	Oldham	A	W	3–1

Football League North Region: Second Championship

	P	W	D	L	F:A	Pts	
Manchester U	21	10	7	4	55:38	27	9th

SEASON 1944–1945 ALL MATCHES

26 Aug	Everton	A	W	2–1
2 Sep	Everton	H	L	1–3
9 Sep	Stockport Co	H	L	3–4
16 Sep	Stockport Co	A	D	4–4
23 Sep	Bury	H	D	2–2
30 Sep	Bury	A	L	2–4
7 Oct	Chester	A	L	0–2
14 Oct	Chester	H	W	1–0
21 Oct	Tranmere R	H	W	6–1
28 Oct	Tranmere R	A	W	4–2
4 Nov	Liverpool	A	L	2–3
11 Nov	Liverpool	H	L	2–5
18 Nov	Manchester C	H	W	3–2
25 Nov	Manchester C	A	L	0–4
2 Dec	Crewe A	A	W	4–1
9 Dec	Crewe A	H	W	2–0
16 Dec	Wrexham	H	W	1–0
23 Dec	Wrexham	A	L	1–2

Football League North Region: First Championship

	P	W	D	L	F:A	Pts	
Manchester U	18	8	2	8	40:40	18	30th

26 Dec	Sheffield U	A	W	4–3
30 Dec	Oldham (Cup Q)	A	W	4–3
6 Jan	Huddersfield T (Cup Q)	H	W	1–0
13 Jan	Huddersfield T (Cup Q)	A	D	2–2
3 Feb	Manchester C (Cup Q)	H	L	1–3
10 Feb	Manchester C (Cup Q)	A	L	0–2
17 Feb	Bury (Cup Q)	H	W	2–0
24 Feb	Bury (Cup Q)	A	L	1–3
3 Mar	Oldham (Cup Q)	H	W	3–2
10 Mar	Halifax T (Cup Q)	A	L	0–1
17 Mar	Halifax T (Cup Q)	H	W	2–0
24 Mar	Burnley (Cup KO)	A	W	3–2
31 Mar	Burnley (Cup KO)	H	W	4–0
2 Apr	Blackpool	A	L	1–4
7 Apr	Stoke C (Cup KO)	H	W	6–1
14 Apr	Stoke C (Cup KO)	A	W	4–1
21 Apr	Doncaster R (Cup KO)	A	W	2–1
28 Apr	Doncaster R (Cup KO)	H	W	3–1
5 May	Chesterfield (Cup SF)	H	D	1–1
12 May	Chesterfield (Cup SF)	A	W	1–0
19 May	Bolton W (Cup F)	A	L	0–1
26 May	Bolton W (Cup F)	H	D	2–2

Football League North Region: Second Championship

	P	W	D	L	F:A	Pts	
Manchester U	22	13	3	6	47:33	29	9th

SEASON 1945–1946 ALL MATCHES

25 Aug	Huddersfield T	A	L	2–3
1 Sep	Huddersfield T	H	L	2–3
8 Sep	Chesterfield	H	L	0–2
12 Sep	Middlesbrough	A	L	1–2
15 Sep	Chesterfield	A	D	1–1
20 Sep	Stoke C	A	W	2–1
22 Sep	Barnsley	A	D	2–2
29 Sep	Barnsley	H	D	1–1
6 Oct	Everton	H	D	0–0
13 Oct	Everton	A	L	0–3
20 Oct	Bolton W	A	D	1–1
27 Oct	Bolton W	H	W	2–1
3 Nov	Preston NE	H	W	6–1
10 Nov	Preston NE	A	D	2–2
17 Nov	Leeds U	A	D	3–3
24 Nov	Leeds U	H	W	6–1
1 Dec	Burnley	H	D	3–3
8 Dec	Burnley	A	D	2–2
15 Dec	Sunderland	H	W	2–1
22 Dec	Sunderland	A	L	2–4
25 Dec	Sheffield U	A	L	0–1
26 Dec	Sheffield U	H	L	2–3
29 Dec	Middlesbrough	H	W	4–1
12 Jan	Grimsby T	H	W	5–0
19 Jan	Grimsby T	A	L	0–1
2 Feb	Blackpool	H	W	4–2
9 Feb	Liverpool	H	W	2–1
16 Feb	Liverpool	A	W	5–0
23 Feb	Bury	A	D	1–1
2 Mar	Bury	H	D	1–1
9 Mar	Blackburn R	H	W	6–2
16 Mar	Blackburn R	A	W	3–1
23 Mar	Bradford	A	L	1–2
27 Mar	Blackpool	A	W	5–1
30 Mar	Bradford	H	W	4–0
6 Apr	Manchester C	H	L	1–4
13 Apr	Manchester C	A	W	3–1
19 Apr	Newcastle U	A	W	1–0
20 Apr	Sheffield Wed	H	W	4–0
22 Apr	Newcastle U	H	W	4–1
27 Apr	Sheffield Wed	A	L	0–1
4 May	Stoke C	H	W	2–1

Football League North

	P	W	D	L	F:A	Pts	
Manchester U	42	19	11	12	98:62	49	4th

1946–1947

SEASON 1946–1947 FOOTBALL LEAGUE (DIVISION 1)

Date	Opponent			Score										
31 Aug	Grimsby T	H	W	2–1	Crompton	Carey	McGlen	Warner	Chilton	Cockburn	Delaney	Pearson[1]	Hanlon	Rowley[1] Mitten[1]
4 Sep	Chelsea	A	W	3–0	..	..	..	..	..	..	..	.. [1]	..	.. [1]
7 Sep	Charlton A	A	W	*3–1	..	..	..	..	..	..	..	.. 3	..	.. [1] .. [1]
11 Sep	Liverpool	H	W	5–0	..	..	..	..	..	..	..	..	..	.. [1]
14 Sep	Middlesbrough	H	W	1–0	..	..	..	..	..	..	..	..	..	..
18 Sep	Chelsea	H	D	1–1	..	..	Chilton[1]	..	Whalley	..	..	Aston	Pearson	..
							McGlen	..	Chilton	..	.. 1	Pearson	Rowley	..
21 Sep	Stoke C	A	L	2–3	..	Walton	..	..	..	Aston	..	.. 2	.. 2	Wrigglesworth[1]
28 Sep	Arsenal	H	W	5–2	..	Carey	..	..	..	Cockburn	..	..	.. 2	.. [1]
5 Oct	Preston NE	H	D	1–1	..	Walton	..	..	..	Carey	..	..	.. 2	
12 Oct	Sheffield U	A	D	2–2	..		..	..	..	Cockburn	.. 1	..		
19 Oct	Blackpool	A	L	1–3	..		..	Carey	..	Cockburn	..	Morris		
26 Oct	Sunderland	H	L	0–3	..		..	Warner	..	..	..	Rowley	Burke Pearson	Rowley Mitten
2 Nov	Aston Villa	A	D	0–0	Collinson	..	..	..	..	..	..		.. 1 .. 2	.. 1
9 Nov	Derby Co	H	W	4–1	..	..	..	..	..	..	..		.. 1 .. 1	
16 Nov	Everton	A	D	2–2	..	..	..	..	..	..	.. 2		.. 1	.. 2
23 Nov	Huddersfield T	H	W	5–2	..	..	..	Carey	..	..	..		Hanlon[1]	
30 Nov	Wolverhampton W	A	L	2–3	..	Worrall	..	..	..	..	.. 1		Rowley[3]	.. 1
7 Dec	Brentford	H	W	4–1	..	Carey	..	Warner	..	..	Hanlon	.. 1		
14 Dec	Blackburn R	A	L	1–2	..		..	..	..	..	..		.. 2	
25 Dec	Bolton W	A	D	2–2	Crompton		..	..	..	..	Delaney			.. 1
26 Dec	Bolton W	H	W	1–0	..		..	..	..	..	..			
28 Dec	Grimsby T	A	D	0–0	..	Whalley	Aston	..	..	..	..			
4 Jan	Charlton A	H	W	4–1	..	Aston	McGlen	..	..	..	.. 1		Burke[2] .. 1	Buckle[1] .. 1
18 Jan	Middlesbrough	A	W	4–2	..		..	..	..	Carey	..	.. 1	Rowley .. 2	
1 Feb	Arsenal	A	L	2–6	Fielding		..	..	..	Cockburn	..	.. 1	Hanlon	.. 1
5 Feb	Stoke C	H	D	1–1	..		Walton	..	..	..	..			.. 1
22 Feb	Blackpool	H	W	3–0	..		..	..	..	Carey	..		.. 1	Rowley[2]
1 Mar	Sunderland	A	D	1–1	..		..	..	..	Cockburn	.. 1			
8 Mar	Aston Villa	H	W	2–1	..		..	..	..	Carey	..		Burke[1] .. 1	.. 1
15 Mar	Derby Co	A	L	3–4	..	Walton	McGlen	..	..	..	.. 1		.. 1	.. 1
22 Mar	Everton	H	W	3–0	Crompton	Carey	..	.. 1	..	Cockburn	.. 1		.. 1	
29 Mar	Huddersfield T	A	D	2–2	..		Aston	Cockburn	..	McGlen	.. 1	Hanlon[1]		.. 2
5 Apr	Wolverhampton W	H	W	3–1	..		..	..	..	..	.. 1		.. 2	
7 Apr	Leeds U	H	W	3–1	..		..	..	..	.. 1	..		.. 1	
8 Apr	Leeds U	A	W	2–0	..		..	..	..	..	..			Mitten
12 Apr	Brentford	A	D	0–0	..		..	Warner	..	Cockburn	Rowley		Morris	.. 2 Rowley[1]
19 Apr	Blackburn R	H	W	*4–0	..		..	..	Whalley	Delaney	.. 1		Burke	
26 Apr	Portsmouth	A	W	1–0	..		..	Cockburn	Chilton	McGlen	..			
3 May	Liverpool	A	L	0–1	..		..	Warner	..	..	..	Morris	.. 1	
10 May	Preston NE	A	D	1–1	..	Walton	..	..	..	Carey	Buckle	.. 1	Rowley[1]	Mitten[1]
17 May	Portsmouth	H	W	3–0	..		..	..	..	McGlen	Hanlon	.. 2	.. 3	.. 1
26 May	Sheffield U	H	W	6–2	..		..	..	..					

FA Cup

Date	Opponent			Score										
11 Jan	Bradford (3)	A	W	3–0	Crompton	Aston	McGlen	Warner	Chilton	Carey	Delaney	Morris	Rowley[2] Pearson	Buckle[1]
25 Jan	Nottingham F (4)	H	L	0–2	Fielding	..	..	..	..	..	..	..	.. ..	..

Appearances (goals)

Aston 21 · Buckle 5 (3) · Burke 13 (9) · Carey 31 · Chilton 41 (1) · Cockburn 32 · Collinson 7 · Crompton 29 · Delaney 37 (8) · Fielding 6 · Hanlon 27 (7) · McGlen 33 (1) · Mitten 20 (8) · Morris 24 (8) · Pearson 42 (19) · Rowley 37 (26) · Walton 15 · Warner 34 (1) · Whalley 3 · Worrall 1 · Wrigglesworth 4 (2) · Own goals 2 · Total 21 players (95)

Football League

	P	W	D	L	F:A	Pts	
Liverpool	42	25	7	10	84:52	57	1st
Manchester U	42	22	12	8	95:54	56	2nd

1947–1948

SEASON 1947–1948 FOOTBALL LEAGUE (DIVISION 1)

Date	Opponent			Score										
23 Aug	Middlesbrough	A	D	2–2	Crompton	Carey	Aston	Warner	Chilton	McGlen	Delaney	Morris[1]	Rowley[2] Pearson[1]	Mitten
27 Aug	Liverpool	H	W	2–0	..	..	..	..	..	..	..	.. 1	.. 4 .. 1	..
30 Aug	Charlton A	H	W	6–2	..	..	..	..	..	..	..		 1	.. 1
3 Sep	Liverpool	A	D	2–2	..	..	..	..	..	..	.. 1			
6 Sep	Arsenal	A	L	1–2	..	..	..	..	..	..	..			
8 Sep	Burnley	A	D	0–0	..	..	..	..	..	..	..			
13 Sep	Sheffield U	H	L	0–1	..	..	..	..	..	..	..	Burke	..	Rowley
20 Sep	Manchester C	A	D	0–0	..	..	..	..	..	..	..	Rowley	..	Mitten
27 Sep	Preston NE	A	L	1–2	..	Aston	McGlen	..	..	Cockburn	Dale	Hanlon .. 1	..	Rowley
4 Oct	Stoke C	H	D	1–1	..	..	..	..	..	Pearson	Delaney	.. 1	Rowley[1]	Mitten[1]
11 Oct	Grimsby T	H	L	3–4	..	..	..	..	..	McGlen	Pearson			
18 Oct	Sunderland	A	L	0–1	..	Walton	Aston	Carey	..	Cockburn	.. 1	Morris	Rowley[1] Pearson[2]	.. 1
25 Oct	Aston Villa	H	W	2–0	..	Aston	Worrall	..	..	..	.. 2	.. 4		
1 Nov	Wolverhampton W	A	W	6–2	..	..	..	..	..	..	.. 1			
8 Nov	Huddersfield T	H	D	4–4	..	..	..	.. 1	..	..	.. 1			
15 Nov	Derby Co	A	D	1–1	Pegg	..	..	..	.. 1	..	.. 1			
22 Nov	Everton	H	D	2–2	..	..	Walton	..	..	..	.. 3	.. 1		
29 Nov	Chelsea	A	W	4–0	Crompton	..	Aston	..	..	..	..	.. 1		
6 Dec	Blackpool	H	D	1–1	..	Walton	Aston	..	..	..	.. 1		.. 2	
13 Dec	Blackburn R	A	D	1–1	..	..	..	..	..	..	..			
20 Dec	Middlesbrough	H	W	2–1	..	..	..	Anderson	..	..	.. 2	.. 1		
25 Dec	Portsmouth	H	W	3–2	..	..	..	Carey	..	..	.. 2	.. 1		.. 2
27 Dec	Portsmouth	A	W	3–1	..	Carey	..	Anderson	..	.. 1	.. 3			
1 Jan	Burnley	H	W	5–0	..	..	..	..	..	.. 1		.. 1		
3 Jan	Charlton A	A	W	2–1	..	..	..	Warner	..	Lynn	.. 1			
17 Jan	Arsenal	H	D	1–1	..	..	..	Anderson	..	Cockburn	.. 1			
31 Jan	Sheffield U	A	L	1–2	Brown	..	..	..	..	..	.. 1			
14 Feb	Preston NE	H	D	1–1	Crompton	..	..	Warner	..	..	.. 1			Buckle[1]
21 Feb	Stoke C	A	W	2–0	..	..	..	Anderson	..	..	.. 1		.. 1	Mitten[1]
6 Mar	Sunderland	H	W	3–1	..	..	..	..	..	..	Hanlon		.. 1	.. 1
17 Mar	Grimsby T	A	D	1–1	..	..	..	..	..	.. 1	Morris[1]			
20 Mar	Wolverhampton W	H	W	3–2	..	..	..	Warner	..	Anderson	.. 1		.. 1	
22 Mar	Aston Villa	A	W	1–0	..	..	..	Anderson	..	Lynn	..			
26 Mar	Bolton W	H	L	0–2	..	..	..	..	..	..	..		.. 1	
27 Mar	Huddersfield T	A	W	2–0	Brown	..	..	Warner	McGlen	Cockburn	..	Burke[1]		
29 Mar	Bolton W	A	W	1–0	..	..	..	Anderson[1]	Chilton	..	Hanlon	Rowley		
3 Apr	Derby Co	H	W	1–0	Crompton	..	..	..	..	..	Delaney	Rowley	Rowley[1]	
7 Apr	Manchester C	H	D	1–1	..	..	..	..	..	Lowrie	Hanlon	Burke	Cassidy	
10 Apr	Everton	A	L	0–2	..	..	Ball	..	..	..	Buckle	..	Rowley[1] Pearson[2]	.. 1
17 Apr	Chelsea	H	W	5–0	..	Carey	..	..	..	Cockburn	Delaney[1]	Rowley[1]		
28 Apr	Blackpool	A	L	0–1	..	..	..	..	..	..	Buckle	Hanlon	.. 3	
1 May	Blackburn	H	W	4–1	..	..	..	..	..	..	Delaney[1]	Burke		

FA Cup

Date	Opponent			Score										
10 Jan	Aston Villa (3)	A	W	6–4	Crompton	Carey	Aston	Anderson	Chilton	Cockburn	Delaney[1]	Morris[2]	Rowley[1] Pearson[2]	Mitten
24 Jan	Liverpool (4) (at Goodison Park)	H	W	3–0	..	..	..	..	..	..	..	.. 1	.. ..	.. 1
7 Feb	Charlton A (5) (at Huddersfield)	H	·W	2–0	..	..	..	Warner[1]	..	..	..	..		.. 1
28 Feb	Preston NE (6) (at Maine Road)	H	W	4–1	..	..	..	Anderson	..	..	..	.. 1	.. 2	.. 1
13 Mar	Derby Co (SF) (at Hillsborough)	N	W	3–1	..	..	..	..	..	..	..	.. 3		
24 Apr	Blackpool (F) (at Wembley)	N	W	4–2	..	..	..	.. 1	..	..	..	.. 2	.. 1	

Appearances (goals)

Anderson 18 (1) · Aston 42 · Ball 1 · Brown 3 · Buckle 3 (1) · Burke 6 (1) · Carey 37 (1) · Cassidy 1 · Chilton 41 · Cockburn 26 (1) · Crompton 37 · Dale 2 · Delaney 36 (8) · Hanlon 8 (1) · Lowrie 2 · Lynn 3 · McGlen 13 · Mitten 38 (8) · Morris 38 (18) · Pearson 40 (18) · Pegg 2 · Rowley 39 (23) · Walton 6 · Warner 15 · Worrall 5 · Total 25 players (81)

Football League

	P	W	D	L	F:A	Pts	
Arsenal	42	23	13	6	81:32	59	1st
Manchester U	42	19	14	9	81:48	52	2nd

SEASON 1948–1949 FOOTBALL LEAGUE (DIVISION 1)

Date	Opponent			Score											
21 Aug	Derby Co	H	L	1–2	Crompton	Carey	Aston	Anderson	Chilton	Cockburn	Delaney	Morris	Rowley[2]	Pearson[1]	Mitten
23 Aug	Blackpool	A	W	3–0	..	Ball	Carey	..	..	McGlen	..	..	..	..	..
28 Aug	Arsenal	A	W	1–0	..	Carey	Aston	..	..	Cockburn	..	..	..	..	.. 1
1 Sep	Blackpool	H	L	3–4	Brown	..	..	..	..	..	..	1	1	..	1
4 Sep	Huddersfield T	H	W	4–1	Crompton	..	..	..	..	McGlen	..	1	..	2	1
8 Sep	Wolverhampton W	A	L	2–3	..	..	..	..	..	..	..	1	1	..	..
11 Sep	Manchester C	A	D	0–0	..	..	..	Cockburn	..	..	..	..	..	..	..
15 Sep	Wolverhampton W	H	W	2–0	..	..	..	Anderson	..	Cockburn	Buckle[1]	..	..	1	..
18 Sep	Sheffield U	A	D	2–2	..	..	..	Cockburn	..	McGlen	1	..	..	1	..
25 Sep	Aston Villa	H	W	3–1	..	..	..	..	..	..	Delaney	Hanlon	..	1	2
2 Oct	Sunderland	A	L	1–2	..	..	..	..	..	..	..	Buckle	1	..	..
9 Oct	Charlton A	H	D	1–1	..	Ball	..	Anderson	..	Warner	..	Morris	Burke[1]	Rowley	..
16 Oct	Stoke C	A	L	1–2	..	Carey	..	..	..	Cockburn	..	1	Rowley	Pearson	..
23 Oct	Burnley	H	D	1–1	..	..	..	..	..	..	..	..	..	..	1
30 Oct	Preston NE	A	W	6–1	..	..	..	Warner	..	..	..	1	1	2	2
6 Nov	Everton	H	W	2–0	..	..	..	..	..	..	1	1	..	..	..
13 Nov	Chelsea	A	D	1–1	..	..	..	Anderson	..	..	..	..	1	..	..
20 Nov	Birmingham C	H	W	3–0	..	..	..	Cockburn	..	McGlen	..	1	1	1	..
27 Nov	Middlesbrough	A	W	4–1	..	..	..	..	..	..	1	..	3	..	..
4 Dec	Newcastle U	H	D	1–1	..	..	..	..	..	..	..	..	..	..	1
11 Dec	Portsmouth	A	D	2–2	..	..	..	..	..	1	..	..	..	..	1
18 Dec	Derby Co	A	W	3–1	..	..	..	..	..	..	..	Pearson[1]	Burke[2]	Rowley	..
25 Dec	Liverpool	H	D	0–0	..	..	..	..	..	..	..	1	1	..	..
26 Dec	Liverpool	A	W	2–0	..	..	..	..	..	..	Buckle	Morris	1	Pearson	..
1 Jan	Arsenal	H	W	2–0	..	..	..	..	..	..	Delaney	Morris	Rowley	1	..
22 Jan	Manchester C	H	D	0–0	..	..	..	..	..	..	..	..	Rowley	..	..
19 Feb	Aston Villa	A	L	1–2	..	..	..	..	..	..	..	Pearson	Burke	Rowley[1]	..
5 Mar	Charlton A	A	W	3–2	..	..	..	..	..	..	..	Downie[1]	Rowley[1]	Pearson[2]	..
12 Mar	Stoke C	H	W	3–0	..	..	..	..	..	..	..	..	..	..	1
19 Mar	Birmingham C	A	L	0–1	..	..	..	..	..	..	..	Anderson	..	..	..
6 Apr	Huddersfield T	A	L	1–2	..	Ball	Anderson	..	..	..	Downie	Burke	Rowley[1]	..
9 Apr	Chelsea	H	D	1–1	..	..	..	..	..	..	Buckle	..	..	..	1
15 Apr	Bolton W	A	W	1–0	..	Ball	Aston	Lowrie	..	Cockburn	Carey[1]	..	Rowley[2]	Pearson	..
16 Apr	Burnley	A	W	2–0	..	..	..	..	..	..	..	..	..	..	..
18 Apr	Bolton W	H	W	3–0	..	..	..	..	..	..	Delaney	Carey	2	..	1
21 Apr	Sunderland	H	L	1–2	..	..	..	..	..	..	..	..	..	..	1
23 Apr	Preston NE	H	D	2–2	..	Carey	..	..	..	..	..	Downie[2]	..	..	..
27 Apr	Everton	A	L	0–2	..	..	..	..	..	..	..	..	Cassidy	..	..
30 Apr	Newcastle U	A	W	1–0	..	..	..	..	..	..	..	..	Burke[1]	..	..
2 May	Middlesbrough	H	W	1–0	..	..	..	..	..	..	..	..	Rowley[1]	..	..
4 May	Sheffield U	H	W	3–2	..	..	..	Cockburn	..	McGlen	..	1	..	1	1
7 May	Portsmouth	H	W	3–2	..	..	..	Anderson	..	Cockburn	..	..	2	..	1

FA Cup

Date	Opponent			Score											
8 Jan	Bournemouth (3)	H	W	6–0	Crompton	Carey	Aston	Cockburn	Chilton	McGlen	Delaney	Pearson[1]	Burke[2]	Rowley[2]	Mitten[1]
29 Jan	Bradford (4)	H	D	1–1	..	..	..	..	..	..	..	Morris	Rowley	Pearson	1
5 Feb	Bradford (4R)	A	D	1–1	..	..	..	..	..	..	Buckle	Pearson	Burke	Rowley	1
7 Feb	Bradford (4R)	H	W	5–0	..	..	..	..	..	..	..	1	2	2	..
12 Feb	Yeovil (5)	H	W	8–0	..	..	..	..	..	..	Delaney	..	2	2	1
26 Feb	Hull C (6)	A	W	1–0	..	Ball	..	..	..	..	..	1	..	..	..
26 Mar	Wolverhampton W (SF) (at Hillsborough)	N	D	1–1	..	Carey	..	..	..	..	..	Anderson	Rowley	Pearson	1
2 Apr	Wolverhampton W (SFR) (at Goodison)	N	L	0–1	..	..	..	..	..	..	..	Pearson	Burke	Rowley	..

Appearances (goals)

Anderson 15 · Aston 39 · Ball 8 · Brown 1 · Buckle 5 (2) · Burke 9 (6) · Carey 41 (1) · Cassidy 1 · Chilton 42 · Cockburn 36 · Crompton 41 · Delaney 36 (4) · Downie 12 (5) · Hanlon 1 · Lowrie 8 · McGlen 23 (1) · Mitten 42 (18) · Morris 21 (6) · Pearson 39 (14) · Rowley 39 (20) · Warner 3 · Total 21 players (77)

Football League

	P	W	D	L	F:A	Pts	
Portsmouth	42	25	8	9	84:42	58	1st
Manchester U	42	21	11	10	77:44	53	2nd

SEASON 1949–1950 FOOTBALL LEAGUE (DIVISION 1)

Date	Opponent			Score											
20 Aug	Derby Co	A	W	1–0	Crompton	Carey	Aston	Warner	Lynn	Cockburn	Delaney	Downie	Rowley[1]	Pearson	Mitten
24 Aug	Bolton W	H	W	3–0	..	..	..	..	..	..	..	..	1	..	1
27 Aug	W B A	H	D	1–2	..	..	..	..	..	..	..	Pearson[1]	..	Birch	..
31 Aug	Bolton W	A	W	2–1	..	..	..	..	..	..	..	1	..	Buckle	1
3 Sep	Manchester C	H	W	2–1	..	..	..	..	..	..	..	2	..	..	..
7 Sep	Liverpool	A	D	1–1	..	..	..	Lowrie	..	Chilton	..	..	..	..	1
10 Sep	Chelsea	A	D	1–1	..	..	..	..	..	..	..	..	1	..	..
17 Sep	Stoke C	H	D	2–2	..	..	..	Chilton	..	Cockburn	..	..	2	..	..
24 Sep	Burnley	A	L	0–1	..	..	..	..	..	..	..	..	..	..	..
1 Oct	Sunderland	H	L	1–3	..	..	..	Lowrie	Chilton	..	..	1	..	..	..
8 Oct	Charlton A	H	W	3–2	..	Ball	..	Warner	..	McGlen	..	Bogan	1	Pearson	2
15 Oct	Aston Villa	A	W	4–0	..	..	Carey	..	Lynn	Cockburn	..	1	1	..	2
22 Oct	Wolverhampton W	H	W	3–0	..	Carey	Aston	..	Chilton	..	..	1	..	2	..
29 Oct	Portsmouth	A	D	0–0	..	..	..	..	..	..	..	..	..	..	..
5 Nov	Huddersfield T	H	W	6–0	Feehan	..	..	Cockburn	..	McGlen	1	..	2	2	1
12 Nov	Everton	A	D	0–0	Crompton	..	..	Warner	..	Cockburn	..	..	..	..	..
19 Nov	Middlesbrough	H	W	2–0	..	..	..	Cockburn	..	McGlen	..	..	1	1	..
26 Nov	Blackpool	A	D	3–3	Feehan	..	..	..	..	..	..	Rowley	Bogan[1]	2	..
3 Dec	Newcastle U	H	D	1–1	Wood	..	..	..	..	..	..	Downie	..	..	1
10 Dec	Fulham	A	L	0–1	Feehan	..	..	..	..	..	..	Bogan	Rowley	..	..
17 Dec	Derby Co	H	L	0–1	..	..	..	..	..	..	..	..	..	..	..
24 Dec	W B A	A	W	2–1	..	..	..	..	..	..	..	1	1	..	..
26 Dec	Arsenal	H	W	2–0	..	..	..	Warner	..	..	..	..	..	2	..
27 Dec	Arsenal	A	D	0–0	..	..	..	..	..	..	..	..	..	..	..
31 Dec	Manchester C	A	W	2–1	..	..	..	..	..	1	..	..	1	..	..
14 Jan	Chelsea	H	W	1–0	Lancaster	..	..	Cockburn	..	..	..	Downie	..	..	1
21 Jan	Stoke C	A	L	1–3	Feehan	..	..	..	..	..	..	Bogan	..	..	1
4 Feb	Burnley	H	W	3–2	Lancaster	..	..	Warner	..	Cockburn	..	..	2	..	1
18 Feb	Sunderland	A	D	2–2	Feehan	..	..	..	..	1	..	Clempson	1	Downie	..
25 Feb	Charlton A	A	W	2–1	Crompton	Ball	..	Carey[1]	..	..	..	Downie	1	Pearson	..
8 Mar	Aston Villa	H	W	7–0	..	..	..	Warner	Carey	..	..	2	1	..	4
11 Mar	Middlesbrough	A	W	3–2	..	..	..	..	Chilton	Carey	..	2	1	..	..
15 Mar	Liverpool	H	D	0–0	..	Carey	..	..	..	Cockburn	..	..	..	..	..
18 Mar	Blackpool	H	L	1–2	..	..	..	..	..	..	..	1	Delaney[1]	..	..
25 Mar	Huddersfield T	A	L	1–3	..	Ball	..	..	..	Bogan	..	Carey	..	..
1 Apr	Everton	H	D	1–1	Feehan	..	..	Carey	..	Delaney	..	Rowley	..	..
7 Apr	Birmingham C	H	L	0–2	..	..	..	..	..	..	1	Pearson	..	Downie	..
8 Apr	Wolverhampton W	A	D	1–1	Crompton	..	..	..	..	..	..	..	1	..	..
10 Apr	Birmingham C	A	D	0–0	..	..	..	..	..	..	..	..	..	..	..
15 Apr	Portsmouth	H	L	0–2	..	McNulty	Ball	Whitefood	..	..	..	..	..	..	..
22 Apr	Newcastle U	A	L	1–2	..	Ball	Aston	Warner	..	..	..	..	..	1	..
29 Apr	Fulham	H	W	3–0	..	McNulty	Ball	Aston	..	..	1	..	2	..	..

FA Cup

Date	Opponent			Score											
7 Jan	Weymouth (3)	H	W	4–0	Feehan	Carey	Aston	Cockburn	Chilton	McGlen	Delaney[1]	Bogan	Rowley[2]	Pearson[1]	Mitten
28 Jan	Watford (4)	A	W	1–0	Lancaster	..	..	Warner	..	Cockburn	..	..	..	1	..
11 Feb	Portsmouth (5)	H	D	3–3	..	..	..	..	..	..	..	..	1	..	2
15 Feb	Portsmouth (5R)	A	W	3–1	Feehan	..	..	..	..	..	1	..	Downie[1]	..	1
4 Mar	Chelsea (6)	A	L	0–2	Crompton	..	..	..	..	..	..	Downie	..	Pearson	..

Appearances (goals)

Aston 40 · Ball 13 · Birch 1 · Bogan 18 (4) · Buckle 7 · Carey 38 (1) · Chilton 35 (1) · Clempson 1 · Cockburn 35 (1) · Crompton 27 · Delaney 42 (4) · Downie 18 (6) · Feehan 12 · Lancaster 2 · Lowrie 3 · Lynn 10 · McGlen 13 · McNulty 2 · Mitten 42 (16) · Pearson 41 (15) · Rowley 39 (20) · Warner 21 · Whitefoot 1 · Wood 1 · Own goals 1 · Total 24 players (69)

Football League

	P	W	D	L	F:A	Pts	
Portsmouth	42	22	9	11	74:38	53	1st
Manchester U	42	18	14	10	69:44	50	4th

SEASON 1950–1951 FOOTBALL LEAGUE (DIVISION 1)

Date	Opponent			Score											
19 Aug	Fulham	H	W	1–0	Allen	Carey	Aston	McIlvenney	Chilton	Cockburn	Delaney	Downie	Rowley[1]	Pearson[1]	McGlen
23 Aug	Liverpool	A	L	1–2					Gibson			1			
26 Aug	Bolton W	A	L	0–1					Gibson						
30 Aug	Liverpool	H	W	1–0							Bogan[1]				
2 Sep	Blackpool	H	W	1–0									2	1	
4 Sep	Aston Villa	A	W	3–1											
9 Sep	Tottenham H	A	L	0–1											
13 Sep	Aston Villa	H	D	0–0							Delaney[1]	Bogan	Cassidy	Pearson[1]	McShane
16 Sep	Charlton A	H	W	3–0								Downie	1	2	
23 Sep	Middlesbrough	A	W	2–1											
30 Sep	Wolverhampton W	A	D	0–0									1	1	1
7 Oct	Sheffield Wed	H	W	3–1			Redman		Jones M	McGlen					
14 Oct	Arsenal	A	L	0–3			Aston		Chilton	Cockburn					
21 Oct	Portsmouth	H	D	0–0				1		McGlen			2	1	
28 Oct	Everton	A	W	4–1	Crompton				Jones M	Cockburn		Bogan			1
4 Nov	Burnley	H	D	1–1	Allen				Chilton			Pearson	Downie		
11 Nov	Chelsea	A	L	0–1									Birch		
18 Nov	Stoke C	H	D	0–0							Bogan			1	
25 Nov	W B A	A	W	1–0		McNulty									
2 Dec	Newcastle U	H	L	1–2		Carey					Birkett[1]		Aston[2]		
9 Dec	Huddersfield T	A	W	3–2		McNulty	McGlen					2		Downie	
16 Dec	Fulham	A	D	2–2								1	1		
23 Dec	Bolton W	H	L	2–3		Carey							1	Birch	Rowley
25 Dec	Sunderland	A	L	1–2									1	Bogan[2]	1
26 Dec	Sunderland	H	L	3–5							McShane			Pearson	
13 Jan	Tottenham H	H	W	2–1			Redman				Birkett[1]	Birch[1]	1		
20 Jan	Charlton A	A	W	2–1	Crompton Allen							Bogan			1
3 Feb	Middlesbrough	H	W	1–0								Pearson	Birch[1]		1
17 Feb	Wolverhampton W	H	W	2–1		McNulty	Carey				McShane[1]	1		Downie[1]	1
26 Feb	Sheffield Wed	A	W	4–0		Carey	McGlen		Jones M				2	1	
3 Mar	Arsenal	H	W	3–1			Redman	Whitefoot							
10 Mar	Portsmouth	A	D	0–0					Chilton	McGlen			1	1	
17 Mar	Everton	H	W	3–0				Gibson					1	1	
23 Mar	Derby Co	H	W	2–0								Clempson	1	1	
24 Mar	Burnley	A	W	2–1						1		1	1		1
26 Mar	Derby Co	A	W	4–2				Cockburn				Pearson[1]	3		
31 Mar	Chelsea	H	W	4–1								1			
7 Apr	Stoke C	A	L	0–2									1	1	
14 Apr	W B A	H	W	3–0				Gibson				1	1		1
21 Apr	Newcastle U	A	W	2–0				Cockburn			2		2	1	1
28 Apr	Huddersfield T	H	W	6–0										1	
5 May	Blackpool	A	D	1–1											

FA Cup

Date	Opponent			Score											
6 Jan	Oldham (3)	H	W	*4–1	Allen	Carey	McGlen	Lowrie	Chilton	Cockburn	Birkett	Pearson[3]	Aston[1]	Birch[1]	McShane Rowley[1]
27 Jan	Leeds U (4)	H	W	4–0		Redman	Gibson					1			
10 Feb	Arsenal (5)	H	W	1–0											
24 Feb	Birmingham C (6)	A	L	0–1		McNulty	Carey								

Appearances (goals)

Allen 40 · Aston 41 (9) · Birch 8 (4) · Birkett 9 (2) · Bogan 11 (3) · Carey 39 · Cassidy 1 · Chilton 38 · Clempson 2 · Cockburn 35 · Crompton 2 · Delaney 13 (1) · Downie 29 (10) · Gibson 32 · Jones M 4 · McGlen 26 · McIlvenney 2 · McNulty 4 · McShane 30 (7) · Pearson 39 (18) · Redman 16 · Rowley 39 (14) · Whitefoot 2 · Total 23 players (74)

Football League

	P	W	D	L	F:A	Pts	
Tottenham H	42	25	10	7	82:44	60	1st
Manchester U	42	24	8	10	74:40	56	2nd

SEASON 1951–1952 FOOTBALL LEAGUE (DIVISION 1)

Date	Opponent			Score											
18 Aug	W B A	A	D	3–3	Allen	Carey	Redman	Cockburn	Chilton	McGlen	McShane	Pearson[1]	Rowley[3]	Downie	Bond
22 Aug	Middlesbrough	H	W	4–2				Gibson		Cockburn			1	1	
25 Aug	Newcastle U	H	W	2–1									1		
29 Aug	Middlesbrough	A	W	4–1											
1 Sep	Bolton W	A	L	0–1							Berry		2	1	
5 Sep	Charlton A	H	W	3–2								1	3		McShane
8 Sep	Stoke C	H	W	4–0										2	
12 Sep	Charlton A	A	D	2–2							1				1
15 Sep	Manchester C	A	W	2–1								Cassidy Rowley			
22 Sep	Tottenham H	A	L	0–2								Walton	Aston[1]	Pearson	Rowley
29 Sep	Preston NE	H	L	1–2							1	Rowley[2]			McShane 1
6 Oct	Derby Co	H	W	2–1								Pearson[2]		Downie	Bond[1]
13 Oct	Aston Villa	A	W	5–2		McNulty				McGlen		Downie		Pearson	McShane
20 Oct	Sunderland	H	L	0–1		Carey				Cockburn	McShane	Pearson[1]	1	Birch	Bond
27 Oct	Wolverhampton W	A	W	2–0											
3 Nov	Huddersfield T	H	D	1–1							Berry	1	Aston	Downie	Rowley[1]
10 Nov	Chelsea	A	L	2–4											
17 Nov	Portsmouth	H	L	1–3										2	
24 Nov	Liverpool	A	D	0–0	Crompton		Byrne	Blanchflower					Rowley		Bond
1 Dec	Blackpool	H	W	3–1		McNulty		Carey			1	1	1		
8 Dec	Arsenal	A	W	*3–1								2	2		
15 Dec	W B A	H	W	5–1	Allen					1	1				1
22 Dec	Newcastle U	A	D	2–2							1				1
25 Dec	Fulham	H	W	3–2				Chilton	Jones M		1	1			
26 Dec	Fulham	A	D	3–3								1			1
29 Dec	Bolton W	H	W	1–0											
5 Jan	Stoke C	A	D	0–0				Carey[1]	Chilton			Aston		Rowley	
19 Jan	Manchester C	H	D	1–1							1	Clempson	1	Pearson[1]	
26 Jan	Tottenham H	H	W	*2–0									1	1	1
9 Feb	Preston NE	A	W	2–1									1		
16 Feb	Derby Co	A	W	3–0	Crompton						1		1		1
1 Mar	Aston Villa	H	D	1–1						1					1
8 Mar	Sunderland	A	W	2–1								1	1		
15 Mar	Wolverhampton W	H	W	2–0								1	1	1	
22 Mar	Huddersfield T	A	L	2–3						Whitefoot		Downie	Rowley	Downie	Bond
5 Apr	Portsmouth	A	L	0–1			Aston			Cockburn				Pearson	Byrne[1]
11 Apr	Burnley	A	D	1–1	Allen					Whitefoot	Downie[1]	Rowley[1]	Pearson		2
12 Apr	Liverpool	H	W	4–0				1			1		1	1	2
14 Apr	Burnley	H	W	6–1						Cockburn	1			1	1
19 Apr	Blackpool	A	D	2–2									3	2	1
21 Apr	Chelsea	H	W	*3–0											
26 Apr	Arsenal	H	W	6–1											

F A Cup

Date	Opponent			Score											
12 Jan	Hull City (3)	H	L	0–2	Allen	McNulty	Byrne	Carey	Chilton	Cockburn	Berry	Pearson	Rowley	Downie	Bond

Appearances (goals)

Allen 33 · Aston 18 (4) · Berry 36 (6) · Birch 2 · Blanchflower 1 · Bond 19 (4) · Byrne 24 (7) · Carey 38 (3) · Cassidy 1 · Chilton 42 · Clempson 8 (2) · Cockburn 38 (2) · Crompton 9 · Downie 31 (11) · Gibson 17 · Jones M 3 · McGlen 2 · McNulty 24 · McShane 12 (1) · Pearson 41 (22) · Redman 18 · Rowley 40 (30) · Walton 2 · Whitefoot 3 · Own goals 3 · Total 24 players (95)

Football League

	P	W	D	L	F:A	Pts	
Manchester U	42	23	11	8	95:52	57	1st

SEASON 1952–1953 FOOTBALL LEAGUE (DIVISION 1)

Date	Opponent			Score	Wood	McNulty	Aston	Carey	Chilton	Gibson	Berry	Downie	Rowley	Pearson	Byrne
23 Aug	Chelsea	H	W	2–0	Wood	McNulty	Aston	Carey	Chilton	Gibson	Berry[1]	Downie[1]	Rowley[1]	Pearson	Byrne
27 Aug	Arsenal	A	L	1–2	Crompton	..	..	..	..	Cockburn	..	..	..	..	..
30 Aug	Manchester C	A	L	1–2	..	..	..	..	..	..	..	..[1]	..	..	..
3 Sep	Arsenal	H	D	0–0	..	Carey	Byrne	Gibson	..	..	..	Clempson	Aston	..	Bond
6 Sep	Portsmouth	A	L	0–2	..	McNulty	..	..	..	..	..	..	..	..	Rowley / Byrne
10 Sep	Derby Co	A	W	3–2	..	..	Aston	Carey	..	Gibson	..[1]	Downie	Rowley	..[3]	Byrne
13 Sep	Bolton W	H	W	1–0	Allen	..	..	..	..	..	..	..[1]	..[2]	..	..
20 Sep	Aston Villa	A	D	3–3	Wood	..	..	..	..	..	..	..	..	..	..
27 Sep	Sunderland	H	L	0–1	..	..	..	Jones M	..	..	..	Clempson	..	..	..
4 Oct	Wolverhampton W	A	L	2–6	Allen	..	..	Carey	..	..	..	Rowley[2]	..	..	Scott
11 Oct	Stoke C	H	L	0–2	Wood	..	..	..	..	..	..	Clempson	Downie	..	..
18 Oct	Preston NE	A	W	5–0	Crompton	Carey	Byrne	Whitefoot	..	..	..	Downie	Aston[2]	Pearson[2]	Rowley[1]
25 Oct	Burnley	H	L	1–3	..	..	..	..	..	..	..[2]	..	..[1]	..	..
1 Nov	Tottenham H	A	W	2–1	..	McNulty	..	..	..	..	..	..	..	..	McShane
8 Nov	Sheffield Wed	H	D	1–1	..	..	..	..	..	..	..	..	..[1]	..[1]	..
15 Nov	Cardiff C	A	W	2–1	..	..	..	Cockburn	..	..	..	..	..[1]	..[1]	..
22 Nov	Newcastle U	H	D	2–2	..	..	..	..	..	..	..	..	..[1]	..[1]	..
29 Nov	W B A	A	L	1–3	..	..	..	..	..	..	..	..	Lewis[1]	..	..
6 Dec	Middlesbrough	H	W	3–2	..	..	..	Carey	..	Cockburn	..	Doherty	Aston[1]	..[2]	Pegg
13 Dec	Liverpool	A	W	2–1	..	Foulkes	..	..	..	..	..	..	..[2]	..[1]	..
20 Dec	Chelsea	A	W	3–2	..	..	..	..	..	..	..	..[2]	..[1]	..	..
25 Dec	Blackpool	A	D	0–0	Wood	McNulty	..	..	..	..	..	..	..	..	..
26 Dec	Blackpool	H	W	2–1	..	..	..	..	..[1]	..	..	Lewis[1]	..	..	..
1 Jan	Derby Co	H	W	1–0	..	Redman	..	..	..	..	..	Aston	Lewis[1]	..	..
3 Jan	Manchester C	H	D	1–1	..	Aston	..	..	..	Whitefoot	..	Doherty	..[1]	..	..
17 Jan	Portsmouth	H	W	1–0	..	..	..	..	..	Cockburn	..	Rowley	..[1]	..	..
24 Jan	Bolton W	A	L	1–2	..	..	..	..	..	..	..	..	..[1]	..	..
7 Feb	Aston Villa	H	W	3–1	..	..	..	..	..	..	..	Lewis[1]	Rowley[2]	..	..
18 Feb	Sunderland	A	D	2–2	Carey	..	..	Gibson	..	..	..	..	..	..	..[1]
21 Feb	Wolverhampton W	H	L	0–3	Wood	..	..	Carey	..	..	..	..	..	..	..
28 Feb	Stoke C	A	L	1–3	Crompton	McNulty	..	Chilton	Jones M	Gibson	..[1]	Aston	..	Downie	..[2]
7 Mar	Preston NE	H	W	5–2	..	Aston	..[1]	Carey	Chilton	Cockburn	..	Rowley[1]	Taylor T[2]	Pearson	..
14 Mar	Burnley	A	L	1–2	..	..	..	..	..	..	..	..	..	..	..[1]
25 Mar	Tottenham H	H	W	3–2	..	..	..	Gibson	..	..	..	..	..	..[2]	..
28 Mar	Sheffield Wed	A	D	0–0	..	..	..	Carey	..	..	..	..	..	..	..
3 Apr	Charlton A	A	D	2–2	..	..	..[1]	..	..	Blanchflower	..[2]	..	..[1]	..	..
4 Apr	Cardiff C	H	L	1–4	..	..	..	Gibson	..	Edwards	..	..	..	..	..
6 Apr	Charlton A	H	W	3–2	..	McNulty	..	Carey	..	Whitefoot	..	Lewis	..[2]	..	Rowley[1]
11 Apr	Newcastle U	A	W	2–1	Olive	..	..	..	..	..	Viollet[1]	Pearson[1]	Aston	Taylor T[2]	..
18 Apr	W B A	H	D	2–2	..	..	..	..	..	..	Berry[1]	Downie	Taylor T	Pearson[1]	..[1]
20 Apr	Liverpool	H	W	3–1	Crompton	Aston	..	..	..	..	..	Downie	Taylor T	Pearson[1]	..
25 Apr	Middlesbrough	A	L	0–5	..	McNulty	..	..	..	..	..	Viollet	Aston	Taylor T	..

FA Cup

Date	Opponent			Score											
10 Jan	Millwall (3)	A	W	1–0	Wood	Aston	Byrne	Carey	Chilton	Cockburn	Berry	Downie	Lewis	Pearson[1]	Rowley
31 Jan	Walthamstow A (4)	H	D	1–1	..	..	..	..	..	..	..	..	..[1]	..	..
5 Feb	Walthamstow A (4R) (at Highbury)	A	W	5–2	..	..	..[1]	..	..	..	..	Lewis[1]	Rowley[2]	..[1]	Pegg
14 Feb	Everton (5)	A	L	1–2	..	..	..	..	..	..	..	..	..[1]	..	..

Appearances (goals)

Allen 2 · Aston 40 (8) · Berry 40 (7) · Blanchflower 1 · Bond 1 · Byrne 40 (2) · Carey 32 (1) · Chilton 42 · Clempson 4 · Cockburn 22 · Crompton 25 · Doherty 5 (2) · Downie 20 (3) · Edwards 1 · Foulkes 2 · Gibson 20 · Jones M 2 · Lewis 10 (7) · McNulty 23 · McShane 5 · Olive 2 · Pearson 39 (16) · Pegg 19 (4) · Redman 1 · Rowley 26 (11) · Scott 2 · Taylor T 11 (7) · Viollet 3 (1) · Whitefoot 10 · Wood 12 · Total 30 players (69)

Football League

	P	W	D	L	F:A	Pts	
Arsenal	42	21	12	9	97:64	54	1st
Manchester U	42	18	10	14	69:72	46	8th

SEASON 1953–1954 FOOTBALL LEAGUE (DIVISION 1)

19 Aug	Chelsea	H	D	1–1	Crompton	Aston	Byrne[1]	Gibson	Chilton	Cockburn	Berry	Rowley[1]	Taylor T[1]	Pearson[1]	Pegg
22 Aug	Liverpool	A	D	4–4	..	..	..	..	..	..	..	..	..[1]	Lewis[1]	..
26 Aug	W B A	H	L	1–3	..	..	..	..	..	..	..	..	..[1]	..	..
29 Aug	Newcastle U	H	D	1–1	Wood	McNulty	Aston	Whitefoot	..[1]	..	..	Byrne	..	..	Rowley
2 Sep	W B A	A	L	0–2	..	Aston	Byrne	..	..	..	..	Lewis	..	Viollet	..
5 Sep	Manchester C	A	L	0–2	..	..	..	..	..	..	..	Viollet	..	Pearson	..
9 Sep	Middlesbrough	H	D	2–2	..	McNulty	..	..	..	..	..	Lewis	Rowley[2]	..	McShane
12 Sep	Bolton W	A	D	0–0	..	..	..	..	..	..	..	Taylor T	..[2]	..	..
16 Sep	Middlesbrough	A	W	4–1	..	..	..[1]	..	..	..	..	..	..[1]	..	..
19 Sep	Preston NE	H	W	1–0	..	Foulkes	..[1]	..	..	..	..	..	..	..	..
26 Sep	Tottenham H	A	D	1–1	..	..	..	..	..	..	..	..	..[1]	..	..
3 Oct	Burnley	H	L	1–2	..	..	..	..	..	..	..	..	..	..[1]	..
10 Oct	Sunderland	H	W	1–0	..	Aston	..	..	..	..	..	..	..[1]	..	..
17 Oct	Wolverhampton W	A	L	1–3	..	Foulkes	..	..	..	..	..[1]	Pearson	Taylor T[1]	Rowley	..
24 Oct	Aston Villa	H	W	1–0	..	..	..	..	..	..	..	..	..[1]	..	..
31 Oct	Huddersfield	A	D	0–0	..	..	..	..	..	Edwards	..	Blanchflower	..	Viollet	Rowley
7 Nov	Arsenal	H	D	2–2	..	..	..	..	..	..	..	..[1]	..[1]	..[2]	..[1]
14 Nov	Cardiff C	A	W	6–1	..	..	..	..	..	..	..	..	..[3]	..[1]	..
21 Nov	Blackpool	H	W	4–1	..	..	..	..	..	..	Webster	..	..[1]	..	..
28 Nov	Portsmouth	A	D	1–1	..	..	..	..	..	..	Berry[1]	..	..	..	..
5 Dec	Sheffield U	H	D	2–2	..	..	..	..	..	..	..	..[2]	..	..	..
12 Dec	Chelsea	A	L	1–3	..	..	..	..	..	..	..	..[2]	..[2]	..[1]	..
19 Dec	Liverpool	H	W	5–1	..	..	..	..	..	..	..	..[1]	..[3]	..[1]	..
25 Dec	Sheffield Wed	H	W	5–2	..	..	..	..	..	..	..	..	..	..[1]	..
26 Dec	Sheffield Wed	H	W	1–0	..	..	..[1]	..	..	..	..	..	..[1]	..	..
2 Jan	Newcastle U	A	W	2–1	..	..	..	..	..	..	..[1]	..	..	..	Pegg
16 Jan	Manchester C	H	D	1–1	..	..	..	..	..	..	..[1]	..	..	..	Pegg
23 Jan	Bolton W	H	L	1–5	..	..	..	..	..	..	..	..[1]	..[1]	..	..
6 Feb	Preston NE	A	W	3–1	Crompton	..	..	..	..	..	..	..[1]	..[1]	..	Rowley[1]
13 Feb	Tottenham H	H	W	2–0	..	..	..	..	..	McFarlane	..	..	..[1]	..	..
20 Feb	Burnley	A	L	0–2	..	..	..	..	..	Berry	..	..	..	..	Pegg
27 Feb	Sunderland	A	W	2–0	Wood	..	..	..	..	..	..	..[1]	..[1]	..	Rowley
6 Mar	Wolverhampton W	H	W	1–0	..	..	..	..	..	..	..[1]	..	..	..	..
13 Mar	Aston Villa	A	D	2–2	Crompton	..	..	..	..	Cockburn	..	..	..[2]	..	..
20 Mar	Huddersfield T	H	W	3–1	..	..	..	..	..	Edwards	..	..[1]	..	..[1]	..
27 Mar	Arsenal	A	L	1–3	..	..	..	Gibson	..	..	..	..	..[1]	..	..
3 Apr	Cardiff C	H	L	2–3	..	..	Redman	Whitefoot	..	..	..	Lewis	..[1]	..	..[1]
10 Apr	Blackpool	A	L	0–2	..	..	Byrne	..	..	..	..	Aston	..	..	..
16 Apr	Charlton A	H	W	2–0	..	..	..	..	..	Gibson	..	..	..[1]	..	Pegg
17 Apr	Portsmouth	H	W	2–0	..	..	..	..	..	..	..	..	..[1]	..[1]	..
19 Apr	Charlton A	A	L	0–1	..	..	..	..	..	Cockburn	..	..	..	..	..
24 Apr	Sheffield U	A	W	3–1	..	..	..	..	..	..	Berry	..	..[1]	..[1]	Rowley

FA Cup

Date	Opponent			Score											
9 Jan	Burnley (3)	A	L	3–5	Wood	Foulkes	Burne	Whitefoot	Chilton	Edwards	Berry	Blanchflower[1]	Taylor T[1]	Viollet[1]	Rowley

Appearances (goals)

Aston 12 (2) · Berry 37 (5) · Blanchflower 27 (13) · Byrne 41 (3) · Chilton 42 (1) · Cockburn 18 · Crompton 15 · Edwards 24 · Foulkes 32 (1) · Gibson 7 · Lewis 6 (1) · McFarlane 1 · McNulty 4 · McShane 9 · Pearson 11 (2) · Pegg 9 · Redman 1 · Rowley 36 (12) · Taylor T 35 (22) · Viollet 29 (11) · Webster 1 · Whitefoot 38 · Wood 27 · Total 23 players (73)

Football League

	P	W	D	L	F:A	Pts	
Wolves	42	25	7	10	96:56	57	1st
Manchester U	42	18	12	12	73:58	48	4th

SEASON 1954–1955 FOOTBALL LEAGUE (DIVISION 1)

Date	Opponent		Res	Score	1	2	3	4	5	6	7	8	9	10	11
21 Aug	Portsmouth	H	L	1–3	Wood	Foulkes	Byrne	Whitefoot	Chilton	Edwards	Berry	Blanchflower	Webster[2]	Viollet[2]	Rowley[1]
23 Aug	Sheffield Wed	A	W	4–2	..	..	..	..	..	..	..	..	[1]	[1]	[1]
28 Aug	Blackpool	A	W	4–2	..	..	..	..	..	..	..	..	..	[2]	
1 Sep	Sheffield Wed	H	W	2–0	..	..	..	..	..	..	..	..			
4 Sep	Charlton A	H	W	3–1	..	..	..	..	..	..	..	..	Taylor[1]		[2]
8 Sep	Tottenham H	A	W	2–0	..	..	..	..	..	..	[1]	..	Webster[1]	..	
11 Sep	Bolton W	A	D	1–1	..	..	..	..	..	..	..	..			
15 Sep	Tottenham H	H	W	2–1	..	..	..	..	..	..	..	..	Taylor	[1]	[1]
18 Sep	Huddersfield T	H	D	1–1	..	..	..	..	..	..	..	..	[1]	[1]	
25 Sep	Manchester C	A	L	2–3	..	..	..	Gibson	..	..	..	..			
2 Oct	Wolverhampton W	A	L	2–4	Crompton	Greaves	Kennedy	..	..	Cockburn	..	Edwards		[1]	[1]
9 Oct	Cardiff C	H	W	5–2	Wood	Foulkes	Byrne	..	..	Edwards	..	Blanchflower[1]	[4]	[3]	
16 Oct	Chelsea	A	W	6–5	..	..	..	..	..	..	..	[2]			
23 Oct	Newcastle U	H	D	*2–2	..	..	..	..	..	..	..	..	[1]		[1]
30 Oct	Everton	A	L	2–4	..	..	..	..	..	..	..	..		[2]	
6 Nov	Preston NE	H	W	2–1	..	..	..	..	..	..	..	..			
13 Nov	Sheffield U	A	L	0–3	..	..	..	..	..	..	..	..			
20 Nov	Arsenal	H	W	2–1	..	..	..	..	..	Goodwin	..	Webster[1]	[1]	..	Scanlon
27 Nov	W B A	A	L	0–2	..	..	..	..	..	Edwards	..	..			
4 Dec	Leicester C	H	W	3–1	..	..	..	..	..	Whitefoot	..	..	Webster[1]	[1]	Rowley[1]
11 Dec	Burnley	A	W	4–2	..	..	Bent	..	..	..	..	..	[3]	[1]	
18 Dec	Portsmouth	A	D	0–0	..	..	Byrne	..	..	Edwards	..	..			
27 Dec	Aston Villa	H	L	0–1	..	..	..	..	..	..	..	..			
28 Dec	Aston Villa	A	L	1–2	..	..	..	..	..	..	[1]	Blanchflower[2]	Webster / Taylor[1]	[1]	Pegg
1 Jan	Blackpool	H	W	4–1	..	..	..	..	..	..	..	..	[1]		
22 Jan	Bolton W	H	D	1–1	..	..	..	..	..	..	..	..	Webster		Rowley
5 Feb	Huddersfield T	A	W	3–1	..	..	..	..	..	Whitefoot	[1]	..	Webster	Edwards[1]	Pegg[1]
12 Feb	Manchester C	H	L	0–5	..	..	..	..	..	..	..	Webster	Viollet / Taylor[1]	[1]	
23 Feb	Wolverhampton W	H	L	2–4	..	..	..	..	..	..	..	Berry	Taylor	[1]	Scanlon[1]
26 Feb	Cardiff C	A	L	0–3	..	..	..	..	Jones	..	..		Webster		
5 Mar	Burnley	H	W	1–0	..	..	..	..	..	..	..	..			
19 Mar	Everton	H	L	1–2	..	..	[1]	..	..	..	[1]	Whelan	Taylor[2]	..	[1]
26 Mar	Preston NE	A	W	2–0	..	..	..	..	..	..	..	..	Viollet[1]		
2 Apr	Sheffield U	H	W	5–0	..	..	Bent	..	..	..	..	..	Edwards[2]	..	[1]
8 Apr	Sunderland	A	L	3–4	..	..	Byrne	..	..	..	..	..	[1]		
9 Apr	Leicester C	A	L	0–1	Crompton	..	..	[1]	..	..	..	..			
11 Apr	Sunderland	H	D	2–2	..	..	..	..	..	..	..	..	[2]	Viollet[1]	
16 Apr	W B A	H	W	3–0	..	..	..	Goodwin	..	..	..	..			
18 Apr	Newcastle U	A	L	0–2	..	..	..	Gibson	..	..	..	..			
23 Apr	Arsenal	A	W	*3–2	Wood	..	..	..	..	Goodwin	..	Blanchflower[2]		[1]	
26 Apr	Charlton A	A	D	1–1	..	..	..	..	..	..	..	..	[1]		[1]
30 Apr	Chelsea	H	W	2–1	..	..	..	..	..	..	..	..			

FA Cup

Date	Opponent		Res	Score											
8 Jan	Reading (3)	A	D	1–1	Wood	Foulkes	Byrne	Gibson	Chilton	Edwards	Berry	Blanchflower	Webster[1]	Viollet[2]	Rowley[1]
12 Jan	Reading (3R)	H	W	4–1	..	..	..	..	..	..	..	..			
29 Feb	Manchester C (4)	A	L	0–2	..	..	..	..	..	..	..	..	Taylor	..	..

Appearances (goals)

Bent 2 · Berry 40 (3) · Blanchflower 29 (10) · Byrne 39 (2) · Chilton 29 · Cockburn 1 · Crompton 5 · Edwards 33 (6) · Foulkes 41 · Gibson 32 · Goodwin 5 · Greaves 1 · Jones 13 · Kennedy 1 · Pegg 6 (1) · Rowley 22 (7) · Scanlon 14 (4) · Taylor 30 (20) · Viollet 34 (20) · Webster 17 (8) · Whelan 7 (1) · Whitefoot 24 · Wood 37 · Own goals 2 · Total 23 players (84)

Football League

	P	W	D	L	F:A	Pts	
Chelsea	42	20	12	10	81:57	52	1st
Manchester U	42	20	7	15	84:74	47	5th

SEASON 1955–1956 FOOTBALL LEAGUE (DIVISION 1)

Date	Opponent		Res	Score	1	2	3	4	5	6	7	8	9	10	11
20 Aug	Birmingham C	A	D	2–2	Wood	Foulkes	Byrne	Whitefoot	Jones	Edwards	Webster	Blanchflower	Taylor	Viollet[2]	Scanlon
24 Aug	Tottenham H	H	D	2–2	..	..	..	..	..	..	Berry[1]	..	Webster[1]	[1]	[1]
27 Aug	W B A	H	W	3–1	..	..	..	..	..	..	Webster	..	Lewis[1]	..	
31 Aug	Tottenham H	A	W	2–1	..	..	..	..	..	[2]		..			
3 Sep	Manchester C	A	L	0–1	..	..	..	..	..	Goodwin	..	..		Edwards	
7 Sep	Everton	H	W	2–1	..	..	..	..	..	..	..	[1]		[1]	
10 Sep	Sheffield U	A	L	0–1	..	..	..	..	..	..	Berry	Whelan	Webster	Blanchflower	Pegg
14 Sep	Everton	A	L	2–4	..	..	..	Whitehurst	..	..	Webster[1]	Blanchflower[1]	Doherty	Berry	
17 Sep	Preston NE	H	W	3–2	..	..	..	Whitefoot	..	..		Blanchflower	Taylor[1]	Viollet[1]	Pegg[1]
24 Sep	Burnley	A	D	0–0	..	..	..	..	..	..	Berry	..			
1 Oct	Luton T	H	W	3–1	..	..	Bent	..	..	..	..	[2]	Webster[1]		
8 Oct	Wolverhampton W	H	W	4–3	..	Byrne	..	..	..	McGuinness	..	Doherty[1]	[2]	[1]	[1]
15 Oct	Aston Villa	A	D	4–4	..	Foulkes	Byrne	..	..	..	[1]	Blanchflower[1]		[1]	[2]
22 Oct	Huddersfield T	H	W	3–0	Crompton	..	Bent	..	..	Edwards	..	[1]	Viollet	[1]
29 Oct	Cardiff C	A	W	1–0	Wood	..	Byrne	..	..	..	..	[1]			
5 Nov	Arsenal	H	D	1–1	..	..	..	..	..	..	..	[1]		Webster	
12 Nov	Bolton W	A	L	1–3	..	..	..	Colman	..	..	..	..		Webster	
19 Nov	Chelsea	H	W	3–0	..	..	[1]	..	..	..	..	Doherty	[2]	Viollet	
26 Nov	Blackpool	A	D	0–0	..	Greaves	..	..	..	..	..			
3 Dec	Sunderland	H	W	2–1	..	Foulkes	..	..	..	..	..	[1]		[1]	
10 Dec	Portsmouth	A	L	2–3	..	..	..	..	..	[1]	..	..	[1]	[1]
17 Dec	Birmingham C	H	W	2–1	..	..	..	..	..	..	..	[1]		[3]	
24 Dec	W B A	A	W	4–1	..	..	[1]	..	..	..	..	[1]		[2]	
26 Dec	Charlton A	H	W	5–1	..	..	..	..	..	..	..	[1]		[1]	
27 Dec	Charlton A	A	L	0–3	..	..	..	..	..	..	..		[1]	
31 Dec	Manchester C	H	W	2–1	..	..	..	..	..	..	[1]	Whelan[1]		
14 Jan	Sheffield U	H	W	3–1	..	..	..	..	..	..	Scott	[1]	Webster	[1]
21 Jan	Preston NE	A	L	1–3	..	..	..	..	..	..	Berry	Taylor[1]	[1]	
4 Feb	Burnley	H	W	2–0	..	Greaves	..	..	..	..	..	[1]	[1]	
11 Feb	Luton T	A	W	2–0	..	..	..	Goodwin	..	Blanchflower	..	[2]		
18 Feb	Wolverhampton W	A	W	2–0	..	..	..	Colman	..	Edwards	..	[1]		
25 Feb	Aston Villa	H	W	1–0	..	..	..	..	..	..	..	[1]	[2]	
3 Mar	Chelsea	A	W	4–2	..	..	[1]	..	..	..	..			[1]
10 Mar	Cardiff C	H	D	1–1	..	..	..	..	..	..	..	[1]		
17 Mar	Arsenal	A	D	1–1	..	..	..	..	..	..	..	[1]	[1]	
24 Mar	Bolton W	H	W	1–0	..	..	..	..	..	..	..	[1]	[2]	[1]
30 Mar	Newcastle U	H	W	5–2	..	..	..	..	..	..	Doherty[1]	[2]		
31 Mar	Huddersfield T	A	W	2–0	..	..	..	..	..	..	[1]		
2 Apr	Newcastle U	A	D	0–0	..	..	..	..	..	Scott	..	[1]		
7 Apr	Blackpool	H	W	2–1	..	..	..	..	..	..	..		
14 Apr	Sunderland	A	D	2–2	..	Bent	..	McGuinness[1]	..	Whelan[1]	Blanchflower	[1]	
21 Apr	Portsmouth	H	W	1–0	..	Byrne	..	Doherty	..	Doherty	Taylor		

FA Cup

Date	Opponent		Res	Score											
7 Jan	Bristol R (3)	A	L	0–4	Wood	Foulkes	Byrne	Colman	Jones	Whitefoot	Berry	Doherty	Taylor	Viollet	Pegg

Appearances (goals)

Bent 4 · Berry 34 (4) · Blanchflower 18 (3) · Byrne 39 (3) · Colman 25 · Crompton 1 · Doherty 16 (4) · Edwards 33 (3) · Foulkes 26 · Goodwin 8 · Greaves 15 · Jones 42 (1) · Lewis 4 (1) · McGuinness 3 (1) · Pegg 35 (9) · Scanlon 6 (1) · Scott 1 · Taylor 33 (25) · Viollet 34 (20) · Webster 15 (4) · Whelan 13 (4) · Whitefoot 15 · Whitehurst 1 · Wood 41 · Total 24 players (83)

Football League

	P	W	D	L	F:A	Pts	
Manchester U	42	25	10	7	83:51	60	1st

SEASON 1956–1957 FOOTBALL LEAGUE (DIVISION 1)

Date	Opponent			Score										
18 Aug	Birmingham C	H	D	2–2	Wood	Foulkes	Byrne	Colman	Jones M	Edwards	Berry	Whelan[1]	Taylor T[2]	Viollet[2]	Pegg
20 Aug	Preston NE	A	W	3–1	..							.. [1]	.. [1]	.. [1]	
25 Aug	W B A	A	W	3–2	..									.. [1]	
29 Aug	Preston NE	H	W	3–2	..						.. [1]			.. [3]	
1 Sep	Portsmouth	H	W	3–0	..							.. [1]	.. [1]		.. [1]
5 Sep	Chelsea	A	W	2–1	..							.. [1]			
8 Sep	Newcastle U	A	D	1–1	..							.. [1]			
15 Sep	Sheffield Wed	H	W	4–1	..						.. [1]	.. [1]		.. [1]	
22 Sep	Manchester C	H	W	2–0	..							.. [1]			
29 Sep	Arsenal	A	W	2–1	..				Cope			.. [1]			
6 Oct	Charlton A	H	W	4–2	..		Bent		Jones M	McGuinness		.. [1]	Charlton[2]		
13 Oct	Sunderland	A	W	*3–1	..		Byrne			Edwards		.. [1]	Taylor T	.. [1]	
20 Oct	Everton	H	L	2–5	..									Charlton[1]	
27 Oct	Blackpool	A	D	2–2	Hawksworth								.. [2]	Viollet	
3 Nov	Wolverhampton W	H	W	3–0	Wood							.. [1]	.. [1]	Charlton	
10 Nov	Bolton W	A	L	0–2	..										.. [1]
17 Nov	Leeds U	H	W	3–2	..					McGuinness			.. [2]		.. [1]
24 Nov	Tottenham H	A	D	2–2	..				.. [1]	Blanchflower		.. [1]		Edwards[1]	
1 Dec	Luton T	H	W	3–1	..				Jones M				.. [1]		
8 Dec	Aston Villa	A	W	3–1	..		Bent			Edwards			.. [2]	Viollet[1]	.. [1]
15 Dec	Birmingham C	A	L	1–3	..							.. [1]	.. [1]	.. [1]	
26 Dec	Cardiff C	H	W	3–1	..		Byrne						.. [1]	.. [1]	
29 Dec	Portsmouth	A	W	3–1	..					McGuinness			Edwards[1]	.. [1]	.. [1]
1 Jan	Chelsea	H	W	3–0	..					Edwards		.. [1]	Taylor T[2]		
12 Jan	Newcastle U	H	W	6–1	..							.. [2]		.. [2]	.. [2]
19 Jan	Sheffield Wed	A	L	1–2	..								.. [1]		
2 Feb	Manchester C	A	W	4–2	..						.. [1]	.. [1]	.. [1]	.. [1]	
9 Feb	Arsenal	H	W	6–2	..						.. [1]	.. [2]	.. [2]	.. [1]	
18 Feb	Charlton A	A	W	5–1	..	Byrne	Bent			McGuinness			.. [2]	Charlton[3]	
23 Feb	Blackpool	H	L	0–2	..	Foulkes	Byrne			Edwards					
6 Mar	Everton	A	W	2–1	..	Byrne	Bent	Goodwin	Blanchflower	McGuinness			Webster[2]	Doherty	
9 Mar	Aston Villa	H	D	1–1	..	Foulkes	Byrne						Edwards	Charlton[1]	
16 Mar	Wolverhampton W	A	D	1–1	Clayton			Colman		Edwards			Webster		
25 Mar	Bolton W	H	L	0–2	Wood					McGuinness			Edwards		.. [1]
30 Mar	Leeds U	A	W	2–1	..					Edwards		.. [1]	Webster		
6 Apr	Tottenham H	H	D	0–0	..		Bent			McGuinness			Taylor T	Viollet	Scanlon
13 Apr	Luton T	A	W	2–0	..		Byrne	Goodwin		Edwards		Viollet	.. [2]	Charlton	
19 Apr	Burnley	A	W	3–1	..						.. [1]	Whelan[3]			Pegg
20 Apr	Sunderland	H	W	4–0	..			Colman				.. [2]	.. [1]		
22 Apr	Burnley	H	W	2–0	..		Greaves	Goodwin	Cope	McGuinness	Webster[1]	Doherty	Dawson[1]	Viollet	Scanlon
27 Apr	Cardiff C	A	W	3–2	..			Colman	Blanchflower			Whelan			.. [2]
29 Apr	W B A	H	D	1–1	Clayton	Greaves	Byrne	Goodwin	Jones M		Berry	Doherty	.. [1]		

FA Cup

Date	Opponent			Score										
5 Jan	Hartlepool U (3)	A	W	4–3	Wood	Foulkes	Byrne	Colman	Jones M	Edwards	Berry[1]	Whelan[2]	Viollet	Pegg
26 Jan	Wrexham (4)	A	W	5–0	..		.. [1]				Webster			
16 Feb	Everton (5)	H	W	1–0	..				.. [1]		Berry			
2 Mar	Bournemouth (6)	A	W	2–1	..					McGuinness	.. [2]	Edwards		
23 Mar	Birmingham C (SF)	N	W	2–0	..					Blanchflower	Edwards	.. [1]	Charlton[1]	
	(at Hillsborough)													
4 May	Aston Villa (F)	N	L	1–2								Taylor T[1]	Charlton	..
	(at Wembley)													

European Cup

Date	Opponent			Score										
12 Sep	RSC Anderlecht (P)	A	W	2–1	Wood	Foulkes	Byrne	Colman	Jones M	Blanchflower	Berry	Whelan[1]	Taylor T[1]	Viollet[1]	Pegg
26 Sep	RSC Anderlecht (P)	†H	W	10–0	..					Edwards	.. [1]	.. [2]	.. [3]	.. [4]	
17 Oct	Borussia D'mund (1)	†H	W	3–2	..									.. [2]	.. [1]
21 Nov	Borussia D'mund (1)	A	D	0–0	..					McGuinness				Edwards	
16 Jan	Athletico Bilbao (2)	A	L	3–5	..					Edwards		.. [1]	.. [1]	Viollet[1]	
6 Feb	Athletico Bilbao (2)	†H	W	3–0	..								.. [1]	.. [1]	
11 Apr	Real Madrid (SF)	A	L	1–3	..					Blanchflower			.. [1]		
25 Apr	Real Madrid (SF)	†H	D	2–2	..								.. [1]	Charlton[1]	
	†at Maine Road													

Appearances (goals)

Bent 6 · Berry 40 (8) · Blanchflower 11 · Byrne 36 · Charlton 14 (10) · Clayton 2 · Colman 36 (1) · Cope 2 · Dawson 3 (3) · Doherty 3 · Edwards 34 (5) · Foulkes 39 · Goodwin 6 · Greaves 3 · Hawksworth 1 · Jones M 29 · McGuinness 13 · Pegg 37 (6) · Scanlon 5 (2) · Taylor T 32 (22) · Viollet 27 (16) · Webster 5 (3) · Whelan 39 (26) · Wood 39 · Own goals 1 · Total 24 players (103)

Football League

	P	W	D	L	F:A	Pts	
Manchester U	42	28	8	6	103:54	64	1st

SEASON 1957–1958 FOOTBALL LEAGUE (DIVISION 1)

Date	Opponent			Score										
24 Aug	Leicester C	A	W	3–0	Wood	Foulkes	Byrne	Colman	Blanchflower	Edwards	Berry	Whelan[3]	Taylor T	Viollet	Pegg
28 Aug	Everton	H	W	*3–0	..						.. [1]	.. [1]		.. [1]	
31 Aug	Manchester C	H	W	4–1	..							.. [1]	.. [1]	.. [1]	
4 Sep	Everton	A	D	3–3	..						.. [2]		.. [2]	.. [1]	
7 Sep	Leeds U	H	W	5–0	..							.. [2]			
9 Sep	Blackpool	A	W	4–1	..						.. [2]			.. [2]	
14 Sep	Bolton W	A	L	0–4	..										
18 Sep	Blackpool	H	L	1–2	..					.. [1]					
21 Sep	Arsenal	H	W	4–2	..								.. [2]	.. [1]	.. [1]
28 Sep	Wolverhampton W	A	L	1–3	..		McGuinness	Goodwin				Doherty[1]		Charlton	
5 Oct	Aston Villa	H	W	*4–1	..		Byrne	Colman	Jones M	McGuinness		Whelan	.. [2]		.. [1]
12 Oct	Nottingham F	A	W	2–1	..				Blanchflower	Edwards		.. [1]		Viollet[1]	
19 Oct	Portsmouth	H	L	0–3	..		Jones M P			McGuinness			Dawson		
26 Oct	W B A	A	L	3–4	..		Byrne	Goodwin		Edwards			Taylor T[2]	Charlton	
													.. [1]	Webster	
2 Nov	Burnley	H	W	1–0	..									.. [2]	
9 Nov	Preston NE	A	D	1–1	..										
16 Nov	Sheffield Wed	H	W	2–1	..			Colman					.. [1]		
23 Nov	Newcastle U	A	W	2–1	..					.. [1]	Scanlon				
30 Nov	Tottenham H	H	L	3–4	Gaskell								Webster	Charlton	.. [2]
7 Dec	Birmingham C	A	D	3–3	Wood				Jones M		Berry		Taylor T[1]	Viollet[2]	
14 Dec	Chelsea	H	L	0–1	..										
21 Dec	Leicester C	H	W	4–0	Gregg						Morgans	Charlton[1]	.. [1]	.. [2]	Scanlon[1]
25 Dec	Luton T	H	W	3–0	..					.. [1]			.. [1]		
26 Dec	Luton T	A	D	2–2	..						Berry		.. [1]		.. [1]
28 Dec	Manchester C	A	D	2–2	..						Morgans		Dawson	.. [1]	
11 Jan	Leeds U	A	D	1–1	..					.. [1]			Taylor T	.. [2]	
18 Jan	Bolton W	H	W	7–2	..					.. [1]		.. [3]		.. [2]	.. [1]
1 Feb	Arsenal	A	W	5–4	..					.. [1]		.. [1]	.. [2]	.. [1]	
22 Feb	Nottingham F	H	D	1–1	..		Greaves	Goodwin	Cope	Crowther	Webster	Taylor E	Dawson	Pearson	Brennan

SEASON 1957–1958 (continued) — FOOTBALL LEAGUE (DIVISION 1)

Date	Opp	V	R	Score	1	2	3	4	5	6	7	8	9	10	11
8 Mar	W B A	H	L	0–4	..	..	..	..	..	Harrop	..	..	..	..	Charlton
15 Mar	Burnley	A	L	0–3	..	..	..	..	..	Crowther	..	Harrop	..	Charlton	Brennan
29 Mar	Sheffield Wed	A	L	0–1	..	..	Cope	..	Greaves	..	..	Taylor E	.. [1]	Charlton	..
31 Mar	Aston Villa	A	L	2–3	..	..	..	..	..	..	..	Pearson	.. [1]	.. [1]	..
4 Apr	Sunderland	H	D	2–2	..	..	Greaves	..	Cope	..	..	Taylor E	..	Webster [2]	Heron
5 Apr	Preston NE	H	D	0–0	..	..	..	..	..	..	Morgans	..	..	..	Pearson
7 Apr	Sunderland	A	W	2–1	..	..	..	..	Harrop	McGuinness	..	..	..	..	..
12 Apr	Tottenham H	A	L	0–1	..	..	..	..	Cope	Crowther	..	..	..	..	..
16 Apr	Portsmouth	A	D	3–3	..	..	..	Crowther	..	McGuinness	Dawson [1]	.. [1]	.. [1]	Pearson	Morgans
19 Apr	Birmingham C	H	L	0–2	..	..	..	Goodwin	..	Crowther	..	..	..	..	..
21 Apr	Wolverhampton W	H	L	0–4	..	..	..	..	..	McGuinness	..	Brennan	..	Viollet	..
23 Apr	Newcastle U	H	D	1–1	..	..	..	Crowther	..	..	..	Taylor E	.. [1]	Charlton	..
26 Apr	Chelsea	A	L	1–2	..	..	..	Goodwin	..	Crowther	..	..	Charlton	Viollet	Webster

FA Cup

Date	Opp	V	R	Score	1	2	3	4	5	6	7	8	9	10	11
4 Jan	Workington T (3)	A	W	3–1	Gregg	Foulkes	Byrne	Colman	Jones M	Edwards	Morgans	Charlton [2]	Taylor T	Viollet [3]	Scanlon
25 Jan	Ipswich T (4)	H	W	2–0	..	..	..	..	..	..	..	..	Dawson [1]	Pearson	Brennan [2] / Charlton
19 Feb	Sheffield Wed (5)	H	W	3–0	..	..	Greaves	Goodwin	Cope	Crowther	Webster	Taylor E [1]	..	Pearson	Charlton
1 Mar	W B A (6)	A	D	2–2	..	..	..	..	..	Harrop	..	.. [1]	..	..	..
5 Mar	W B A (6R)	H	W	1–0	..	..	..	..	..	Crowther	..	..	..	Charlton [2]	Pearson
22 Mar	Fulham (SF) (at Villa Park)	N	D	2–2	..	..	..	..	..	..	..	..	Charlton [3]	.. [1]	Brennan [1]
26 Mar	Fulham (SFR) (at Highbury)	N	W	5–3	..	..	..	..	..	..	..	Charlton	..	..	..
3 May	Bolton W (F) (at Wembley)	N	L	0–2	..	..	..	..	..	..	Dawson	..	..	Viollet	Webster

European Cup

Date	Opp	V	R	Score	1	2	3	4	5	6	7	8	9	10	11
25 Sep	Shamrock R (P)	A	W	6–0	Wood	Foulkes	Byrne	Goodwin	Blanchflower	Edwards	Berry [1]	Whelan [2]	Taylor T [2]	Viollet [2]	Pegg [1]
2 Oct	Shamrock R (P)	H	W	3–2	..	..	..	Colman	Jones M	McGuinness	..	Webster	.. [1]	Webster [1]	.. [1]
21 Nov	Dukla Prague (1)	H	W	3–0	..	..	..	..	Blanchflower	Edwards	..	Whelan	..	..	..
4 Dec	Dukla Prague (1)	A	L	0–1	..	..	..	.. [1]	Jones M	Scanlon	..	..	..	..	..
14 Jan	Red Star Belgrade (2)	H	W	2–1	Gregg	..	..	..	..	..	Morgans	Charlton [1] [2]	..	Viollet [1]	Scanlon
5 Feb	Red Star Belgrade (2)	A	D	3–3	..	..	..	..	..	..	..	Taylor E [1]	Webster	.. [1]	Pearson
8 May	A C Milan (SF)	H	W	2–1	..	..	Greaves	Goodwin	Cope	Crowther	..	..	..	..	..
14 May	A C Milan (SF)	A	L	0–4	..	..	..	..	..	..	..	..	..	..	..

Appearances (goals)

Berry 20 (4) · Blanchflower 18 · Brennan 5 · Byrne 26 · Charlton 21 (8) · Colman 24 · Cope 13 · Crowther 11 · Dawson 12 (5) · Doherty 1 (1) · Edwards 26 (6) · Foulkes 42 · Gaskell 3 · Goodwin 16 · Greaves 12 · Gregg 19 · Harrop 5 · Heron 1 · Jones M 10 · Jones P 1 · McGuinness 7 · Morgans 13 · Pearson 8 · Pegg 21 (4) · Scanlon 9 (3) · Taylor E 11 (2) · Taylor T 25 (16) · Viollet 22 (16) · Webster 20 (6) · Whelan 20 (12) · Wood R 20 · Own goals 2 · Total 31 players (85)

Football League

	P	W	D	L	F:A	Pts	
Wolverhampton W	42	28	8	6	103:47	64	1st
Manchester U	42	16	11	15	85:75	43	9th

1958–1959

SEASON 1958–1959 FOOTBALL LEAGUE (DIVISION 1)

Date	Opp	V	R	Score	1	2	3	4	5	6	7	8	9	10	11
23 Aug	Chelsea	H	W	5–2	Gregg	Foulkes	Greaves	Goodwin	Cope	McGuinness	Dawson	Taylor E	Viollet	Charlton [3] [2]	Scanlon [1]
27 Aug	Nottingham F	A	W	3–0	..	..	..	..	..	..	..	..	.. [1]	.. [1]	..
30 Aug	Blackpool	A	L	1–2	..	..	..	..	..	..	..	..	..	.. [1]	..
3 Sep	Nottingham F	H	D	1–1	..	..	..	..	..	..	Webster [1]	..	.. [2]	.. [2]	.. [1]
6 Sep	Blackburn R	H	W	6–1	..	..	..	..	..	..	..	..	..	..	..
8 Sep	West Ham U	A	L	2–3	..	..	..	..	..	..	.. [1]	..	..	.. [1]	..
13 Sep	Newcastle U	A	D	1–1	..	..	..	..	..	Crowther	..	..	..	..	.. [3]
17 Sep	West Ham U	H	W	4–1	..	..	..	..	..	McGuinness	.. [2]	Dawson	..	..	..
20 Sep	Tottenham H	H	D	2–2	..	..	..	..	..	..	..	Quixall	..	..	..
27 Sep	Manchester C	A	D	1–1	..	..	..	..	..	Viollet	..	..	Webster	.. [1]	..
4 Oct	Wolverhampton W	A	L	0–4	Wood	..	..	..	Harrop	Crowther	..	..	..	Pearson	..
8 Oct	Preston NE	H	L	0–2	Gregg	..	..	..	Cope	McGuinness	..	Taylor E	Dawson	Charlton	..
11 Oct	Arsenal	H	D	1–1	..	..	..	..	.. [2]	..	.. [1]	Quixall	Charlton	Taylor E	..
18 Oct	Everton	A	L	2–3	..	..	..	.. [1]	..	..	..	..	..	..	..
25 Oct	W B A	H	L	1–2	..	..	..	.. [1]	Harrop	..	..	..	Dawson	Charlton	..
1 Nov	Leeds U	A	W	2–1	..	..	..	..	..	..	Morgans	..	..	..	.. [1]
8 Nov	Burnley	H	L	1–3	..	..	..	..	..	..	.. [1]	..	.. [2]	.. [1]	..
15 Nov	Bolton W	A	L	3–6	..	..	..	..	Cope	..	Bradley	..	..	.. [2]	..
22 Nov	Luton T	H	W	2–1	..	..	Carolan	..	..	.. [1]	..	..	Viollet [1]	.. [1]	..
29 Nov	Birmingham C	A	W	4–0	..	..	..	..	..	.. [1]	..	..	.. [1]	.. [1]	.. [1]
6 Dec	Leicester C	H	W	4–1	..	..	..	..	..	.. [1]	..	..	.. [1]	.. [1]	.. [1]
13 Dec	Preston NE	A	W	4–3	..	..	..	.. [1]	..	..	..	..	..	Pearson [1]	..
20 Dec	Chelsea	A	W	3–2	..	..	..	..	..	..	..	.. [1]	.. [1]	..	..
26 Dec	Aston Villa	H	W	2–1	..	..	Greaves	..	..	..	Hunter	..	.. [1]	Charlton [2]	..
27 Dec	Aston Villa	A	W	2–0	..	..	Carolan	..	..	..	Bradley	..	.. [1]	..	..
3 Jan	Blackpool	H	W	3–1	..	..	..	..	..	..	..	.. [1]	..	.. [2]	.. [1]
31 Jan	Newcastle U	H	D	4–4	..	..	..	Harrop	Goodwin	..	..	..	.. [1]	.. [1]	.. [1]
7 Feb	Tottenham H	A	W	3–1	..	Greaves	..	Goodwin [1]	Cope	..	.. [2]	..	.. [1]	.. [1]	..
16 Feb	Manchester C	H	W	4–1	..	..	..	..	..	..	..	..	.. [1]	..	..
21 Feb	Wolverhampton W	H	W	2–1	..	..	..	..	..	..	.. [1]	..	..	..	..
28 Feb	Arsenal	A	L	2–3	..	..	..	..	..	..	.. [2]	..	..	..	.. [1]
2 Mar	Blackburn R	A	W	3–1	..	..	..	..	..	..	..	..	.. [1]	..	.. [1]
7 Mar	Everton	H	W	2–1	..	..	..	..	..	..	.. [1]	..	.. [3]	..	.. [1]
14 Mar	W B A	A	W	3–1	..	..	..	..	..	..	..	..	.. [2]	.. [1]	..
21 Mar	Leeds U	H	W	4–0	..	..	..	..	..	..	.. [1]	..	.. [1]	.. [2]	..
27 Mar	Portsmouth	H	W	6–1	..	..	..	.. [1]	..	..	..	..	..	..	..
28 Mar	Burnley	A	L	2–4	..	..	..	..	..	..	..	..	..	.. [2]	..
30 Mar	Portsmouth	A	W	3–1	..	..	..	..	Foulkes	..	..	..	..	.. [1]	.. [1]
4 Apr	Bolton W	H	W	3–0	..	..	..	..	..	..	..	..	..	Pearson	..
11 Apr	Luton T	A	D	0–0	..	..	..	..	..	..	..	.. [1]	..	Charlton	..
18 Apr	Birmingham C	H	W	1–0	..	..	..	..	..	..	.. [1]	..	..	..	..
25 Apr	Leicester C	A	L	1–2	..	..	..	..	..	Brennan	..	..	..	..	..

FA Cup

Date	Opp	V	R	Score	1	2	3	4	5	6	7	8	9	10	11
10 Jan	Norwich C (3)	A	L	0–3	Gregg	Foulkes	Carolan	Goodwin	Cope	McGuinness	Bradley	Quixall	Viollet	Charlton	Scanlon

Appearances (goals)

Bradley 24 (12) · Brennan 1 · Carolan 23 · Charlton 38 (29) · Cope 32 (2) · Crowther 2 · Dawson 11 (4) · Foulkes 32 · Goodwin 42 (6) · Greaves 34 · Gregg 41 · Harrop 5 · Hunter 1 · McGuinness 39 (1) · Morgans 2 · Pearson 4 (1) · Quixall 33 (4) · Scanlon 42 (16) · Taylor E 11 · Viollet 37 (21) · Webster 7 (5) · Wood 1 · Own goals 2 · Total 22 players (103)

Football League

	P	W	D	L	F:A	Pts	
Wolves	42	28	5	9	110:49	61	1st
Manchester U	42	24	7	11	103:66	55	2nd

SEASON 1959–1960 FOOTBALL LEAGUE (DIVISION 1)

Date	Opponent			Score	1	2	3	4	5	6	7	8	9	10	11
22 Aug	W B A	A	L	2–3	Gregg	Greaves	Carolan	Goodwin	Foulkes	McGuinness	Bradley	Quixall	Viollet[2]	Charlton	Scanlon
26 Aug	Chelsea	H	L	0–1	..	..	..	..	..	..	..	..	Dawson	Viollet	Charlton
29 Aug	Newcastle U	H	W	3–2	..	Cope	..	Brennan	..	..	..	..2	Viollet[2]	Charlton[1]	Scanlon
2 Sep	Chelsea	A	W	6–3	..	..	..	..	..	..	..	..1	..2	..1	..1
5 Sep	Birmingham C	A	D	1–1	..	..	..	..	..	..	..	..	..1	..	..
9 Sep	Leeds U	H	W	6–0	..	..	..	..	..	..	..	..2	..1	..2	..1
12 Sep	Tottenham H	H	L	1–5	..	..	..	Goodwin	..	..	..	Giles	..1	..	..
16 Sep	Leeds U	A	D	*2–2	..	Foulkes	..	Brennan	Cope	..	..	Quixall	..	..1	..
19 Sep	Manchester C	A	L	0–3	..	..	..	..	..	..	..	..	..	..	..
26 Sep	Preston NE	A	L	0–4	..	..	..	Viollet	..	..	..	..	Dawson	..	..
3 Oct	Leicester C	H	W	4–1	Gaskell	..	..	Goodwin	..	..	..	..1	Viollet[2]	..1	..
10 Oct	Arsenal	H	W	*4–2	Gregg	..	..	..	..	..	..	..1	..1	..1	..
17 Oct	Wolverhampton W	A	L	*2–3	..	..	..	..	..	..	..	Giles	..1	Pearson	..
24 Oct	Sheffield Wed	H	W	3–1	..	..	..	..	..	..	..1	Quixall	..2	Charlton	..
31 Oct	Blackburn R	A	D	1–1	..	..	..	..	..	..	..	..1	..	..	..
7 Nov	Fulham	H	D	3–3	..	..	..	..	..	..	..	..	..1	..	..1
14 Nov	Bolton W	A	D	1–1	..	..	..	..	..	..	..	..	..	..	Dawson[1]
21 Nov	Luton T	H	W	4–1	..	..	..	..	..1	..	..	..1	..2	..	Scanlon
28 Nov	Everton	A	L	1–2	..	..	..	..	..	..	..	..	..1	..	..
5 Dec	Blackpool	H	W	3–1	Gaskell	..	..	..	..	..	Brennan	Dawson	..2	Pearson[1]	..
12 Dec	Nottingham F	A	W	5–1	..	..	..	..	..	..	..	..1	..3	..	..1
19 Dec	W B A	H	L	2–3	..	..	..	..	..	..	..1	..1	..	..	..
26 Dec	Burnley	H	L	1–2	..	..	..	..	..	..	..	..1	..	Charlton	..
28 Dec	Burnley	A	W	4–1	..	..	..	..	..	..	..	..	..2	..	..2
2 Jan	Newcastle U	A	L	3–7	..	..	..	..	..	..	..	..2	..	..	..
16 Jan	Birmingham C	H	W	2–1	Gregg	..	..	Setters	..	..	Bradley	..1	..1	..	..
23 Jan	Tottenham H	A	L	1–2	..	..	..	..	..	..	..1	..	..	..	..
6 Feb	Manchester C	H	D	0–0	..	..	..	..	..	..	..	..	..	..	..
13 Feb	Preston NE	H	D	1–1	..	..	..	..	..	..	..	..	..1	..	..
24 Feb	Leicester C	A	L	1–3	..	..	..	..	..	..	Viollet	..	Dawson	..	..1
27 Feb	Blackpool	A	W	6–0	..	..	..	..	..	..	..2	..	..	..3	..1
5 Mar	Wolverhampton W	H	L	0–2	..	..	..	..	..	..	..	..	..	..	..
19 Mar	Nottingham F	H	W	3–1	..	..	..	..	..	..	Giles	Viollet	..1	Pearson[1]	Charlton[2]
26 Mar	Fulham	A	W	5–0	..	..	..	..	..	..	..1	..2	..	..	..
30 Mar	Sheffield Wed	A	L	2–4	Gaskell	..	Heron	..	..	..	Bradley	..1	..	..	..1
7 Apr	Bolton W	H	W	2–0	..	..	Carolan	..	..	..	..	Giles	..	..	..2
9 Apr	Luton T	A	W	3–2	Gregg	..	..	..	..	..	..1	..	..2	Lawton	Scanlon
15 Apr	West Ham U	A	L	1–2	..	..	..	..	..	..	..	..	..1	..	Charlton
16 Apr	Blackburn R	H	W	1–0	..	..	..	..	..	..	..	..	..1	..	..
18 Apr	West Ham U	H	W	5–3	..	..	..	..	..	..	Giles	Quixall[1]	..2	Viollet	..2
23 Apr	Arsenal	A	L	2–5	..	..	..	..	..	..	..1	..	..	Pearson[1]	..
30 Apr	Everton	H	W	5–0	..	..	..	..	..	..	Bradley[1]	..1	..3	..	..

FA Cup

Date	Opponent			Score											
9 Jan	Derby Co (3)	A	W	*4–2	Gregg	Foulkes	Carolan	Goodwin[1]	Cope	Brennan	Dawson	Quixall	Viollet	Charlton[1]	Scanlon[1]
30 Jan	Liverpool (4)	H	W	3–1	..	..	..	Setters	..	..	Bradley[1]	..	..	..	..2
20 Feb	Sheffield Wed (5)	A	L	0–1	..	..	..	..	..	..	..	..	..	..	..

Appearances (goals)

Bradley 29 (8) · Brennan 29 · Carolan 41 · Charlton 37 (18) · Cope 40 · Dawson 22 (15) · Foulkes 42 · Gaskell 9 · Giles 10 (2) · Goodwin 18 (1) · Greaves 2 · Gregg 33 · Heron 1 · Lawton 3 · McGuinness 19 · Pearson 10 (3) · Quixall 33 (13) · Scanlon 31 (7) · Setters 17 · Viollet 36 (32) · Own goals 3 · Total 20 players (102)

Football League

	P	W	D	L	F:A	Pts	
Burnley	42	24	7	11	85:61	55	1st
Manchester U	42	19	7	16	102:80	45	7th

SEASON 1960–1961 FOOTBALL LEAGUE (DIVISION 1)

Date	Opponent			Score	1	2	3	4	5	6	7	8	9	10	11
20 Aug	Blackburn R	H	L	1–3	Gregg	Cope	Carolan	Setters	Haydock	Brennan	Giles	Quixall	Viollet	Charlton[1]	Scanlon
24 Aug	Everton	A	L	0–4	..	Brennan	..	..	..	Nicholson	..	..	..	..	..
31 Aug	Everton	H	W	4–0	..	Foulkes	Brennan	..	..1	..	Giles	Dawson[2]	Viollet	Charlton[1]	
3 Sep	Tottenham H	A	L	1–4	..	..	..	..	..	..	Quixall	Giles	..	..1	..
5 Sep	West Ham U	A	L	1–2	..	..	..	Cope	..	..	..1	..	..	..	..
10 Sep	Leicester C	H	D	1–1	..	..	..	..	..	..	..	..1	..	..	..
14 Sep	West Ham U	H	W	6–1	..	..	..	..	..	..	..1	..	Viollet[2]	Charlton[2]	Scanlon[1]
17 Sep	Aston Villa	A	L	1–3	..	..	..	..	..	..	Giles	Quixall	..1	..	..
24 Sep	Wolverhampton W	H	L	1–3	..	..	..	..	..	..	..	..	..	..1	..
1 Oct	Bolton W	A	D	1–1	..	Setters	..	Stiles	Foulkes	..	Moir	Giles[1]	Dawson	..	..
15 Oct	Burnley	A	L	3–5	..	..	Dunne A	..	..	..	Quixall	..	Viollet[3]	Pearson	Charlton
22 Oct	Newcastle U	H	W	3–2	..	..1	Brennan	..	..	..	Dawson[1]	..	..2	Charlton	Scanlon
24 Oct	Nottingham F	H	W	2–1	..	Dunne A	..	..	..	..	..	..	..2	Pearson	..
29 Oct	Arsenal	A	L	1–2	..	Brennan	Heron	..	..	..	..	..	..	Quixall[1]	Charlton
5 Nov	Sheffield Wed	H	D	0–0	..	Setters	Brennan	..	..	..	..	..	..	..	..
12 Nov	Birmingham C	A	L	1–3	..	..	..	..	..	..	..	..	..	Pearson	..1
19 Nov	W B A	H	W	3–0	..	..	..	..	..	Bradley	Quixall[1]	Dawson[1]	Viollet[1]	..	
26 Nov	Cardiff C	A	L	0–3	..	Brennan	Cantwell	Setters	..	..	..	..	..1	Pearson	..
3 Dec	Preston NE	H	W	1–0	..	..	..	..	..	..	..	..	..2	..	..1
10 Dec	Fulham	A	D	4–4	..	..	..	..	..	..	..	..	..1	..	..
17 Dec	Blackburn R	A	W	2–1	..	..	..	..	..	..	Quixall	Stiles	..	..2	..
24 Dec	Chelsea	A	W	2–1	..	..	..	..	..	..	..	..	..1	..	..1
26 Dec	Chelsea	H	W	6–0	..	..	..	..	..	..	..2	..	..3	..	..1
31 Dec	Manchester C	H	W	5–1	..	..	..	..	..	..	..	..	..3	..	..2
14 Jan	Tottenham H	H	W	2–0	..	..	..	..	..	..	..	..1	..	..1	..
21 Jan	Leicester C	A	L	0–6	Briggs	..	..	..	..	..	..	..	..	..	..
4 Feb	Aston Villa	H	D	1–1	Pinner	..	..	..	..	..1	..	..	Pearson	..	..
11 Feb	Wolverhampton W	A	L	1–2	..	..	..	..	..	..	..	..	..1	..	..
18 Feb	Bolton W	H	W	3–1	..	..	..	Stiles	..	Setters	Morgans	Quixall[1]	..2	..	..
25 Feb	Nottingham F	A	L	2–3	Gregg	..	..	Setters	..	Nicholson	..	..	..1	..1	..1
4 Mar	Manchester C	A	W	3–1	..	..	..	..	..	Stiles	Moir	..	..	..2	..
11 Mar	Newcastle U	A	D	1–1	Pinner	..	..	..	..	..	..	..	Lawton	..	..1
18 Mar	Arsenal	H	W	1–1	Gaskell	..	..	..	..	..	..1	..	Dawson	..	..
25 Mar	Sheffield Wed	A	L	1–5	..	..	..	..	..	..	..	..	..	..	..1
31 Mar	Blackpool	A	L	0–2	..	..	..	..	..	..	..	..	..	..	..
1 Apr	Fulham	H	W	3–1	..	..	..	..	Nicholson	Giles	..1	Viollet[1]	..	..1	
3 Apr	Blackpool	H	W	*2–0	..	..	..	..	..1	..	..	..	..	..	..
8 Apr	W B A	A	D	1–1	..	..	..	..	..	..	..	..	..	..1	..
12 Apr	Burnley	H	W	6–0	..	..	..	..	Stiles	..	..3	..3	..	..	Moir
15 Apr	Birmingham C	H	W	4–1	..	..	..	..	..	..	..1	..1	..	..2	..
22 Apr	Preston NE	A	W	4–2	..	Dunne A	Brennan	..2	..	..	..	..	..	..	Charlton[2]
29 Apr	Cardiff C	H	D	3–3	..	Brennan	Cantwell	..1	..	..	..	..	..	..	..2

FA Cup

Date	Opponent			Score											
7 Jan	Middlesbrough (3)	H	W	3–0	Gregg	Brennan	Cantwell[1]	Setters	Foulkes	Nicholson	Quixall	Stiles	Dawson[2]	Pearson	Charlton
28 Jan	Sheffield Wed (4)	A	D	1–1	Briggs	..	..1	..	..	..	Viollet	..	..	..	..
1 Feb	Sheffield Wed (4)R	H	L	2–7	..	..	..	..	..	..	Quixall	..	..1	..1	..

Football League Cup

Date	Opponent			Score											
19 Oct	Exeter C (1)	A	D	1–1	Gregg	Setters	Brennan	Stiles	Foulkes	Nicholson	Dawson[1]	Lawton	Viollet	Pearson	Scanlon
26 Oct	Exeter C (1R)	H	W	4–1	Gaskell	Dunne A	Carolan	..	Cope	..	..	Giles[1]	Quixall[2]	..	..
2 Nov	Bradford C (2)	A	L	1–2	Gregg	Setters	Brennan	Bratt	Foulkes	..	..	..	Viollet[1]	..	..

Appearances (goals)

Bradley 4 · Brennan 41 · Briggs 1 · Cantwell 24 · Carolan 2 · Charlton 39 (21) · Cope 6 · Dawson 28 (16) · Dunne A 3 · Foulkes 40 · Gaskell 10 · Giles 23 (2) · Gregg 27 · Haydock 4 · Heron 1 · Lawton 1 · Moir 8 (1) · Morgans 2 · Nicholson 31 (5) · Pearson 27 (7) · Pinner 4 · Quixall 38 (13) · Scanlon 8 (1) · Setters 40 (4) · Stiles 26 (2) · Viollet 24 (15) · Own goals 1 · Total 26 players (88)

Football League

	P	W	D	L	F:A	Pts	
Tottenham H	42	31	4	7	115:55	66	1st
Manchester U	42	18	9	15	88:76	45	7th

1961–1962

SEASON 1961–1962 FOOTBALL LEAGUE (DIVISION 1)

19 Aug	West Ham U	A	D	1–1	Gregg	Brennan	Cantwell	Stiles[1]	Foulkes	Setters	Quixall	Viollet	Herd	Pearson	Charlton
23 Aug	Chelsea	H	W	3–2	..	..	..	..	..	..	..	..	.. [1]	.. [1]	.. [1]
26 Aug	Blackburn R	H	W	6–1	..	..	..	..	..	.. [1]	.. [2]	..	.. [2]	..	.. [1]
30 Aug	Chelsea	A	L	0–2	..	..	..	..	..	..	..	..	..	..	..
2 Sep	Blackpool	A	W	3–2	..	..	..	..	..	..	Bradley	.. [2]	..	..	.. [1]
9 Sep	Tottenham H	H	W	1–0	..	..	..	..	..	..	Quixall[1]	..	..	..	..
16 Sep	Cardiff C	A	W	2–1	..	..	..	..	..	..	.. [1]	..	Dawson[1]	..	..
18 Sep	Aston Villa	A	D	1–1	Gaskell	..	Dunne A	.. [1]	..	..	..	..	Herd	..	..
23 Sep	Manchester C	H	W	*3–2	Gregg	..	..	.. [1]	..	..	..	.. [1]	..	..	..
30 Sep	Wolverhampton W	H	L	0–2	..	..	Cantwell	..	..	Lawton	..	Giles	Dawson	..	..
7 Oct	W B A	A	D	1–1	Gaskell	..	..	..	..	..	Moir	Quixall	.. [1]	Giles	..
14 Oct	Birmingham C	H	L	0–2	Gregg	..	..	..	Haydock	..	Bradley	Giles	..	Herd	Moir
21 Oct	Arsenal	A	L	1–5	..	..	..	Nicholson	Foulkes	..	Moir	..	Herd	Viollet[1]	Charlton
28 Oct	Bolton W	H	L	0–3	..	..	Dunne A	..	..	Setters	..	Quixall	..	..	..
4 Nov	Sheffield Wed	A	L	1–3	..	..	Cantwell	Stiles	..	..	Bradley	Giles	Viollet[1]	Charlton	McMillan
11 Nov	Leicester C	H	D	2–2	Gaskell	..	..	..	..	..	..	.. [1]	.. [1]	..	..
18 Nov	Ipswich T	A	L	1–4	..	..	Dunne A	..	..	..	..	..	Herd	..	.. [1]
25 Nov	Burnley	H	L	1–4	..	..	..	..	..	..	..	..	.. [1]	Quixall	Charlton
2 Dec	Everton	A	L	1–5	..	..	..	Nicholson	..	..	Chisnall	..	.. [1]	Lawton	..
9 Dec	Fulham	H	W	3–0	..	..	..	..	..	..	..	..	.. [2]	.. [1]	..
16 Dec	West Ham U	H	L	1–2	..	..	..	..	..	..	..	..	.. [1]	..	..
26 Dec	Nottingham F	H	W	6–3	..	.. [1]	..	..	..	..	..	..	.. [1]	.. [3]	.. [1]
13 Jan	Blackpool	H	L	0–1	..	..	..	..	..	..	..	..	..	..	..
15 Jan	Aston Villa	H	W	2–0	..	..	..	..	..	..	..	..	Quixall[1]	..	.. [1]
20 Jan	Tottenham H	A	D	2–2	..	..	..	..	..	..	..	Stiles[1]	Lawton	Giles	.. [1]
3 Feb	Cardiff C	H	W	3–0	..	..	..	..	..	..	..	.. [1]	.. [1]	.. [1]	..
10 Feb	Manchester C	A	W	2–0	..	..	..	Stiles	Setters	Nicholson	.. [1]	Giles	Herd[1]	Lawton	..
24 Feb	W B A	H	W	4–1	Briggs	..	..	..	Foulkes	Setters[1]	Quixall[1]	..	..	..	.. [2]
28 Feb	Wolverhampton W	A	D	2–2	..	..	..	Setters	..	Nicholson	..	Stiles	.. [1]	.. [1]	..
3 Mar	Birmingham C	A	D	1–1	..	..	..	Stiles	..	Setters	..	Giles	.. [1]	..	..
17 Mar	Bolton W	A	L	0–1	..	..	..	Nicholson	..	..	..	..	Lawton	Stiles	..
20 Mar	Nottingham F	A	L	0–1	..	..	..	..	..	..	..	..	..	..	Moir
24 Mar	Sheffield Wed	H	D	1–1	Gaskel	..	..	Stiles	..	..	Moir	..	Viollet	Lawton	Charlton[1]
4 Apr	Leicester C	A	L	3–4	..	Setters	..	..	..	Nicholson	..	Quixall[1]	Herd	..	McMillan[2]
7 Apr	Ipswich T	H	W	5–0	Briggs	Brennan	..	.. [1]	..	Setters[1]	..	Giles	Quixall[3]	McMillan	Charlton
10 Apr	Blackburn R	A	L	0–3	Gaskell	..	..	..	..	..	..	..	Cantwell	Pearson	McMillan
14 Apr	Burnley	A	W	3–1	Briggs	.. [1]	..	..	..	..	Giles	Pearson	.. [1]	Herd[1]	..
16 Apr	Arsenal	H	L	2–3	..	..	Cantwell[1]	..	..	..	..	..	Herd	McMillan[1]	Charlton
21 Apr	Everton	H	D	1–1	Gaskell	..	Dunne A	..	..	..	..	..	Cantwell	Herd[1]	..
23 Apr	Sheffield U	H	L	0–1	..	..	..	..	..	..	..	..	Herd	McMillan	..
24 Apr	Sheffield U	A	W	3–2	..	..	..	Nicholson	..	..	..	..	McMillan[2]	Stiles[1]	..
28 Apr	Fulham	A	L	0–2	..	..	..	Setters	..	Nicholson	..	..	..	..	..
	FA Cup														
6 Jan	Bolton W (3)	H	W	2–1	Gaskell	Brennan	Dunne A	Nicholson[1]	Foulkes	Setters	Chisnall	Giles	Herd[1]	Lawton	Charlton
31 Jan	Arsenal (4)	H	W	1–0	..	..	..	..	..	.. [1]	..	Stiles	Lawton	Giles	..
17 Feb	Sheffield Wed (5)	H	D	0–0	..	..	..	Setters	..	Nicholson	..	Giles	Herd	Lawton	..
21 Feb	Sheffield Wed (5R)	A	W	2–0	..	..	..	Stiles	..	Setters	Quixall	.. [1]	..	..	.. [1]
10 Mar	Preston NE (6)	A	D	0–0	..	..	..	Nicholson	..	..	Chisnall	..	Cantwell	..	..
14 Mar	Preston NE (6R)	H	W	2–1	..	..	..	Stiles	..	..	Quixall	..	Herd[1]	..	.. [1]
31 Mar	Tottenham H (SF) (at Hillsborough)	N	L	1–3	..	Dunne A	Cantwell	..	..	..	..	..	.. [1]	..	..

Appearances (goals)

Bradley 6 · Brennan 41 (2) · Briggs 8 · Cantwell 17 (2) · Charlton 37 (8) · Chisnall 9 (1) · Dawson 4 (2) · Dunne A 28 · Foulkes 40 · Gaskell 21 · Giles 30 (2) · Gregg 13 · Haydock 1 · Herd 27 (14) · Lawton 20 (6) · McMillan 11 (6) · Moir 9 · Nicholson 17 · Pearson 17 (1) · Quixall 21 (10) · Setters 38 (3) · Stiles 34 (7) · Viollet 13 (7) · Own goals 1 · Total 23 players (72)

Football League

	P	W	D	L	F:A	Pts	
Ipswich	42	24	8	10	93:67	56	1st
Manchester U	42	15	9	18	72:75	39	15th

1962–1963

SEASON 1962–1963 FOOTBALL LEAGUE (DIVISION 1)

18 Aug	W B A	H	D	2–2	Gaskell	Brennan	Dunne A	Stiles	Foulkes	Setters	Giles	Quixall	Herd[1]	Law[1]	Moir
22 Aug	Everton	A	L	1–3	..	..	..	..	..	..	..	Pearson	..	..	.. [1]
25 Aug	Arsenal	A	W	3–1	..	..	..	Nicholson	..	Lawton	..	Chisnall[1]	.. [2]	..	..
29 Aug	Everton	H	L	0–1	..	..	..	..	..	..	..	..	..	..	..
1 Sep	Birmingham C	H	W	2–0	..	..	..	..	..	..	.. [1]	..	.. [1]	..	..
5 Sep	Bolton W	A	L	0–3	..	..	..	..	..	..	..	Quixall	..	..	..
8 Sep	Leyton O	A	L	0–1	..	..	..	..	..	..	Moir	Setters	..	..	McMillan
12 Sep	Bolton W	H	W	3–0	..	..	..	Stiles	..	Setters	Giles	Lawton	.. [2]	..	Cantwell[1]
15 Sep	Manchester C	H	L	2–3	..	..	..	..	..	Nicholson	..	..	..	.. [2]	..
22 Sep	Burnley	H	L	2–5	..	..	..	..	..	Lawton	..	Law[2]	..	Pearson	Moir
29 Sep	Sheffield Wed	A	L	0–1	Gregg	..	..	..	..	..	..	..	Quixall	Chisnall	McMillan
6 Oct	Blackpool	A	D	2–2	..	..	..	..	..	Nicholson	..	..	Herd[2]	Lawton	..
13 Oct	Blackburn R	H	L	0–3	..	..	..	..	..	..	..	..	..	Charlton	..
20 Oct	Tottenham H	A	L	2–6	..	..	Cantwell	..	..	Setters	..	Quixall[1]	.. [1]	Law	Charlton
27 Oct	West Ham U	H	W	3–1	..	..	..	..	..	..	..	.. [2]	..	.. [1]	..
3 Nov	Ipswich T	A	W	5–3	..	..	..	..	..	..	..	..	.. [1]	.. [4]	..
10 Nov	Liverpool	H	D	3–3	..	..	..	..	..	..	.. [1]	.. [1]	.. [1]	..	..
17 Nov	Wolverhampton W	A	W	3–2	..	..	..	..	..	..	..	..	.. [1]	.. [2]	..
24 Nov	Aston Villa	H	D	2–2	..	..	..	..	..	..	..	.. [2]	..	..	..
1 Dec	Sheffield U	A	D	1–1	..	..	..	..	..	..	..	..	..	Lawton	.. [1]
8 Dec	Nottingham F	H	W	5–1	..	..	..	Nicholson	..	Lawton	.. [1]	..	.. [2]	Law[1]	.. [1]
15 Dec	W B A	A	L	0–3	..	..	..	Stiles	..	Nicholson	..	..	..	..	Moir
26 Dec	Fulham	A	W	1–0	..	..	..	..	..	Setters	..	..	..	..	Charlton[1]
23 Feb	Blackpool	H	D	1–1	..	..	..	Crerand	..	..	..	..	.. [1]	Chisnall	..
2 Mar	Blackburn R	A	D	2–2	..	..	..	..	..	..	..	..	..	Law[1]	.. [1]
9 Mar	Tottenham H	H	L	0–2	..	..	..	..	..	Stiles	..	..	..	..	..
18 Mar	West Ham U	A	L	1–3	..	..	..	..	..	Setters	..	Stiles	.. [1]	..	..
23 Mar	Ipswich T	H	L	0–1	..	..	..	..	..	..	..	Quixall	..	..	..
1 Apr	Fulham	H	L	0–2	..	..	Dunne A	..	..	..	..	Chisnall	Quixall	..	..
9 Apr	Aston Villa	A	W	2–1	..	..	Cantwell	..	..	..	..	Stiles[1]	Herd	Quixall	.. [1]
13 Apr	Liverpool	A	L	0–1	..	..	Dunne A	..	..	..	..	..	Quixall	Law	..
15 Apr	Leicester C	H	D	2–2	..	..	..	..	..	..	Quixall	..	Herd[1]	..	.. [1]
16 Apr	Leicester C	A	L	3–4	..	..	..	..	..	..	..	..	..	.. [3]	..
20 Apr	Sheffield U	H	D	1–1	..	..	..	..	..	..	..	..	..	.. [1]	..
22 Apr	Wolverhampton W	H	W	2–1	Gaskell	..	..	..	..	..	..	..	.. [1]	.. [1]	..
1 May	Sheffield Wed	H	L	1–3	..	..	Cantwell	..	..	.. [1]	..	..	..	..	..
4 May	Burnley	A	W	1–0	..	Dunne A	..	..	..	..	Giles	..	Quixall	.. [1]	..
6 May	Arsenal	H	L	2–3	..	..	..	..	..	..	..	..	..	.. [2]	..
10 May	Birmingham C	A	L	1–2	..	..	..	..	..	Stiles	Quixall	Giles	Herd	.. [1]	..
15 May	Manchester C	A	D	1–1	..	..	..	..	..	..	.. [1]	..	..	..	..
18 May	Leyton O	H	W	*3–1	..	..	..	..	..	Setters	..	..	..	.. [1]	.. [1]
20 May	Nottingham F	A	L	2–3	..	..	..	..	Haydock	Brennan	..	Stiles	..	Giles	Walker
	FA Cup														
4 Mar	Huddersfield T (3)	H	W	5–0	Gregg	Brennan	Cantwell	Stiles	Foulkes	Setters	Giles[1]	Quixall[1]	Herd	Law[3]	Charlton
11 Mar	Aston Villa (4)	H	W	1–0	..	..	..	..	..	..	..	.. [1]	..	..	..
16 Mar	Chelsea (5)	H	W	2–1	..	..	..	..	..	..	..	.. [1]	..	.. [1]	..
30 Mar	Coventry C (6)	A	W	3–1	..	..	Dunne A	Crerand	..	..	..	.. [1]	..	..	.. [2]
27 Apr	Southampton (SF) (at Villa Park)	N	W	1–0	Gaskell	Dunne A	Cantwell	..	..	..	..	Stiles	..	.. [1]	..
25 May	Leicester C (F) (at Wembley)	N	W	3–1	..	..	..	..	..	..	..	Quixall	.. [2]	.. [1]	..

Appearances (goals)

Brennan 37 · Cantwell 25 (1) · Charlton 28 (7) · Chisnall 6 (1) · Crerand 19 · Dunne A 25 · Foulkes 41 · Gaskell 18 · Giles 36 (4) · Gregg 24 · Haydock 1 · Herd 37 (19) · Law 38 (23) · Lawton 12 · McMillan 4 · Moir 9 (1) · Nicholson 10 · Pearson 2 · Quixall 31 (7) · Setters 27 (1) · Stiles 31 (2) · Walker 1 · Own goals 1 · Total 22 players (67)

Football League

	P	W	D	L	F:A	Pts	
Everton	42	25	11	6	84:42	61	1st
Manchester U	42	12	10	20	67:81	34	19th

SEASON 1963–1964 FOOTBALL LEAGUE (DIVISION 1)

Date	Opponent		R	Score	1	2	3	4	5	6	7	8	9	10	11
24 Aug	Sheffield Wed	A	D	3–3	Gregg	Dunne A	Cantwell	Crerand	Foulkes	Setters	Moir[1]	Chisnall	Sadler	Law[2]	Charlton[2]
28 Aug	Ipswich T	H	W	2–0	..	..	..	..	..	..	..	..	..	..[2]	..
31 Aug	Everton	H	W	5–1	..	..	..	..	..	Stiles	..	..[2]	..[1]	..[2]	..
3 Sep	Ipswich T	A	W	7–2	..	..	..	..	..	Setters[1]	..[1]	..[1]	..[1]	..[3]	..
7 Sep	Birmingham C	A	D	1–1	..	..	..	..	..	..	..	..[1]	..	..	..
11 Sep	Blackpool	H	W	3–0	..	..	..	..	..	..	..	..	..	..[1]	..[2]
14 Sep	W B A	H	W	1–0	..	..	..	..	..	..	Best	Stiles	..	Chisnall[1]	..
16 Sep	Blackpool	A	L	0–1	..	..	..	..	..	..	Moir	..	..	..	..
21 Sep	Arsenal	A	L	1–2	..	..	..	..	..	..	Herd[1]	Chisnall	..	Law	..
28 Sep	Leicester C	H	W	3–1	..	..	..	..	..	..[1]	Moir	..	..	Herd[2]	..
2 Oct	Chelsea	A	D	1–1	..	..	..	..	..	..	..[1]	..	..	..	..
5 Oct	Bolton W	A	W	1–0	..	..	..	..	..	..	Herd[1]	..	..	Stiles	..
19 Oct	Nottingham F	A	W	2–1	..	..	..	..	..	..	Quixall[1]	..[1]	Herd	Law	..
26 Oct	West Ham U	H	L	0–1	..	..	..	..	..	..	Moir	..	..	..	..
28 Oct	Blackburn R	H	D	2–2	..	..	..	..	..	Stiles	..	..	Quixall[2]	..	..
2 Nov	Wolverhampton W	A	L	0–2	..	..	..	..	..	Setters	..	..	..	..	..
9 Nov	Tottenham H	H	W	4–1	..	..	..	..	..	..	Quixall	Moore	Herd[1]	..[3]	..
16 Nov	Aston Villa	A	L	0–4	..	..	..	..	..	..	..	..	..	..	..
23 Nov	Liverpool	H	L	0–1	..	..	..	..	..	..	..	..	..	..	..
30 Nov	Sheffield U	A	W	2–1	Gaskell	..	..	..	..	..	..	..	..	..[2]	..
7 Dec	Stoke C	H	W	5–2	..	..	..	..	..	..	..	..	..[1]	..[4]	..
14 Dec	Sheffield Wed	H	W	3–1	..	Brennan	Dunne A	..	..	..	..	Chisnall	Sadler	Herd[3]	..
21 Dec	Everton	A	L	0–4	..	Dunne A	Cantwell	..	..	..	Moir	..	..	..	..
26 Dec	Burnley	A	L	1–6	..	..	..	..	..	..	Quixall	..	Charlton	..[1]	Brennan
28 Dec	Burnley	H	W	5–1	..	..	..	..	..	..	Anderson	..[2]	..[2]	..	Best[1]
11 Jan	Birmingham C	H	L	1–2	..	..	..	..	..	..	Herd	..	Sadler[1]	Law	..
18 Jan	W B A	A	W	4–1	..	..	..	..	..	..	..	..	Charlton[1]	..[2]	..[1]
1 Feb	Arsenal	H	W	3–1	..	Brennan	Dunne A	Stiles	..	..[1]	..[1]	..	..[1]	..	..
8 Feb	Leicester C	A	L	2–3	..	..	..	Crerand	..	..	..[1]	..	..[1]	..	..
19 Feb	Bolton W	H	W	5–0	..	..	..	..	..	..	..[2]	Stiles	..[1]	..[2]	..
22 Feb	Blackburn R	A	W	3–1	..	..	..	..	..	..	Chisnall[1]	..	..[2]	..	..
7 Mar	West Ham U	A	W	2–0	..	..	..	Tranter	Stiles	Anderson	..	Sadler[1]	Herd[1]	Moir	..
21 Mar	Tottenham H	A	W	3–2	..	..	..	Foulkes	..	Best	Moore[1]	Law[1]	Charlton[1]	..	..
23 Mar	Chelsea	H	D	1–1	..	..	..	..	..	..	..	..	..[1]	..	..
27 Mar	Fulham	A	D	2–2	..	..	..	..	..	..	..	Herd[1]	..[1]	..	..
28 Mar	Wolverhampton W	H	D	2–2	Gregg	..	Cantwell	..	..	..	..	Chisnall	..[1]	Setters	..[1]
30 Mar	Fulham	H	W	3–0	..	..	Dunne A	..[1]	..	..[1]	Moir	Moore	..[1]	Law	..
4 Apr	Liverpool	A	L	0–3	..	..	..	..	..	Setters	Best	Stiles	..	..	..
6 Apr	Aston Villa	H	W	1–0	..	..	..	..	..	Stiles	Charlton	..	..	..[1]	Moir[1]
13 Apr	Sheffield U	H	W	2–1	..	..	Cantwell	..	..	..	..	..[1]	Sadler	..[1]	..[1]
18 Apr	Stoke C	A	L	1–3	..	..	Dunne A	..	..	..	..	..[1]	Sadler	Herd	..
25 Apr	Nottingham F	H	W	3–1	Gaskell	..	..	..	..	Setters	Moore[1]	Herd	Law[2]	Charlton	

FA Cup

Date	Opponent		R	Score	1	2	3	4	5	6	7	8	9	10	11
4 Jan	Southampton (3)	A	W	3–2	Gaskell	Dunne A	Cantwell	Crerand[1]	Foulkes	Setters	Anderson	Moore[1]	Charlton	Herd[1]	Best
25 Jan	Bristol R (4)	H	W	4–1	..	..	..	..	..	..	Herd[1]	Chisnall	..	Law[3]	..
15 Feb	Barnsley (5)	A	W	4–0	..	Brennan	Dunne A	..	..	..	..	Stiles	..[2]	..	..[1]
29 Feb	Sunderland (6)	H	D	3–3	..	..	..	..	..	..	..	..[1]	..[1]	..[1]	
4 Mar	Sunderland (6R)	A	D	2–2	..	..	..	..	..	..	..	Chisnall	..[1]	..[1]	..
9 Mar	Sunderland (6R) (at Huddersfield)	N	W	5–1	..	..	..	..	..	..	..[1]	..	..[1]	..[3]	..
14 Mar	West Ham U (SF) (at Hillsborough)	N	L	1–3	..	..	..	..	..	..	..	..	..	..[1]	..

European Cup Winners' Cup

Date	Opponent		R	Score	1	2	3	4	5	6	7	8	9	10	11
25 Sep	Willem II (1)	A	D	1–1	Gregg	Dunne A	Cantwell	Crerand	Foulkes	Setters[1]	Herd[1]	Chisnall	Sadler	Law	Charlton
15 Oct	Willem II (1R)	H	W	6–1	..	..	..	..	..	..	Quixall	..[1]	Herd	..[3]	..[1]
3 Dec	Tottenham H (2)	A	L	0–2	Gaskell	..	..	..	..	..	..	Stiles	..	..	..
10 Dec	Tottenham H (2)	H	W	4–1	..	..	..	..	..	..	..	Chisnall	..	..[2]	..[2]
26 Feb	Sporting Lisbon (3)	H	W	4–1	..	Brennan	Dunne A	..	..	..	Herd	Stiles	Sadler	Herd[2]	Law[3]	Best
18 Mar	Sporting Lisbon (3)	A	L	0–5	..	..	..	..	..	..	..	Chisnall	..	..	..

Appearances (goals)

Anderson 2 · Best 17 (4) · Brennan 17 · Cantwell 28 · Charlton 40 (9) · Chisnall 20 (6) · Crerand 41 (1) · Dunne A 40 · Foulkes 41 (1) · Gaskell 17 · Gregg 25 · Herd 30 (20) · Law 30 (30) · Moir 18 (3) · Moore 18 (4) · Quixall 9 (3) · Sadler 19 (5) · Setters 32 (4) · Stiles 17 · Tranter 1 · Total 20 players (90)

Football League

	P	W	D	L	F:A	Pts	
Liverpool	42	26	5	11	92:45	57	1st
Manchester U	42	23	7	12	90:62	53	2nd

SEASON 1964–1965 FOOTBALL LEAGUE (DIVISION 1)

Date	Opponent		R	Score	1	2	3	4	5	6	7	8	9	10	11
22 Aug	W B A	H	D	2–2	Gaskell	Brennan	Dunne A	Setters	Foulkes	Stiles	Connelly	Charlton[1]	Herd	Law[1]	Best
24 Aug	West Ham U	A	L	1–3	..	..	..	..	..	..	..	..	..	..[1]	..[1]
29 Aug	Leicester C	A	D	2–2	..	..	..	Crerand	..	..	..	..	Sadler[1]	..[1]	..
2 Sep	West Ham U	H	W	3–1	..	..	..	..	..	..	..[1]	..	..	..[1]	..
5 Sep	Fulham	A	L	1–2	..	..	..	..	..	..	..[1]	..	..	..	..
8 Sep	Everton	A	D	3–3	..	..	Dunne P	..	..	..	..[1]	..	Herd[1]	..[1]	..
12 Sep	Nottingham F	H	W	3–0	..	..	..	..	..	Setters	..[1]	..[2]	..	Stiles	..
16 Sep	Everton	H	W	2–1	..	..	..	..	..	Stiles	..	..	..	Law	..
19 Sep	Stoke C	A	W	2–1	..	..	..	..	..	Setters	..[1]	..	..	Stiles	..
26 Sep	Tottenham H	H	W	4–1	..	..	..	..	..	..[2]	..	Stiles	..	Law[2]	..
30 Sep	Chelsea	A	W	2–0	..	..	..	..	..	..	..	..	..[1]	..	..[1]
6 Oct	Burnley	A	D	0–0	..	..	..	..	..	..	..	..	..	..	..
10 Oct	Sunderland	H	W	1–0	..	..	..	..	..	..	..	..	..[1]	..	..
17 Oct	Wolverhampton W	A	W	4–2	..	..	..	..	..	..	..	..	..[1]	..[2]	..
24 Oct	Aston Villa	H	W	7–0	..	..	..	..	..	Setters	..[1]	Stiles	..[2]	..[4]	..
31 Oct	Liverpool	A	W	2–0	..	..	..	..[1]	..	Stiles	..	Charlton	..[1]	..	..
7 Nov	Sheffield Wed	H	W	1–0	..	..	..	..	..	..	..	..	..[1]	..	..
14 Nov	Blackpool	A	W	2–1	..	..	..	..	..	..	..[1]	..	..[1]	..	Moir
21 Nov	Blackburn R	H	W	3–0	..	..	..	..	..	..	..[1]	..	..[1]	..	Best[1]
28 Nov	Arsenal	A	W	3–2	..	..	..	..	..	..	..[1]	..	..	..[2]	..
5 Dec	Leeds U	H	L	0–1	..	..	..	..	..	..	..	..	..	..	..
12 Dec	W B A	A	D	1–1	..	..	..	..	..	..	..	..	..	..[1]	..
16 Dec	Birmingham C	H	D	1–1	..	..	..	..	..	..	..	..[1]	Sadler	Herd	..
26 Dec	Sheffield U	A	W	1–0	..	..	..	..	..	..	..	..	..	..	..[1]
28 Dec	Sheffield U	H	D	1–1	..	..	..	..	..	..	..	..	..	..	..[1]
16 Jan	Nottingham F	A	D	2–2	..	..	..	..	..	..	..	..	Herd	Law[2]	..
23 Jan	Stoke C	H	D	1–1	..	..	..	..	..	..	..	..	..	..[1]	..
6 Feb	Tottenham H	A	L	0–1	..	..	..	..	..	..	..	..	..	..	..
13 Feb	Burnley	H	W	3–2	..	..	..	..	..	..	..	..[1]	..[1]	..	..[1]
24 Feb	Sunderland	A	L	0–1	..	..	..	..	..	Fitzpatrick	..	..	..	..	..
27 Feb	Wolverhampton W	H	W	3–0	..	..	..	..	..	Stiles	..[1]	..[2]	..	..	..
13 Mar	Chelsea	H	W	4–0	..	..	..	..	..	..	..	..	..[2]	..[1]	..[1]
15 Mar	Fulham	H	W	4–1	..	..	..	..	..	..	..[2]	..	..[2]	..	..
20 Mar	Sheffield Wed	A	L	0–1	..	..	..	..	..	..	..	..	..	..[2]	..
22 Mar	Blackpool	H	W	2–0	..	..	..	..	..	..	..	..	..	..[2]	..
3 Apr	Blackburn R	A	W	5–0	..	..	..	..	..	..	..[3]	..[1]	..[1]	..	..
12 Apr	Leicester C	H	W	1–0	..	..	..	..	..	..	..	..	..	Best	Aston
17 Apr	Leeds U	A	W	1–0	..	..	..	..	..	..	..	..	..	Law	Best
19 Apr	Birmingham C	A	W	4–2	..	..	..	..	..	..	..	..[1]	Cantwell[1]	..[2]	..[2]
24 Apr	Liverpool	H	W	3–0	..	..	..	..	..	..	..[1]	..	Herd	..[2]	..
26 Apr	Arsenal	H	W	3–1	..	..	..	..	..	..	..	..	..	..[2]	..[1]
28 Apr	Aston Villa	A	L	1–2	..	..	..	..	..	Fitzpatrick	..	..[1]	..	..	..

FA Cup

Date	Opponent			Score										
					Dunne P	Brennan	Dunne A	Crerand	Foulkes	Stiles	Connelly	Charlton	Herd	Kinsey[1]	Best[1]
9 Jan	Chester (3)	H	W	2–1											Law
30 Jan	Stoke C (4)	A	D	0–0	..	..	..		..	..	..	..	..[1]		
3 Feb	Stoke C (4R)	H	W	1–0				..[1]						..[1]	
20 Feb	Burnley (5)	H	W	2–1				..[1]						..[2]	
10 Mar	Wolverhampton W (6)	A	W	5–3											..[1]
27 Mar	Leeds U (SF)	N	D	0–0	..	..	..								
	(at Hillsborough)														
31 Mar	Leeds U (SFR)	N	L	0–1	..	..	..	..							
	(at City Ground)														

Inter-Cities Fairs Cup

Date	Opponent			Score	Dunne P	Brennan	Dunne A	Crerand	Foulkes	Stiles	Connelly	Charlton	Herd[1]	Setters	Best[1]
23 Sep	Djurgaarden (1)	A	D	1–1								..[2]		Law[3]	..[1]
27 Oct	Djurgaarden (1)	H	W	6–1								..[3]	..[1]		
11 Nov	Borussia Dortmund (2)	A	W	6–1							..[1]	..[2]		..[1]	
2 Dec	Borussia Dortmund (2)	H	W	4–1							..[1]			..[1]	
20 Jan	Everton	H	D	1–1							..[1]		..[1]		
9 Feb	Everton	A	W	2–1							..[1]	..[1]	..[1]	..[2]	
12 Mar	Racing Strasbourg (4)	A	W	5–0									..[1]		
19 May	Racing Strasbourg (4)	H	D	0–0									..[2]	..[1]	
31 May	Ferencvaros (5)	H	W	3–2											
6 Jun	Ferencvaros (5)	A	L	0–1											
16 Jun	Ferencvaros (5)	A	L	1–2							..[1]				

Appearances (goals)

Aston 1 · Best 41 (10) · Brennan 42 · Cantwell 2 (1) · Charlton 41 (10) · Connelly 42 (15) · Crerand 39 (3) · Dunne A 42 · Dunne P 37 · Fitzpatrick 2 · Foulkes 42 · Gaskell 5 · Herd 37 (20) · Law 36 (28) · Moir 1 · Sadler 6 (1) · Setters 5 · Stiles 41 · Own goals 1 · Total 18 players (89)

Football League

	P	W	D	L	F:A	Pts	
Manchester U	42	26	9	7	89:39	61	1st

1965–1966

SEASON 1965–1966 FOOTBALL LEAGUE (DIVISION 1)

21 Aug	Sheffield Wed	H	W	1–0	Dunne P	Brennan	Dunne A	Crerand	Foulkes	Stiles	Anderson	Charlton	Herd[1]	Best	Aston[1]
24 Aug	Nottingham F	A	L	2–4							Connelly			Law	Best
28 Aug	Northampton T	A	D	1–1	Gaskell	Dunne A	Cantwell				..[1]			Law	Best
1 Sep	Nottingham F	H	D	0–0		Brennan	Dunne A					..[1]			
4 Sep	Stoke C	H	D	1–1								..[1]	..[1]		
8 Sep	Newcastle U	A	W	2–1											
11 Sep	Burnley	A	L	0–3						..[1]					
15 Sep	Newcastle U	H	D	1–1								..[1]		..[3]	
18 Sep	Chelsea	H	W	4–1								..[1]			Aston[1]
25 Sep	Arsenal	A	L	2–4	Dunne P								..[1]		
9 Oct	Liverpool	H	W	2–0								Best[1]	Charlton[1]		Fitzpatrick for Law
16 Oct	Tottenham H	A	L	1–5									..[1]	Herd[3]	
23 Oct	Fulham	H	W	4–1									..[1]	..[2]	
30 Oct	Blackpool	A	W	2–1	Gregg						Best[1]	Law[1]	..[1]		Connelly for Aston
6 Nov	Blackburn R	H	D	2–2							..[2]	..[1]	..[2]	Connelly[1]
13 Nov	Leicester C	A	W	5–0		Dunne A	Cantwell			Sadler					
20 Nov	Sheffield U	H	W	3–1						Foulkes	..[2]		..[1]	
4 Dec	West Ham U	H	D	0–0	Dunne P						..[1]		..[1]	
11 Dec	Sunderland	A	W	3–2									..[1] ..[1]	
15 Dec	Everton	H	W	3–0	Gregg							..[2]	..[1] ..[1]	
18 Dec	Tottenham H	H	W	*5–1								..[1]		
27 Dec	W B A	H	D	1–1								..[1]		
1 Jan	Liverpool	A	L	1–2						..[1]				Aston
8 Jan	Sunderland	H	D	1–1									..[1]	
12 Jan	Leeds U	A	D	1–1									..[1]	
15 Jan	Fulham	A	W	1–0										
29 Jan	Sheffield Wed	A	D	0–0								..[2]	..[3]	Connelly[1]
5 Feb	Northampton T	H	W	6–2									..[1]	Aston
19 Feb	Stoke C	A	D	2–2		Brennan	Dunne A				Connelly[1]	Best	..[1] ..[3]	Aston
26 Feb	Burnley	H	W	4–2							Best	Law		Connelly
12 Mar	Chelsea	A	L	0–2						..[1]		..[1]		
19 Mar	Arsenal	H	W	2–1						Fitzpatrick	Connelly		Cantwell[1]	..[1]
6 Apr	Aston Villa	A	D	1–1	Gaskell		Noble		Sadler	Stiles	Best	Anderson	Herd	
9 Apr	Leicester C	H	L	1–2	Gregg		Cantwell	Fitzpatrick	Foulkes		Connelly	Charlton	Sadler[1]	Aston
16 Apr	Sheffield U	A	L	1–3			Dunne A	Crerand	Cantwell		Anderson	Law		Charlton[1]
25 Apr	Everton	A	D	0–0							Connelly			
27 Apr	Blackpool	H	W	2–1						..[1]			..[1]	Herd for Dunne A
30 Apr	West Ham U	A	L	2–3			..[1]			Fitzpatrick	Ryan		Herd[1] ..[2]	Anderson for Fitzpatrick
4 May	W B A	A	D	3–3						Stiles		Charlton[1] ..[1]		
7 May	Blackburn R	A	W	4–1							..[1]	Herd[2] ..[2]	Charlton[1]	
9 May	Aston Villa	H	W	6–1								..[1]	Charlton[1]	
19 May	Leeds U	H	D	1–1			Noble			Dunne A			Law	

FA Cup

22 Jan	Derby Co	A	W	5–2	Gregg	Dunne A	Cantwell	Crerand	Foulkes	Stiles	Best[2]	Law[2]	Charlton	Herd[1]	Aston
12 Feb	Rotherham U (4)	H	D	0–0											Connelly[1]
15 Feb	Rotherham U (4R)	A	W	1–0		Brennan	Dunne A				..[1]	..[2]		..[1]	
5 Mar	Wolverhampton W (5)	A	W	4–2								..[2]			
26 Mar	Preston NE (6)	A	D	1–1							Connelly[1]	..[2]			Aston
30 Mar	Preston NE (6R)	H	W	3–1							Anderson				Connelly
23 Apr	Everton (SF)	N	L	0–1											
	(at Burnden Park)														

European Cup

22 Sep	HJK Helsinki (P)	A	W	3–2	Gaskell	Brennan	Dunne A	Fitzpatrick	Foulkes	Stiles	Connelly[1] ..[3]	Charlton	Herd[1]	Law[1]	Aston
6 Oct	HJK Helsinki (P)	H	W	6–0	Dunne P			Crerand			Best[2]	Charlton[1]			
17 Nov	ASK Vorwaerts (1)	A	W	2–0	Gregg	Dunne A	Cantwell				Best	Law[1]	Herd[3]		Connelly
1 Dec	ASK Vorwaerts (1)	H	W	3–1	Dunne P					..[1]	..[1]				
2 Feb	Benfica (2)	H	W	3–2	Gregg						..[2]		..[1]		..[1]
9 Mar	Benfica (2)	A	W	5–1		Brennan	Dunne A		..[1]						
13 Apr	FK Partizan	A	L	0–2							Anderson				
	Belgrade (SF)														
20 Apr	FK Partizan	H	W	1–0						..[1]					
	Belgrade (SF)														

Appearances (goals)

Anderson 23 (4) · Aston 22 (4) · Best 31 (9) · Brennan 28 · Cantwell 23 (2) · Charlton 38 (16) · Connelly 31 (5) · Crerand 41 · Dunne A 40 (1) · Dunne P 8 · Fitzpatrick 3 · Foulkes 33 · Gaskell 8 · Gregg 26 · Herd 36 (24) · Law 33 (15) · Noble 2 · Ryan 4 (1) · Sadler 10 (4) · Stiles 39 (2) · Own goals 1 · Total 20 players (84)

Football League

	P	W	D	L	F:A	Pts	
Liverpool	42	26	9	7	79:34	61	1st
Manchester U	42	18	15	9	84:59	51	4th

SEASON 1966–1967 FOOTBALL LEAGUE (DIVISION 1)

Date	Opponent			Score	1	2	3	4	5	6	7	8	9	10	11	Subs
20 Aug	W B A	H	W	5–3	Gaskell	Brennan	Dunne A	Fitzpatrick	Foulkes	Stiles[1]	Best[1]	Law[2]	Charlton	Herd[1]	Connelly	
23 Aug	Everton	A	W	2–1	..	..	..	..	..	..	..	..	..	..	..	
27 Aug	Leeds U	A	L	1–3	..	..	..	..	..	..	..	..	..	..	..	
31 Aug	Everton	H	W	3–0	..	..	..	Crerand	..	1	..	Connelly[1]	1	..	Best	
3 Sep	Newcastle U	H	W	3–2	Gregg	..	..	..	..	..	..	1	1	1	..	
7 Sep	Stoke C	A	L	0–3	..	..	..	..	..	..	..	..	..	..	..	
10 Sep	Tottenham H	A	L	1–2	Gaskell	..	..	..	..	..	Best	1	Sadler	..	Charlton	Aston for Sadler
17 Sep	Manchester C	H	W	1–0	Stepney	..	..	..	..	..	..	1	..	Charlton	Aston	
24 Sep	Burnley	H	W	4–1	..	..	..	1	..	..	Herd[1]	1	1	Best	..	Aston for Law
1 Oct	Nottingham F	A	L	1–4	..	..	..	..	..	..	Best	Charlton[1]	..	Herd	Aston	
8 Oct	Blackpool	A	W	2–1	..	Dunne A	Noble	..	Cantwell	..	Herd	Law[2]	..	Charlton	Best	
15 Oct	Chelsea	H	D	1–1	..	..	..	..	..	..	..	1	..	..	..	
29 Oct	Arsenal	H	W	1–0	..	..	..	..	..	..	..	..	1	..	..	
5 Nov	Chelsea	A	W	3–1	..	Brennan	..	..	Foulkes	..	..	Aston[2]	..	..	1	
12 Nov	Sheffield Wed	H	W	2–0	..	Dunne A	..	..	..	..	1	Law	..	1	..	Aston for Foulkes
19 Nov	Southampton	A	W	2–1	..	..	..	..	Cantwell	..	..	2	..	..	..	Aston for Cantwell
26 Nov	Sunderland	H	W	5–0	..	..	..	..	Sadler	..	Best	1	Charlton	Herd[4]	Aston	
30 Nov	Leicester C	A	W	2–1	..	..	..	..	..	..	..	1	..	1	..	
3 Dec	Aston Villa	A	L	1–2	..	..	..	..	..	..	..	..	1	..	..	
10 Dec	Liverpool	H	D	2–2	..	Brennan	..	..	..	Dunne A	2	Ryan	..	..	..	Anderson for Dunne A
17 Dec	W B A	A	W	4–3	..	..	..	..	..	Stiles	..	Law[1]	..	3	..	
26 Dec	Sheffield U	A	L	1–2	..	Dunne A	..	..	Foulkes	Sadler	..	..	..	1	..	
27 Dec	Sheffield U	H	W	2–0	..	..	..	1	..	..	..	..	..	1	..	
31 Dec	Leeds U	H	D	0–0	..	..	..	..	..	..	..	..	..	..	..	
14 Jan	Tottenham H	H	W	1–0	..	..	..	..	..	..	..	Ryan	..	1	..	
21 Jan	Manchester C	A	D	1–1	..	..	..	1	..	Stiles	Ryan	Charlton	Sadler	..	Best	
4 Feb	Burnley	A	D	1–1	..	..	..	..	..	..	Best	Law	..	1	Charlton	
11 Feb	Nottingham F	H	W	1–0	..	..	..	..	..	..	..	1	..	..	..	Ryan for Foulkes
25 Feb	Blackpool	H	W	*4–0	..	..	..	..	..	..	..	..	Charlton[2]	Aston	1	
3 Mar	Arsenal	A	D	1–1	..	..	..	..	..	..	..	..	..	..	..	
11 Mar	Newcastle U	A	D	0–0	..	..	..	..	..	..	..	..	..	..	..	
18 Mar	Leicester C	H	W	5–2	..	..	..	..	..	..	..	1	Charlton[1]	Herd[1]	1	Sadler[1] for Herd
25 Mar	Liverpool	A	D	0–0	..	..	..	..	..	..	..	..	Sadler	Charlton	..	
27 Mar	Fulham	A	D	2–2	..	..	..	..	..	1	1	..	..	..	..	
28 Mar	Fulham	H	W	2–1	..	..	..	..	..	1	1	..	..	..	..	
1 Apr	West Ham U	H	W	3–0	..	..	..	..	..	..	1	1	..	1	..	
10 Apr	Sheffield Wed	A	D	2–2	..	..	..	..	..	..	..	..	..	2	..	
18 Apr	Southampton	H	W	3–0	..	..	..	..	..	..	..	1	1	1	..	
22 Apr	Sunderland	A	D	0–0	..	..	..	..	..	..	..	..	..	..	..	
29 Apr	Aston Villa	H	W	3–1	..	Brennan	Dunne A	..	..	..	1	1	..	..	1	
6 May	West Ham U	A	W	6–1	..	..	..	..	1	1	1	2	..	1	..	
13 May	Stoke C	H	D	0–0	..	..	..	..	..	..	..	Ryan	..	..	..	

FA Cup

Date	Opponent			Score	1	2	3	4	5	6	7	8	9	10	11	Subs
28 Jan	Stoke C (3)	H	W	2–0	Stepney	Dunne A	Noble	Crerand	Foulkes	Stiles	Best	Law[1]	Sadler	Herd[1]	Charlton	
18 Feb	Norwich C (4)	H	L	1–2	..	..	..	..	Sadler	..	Ryan	1	Charlton	..	Best	

Football League Cup

Date	Opponent			Score	1	2	3	4	5	6	7	8	9	10	11
14 Sep	Blackpool (2)	A	L	1–5	Dunne P	Brennan	Dunne A	Crerand	Foulkes	Stiles	Connelly	Best	Sadler	Herd[1]	Aston

Appearances (goals)

Aston 26 (5) · Best 42 (10) · Brennan 16 · Cantwell 4 · Charlton 42 (12) · Connelly 6 (2) · Crerand 39 (3) · Dunne A 40 · Fitzpatrick 3 · Foulkes 33 (4) · Gaskell 5 · Gregg 2 · Herd 28 (16) · Law 36 (23) · Noble 29 · Ryan 4 · Sadler 35 (5) · Stepney 35 · Stiles 37 (3) · Own goals 1 · Total 19 players (84)

Football League

	P	W	D	L	F:A	Pts	
Manchester U	42	24	12	6	84:45	60	1st

SEASON 1967–1968 FOOTBALL LEAGUE (DIVISION 1)

Date	Opponent			Score	1	2	3	4	5	6	7	8	9	10	11	Subs
19 Aug	Everton	A	L	1–3	Stepney	Brennan	Dunne A	Crerand	Foulkes	Stiles	Best	Law	Charlton[1]	Kidd	Aston	Sadler for Crerand
23 Aug	Leeds U	H	W	1–0	..	..	..	..	..	..	Ryan	..	..	..	..	
26 Aug	Leicester C	H	D	1–1	..	..	..	Sadler	..	1	Best	..	..	..	..	
2 Sep	West Ham U	A	W	3–1	..	Dunne A	Burns	Crerand	..	..	Ryan[1]	Sadler[1]	..	1	Best	
6 Sep	Sunderland	A	D	1–1	..	..	..	..	..	..	..	..	..	1	..	Fitzpatrick for Stiles
9 Sep	Burnley	H	D	2–2	..	..	1	..	1	Fitzpatrick	..	..	..	..	..	Kopel for Fitzpatrick
16 Sep	Sheffield Wed	A	D	1–1	..	..	..	..	..	Stiles	Best[1]	..	Law	Kidd	..	
23 Sep	Tottenham H	H	W	3–1	..	..	..	..	..	..	2	..	..	1	..	
30 Sep	Manchester C	A	W	2–1	..	..	..	..	..	..	..	..	2	..	..	Aston for Foulkes
7 Oct	Arsenal	H	W	1–0	..	..	..	..	Sadler	..	..	Kidd	..	Aston[1]	..	
14 Oct	Sheffield U	A	W	3–0	..	..	..	..	..	..	..	1	..	1	..	Fitzpatrick for Stiles
25 Oct	Coventry C	H	W	4–0	..	..	..	..	Fitzpatrick	1	1	..	2	..	..	
28 Oct	Nottingham F	A	L	1–3	Kopel	..	..	..	..	1	..	..	..	..	..	
4 Nov	Stoke C	H	W	1–0	..	Dunne A	..	..	Foulkes	Sadler	Ryan	..	1	Best	..	
8 Nov	Leeds U	A	L	0–1	..	..	..	..	..	..	..	..	..	..	..	
11 Nov	Liverpool	A	W	2–1	..	..	..	..	..	Fitzpatrick	..	1	1	2	..	Fitzpatrick for Ryan
18 Nov	Southampton	H	W	3–2	..	..	..	..	..	..	..	1	1	..	1	
25 Nov	Chelsea	A	D	1–1	..	Brennan	Dunne A	..	..	Burns	..	1	..	..	..	
2 Dec	W B A	H	W	2–1	..	..	..	..	..	..	..	..	..	2	..	
9 Dec	Newcastle U	A	D	2–2	..	..	..	1	..	..	..	..	1	..	..	
16 Dec	Everton	H	W	3–1	..	Dunne A	Burns	..	..	..	Best	..	Law[1]	1	..	
23 Dec	Leicester C	A	D	2–2	..	..	..	..	..	..	2	1	1	1	..	
26 Dec	Wolverhampton W	H	W	4–0	..	..	..	..	..	..	..	1	1	1	..	
30 Dec	Wolverhampton W	A	W	3–2	..	..	..	..	..	..	1	1	1	..	1	
6 Jan	West Ham U	H	W	3–1	..	..	..	..	Sadler	Fitzpatrick	1	1	1	1	..	
20 Jan	Sheffield Wed	H	W	4–2	..	..	..	..	..	..	2	1	1	..	..	
3 Feb	Tottenham H	A	W	2–1	..	..	..	..	..	..	1	..	1	Herd	..	
17 Feb	Burnley	A	L	1–2	..	..	..	..	..	Stiles	1	..	..	Law	..	
24 Feb	Arsenal	A	W	*2–0	..	..	..	..	..	..	1	Fitzpatrick	..	..	..	
2 Mar	Chelsea	H	L	1–2	..	..	..	..	..	1	Charlton	Ryan	..	..	..	
16 Mar	Coventry C	A	L	0–2	..	Brennan	..	..	..	..	Fitzpatrick	Herd	..	Aston for Kidd	
23 Mar	Nottingham F	H	W	3–0	..	1	1	..	..	Fitzpatrick	Herd[1]	..	Best	Aston	
27 Mar	Manchester C	H	L	1–3	..	..	..	..	..	..	Law	..	..	Herd	Aston for Herd
30 Mar	Stoke C	A	W	4–2	..	..	..	..	Fitzpatrick	Best[1]	Gowling[1]	..	Herd	Aston[1]	Ryan[1] for Gowling
6 Apr	Liverpool	H	L	1–2	..	Dunne A	..	..	..	..	..	..	..	..	
12 Apr	Fulham	A	W	4–0	..	..	..	..	Stiles	2	Kidd[1]	..	Law[1]	..	
13 Apr	Southampton	A	D	2–2	..	..	..	Foulkes	Sadler	1	..	1	Gowling	..	
15 Apr	Fulham	H	W	3–0	Rimmer	..	..	..	..	1	..	1	Law	1	
20 Apr	Sheffield U	H	W	1–0	Stepney	Brennan	Dunne A	..	Sadler	Stiles	..	..	1	..	
27 Apr	W B A	A	L	3–6	..	Dunne A	Burns	..	..	..	2	..	1	..	
4 May	Newcastle U	H	W	6–0	..	Brennan	Dunne A	..	Foulkes	Sadler[1]	3	2	Gowling	..	
11 May	Sunderland	H	L	1–2	..	..	..	..	..	Stiles	1	..	Sadler	..	Gowling for Foulkes

FA Cup

Date	Opponent			Score	1	2	3	4	5	6	7	8	9	10	11
27 Jan	Tottenham H (3)	H	D	2–2	Stepney	Dunne A	Burns	Crerand	Sadler	Fitzpatrick	Best[1]	Kidd	Charlton[1]	Law	Aston
31 Jan	Tottenham H (3R)	A	L	0–1	..	..	..	..	..	..	..	..	..	Herd	..

European Cup

Date	Opponent	H/A	Res	Score	Stepney	Dunne A	Burns	Crerand	Foulkes	Stiles	Best	Sadler	Charlton	Law	Kidd
20 Sep	Hibernians (Malta) (1)	H	W	4-0	Stepney	Dunne A	Burns	Crerand	Foulkes	Stiles	Best	Sadler[2]	Charlton	Law[2]	Kidd
27 Sep	Hibernians (1)	A	D	0-0	..	..	..	..	..	Sadler	Fitzpatrick	Kidd	..	Best	Aston
15 Nov	FK Sarajevo (2)	A	D	0-0	..	..	..	..	..	..	Burns	..	..	Best[1]	Aston[1]
29 Nov	FK Sarajevo (2)	H	W	2-1	..	Brennan	Dunne A	..	..	..	Best[1]	..	..	..	..
28 Feb	Gornik Zabrze (3)	H	W	*2-0	..	Dunne A	Burns	..	Sadler	Stiles	Best	..	..	Ryan	..
13 Mar	Gornik Zabrze (3)	A	L	0-1	..	..	..	..	..	..	Fitzpatrick	Charlton	Herd	Kidd	Best
24 Apr	Real Madrid (SF)	H	W	1-0	..	..	..	..	..	..	Best[1]	Kidd	Charlton	Law	Aston
15 May	Real Madrid (SF)	A	D	*3-3	..	Brennan	Dunne A	..	Foulkes[1]	..	..	..	..	Sadler[1]	..
29 May	Benfica (F) (at Wembley)	N	W	4-1	..	..	..	..	..	..	..	[1]	[1]	[2]	..

Appearances (goals)

Aston 34 (10) · Best 41 (28) · Brennan 13 (1) · Burns 36 (2) · Charlton 41 (15) · Crerand 41 (1) · Dunne A 37 (1) · Fitzpatrick 14 · Foulkes 24 (1) · Gowling 4 (1) · Herd 6 (1) · Kidd 34 (15) · Kopel 1 · Law 23 (7) · Rimmer 1 · Ryan 7 (2) · Sadler 40 (3) · Stepney 41 · Stiles 20 · Own goals 1 · Total 19 players (89)

Football League

	P	W	D	L	F:A	Pts	
Manchester C	42	26	6	10	86:43	58	1st
Manchester U	42	24	8	10	89:55	55	2nd

1968–1969

SEASON 1968–1969 FOOTBALL LEAGUE (DIVISION 1)

Date	Opponent	H/A	Res	Score	Stepney	Brennan	Dunne A	Crerand	Foulkes	Stiles	Best	Kidd	Charlton	Law	Aston	Subs / Notes
10 Aug	Everton	H	W	2-1	Stepney	Brennan	Dunne A	Crerand	Foulkes	Stiles	Best[1]	Kidd	Charlton[1]	Law	Aston	
14 Aug	W B A	A	L	1-3	..	..	..	..	..	..	..	..	..	Kidd[1]	..	Sadler for Foulkes
17 Aug	Manchester C	A	D	0-0	..	Kopel	..	Fitzpatrick	Sadler	..	..	Gowling	..	Kidd	..	Burns for Aston
21 Aug	Coventry C	H	W	1-0	..	..	..	..	..	..	Ryan[1]	Kidd	..	Burns	Best	
24 Aug	Chelsea	H	L	0-4	..	..	..	Crerand	..	..	..	..	..	..	..	
28 Aug	Tottenham H	H	W	3-1	..	Brennan	..	Fitzpatrick[2]	..	..	Morgan	..	..	Law[2]	[1]	
31 Aug	Sheffield Wed	A	L	4-5	..	..	..	..	..	..	..	..	[1]	..	..	Burns for Dunne A
7 Sep	West Ham U	H	D	1-1	..	..	Dunne A	Burns	Foulkes	..	..	Sadler	..	[1]	..	
14 Sep	Burnley	A	L	0-1	..	..	..	..	..	..	..	..	..	..	..	
21 Sep	Newcastle U	H	W	3-1	..	..	..	Crerand	Sadler	..	..	Fitzpatrick	..	[1]	[2]	Kidd for Crerand
5 Oct	Arsenal	H	D	0-0	..	..	..	..	Foulkes	..	..	..	..	[1]	..	
9 Oct	Tottenham H	A	D	2-2	..	..	..	[1]	..	..	..	..	..	[1]	..	Sartori for Burns
12 Oct	Liverpool	A	L	0-2	..	Brennan	Kopel	..	..	..	James	Ryan	..	Gowling	Sartori	
19 Oct	Southampton	H	L	1-2	..	Kopel	Dunne A	..	Foulkes	..	Morgan	Sadler	..	Sartori	Best[1]	Fitzpatrick for Foulkes
26 Oct	Q P R	A	W	3-2	..	Brennan	..	..	Sadler	..	..	Kidd	..	Law[1]	[2]	
2 Nov	Leeds U	H	D	0-0	..	..	..	..	..	..	..	..	..	..	..	
9 Nov	Sunderland	A	D	1-1	..	..	..	..	..	..	..	..	..	Sartori	..	
16 Nov	Ipswich T	H	D	0-0	..	..	..	..	..	..	James	..	..	..	..	Kopel for Kidd
23 Nov	Stoke C	A	D	0-0	..	Kopel	..	..	..	..	..	Best	..	Fitzpatrick	Sartori	
30 Nov	Wolverhampton W	H	W	2-0	..	..	..	..	Sadler	..	..	Sartori	..	Law[1]	Best[1]	Fitzpatrick for Stiles
7 Dec	Leicester C	A	L	1-2	..	..	Dunne A	Burns	..	..	..	..	..	[1]	..	
14 Dec	Liverpool	H	W	1-0	..	..	..	..	James	..	Best	Sadler	..	[1]	Sartori	
21 Dec	Southampton	A	L	0-2	..	..	..	..	..	..	..	..	..	..	Kidd	
26 Dec	Arsenal	A	L	0-3	..	..	..	..	..	..	..	Fitzpatrick	[1]	..	Sartori	Sartori for Crerand
11 Jan	Leeds U	A	L	1-2	..	..	..	..	..	..	..	..	[3]	Sartori	Best[1]	
18 Jan	Sunderland	H	W	4-1	Rimmer	..	..	Fitzpatrick	..	..	Morgan	Sartori	..	[3]	..	
1 Feb	Ipswich T	A	L	0-1	Stepney	Fitzpatrick	Dunne A	Crerand	..	..	..	Kidd	..	[1]	[1]	Foulkes for Sartori
15 Feb	Wolverhampton W	A	D	2-2	..	..	..	..	..	Sadler	..	..	..	Sartori	Sadler	
8 Mar	Manchester C	H	L	0-1	..	Brennan	Fitzpatrick	..	Foulkes	Stiles	..	..	..	..	Aston	Foulkes for Brennan
10 Mar	Everton	A	D	0-0	..	..	Dunne A	..	James[1]	..	Best	..	Fitzpatrick	Law[1]	Best[2]	Sadler for Morgan
15 Mar	Chelsea	A	L	2-3	..	Fitzpatrick	..	..	..	..	Morgan[3]	Sadler	..	Aston[1]	[2]	
19 Mar	Q P R	H	W	8-1	..	..	..	..	..	..	..	..	Best[1]	Aston[1]	[2]	
22 Mar	Sheffield Wed	H	W	1-0	..	..	..	..	..	..	..	..	Best[1]	..	Aston	
24 Mar	Stoke C	H	D	1-1	..	..	..	..	..	..	..	..	Aston[1]	..	Best	Sadler for Morgan
29 Mar	West Ham U	A	D	0-0	..	..	..	..	..	..	Ryan	..	..	..	[1]	Sadler for Dunne A
31 Mar	Nottingham F	A	W	1-0	..	..	Stiles	..	Sadler	..	..	..	..	..	[2]	
2 Apr	W B A	H	W	2-1	..	..	..	..	..	..	Morgan[2]	Ryan	..	Kidd	[1]	Foulkes for Ryan
5 Apr	Nottingham F	H	W	3-1	..	..	..	..	..	..	[2]	Kidd	..	Law	[1]	
8 Apr	Coventry C	A	L	1-2	..	..	[1]	..	..	..	..	..	..	Charlton	..	
12 Apr	Newcastle U	A	L	0-2	Rimmer	..	..	..	..	..	..	..	Charlton	Law	..	
19 Apr	Burnley	H	W	*2-0	..	Brennan	Fitzpatrick	..	Foulkes	Stiles	..	[1]	Charlton	Aston	[1]	
17 May	Leicester C	H	W	3-2	..	..	Burns	..	..	..	..	..	Charlton	[1]	[1]	

FA Cup

Date	Opponent	H/A	Res	Score	Stepney	Dunne A	Burns	Crerand	James	Stiles	Best	Kidd	Charlton	Law	Sartori	Subs / Notes
4 Jan	Exeter C (3)	A	W	*3-1	Stepney	Dunne A	Burns	Fitzpatrick[1]	James	Stiles	Best	Kidd[1]	Charlton	Law[1]	Sartori	Sadler for Best
25 Jan	Watford (4)	H	D	1-1	Rimmer	Kopel	Dunne A	..	..	..	..	Morgan	Best	Law[2]	Best	
3 Feb	Watford (4R)	A	W	2-0	Stepney	Fitzpatrick	..	Crerand	..	..	..	Kidd	..	Law[1]	Best[1]	
8 Feb	Birmingham C (5)	A	D	2-2	..	..	..	[1]	..	..	..	..	..	Law[3]	..	
24 Feb	Birmingham C (5R)	H	W	6-2	..	..	..	..	..	..	[1]	[1]	..	Law[3]	..	
1 Mar	Everton (6)	H	L	0-1	..	..	..	..	..	..	..	..	..	..	..	

European Cup

Date	Opponent	H/A	Res	Score	Stepney	Dunne A	Burns	Crerand	Foulkes	Stiles	Best	Law	Charlton	Sadler	Kidd	Subs / Notes
18 Sep	Waterford (1)	A	W	3-1	Stepney	Dunne A	Burns[1]	Crerand	Foulkes	Stiles[1]	Best	Law[3]	Charlton	Sadler	Kidd	Rimmer for Stepney
2 Oct	Waterford (1)	H	W	7-1	..	..	[1]	..	..	[1]	..	Law[4]	..	..	..	
13 Nov	RSC Anderlecht (2)	H	W	3-0	..	Brennan	Dunne A	..	Sadler	..	Ryan	Kidd[1]	..	Law[2]	Sartori	
27 Nov	RSC Anderlecht (2)	A	L	1-3	..	Kopel	..	..	Foulkes	..	Fitzpatrick	Law	..	Sadler	Best[2]	
26 Feb	Rapid Vienna (3)	H	W	3-0	..	Fitzpatrick	..	..	James	..	Morgan[1]	Kidd	..	Law	Best[2]	
5 Mar	Rapid Vienna (3)	A	D	0-0	..	..	..	..	..	..	..	Sadler	..	Law	..	
23 Apr	AC Milan (SF)	A	L	0-2	Rimmer	Brennan	Fitzpatrick	..	Foulkes	..	..	..	..	..	..	Burns for Stiles
15 May	AC Milan (SF)	H	W	1-0	..	..	Burns	..	..	..	..	..	[1]	..	..	

World Club Championship

Date	Opponent	H/A	Res	Score	Stepney	Dunne A	Burns	Crerand	Foulkes	Stiles	Morgan	Sadler	Charlton	Law	Best	Subs / Notes
25 Sep	Estudiantes	A	L	0-1	Stepney	Dunne A	Burns	Crerand	Foulkes	Stiles	Morgan	Sadler	Charlton	Law	Best	
16 Oct	Estudiantes	H	D	1-1	..	Brennan	Dunne A	..	..	Sadler	..	Kidd	..	[1]	..	Sartori for Law

Appearances (goals)

Aston 13 (2) · Best 41 (19) · Brennan 13 · Burns 14 · Charlton 32 (5) · Crerand 35 (1) · Dunne A 33 · Fitzpatrick 28 (3) · Foulkes 10 · Gowling 2 · James 21 (1) · Kidd 28 (1) · Kopel 7 · Law 30 (14) · Morgan 29 (6) · Rimmer 4 · Ryan 6 (1) · Sadler 26 · Sartori 11 · Stepney 38 · Stiles 41 (1) · Own goals 3 · Total 21 players (57)

Football League

	P	W	D	L	F:A	Pts	
Leeds U	42	27	13	2	66:26	67	1st
Manchester U	42	15	12	15	57:53	42	11th

SEASON 1969–1970 FOOTBALL LEAGUE (DIVISION 1)

1969–1970

9 Aug	Crystal Palace	A	D	2–2	Rimmer	Dunne A	Burns	Crerand	Foulkes	Sadler	Morgan[1]	Kidd	Charlton[1]	Law	Best	Givens for Dunne A
13 Aug	Everton	H	L	0–2	..	Brennan	..	..	..	..	..	..	..	..	..	Givens for Foulkes
16 Aug	Southampton	H	L	1–4	..	..	..	..	..	..	..[1]	..	..	..	..	
19 Aug	Everton	A	L	0–3	Stepney	Fitzpatrick	..	..	Edwards	..	..	..	Givens	Best	Aston	
23 Aug	Wolverhampton W	A	D	0–0	..	..	..	..	Ure	..	..	..	Charlton	Law	Best	Givens for Law
27 Aug	Newcastle U	H	D	0–0	..	..	Dunne A	..	..	..	..	..	..	Givens	..	
30 Aug	Sunderland	H	W	3–1	..	..	..	..	..	..	..	..[1]	..	..[1]	..[1]	
6 Sep	Leeds U	A	D	2–2	..	..	..	Burns	..	..	..	Givens	..	Gowling	..[2]	
13 Sep	Liverpool	H	W	1–0	..	..	..	..	..	..	..[1]	Kidd	..	..	..	
17 Sep	Sheffield Wed	A	W	3–1	..	..	..	..	..	..	..	..[1]	..	..	..[2]	Aston for Gowling
20 Sep	Arsenal	A	D	2–2	..	..	..	..	..	..[1]	..	..	..	Aston	..[1]	
27 Sep	West Ham U	H	W	5–2	..	..	..	..[1]	..	..	..	..[1]	..[1]	..	..[2]	
4 Oct	Derby Co	A	L	0–2	..	..	..	..	..	..	..	..	..	..	..	Sartori for Aston
8 Oct	Southampton	A	W	3–0	..	..	..	..[1]	..	..	..	..[1]	..	..	..[1]	
11 Oct	Ipswich T	H	W	2–1	..	..	..	..	..	..	..	..[1]	..	..	..[1]	Brennan for Best
18 Oct	Nottingham F	H	D	1–1	..	..	..	..	..	..	..	..	..	..	..[1]	
25 Oct	W B A	A	L	1–2	..	Brennan	..	..	..	..	Sartori	..[1]	..	..	..	Givens for Aston
1 Nov	Stoke C	H	D	1–1	..	..	..	..	..	..	Law	..	..[1]	..	..	
8 Nov	Coventry C	A	W	2–1	..	..	..	..	..	..	Sartori	Best	..	Law[1]	Aston[1]	
15 Nov	Manchester C	A	L	0–4	..	..	..	..	..	..	..	..	..	..	..	Kidd for Sartori
22 Nov	Tottenham H	H	W	3–1	..	Fitzpatrick	..	..[1]	..	..	..	Kidd	..[2]	Best	..	Edwards for Fitzpatrick
29 Nov	Burnley	A	D	1–1	..	Edwards	..	..	..	..	Best[1]	..	..	Stiles	..	
6 Dec	Chelsea	H	L	0–2	..	..	..	..	..	..	..	..	..	..	..	Ryan for Kidd
13 Dec	Liverpool	A	W	*4–1	..	Brennan	..	..	..[1]	..	Morgan[1]	Best	..[1]	Crerand	..	Sartori for Aston
26 Dec	Wolverhampton W	H	D	0–0	..	Edwards	..	..	..	..	..	Crerand	..	Kidd	Best	
27 Dec	Sunderland	A	D	1–1	..	..	Brennan	..	..	..	..	..	..	..[1]	..	
10 Jan	Arsenal	H	W	2–1	..	..	Dunne A	..	..	..	..[1]	..	..	..	Aston	Sartori[1] for Dunne A
17 Jan	West Ham U	A	D	0–0	Rimmer	..	Burns	Crerand	..	..	..	Sartori	..	..	..	
26 Jan	Leeds U	H	D	2–2	Stepney	..	..	..	..	..[1]	..	..	..	..[1]	..	
31 Jan	Derby C	H	W	1–0	..	..	..	..	..	..	..	..	..[1]	..	..	
10 Feb	Ipswich T	A	W	1–0	..	..	Dunne A	..	..	..	..	..	..	..[1]	Best	
14 Feb	Crystal Palace	H	D	1–1	..	..	..	..	..	..	..	..	..	..[1]	..	
28 Feb	Stoke C	A	D	2–2	..	..	..	..	..	..	..[1]	..[1]	..	..	..	Burns for Sadler
17 Mar	Burnley	H	D	3–3	Rimmer	..	..	..[1]	..	..	..	..	..	Law[1]	..[1]	
21 Mar	Chelsea	A	L	1–2	Stepney	..	Burns	..	..	Stiles	..[1]	..	..	..	..	
28 Mar	Manchester C	H	L	1–2	..	..	Dunne A	..	Sadler	Burns	..	..	..	Kidd[1]	..	Law for Sartori
30 Mar	Coventry C	H	D	1–1	..	..	..	Fitzpatrick	Ure	Sadler	..	Best	Law	..[1]	Aston	Burns for Kidd
31 Mar	Nottingham F	A	W	2–1	..	Stiles	..	Crerand	James	..	..	Fitzpatrick	Charlton[1]	Gowling	Best	
4 Apr	Newcastle U	A	L	1–5	..	Fitzpatrick	..	..	..	..	..	Gowling	..[1]	Stiles	Aston	Sartori for Aston
8 Apr	W B A	H	W	7–0	..	Stiles	..	..	Ure	..	..	Fitzpatrick[2]	..[2]	Gowling[2]	Best[1]	
13 Apr	Tottenham H	A	L	1–2	..	Edwards	..	..	..	Stiles	..	..[1]	..	Kidd	..	Gowling for Morgan
15 Apr	Sheffield Wed	H	D	2–2	..	..	..	..	Sadler	..	..	..	..[1]	..	..[1]	

FA Cup

3 Jan	Ipswich T (3)	A	W	*1–0	Stepney	Edwards	Brennan	Burns	Ure	Sadler	Morgan	Crerand	Charlton	Kidd	Best	Aston for Morgan
24 Jan	Manchester C (4)	H	W	3–0	..	..	Burns	Crerand	..	..	..[1]	Sartori	..	..[2]	Aston	
7 Feb	Northampton T (5)	A	W	8–2	..	..	Dunne A	..	..	..	..	..	..	..[2]	Best[6]	Burns for Charlton
21 Feb	Middlesbrough (6)	A	D	1–1	..	..	..	..	..	..	..	..[1]	..	..	..	
25 Feb	Middlesbrough (6R)	H	W	2–1	..	Dunne A	Burns	..	..	..	..[1]	..	..[1]	..	..	
14 Mar	Leeds U (SF) (at Hillsborough)	N	D	0–0	..	Edwards	Dunne A	..	..	..	..	..	..	..	..	
23 Mar	Leeds U (SFR) (at Villa Park)	N	D	0–0	..	..	..	..	Sadler	Stiles	..	..	..	..	..	Law for Sartori
26 Mar	Leeds U (SFR) (at Burnden Park)	N	L	0–1	..	..	..	..	..	..	..	..	..	..	..	Law for Sartori
10 Apr	Watford (playoff) (at Highbury)	N	W	2–0	..	Stiles	..	..	Ure	Sadler	..	Fitzpatrick	..	..[2]	..	

League Cup

3 Sep	Middlesbrough (2)	H	W	1–0	Stepney	Fitzpatrick	Dunne A	Crerand	James	Sadler[1]	Morgan	Kidd	Charlton	Givens	Best	Gowling for Kidd
23 Sep	Wrexham (3)	H	W	2–0	..	..	..	Burns	Ure	..	..	..[1]	..	Aston	..[1]	
14 Oct	Burnley (4)	A	D	0–0	..	..	..	..	..	..	..	..	..	..	..	
20 Oct	Burnley (4R)	H	W	1–0	..	..	..	..	..	..	..	..	..	..	..[1]	Sartori for Fitzpatrick
12 Nov	Derby Co (5)	A	D	0–0	..	Brennan	..	..	..	..	Sartori	Best	..	Law	Aston	
19 Nov	Derby Co (5R)	H	W	1–0	..	Fitzpatrick	..	..	..	..	Best	Kidd[1]	..	..	..	Sartori for Law
3 Dec	Manchester C (SF)	A	L	1–2	..	Edwards	..	..	..	..	..	..	..[1]	Stiles	..	
17 Dec	Manchester C (SF)	H	D	2–2	..	..[1]	..	Stiles	..	..	Morgan	Crerand	..	Law[1]	Best	

Appearances (goals)

Aston 21 (1) · Best 37 (15) · Brennan 8 · Burns 30 (3) · Charlton 40 (12) · Crerand 25 (1) · Dunne A 33 · Edwards 18 · Fitzpatrick 20 (3) · Foulkes 3 · Givens 4 (1) · Gowling 6 (3) · James 2 · Kidd 33 (12) · Law 10 (2) · Morgan 35 (7) · Rimmer 5 · Sadler 40 (2) · Sartori 13 (2) · Stepney 37 · Stiles 8 · Ure 34 (1) · Own goals 1 · Total 22 players (66)

Football League

	P	W	D	L	F:A	Pts	
Everton	42	29	8	5	72:34	66	1st
Manchester U	42	14	17	11	66:61	45	8th

SEASON 1970–1971 FOOTBALL LEAGUE (DIVISION 1)

1970–1971

15 Aug	Leeds U	H	L	0–1	Stepney	Edwards	Dunne A	Crerand	Ure	Sadler	Fitzpatrick	Stiles	Charlton	Kidd	Best	Gowling for Stiles
19 Aug	Chelsea	H	D	0–0	..	..	..	..	..	..	Morgan	Fitzpatrick	..	Stiles	..	
22 Aug	Arsenal	A	L	0–4	..	Stiles	..	..	..	..	..	..	..	Law	..	Edwards for Stepney
25 Aug	Burnley	A	W	2–0	Rimmer	Edwards	..	Fitzpatrick	..	..	..	Law[2]	..	Stiles	..	
29 Aug	West Ham U	H	D	1–1	..	..	..	..[1]	..	..	..	..	..	..	..	Gowling for Stiles
2 Sep	Everton	H	W	2–0	..	..	..	..	..	..	Stiles	..	..[1]	Kidd	..[1]	
5 Sep	Liverpool	A	D	1–1	..	..	..	..	..	..	..	..	..	..[1]	..	
12 Sep	Coventry C	H	W	2–0	..	..	..	..	..	..	..	..	..[1]	..	..[1]	
19 Sep	Ipswich T	A	L	0–4	..	..	..	..	..	..	..	..	..	Gowling	..	Young for Dunne A
26 Sep	Blackpool	H	D	1–1	..	Watson	Burns	..	James	..	Morgan	Gowling	..	Kidd	..[1]	
3 Oct	Wolverhampton W	A	L	2–3	..	..	..	..	..	..	..	..[1]	..	..[1]	..	Sartori for James
10 Oct	Crystal Palace	H	L	0–1	..	Edwards	Dunne A	..	Ure	Stiles	..	Best	..	..	Aston	
17 Oct	Leeds U	A	D	2–2	..	..	..	..[1]	..	..	Burns	..	..[1]	..	..	Sartori for Stiles
24 Oct	W B A	H	W	2–1	..	..	..	..	..	Burns	Law[1]	..	..	..[1]	..	
31 Oct	Newcastle U	A	L	0–1	..	..	..	..	James	Sadler	Burns	..	..	..	..	
7 Nov	Stoke C	H	D	2–2	..	..	Burns	..	..	..[1]	Law[1]	..	..	..	..	
14 Nov	Nottingham F	A	W	2–1	..	Watson	Dunne A	..	..	..	..	..	..	Gowling[1]	Sartori[1]	
21 Nov	Southampton	A	L	0–1	..	..	..	..	..	..	..	..	..	Kidd	Aston	Sartori for Fitzpatrick
28 Nov	Huddersfield T	H	D	1–1	..	..	..	..	..	..	..	..[1]	..	..	..	
5 Dec	Tottenham H	A	D	2–2	..	..	..	..	..	..	..[1]	..[1]	..	..	..	
12 Dec	Manchester C	H	L	1–4	..	..	..	..	..	Stiles	..	..	..	..[1]	..	Sartori for Law
19 Dec	Arsenal	H	L	1–3	..	..	..	Crerand	..	Fitzpatrick	Morgan	..	..	..	Sartori[1]	
26 Dec	Derby Co	A	D	4–4	..	Fitzpatrick	..	..	Ure	Sadler	..	..[1]	..	..[1]	Law[2]	
9 Jan	Chelsea	A	W	2–1	Stepney	..	..	..	Edwards	Stiles	..[1]	Law	..	Gowling[1]	Aston	
16 Jan	Burnley	H	D	1–1	..	..	..	..	..	..	..	..	..	..	..[1]	
30 Jan	Huddersfield	A	W	2–1	..	..	Burns	..	..	Sadler	..	..[1]	..	..	Best	Aston[1] for Law
6 Feb	Tottenham H	H	W	2–1	..	..	..	..	..	..	..[1]	Kidd	..	..	..[1]	
20 Feb	Southampton	H	W	5–1	..	..	..	..	..	..	..[1]	Best	..	..[4]	Aston	
23 Feb	Everton	A	L	0–1	..	..	Dunne A	..	..	..	..	..	..	..	..	Burns for Gowling
27 Feb	Newcastle U	H	W	1–0	..	..	..	..	..	..	..	..	..	Kidd	..	
6 Mar	W B A	A	L	3–4	..	..	..	..	..	..	..	..[1]	..	..[1]	..[1]	
13 Mar	Nottingham F	H	W	2–0	..	..	..	..	..	..	..	..[1]	..	Law[1]	..	Burns for Aston
20 Mar	Stoke C	A	W	2–1	..	..	..	..	..	..	..	..[2]	..	..	..	
3 Apr	West Ham U	A	L	1–2	..	..	..	..	..	..	..	..[1]	..	..	..	Burns for Sadler
10 Apr	Derby Co	H	L	1–2	..	Dunne A	Burns	..	..	Stiles	..	..	..	..[1]	..	Gowling for Aston

Date	Opponent			Score												Substitutes
12 Apr	Wolverhampton W	H	W	1–0	..	..	..	..	..	..	Best	Gowling[1]	..	..	Morgan	Kidd for Law
13 Apr	Coventry C	A	L	1–2	..	..	..	..	..	Sadler	.2	..	..	Kidd	..	
17 Apr	Crystal Palace	A	W	5–3	..	Fitzpatrick	Dunne A	..	..	..	..	..	..	Law3	..	Burns for Crerand
19 Apr	Liverpool	H	L	0–2	..	Dunne A	Burns	..	..	..	..	..	..	..	..	
24 Apr	Ipswich T	H	W	3–2	..	..	..	..	James	..	Law	..	1	Kidd1	Best1	Sartori for Sadler
1 May	Blackpool	A	D	1–1	..	..	..	..	..	..	.1	..	1	..	.2	
5 May	Manchester C	A	W	4–3	..	O'Neil	..	..	..	..	..	..	1	..	.2	

FA Cup

Date	Opponent			Score												Substitutes
2 Jan	Middlesbrough (3)	H	D	0–0	Rimmer	Fitzpatrick	Dunne A	Crerand	Ure	Sadler	Morgan	Best	Charlton	Kidd	Law	
5 Jan	Middlesbrough (3R)	A	L	1–2	..	..	..	..	Edwards	..	..	.1	..	..	..	Gowling for Kidd

League Cup

Date	Opponent			Score												Substitutes
9 Sep	Aldershot (2)	A	W	3–1	Rimmer	Edwards	Dunne A	Fitzpatrick	Ure	Sadler	Stiles	Law1	Charlton	Kidd1	Best1	James for Dunne A
7 Oct	Portsmouth (3)	H	W	1–0	..	Donald	Burns	..	..	..	Morgan	Gowling	.1	.1	Aston	Aston for Sadler
28 Oct	Chelsea (4)	H	W	2–1	..	Edwards	Dunne A	..	James	..	Law	Best1	..	..	Aston	Burns for Law
18 Nov	Crystal Palace (5)	H	W	4–2	..	Watson	..	.1	..	..	..	..	..	..	.2 .1	
16 Dec	Aston Villa (SF)	H	D	1–1	..	..	..	..	..	Stiles	Sartori	..	..	..	..	
23 Dec	Aston Villa (SF)	A	L	1–2	..	Fitzpatrick	..	Crerand	Ure	Sadler	Morgan	..	..	.1	Law	

Appearances (goals)

Aston 19 (3) · Best 40 (18) · Burns 16 · Charlton 42 (5) · Crerand 24 · Dunne A 35 · Edwards 29 · Fitzpatrick 35 (2) · Gowling 17 (8) · James 13 · Kidd 24 (8) · Law 28 (15) · Morgan 25 (3) · O'Neil 1 · Rimmer 20 · Sadler 32 (1) · Sartori 2 (2) · Stepney 22 · Stiles 17 · Ure 13 · Watson 8 · Total 21 players (65)

Football League

	P	W	D	L	F:A	Pts	
Arsenal	42	29	7	6	71:29	65	1st
Manchester U	42	16	11	15	65:66	43	8th

1971–1972

SEASON 1971–1972 FOOTBALL LEAGUE (DIVISION 1)

Date	Opponent			Score												Substitutes
14 Aug	Derby Co	A	D	2–2	Stepney	O'Neil	Dunne A	Gowling1	James	Sadler	Morgan1	Kidd	Charlton	Law1	Best	
18 Aug	Chelsea	A	W	3–2	..	Fitzpatrick	..	..	..	..	..	.1	.1	..	..	Aston for Best
20 Aug	Arsenal (Anfield)	H	W	3–1	..	O'Neil	..	.1	..	..	..	..	..	Best2	Aston	Burns for Charlton
23 Aug	WBA (Stoke)	H	W	3–1	..	..	..	.1	..	..	..	..	..	Law	Best	
28 Aug	Wolverhampton W	A	D	1–1	..	..	..	..	..	..	..	..	..	..	.1	
31 Aug	Everton	A	L	0–1	..	..	..	..	..	..	..	..	..	..	..	Aston for Law
4 Sep	Ipswich T	H	W	1–0	..	..	..	..	..	..	..	.1	..	.2	..	Aston for Gowling
11 Sep	Crystal Palace	A	W	3–1	..	..	..	..	..	..	..	..	.1	..	.3	
18 Sep	West Ham U	H	W	4–2	..	..	..	..	..	..	..	1	1	..	..	
25 Sep	Liverpool	A	D	2–2	..	..	Burns	..	..	..	..	..	..	Best1	Aston	Burns for Dunne A
2 Oct	Sheffield U	H	W	2–0	..	..	Dunne A	.1	..	..	..	..	1	Law1	Best1	
9 Oct	Huddersfield T	A	W	3–0	..	..	..	..	..	..	..	..	..	..	.1	
16 Oct	Derby Co	H	W	1–0	..	..	..	..	..	..	..	..	..	..	.1	Aston for Gowling
23 Oct	Newcastle U	A	W	1–0	..	..	..	.1	..	..	..	..	..	McIlroy1	..	Sartori for Kidd
30 Oct	Leeds U	H	L	0–1	..	..	..	..	..	..	..	.1	..	Law2	..	Aston for Dunne A
6 Nov	Manchester C	A	D	3–3	..	..	..	..	..	..	..	.1	..	.2	..	McIlroy for Law
13 Nov	Tottenham H	H	W	3–1	..	..	Burns	..	Edward	..	McIlroy1	Kidd1	..	McIlroy1	.3	Aston for Best
20 Nov	Leicester C	H	W	3–2	..	..	..	..	Sadler	..	.1	..	..	Law1	..	
27 Nov	Southampton	A	W	5–2	..	..	..	..	..	,	.2	..	..	.1	..	McIlroy for Kidd
4 Dec	Nottingham F	H	W	3–2	..	..	..	..	..	..	..	..	..	.1	..	
11 Dec	Stoke C	A	D	1–1	..	Dunne A	..	..	..	..	..	..	..	.1	..	
18 Dec	Ipswich T	A	D	0–0	..	..	..	..	.1	..	..	..	..	..	..	
27 Dec	Coventry C	H	D	2–2	..	..	..	..	Edwards	..	..	..	..	McIlroy1	..	Sartori for Gowling
1 Jan	West Ham U	A	L	0–3	..	..	..	..	..	..	McIlroy	..	..	..	Best	Aston for McIlroy
8 Jan	Wolverhampton W	H	L	1–3	..	O'Neil	..	..	James	..	..	Kidd1	..	..	..	
22 Jan	Chelsea	H	L	0–1	..	..	Dunne A	Burns	..	..	..	..	..	..	..	
29 Jan	WBA	A	L	1–2	..	..	Burns	Gowling	..	..	..	..	..	Gowling	..	
12 Feb	Newcastle U	H	L	0–2	..	..	Dunne A	Burns1	..	..	..	Gowling	..	Law	..	McIlroy for Kidd
19 Feb	Leeds U	A	L	1–5	..	..	..	Buchan	..	Burns	..	Kidd	Kidd	Best1	Storey-Moore1	McIlroy for Gowling
4 Mar	Tottenham H	A	L	0–2	..	..	..	..	..	Morgan	..	..	..	..	..	McIlroy for Kidd
8 Mar	Everton	H	D	0–0	..	..	..	..	..	Gowling1	Best	Charlton1	Law1	.1	..	McIlroy for Kidd
11 Mar	Huddersfield T	H	W	2–0	..	..	..	..	..	..	Morgan	Best1	..	..	..	Young for Law
25 Mar	Crystal Palace	H	W	4–0	..	..	..	..	Sadler1	Best	McIlroy	..	Young	..	..	Gowling for McIlroy
1 Apr	Coventry C	A	W	3–2	Connaughton	..	..	..	Sadler	Morgan	..	..	Kidd	..	..	Law for Gowling
3 Apr	Liverpool	H	L	0–3	..	..	..	.1	James	Sadler	Gowling	..	Young	.1	..	Young for James
4 Apr	Sheffield U	A	D	1–1	..	..	..	..	..	..	Morgan	Kidd	Kidd1	Kidd	..	McIlroy for Young
8 Apr	Leicester C	A	L	0–2	..	..	..	..	Sadler	Gowling	Best	Young	Charlton	Kidd	..	
12 Apr	Manchester C	H	L	1–3	Stepney	..	..	..	James	Young	.1	McIlroy	.1	Law	.1	Gowling for Charlton
15 Apr	Southampton	H	W	3–2	..	..	..	..	..	..	Morgan	Kidd	Charlton1	Law	Best	
22 Apr	Nottingham F	A	D	0–0	..	..	..	..								
25 Apr	Arsenal	A	L	0–3	..	..	..	..								
29 Apr	Stoke C	H	W	3–0	..	..	..	..								

FA Cup

Date	Opponent			Score												Substitutes
15 Jan	Southampton (3)	A	D	1–1	Stepney	O'Neil	Burns	Gowling	Edwards	Sadler	Morgan	Kidd	Charlton1	Law	Best	McIlroy for Kidd
19 Jan	Southampton (3R)	H	W	4–1	..	..	..	..	..	.1	..	McIlroy	..	..	.2	Aston1 for McIlroy
5 Feb	Preston NE (4)	A	W	2–0	..	..	Dunne A	.2	James	..	..	Kidd	..	..	..	
26 Feb	Middlesbrough (5)	H	D	0–0	..	O'Neil	Dunne A	Burns	..	..	..	Gowling	1	..	.1	
29 Feb	Middlesbrough (5R)	A	W	3–0	..	..	..	..	..	..	.1	..	..	..	.1	
18 Mar	Stoke C (6)	H	D	1–1	..	..	..	Buchan	..	..	Kidd	..	..	.1	Gowling for Sadler
22 Mar	Stoke C (6R)	A	L	1–2	..	..	..	Gowling	..	Buchan	..	..	..	.1	McIlroy for Morgan

League Cup

Date	Opponent			Score												Substitutes
7 Sep	Ipswich T (2)	A	W	3–1	Stepney	O'Neil	Dunne A	Gowling	James	Sadler	Morgan1	Kidd	Charlton	Best2	Aston	
6 Oct	Burnley (3)	H	D	1–1	..	..	..	..	..	..	..	..	.1	Law	Best	
18 Oct	Burnley (3R)	A	W	1–0	..	..	..	..	..	..	..	..	..	..	..	Aston for Kidd
27 Oct	Stoke C (4)	H	D	1–1	..	..	Burns	.1	..	..	..	..	..	..	..	Aston for Kidd
8 Nov	Stoke C (4R)	A	D	0–0	..	..	..	..	..	..	..	..	..	McIlroy	..	
15 Nov	Stoke C (4R)	A	L	1–2	..	..	..	..	..	..	..	McIlroy	..	Sartori	.1	

Appearances (goals)

Aston 2 · Best 40 (18) · Buchan 13 (1) · Burns 15 (1) · Charlton 40 (8) · Connaughton 3 · Dunne A 34 · Edwards 4 · Fitzpatrick 1 · Gowling 35 (6) · James 37 (1) · Kidd 34 (10) · Law 32 (13) · McIlroy 8 (4) · Morgan 35 (1) · O'Neil 37 · Sadler 37 (1) · Stepney 39 · Storey-Moore 11 (5) · Young 5 · Total 20 players (69)

Football League

	P	W	D	L	F:A	Pts	
Derby Co	42	24	10	8	69:33	58	1st
Manchester U	42	19	10	13	69:61	48	8th

SEASON 1972–1973 FOOTBALL LEAGUE (DIVISION 1)

Date	Opponent	V	R	Score	1	2	3	4	5	6	7	8	9	10	11	Substitutes
12 Aug	Ipswich T	H	L	1–2	Stepney	O'Neil	Dunne A	Morgan	James	Buchan	Best	Kidd	Charlton	Law[1]	Storey-Moore	McIlroy for Charlton
15 Aug	Liverpool	A	L	0–2				Young			Morgan			Best		McIlroy for Kidd
19 Aug	Everton	A	L	0–2					Buchan	Sadler		Fitzpatrick	Kidd	.[1]		McIlroy for James
23 Aug	Leicester C	H	D	1–1									McIlroy[1]			Kidd for McIlroy
26 Aug	Arsenal	H	D	0–0								Young				
30 Aug	Chelsea	H	D	0–0								Fitzpatrick	Law			Charlton for Storey-Moore
2 Sep	West Ham U	A	D	2–2								Law	Charlton	.[1]	.[1]	McIlroy for Law
9 Sep	Coventry C	H	L	0–1				Buchan	Fitzpatrick		McIlroy					Young for Charlton
16 Sep	Wolverhampton W	A	L	0–2		Buchan	Dunne A				Young	McIlroy				Kidd for Sadler
23 Sep	Derby Co	H	W	3–0		Donald		Young		Buchan	Morgan[1]	Davies[1]				
30 Sep	Sheffield U	A	L	0–1												McIlroy for Storey-Moore
7 Oct	W B A	A	D	2–2								Macdougall[1]	Davies	.[1]		
14 Oct	Birmingham C	H	W	1–0		Watson			Sadler							
21 Oct	Newcastle U	A	L	1–2											.[1]	Charlton for Storey-Moore
28 Oct	Tottenham H	H	L	1–4				Law						Charlton[1]		
4 Nov	Leicester C	A	D	2–2		Donald		Morgan			Best[1]		Charlton	Storey-Moore		
11 Nov	Liverpool	H	W	2–0		O'Neil							.[1] Charlton	Davies[1]		McIlroy for Dunne A
18 Nov	Manchester C	A	L	0–3												Kidd for Morgan
25 Nov	Southampton	H	W	2–1					Edwards			.[1]		.[1]		
2 Dec	Norwich C	A	W	2–0					Sadler		Young	.[1]			.[1]	
9 Dec	Stoke C	H	L	0–2				Young			Morgan					Law for Young
16 Dec	Crystal Palace	A	L	0–5									Kidd			Law for Dunne A
23 Dec	Leeds U	H	D	1–1				Law				.[1] Charlton				Kidd for Law
26 Dec	Derby Co	A	L	1–3				Kidd							.[1]	Young for Dunne A
6 Jan	Arsenal	A	L	1–3	Young	Forsyth	Graham				Kidd[1]		Law			
20 Jan	West Ham U	H	D	2–2				Law	Holton		Macdougall		Macari[1]	Graham		Davies for Law
24 Jan	Everton	H	D	0–0				Martin								Kidd for Macdougall
27 Jan	Coventry C	A	D	1–1				Graham	.[1]					Martin		
10 Feb	Wolverhampton W	H	W	2–1									.2			
17 Feb	Ipswich T	A	L	1–4	Forsyth	Dunne A			Martin				.[1]	Kidd		
3 Mar	W B A	H	W	2–1	Young	Forsyth		James		Morgan	Kidd[1]		.[1]	Storey-Moore		Martin for Storey-Moore
10 Mar	Birmingham C	A	L	1–3	Rimmer								.[1]			Martin for Storey-Moore
17 Mar	Newcastle U	H	W	2–1		James		Holton[1]						Martin[1]		
24 Mar	Tottenham H	A	D	1–1			.[1]									
31 Mar	Southampton	A	W	2–0								.[1]		.[1]		Anderson for Kidd
7 Apr	Norwich C	H	W	1–0	Stepney								Law			Anderson for Kidd
11 Apr	Crystal Palace	H	W	2–0							.[1]	.[1]	Macari	.[1]		Anderson for Kidd
14 Apr	Stoke C	A	D	*2–2								Anderson	.[1]			Fletcher for Anderson
18 Apr	Leeds U	A	W	1–0												Fletcher for Anderson
21 Apr	Manchester C	H	D	0–0							Kidd					Anderson for James
23 Apr	Sheffield U	H	L	1–2		Sidebottom					.[1]					
28 Apr	Chelsea	A	L	0–1												Anderson for Kidd

FA Cup

Date	Opponent	V	R	Score	1	2	3	4	5	6	7	8	9	10	11	Substitutes
13 Jan	Wolverhampton W (3)	A	L	0–1	Stepney	Young	Forsyth	Law	Sadler	Buchan	Morgan	Davies	Charlton	Kidd	Graham	Dunne A for Kidd

League Cup

Date	Opponent	V	R	Score	1	2	3	4	5	6	7	8	9	10	11	Substitutes
6 Sep	Oxford U (2)	A	D	2–2	Stepney	O'Neil	Dunne A	Buchan	James	Sadler	Morgan	Charlton	Law[1]	Best	Storey-Moore	McIlroy for Dunne A
12 Sep	Oxford U (2R)	H	W	3–1		Fitzpatrick	Buchan	Young				Law	Charlton	.2		McIlroy for Law
3 Oct	Bristol R (3)	A	D	1–1		Donald	Dunne A			Buchan		.[1]	Kidd			
11 Oct	Bristol R (3R)	H	L	1–2		Watson										McIlroy[1] for Kidd

Appearances (goals)

Anderson 2 (1) · Best 19 (4) · Buchan 42 · Charlton 34 (6) · Davies 15 (4) · Donald 4 · Dunne A 24 · Edwards 1 · Fitzpatrick 5 · Forsyth 8 · Graham 18 (1) · Holton 15 (3) · James 22 · Kidd 17 (4) · Law 9 (1) · Macari L 16 (5) · Macdougall 18 (5) · McIlroy 4 · Martin 14 (2) · Morgan 39 (2) · O'Neil 16 · Rimmer 4 · Sadler 19 · Sidebottom 2 · Stepney 38 · Storey-Moore 26 (5) · Watson 3 · Young 28 · Own goals 1 · Total 28 players (44)

Football League

	P	W	D	L	F:A	Pts	
Liverpool	42	25	10	7	72:42	60	1st
Manchester U	42	12	13	17	44:60	37	18th

SEASON 1973–1974 FOOTBALL LEAGUE (DIVISION 1)

Date	Opponent	V	R	Score	1	2	3	4	5	6	7	8	9	10	11	Substitutes
25 Aug	Arsenal	A	L	0–3	Stepney	Young	Buchan M	Daly	Holton	James	Morgan	Anderson	Macari	Graham	Martin	McIlroy for Daly
29 Aug	Stoke C	H	W	1–0				Martin				.[1]			McIlroy	Fletcher for James
1 Sep	Q P R	H	W	2–1						.[1]					.[1]	Fletcher for Martin
5 Sep	Leicester C	A	L	0–1				Daly		Sidebottom			Kidd			Martin for Daly
8 Sep	Ipswich T	A	L	1–2					Sadler	Greenhoff		.[1]				Macari for Kidd
12 Sep	Leicester C	H	L	1–2	.[1]	Buchan M	Young	Martin	Holton	James			Macari		Storey-Moore	
15 Sep	West Ham U	H	W	3–1								Kidd[1]	Anderson		.[1]	Buchan G for Holton
22 Sep	Leeds U	A	D	0–0					Greenhoff			Anderson	Macari	Kidd	Graham	Buchan G for Macari
29 Sep	Liverpool	H	D	0–0												Buchan G for Graham
6 Oct	Wolverhampton W	A	L	1–2												McIlroy[1] for Anderson
13 Oct	Derby Co	H	L	0–1			Forsyth					Young	Kidd	Anderson		
20 Oct	Birmingham C	H	W	1–0	.[1]		Young					Kidd	Macari	Graham	Best	Martin for Best
27 Oct	Burnley	A	D	0–0						James	Griffiths					Sadler for Kidd
3 Nov	Chelsea	H	D	2–2			.[1]		.[1]			Macari	Kidd		.[1]	
10 Nov	Tottenham H	A	L	1–2					Holton	James					.[1]	
17 Nov	Newcastle U	A	L	2–3								.[1]		.[1]		
24 Nov	Norwich C	H	D	0–0												Fletcher for Morgan
8 Dec	Southampton	H	D	0–0			Forsyth		James	Griffiths		Young		McIlroy		Anderson for Kidd
15 Dec	Coventry C	H	L	2–3							.[1]	Macari	McIlroy	Young	.[1]	Martin for James
22 Dec	Liverpool	A	L	0–2			Young		Sidebottom			Kidd	Graham			McIlroy for Kidd
26 Dec	Sheffield U	H	L	1–2		Young	Griffiths		Holton	Buchan M	.[1]	McIlroy				
29 Dec	Ipswich T	H	W	2–0			Houston				.[1]					
1 Jan	Q P R	A	L	0–3			Houston									
12 Jan	West Ham U	A	L	1–2			Forsyth					Kidd	Young	Graham		McIlroy[1] for Kidd
19 Jan	Arsenal	H	D	1–1			Buchan M			James[1]		McIlroy		Martin		
2 Feb	Coventry C	A	L	0–1								Kidd	Young			Forsyth for McIlroy
9 Feb	Leeds U	H	L	0–2								Kidd	Young	Forsyth		McIlroy for Forsyth
16 Feb	Derby Co	A	D	2–2			Forsyth	.[1]	.[1]		Buchan M	Fletcher		Macari	McIlroy	Daly for Morgan
23 Feb	Wolverhampton W	H	D	0–0												Daly for McIlroy
2 Mar	Sheffield U	A	W	1–0								Macari[1]	McIlroy	Daly	Martin	
13 Mar	Manchester C	A	D	0–0					Martin				Greenhoff		Bielby	Graham for Martin
16 Mar	Birmingham C	A	L	0–1							McCalliog			Graham		
23 Mar	Tottenham H	H	L	0–1					Greenhoff	James	Morgan	McIlroy	Kidd	McCalliog	Daly	Bielby for Kidd
30 Mar	Chelsea	A	W	3–1					Daly[1]		.[1]		.[1]	Greenhoff	Martin	Bielby for James
3 Apr	Burnley	H	D	3–3						Holton[1]						
6 Apr	Norwich C	A	W	2–0					Greenhoff[1]			Macari[1]	McIlroy		Daly	
13 Apr	Newcastle U	H	W	1–0								Daly	McCalliog[1]	Macari	McIlroy	
15 Apr	Everton	H	W	3–0		Young		.[1]				Macari	McIlroy	McCalliog[2]	Daly	Martin for McIlroy
20 Apr	Southampton	A	D	1–1												
23 Apr	Everton	A	L	0–1*		Forsyth										
27 Apr	Manchester C	H	L	0–1												
29 Apr	Stoke C	A	L	0–1											Martin	

FA Cup

Date	Opponent	V	R	Score	1	2	3	4	5	6	7	8	9	10	11	Substitutes
5 Jan	Plymouth A (3)	H	W	1–0	Stepney	Young	Forsyth	Greenhoff	Holton	Buchan M	Morgan	Macari[1]	Kid	Graham	Martin	McIlroy for Martin
26 Jan	Ipswich T (4)	H	L	0–1		Buchan M				James			McIlroy	Young		Kidd for Macari

League Cup

Date	Opponent	V	R	Score	1	2	3	4	5	6	7	8	9	10	11	Substitutes
8 Oct	Middlesbrough (2)	H	L	0–1	Stepney	Buchan M	Young	Greenhoff	Holton	James	Morgan	Daly	Macari	Kidd	Graham	Buchan G for Macari

Appearances (goals)

Anderson 11 (1) · Best 12 (2) · Bielby 2 · Buchan M 42 · Daly 14 (1) · Fletcher 2 · Forsyth 18 (1) · Graham 23 (1) · Greenhoff 36 (3) · Griffiths C 7 · Holton 34 (2) · Houston 20 (2) · James 21 (2) · Kidd B 21 (2) · Macari 34 (5) · McCalliog 11 (4) · McIlroy 24 (6) · Martin 12 · Morgan 41 (2) · Sadler 2 · Sidebottom 2 · Stepney 42 (2) · Storey-Moore 2 (1) · Young 29 (1) · Total 24 players (38)

Football League

	P	W	D	L	F:A	Pts	
Leeds U	42	24	14	4	66:31	62	1st
Manchester U	42	10	12	20	38:48	32	21st

1974–1975

SEASON 1974–1975 FOOTBALL LEAGUE (DIVISION 2)

Starting line-up (17 Aug): Stepney · Forsyth · Houston · Greenhoff B · Holton · Buchan M · Morgan · Macari · Pearson · McCalliog · Daly

Date	Opponent	V	Res	Score	Substitution
17 Aug	Orient	A	W	2–0	McIlroy for Macari
24 Aug	Millwall	H	W	4–0	
28 Aug	Portsmouth	H	W	2–1	
31 Aug	Cardiff C	A	W	1–0	Young for Pearson
7 Sep	Nottingham F	H	D	2–2	Macari for Greenhoff B
14 Sep	W B A	A	D	1–1	Greenhoff B for Martin
16 Sep	Millwall	A	W	1–0	Young for Daly
21 Sep	Bristol R	H	W	*2–0	Young for McCalliog
25 Sep	Bolton W	H	W	*3–0	
28 Sep	Norwich C	A	L	0–2	Young for Morgan
5 Oct	Fulham	A	W	2–1	Macari for Daly
12 Oct	Notts Co	H	W	1–0	Young for McCalliog
15 Oct	Portsmouth	A	D	0–0	McCreery for Morgan
19 Oct	Blackpool	A	W	3–0	McCreery for Daly
26 Oct	Southampton	H	W	1–0	Pearson for Morgan
2 Nov	Oxford U	H	W	4–0	Morgan for Greenhoff B
9 Nov	Bristol C	A	L	0–1	Graham for Daly
16 Nov	Aston Villa	H	W	2–1	Greenhoff B for Pearson
23 Nov	Hull C	A	L	0–2	
30 Nov	Sunderland	H	W	3–2	Davies for Greenhoff B
7 Dec	Sheffield Wed	A	D	4–4	Davies for Holton
14 Dec	Orient	H	D	0–0	Davies for Greenhoff B
21 Dec	York C	A	W	1–0	Davies for Sidebottom
26 Dec	W B A	H	W	2–1	
28 Dec	Oldham	A	L	0–1	Davies for Greenhoff B
11 Jan	Sheffield Wed	H	W	2–0	Daly for Morgan
18 Jan	Sunderland	A	D	0–0	
1 Feb	Bristol C	H	L	0–1	Young for Daly
8 Feb	Oxford U	A	L	0–1	Davies for Morgan
15 Feb	Hull C	H	W	2–0	Davies for James
22 Feb	Aston Villa	A	L	0–2	Davies for Martin
1 Mar	Cardiff C	H	W	4–0	Coppell for Morgan
8 Mar	Bolton W	A	W	1–0	Young for Houston
15 Mar	Norwich C	H	D	1–1	Young for Coppell
22 Mar	Nottingham F	A	W	1–0	
28 Mar	Bristol R	A	D	1–1	Morgan for James
29 Mar	York C	H	W	2–1	
31 Mar	Oldham	H	W	3–2	Martin for Daly
5 Apr	Southampton	A	W	1–0	Nicholl for Buchan M
12 Apr	Fulham	H	W	1–0	
19 Apr	Notts Co	A	D	2–2	
26 Apr	Blackpool	H	W	4–0	

FA Cup

Date	Opponent	V	Res	Score	Substitution
4 Jan	Walsall (3)	H	D	0–0	Davies for Morgan
7 Jan	Walsall (3R)	A	L	2–3	Davies for Daly

League Cup

Date	Opponent	V	Res	Score	Substitution
11 Sep	Charlton A (2)	H	W	*5–1	Young for Forsyth
9 Oct	Manchester C (3)	H	W	1–0	Macari for Pearson
13 Nov	Burnley (4)	H	W	3–2	Morgan for Greenhoff B
4 Dec	Middlesbrough (5)	A	D	0–0	Young for Morgan
18 Dec	Middlesbrough (5R)	H	W	3–0	McCalliog for Greenhoff B
15 Jan	Norwich C (SF)	H	D	2–2	Young for Daly
22 Jan	Norwich C (SF)	A	L	0–1	Young for James

Appearances (goals)

Albiston 2 · Baldwin 2 · Buchan M 41 · Connell 9 (1) · Daly 36 (11) · Forsyth 39 (1) · Greenhoff B 39 (4) · Holton 14 · Houston 40 (6) · James 13 · Macari 36 (11) · McCalliog 20 (3) · McIlroy 41 (7) · Martin 7 · Morgan 32 (3) · Pearson 30 (17) · Roche 2 · Sidebottom 12 · Stepney 40 · Young 7 · Own goals 2 · Total 20 players (66)

Football League

	P	W	D	L	F:A	Pts	
Manchester U	42	26	9	7	66:30	61	1st

SEASON 1975–1976 FOOTBALL LEAGUE (DIVISION 1)

Date	Opponent			Score											Substitute
16 Aug	Wolverhampton W	A	W	2–0	Stepney	Forsyth	Houston	Jackson	Greenhoff B	Buchan M	Coppell	McIlroy	Pearson	Macari[2]	Daly	Nicholl for Pearson
19 Aug	Birmingham C	A	W	2–0								[2]	McCreery			Nicholl for Stepney
23 Aug	Sheffield U	H	W	5–1								[1]	Pearson[2]	[1]	[1]	Nicholl for Forsyth
27 Aug	Coventry C	H	D	1–1												
30 Aug	Stoke C	A	W	*1–0												
6 Sep	Tottenham H	H	W	*3–2	Nicholl										[2]	
13 Sep	QPR	A	L	0–1			Albiston		Houston							Young for Jackson
20 Sep	Ipswich T	H	W	1–0			Houston[1]	McCreery	Greenhoff B						[1]	
24 Sep	Derby Co	A	L	1–2												
27 Sep	Manchester C	A	D	2–2					[1]					[1]		
4 Oct	Leicester C	H	D	0–0				Jackson				[2]				
11 Oct	Leeds U	A	W	2–1							[2]					Grimshaw for Houston
18 Oct	Arsenal	H	W	3–1								[1]				
25 Oct	West Ham U	A	L	1–2									[1]			McCreery for Daly
1 Nov	Norwich C	H	W	1–0	Roche								[1]			
8 Nov	Liverpool	A	L	1–3							[1]					McCreery for Jackson
15 Nov	Aston Villa	H	W	2–0				Daly			[1]	[1]		[1]	Hill	
22 Nov	Arsenal	A	L	1–3				[1]								McCreery for McIlroy
29 Nov	Newcastle U	H	W	1–0	Stepney	Forsyth										McCreery for Pearson
6 Dec	Middlesbrough	A	D	0–0		Forsyth										Nicholl for Forsyth
13 Dec	Sheffield U	A	W	4–1									[2]	[1]	[1]	McCreery for McIlroy
20 Dec	Wolverhampton W	H	W	1–0										[1]	[1]	Kelly for Greenhoff B
23 Dec	Everton	A	D	1–1										[1]		
27 Dec	Burnley	H	W	2–1								[1]				McCreery for Pearson
10 Jan	QPR	H	W	2–1								[1]			[1]	
17 Jan	Tottenham H	A	D	1–1								[1]		[1]		McCreery for McIlroy
31 Jan	Birmingham C	H	W	3–1			[1]					[1]		[1]		McCreery for Pearson
7 Feb	Coventry C	A	D	1–1										[1]		McCreery for Pearson
18 Feb	Liverpool	H	D	0–0												McCreery for McIlroy
21 Feb	Aston Villa	A	L	1–2										[1]		Coyne for Macari
25 Feb	Derby Co	H	D	1–1										[1]		McCreery for Hill
28 Feb	West Ham U	H	W	4–0			[1]							[1]	[1]	McCreery[1] for McIlroy
13 Mar	Leeds U	H	W	3–2				[1]	[1]					[1]	McCreery	[1]
16 Mar	Norwich C	A	D	1–1											[1]	
20 Mar	Newcastle U	A	W	*4–3										[2]		
27 Mar	Middlesbrough	H	W	3–0				[1]						[1]	[1]	
10 Apr	Ipswich T	A	L	0–3												
17 Apr	Everton	H	W	*2–1										Macari		McCreery[1] for Coppell
19 Apr	Burnley	A	W	1–0							McCreery			[1]		Jackson for Pearson
21 Apr	Stoke C	H	L	0–1							Jackson		McCreery			Nicholl for Jackson
24 Apr	Leicester C	A	L	1–2				Nicholl				McCreery	Coyne[1]			Albiston for Houston
4 May	Manchester C	H	W	2–0				Daly	Albiston		Coppell	McIlroy[1]	Pearson	Jackson	[1]	McCreery for Pearson

FA Cup

Date	Opponent			Score											Substitute
3 Jan	Oxford U (3)	H	W	2–1	Stepney	Forsyth	Houston	Daly[2]	Greenhoff B	Buchan M	Coppell	McIlroy	Pearson	Macari	Hill	Nicholl for Forsyth
24 Jan	Peterborough (4)	H	W	3–1		[1]						[1]			[1]	
14 Feb	Leicester C (5)	A	W	2–1				[1]						[1]		McCreery for Hill
6 Mar	Wolverhampton W (6)	H	D	1–1				[1]								
9 Mar	Wolverhampton W (6R)	A	W	3–2					[1]			[1]	[1]			Nicholl for Macari
3 Apr	Derby Co (SF) (at Hillsborough)	N	W	2–0										McCreery	[2]	
1 May	Southampton (F) (at Wembley)	N	L	0–1										Macari		McCreery for Hill

League Cup

Date	Opponent			Score											Substitute
10 Sep	Brentford (2)	H	W	2–1	Stepney	Nicholl	Houston	Jackson	Greenhoff B	Buchan M	Coppell	McIlroy[1]	Pearson	Macari[1]	Daly	Grimshaw for Jackson
8 Oct	Aston Villa (3)	A	W	2–1								[1]		[1]		
12 Nov	Manchester C (4)	A	L	0–4	Roche											

Appearances (goals)

Albiston 2 · Buchan M 42 · Coppell 39 (4) · Coyne 1 (1) · Daly 41 (7) · Forsyth 28 (2) · Greenhoff B 40 · Hill 26 (7) · Houston 42 (2) · Jackson 16 · Macari 36 (13) · McCreery 12 (4) · McIlroy 41 (10) · Nicholl 15 · Pearson 39 (13) · Roche 4 · Stepney 38 · Own goals 5 · Total 17 players (68)

Football League

	P	W	D	L	F:A	Pts	
Liverpool	42	23	14	5	66:31	60	1st
Manchester U	42	23	10	9	68:42	56	3rd

SEASON 1976–1977 FOOTBALL LEAGUE (DIVISION 1)

Date	Opponent			Score											Substitute
21 Aug	Birmingham C	H	D	2–2	Stepney	Nicholl	Houston	Daly	Greenhoff B	Buchan M	Coppell[1]	McIlroy	Pearson[1]	Macari	Hill	Foggon for Daly
24 Aug	Coventry C	A	W	2–0										[1]	[1]	
28 Aug	Derby Co	A	D	0–0												
4 Sep	Tottenham H	H	L	2–3							[1]			[1]		McCreery for McIlroy
11 Sep	Newcastle U	A	D	2–2						[1]				[1]		Foggon for Hill
18 Sep	Middlesbrough	H	W	*2–0										[1]		Foggon for Daly
25 Sep	Manchester C	A	W	3–1				[1]			[1]					McCreery[1] for Pearson
2 Oct	Leeds U	A	W	2–0				[1]			[1]					McCreery for Pearson
16 Oct	W B A	A	L	0–4					Waldron							McCreery for Macari
23 Oct	Norwich C	H	D	2–2				[1]							[1]	McGrath for McIlroy
30 Oct	Ipswich T	H	L	0–1			Albiston		Houston							McCreery for Macari
6 Nov	Aston Villa	A	L	2–3							McGrath			[1]	Coppell	[1]
10 Nov	Sunderland	H	D	3–3	Roche	Albiston	Houston		Paterson	Waldron	Coppell	Greenhoff B[1]		Macari	[1]	Clark for Waldron
20 Nov	Leicester C	A	D	1–1	Stepney	Nicholl	Albiston	[1]	Greenhoff B	Paterson		McIlroy		Greenhoff J		
27 Nov	West Ham U	H	L	0–2			Forsyth			Houston						
18 Dec	Arsenal	A	L	1–3			Houston	McIlroy[1]		Buchan M	McCreery	Greenhoff J		Macari		McGrath for Greenhoff B
27 Dec	Everton	H	W	4–0		Nicholl					Coppel			[1]	[1]	McCreery for Coppell
1 Jan	Aston Villa	H	W	2–0										[2]		McCreery for Pearson
3 Jan	Ipswich T	A	L	1–2			Albiston				McCreery			[1]		McGrath for Pearson
15 Jan	Coventry C	H	W	2–0			Houston				Coppell			[1]		McCreery for Hill
19 Jan	Bristol C	A	W	2–1						[1]				[1]		
22 Jan	Birmingham C	A	W	3–2			[1]						[1]			
5 Feb	Derby Co	H	W	*3–1			[1]							[1]	Daly	
12 Feb	Tottenham H	A	W	3–1				[1]						[1]	Hill[1]	
16 Feb	Liverpool	H	D	0–0												
19 Feb	Newcastle U	H	W	3–1								[3]		[1]		Albiston for Hill
5 Mar	Manchester C	H	W	3–1							[1]			[1]		McCreery for Hill
12 Mar	Leeds U	H	W	1–0												McCreery for Hill
23 Mar	W B A	H	D	2–2			Albiston		Houston						[1]	McCreery for McIlroy
2 Apr	Norwich C	A	L	*1–2			Houston		Greenhoff B				McCreery			McGrath for Hill
5 Apr	Everton	A	W	2–1			Albiston						Pearson	McCreery	[2]	McGrath for Hill
9 Apr	Stoke C	H	W	3–0			Houston[1]							Macari[1]		McCreery for Greenhoff J
11 Apr	Sunderland	A	L	1–2							McCreery					Albiston for Macari
16 Apr	Leicester C	H	D	1–1			Albiston				Greenhoff J[1]				McCreery	Hill for McCreery
13 Apr	QPR	A	L	0–4					Houston							Forsyth for Greenhoff B
26 Apr	Middlesbrough	A	L	0–3			Houston		Buchan M						Hill	
30 Apr	QPR	H	W	1–0										[1]		McCreery for Hill
3 May	Liverpool	A	L	0–1				Forsyth	Albiston							McCreery for Greenhoff J
7 May	Bristol C	A	D	1–1			Jackson	Greenhoff B	Buchan M		McCreery			Albiston	McIlroy for Houston
11 May	Stoke C	A	D	3–3			Albiston				McCreery[1]	McGrath		Hill[2]	
14 May	Arsenal	H	W	3–2			McIlroy				Greenhoff J[1]	Pearson	[1]	[1]	McCreery for Pearson
16 May	West Ham U	A	L	2–4	Roche									[1]	McCreery for Greenhoff J

FA Cup

Date	Opponent			Score												Substitute
8 Jan	Walsall (3)	H	W	1–0	Stepney	Nicholl	Houston	McIlroy	Greenhoff B	Buchan M	Coppell	Greenhoff J	Pearson	Macari	Hill[1]	McCreery for Hill
29 Jan	Q P R (4)	H	W	1–0	..	..	..	..	..	..	..	..	..	..[1]	..[1]	McCreery for Greenhoff J
26 Feb	Southampton (5)	A	D	2–2	..	..	..	..	..	..	..	..2	..	..[1]	..	McCreery for Greenhoff B
8 Mar	Southampton (5R)	H	W	2–1	..	..	..	..[1]	..	..	..	..	..	..[1]	..	
19 Mar	Aston Villa (6)	H	W	2–1	..	..	..	..	..	..	..[1]	..[1]	..	..	..	
23 Apr	Leeds U (SF) (at Hillsborough)	N	W	2–1	..	..	..	..	..	..	..	..	..[1]	..[1]	..	
21 May	Liverpool (F) (at Wembley)	N	W	2–1	..	Albiston	..	..	..	..	..[1]	..[1]	..	..	..	McCreery for Hill

League Cup

Date	Opponent			Score												Substitute
1 Sep	Tranmere R (2)	H	W	5–0	Stepney	Nicholl	Houston	Daly2	Greenhoff B	Buchan M	Coppell	McIlroy	Pearson[1]	Macari[1]	Hill[1]	McCreery for McIlroy
22 Sep	Sunderland (3)	H	D	*2–2	..	..	..	..			McCreery Coppell	..				
4 Oct	Sunderland (3R)	A	D	2–2	..	..	..	..[1]	Waldron	..	Coppell	..	McCreery	Greenhoff B[1]	..	Albiston for Greenhoff B
6 Oct	Sunderland (3R)	H	W	1–0	..	..	..	..	Greenhoff B[1]	..	..	..	..	Macari	..	Albiston for Hill
27 Oct	Newcastle U (4)	H	W	7–2	..	..[1]	Albiston	..	..	Houston[1]	..[1]	..	Pearson[1]	..	..3	McGrath for Pearson
1 Dec	Everton (5)	H	L	0–3	..	Forsyth	..	..	Paterson	Greenhoff B	..	..	..	Jackson	..	McCreery for Daly

UEFA Cup

Date	Opponent			Score												Substitute
15 Sep	Ajax (1)	A	L	0–1	Stepney	Nicholl	Houston	Daly	Greenhoff B	Buchan M	Coppell	McIlroy	Pearson	Macari	Hill	McCreery for Daly
29 Sep	Ajax (1)	H	W	2–0	..	..	..	..	..	..	..	..[1]	McCreery	..[1]	..	Albiston for Daly, Paterson for Hill
20 Oct	Juventus (2)	H	W	1–0	..	..	Albiston	..	..	Houston	..	..	Pearson	..	..[1]	McCreery for Daly
3 Nov	Juventus (2)	A	L	0–3	..	..	..	..	..	..	..	..	..	..	..	McCreery for McIlroy, Paterson for Macari

Appearances (goals)

Albiston 14 · Buchan M 33 · Coppell 40 (7) · Daly 16 (4) · Forsyth 3 · Greenhoff B 40 (3) · Greenhoff J 27 (8) · Hill 38 (15) · Houston 37 (3) · Jackson 2 · Macari 38 (9) · McCreery 9 (2) · McGrath 2 · McIlroy 39 (2) · Nicholl 39 · Paterson 1 · Pearson 39 (15) · Roche 2 · Stepney 40 · Waldron 3 · Own goals 3 · Total 20 players (71)

Football League

	P	W	D	L	F:A	Pts	
Liverpool	42	23	11	8	62:33	57	1st
Manchester U	42	18	11	13	71:62	47	6th

1977–1978

SEASON 1977–1978 FOOTBALL LEAGUE (DIVISION 1)

Date	Opponent			Score												Substitute
20 Aug	Birmingham C	A	W	4–1	Stepney	Nicholl	Albiston	McIlroy	Greenhoff B	Buchan M	Coppell	McCreery[1]	Pearson	Macari2	Hill[1]	Grimes for Pearson
24 Aug	Coventry C	H	W	2–1	..	..	..	..	..	..	McGrath	..	Coppell	..	..	Grimes for McIlroy
27 Aug	Ipswich T	H	D	0–0	..	..	..	..	..	..	Coppell	..	Pearson	..[1]	..	
3 Sep	Derby Co	A	W	1–0	..	Forsyth	..	..	Nicholl	..	Coppell	..	..	..	..	McGrath for Macari
10 Sep	Manchester C	A	L	1–3	..	..	..	..	..	..	..	..	..	..	..	McGrath for Buchan M
17 Sep	Chelsea	H	L	0–1	..	Nicholl	..	..	Greenhoff B	..	..	..	..	..	..[1]	
24 Sep	Leeds U	A	D	1–1	..	..	..	..	..	Houston	McGrath	Coppell	..	..	..	
1 Oct	Liverpool	H	W	2–0	..	..	..	..[1]	..	Buchan M	..	Greenhoff J	Greenhoff J	..[1]	..	
8 Oct	Middlesbrough	A	L	1–2	..	..	..	McCreery	..	..	..	Coppell[1]	..[1]	..	..	
15 Oct	Newcastle U	H	W	3–2	..	..	..	McIlroy	Houston	..	..	..	..[1]	..	..	
22 Oct	W B A	A	L	0–4	..	Forsyth	Rogers	..	Nicholl	..	Coppell	McCreery	Pearson	..	..	McGrath for McCreery
29 Oct	Aston Villa	A	L	1–2	..	Nicholl[1]	Albiston	..	Houston	..	McGrath	Coppell	..	McCreery	..[1]	Grimes for Hill, Grimes for McGrath
5 Nov	Arsenal	H	L	1–2	..	..	..	..	..	..	..	..	..	..[1]	..	
12 Nov	Nottingham F	A	L	1–2	Roche	..	Houston	..	Greenhoff B	..	..	..	..	Macari	..[1]	McCreery for McIlroy
19 Nov	Norwich C	H	W	1–0	..	..	..	..	..	..	Coppell	Greenhoff J	..[1]	..	..2	McGrath for Macari
26 Nov	Q P R	A	D	2–2	..	..	..	Grimes	..	..	..	..[1]	..[1]	Grimes	..	McGrath for Grimes
3 Dec	Wolverhampton W	H	W	3–1	..	..	Albiston	McIlroy[1]	..	Houston	..	..	..	..	..	
10 Dec	West Ham U	A	L	1–2	..	..	..	Coppell	..	..	McGrath[1]	..	..	Macari	..[1]	Grimes for Pearson
17 Dec	Nottingham F	H	L	0–4	..	..	Houston	McIlroy	..	Buchan M	Coppell	..	..	..2	..[1]	
26 Dec	Everton	A	W	6–2	..	..	..	..[1]	..	..	..[1]	..	..[1] Ritchie	..	..[1]	
27 Dec	Leicester C	H	W	3–1	..	..	Albiston	..	Houston	..	..[1]	..	..	..	..	
31 Dec	Coventry C	A	L	0–3	..	..	Houston	..	Greenhoff B	..	..	..	..	..	..	McGrath for Buchan M
2 Jan	Birmingham C	H	L	1–2	..	..	..	..	..	..	..	..[1]	..	..	..	
14 Jan	Ipswich T	A	W	2–1	..	..	Albiston	..[1]	Houston	..	..	..	Pearson[1]	..	..2	
21 Jan	Derby Co	H	W	4–0	..	..	..	..	..	..[1]	..	..	..[1]	..	..[1]	Greenhoff for Buchan M
8 Feb	Bristol C	H	D	1–1	..	..	..	..	..	..	Jordan	..	..	..	..[1]	
11 Feb	Chelsea	A	D	2–2	..	..	..	..[1]	..	Greenhoff B	..	..	..	..	..[1]	
25 Feb	Liverpool	A	L	1–3	..	..	..	..[1]	McQueen	Houston	..	..	..	..	..	
1 Mar	Leeds U	H	L	0–1	..	..	..	..	Greenhoff B	..	..	Greenhoff J	Jordan	..	..	McGrath for Hill
4 Mar	Middlesbrough	H	D	0–0	..	..	Houston	..	McQueen	Greenhoff B	..	..	..[1]	..	..[1]	
11 Mar	Newcastle U	A	D	2–2	Stepney	..	..	..	..	..	..	..	..	..	..2	Albiston for Jordan
15 Mar	Manchester C	H	D	2–2	Stepney	..	..	..	..	..	..	..	Pearson	..	..[1]	
18 Mar	W B A	H	D	1–1	..	..	..	..	..[1]	..	..	..	..[1]	..	..[1]	
25 Mar	Leicester C	A	W	3–2	..	..	..	..	..	..	..	..	..	..	..[1]	
27 Mar	Everton	H	L	1–2	..	..	Albiston	..	..	..	..	..	..	..	Jordan	
29 Mar	Aston Villa	H	D	1–1	..	..	Greenhoff B	Houston	..[1]	Buchan M	..	Jordan[1]	..	..	Hill	
1 Apr	Arsenal	A	L	1–3	..	..	..	..	..	..	..[1]	..	..2	Grimes[1]	McCreery	
8 Apr	Q P R	H	W	3–1	..	..	..	..	..	..	..	..[1]	..	Greenhoff B Grimes[1]	McIlroy[1]	
15 Apr	Norwich C	A	W	3–1	..	Albiston	..	..	..	..	..	..	..[1]	..	Greenhoff B	
22 Apr	West Ham U	H	W	3–0	..	..	..	Greenhoff B	..	..	..	..	..[1]	Greenhoff B[1]	Grimes	McCreery for Greenhoff B
25 Apr	Bristol City	A	W	1–0	Roche	..	..	McIlroy	..	Nicholl	..	..	..	..	..	
29 Apr	Wolverhampton W	A	L	1–2	Stepney	..	..	..	..	..	..	..	..	..	..	

FA Cup

Date	Opponent			Score												Substitute
7 Jan	Carlisle U (3)	A	D	1–1	Roche	Nicholl	Albiston	McIlroy	Greenhoff B	Buchan M	Coppell	Greenhoff J	Pearson	Macari[1]	Grimes	McCreery for Grimes
10 Jan	Carlisle U (3R)	H	W	4–2	..	..	..	..	Houston	..	..	..2	..2	..2	Hill	
28 Jan	W B A (4)	H	D	1–1	..	..	..	..	..	..	..[1]	Jordan	..	..	..	
1 Feb	W B A (4R)	A	L	2–3	..	..	..	..	..	..	..	..	..[1]	..	..[1]	Greenhoff for Albiston

League Cup

Date	Opponent			Score												Substitute
30 Aug	Arsenal (2)	A	L	2–3	Stepney	Nicholl	Albiston	Grimes	Greenhoff B	Buchan M	Coppell	McCreery[1]	Pearson[1]	Macari	Hill	McGrath for Greenhoff B

European Cup-Winners' Cup

Date	Opponent			Score												Substitute
14 Sep	St Etienne (1)	A	D	1–1	Stepney	Nicholl	Albiston	McIlroy	Greenhoff B	Buchan M	McGrath	McCreery	Pearson	Coppell	Hill[1]	McGrath for Pearson
5 Oct	St Etienne (1) (at Plymouth)	N	W	2–0	..	..	..	..	..	..	Coppell[1]	Greenhoff J	..[1]	Macari	..	
19 Oct	F C Porto (2)	A	L	0–4	..	..	..	..	Houston	..	McGrath	McCreery	Coppell	..	..	Forsyth for Houston, Grimes for Coppell
2 Nov	F C Porto (2)	H	W	*5–2	..	..[1]	..	..	..	..	..	Coppell2	Pearson	McCreery	..	

Appearances (goals)

Albiston 27 · Buchan M 28 (1) · Coppell 42 (5) · Greenhoff B 31 (1) · Greenhoff J 22 (6) · Grimes 7 (2) · Hill 37 (17) · Houston 30 · Jordan 14 (3) · Macari 32 (8) · McCreery 13 (1) · McGrath 9 (1) · McIlroy 39 (9) · McQueen 14 (1) · Nicholl 37 (2) · Pearson 30 (10) · Ritchie 4 · Roche 19 · Rogers 1 · Stepney 23 · Total 20 players (67)

Football League

	P	W	D	L	F:A	Pts	
Nottingham F	42	25	14	3	69:24	64	1st
Manchester U	42	16	10	16	67:63	42	10th

SEASON 1978–1979 FOOTBALL LEAGUE (DIVISION 1)

Date	Opponent	H/A	Res	Score	Players / Notes
19 Aug	Birmingham C	H	W	1–0	Roche · Greenhoff B · Albiston · McIlroy[1] · McQueen[1] · Buchan M · Coppell · Greenhoff J · Jordan[1] · Macari[1] · McCreery
23 Aug	Leeds United	A	W	3–2	
26 Aug	Ipswich T	A	L	0–3	McGrath for McCreery / Grimes for McCreery
2 Sep	Everton	H	D	1–1	Nicholl · Greenhoff B[1]
9 Sep	Q P R	A	D	1–1	Greenhoff B · McQueen
16 Sep	Nottingham F	H	D	1–1	Grimes for McCreery
23 Sep	Arsenal	A	D	1–1	Albiston · Houston · Greenhoff B · McIlroy
30 Sep	Manchester C	H	W	1–0	
7 Oct	Middlesbrough	H	W	3–2	McCreery[2] · Grimes for Greenhoff J
14 Oct	Aston Villa	A	D	2–2	McIlroy[1] · Grimes
21 Oct	Bristol C	H	L	1–3	Greenhoff B for McIlroy
28 Oct	Wolverhampton W	A	W	4–2	Nicholl · Greenhoff B[1] · [2] · [1] · McIlroy · Grimes for McQueen
4 Nov	Southampton	H	D	1–1	McIlroy · Greenhoff B · Grimes
11 Nov	Birmingham C	A	L	1–5	McCreery · McIlroy · Albiston for Nicholl
18 Nov	Ipswich T	H	W	2–0	Bailey · Albiston · Greenhoff B · McQueen · Sloan · McGrath for Sloan / Macari for Sloan
21 Nov	Everton	A	L	0–3	
25 Nov	Chelsea	A	W	1–0	Greenhoff B · McIlroy · Macari · Thomas
9 Dec	Derby Co	A	W	3–1	[1] Ritchie[1]
16 Dec	Tottenham H	H	W	2–0	[1] · Paterson for Houston
22 Dec	Bolton W	A	L	0–3	Connell · Nicholl for Greenhoff J
26 Dec	Liverpool	H	L	0–3	
30 Dec	W B A	H	L	3–5	[1] Houston · [1] · [1] · McCreery · Sloan for Greenhoff J
3 Feb	Arsenal	H	L	0–2	Nicholl · Macari · McIlroy · Ritchie for Greenhoff J
10 Feb	Manchester C	A	W	3–0	Albiston · McIlroy · [2] · Ritchie[1] · Macari
24 Feb	Aston Villa	H	D	1–1	Nicholl for Macari
28 Feb	Q P R	H	W	2–0	[1] · [1] · Nicholl · Grimes
3 Mar	Bristol C	A	W	2–1	Nicholl · [1] · Grimes
20 Mar	Coventry C	A	L	3–4	[1] · [2] · Jordan · Greenhoff B
24 Mar	Leeds U	H	W	4–1	[1] · Ritchie[3] · [1] · Paterson for Greenhoff J
27 Mar	Middlesbrough	A	D	2–2	[1] · [1] · Jordan · Macari[1]
7 Apr	Norwich C	A	D	2–2	Albiston · Houston · [1] · Macari[1]
11 Apr	Bolton W	H	L	1–2	Nicholl · Albiston · [1] · Ritchie · Houston for Ritchie
14 Apr	Liverpool	A	L	0–2	Greenhoff B · McCreery for Ritchie
16 Apr	Coventry C	H	D	0–0	McQueen · McCreery · Greenhoff B · Grimes for Buchan M
18 Apr	Nottingham F	A	D	1–1	[1] · Grimes for Thomas
21 Apr	Tottenham H	A	D	1–1	[1] · Greenhoff B · Buchan M · Macari · Grimes for Buchan M
25 Apr	Norwich C	H	W	1–0	Houston · Buchan M · Nicholl · Ritchie · [1] · Grimes for Ritchie
28 Apr	Derby Co	H	D	0–0	McCreery · Houston · Nicholl · Paterson · Grimes for Ritchie
30 Apr	Southampton	A	D	1–1	Albiston · Houston · Sloan · McQueen · Moran · Paterson · Ritchie[1] · Grimes
5 May	W B A	A	L	0–1	McIlroy · Greenhoff B · Greenhoff J · Jordan · Thomas · Grimes for Thomas
7 May	Wolverhampton W	A	W	3–2	Nicholl · Albiston · Greenhoff B · Houston · Buchan M · [1] · Ritchie[1] · [1] · Grimes for Greenhoff B
16 May	Chelsea	H	D	1–1	Albiston · Houston · McIlroy · McQueen · Nicholl · [1] · Greenhoff J · McCreery · Grimes for Greenhoff J

FA Cup

Date	Opponent	H/A	Res	Score	Players / Notes
15 Jan	Chelsea (3)	H	W	3–0	Bailey · Greenhoff B · Houston · McIlroy · McQueen · Buchan M · Coppell[1] · Greenhoff J[1] · Pearson · Nicholl · Grimes[1]
31 Jan	Fulham (4)	A	D	1–1	Macari · Thomas · Nicholl for Pearson
12 Feb	Fulham (4R)	H	W	1–0	Albiston · [1] · Ritchie
20 Feb	Colchester (5)	A	W	1–0	[1]
10 Mar	Tottenham H (6)	A	D	1–1	Nicholl · Grimes · [1] · Nicholl for Greenhoff B / Jordan for Titchie
14 Mar	Tottenham H (6R)	H	W	2–0	Jordan[1] · Jordan for Titchie
31 Mar	Liverpool (SF) (at Maine Road)	N	D	2–2	Greenhoff B[1]
4 Apr	Liverpool (SFR) (at Goodison Park)	N	W	1–0	[1] · Macari · Ritchie for Macari
12 May	Arsenal (F) (at Wembley)	N	L	2–3	[1] · [1]

League Cup

Date	Opponent	H/A	Res	Score	Players / Notes
30 Aug	Stockport Co (2)	H	W	3–2	Roche · Greenhoff B · Albiston · McIlroy[1] · McQueen · Buchan M · Coppell · Greenhoff J[1] · Jordan[1] · Macari · Grimes
4 Oct	Watford (3)	H	L	1–2	Albiston · Houston · Greenhoff B · McIlroy · McCreery for Greenhoff B

Appearances (goals)

Albiston 32 · Bailey 28 · Buchan M 37 (2) · Connell 2 · Coppell 42 (11) · Greenhoff B 32 (2) · Greenhoff J 33 (11) · Grimes 5 · Houston 21 · Jordan 30 (6) · Macari 31 (6) · McCreery 14 · McIlroy 40 (6) · McQueen 36 (6) · Moran 1 · Nicholl 19 · Paterson 1 · Ritchie 16 (9) · Roche 14 · Sloan 3 · Thomas 25 (1) · Total 21 players (60)

Football League

	P	W	D	L	F:A	Pts	
Liverpool	42	30	8	4	85:16	68	1st
Manchester U	42	15	15	12	60:63	45	9th

SEASON 1979–1980 FOOTBALL LEAGUE (DIVISION 1)

Date	Opponent	H/A	Res	Score	Players / Notes
18 Aug	Southampton	A	D	1–1	Bailey · Nicholl · Albiston · McIlroy · McQueen[1] · Buchan M · Coppell[1] · Wilkins · Jordan · Macari · Thomas
22 Aug	W B A	H	W	2–0	Ritchie for McIlroy
25 Aug	Arsenal	A	D	0–0	Paterson for Coppell
1 Sep	Middlesbrough	H	W	2–1	[2]
8 Sep	Aston Villa	A	W	3–0	[1] · [1] · Grimes[1] for Jordan
15 Sep	Derby Co	H	W	*1–0	Ritchie · Grimes
22 Sep	Wolverhampton W	A	L	1–3	Grimes · Coppell · [1] · Thomas
29 Sep	Stoke C	H	W	4–0	[1] · [2] · [1] · [1]
6 Oct	Brighton	H	W	2–0	[1] · [1] · Sloan for Macari
10 Oct	W B A	A	L	0–2	
13 Oct	Bristol C	A	D	1–1	[1]
20 Oct	Ipswich T	H	W	1–0	[1]
27 Oct	Everton	A	D	0–0	Sloan for Albiston
3 Nov	Southampton	H	W	1–0	Houston · Moran · [1]
10 Nov	Manchester C	A	L	0–2	
17 Nov	Crystal Palace	H	D	1–1	Coppell · Jordan[1] · Grimes for Thomas
24 Nov	Norwich C	H	W	5–0	Grimes · [1] · [2] · [1]
1 Dec	Tottenham H	A	W	2–1	[1] · [1]
8 Dec	Leeds U	H	D	1–1	[1]
15 Dec	Coventry C	A	W	2–1	Houston · McQueen[1] · [1]
22 Dec	Nottingham F	H	W	3–0	[2]
26 Dec	Liverpool	A	L	0–2	Grimes for Thomas
29 Dec	Arsenal	H	W	3–0	[1] · [1] · [1]
12 Jan	Middlesbrough	A	D	1–1	[1] · McGrath for Thomas
2 Feb	Derby Co	A	W	*3–1	[1] · Jovanovic · [1] · Grimes for Jovanovic
9 Feb	Wolverhampton W	H	L	0–1	Wilkins · Grimes for Wilkins
16 Feb	Stoke C	A	D	1–1	[1] · Grimes · Ritchie for Macari
23 Feb	Bristol C	H	W	*4–0	[1] · [2] · Ritchie for McQueen
27 Feb	Bolton W	H	W	2–0	[1] · Sloan for Wilkins
1 Mar	Ipswich T	A	L	0–6	Sloan · Jovanovic for Nicholl
12 Mar	Everton	H	D	0–0	Albiston · Wilkins · Greenhoff for Macari
15 Mar	Brighton	A	D	0–0	
22 Mar	Manchester C	H	W	1–0	Thomas[1] · Grimes for Thomas
29 Mar	Crystal Palace	A	W	2–0	[1]
2 Apr	Nottingham F	A	L	0–2	
5 Apr	Liverpool	H	W	2–1	Greenhoff[1] · [1]
7 Apr	Bolton W	A	W	3–1	McIlroy · [1] · [1] · Grimes · [1] · Ritchie for Wilkins
12 Apr	Tottenham H	H	W	4–1	[1] · Ritchie[2]
19 Apr	Norwich C	A	W	2–0	Moran · [2]
23 Apr	Aston Villa	H	W	2–1	Greenhoff · [2] · Macari
26 Apr	Coventry C	H	W	2–1	[2] · Sloan for Greenhoff
3 May	Leeds U	A	L	0–2	McQueen · Ritchie for Buchan M

FA Cup

Date	Match			Score	1	2	3	4	5	6	7	8	9	10	11	Substitutes
5 Jan	Tottenham H (3)	A	D	1–1	Bailey	Nicholl	Houston	McIlroy[1]	McQueen	Buchan M	Coppell	Wilkins	Jordan	Macari	Thomas	
9 Jan	Tottenham H (3R)	H	L	0–1	..	..	..	..	..	..	..	..	..	..	..	

League Cup

Date	Match			Score	1	2	3	4	5	6	7	8	9	10	11	Substitutes
29 Aug	Tottenham H (2)	A	L	1–2	Bailey	Nicholl	Albiston	Paterson	McQueen	Buchan M	Ritchie	Wilkins	Jordan	Macari	Thomas[1]	
5 Sep	Tottenham H (2)	H	W	*3–1	..	..	..	McIlroy	Houston	..	Coppell[1]	..	..	..	..[1]	Ritchie for Houston
26 Sep	Norwich C (3)	A	L	1–4	..	..	..	..[1]	McQueen	..	Grimes	..	Coppell	..	..	Ritchie for McIlroy

Appearances (goals)

Albiston 25 · Bailey 42 · Buchan M 42 · Coppell 42 (8) · Greenhoff J 4 (1) · Grimes 20 (2) · Houston 14 · Jordan 32 (13) · Jovanovic 1 · Macari 39 (9) · McIlroy 41 (6) · McQueen 33 (9) · Moran 9 (1) · Nicholl 42 · Ritchie 3 (3) · Sloan 1 · Thomas 35 (8) · Wilkins 37 (2) · Own goals 3 · Total 18 players (65)

Football League

	P	W	D	L	F:A	Pts	
Liverpool	42	25	10	7	81:30	60	1st
Manchester U	42	24	10	8	65:35	58	2nd

1980–1981

SEASON 1980–1981 FOOTBALL LEAGUE (DIVISION 1)

Date	Opponent			Score	1	2	3	4	5	6	7	8	9	10	11	Substitutes
16 Aug	Middlesbrough	H	W	3–0	Bailey	Nicholl	Albiston	McIlroy	Moran	Buchan M	Coppell	Greenhoff J	Jordan	Macari[1]	Thomas[1]	Grimes[1] for Jordan
19 Aug	Wolverhampton W	A	L	0–1	Roche	..	..	..	..	..	Grimes	..	Coppell	..	..	Ritchie for Grimes
23 Aug	Birmingham C	A	D	0–0	..	..	..	..	..	..	McGrath	Coppell	Ritchie	..	..	Duxbury for Moran
30 Aug	Sunderland	H	D	1–1	Bailey	..	..	..	Jovanovic[1]	..	Coppel	Greenhoff J	..	..	..	
6 Sep	Tottenham H	A	D	0–0	..	..	..	..	..	..	..	..	..	..	..	Duxbury for Ritchie
13 Sep	Leicester C	H	W	5–0	..	..	..	..	2	..	Grimes[1]	..	Coppell[1]	..[1]	..	McGarvey for Macari
20 Sep	Leeds U	A	D	0–0	..	..	..[1]	..	..	..	..	..	..[1]	Duxbury	..	Duxbury for Macari
27 Sep	Manchester C	H	D	2–2	..	..	..	..[1]	McQueen	..	Duxbury	Coppell[1]	Jordan	Macari[1]	..	Sloan for Duxbury
4 Oct	Nottingham F	A	W	2–1	..	..	..	..[2]	Jovanovic	Moran	..	..[1]	..	..	..	
8 Oct	Aston Villa	H	D	3–3	..	..	..	..	..	..	..	..	..	..	..	Greenhoff J for Macari
11 Oct	Arsenal	H	D	0–0	..	..	..	..[1]	..	..	Grimes	..	..	Duxbury	..	
18 Oct	Ipswich T	A	D	1–1	..	..	..	..	..	..	Coppell	Duxbury	..[1]	Macari	..	Duxbury for Jovanovic
22 Oct	Stoke C	A	W	2–1	..	..	..	..	..	..	..	Birtles	..[1]	..[1]	..	
25 Oct	Everton	H	W	2–0	..	..	..	..	Moran	Duxbury	..[1]	..	..	..	..	
1 Nov	Crystal Palace	A	L	0–1	..	..	..	..	Jovanovic	Moran	..	..	..	..	..	
8 Nov	Coventry C	H	D	0–0	..	..	..	..	..	..	..	..	..	..	..	Sloan for Jovanovic
12 Nov	Wolverhampton W	H	D	0–0	..	..	..	..	Moran	Duxbury	..	..	..[1]	..	..	
15 Nov	Middlesbrough	A	D	1–1	..	..	..	..[1]	Jovanovic	Moran	..	..	..[2]	Duxbury[1]	..	Grimes for Birtles
22 Nov	Brighton	A	W	4–1	..	..	Jovanovic	..	Moran	Duxbury	..	..	..[1]	Macari	Grimes	Whelan for Birtles
29 Nov	Southampton	H	D	1–1	..	..	Nicholl	..	Moran	Duxbury	..	Greenhoff J	..[1]	..	Duxbury	
6 Dec	Norwich C	A	D	*2–2	..	..	..	..	Jovanovic	Buchan M	..[1]	Duxbury	..[1]	..[1]	Thomas	
13 Dec	Stoke C	H	D	2–2	..	..	..	..	..	Moran	..	..	..	..	..	
20 Dec	Arsenal	A	L	1–2	..	..	..	..	..	..	..	..	..	..	..	
26 Dec	Liverpool	H	D	0–0	..	..	..	..	..	1	..	..	..	..	..	
27 Dec	W B A	A	L	1–3	..	..	..	..	..	..	..	..	..	..[1]	..	
10 Jan	Brighton	H	W	2–1	..	..	..	Wilkins	McQueen[1]	Buchan M	..	Birtles	..	..[1]	..	Duxbury for Wilkins
28 Jan	Sunderland	A	L	0–2	..	..	..	Duxbury	..	..	..	..	..[1]	..[1]	..	McIlroy for Thomas
31 Jan	Birmingham C	H	W	2–0	..	..	..	..	..	..	..	..	..	..	..	Wilkins for Jovanovic
7 Feb	Leicester C	A	L	0–1	..	..	..	..	Jovanovic	..	..	..	..	..	..	
17 Feb	Tottenham H	H	D	0–0	..	..	..	..	Moran	..	..	Wilkins	Birtles	..	McIlroy	McGarvey for Duxbury
21 Feb	Manchester C	A	L	0–1	..	..	..	..	..	..	..	..	..	..	..	
28 Feb	Leeds U	H	L	0–1	..	..	..	Wilkins	..	..	..	Birtles	Jordan	..	..	
7 Mar	Southampton	A	L	0–1	..	..	..	..	..	..	..	..	..[2]	..	..[1]	
14 Mar	Aston Villa	A	D	3–3	..	..	..	..	..	..	..	..	..	..	..	Duxbury for McIlroy
18 Mar	Nottingham F	H	D	*1–1	..	..[1]	..	Moran	McQueen	..	..	..	..	Duxbury	Thomas[1]	
21 Mar	Ipswich T	H	W	2–1	..	..[1]	..	Moran	McQueen	..	..	..	..[1]	Macari	..	Macari for Nicholl
28 Mar	Everton	A	W	1–0	..	..	..	..	..	..	..	..	..[1]	..	..	Wilkins for Thomas
4 Apr	Crystal Palace	H	W	1–0	Duxbury[1]	..	..	..	..	..	..	..	..[2]	Macari	..	
11 Apr	Coventry C	A	W	2–0	..	..	..	..	..	..[1]	..	..	..	..	Wilkins	
14 Apr	Liverpool	A	W	1–0	..	..	..	..	..	..	..	..	..[1]	..[1]	..	
18 Apr	W B A	H	W	2–1	..	..	..	..	..	..	..	..	..[1]	..	..	
25 Apr	Norwich C	H	W	1–0	..	..	..	..	..	..	..	..	..[1]	..	..	

FA Cup

Date	Match			Score	1	2	3	4	5	6	7	8	9	10	11	Substitutes
3 Jan	Brighton (3)	H	D	2–2	Bailey	Nicholl	Albiston	McIlroy	Jovanovic	Moran	Coppell	Birtles	Jordan	Macari	Thomas[1]	Duxbury[1] for McIlroy
7 Jan	Brighton (3R)	A	W	2–0	..	..[1]	..	Wilkins	McQueen	Buchan M	..	..[1]	..	..	..	Duxbury for Wilkins
24 Jan	Nottingham F(4)	A	L	0–1	..	..	..	..	..	..	..	..	..	..	..	

League Cup

Date	Match			Score	1	2	3	4	5	6	7	8	9	10	11	Substitutes
27 Aug	Coventry C (2)	H	L	0–1	Bailey	Nicholl	Albiston	McIlroy	Jovanovic	Buchan M	Coppell	Greenhoff J	Ritchie	Macari	Thomas	Sloan for Greenhoff J
2 Sep	Coventry C (2)	A	L	0–1	..	..	..	..	..	..	..	..	..	..	..	

UEFA Cup

Date	Match			Score	1	2	3	4	5	6	7	8	9	10	11	Substitutes
17 Sep	Widzew Lodz (1)	H	D	1–1	Bailey	Nicholl	Albiston	McIlroy[1]	Jovanovic	Buchan M	Grimes	Greenhoff J	Coppell	Macari	Thomas	Duxbury for Nicholl
1 Oct	Widzew Lodz (1)	A	D	0–0	..	..	..	..	..	..	..	Coppell	Jordan	Duxbury	..	Moran for Buchan M

Appearances (goals)

Albiston 42 (1) · Bailey 40 · Birtles 25 · Buchan M 26 · Coppell 42 (6) · Duxbury 27 (2) · Greenhoff J 8 · Grimes 6 (2) · Jordan 33 (15) · Jovanovic 19 (4) · Macari 37 (9) · McGrath 1 · McIlroy 31 (5) · McQueen 11 (2) · Moran 32 · Nicholl 36 (1) · Ritchie 3 · Roche 2 · Thomas 30 (2) · Wilkins 11 · Own goals 2 · Total 20 players (51)

Football League

	P	W	D	L	F:A	Pts	
Aston Villa	42	26	8	8	72:40	60	1st
Manchester U	42	15	18	9	51:36	48	8th

SEASON 1981–1982 FOOTBALL LEAGUE (DIVISION 1)

29 Aug	Coventry C	A	L	1–2	Bailey	Gidman	Albiston	Wilkins	McQueen	Buchan M	Coppell	Birtles	Stapleton	Macari [1]	McIlroy	
31 Aug	Nottingham F	H	D	0–0	..	..	..	..	..	..	..	..	..	..	..	
5 Sep	Ipswich T	H	L	1–2	..	..	..	..	..	..	..	..	.. [1]	..	..	Duxbury for McIlroy
12 Sep	Aston Villa	A	D	1–1	..	..	..	..	..	..	..	..	.. [1]	..	..	
19 Sep	Swansea	H	W	1–0	..	..	..	..	..	..	..	.. [1]	..	..	..	Moses for McIlroy
22 Sep	Middlesbrough	A	W	2–0	..	..	..	..	..	..	..	.. [1]	.. [1]	..	Moses	Duxbury for Buchan M
26 Sep	Arsenal	A	D	0–0	..	..	..	..	..	..	..	..	..	..	..	
30 Sep	Leeds U	H	W	1–0	..	..	..	..	..	..	..	..	.. [1]	McIlroy	..	Duxbury for McQueen
3 Oct	Wolverhampton W	H	W	5–0	..	..	..	..	Moran	..	..	.. [1]	.. [1]	.. [3]	..	
10 Oct	Manchester C	A	D	0–0	..	..	..	..	..	..	Robson	..	..	..	..	Coppell for Birtles
17 Oct	Birmingham C	H	D	1–1	..	..	..	..	..	..	..	..	..	Moses	Coppell [1]	
21 Oct	Middlesbrough	H	W	1–0	..	..	..	..	Duxbury	..	..	..	..	.. [1]	..	
24 Oct	Liverpool	A	W	2–1	..	..	.. [1]	..	Moran [1]	..	..	..	..	..	..	
31 Oct	Notts Co	H	W	2–1	..	..	..	..	Duxbury	..	..	.. [1]	..	.. [1]	..	
7 Nov	Sunderland	A	W	5–1	..	..	..	..	Moran [1]	..	.. [1]	.. [1]	.. [2]	..	..	Macari for Robson
21 Nov	Tottenham H	A	L	1–3	Roche	Duxbury	..	..	..	..	..	.. [1]	..	..	McIlroy	Duxbury for Gidman
28 Nov	Brighton	H	W	2–0	..	Gidman	..	..	..	McQueen	..	.. [1]	.. [1]	..	..	Nicholl for Buchan M
5 Dec	Southampton	A	L	2–3	..	..	..	..	..	..	.. [1]	..	.. [1]	..	..	
6 Jan	Everton	H	D	1–1	Bailey	..	..	..	..	Buchan M	..	McGarvey	.. [1]	McIlroy	Coppell	
23 Jan	Stoke C	A	W	3–0	..	Duxbury	..	..	..	McQueen	..	Birtles [1]	.. [1]	Macari	.. [1]	
27 Jan	West Ham U	H	W	1–0	..	..	..	..	..	..	..	..	..	.. [1]	..	
30 Jan	Swansea	A	L	0–2	..	..	..	..	..	..	..	..	..	..	..	
6 Feb	Aston Villa	H	W	4–1	..	Gidman	..	..	.. [2]	Buchan M	.. [1]	..	..	Duxbury	.. [1]	Gidman for McQueen
13 Feb	Wolverhampton W	A	W	1–0	..	..	..	..	..	..	..	.. [1]	..	..	..	McGarvey for Birtles
20 Feb	Arsenal	H	D	0–0	..	..	..	..	..	..	..	..	..	..	..	
27 Feb	Manchester C	H	D	1–1	..	..	..	..	.. [1]	..	..	..	..	..	..	
6 Mar	Birmingham C	A	W	1–0	..	..	..	..	..	..	..	.. [1]	..	..	..	
17 Mar	Coventry C	H	L	0–1	..	..	..	..	..	..	..	..	..	Moses	..	McGarvey for Moran
20 Mar	Notts Co	A	W	3–1	..	..	..	..	..	..	..	..	.. [1]	..	.. [2]	Duxbury for Robson
27 Mar	Sunderland	H	D	0–0	..	..	..	..	McQueen	..	..	..	..	..	..	McGarvey for Moran
3 Apr	Leeds U	A	D	0–0	..	Duxbury	..	..	Moran	..	..	McGarvey	..	..	..	McGarvey for Birtles
7 Apr	Liverpool	H	L	0–1	..	..	..	..	..	..	..	..	..	..	..	
10 Apr	Everton	A	D	3–3	..	Gidman	..	..	..	Duxbury	..	..	..	..	.. [2]	Grimes for Buchan M
12 Apr	W B A	H	W	1–0	..	..	..	..	.. [1]	McQueen	..	..	..	Grimes	..	Grimes [1] for Moses
17 Apr	Tottenham H	H	W	2–0	..	..	..	..	..	..	..	.. [1]	..	..	.. [1]	
20 Apr	Ipswich T	A	L	1–2	..	.. [1]	..	..	..	..	..	..	..	..	Duxbury	
24 Apr	Brighton	A	W	1–0	..	..	..	.. [1]	..	..	..	..	..	..	..	Birtles for Wilkins
1 May	Southampton	H	W	1–0	..	..	..	..	Duxbury	..	..	.. [1]	..	..	Davies	Whiteside for Duxbury
5 May	Nottingham F	A	W	1–0	..	..	..	..	Moran	Duxbury	..	..	.. [1]	..	Coppell	
8 May	West Ham U	A	D	1–1	..	..	..	..	.. [1]	..	Moses	Birtles	..	..	..	McGarvey for Birtles
12 May	W B A	A	W	3–0	..	..	..	..	..	McQueen	Robson [1]	.. [1]	..	..	.. [1]	
15 May	Stoke C	H	W	2–0	..	..	..	..	..	..	.. [1]	..	Whiteside [1]	..	..	McGarvey for Birtles
	FA Cup															
2 Jan	Watford (3)	A	L	0–1	Bailey	Gidman	Albiston	Wilkins	Moran	Buchan M	Robson	Birtles	Stapleton	Moses	McIlroy	Macari for Moses
	Milk Cup															
7 Oct	Tottenham H (2)	A	L	0–1	Bailey	Gidman	Albiston	Wilkins	Moran	Buchan M	Coppell	Birtles	Stapleton	McIlroy	Robson	Duxbury for Birtles
28 Oct	Tottenham H (2)	H	L	0–1	..	..	..	..	..	..	Robson	..	..	Moses	Coppell	

Appearances (goals)

Albiston 42 (1) · Bailey 39 · Birtles 32 (11) · Buchan M 27 · Coppell 35 (9) · Davies 1 · Duxbury 19 · Gidman 36 (1) · Grimes 9 (1) · Macari 10 (2) · McGarvey 10 (2) · McIlroy 12 (3) · McQueen 21 · Moran 30 (7) · Moses 20 (2) · Robson 32 (5) · Roche 3 · Stapleton 41 (13) · Whiteside 1 (1) · Wilkins 42 (1) · Total 20 players (59)

Football League

	P	W	D	L	F:A	Pts	
Liverpool	42	26	9	7	80:32	87	1st
Manchester U	42	22	12	8	59:29	78	3rd

SEASON 1982–1983 FOOTBALL LEAGUE (DIVISION 1)

28 Aug	Birmingham C	H	W	3–0	Bailey	Duxbury	Albiston	Wilkins	Moran [1]	McQueen	Robson	Muhren	Stapleton [1]	Whiteside	Coppell [1]	
1 Sep	Nottingham F	A	W	3–0	..	..	..	.. [1]	..	..	.. [1]	..	..	.. [1]	..	
4 Sep	W B A	A	L	1–3	..	..	..	..	..	..	.. [1]	..	..	..	..	
8 Sep	Everton	H	W	2–1	..	..	..	..	..	..	.. [1]	..	..	.. [1]	..	
11 Sep	Ipswich T	H	W	3–1	..	..	..	..	..	..	..	..	..	.. [2]	.. [1]	
18 Sep	Southampton	A	W	1–0	..	..	..	..	Buchan M	..	..	Grimes	..	..	..	Macari [1] for Coppell
25 Sep	Arsenal	H	D	0–0	..	..	..	..	Moran	..	..	..	..	..	Macari	
2 Oct	Luton T	A	D	1–1	..	..	..	..	..	..	..	.. [1]	..	..	Moses	
9 Oct	Stoke C	H	W	1–0	..	..	..	..	..	..	.. [1]	..	..	..	..	
16 Oct	Liverpool	A	D	0–0	..	..	..	..	..	..	..	..	..	..	Coppell	
23 Oct	Manchester C	H	D	2–2	..	..	..	..	..	..	..	Muhren	.. [2]	..	..	Macari for Muhren
30 Oct	West Ham U	A	L	1–3	..	..	..	Grimes	.. [1]	Buchan M	..	..	..	..	..	
6 Nov	Brighton	A	L	0–1	..	..	..	Moses	..	McQueen	..	..	..	..	..	Macari for Moran
13 Nov	Tottenham H	H	W	1–0	..	..	..	..	McGrath	..	..	.. [1]	..	..	..	
20 Nov	Aston Villa	A	L	1–2	..	..	..	..	Moran	..	..	..	.. [1]	..	..	McGarvey for Whiteside
27 Nov	Norwich C	H	W	3–0	..	..	..	..	..	..	.. [2]	.. [1]	..	..	..	
4 Dec	Watford	A	W	1–0	..	..	..	..	Buchan M	..	..	..	..	.. [1]	..	
11 Dec	Notts Co	H	W	4–0	..	.. [1]	..	..	Moran	..	.. [1]	..	.. [1]	.. [1]	..	Grimes for Robson
18 Dec	Swansea	A	D	0–0	..	..	..	..	..	..	..	..	..	..	..	
27 Dec	Sunderland	H	D	0–0	..	..	..	..	..	..	..	..	..	..	..	
28 Dec	Coventry C	A	L	0–3	..	..	..	..	..	..	..	Wilkins	..	McGarvey	Grimes	
1 Jan	Aston Villa	H	W	3–1	..	..	..	..	..	..	..	Muhren	.. [2]	Whiteside	Coppell [1]	
3 Jan	W B A	H	D	0–0	..	..	..	..	..	..	..	..	..	..	..	
15 Jan	Birmingham C	A	W	2–1	..	..	..	..	..	..	.. [1]	..	..	.. [1]	..	
22 Jan	Nottingham F	H	W	2–0	..	..	..	..	..	..	..	.. [1]	..	..	.. [1]	
5 Feb	Ipswich T	A	D	1–1	..	..	..	..	..	..	..	..	.. [1]	..	..	
26 Feb	Liverpool	H	D	1–1	..	..	..	..	..	..	Wilkins	.. [1]	..	..	..	Macari for Moran
2 Mar	Stoke C	A	L	0–1	..	..	..	..	McGrath	..	..	..	..	..	..	
5 Mar	Manchester C	A	W	2–1	..	..	..	..	..	..	..	..	.. [2]	..	..	
19 Mar	Brighton	H	D	1–1	..	Gidman	.. [1]	Grimes	..	Duxbury	..	..	..	..	..	Macari for Wilkins
22 Mar	West Ham U	H	W	2–1	..	..	..	Moses	..	..	..	..	.. [1]	McGarvey [1]	..	Macari for Stapleton
2 Apr	Coventry C	H	W	*3–0	Wealands	Duxbury	..	..	..	McQueen	..	..	.. [1]	Whiteside	..	Macari [1] for Whiteside
4 Apr	Sunderland	A	D	0–0	..	..	..	..	..	..	..	..	..	Macari	..	McGarvey for Macari
9 Apr	Southampton	H	D	1–1	Bailey	..	..	..	..	..	Robson [1]	..	..	Whiteside	Wilkins	
19 Apr	Everton	A	L	0–2	Wealands	..	..	..	..	..	..	Wilkins	..	..	Grimes [1]	Cunningham for Whiteside
23 Apr	Watford	H	W	2–0	Wealands	..	..	..	..	..	..	..	..	..	..	Cunningham [1] for Albiston
30 Apr	Norwich C	A	D	1–1	Bailey	..	Grimes	..	Moran	..	..	..	..	.. [1]	Cunningham	
2 May	Arsenal	A	L	0–3	..	..	..	..	..	..	McGrath	..	McGarvey	..	..	
7 May	Swansea	H	W	2–1	..	..	..	Wilkins	..	..	Robson [1]	Muhren	Stapleton [1]	..	..	Davies for Muhren
9 May	Luton T	H	W	3–0	..	..	..	McGrath [2]	..	..	..	..	.. [1]	..	Davies	McGarvey for Whiteside
11 May	Tottenham H	A	L	0–2	..	..	Albiston	Moses	..	McGrath	..	..	..	..	Grimes	McGarvey for Robson
14 May	Notts Co	A	L	2–3	Wealands	Gidman	..	..	McGrath [1]	Duxbury	Wilkins	.. [1]	..	..	Davies	
	FA Cup															
8 Jan	West Ham U (3)	H	W	2–0	Bailey	Duxbury	Albiston	Moses	Moran	McQueen	Robson	Muhren	Stapleton [1]	Whiteside	Coppell [1]	
29 Jan	Luton T (4)	A	W	2–0	..	..	..	.. [1]	.. [1]	..	..	..	..	..	..	
19 Feb	Derby Co (5)	A	W	1–0	..	..	..	..	..	..	..	..	..	.. [1]	..	
12 Mar	Everton (6)	H	W	1–0	..	..	..	..	..	..	Wilkins	..	.. [1]	..	..	Macari for Duxbury
16 Apr	Arsenal (SF) (at Villa Park)	N	W	2–1	..	..	..	..	..	..	Robson [1]	Wilkins	..	.. [1]	Grimes	McGrath for Moran
21 May	Brighton (F) (at Wembley)	N	D	2–2	..	..	..	Wilkins [1]	..	..	..	Muhren	.. [1]	..	Davies	
26 May	Brighton (FR) (at Wembley)	N	W	4–0	..	..	..	..	..	..	.. [2]	.. [1]	..	.. [1]	..	

Milk Cup

Date	Opponent			Score	1	2	3	4	5	6	7	8	9	10	11	Subs
6 Oct	Bournemouth (2)	H	W	*2–0	Bailey	Duxbury	Albiston	Wilkins	Moran	McQueen	Robson	Grimes	Stapleton[1]	Beardsley	Moses	Whiteside for Beardsley
26 Oct	Bournemouth (2)	A	D	2–2	..	..	..	..	Grimes	Buchan M	..	Muhren[1]	..	Whiteside	Coppell[1]	Macari for Wilkins
10 Nov	Bradford C (3)	A	D	0–0	..	..	..	Moses	McGrath	McQueen	..	..	..	..	..	
24 Nov	Bradford C (3R)	H	W	4–1	..	..	..[1]	..	Moran[1]	..	..	..	..	Macari	..[1]	Whiteside for Coppell
1 Dec	Southampton (4)	H	W	2–0	..	..	..	..	..	..[1]	..[1]	..	..	Whiteside[1]	..[1]	
19 Jan	Nottingham F (5)	H	W	4–0	..	..	..	..	..	..[2]	..[1]	..	..	..[1]	..[2]	
15 Feb	Arsenal (SF)	A	W	4–2	..	..	..	..	..[1]	..	..	..	..	..	..[1]	
23 Feb	Arsenal (SF)	H	W	2–1	..	..	..	..	..	..	..	..	..	..[1]	..[1]	
26 Mar	Liverpool (F) (at Wembley)	N	L	1–2	..	..	..	..	..	..	Wilkins	..	..	..	..[1]	Wilkins for Robson

UEFA Cup

Date	Opponent			Score	1	2	3	4	5	6	7	8	9	10	11	Subs
15 Sep	Valencia (1)	H	D	0–0	Bailey	Duxbury	Albiston	Wilkins	Buchan M	McQueen	Robson	Grimes	Stapleton	Whiteside	Coppell	Coppell for Moses,
29 Oct	Valencia (1)	A	L	1–2	..	..	..	..	Moran	Buchan M	..[1]	..	..	..	Moses	Macari for Buchan M

Appearances (goals)

Albiston 38 (1) · Bailey 37 · Buchan M 3 · Coppell 29 (4) · Cunningham 3 (1) · Davies 2 · Duxbury 42 (1) · Gidman 3 · Grimes 15 (2) · Macari 2 (2) · McGarvey 3 (1) · McGrath 14 (3) · McQueen 37 · Moran 29 (2) · Moses 29 · Muhren 32 (5) · Robson 33 (10) · Stapleton 41 (14) · Wealands 5 · Whiteside 39 (8) · Wilkins 26 (1) · Own goals 1 · Total 21 players (56)

Football League

	P	W	D	L	F:A	Pts	
Liverpool	42	24	10	8	87:37	82	1st
Manchester U	42	19	13	10	56:38	70	3rd

1983–1984

SEASON 1983–1984 FOOTBALL LEAGUE (DIVISION 1)

Date	Opponent			Score	1	2	3	4	5	6	7	8	9	10	11	Subs
27 Aug	Q P R	H	W	3–1	Bailey	Duxbury	Albiston	Wilkins	Moran	McQueen	Robson	Muhren[2]	Stapleton[1]	Whiteside	Graham	Macari for Whiteside
29 Aug	Nottingham F	H	L	1–2	..	Gidman	..	..	..[1]	..	..	..[1]	..	..	..	Macari for Duxbury
3 Sep	Stoke C	A	W	1–0	..	Gidman	..	..	..[1]	..	..[1]	..	..[1]	..	..	
6 Sep	Arsenal	A	W	3–2	..	..	..	..[1]	..	..	..[1]	..[1]	..	..	..	Moses for Graham
10 Sep	Luton T	H	W	2–0	..	..	..	..	..	..	..	..	..	..	..	Moses for Robson
17 Sep	Southampton	A	L	0–3	..	Duxbury	..	..	..	..	Moses	..	..	..	..	
24 Sep	Liverpool	H	W	1–0	..	..	..	..	..	..	Robson	..	..[1]	..	..	
1 Oct	Norwich C	A	D	3–3	..	..	..	..[1]	..	McGrath	..	..	..[1]	..[2]	..	Moses for Muhren
15 Oct	W B A	H	W	3–0	..	..	..	..	..[1]	McQueen	..	..	..	..[1]	..[1]	
22 Oct	Sunderland	A	W	1–0	..	..	..	..	..	..	..	Moses	..	..	..	Macari for McQueen
29 Oct	Wolverhampton W	H	W	3–0	..	Gidman	..	..	Duxbury	..	..[1]	Muhren	..[2]	..	..	Moses for Gidman
5 Nov	Aston Villa	H	L	1–2	..	Duxbury	..	..	Moran	..	..[1]	Moses	..	..	..	Macari for Whiteside
12 Nov	Leicester C	A	D	1–1	..	..	..	..	..	..	..[1]	..	..	..	..	
19 Nov	Watford	H	W	4–1	..	Moses	..	..	Duxbury	..	..[1]	Muhren	..[3]	Crooks	..	
27 Nov	West Ham U	A	D	1–1	..	..	..	..	..[1]	..	..	..	..	..	..	Whiteside for Muhren
3 Dec	Everton	H	L	0–1	..	Duxbury	..	..	Moran	..	..	Moses	..	..	Whiteside	
10 Dec	Ipswich T	A	W	2–0	..	..	..	..	..	..	..	..	..[1]	..	Graham[1]	
16 Dec	Tottenham H	H	W	4–2	..	Moses	..	..	..[2]	Duxbury	..	Muhren	..	Whiteside	..[2]	Macari for Stapleton
26 Dec	Coventry C	A	D	1–1	..	Duxbury	..	..	..[1]	McQueen	Moses	..	..	Crooks	..[1]	
27 Dec	Notts Co	H	D	3–3	Wealands	..	..	..	..[1]	..	..	..[1]	..	Whiteside	..[1]	Whiteside for Crooks
31 Dec	Stoke City	H	W	1–0	..	..	..	..	..	..	..	..	..	..[1]	..	
2 Jan	Liverpool	A	D	1–1	Bailey	..	..	..	..	..	..	..	..	..	..[1]	Crooks for McQueen
13 Jan	Q P R	A	D	1–1	..	..	Moses	..	..	Hogg	Robson[1]	..	..[1]	..	..	Hughes for Whiteside
21 Jan	Southampton	H	W	3–2	..	..	Moses	Albiston	..	Duxbury	..	..	..[1]	..	..	
4 Feb	Norwich C	H	D	0–0	..	..	Moses	Albiston	..	Duxbury	..	..	..	..	..[1]	
7 Feb	Birmingham C	A	D	2–2	..	Duxbury	..	..	..	Hogg[1]	..	Moses	..	..[2]	Moses	Graham for Robson
12 Feb	Luton T	A	W	5–0	..	..	..	..	..	..	..[2]	Muhren	..[1]	..[1]	..	Graham for Wilkins
18 Feb	Wolverhampton W	A	D	1–1	..	..	..	..	..[2]	..	..	..	..	..	..	Graham for Moran
25 Feb	Sunderland	H	W	2–1	..	..	..	..	..	..	..[1]	..	..	..[1]	..[1]	Graham for Whiteside
3 Mar	Aston Villa	A	W	3–0	..	..	..	..	McGrath	..	..	..	Hughes[1]	..	..[1]	
10 Mar	Leicester C	H	W	2–0	..	..	..	..	Moran	..	..[1]	..[2]	Whiteside	..	..	Hughes for Whiteside
17 Mar	Arsenal	H	W	4–0	..	..	..	..	..	..	..	Graham	..	..	..	
31 Mar	W B A	A	L	0–2	..	..	..	..	..	..	..[1]	..	..	..	..	Hughes for Whiteside
7 Apr	Birmingham C	H	W	1–0	..	..	..	..	..	..	McGrath	Moses	..	..	Davies	Hughes for Davies
14 Apr	Notts Co	A	L	0–1	..	..	..	..	..	..	Davies	McGrath	..	..	Graham	
17 Apr	Watford	A	D	0–0	..	..	..	..[1]	..	..	McGrath[1]	Moses	..	Hughes[2]	..	Whiteside for Wilkins
21 Apr	Coventry C	H	W	4–1	..	..	..	..	..	..	..	..	..	..	..	Whiteside for McGrath
28 Apr	West Ham U	H	D	0–0	..	..	..	..	..	..	Robson	..	..	..	Davies	Whiteside for Davies
5 May	Everton	A	D	1–1	..	..	..	..	..	..	..	..	..[1]	..	Davies	Whiteside[1] for Stapleton
7 May	Ipswich T	H	L	1–2	..	..	..	..	McGrath	..	..	..	..	..[1]	Graham	Whiteside for Graham
12 May	Tottenham H	A	D	1–1	..	..	..	..	..	..	..	..	..	..	..	
16 May	Nottingham F	A	L	0–2	..	..	..	..	..	..	Blackmore	..	..	..	..	

FA Cup

Date	Opponent			Score	1	2	3	4	5	6	7	8	9	10	11	Subs
7 Jan	Bournemouth (3)	A	L	0–2	Bailey	Moses	Albiston	Wilkins	Hogg	Duxbury	Robson	Muhren	Stapleton	Whiteside	Graham	Macari for Albiston

Milk Cup

Date	Opponent			Score	1	2	3	4	5	6	7	8	9	10	11	Subs
3 Oct	Port Vale (2)	A	W	1–0	Bailey	Duxbury	Albiston	Wilkins	Moran	McGrath	Robson	Muhren	Stapleton[1]	Whiteside	Graham	Moses for Duxbury
26 Oct	Port Vale (2)	H	W	2–0	..	Gidman	..	..[1]	Duxbury	McQueen	..	Moses	..	..[1]	..	Hughes for Whiteside
8 Nov	Colchester U (3)	A	W	2–0	..	Duxbury	..	..	Moran	..[1]	..	..	..	..	..	Macari for Whiteside
30 Nov	Oxford U (4)	A	D	1–1	..	..	..	..	..	..	..	..	..	..	Hughes[1]	
7 Dec	Oxford U (4R)	H	D	1–1	..	..	..	..	..	..	..	..	..[1]	..	Graham	
19 Dec	Oxford U (4R)	A	L	1–2	Wealands	Moses	..	..	..	Duxbury	..	Muhren	..	..	..[1]	Macari for Robson

European Cup-Winners' Cup

Date	Opponent			Score	1	2	3	4	5	6	7	8	9	10	11	Subs
14 Sep	Dukla Prague (1)	H	D	1–1	Bailey	Duxbury	Albiston	Wilkins[1]	Moran	McQueen	Robson	Muhren	Stapleton	Macari	Graham	Moses for Muhren, Gidman for Robson
27 Sep	Dukla Prague (1)	A	D	2–2	..	..	..	..	..	..	..	..[1]	..[1]	Whiteside	..[1]	
19 Oct	Spartak Varna (2)	A	W	2–1	..	..	..	..	..	..	..	..	..	..	..[1]	
2 Nov	Spartak Varna (2)	H	W	2–0	..	..	..	Moses	..	..	..	Macari	..[2]	..	..	Dempsey for Moran, Hughes for Whiteside
7 Mar	Barcelona (3)	A	L	0–2	..	..	..	Wilkins	..	Hogg	..	Muhren	..	Hughes	Moses	
21 Mar	Barcelona (3)	H	W	3–0	..	..	..	..	..	..	..	..[2]	..[1]	Whiteside	..	Hughes for Whiteside
11 Apr	Juventus (SF)	H	D	1–1	..	..	..	McGrath	..	..	Graham	Moses	..	..	Gidman	Davies[1] for Gidman
25 Apr	Juventus (SF)	A	L	1–2	..	..	..	Wilkins	..	..	McGrath	..	..	Hughes	Graham	Whiteside[1] for Stapleton

Appearances (goals)

Albiston 40 (2) · Bailey 40 · Blackmore 1 · Crooks 6 (2) · Davies 3 · Duxbury 39 · Gidman 4 · Graham 33 (5) · Hogg 16 (1) · Hughes 7 (4) · McGrath 9 (1) · McQueen 20 (1) · Moran 38 (7) · Moses 31 (2) · Muhren 26 · Robson 33 (12) · Stapleton 42 (13) · Wealands 2 · Whiteside 30 (10) · Wilkins 42 (3) · Total 20 players (71)

Football League

	P	W	D	L	F:A	Pts	
Liverpool	42	22	14	6	73:32	80	1st
Manchester U	42	20	14	8	71:41	74	4th

SEASON 1984–1985 FOOTBALL LEAGUE (DIVISION 1)

1984–1985

25 Aug	Watford	H	D	1–1	Bailey	Duxbury	Albiston	Moses	Moran	Hogg	Robson	Strachan[1]	Hughes	Brazil	Olsen	Whiteside for Brazil
28 Aug	Southampton	A	D	0–0	..	..	..	..	..	..	..	..	..	..	..	
1 Sep	Ipswich T	A	D	1–1	..	..	..	..	..	..	..	..	..[1]	..	..	Whiteside for Brazil
5 Sep	Chelsea	H	D	1–1	..	..	..	..	..	..	..	..	..	Whiteside	..[1]	
8 Sep	Newcastle U	H	W	5–0	..	..	..	..[1]	..	..	..	..[2]	..[1]	..	..[1]	
15 Sep	Coventry C	A	W	3–0	..	..	..	..	..	..	..[1]	..	..	..[2]	..	
22 Sep	Liverpool	H	D	1–1	..	..	..	..	..	..	..	..[1]	..	..	..	Muhren for Moran
29 Sep	W B A	A	W	2–1	..	..	..	..	..	..	..[1]	..[1]	..	Brazil	..	
6 Oct	Aston Villa	A	L	0–3	..	..	..	..	..	..	Strachan	Muhren	..	..	..	
13 Oct	West Ham U	H	W	5–1	..	..	..	..[1]	McQueen[1]	..	Robson	Strachan	..[1]	..[1]	..	
20 Oct	Tottenham H	H	W	1–0	..	Gidman	..	..	Moran	..	..	..	..[1]	..	..	
27 Oct	Everton	A	L	0–5	..	Moran	..	..	McQueen	..	..	..	..	..	..	Stapleton for Moran
2 Nov	Arsenal	H	W	4–2	..	Gidman	..	..	Moran	..	..[1]	..[2]	..[1]	Stapleton	..	
10 Nov	Leicester C	A	W	3–2	..	..	..	..	Garton	..	..	..[1]	..[1]	Brazil[1]	..	Whiteside for Olsen
17 Nov	Luton T	H	W	2–0	..	..	..	..	McQueen	Duxbury	..	..	..	Whiteside[2]	..	Stapleton for Robson
24 Nov	Sunderland	A	L	2–3	..	..	Duxbury	..	..	Garton	..[1]	..	..[1]	..	..	Muhren for Olsen
1 Dec	Norwich C	H	W	2–0	..	..	..	..	..	McGrath	..[1]	..	..[1]	..	..	
8 Dec	Nottingham F	A	L	2–3	..	Duxbury	Blackmore	..	..	..	..	..[2]	Stapleton	Brazil	Muhren	
15 Dec	Q P R	H	W	3–0	..	Gidman[1]	Albiston	..	..	Duxbury[1]	..	..	..	..[1]	Olsen	
22 Dec	Ipswich T	H	W	3–0	..	..[1]	..	..	..	..	..[1]	..[1]	Hughes	Stapleton	..	
26 Dec	Stoke C	A	L	1–2	..	..	..	..	..	..	..	..	..	..[1]	Muhren	Brazil for Strachan
29 Dec	Chelsea	A	W	3–1	..	Duxbury	..	..[1]	..	McGrath	..	..	Stapleton[1]	Hughes[1]	..	
1 Jan	Sheffield Wed	H	L	1–2	..	..	..	..	..	..	..	..	Hughes[1]	Brazil	..	
12 Jan	Coventry C	H	L	0–1	Pears	..	..	..	..	..	..	..	Stapleton	Hughes	..	Brazil for Robson
2 Feb	W B A	H	W	2–0	..	Gidman	..	..	Moran	Hogg	McGrath	..[2]	Hughes	Whiteside	Olsen	
9 Feb	Newcastle U	A	D	1–1	..	..	..	..	..[1]	..	..	..	..	..	..	Stapleton for Olsen
23 Feb	Arsenal	A	W	1–0	Bailey	..	..	Duxbury	..	..	..	..	..	Stapleton	..	Whiteside[1] for Moran
2 Mar	Everton	H	D	1–1	..	..	..	..	McGrath	..	Strachan	Brazil	..	Whiteside	..[1]	
12 Mar	Tottenham H	A	W	2–1	..	..	..	..	..	..	..	Whiteside[1]	..[1]	Stapleton	..	
15 Mar	West Ham U	A	D	2–2	..	..	..	..	..	..	..	..	..	..[1]	..	Robson[1] for Whiteside
23 Mar	Aston Villa	H	W	4–0	..	..	..	Whiteside[1]	..	..	Robson	Strachan	..[3]	..	..	
31 Mar	Liverpool	A	W	1–0	..	..	..	..	..	..	..	..	..	..[1]	..	
3 Apr	Leicester C	H	W	2–1	..	..	..	..	..	..	..[1]	..	..	..[1]	..	
6 Apr	Stoke C	H	W	5–0	..	..	..	..[1]	..	..	..	..	..[2]	..	..[2]	Duxbury for Robson
9 Apr	Sheffield Wed	A	L	0–1	Pears	..	..	Duxbury	..	..	..	..	..	..	..	Brazil for Duxbury
21 Apr	Luton T	A	L	1–2	Bailey	..	..	Whiteside[1]	..	..	..	Muhren	..	..	..	
24 Apr	Southampton	H	D	0–0	..	..	..	..	..	..	..	Strachan	..	..	..	Duxbury for Stapleton
27 Apr	Sunderland	H	D	2–2	..	..	..	..	..	Moran[1]	..[1]	..	..	Brazil	..	Duxbury for Gidman
4 May	Norwich C	A	W	1–0	..	..	..	..	..	..[1]	..	..	..	Stapleton	..	
6 May	Nottingham F	H	W	2–0	..	..[1]	..	..	Moran	Hogg	McGrath	..	Stapleton[1]	Brazil	..	Muhren for Moran
11 May	Q P R	A	W	3–1	..	..	..	..	McGrath	..	Duxbury	..[1]	..	..[2]	..	Muhren for Hogg
13 May	Watford	A	L	1–5	..	..	..	..	..	Moran[1]	..	..	Hughes	Stapleton	Brazil	Muhren for Whiteside

FA Cup

5 Jan	Bournemouth (3)	H	W	3–0	Bailey	Duxbury	Albiston	Moses	McQueen[1]	McGrath	Robson	Strachan[1]	Stapleton[1]	Hughes	Muhren	
26 Jan	Coventry C (4)	H	W	2–1	Pears	Gidman	..	..	Moran	Hogg	McGrath[1]	..	Whiteside	..[1]	Olsen	Brazil for Hughes
15 Feb	Blackburn R (5)	A	W	2–0	Bailey	..	..	..	..	..	..[1]	..[1]	Hughes	Whiteside	..	
9 Mar	West Ham U (6)	H	W	4–2	..	..	..	Duxbury	McGrath	..	Strachan	Whiteside[3]	..[1]	Stapleton	..	
13 Apr	Liverpool (SF) (at Goodison Park)	N	D	2–2	..	..	..	Whiteside	..	..	Robson	Strachan	..[1]	..[1]	..	
17 Apr	Liverpool (SFR) (at Maine Road)	N	W	2–1	..	..	..	..	..	..	..[1]	..	..[1]	..	..	
18 May	Everton (F)† (at Wembley)	N	W	1–0	..	..	..	..[1]	..	Moran	..[1]	..	..	..	..	Duxbury for Albiston

† after extra time

Milk Cup

26 Sep	Burnley (2)	H	W	4–0	Bailey	Duxbury	Albiston	Moses	Garton	Hogg	Robson[1]	Graham	Hughes[3]	Whiteside	Muhren	Brazil for Whiteside
9 Oct	Burnley (2)	A	W	3–0	..	..	..	..	Moran	..	Strachan	Blackmore	Stapleton	Brazil[2]	Olsen[1]	
30 Oct	Everton (3)	H	L	1–2	..	Gidman	..	..	..	..	Robson	Strachan	Hughes	..[1]	..	Stapleton for Olsen

UEFA Cup

19 Sep	Raba Gyor (1)	H	W	3–0	Bailey	Duxbury	Albiston	Moses	Moran	Hogg	Robson[1]	Muhren[1]	Hughes[1]	Whiteside	Olsen	
3 Oct	Raba Gyor (1)	A	D	2–2	..	..	..	..	..	..	..	..[1]	..	Brazil[1]	..	Gidman for Robson
24 Oct	Eindhoven (2)	A	D	0–0	..	Gidman	..	..	..	..	..	Strachan	..	..	..	
7 Nov	Eindhoven (2)	H	W	1–0	..	..	..	..	..	..	..	..[1]	..	Stapleton	..	Garton for Moran, Whiteside for Stapleton
28 Nov	Dundee U (3)	H	D	2–2	..	..	..	..	McQueen	Duxbury	..[1]	..[1]	..	Whiteside	..	Stapleton for Whiteside
12 Dec	Dundee U (3)	A	W	*3–2	..	..	..	..	..	..	..	..	Stapleton	Hughes[1]	Muhren[1]	
6 Mar	Videoton (4)	H	W	1–0	..	..	..	Duxbury	McGrath	Hogg	Strachan	Whiteside	Hughes	Stapleton[1]	Olsen	
20 Mar	Videoton (4)	A	L	0–1	..	..	..	..	..	..	Robson	Strachan	..	..	Whiteside	Olsen for Robson

(4–5 pens after extra time)

Appearances (goals)

Albiston 39 · Bailey 38 · Blackmore 1 · Brazil 17 (5) · Duxbury 27 (1) · Garton 2 · Gidman 27 (3) · Hogg 29 · Hughes 38 (16) · McGrath P 23 · McQueen 12 (1) · Moran 19 (4) · Moses R 26 (3) · Muhren 7 · Olsen 36 (5) · Pears 4 · Robson 32 (9) · Stapleton 21 (6) · Strachan 41 (15) · Whiteside 23 (9) · Total 20 players (77)

Football League

	P	W	D	L	F:A	Pts	
Everton	42	28	6	8	88:43	90	1st
Manchester U	42	22	10	10	77:47	76	4th

SEASON 1985–1986 FOOTBALL LEAGUE (DIVISION 1)

1985–1986

17 Aug	Aston Villa	H	W	4–0	Bailey	Gidman	Albiston	Whiteside[1]	McGrath	Hogg	Robson	Moses	Hughes[2]	Stapleton	Olsen[1]	Duxbury for Moses
20 Aug	Ipswich T	A	W	1–0	..	..	..	..	..	..	..[1]	Strachan	..	..	..	Duxbury for Gidman
24 Aug	Arsenal	A	W	2–1	..	Duxbury	..	..	..[1]	..	..	..	..[1]	..	..	
26 Aug	West Ham U	H	W	2–0	..	..	..	..	..	..	..	..[1]	..[1]	..	..	
31 Aug	Nottingham F	A	W	3–1	..	..	..	..	..	..	..	..	..[1]	..[1]	Barnes[1]	Brazil for Strachan
4 Sep	Newcastle U	H	W	3–0	..	..	..	..	..	..	..	..	..[1]	..[2]	..	Brazil for Stapleton
7 Sep	Oxford U	H	W	3–0	..	..	..	..[1]	..	..	..[1]	..	..	..	..[1]	Brazil for Stapleton
14 Sep	Manchester C	A	W	3–0	..	..[1]	..[1]	..	..	..	..[1]	..	..	..	..	Brazil for Stapleton
21 Sep	W B A	A	W	5–1	..	..	..	..	..	..	..	..[1]	Brazil[2]	..[1]	Blackmore[1]	Moran for Strachan
28 Sep	Southampton	H	W	1–0	..	..	..	..	..	Moran	..	Moses	Hughes[1]	..	Barnes,	Brazil for Whiteside
5 Oct	Luton T	A	D	1–1	..	..	..	..	..	..	..	..	..[1]	..	..	
12 Oct	Q P R	H	W	2–0	..	..	..	..	..	..	..	Olsen[1]	..[1]	..	..	
19 Oct	Liverpool	H	D	1–1	..	..	..	..	Moran	Hogg	McGrath[1]	Moses	..	..	Olsen	Barnes for Moses
26 Oct	Chelsea	A	W	2–1	..	..	..	..	..	..	..	Olsen[1]	..[1]	..	Barnes	
2 Nov	Coventry C	H	W	2–0	..	Garton	..	..	..	..	..	..[2]	..	..	..	
9 Nov	Sheffield Wed	A	L	0–1	..	Gidman	..	..	McGrath	Moran	Robson	..	..	..	..	Strachan for Robson
16 Nov	Tottenham H	H	D	0–0	..	..	..	..	..	..	Strachan	..	..	..	..	
23 Nov	Leicester C	A	L	0–3	..	..	..	..	Moran	Hogg	McGrath	Strachan	..	..	Olsen	Brazil for Albiston
30 Nov	Watford	H	D	1–1	..	..	Gibson C	..	..	..	..	..	..	..	..	Brazil[1] for Moran
7 Dec	Ipswich T	H	W	1–0	..	..	..	..	McGrath	..	Dempsey	..	..	..[1]	..	Brazil for Hughes
14 Dec	Aston Villa	A	W	3–1	Turner	..	..	..	..	Garton	Blackmore[1]	..[1]	..[1]	..	..	Brazil for Stapleton
21 Dec	Arsenal	H	L	0–1	Bailey	..	..	..	..	..	..	..	..	..	..	
26 Dec	Everton	A	L	1–3	..	..	..	..	..	Hogg	..	..	..	..[1]	..	Wood for Olsen
1 Jan	Birmingham C	H	W	1–0	Turner	..	Albiston	..	..	Garton	..	..	..	..	Gibson C[1]	Brazil for McGrath
11 Jan	Oxford U	A	W	3–1	Bailey	..	..	..[1]	Moran	..	..	..	..[1]	..	..[1]	
18 Jan	Nottingham F	H	L	2–3	..	..	..	..	..	..	Olsen[2]	..	..	..	..	
2 Feb	West Ham U	A	L	1–2	..	..	..	..	McGrath	Moran	Robson[1]	Olsen	..	..	..	Gibson T for Robson
9 Feb	Liverpool	A	D	1–1	Turner	..	..	..	..	..	Sivebaek	Gibson T	..	Gibson C[1]	Olsen	Stapleton for Olsen
22 Feb	W B A	H	W	3–0	..	..	..	Blackmore	..	..	Strachan	Gibson C	..	Stapleton	..[3]	Gibson T for Gidman
1 Mar	Southampton	A	L	0–1	..	Duxbury	..	Gibson C	..	..	Robson	Strachan	..	..	..	Gibson T for Olsen

SEASON 1986–1987 — (continued from previous season, 1985–1986)

Date	Opponent	Venue	Result	Score	Notes
15 Mar	Q P R	A	L	0–1	Gibson T for Olsen
19 Mar	Luton T	H	W	2–0	Stapleton for Moran
22 Mar	Manchester C	H	D	2–2	Stapleton for Barnes
29 Mar	Birmingham C	A	D	1–1	Stapleton for Gibson C
31 Mar	Everton	H	D	0–0	Stapleton for Davenport
5 Apr	Coventry C	A	W	3–1	Stapleton for Gibson C
9 Apr	Chelsea	H	L	1–2	Stapleton for Strachan
13 Apr	Sheffield Wed	H	L	0–2	Gibson T for Davenport
16 Apr	Newcastle U	A	W	4–2	Sivebaek for Gibson T
19 Apr	Tottenham H	A	D	0–0	Olsen for Davenport
26 Apr	Leicester C	H	W	4–0	Olsen for Whiteside
3 May	Watford	A	D	1–1	Olsen for Davenport

FA Cup

Date	Opponent	Venue	Result	Score	Notes
9 Jan	Rochdale (3)	H	W	2–0	Olsen for Hughes
25 Jan	Sunderland (4)	A	D	0–0	
29 Jan	Sunderland (4R)	H	W	3–0	Blackmore for Strachan
5 Mar	West Ham U (5)	A	D	1–1	Olsen for Robson
9 Mar	West Ham U (5R)	H	L	0–2	Blackmore for Higgins

Milk Cup

Date	Opponent	Venue	Result	Score	Notes
24 Sep	Crystal Palace (2)	A	W	1–0	Brazil for Hughes
9 Oct	Crystal Palace (2)	H	W	1–0	Brazil for Duxbury
29 Oct	West Ham U (3)	H	W	1–0	
26 Nov	Liverpool (4)	A	L	1–2	

Appearances (goals)

Albiston 37 (1) · Bailey 25 · Barnes 12 (2) · Blackmore 12 (3) · Brazil 1 (3) · Davenport 11 (1) · Dempsey 1 · Duxbury 21 (1) · Garton 10 · Gibson C 18 (5) · Gibson T 2 · Gidman 24 · Higgins 6 · Hughes 40 (17) · Hogg 17 · McGrath 40 (3) · Moran 18 · Moses 4 · Olsen 25 (11) · Robson 21 (7) · Sivebaek 2 · Stapleton 34 (7) · Strachan 27 (5) · Turner 17 · Whiteside 37 (4) · Total 25 players (70)

Football League

	P	W	D	L	F:A	Pts	
Liverpool	42	26	10	6	89:37	88	1st
Manchester U	42	22	10	10	70:36	76	4th

SEASON 1986–1987 FOOTBALL LEAGUE (DIVISION 1)

Date	Opponent	Venue	Result	Score	Notes
23 Aug	Arsenal	A	L	0–1	Olsen for Gibson C
25 Aug	West Ham U	H	L	2–3	Olsen for Gibson C
30 Aug	Charlton A	H	L	0–1	Gibson T for Whiteside
6 Sep	Leicester C	A	D	1–1	Davenport for Gibson T
13 Sep	Southampton	H	W	5–1	Gibson T for Strachan
16 Sep	Watford	A	L	0–1	
21 Sep	Everton	A	L	1–3	Olsen for Whiteside
28 Sep	Chelsea	H	L	0–1	Olsen for Whiteside
4 Oct	Nottingham F	A	D	1–1	
11 Oct	Sheffield Wed	H	W	3–1	Gibson T for Strachan
18 Oct	Luton T	H	W	1–0	
26 Oct	Manchester C	A	D	1–1	Moses for Robson
1 Nov	Coventry C	H	D	1–1	Olsen for McGrath
8 Nov	Oxford U	A	L	0–2	Moran for Sivebaek
15 Nov	Norwich C	A	D	0–0	Strachan for Barnes
22 Nov	Q P R	H	W	1–0	Robson for Barnes
29 Nov	Wimbledon	A	L	0–1	Stapleton for McGrath
7 Dec	Tottenham H	H	D	3–3	Stapleton for Davenport
13 Dec	Aston Villa	A	D	3–3	Stapleton for O'Brien
20 Dec	Leicester C	H	W	2–0	
26 Dec	Liverpool	A	W	1–0	O'Brien for Robson
27 Dec	Norwich C	H	L	0–1	Stapleton for Whiteside
1 Jan	Newcastle U	H	W	*4–1	Davenport for Gill
3 Jan	Southampton	A	D	1–1	McGrath for Duxbury
24 Jan	Arsenal	H	W	2–0	Davenport for Gibson T
7 Feb	Charlton A	A	D	0–0	Stapleton for Garton
14 Feb	Watford	H	W	3–1	Stapleton for Olsen
21 Feb	Chelsea	A	D	1–1	O'Brien for Davenport
28 Feb	Everton	H	D	0–0	Davenport for Strachan
7 Mar	Manchester C	H	W	*2–0	Davenport for Gibson C
14 Mar	Luton T	A	L	1–2	Gibson T for Garton
21 Mar	Sheffield Wed	A	L	0–1	Albiston for Wood
28 Mar	Nottingham F	H	W	2–0	Albiston for Wood
4 Apr	Oxford U	H	W	3–2	Albiston for Robson
14 Apr	West Ham U	A	D	0–0	Stapleton for Gibson T
18 Apr	Newcastle U	A	L	1–2	Stapleton for Albiston
20 Apr	Liverpool	H	W	1–0	Sivebaek for Moses
25 Apr	Q P R	A	D	1–1	Stapleton for Moses
2 May	Wimbledon	H	L	0–1	Blackmore for Sivebaek
4 May	Tottenham H	A	L	0–4	Blackmore for Strachan
6 May	Coventry C	A	D	1–1	Olsen for Whiteside
9 May	Aston Villa	H	W	3–1	

FA Cup

Date	Opponent	Venue	Result	Score	Notes
10 Jan	Manchester C (3)	H	W	1–0	Gibson T for Davenport
31 Jan	Coventry C (4)	H	L	0–1	Davenport for Stapleton, McGrath for Blackmore

Littlewoods Cup

Date	Opponent	Venue	Result	Score	Notes
24 Sep	Port Vale (2)	H	W	2–0	Whiteside for Moran, Gibson T for Stapleton
7 Oct	Port Vale (2)	A	W	5–2	Olsen for Moses, Gibson T for Davenport
29 Oct	Southampton (3)	H	D	0–0	Moran for Gibson C, Wood for Whiteside
4 Nov	Southampton (3R)	A	L	1–4	

Appearances (goals)

Albiston 19 · Bailey 5 · Barnes 7 · Blackmore 10 (1) · Davenport 34 (14) · Duxbury 32 (1) · Garton 9 · Gibson C 24 (1) · Gibson T 12 (1) · Gill 1 · Hogg 11 · McGrath 34 (2) · Moran 32 · Moses 17 · O'Brien 9 · Olsen 22 (3) · Robson 29 (7) · Sivebaek 27 (1) · Stapleton 25 (7) · Strachan 33 (4) · Turner 23 · Walsh 14 · Whiteside 31 (8) · Wood 2 · Own goals 2 · Total 24 players (52)

Football League

	P	W	D	L	F:A	Pts	
Everton	42	26	8	8	76:31	86	1st
Manchester U	42	14	14	14	52:45	56	11th

Date	Opponent	V	R	Score	GK	Anderson	Duxbury	Moses	McGrath	Moran	Robson	Strachan	McClair	Whiteside	Olsen	Substitutes
15 Aug	Southampton	A	D	2-2	Walsh	Anderson	Duxbury	Moses	McGrath	Moran	Robson	Strachan	McClair	Whiteside[2]	Olsen	Albiston for Moses, Davenport for Olsen
19 Aug	Arsenal	H	D	0-0	..	..	..	..	..	..	..	..	..	..	..	
22 Aug	Watford	H	W	2-0	..	..	..	..	..[1]	..	..	..	..[1]	..	..	Albiston for Olsen, Davenport for Strachan
29 Aug	Charlton A	A	W	3-1	..	..	..	..	..[1]	..	..	..	..[1]	..[1]	..	Gibson C for Duxbury, Davenport for Olsen
31 Aug	Chelsea	H	W	3-1	..	..	Albiston	..	..	..	Duxbury	..[1]	..[1]	..[1]	..	Gibson C for Albiston
5 Sep	Coventry C	A	D	0-0	..	..	..	..	..	..	..	..	..	..	..	Gibson C for Albiston, Davenport for Olsen
12 Sep	Newcastle U	H	D	2-2	..	..	Duxbury	..	..	..	Robson	..	..[1]	..	..[1]	Davenport for Olsen
19 Sep	Everton	A	L	1-2	..	..	..	..	..	Hogg	..	..	..[1]	..	..	Garton for Hogg, Davenport for Strachan
26 Sep	Tottenham H	H	W	1-0	..	..	Gibson C	Garton	..	Duxbury	..	..	..[1]	..	..	Blackmore for Anderson, Davenport for Strachan
3 Oct	Luton T	A	D	1-1	..	Blackmore	..	..	..	..	..	..	..[1]	..	..	O'Brien for Blackmore
10 Oct	Sheffield W	H	W	4-2	..	Garton	..	Duxbury	..	Moran	..	..	..[2]	..	..	Blackmore[1] for Moran, Davenport for Strachan
17 Oct	Norwich C	H	W	2-1	..	..	..	..[1]	..	Davenport[1]	..[1]	Blackmore	..	..	..	Moran for Gibson C, O'Brien for Blackmore
25 Oct	West Ham U	A	D	1-1	..	Anderson	..	..[1]	..	Moran	..	Strachan	..	..	Davenport	Blackmore for Strachan
31 Oct	Nottingham F	H	D	2-2	..	..	..	..	Garton	..	..[1]	Davenport	..	Whiteside[1]	..	Strachan for Whiteside
15 Nov	Liverpool	H	D	1-1	..	..	..	..	Blackmore	..	..	Strachan	..	..	..	Davenport for Moran
21 Nov	Wimbledon	A	L	1-2	..	..	Duxbury	Moses	..	..	..[1]	Graham	..	..	..	Albiston for Duxbury, O'Brien for Graham
5 Dec	Q P R	A	W	2-0	Turner	Duxbury	Albiston	..	Moran	O'Brien	..	Strachan	..	Davenport[1]	..	Albiston for Robson
12 Dec	Oxford United	H	W	3-1	..	..	Gibson C	..	..	Davenport	..	..[2]	..	Whiteside	..[1]	Davenport for Olsen
19 Dec	Portsmouth	A	W	2-1	..	..	..	Bruce	..	Moses	..[1]	..	..[1]	..	..	Anderson for Gibson C, Olsen for Moses
26 Dec	Newcastle U	A	L	0-1	..	..	..	..	..	..	..	..	..	..	Davenport	Davenport for Whiteside, Moses for Strachan
28 Dec	Everton	H	W	2-1	..	Anderson	..	..	..	Duxbury	..	..	..[2]	..	Olsen	Blackmore for Olsen, O'Brien for Moses
1 Jan	Charlton A	H	D	0-0	..	..	..	..	Duxbury	Moses	..	..	..	..	Davenport	Davenport for Albiston, O'Brien for Moran
2 Jan	Watford	A	W	1-0	..	..	Albiston	..	Moran	Duxbury	..	..	..[1]	Whiteside	Gibson C	Davenport for Albiston, O'Brien for Moran
16 Jan	Southampton	H	L	0-2	..	..	Gibson C	..	Moses	..	..	Duxbury	..	Davenport	Olsen	Strachan for Gibson C, O'Brien for Moran
24 Jan	Arsenal	A	W	2-1	..	..	Duxbury	..	Blackmore	Hogg	..	Strachan[1]	..[1]	Whiteside	..	O'Brien for Blackmore
6 Feb	Coventry C	H	W	1-0	..	..	..	..	O'Brien[1]	..	..	..	..	..	..	Albiston for O'Brien
10 Feb	Derby Co	A	W	2-1	..	..	Albiston	..	..	..	..	..[1]	..	..[1]	Davenport	Albiston for Duxbury, Davenport for Olsen
13 Feb	Chelsea	A	W	2-1	..	..	Albiston	..	..[1]	..[1]	..	Davenport	..	..	Gibson C	Blackmore for Gibson C
23 Feb	Tottenham H	A	D	1-1	..	..	Duxbury	..	..	..	Davenport	Blackmore	..[1]	..	..	Strachan for Hogg, Olsen for Anderson
5 Mar	Norwich C	A	L	0-1	..	Blackmore	..	..	..	Moran	Robson	Strachan	..	Davenport	..	Olsen for Duxbury
12 Mar	Sheffield W	H	W	4-1	..	..[1]	Gibson C	..	..	Duxbury	..	Hogg	..[2]	..	Olsen	O'Brien for Gibson C, McGrath for Hogg
19 Mar	Nottingham F	A	D	0-0	..	Anderson	Blackmore	..	..	..	Whiteside	Olsen	..	..	Gibson C	Olsen for Strachan
26 Mar	West Ham U	H	W	3-1	..	..[1]	..	..	McGrath	Duxbury	Robson[1]	Strachan[1]	..	..	..	[1]Olsen for Davenport, O'Brien for McGrath
2 Apr	Derby Co	H	W	4-1	..	..	..	Duxbury	..	Hogg	..	..	..[3]	..	..	Olsen for Blackmore, Whiteside for McGrath
4 Apr	Liverpool	A	D	3-3	..	..	..	Bruce	..	Duxbury	..[2]	..[1]	..	..	..	Olsen for Gibson C
12 Apr	Luton T	H	W	3-0	..	..	..	..[1]	..	..	..[1]	..	..[1]	..	..	Blackmore for Anderson
30 Apr	Q P R	H	W	*2-1	..	..	..	..	..	..	..	..	..[1]	..	Olsen	O'Brien for Blackmore
2 May	Oxford U	A	W	2-0	..	..	Gibson C	..	..	..	..[1]	..	..	..[2]	..	Blackmore for Anderson
7 May	Portsmouth	H	W	4-1	..	..	..	..	..	..	..	..	..[2]	..	..	Blackmore for Anderson, Hogg for McGrath
9 May	Wimbledon	H	W	2-1	Duxbury	Blackmore	..	..	..	Moses	..	..[2]	..	Gibson C		Martin for Moses

FA Cup

Date	Opponent	V	R	Score												Substitutes
10 Jan	Ipswich Town (3)	A	W	*2-1	Turner	Anderson[1]	Duxbury	Bruce	Moran	Moses	Robson	Strachan	McClair	Whiteside	Gibson C	Davenport for Moses, Olsen for Gibson C
30 Jan	Chelsea (4)	H	W	2-0	..	..	..	..	Blackmore	Hogg	..	..	..[1]	..[1]	Olsen	O'Brien for Blackmore
20 Feb	Arsenal (5)	A	L	1-2	..	..	Gibson C	..	..	Duxbury	..	Davenport	..	..	..	O'Brien for Hogg, Blackmore for Olsen

Littlewoods Cup

Date	Opponent	V	R	Score												Substitutes
23 Sep	Hull C (2)	H	W	5-0	Walsh	Anderson	Gibson C	Moses	McGrath[1]	Duxbury	Robson	Strachan	McClair[1]	Whiteside[1]	Davenport[1]	Garton for Moses
7 Oct	Hull C (2)	A	W	1-0	Turner	Blackmore	..	Garton	..	..	..	..	..[1]	..	Olsen	O'Brien for Gibson C, Graham for Duxbury
28 Oct	Crystal Palace (3)	H	W	2-1	..	Anderson	..	Duxbury	Garton	Moran	..	..	..[2]	..	Davenport	Blackmore for Robson, Olsen for Davenport
18 Nov	Bury (4)	H	W	2-1	..	Walsh	..	..	Blackmore	Davenport	..	..	..[1]	..	Olsen	O'Brien for Gibson C, Moses for Davenport
20 Jan	Oxford U (5)	A	L	0-2	Turner	..	..	Blackmore	Moran	Duxbury	..	..	..	..	..	Hogg for Moran, Davenport for Strachan

Appearances (Goals)

Albiston 5 · Anderson 30 (2) · Blackmore 15 (3) · Bruce 21 (2) · Davenport 21 (5) · Duxbury 39 · Garton 5 · Gibson C 26 (2) · Graham 1 · Hogg 9 · McClair 40 (24) · McGrath 21 (2) · Moran 20 · Moses 16 · O'Brien 6 (2) · Olsen 31 (2) · Robson 36 (11) · Strachan 33 (8) · Turner 24 · Walsh 16 · Whiteside 25 (7) · Own goals 1 · Total 21 players (71)

Football League

	P	W	D	L	F:A	Pts	
Liverpool	40	26	12	2	87:24	90	1st
Manchester U	40	23	12	5	71:38	81	2nd

Index

Figures in italics refer to illustrations

239